The Effective Change Manager's Handbook

Publisher's note

Every possible effort has been made to ensure that the information contained in this book is accurate at the time of going to press, and the publishers and authors cannot accept responsibility for any errors or omissions, however caused. No responsibility for loss or damage occasioned to any person acting, or refraining from action, as a result of the material in this publication can be accepted by the editor, the publisher or any of the authors.

First published in Great Britain and the United States in 2015 by Kogan Page Limited

2nd Floor, 45 Gee Street
London EC1V 3RS
United Kingdom
www.koganpage.com

1518 Walnut Street, Suite 1100
Philadelphia PA 19102
USA

4737/23 Ansari Road
Daryaganj
New Delhi 110002
India

ISBN 978 0 7494 7307 5
E-ISBN 978 0 7494 7308 2

British Library Cataloguing-in-Publication Data

A CIP record for this book is available from the British Library.

Library of Congress Cataloging-in-Publication Data

The effective change manager's handbook : essential guidance to the change management body of knowledge / edited by Richard Smith and the APMG.
pages cm
ISBN 978-0-7494-7307-5 (paperback) – ISBN 978-0-7494-7308-2 (ebk) 1. Organizational change–Management. I. Smith, Richard, 1953 December 29-
HD58.8.E36 2014
658.4'06–dc23

2014030706

Typeset by Graphicraft Limited, Hong Kong
Print production managed by Jellyfish
Printed and bound by CPI Group (UK) Ltd, Croydon, CR0 4YY

The Effective Change Manager's Handbook

Essential guidance to the change management body of knowledge

Edited by Richard Smith, David King, Ranjit Sidhu and Dan Skelsey

KoganPage

LONDON PHILADELPHIA NEW DELHI

CONTENTS

PREFACE
Change management in context

It is less than a year since I wrote the preface to the Change Management Institute's *The Effective Change Manager: The Change Management Body of Knowledge* (CMBoK). At the time I had little idea that I would be writing another preface so soon. However, a need has become apparent for a robust examinable text that follows the content and structure of that body of knowledge. In the preface to *The Effective Change Manager* I described change management as:

- an emergent profession;
- an interdisciplinary profession;
- a developing profession.

Change management is an *emergent* profession in the sense that no one set out to invent it. The rapidly changing demands on organizations in the latter part of the 20th century and the beginning of the 21st placed a premium on effective organizational change management. Success in delivering organizational change initiatives has been patchy at best, and research has begun to identify the range of factors that predispose an initiative to succeed. A need has become clear for people with a particular range of knowledge and competence to help organizations apply these insights effectively.

For this reason, change management is also an *interdisciplinary* profession. Insights about successful change draw on a wide range of academic research and practitioner expertise, and require effective interfaces with many other disciplines. The change management 'nation' is composed of many 'tribes'. In particular, those who have come to change management practice from an organizational development (OD) background have long used more than half a century of social science research to engage the commitment of people, helping them to invest personally in change to their working lives. But in addition to the 'OD tribe' there are project and programme managers, who have used their specialist knowledge of operational management, applying their structured approaches, tools and techniques to support successful change.

It has taken time for people with the appropriate set of interdisciplinary insights to emerge. They have been guided by far-sighted academics who have for many years researched and run courses in change management, or who have included this as an explicit module in MBA programmes. However, the emergence of this interdisciplinary profession is taking time – it is a *developing* profession. No longer embryonic or in its infancy, change management is clearly 'out there' in the world. It is finding a distinctive voice and making its own impact. Its final 'mature' form remains to be seen, so perhaps in developmental terms the change management profession could be said to be 'adolescent'. It may sometimes be susceptible to a passing fashion or to the influence of a single, charismatic figure. However, it is increasingly firm in its sense of itself. It possesses the energy, enthusiasm and, increasingly, the wisdom to make a positive difference in the world.

This book, and the well-researched structure of *The Effective Change Manager* that lies behind it, are a contribution to the maturing of change management. In a remarkably short period a team of 17 authors, each with relevant specialisms, has collaborated to develop this current text. It covers fully the knowledge expected of effective change managers. It covers key elements of the Change Management Institute's accreditation process for change managers, and can be used as the basis for courses and examinations that support that process, including the APMG International syllabus from 2015 onwards.

In this current book – *The Effective Change Manager's Handbook* – we have sought to reflect both the breadth and depth of knowledge needed by change managers across the variety of challenges they face. Our understanding of change management has been based on several years' worldwide research by the Change Management Institute (CMI) about what change managers actually do. Rather than offering an academic definition of 'change management' the book as a whole reflects this research.

Most importantly, however, this is a *handbook*. We are not seeking to break new ground in what we cover here. Our aim is to make existing change management knowledge both accessible and practical. Given the impact of change on leaders and managers of many backgrounds and across organizational life, this book is not written for people in a narrow professional 'ghetto'. It is designed to address the needs of many who need to do the work of managing change, even though this is not their job title. See the following section on 'Who is this book for?'

In the following pages we offer applications, techniques, checklists and frameworks that will, we hope, encourage and support excellent practice. If readers return to this book frequently, dipping into it to find fresh insights or tools to address a current challenge, we shall have succeeded in our purpose.

Richard Smith, June 2014
on behalf of the editorial team

WHO IS THIS BOOK FOR?

The Effective Change Manager's Handbook refers frequently to the 'change managers' for whom it has been written. We express it this way (with a lower case 'c' and 'm') because change managers have many job titles! They may be called Business Change Manager, Project Manager, Programme Manager, OD Specialist, Innovations Manager – or any of a hundred other job titles. For the editors and authors of this book, change managers are all those who contribute in various ways to the process of:

- recognizing the need for change and defining that change;
- assessing the organization's capability and capacity for change;
- acquiring resources, planning change and assessing its impact;
- developing a stakeholder strategy;
- engaging people with the change process;
- equipping people with appropriate knowledge, skills and attitudes;
- communicating change;
- managing change projects and measuring change progress;
- facilitating groups working on change initiatives;
- sustaining and embedding change in the organization.

Anyone involved in any aspect of this process is fulfilling, at least in part, the role of 'change manager'. We hope that all those who in this sense are managing change will find practical value in this book.

EDITORIAL AND PRACTICAL INFORMATION ABOUT THIS BOOK

Organization of *The Effective Change Manager's Handbook*

The book's 13 chapters reflect the 13 'knowledge areas' of the Change Management Institute's CMBoK. In many cases, the major sections into which the chapters are divided (each designated by a letter – A, B, C etc) reflect the next level of CMBoK structure, the 'knowledge component'. However, this has not been appropriate in every case, and the authors have had the freedom to address in this book themes that may run across multiple CMBoK knowledge components.

Cross-references between chapters refer to the Chapter, Section and, where appropriate, subsection concerned thus: Chapter 1, Section A1.1. References within a chapter omit the chapter number and begin with the Section letter.

Common terms used in particular ways

Organizations use a wide variety of terms when describing the plans associated with change processes. This is influenced by their approach to project, programme and portfolio management. For consistency we have adopted the following terminology:

- *Change initiative*: except where the context requires an alternative, we have used this term as a general expression to include any intentional change process, including those constituted formally as a change portfolio, change programme or change project.
- *Change management plan*: we have used this term for a plan that typically includes change impact, the organization's change readiness, capability and capacity for change, meeting key learning needs and achievement of outcomes.
- *Benefits realization plan*: we have used this term for a plan that typically identifies the benefit owners, includes a summary of the benefits of a change initiative, states the timing of their expected realization and schedules benefit reviews.
- *Delivery plan*: our use of this term applies to a plan that can be created at various levels of a change initiative (programme or project) and typically includes the timing and sequence of key implementation tasks, delivery of outputs and transition to the business.

THOSE WHO HAVE MADE THIS BOOK POSSIBLE

APMG International (APMG)

APMG International is a leading international examination institute that accredits training and consulting organizations using a meticulous assessment process, and manages certification schemes for professionals. It is itself externally accredited to the highest international standards by the United Kingdom Accreditation Service (UKAS). Examinations set by APMG International are rigorous, challenging and consistent, so candidates can be proud of their achievement.

APMG began offering foundation examinations in change management in 2006, focusing on candidates' ability to remember and understand key concepts. In 2010 practitioner examinations were added, requiring candidates to analyse case studies and apply their change management knowledge appropriately. Thousands of candidates have passed the APMG Change Management Foundation and Practitioner-level examinations. APMG has sponsored *The Effective Change Manager's Handbook* as part of its commitment to develop and maintain its examinations against the most rigorous and respected global standards.

Change management examinations offered by APMG use this book as an examinable text, and candidates will need to refer to it. More information about the APMG Change Management examinations, and about the approved training organizations that offer them, can be found at: **www.apmg-international.com/en/qualifications/change management/**

The Change Management Institute (CMI)

The Change Management Institute (CMI) is a global, independent, not-for-profit organization set up in 2005 to promote and develop the profession of change management through education, networking and accreditation. CMI provides and supports professional education and networking opportunities for change management professionals, developing their capability as change practitioners. It also provides a professional accreditation scheme for change managers at both Foundation and Master level.

In response to a need for standards, the CMI launched the Change Management Practitioner Competency Model in 2008. This has been regularly updated every two years. In 2013 CMI published the Change Management Body of Knowledge (CMBoK) *The Effective Change Manager*. Informed by international research and peer review, the CMBoK describes and defines the knowledge required for a change manager to practise effectively across a wide range of situations. It is a key resource for change managers and those using their services.

This book, *The Effective Change Manager's Handbook*, is fully aligned with the CMI's CMBoK, and provides a convenient reference for those seeking accreditation under the CMI's professional accreditation scheme. The CMI website provides more information about their professional accreditation: **www.change-management-institute.com/accreditation**

Acknowledgements

The editorial team would like to thank APMG International for supporting the development of this book, and the Change Management Institute for allowing us unrestricted access to the material we wrote for their CMBoK. The partnership between these two independent organizations has proved most fruitful.

We would also like to express our thanks to the authors (17 contributors in total) who gave their time freely to write chapters of this book. They have met challenging deadlines and been generous with their forgiveness when publishing constraints have required us to edit or omit aspects of their work.

A number of senior change professionals read an early draft of this book. They made invaluable and constructive comments, and the book is a very much better publication as a result. The editors would particularly like to acknowledge the detailed and thoughtful reviews provided by Ira Blake, Helen Campbell, Robert Cole, Melanie Franklin and Caroline Perkins.

The editorial team at Kogan Page has been enormously supportive in bringing this book to publication, solving with great patience the various problems with which we have confronted them. We would like to mention particularly Liz Barlow, who first believed in the book, and Geraldine Collard and Melody Dawes who have borne the brunt of our inexperience of the publication process and our tight schedules!

Trade marks and permissions

Prosci® is a registered trade mark of Prosci Inc.

The Myers-Briggs Type Indicator® and MBTI® are registered trade marks of the MBTI Trust Inc.

MIND MAPS® is a registered trademark of The Buzan Organization Ltd.

SCRUM™ (the Agile methodology) is a trademark of Jeff Sutherland.

GROW™ is a trademark of Sir John Whitmore.

ADKAR® is a registered trademark of Prosci, Inc.

It is the nature of a book such as this that it draws heavily on existing publications. In producing it we have truly been 'standing on the shoulders of giants'! We have made every effort to honour the sources of all the ideas we have used and have sought permission from all copyright holders we have been able to identify. If we have inadvertently missed any of these we are truly sorry and will gladly put the matter right in a future edition.

AUTHOR BIOGRAPHIES

Chapter 1

Richard Smith

Richard's career has focused on organizational development and related people development issues. This has included both strategic change for organizations and tactical change for individuals and teams. He worked for a range of 'blue chip' organizations before establishing a niche consulting practice aimed at releasing potential, equipping leaders and facilitating change. This consulting work has taken him to 40 countries across six continents, working with global clients as diverse as Unilever, GKN, Nestlé, Mars and Harvard Business School, as well as with many more local businesses. He is a chief examiner for APMG Change Management products, and led the authoring team for the first global *Change Management Body of Knowledge*, written on behalf of the Change Management Institute.

Contact: **richard.smith@richardsmithassociates.com**

Chapter 2

Robert Cole, David King and Rod Sowden

Robert Cole

Having worked in Hewlett-Packard's research laboratories as a change manager and strategist Robert left at the end of the dot-com boom to become a consultant and trainer. Since then he has worked on a number of engagements, mostly as a change consultant and mentor to internal change managers in local and central government, as well as medium and large companies in many industries. Robert teaches a course on strategy at the Bristol Management Centre. He is the author of a number of online courses in change, and runs a business offering vocational qualifications in Managing Change.

Contact: **robert.cole@c4cm.co.uk**

David King

An independent consultant and trainer for over 25 years, David specializes in designing and delivering change programmes, projects and related learning solutions to organizations in public, private and third sectors. David is an examiner in Change Management for global qualifications body APM Group International and a co-author of the Change Management Institute's *Change Management Body of Knowledge* (CMBoK), published in September 2013. David is also author of *Think,*

Learn, Improve!: Turn your business vision into reality, which sets out a practitioner's framework of tools and techniques for designing and developing a comprehensive change programme.

Contact: **david.king@systemic.ltd.uk**

Rod Sowden

Rod is a certified management consultant who specializes in strategic change programme design and recovery. As lead author of Managing Successful Programmes® (2007 and 2011), he is one of the leading architects of programme management best practice. His work as lead author designing and developing the P3M3 maturity model (2008 and 2014) has developed the industry's ability to understand and model what successful organizations do. Rod also wrote the MSP® Survival Guide for Business Change Managers. In 2004 he founded Aspire Europe as an organization dedicated to delivering programmes and improving organizations' programme delivery. Rod has worked in a variety of industry sectors including central government, health, finance and logistics sectors.

Contact: **rod.sowden@aspireeurope.com**

Chapter 3

Stephen Jenner

Steve is author of, and chief examiner for, Managing Benefits™ and co-author of, and chief examiner for, the OGC's (now Axelos) 'Management of Portfolios®'. He designed, implemented and operated the approach to portfolio and benefits management that won the UK's 2007 Civil Service Financial Management Award. Steve also worked on the development of Project Portfolio and Benefits Management for the UK government as part of the Transformational Government and Service Transformation agendas. He is currently working at Queensland University of Technology in Brisbane. A professionally qualified management accountant and a Fellow of the APM, Steve also holds an MBA and a Masters of Studies degree from Cambridge University.

Contact: **stephen.jenner5@btinternet.com**

Chapter 4

Patrick Mayfield

Patrick Mayfield has had a career spanning over 38 years in IT-based change and leadership, in both the public and private sectors. He has worked on frameworks that were adaptive yet resilient to change of all types and scales. In 2001 he set up pearcemayfield, an international consultancy and training business. Patrick authored the chapter on 'Leadership and stakeholder engagement', part of the 1997 revised edition of the programme management framework, Managing Successful Programmes® (MSP®). More recently he has led research into high-performing programme and project managers, and in 2013 he published his book, *Practical*

People Engagement: Leading change through the power of relationships. APMG International has since adopted this book as the core reference for its new qualification in Stakeholder Engagement.

Contact: **patrick.mayfield@pearcemayfield.com**

Chapter 5

Ranjit Sidhu

Ranjit is a trainer, facilitator and change management consultant with over 20 years' experience on a variety of projects spanning Europe, North America and Africa. Her credentials include being an accredited trainer for APMG International's Change Management, AgilePM, and Facilitation qualifications, and the AXELOS PRINCE2® certification. Ranjit is also a certified trainer of NLP, and an assessor for the APM Practitioner. She is a contributing author for the *Gower Handbook of People in Project Management* and *The Effective Change Manager* (CMBoK) from the Change Management Institute. Her book, *Titanic Lessons in Project Leadership*, uses that tragic case study to highlight guidelines for effective communication and team building.

Contact: **ranjit@changequest.co.uk**

Chapter 6

Caroline Perkins

Caroline Perkins founded the Change Management Institute (CMI) and is its president and spokesperson. CMI is a global, voluntary, 'not for profit' professional organization that promotes and professionalizes change management, providing networking, education and accreditation services. Under Caroline's leadership CMI has opened active chapters across Australia, the UK, New Zealand, China and Brazil, rolled out the first global professional accreditation programme for change managers, and developed the *Change Management Body of Knowledge* (CMBoK). Caroline also owns and manages Carbon Group, a specialist international change consultancy that helps organizations to develop change strategies and manage change programmes. Caroline's book *The Agile Change Management Methodology* outlines her researched-based organizational change maturity model, providing a road map to organizational agility. She is an accredited change manager (ACM) and an accomplished speaker on the subject of organizational change.

Contact: **cperkins@carbon-group.com**

Chapter 7

Nicola Busby

Nicola specializes in planning, implementing and embedding change initiatives in the non-profit and public sector in the UK. She has supported thousands of individuals, from chief executives to catering staff, through significant change in a number of major public institutions including the Houses of Parliament and the Financial Ombudsman Service. In 2006 Nicola was awarded a scholarship to study for an MBA at the University of Westminster for which she was awarded a distinction.

Contact: **njbusby@googlemail.com** or on LinkedIn.

Chapter 8

Ira Blake

Ira has expertise in transformational change, specializing in organization effectiveness and capability. Over 13 years, Ira has led change initiatives in multiple industries including pharmaceuticals, not-for-profit, central and local government, retail banking, travel, retail and transport. She has worked as an internal consultant and external consultant – for a big-five consultancy and now as director of her own company. Ira is the author of *Project Managing Change* and has written articles for *Project Management News* and *Business Reporter*. Ira is an accredited change manager (ACM), MCIPD qualified and holds an MBA from Cranfield University. She is the co-lead for the Change Management Institute UK and a contributor to the first global *Change Management Body of Knowledge*.

Contact: **ira.blake@uncommonexpertise.co.uk**

Chapter 9

Richard Smith

See Chapter 1.

Chapter 10

Dan Skelsey

Dan's career as a programme manager, change manager and educator has spanned five continents. He has used facilitation as a tool in every role, and realized that this was a learnable and vital skill for all forms of management. In 2007, he established Project Laneways with a mission to provide quality learning experiences in change management, project management and related topics. He was the first to offer the APMG Facilitation Practitioner certification training in Australasia. Dan is an examiner for the APMG change management qualifications, and was one of four authors for the first global *Change Management Body of Knowledge*. He has a Masters from Cambridge and is a graduate of the Australian Institute of Company Directors.

Contact: **dan.skelsey@project-laneways.com.au**

Chapter 11

Helen Campbell

Helen specializes in building organizational change capability in project, business and leadership teams. She has worked in the UK, Europe and Australia managing a wide range of changes, from a terrorist bombing to anti-money-laundering regulation. She is a Master-accredited change manager and has specialized in change management for over 15 years in private, public and not-for-profit sector clients such as Ernst & Young, BT Financial Group, NSW Government, British Telecom, NatWest Bank and Westpac. Helen is co-founder and chief assessor for the Change Management Institute. She is author of *Managing Organizational Change* (Kogan Page, London, May 2014) (**www.cycleofchangemodel.com**), was a guest lecturer at University of Sydney and is frequently invited to speak at conferences and on expert panels.

Contact: **helen@catalyst-solutions.com.au**

Chapter 12

Ray Wicks

Ray's consultancy career has been focused on designing and facilitating leadership and management development solutions. His particular expertise is in helping leaders and managers to understand and deal with the people side of change. He is accredited to train trainers in transition management (William Bridges), which provides perspectives in helping organizations to successfully implement their change agendas. Ray's consulting work has taken him to 23 countries across Europe, North America, Asia and Australia, working across a range of organizations, sectors and cultures.

Contact: **ray.wicks1@btinternet.com**

Chapter 13

Tim Cole, Martin Lunn, Una McGarvie and Eric Rouhof

Tim Cole

Following a degree in accountancy and training as a chartered accountant, Tim's career has focused on the development and assessment of people. He has used business and financial simulations as a key methodology, offering blended learning and development and experiential assessment processes. He worked for a range of 'blue chip' multinational organizations before establishing and directing niche consulting practices aimed at recognizing and nurturing talent. His consulting work has taken him to around 40 countries across most continents, working with global clients as diverse as Unilever, Heinz, Cazenove and Rolls-Royce, as well as with many local businesses. Tim also provides global search and recruitment services, and coaches individuals on personal marketing and career matters.

Contact: **tim@timcole.com**

Martin Lunn

Martin has worked in manufacturing engineering and subsequently in operations management for more than 20 years. He has experience in automotive, service and distribution industries. Now working for GKN plc as a global continuous improvement leader Martin works with leadership teams from 140 sites across the world. He provides support in all aspects of lean deployment, covering strategy and vision, lean education and implementation support in the areas of production, business process and employee involvement.

Contact: **martin.lunn@gkn.com**

Una McGarvie

Una's career has focused on the challenges of managing organizational change, including advising major change programmes on the impact of change from a HR perspective. Her experience includes delivery of a variety of transformational change initiatives including national police IT systems, government policy, employee engagement, procurement, mergers and organizational redesign. She is a director of Connecting the Dots Ltd, providing learning and consultancy across a range of sectors including coaching senior leaders of major UK government change programmes. She has an MSc in Project Management, a post-graduate qualification in Leadership and is a member of the APM, BCS, CMI and European Mentoring and Coaching Council. Una is also a Chartered Fellow of the CIPD.

Contact: **una@connectingdots.co.uk**

Eric Rouhof

Eric is a passionate SHE professional with Masters degrees in Chemical Engineering and SHE Management. He respects the paradox of SHE Management: it is by nature a form of risk management, but it is also a value – 'nobody gets hurt here'. For him, the key to sustainable SHE results is to win the 'hearts and minds' of employees, while ensuring that management defines appropriate norms and values. Eric's functional experience includes research and development, project management and plant management. Currently 'Director Quality and SHE' at a life sciences and material sciences multinational, he covers sites in Europe, America and Asia. Eric also runs a small SHE consultancy, serving various industry sectors, including hospital patient safety.

Contact: **rouhofconsultinggroup@gmail.com**

A change management perspective

01

RICHARD SMITH

Introduction

Change is a necessity for survival. This was brought home to me many years ago as I read Charles Handy's book *The Empty Raincoat: Making sense of the future* (Handy, 1994). He describes a pattern, the 'sigmoid curve' (shaped somewhat like a Greek letter 's': see Figure 1.1). It is a classic life cycle that traces the stumbling start, the rise and success, and the eventual decay of empires, organizations, products, processes and even an individual person or career. Handy points out that the timescale is becoming ever more compressed. 'New' products, processes, organizations and initiatives rise and decay at an ever-faster rate.

FIGURE 1.1 The sigmoid curve

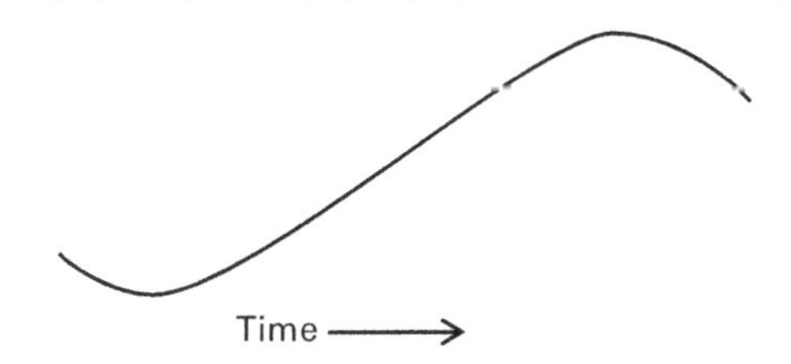

SOURCE: From *The Empty Raincoat* by Charles Handy, published by Hutchinson. Reprinted by permission of The Random House Group Limited.

This sounds depressing, but change is possible (Figure 1.2). A new curve can be begun. As Handy puts it: 'The right place to start that second curve is at point A, where there is the time, as well as the resources and the energy to get the new curve through its initial explorations and floundering before the first curve begins to dip downwards.' The difficulty is that at point A there is no apparent and urgent need for change. That tends to come at point B, when disaster is imminent. By this stage, however, the time, energy and resources to support the needed 'new beginning' are no longer available.

FIGURE 1.2 The sigmoid curve – the second curve

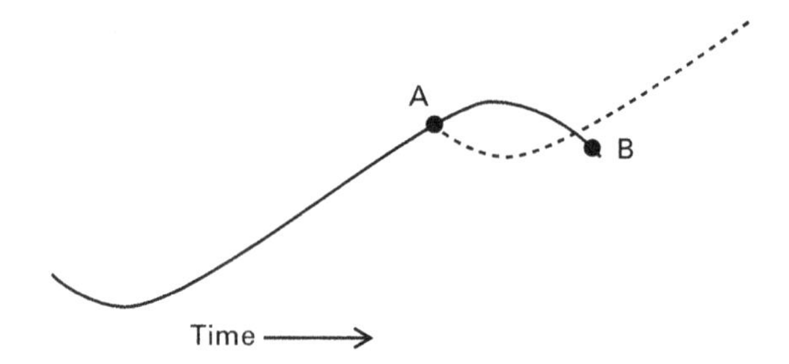

SOURCE: From *The Empty Raincoat* by Charles Handy, published by Hutchinson. Reprinted by permission of The Random House Group Limited.

So as we begin our thinking about organizational change, we recognize the necessity of a restless searching for change that will enable the health and success of an organization – and its people – to be continually renewed as it transfers from one sigmoid curve to the next... and the next.

This chapter is the least 'handbook-like' of the 13 chapters in this book. Other chapters will each take a particular aspect of the discipline of change management and explore it practically, offering tools, templates and techniques to help the practising change manager perform effectively. This chapter offers no tools and few prescriptions (some may have slipped in through lack of self-restraint by the author!). Its purpose is to set a context for the discipline of change management, based on the wide and growing body of published research and thinking.

The chapter introduces a selection of influential models and perspectives on change. These are drawn from the wide and still-growing body of research and thought about change since the mid-20th century. All of us involved in change management have our favourite approaches and models – and it is inevitable that those I have selected and referred to will miss some of the favourites of each reader. My hope is that the way I have described and presented this selection will encourage readers to explore further, using the references to build their own change management perspective.

CHAPTER CONTENTS

Section A: Why change management matters

Introduction

This section sets out to assess why effective change management is important. It describes 'the knowledge required to offer clear, concise and well-evidenced information about the role of effective change management in enabling successful change in organizations' (CMI CMBoK, 2013).

I shall mention some of the research showing how often and how seriously change initiatives fail. More encouragingly I outline key research findings that show how a range of factors can be managed to increase the chances of successful change. The research offers change managers valuable evidence to use when advocating good practice.

1. Organizations' experiences of change

It is easy for leaders and managers in organizations to assume that change is straightforward. We are educated and trained to approach problems logically and rationally. We see an opportunity to make an improvement – large or small – and can formulate plans to make that improvement.

It sometimes comes as a shock that our wholly rational plan does not meet with the immediate approval (and applause) of colleagues. A greater shock awaits; having convinced colleagues that the plan is absolutely what is needed, it simply does not work in practice. So many structural, technical and organizational factors seem to resist progress that implementation, we say, feels like 'wading through treacle'. Within a few months the plan is consigned to history and the organization continues as before.

This is a caricature, of course. However, like any caricature it contains elements of the experience of many managers and leaders. Research over several decades records a depressingly high failure rate for change initiatives. Failure rates of change initiatives – more particularly, where change achieves substantially less than the expected value – have been reported as high as 70–80 per cent (King and Peterson, 2007). However, a few top-performing organizations experience success rates in excess of 80 per cent (IBM, 2008b). The variable criteria and measures typically used in these studies make it difficult to draw definitive conclusions about the failure rates and their causes (Hughes, 2011). Nevertheless, the continuing consistent, accumulated evidence from CEOs, project and change managers through a wide range of sources does point to the reality that very many change efforts do fail.

Further reading

Research on the successes and failures of change initiatives includes:

Beer, M and Nohria, N (2000) *Cracking the code of change*

Hughes, M (2011) *Do 70 per cent of all organizational change initiatives really fail?*

IBM (2008b) *Making Change Work*

King, S and Peterson, L (2007) *How effective leaders achieve success in critical change initiatives*

Laclair, JA and Rao, RP (2002) *Helping employees embrace change*

Kotter, JP (1995) *Leading change: why transformation efforts fail*

Moorhouse Consulting (2013) *Barometer on Change 2013*

2. Factors contributing to success in change management

2.1 What the research suggests

The failure of many change initiatives to deliver what they promise is serious, but not inevitable. There is a strong and growing body of evidence that demonstrates the value of well-established change management practices in improving the success rate:

- A study by Laclair and Rao (2002) found a close relationship between 12 change management factors (at three levels: senior, mid- and front line) and the value captured from change initiatives. Companies effective at all three levels captured an average of 143 per cent of the expected value. Laclair and Rao measured general management factors that, followed effectively, contribute powerfully to success. Examples include executive and line management fulfilling their functions effectively and providing training, resource and empowerment for the front line.
- PriceWaterhouseCoopers published a study (PwC, 2004) on project and programme management practices. They conclude, amongst other things: 'The survey reveals an undeniable correlation between project performance, maturity level and change management. The majority of the best performing and most mature organisations always or frequently apply change management to their projects.' This highlights the need for alignment of change and project management practices and for ensuring appropriate organizational structure.
- An IBM study (2008b) highlights four key activities that make change effective:
  - prepare by gaining deep, realistic insight into the complexity of the change, and plan accordingly;

  - use a robust change methodology aligned with a project management methodology;
  - build and apply skills in sponsors, change managers and empowered staff;
  - invest appropriately in change management.

  They also found that the success rate of change projects using a dedicated change manager rose by 19 per cent compared to those that did not.

- Prosci studies over several years (Prosci, 2012) have demonstrated a close relationship between effectiveness of change management programmes and the proportion of projects that meet or exceed objectives. Those change management programmes rated 'good' or 'excellent' had an above 80 per cent success rate. Those rated 'poor' or 'fair' achieve less than 50 per cent. They highlight particularly the importance for change success of effective sponsorship, consistent communication, appropriate methodology, properly resourced change support and employee engagement.
- A paper on the change management of IT service management projects (Ferris, 2013) points out that project management as such is not the reason why many such initiatives fail. She writes: 'There is no consideration given to the need for an organisational change management (OCM) capability on the project that will ensure the changes being brought about through the introduction of new technology become truly embedded into the organisation.' Ferris says that for these initiatives effective change management delivers improved adoption speed, utilization rate and employee proficiency. She stresses the importance of effective preparation for change, disciplined management, clear reinforcement and careful handover.
- A study of over 2,500 people in change management roles across 120 organizations was conducted by ChangeFirst Limited in 2010. It found that six to nine months after project launch, projects with change management input were delivering significant performance improvements, financial results and behavioural change. A majority of the respondents attributed over 20 per cent of the success directly to effective change management. The calculated return on investment (ROI) on large projects was calculated as a 650 per cent return on current levels of investment in change management.
- A number of the studies demonstrated that consistent application of an appropriate methodology was a further factor consistently associated with greater success.

2.2 Improving success rates

This book is dedicated to sharing the kinds of insights and practices that lead to these improvements in success rates, especially:

- The need for the organization's executive leadership (or an equivalent local group relevant to more localized change) to define and understand deeply:
  - the nature and impact of a proposed change;
  - the organization's capacity and capability to undertake it.

- The importance of clarity about the various ways in which the organization expects to benefit from the change.
- The way that stakeholders are identified and strongly connected to the change through a variety of communication practices.
- The way that change and project management practices are aligned and managed, making them appropriate to the size and structure of the organization.
- How individuals and teams can be supported through the change by good leadership, appropriate training and great facilitation.
- Advocacy of best practice across the organization, supported by effective information gathering, relevant case studies and application of lessons learned from past change initiatives.

2.3 Change and the organizational context

Balogun and Hope Hailey (2008) describe what they call the 'design choices' to be considered in planning a change:

- *Change path*: will the change be introduced 'overnight' or as a journey over a period of time?
- *Change start-point*: will it roll out following the hierarchy (up or down), or grow from local 'pockets'?
- *Change style*: will it be introduced more directively or more collaboratively?
- *Change target*: does it focus on performance, people or culture?
- *Change levers*: what levers will be most appropriate? (See the McKinsey '7-S model' in Chapter 6, Section A1.2.)
- *Change roles*: who will sponsor and support the change, and how?

These choices cannot be made appropriately if considering the change in isolation. The change exists in a particular organizational context, and there are many factors in that wider context that should shape the design choices for a change process. Factors listed by Balogun and Hope Hailey include:

- *Power*
  How concentrated or diffuse is power in the organization? How much local or individual empowerment do people experience? What power lies with different stakeholder groups? (Chapter 4)
- *Time*
  Is the change urgent – the result of a crisis? Is it possible to take a long-term view? (Chapter 2)
- *Scope*
  How widespread is the change? What are its impacts? (Chapter 6)
- *Preservation*
  What elements of the past should be preserved? Which must be destroyed? (Consider physical icons, such as buildings, locations and technologies, and

intangibles such as values, ways of working and relationship networks.) (Section B and Chapter 11)

- *Diversity*
  How homogeneous is the organization? Is diversity amongst people an obstacle to achieving alignment? Is inadequate diversity an obstacle to creativity and change? (Section E and Chapter 12)
- *Capability*
  Do individuals have the range of skills required, both for the change process and for the demands they will face after the change? How good is the organization at managing change? Does it have access to suitably skilled people? (Chapters 7 and 9)
- *Capacity*
  Does the organization have the cash, time and people it needs for change to succeed? (Chapter 2)
- *Readiness*
  Is there a critical mass of people in the organization who see the need for change? How committed are they to change? (Chapters 5, 7 and 11)

The impact and influence of each of the contextual factors on the various design choices can be considered and documented. Informed and intentional decisions about the design choices form a strong foundation for any planned change.

However good the plans for change, it is important to retain flexibility. Good planning is vital – but mechanistic, rigid planning is dangerous, because the course of change is seldom smooth. The unexpected will occur and the plan must be adapted to accommodate both problems and opportunities that arise.

3. Preparing the organization and seeing it through

As will be seen on many occasions throughout this book, change depends on people. The earlier and more thoroughly that people across the organization (or those parts of it affected) can be prepared for the change, the more likely it is that the change will succeed.

According to Prosci (2012), with its focus on project change management, the top two 'lessons learnt' from previous change initiatives were both about preparation: 1) to get change sponsors actively involved at an earlier stage – from the very start of a project; and 2) to start change management activity sooner, right from project initiation.

For strategic change projects, however, much of the research points to change management involvement from an even earlier point. Change management input can help executive leadership to think through the context and approach to change and its implications even before explicit projects are defined.

Summary

This brief section has highlighted the difficulty of making change initiatives effective and some of the factors that can help. Change managers who know this research are better able to influence their colleagues to apply good change management practices.

Further reading

Balogun, J and Hope Hailey, V (2008) *Exploring Strategic Change*

IBM (2008b) *Making Change Work*

Prosci (2012) *Best Practices in Change Management* – or a more recent report if available

Questions to think about

1. What data do I have on the success of change initiatives in my own organization?
2. What information would help me to evaluate our change better?

Section B: Change and the individual

Introduction

This section begins by introducing two significant and widely respected models of individual change. Both offer insights into change as a human process, and have direct, practical application for those seeking to lead and manage change. It then introduces other reasons why people may embrace or resist change – the impact of motivations and of personality – before concluding with some wider observations about resistance to change.

1. The impact of the 'change curve'

One very helpful way of understanding the process of change for individuals or groups is the 'change curve', also sometimes referred to as the 'transition curve', the 'coping cycle' or the 'human response to change'. It derives from the work of Elisabeth Kübler-Ross (1969) who observed people in the process of coping with death and bereavement. All change involves the elements of letting go of the past and engaging with a different future; as a result, the patterns she observed offer valuable insights into people facing change. Other authors – notably Adams, Hayes and Hopson (1976), and Parker and Lewis (1981) – have developed Kübler-Ross's thinking for various life changes. The discussion here applies her approach in a way relevant to a variety of change situations.

Although some challenge the research applying this model to organizational situations, it remains a helpful way of looking at change. It is easily communicated and helps to explain many characteristic patterns of response observed in change processes. Figure 1.3 shows how personal performance, energy and, characteristically, mood vary through the normal process of human change.

FIGURE 1.3 The human response to change

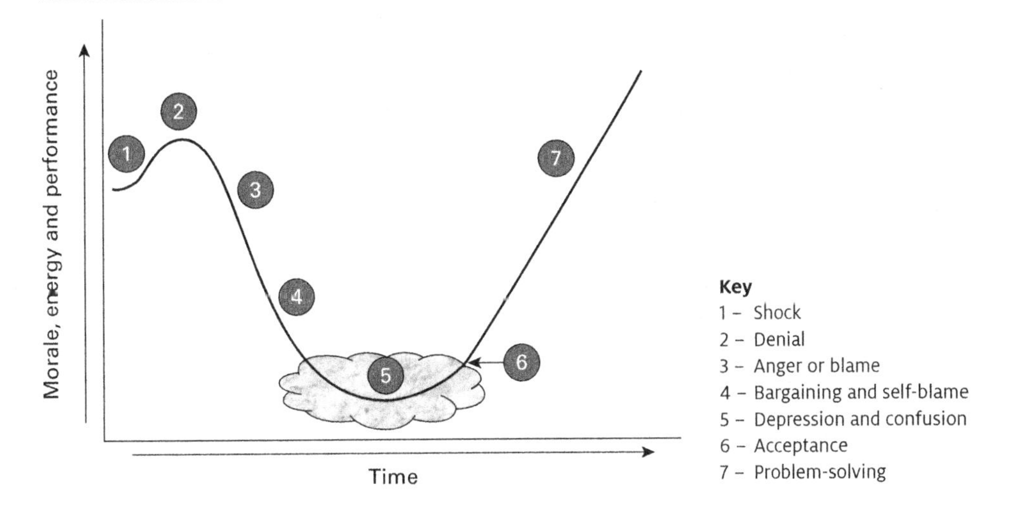

1.1 The stages of the curve

Shock and denial

After the initial 'shock' (1) of being confronted with a change, an individual (or group) often resists engaging with the change, as if trying to prove that the change is either unreal or unnecessary. This 'denial' phase (2) is characterized by a burst of additional (defensive) energy, which tends to increase temporarily both performance and mood.

The shock element is minimized by effective and early communication. If at all possible, involve people in the planning process. Once change is announced, be aware of signs that people are not taking it fully seriously, demonstrating both empathy and firmness of resolve.

Anger and blame

Assuming the change is real and will continue there comes a point at which those experiencing the change can no longer avoid engaging with it. At this point denial often gives way to anger or blame (3). The idea that 'It's not fair!' may take hold. 'The management', 'the market', 'the people in suits' – always 'they' – are blamed for the change.

This is a time for empathy, and for helping people to consider realistically the impact that the changes will have on them individually. Don't try to minimize the losses that people will experience – they need to know that the cost of the change to them personally has been well understood.

Bargaining and self-blame

As mood and performance decline further, blame may turn towards self, and elements of bargaining emerge (4). In fear of bereavement, people try to do deals with God to preserve the life of their loved one. Faced with imminent redundancy, people may take on additional work to delay or avert the threat.

Personal support and empathy remain important. An effective response will include effective line management, sharing concerns in peer groups and opportunities to contribute to planning how changes are implemented. Good active listening can be a powerful tool to help people deal with any unwelcome consequences of change.

Depression and confusion

The process to this point has been characterized by a drive to hold on to – or to revert to – the existing or former situation. Energy, morale and performance may fluctuate – but all relate to the 'downswing' side of the curve, between anger/blaming others and self-blame/bargaining. The realization that all such efforts are failing leaves people at their lowest point of performance, energy and morale. Confusion, sadness, even depression are characteristics of this period (5). Empathy, active listening and good support structures are probably the most effective responses to this phase of change.

Acceptance and problem solving

For someone to come through this period requires a point of acceptance. It is a point at which the person accepts at a deep level that change is happening and resolves to address this 'new future' (6). For significant changes, a person may not reach this point quickly – and in some cases may not reach it at all – but no real future-oriented behaviour will begin until there is true acceptance of what has changed. This insight is like the first light of dawn, by which individuals see that they have a future beyond the change.

Following this point, people begin to engage in problem-solving behaviour (7): how I live without my loved one, how I can find a new job, how I can configure this new work system to make my life easier. This allows people to try out new approaches, make new discoveries and eventually to integrate these into their new 'way of being'.

1.2 Practical observations for leading and managing change

1. People sometimes get stuck in one stage, or oscillate between two – often around 'blame'. Sometimes people regress through this process. However, the stages it describes – where people progress through them – are normal human responses to change and should be respected as such.
2. The length and depth of the personal change curve can be anything from a brief and minor 'wobble' (fluctuation) to a major 'roller-coaster' lasting for months. Some factors that tend to affect this length and depth – and the probability of emerging successfully on the upside – include:
   - How deeply an individual is affected by the change. Understanding the change from the perspectives of various stakeholders and stakeholder groups is therefore critical, so that the impact on each can be calibrated.
   - The personal confidence and resilience of the individual. The contribution of supervisors and local line managers is vital. They are best placed to assess how different people are likely to handle the level of change expected.
   - The interaction between one change and another in the life of an individual. Someone who possesses a stable and strong network of friends and family may cope with redundancy better than another person who is currently undergoing a messy family breakup. Again, if supervisors and line managers know their people well, they can help to asses such impacts.
   - How much control or influence people feel they have over the change. This is why involving people as early as possible, and as deeply as possible, improves the prospects for successful change. Note that this may go a long way towards explaining the relatively small disturbance that follows 'positive changes'; in many cases these are changes that we have initiated ourselves and feel more in control of.
3. The change curve is a function of time. Some apparent 'resistance' simply reflects a difference between the position of those announcing a change and those receiving it. Those announcing the change have had a greater involvement in the process to this point, so their personal change curve is shallower and shorter. They have also had more time to process the impact of change on themselves, so are typically further through the curve. At the point of announcement those receiving the change are right at the start of their curve. Judging their early reactions too harshly as 'inappropriate resistance' simply fails to recognize the natural process of human change.
4. When people become angry about the change in general, or about particular aspects of it, and when they blame those announcing the change they are (at least in part) expressing their own process of adjustment to the change. Of course, all feedback should be listened to and taken seriously – but anger

and blame from the recipients of change are not necessarily evidence that change is being managed badly. It is wise not to take such anger and blame too personally!

5 It is important to note that this characteristic pattern of human response to change remains true for the positive changes in life as well as for unwelcome ones. Most people who have accepted a new 'dream job' will be able to trace their experience over the first six months through this curve! Of course not everyone will experience these things in exactly the same way, but many will recognize – from their own experience – elements of these descriptions.

Tip

The change curve is a personal journey. Don't expect all members of a peer group to experience change in the manner of synchronized swimmers! Different personalities, different life experiences, different personal circumstances at the time of the change – all these and more will affect the way that different individuals respond – and how quickly.

2. Starting with 'endings'

The second of our two models of individual change was developed in the early 1990s by William Bridges. In his book *Managing Transitions* Bridges (2009) makes a key distinction between 'change' and 'transition':

Change: the actual events, activities and steps that can be put into a diary or project plan.

Transition: the human, psychological process of letting go of one pattern and engaging with a new one.

It is clear from the discussion of the change curve that 'transition' will be a personal process. People will vary as to how quickly they will be ready to let go of the past and truly engage with a new future. Bridges describes three phases (or as he later says, processes) that have to be completed in order for personal transition to be successful (Figure 1.4). He summarizes these phases in this way (my italics):

1 Letting go of the old ways and the old identity people had. This first phase of transition is an *ending*, and the time when you need to help people to deal with their losses.

2 Going through an in-between time when the old is gone but the new isn't fully operational. We call this time the '*neutral zone*': it is when the critical psychological realignments and repatternings take place.

3 Coming out of the transition and making a *new beginning*. This is when people develop the new identity, experience the new energy, and discover the new sense of purpose that make the change begin to work.

(Bridges, 2009)

FIGURE 1.4 Bridges' stages of transition

It will be clear how closely this 'transition' process mirrors the change curve described above. It is also helpful to notice two key developments that Bridges' thinking highlights. First, he sees these three 'phases' as sequential but overlapping processes: each of these needs attention at the right time, to ensure that planned changes are actually implemented by people. These processes are explored in more detail below. Second, he focuses on the creative potential of the 'neutral zone', not just as a time of confusion and depression but as a time when there is sufficient fluidity for experimentation, a time when genuinely new attitudes and behaviours can be developed.

2.1 Endings

The principal business of this stage is for people to be clear about what particular details of their working life will come to an end as a result of the change. To 'let go' of something I must first realize that I'm holding it. Things to consider, for example:

- The people in the work process – upstream and downstream – may be different.
- Communication may be more through clicks on a screen, less by telephone.
- The location of desks and the community around the coffee machine may change.

These issues and many like them are easily forgotten as we debate change strategies – but each is an ending for those affected. Some (not necessarily all) will feel like losses.

Tip

You can ask people to help you identify endings and losses: 'What would change for you if we...?'

The advice offered by Bridges to managers and leaders on how to help people through this process of *'letting go of the old ways and the old identity people had'* would include:

- Describe the change in very specific terms, so that people are clear what precisely will be different.
- Do not dismiss as trivial *anything* that people are losing. Acknowledge them as losses – large and small – with genuine empathy.
- Let people know what will *not* change. For example, a statement that existing workgroups will be kept close together in the new office configuration may make a big difference to the people in those groups.
- Identify the reasons why the current situation cannot continue. There will be gains amongst the losses.

CASE STUDY

A food company was automating a packing line, which would require only one operator after the change instead of 17 prior to the change. This would clearly break up established work groups, but guarantees were given to affected staff about continuity of employment. Further commitments were given that posts on the new, technologically advanced line would be filled from existing junior staff, who would be provided with the training required.

- Don't confuse problems that people raise about the content of the change with those arising from people going through the change process. Problems raised about the content are valuable input and will improve the change.
- Show respect for all that has gone before. Help people to see how the best aspects of the past – its successes and, most importantly, its values – will be preserved and enhanced by the change.
- Communicate prodigiously. Even if you've already done so, do it again. It is difficult to communicate too much!

2.2 *Neutral zone*

Bridges coins the term 'neutral zone' for the time when those affected have let go (or made substantial progress on letting go) of the way things were. He acknowledges that this 'in-between time' is often difficult, strange, stressful and disorientating for those affected, but asserts that precisely for these reasons it opens the possibility of experimentation and for developing genuinely new patterns.

Think of the neutral zone as a journey from one place to another. Here are some implications:

- Except in science-fiction films I cannot be 'beamed' from one place to another. The journey is inevitable. However, I can choose to see any journey as a mere inconvenience – an unwelcome interruption to my life, to be kept as short as possible – or as an opportunity to look around, to learn, to see new things. Using an image such as this can help people to give meaning to this period. It can legitimize the opportunities that may occur if we look for them.
- During a journey I am likely to be 'living out of a suitcase'. My normal routines are disrupted and I need new ones to fit in with the timings of flights, transfers, overnight hotels and the inevitable delays. In adapting myself to these new routines I may learn better ways of managing myself when I am settled. In the same way, individuals and teams passing through their neutral zone need temporary solutions to the problems of transition. Some of these adaptations will prove to be useful innovations once the transition draws to a close. Notice these and celebrate them.
- A journey can be a lonely time. Encourage those in the neutral zone to connect more intentionally with other people and other teams (other travellers or those now securely arrived at their destination). Even planned social events that bring people together outside their routine work can help people to remain 'grounded'. Consider including the friends or family who are their key personal support systems.
- Providing guidance to many people on their own individual journeys can be difficult. Travel agents have helpline numbers to ensure that they receive feedback from travellers and can revise travel arrangements where necessary. When you and your people are in the neutral zone, it is very valuable to set up temporary feedback and communication systems that will ensure you know the impacts that a range of organizational decisions will have on your 'travellers'. Conventional 'chain of command' communication may not be sufficient during this period.

2.3 New beginnings

> *'Starts take place on a schedule as a result of decisions... Beginnings on the other hand are the final phase of this organic process that we call "transition," and their timing is not set by the dates written on the implementation schedule. Beginnings follow the timing of the mind and heart.'*
>
> Bridges, 2009

Making a new beginning is a risk time. It means committing to a new kind of future. Bridges recommends four things that encourage such commitment. He suggests that people need:

A *purpose* for the future after the change, which encourages people to focus on making it work.

A *picture* that will engage the creative imagination of those affected, so that they can already 'touch and feel' the positive situation after the change.

A *plan* that is credible, and that gives people a clear route to success in implementing the change.

A *part to play*, both in the execution of the plan and in the 'new world' after the change is accomplished.

Advising leaders and managers on change, Bridges suggests that making new beginnings into a reality requires:

- Consistency in behaviour and messaging from all seen as influential in the situation after the change. This includes recognizing the importance of symbolic decisions.
- Visible early successes to encourage and reassure people: make these widely known.
- Celebration of key milestones on the change journey – especially journey's end!

2.4 Summary

The human change-wisdom of William Bridges brings together many elements of practical advice found in other writers on change, and is a sound basis for coaching business change leaders on effective approaches. Bridges summarizes his thinking like this:

> Letting go, repatterning and making a new beginning: together these processes reorient and renew people when things are changing all around them. You need the transition that they add up to for the change to get under the surface of things and affect how people actually work. (Bridges, 2009)

3. Why people embrace or resist change – motivation

We have already seen that people respond to change through a psychological process of transition, and have noted that people respond differently, as individuals, to a given change. To explore these differences, we need to understand what drives or motivates people.

This is a complex field of study. In the space we can allow here, our aim will be to offer a view of the practical implications of a few key perspectives. These are drawn from foundational work on human motivation dating back to the middle of the 20th century.

3.1 Maslow and the hierarchy of needs

Many people have come across Maslow's concept of the 'hierarchy of needs' (Maslow, 1943) either in academic studies or in business settings.

As shown in Figure 1.5, Maslow suggested that people have five 'basic needs':

- At the most basic level people need food, water, sleep and shelter – the *physiological needs*.
- *Safety needs* (sometimes called 'security needs') represent the need for an orderly, secure world with a low level of perceived threat to life and the future. This includes the reasonable expectation that my physiological needs will be met tomorrow as well as today. It is symbolized for many in personal and work routines.
- Maslow refers to the next level of his hierarchy as '*love needs*' (sometimes called 'social needs'). By this he means the craving for love, affection, social interaction and 'belongingness'.
- *Esteem needs* are satisfied by a combination of self-esteem, strongly anchored in real achievements and capabilities, and respect and recognition from others, together with the status this frequently grants. These support self-confidence and feelings of self-worth.
- Maslow's final 'basic need' is expressed as a '*need for self-actualization*'. This is a desire to 'be the best that I can be', a longing to fulfil my potential and to use my creativity in accordance with my particular talents. Maslow writes: 'A musician must make music, an artist must paint, a poet must write... to be ultimately happy. This need we may call self-actualization.'

FIGURE 1.5 A hierarchy of needs (Maslow, 1943)

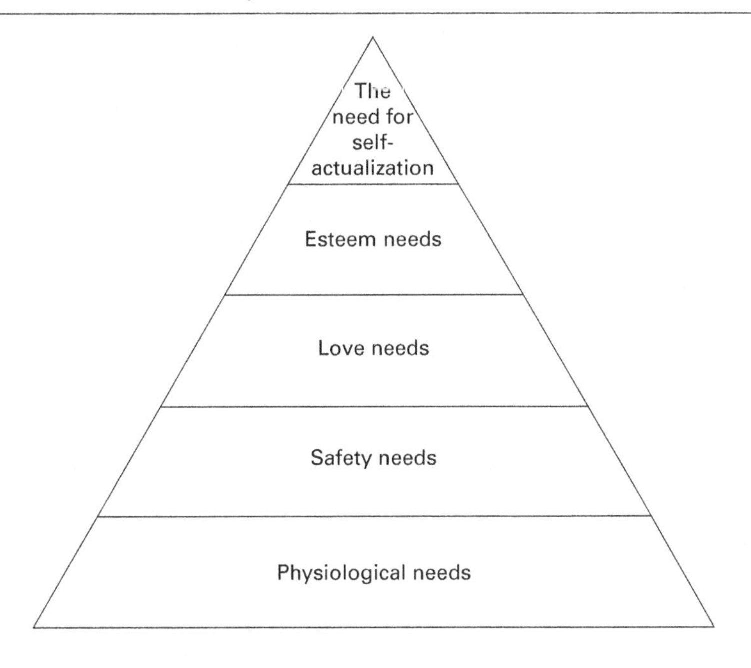

The point that Maslow makes about these basic needs is that they tend to be hierarchically ordered. That is, it is only after physiological needs are sufficiently satisfied that individual concern focuses on safety needs and so on up the hierarchy. In other words, a lower-level need has power to motivate behaviour until it is sufficiently satisfied, then the next higher category of need tends to take over.

Tip

Work – at its best – has the possibility of addressing all these 'basic needs'. In view of our earlier discussion about 'endings' this framework can be used by leaders and managers to assess the likely impacts of endings and losses on different people.

3.2 *Rewards and punishments*

Early experiments with animal models were based on simple ideas about modifying behaviour using schedules of reward and punishment. Some of these are described briefly in Chapter 9, Section A. 'Rewards' were usually food items, and punishments typically mild electric shocks or cold water. Some key conclusions can be summarized thus:

- A specific behaviour that is rewarded tends to be repeated more frequently, but when the pattern of rewarding the behaviour is withdrawn, frequency tends to reduce.
- If a particular behaviour is rewarded only sometimes (say one time in three), the frequency of the behaviour tends to increase more slowly, but it also dies away more slowly when the reward schedule is withdrawn.
- Punishment associated with a specific behaviour tends to reduce the frequency of that behaviour, but less strongly than rewarding an alternative behaviour.

Clearly this way of thinking is associated strongly with the physiological and safety needs. This 'behaviourist' approach to reward schedules tended to lead to a simplistic view of how to get people to behave in a particular way: reward it and/or punish the alternatives. Although a 21st-century Western culture rebels at the thought, much of our thinking about motivation is still influenced by such models – consider the prevalence of 'performance-related pay'. However, it remains true that human motivation, while it includes responses to reward and punishment, is much more complex than this model suggests.

3.3 *People are not the same as experimental animals*

There are, of course, dangers in taking animal experiments and applying the results to people. One 'thread' of psychological research that explores the importance of thinking in specifically human motivation is known as 'expectancy theory'. The originators of this theory include Edward Tolman and Victor Vroom, and a clear outline of their thinking is set out in Huczinsky and Buchanan (2007).

The idea is that the motivating force to do anything is a function of three things:

- how much I value a particular outcome (this '*valency*' could of course be negative as well as positive!);
- how strongly I believe that my efforts will lead to good performance ('*expectancy*') – notice that this is a personal and subjective judgement;
- how strongly I believe that good performance by me will lead to rewarding outcomes ('*instrumentality*') – another personal and subjective judgement.

In a change situation, understanding the value (positive or negative) of the change from the perspective of different stakeholders is important. It is also important to do all that is possible to influence the strength of their belief that their discretionary effort can affect their performance, and that their performance can affect the outcome of the change. If the change has positive value to the stakeholders, this encourages their belief that they can make a difference. If the stakeholders concerned believe the change to be 'the work of the devil', the less they believe they can make a difference, the better! An application of expectancy theory is described in Chapter 7, Section A2.

3.4 Satisfaction and growth

Frederick Herzberg famously researched job satisfaction as a component of human motivation (Herzberg, 2003). He and his team interviewed hundreds of people, asking them to describe critical incidents that had led them to feel good about their work. The results of these interviews produced a list of factors that lead to positive job satisfaction such as that shown on the right in Table 1.1 (approximately in that order of significance). The research team also asked the reverse question: what had led people to feel less satisfied with their jobs? The results of these enquiries are listed on the left in Table 1.1.

What Herzberg and his colleagues noticed was that 'dissatisfiers' were different in kind to the 'satisfiers'. Dissatisfiers were all about the context of the job ('extrinsic'), whilst the satisfiers were in various ways built into the job itself ('intrinsic'). He also noted that beyond a certain level, the dissatisfiers could no more create positive motivation than good drains could create positive health. If in poor condition they lead to poor outcomes, but in themselves they do not create good ones. Satisfiers, on the other hand, were directly associated with job satisfaction and increased motivation to work.

The implications of Herzberg's work caused some large organizations to restructure jobs. They moved away from production-line thinking towards autonomous work groups that followed a product through the production process, seeing the completed results of their work. For our present purpose it is important to consider the impact of change initiatives on both satisfiers and dissatisfiers. Will the outcomes for key stakeholders increase dissatisfaction? Will they promote positive satisfaction?

Confirmation of Herzberg's general findings comes from the author Dan Pink (Pink, 2011 and undated pdf). He cites MIT research showing that for tasks requiring

TABLE 1.1 Hygiene factors and motivators

Factors Tending to Lead to LOWER Job Satisfaction (Dissatisfiers – 'Hygiene Factors')	Factors Tending to Lead to HIGHER Job Satisfaction (Satisfiers – 'Motivators')
• Company policy and administration • Supervision (technical quality of oversight) • Supervision (relationship with supervisor) • Working conditions • Salary • Relationship with peers • Personal life • Relationship with subordinates • Status • Security	• Achievement • Recognition • The work itself (job content) • Responsibility • Advancement (promotion) • Growth (personal/professional development)

even a modest amount of cognitive skill, increases in financial reward are not related to increased performance. Indeed the reverse may be true. This implies that organizations need to pay people sufficient that pay is no longer an issue (in Herzberg's terms, not a 'dissatisfier'), but that beyond that financial reward may have limited value. Instead, Pink suggests that there are three key motivators for 'knowledge work':

Autonomy: people like to be self-directed, with a high degree of freedom to decide the direction, methods and circumstances of their work.

Mastery: people like to do things well, and to get better at doing things they value, so opportunities to grow, develop and excel at their work are intrinsically motivating.

Purpose: people like to feel that their work has meaning and value, and will choose to invest themselves in activities they consider worthwhile.

Tip

Any change initiative run in a way that encourages autonomy, mastery and purpose will be more likely to motivate people and engage their discretionary effort.

3.5 Theory X and theory Y

Douglas McGregor posed a key question (McGregor, 1960): 'What are your assumptions (implicit as well as explicit) about the most effective way to manage people?' He answered this question by outlining two different sets of assumptions that he observed in practice – and to avoid labelling them in any prejudicial way he simply called them 'theory X' and 'theory Y', labels that they have had ever since.

Table 1.2 summarizes these two contrasting sets of assumptions, which are both based on the premise that 'management is responsible for organizing the elements of productive enterprise... in the interest of economic ends' (McGregor, 1957).

TABLE 1.2 Theory X and Theory Y (based on McGregor, 1957)

Theory X	Theory Y
1 Human behaviour must be externally controlled.	**1** People can be self-controlled and self-directed.
2 Management must direct, motivate and control people and their behaviour.	**2** Motivation is a built-in human characteristic that managers can recognize and develop.
3 Most people are not very clever, lack ambition, dislike responsibility and prefer to be led.	**3** People have great potential for development and are capable of assuming responsibility.
4 People are lazy, work as little as possible and are passive or resistant to the organization's needs.	**4** People are not passive or resistant to organizational needs; experience of organizations may make them so.
5 Most people are self-centred, resistant to change and indifferent to organizational needs.	**5** People willingly support organizational goals, especially if these are aligned with their own.

One way of looking at McGregor's observations and conclusions is that, in general, people will tend to prove you right whichever view you hold – this is because people tend to behave according to the way they are treated, though in the long term theory Y assumptions seem to yield better results.

Most business leaders I have worked with, when asked to position their own beliefs about people on a spectrum between these two poles (as shown in Figure 1.6), place themselves much closer to theory Y than to theory X. However, presented with versions of these statements in questionnaire format, asking how they would

FIGURE 1.6 A spectrum of beliefs

respond to particular leadership situations, those same business leaders are more evenly balanced between the two poles. This suggests that under the pressure of real-life situations, behaviour and actions might not always align well with intentions and words. Trust is very important in managing change, and this illustrates the importance of ensuring that the leaders, especially senior leaders, in any change plan behave consistently with the culture and norms they espouse.

3.6 Survival and learning anxieties

Describing the process of change, Schein (1993) compares two types of anxiety as motivators of behaviour. These are learning anxiety and survival anxiety.

Most people have, through their lives, developed a level of *learning anxiety*. They have struggled with the frustration of trying to work out a problem that seems intractable. They have experienced the feeling of incompetence whilst trying to learn (or improve) a new skill – say a golf swing or yet another new version of their computer's operating system. They have made mistakes and experienced the emotional penalty as they are criticized by others. All these create a learning anxiety that makes change inherently difficult. Of course, some people have high levels of such anxiety and some much lower levels, but the experience of learning anxiety is widely shared.

Change will require unlearning old ways and learning new ones, and the result of learning anxiety is to inhibit change to a greater or lesser degree. Calling on Kurt Lewin's concept of 'unfreezing' as a part of the change process (Section C2.1 below), Schein suggests that for organizations to change at an acceptable pace, they have to learn to 'unfreeze' by creating a competing and greater anxiety – '*survival anxiety*'. Unfreezing requires three elements in order to be managed effectively:

- *Disconfirmation*: creating the disturbing belief that the current position is not sustainable, that it is not working any more.
- *Creation of guilt or anxiety*: the belief that if I do not change I shall fail to achieve my goals and that the negative consequences of this will be serious (ranging from experiencing disapproval to seeing my team disbanded, seeing the organization fail or losing my job).
- *Creation of psychological safety*: through a clear plan with suitable support and coaching. This sounds at variance with the two preceding elements, and is designed to prevent the 'survival anxiety' becoming too great, leaving people paralysed by anxiety. It offers a safe way forward.

To motivate people to make a desired change, it is necessary to create sufficient survival anxiety to destabilize the current situation and drive them forward. At the same time it is necessary to support people in such a way that they feel safe enough to learn effectively – that their learning anxiety (which would hold them back) is kept as low as possible, and certainly lower than the survival anxiety. This psychological safety is created through provision of:

- training and practice;
- support and encouragement;

- a non-judgemental approach that does not punish errors;
- coaching;
- acknowledgement and reward for effort in the right direction and for experimentation.

Tip

Organization leaders can model the norms of trying things differently, not judging one another, and accepting feedback, training and coaching. This considerably increases the sense of psychological safety and encourages others in the organization to engage with change.

3.7 Personal growth

In Maslow's hierarchy, the highest level is represented by 'self-actualization', which represents the need people have for personal development and growth. Carl Rogers studied the conditions that facilitate personal growth. In his work as a clinical psychologist he discovered that what most helped clients move forward in their lives was a particular quality of relationship. This is summed up by his three 'core conditions' for personal growth and change (Rogers, 1957):

- *Congruence:* being authentic and genuine in the relationship. This means being aware enough of one's own thoughts and feelings that people experience integrity – that they can trust you.
- *Unconditional positive regard:* an attitude of acceptance of and respect for a person as he or she is, without judgement and without suggesting conditions or expectations to make them 'acceptable'.
- *Empathy:* a willingness to understand another person within his or her own frame of reference, communicating by word and action that one understands their thoughts and feelings.

Rogers's initial interest was in the context of psychotherapy, but he also applied his ideas about this quality of relationship in group work, the field of education and in the wider world of politics. Notably, Rogers held gatherings of both sides in conflict situations, specifically in South Africa and Northern Ireland, where people were able to begin to hear one another's points of view in a safe environment.

For any leader or manager of people through change, or for any agent of change, offering these 'core conditions' to colleagues and subordinates will play a major part in creating the psychological safety discussed by Schein, and as a result will support people in making the personal changes upon which the success of the wider change initiative will depend.

4. Why people embrace or resist change – individual differences

We have explored some aspects of motivation and how this can affect the willingness of people to embrace change. Understanding these aspects is part of a picture. At a deeper level people seem to be 'wired' differently from each other. What we may describe as 'personality' or 'temperament' means that one person will react to change in a way that differs systematically from the way another person will respond.

Understanding some of these systematic differences between people allows us to manage our relationships with a wide range of people more effectively. This understanding can inform the content, styles and channels of communication that we choose, enabling us to connect effectively with as many people as possible. It can also help us to interpret the responses we receive more appropriately.

Two particular ways of describing the differences between people are highlighted below: people of different 'types' and the recognition of different 'learning styles'. In neither case will our comments here make you an 'expert' in the tools concerned. They are intended to offer some practical points to consider, based on the particular tools, and to show the wider value of having such a framework to use in leading or managing change.

4.1 People of different 'types'

The best known example of 'type' theory is based on original research by the psychologist Carl Jung, and made operational through a psychological questionnaire, the Myers-Briggs Type Indicator® (MBTI®). This instrument is available only to qualified users; those who wish to explore the use of this tool are advised to seek appropriate training and accreditation. However, the model that underlies the MBTI® offers valuable insights into the behaviour we see around us and is described below. The Myers & Briggs Foundation website is a further source of information (**http://www.myersbriggs.org**).

The MBTI® model is based on four pairs of opposite 'preferences' that people show. In each case, neither preference is better than its opposite; they simply lead to different choices. The analogy of being right- or left-handed is often used: we can do most things with either hand, but one feels more comfortable than the other, and through regular use has become stronger. The four pairs of preferences (described in more detail in Table 1.3) are:

- Extravert – Introvert (abbreviated as 'E' or 'I').

  NOTE: This description is not the same as the way these terms are often used. Commonly we judge people to be extraverts by the way they *use* their energy – for example to be the 'life and soul of the party'. In terms of this model, the question is 'where do I *gain* energy from?' Either an introvert or an extravert can choose to act as the life and soul of a party, but the extravert would be energized by doing so whilst the introvert would be drained and need time alone to recover energy.

- Sensing – iNtuiting (abbreviated as 'S' or 'N' – the N avoids confusion with 'Introvert').

TABLE 1.3 A summary of types

Extravert – Introvert (abbreviated as 'E' or 'I')	
E people are energized by the external world: • Like talking to people/being sociable • Like to learn by activity and talk • Lots of interests • Speak first, think about it later • Like starting new things	**I** people are energized by their own inner world: • Enjoy their own thoughts and feelings • Prefer writing to express ideas • A reflective learner • Fewer, more serious interests • Think before they speak
Sensing – iNtuiting (abbreviated as 'S' or 'N' – the N avoids confusion with 'Introvert')	
S people focus on sensory data: • Focus on what their senses tell them • Pay attention to definite, detailed facts • Notice things in an orderly way • Like getting information in clear stages • 'Here and now' approach, trust experience	**N** people focus on interpretations and intuitions: • A 'big picture' person • Enjoy concepts and theory • Look behind facts for meaning • Future-oriented • Willing to trust intuitions
Thinking – Feeling (abbreviated as 'T' or 'F')	
T people make decisions through rational thought: • Treating problems with logic • Cause-and-effect reasoning • Tough minded • Look for the objectively 'right' answer • Appreciate just solutions	**F** people make decisions through sensitive feelings: • With empathy/consideration for others • With compassion • Based on values and beliefs • Seeking a widely accepted outcome • Open to and accepting of others
Judging – Perceiving (abbreviated as 'J' or 'P')	
J people prefer situations to be 'cut and dried' and clear: • Working to a timetable • Systematic and methodical • Like to plan • Appreciate 'closure' on decisions • Dislike the pressure of leaving things late	**P** people prefer more 'open-ended' ambiguous situations: • Spontaneous • Happy with ambiguity • Like to be flexible and adaptable • Dislike restrictive systems, detailed plans • Positively enjoy 'urgent' work

SOURCE: Modified and reproduced by special permission of the Publisher, CPP, Inc, Mountain View, CA 94043 from *Introduction to Type*, Sixth Edition by Isabel Briggs Myers.

- Thinking – Feeling (abbreviated as 'T' or 'F').
- Judging – Perceiving (abbreviated as 'J' or 'P').

NOTE: The use of the term 'Judging' here does not have the negative connotation it sometimes has in everyday speech. It is used here to describe someone with a preference for getting decisions made, whether by head or heart, in contrast to another person who prefers to focus on exploring the available information. 'J' people focus on the *use* of information; 'P' people focus on *gathering* it.

Those who know the MBTI® instrument would take the four letters representing a person's four preferences between the individual pairs to make a summary such as ESTJ, ISTJ, ENTJ, INTJ and so on – there are 16 possible combinations. These four-letter type summaries create a rich picture of the way that someone is likely to behave across a range of situations, and towards a variety of different people. This model can help people to clarify their own preferences and to understand how they differ from other people.

Conflicts and complementarity

From the descriptions of these types it is easy to see how different people might misunderstand one another, especially when they have opposing preferences. They may end up in conflict, not because of the *content* of an issue but because of their *different ways of seeing things*. The ideal is to look for the strengths that each person can contribute to a given situation. For example, the objectivity, rationality and care for fairness of the 'Thinking' person will be of great importance to a good outcome from a meeting to discuss the impact of change on a work group. So will be the natural sense of humanity and sensitive understanding of the people involved, which will be natural to the 'Feeling' colleague. Ideally we value both, whilst respecting the different preferences from which they come. And if the two individuals can begin to understand and respect each others' contribution they could begin to make a great team.

Questions to think about

As an exercise you might like to think of the ways in which it would be different for you to plan a change initiative:

- with someone who likes to get decisions taken promptly and in an organized way (Judging) and who is also very rational, logical and objective (Thinking); or
- with someone who likes to get decisions taken promptly and in an organized way (Judging) and who is also very sensitive to people, tender hearted and compassionate (Feeling).

1. What would be the advantages of each?
2. What would be the risks?
3. How is your own set of preferences influencing your judgement?

Preferences at work in learning

People with a strong 'Sensing' preference are likely to appreciate more detailed instruction; those with an opposite 'iNtuiting' preference will prefer more open-ended approaches. Those with a strong 'Thinking' preference typically seek more rigorous logic in their learning and less personal support than those with the opposite 'Feeling' preference.

Preferences at work in change situations

Type preferences will also affect the attitude to change. For example, someone with strong 'Introvert' and 'Sensing' preferences will display a thoughtful and down-to-earth approach that supports only careful, incremental change. By contrast, a person with strong 'Extravert' and 'iNtuitive' preferences is likely to favour engaging with others in dramatic and immediate change. An 'Introverted iNtuitive' person will favour ideas and vision, whilst an 'Extraverted Sensing' person will want to organize immediate action (Hirsh and Kummerow, 1994).

Summary

The differences between people highlighted by considering personality 'type' have implications for many aspects of change. For example:

- In facilitating a working group, using a format that allows time for those who are more 'Introverted' to think before they speak will prevent their ideas being lost in the more 'in the moment' flow of ideas from the 'Extravert' members of the group. Chapter 10, Section C3 says more about working with different 'types' in a facilitation setting.
- When communicating information during a change initiative we can ensure that the big picture, the vision for the change, is clear (meeting the needs of those with an 'iNtuitive' preference), whilst providing a backup resource of data and facts (to meet the needs of those with a 'Sensing' preference).

For anyone involved in facilitating change it is important to learn to observe, engage with and get the best from a variety of people. This is a key element of ongoing personal and professional development. A framework such as that used in the MBTI® can provide a useful structure for such observations.

4.2 Learning styles

The recognition of different 'learning styles' (Honey and Mumford, 1992) offers another helpful way to think about the differences between people. Their approach is based on different preferences that people have about how they receive information and learning (described in Chapter 9, Section A3.1). When planning a change initiative, and particularly the communications and learning elements around it, this learning styles framework can act as a helpful checklist to ensure that as many people as possible are being reached through their own preferred medium of communication.

5. Why people embrace or resist change – some findings from neuroscience

FIGURE 1.7 Areas of the brain

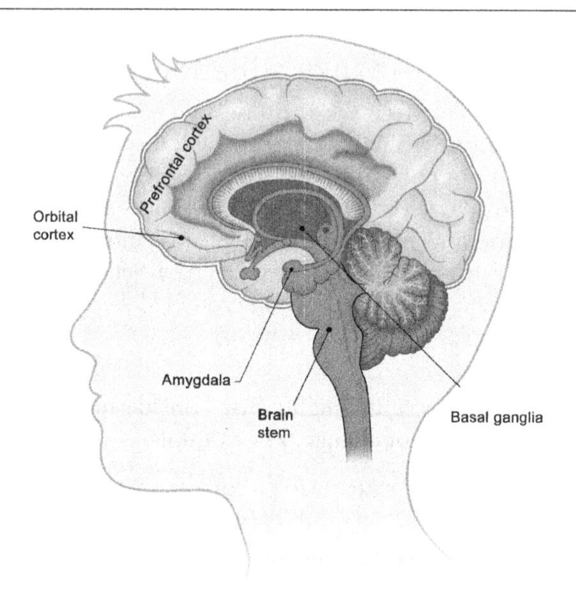

SOURCE: istockphoto.com

The findings of neuroscience are increasingly illuminating aspects of the human response to change. Here are three examples of neuroscience observations relating to change resistance:

- The area of our brain that handles tried-and-tested routines (the basal ganglia, see Figure 1.7) requires little energy to operate effectively. Much of everyday life, including working life, is run from this 'operations room'. However, it is a different part of the brain (the prefrontal cortex) that is used to process new information or options. In a change situation this area is being used very much more – and it is very energy-intensive. Continued demands upon its resources are uncomfortable – indeed we speak of 'being out of our comfort zone'. As a result we are to a degree 'hard-wired' to avoid or minimize the amount of change to which we are exposed (Rock and Schwarz, 2006).
- Human brains are particularly responsive to mismatches between actual events and what they expect – what neuroscience calls 'errors'. A period of change will create many such 'mismatch' signals from the environment. The area of the brain that generates these signals (the orbital frontal cortex) is closely connected to the part that operates the 'fight, flight or freeze' response (the amygdala). These parts of the brain requisition energy that would normally be used by the 'thinking brain' (the prefrontal cortex). This

leads to a 'double whammy': emotional (fight, flight or freeze) responses are enabled and rational thought is (at least somewhat) disabled. This helps us to understand why apparently emotional and irrational responses are common during change (Rock and Schwarz, 2006).

- Ringleb and Rock (2008) cite Ochsner and Lieberman (2001) as saying that the brain is 'deeply social'. 'Social pain', like other examples of pain or lack (physical pain, hunger, thirst) operates as 'a signal to change behaviour' and 'if... unheeded takes a toll on mind and biology' (Ringleb and Rock, 2008). Organizational changes often disrupt valued social contact, and this affects clear thinking.

Rock and Schwarz (2006) also highlight two key threads of neuroscience research relevant to helping people embrace change:

- People operate on the basis of 'mental maps' of the world around them – sets of assumptions and beliefs that guide behaviour. Changing these is difficult and requires 'lightbulb moments' – 'moments of insight' – which have been shown to create a whole web of new neural connections in the brain. These insights 'need to be generated from within, not given to individuals as conclusions'. They can open a whole range of new possibilities for people, transforming their attitude to a change. To generate lasting change we must ask insight-provoking questions rather than giving prescriptions, and we must use experiential rather than didactic learning processes to support change.
- We become what we pay attention to. The 'moments of insight' mentioned above need to be held in focus over a period of time if they are to make a permanent difference. These authors write of 'attention density', by which they mean the 'amount of attention given to a particular mental experience over a specific time'. Their point is that high attention density actually adapts and changes the internal 'wiring' of the brain so that new ways of thinking (and behaving) become natural and routine. Reminding people gently but frequently of their insights (through coaching or affirming feedback) creates permanent changes in attitudes and behaviour.

6. A word about resistance to change

Resistance to change can take many forms. Objections to proposed change may be very vocal and explicit or may be expressed in silent truculence and dissent. Symptoms may range from reluctance and underperformance, through to industrial conflict or even sabotage. Some resistance will be to the content and nature of the change, some to the process by which the change is implemented.

6.1 Individual responses to change

Cameron and Green (2012), in their book *Making Sense of Change Management*, identify five factors likely to influence an individual's response to change:

1. *The nature of the change*
   This factor includes issues such as the scale of the change, the values underlying it, the perceived purpose it is seeking to achieve, the speed with which it is applied and whether or not it is part of a series of changes.
2. *The consequences of the change*
   For most people this will not be an abstract question but a practical one: 'How will this affect me?' Clearly, change that will have greater impact on the individual – positive or negative – is likely to evoke a greater response.
3. *The organizational history*
   Fundamentally this factor is about accumulated trust. Individuals will consider past changes, and whether they consider that the organization has a good or bad record of implementing them.
4. *The type of individual*
   This relates to the personality and current motivations of an individual. People with different MBTI® profiles or different learning preferences will respond differently to change. Those whose 'basic needs' are satisfied and secure will respond differently from those for whom this is not the case.
5. *The individual history*
   The way people have experienced previous changes will also have an effect on how they respond to further change. Some will have built confidence, strength and resilience through their experiences of change, others will have felt damaged by them.

All these factors will have an impact on an individual's openness to change in general. These factors will also influence the individual's resistance (or otherwise) to a particular change.

6.2 Applying individual change theories to change resistance

The topic of resistance to change is addressed more fully in Chapter 7, Section C. However, a few summary observations are relevant here:

- Observations based on the 'change curve' tell us that people who feel involved in planning or implementing a change show a shallower and shorter decline in morale – and performance – than those who feel that change has been 'done to' them. Accordingly, resistance of all kinds is lowered.
- William Bridges' thinking about change places considerable emphasis on the skill of those leading people through the change process, helping them to identify and deal with endings, to navigate the neutral zone and to engage with the new beginnings they will experience.
- Maslow would encourage those initiating change to consider the needs or drives of those facing change. To the extent that the changes have positive or negative impacts on the satisfaction of these needs, they will provoke a greater or lesser response.
- Behaviourist thinking encourages thought about the rewards or penalties associated with change. It also warns that previous changes may have conditioned people to respond in a particular way – which may be disproportionate to the change they are currently experiencing.

- Expectancy theory suggests that engagement with or resistance to change will be impacted by the way a person values the outcome (positive or negative), and whether they believe they can make a difference to that outcome.
- Herzberg's motivation-hygiene theory suggests that change which degrades people's experience of the 'hygiene factors' will reduce their job satisfaction, and is likely to be met with resistance.
- Combined with McGregor's 'theory X' and 'theory Y', Herzberg's research and the views expressed by Pink suggest that resistance might be reduced by giving people increased autonomy and respect – the opportunity to achieve and grow, both personally and professionally.
- Rogers's writing about personal growth supports this. His writing further suggests the great value of facilitative leadership offering congruence, empathy and unconditional positive regard for people. This supports the desire people have to develop and grow, and as a result encourages a positive response to change.
- Schein's concept of 'learning anxiety' describes another potential source of resistance to change. He suggests practical ways to reduce such anxiety and the associated resistance.
- People are different – and seem to be 'wired' to respond in different ways to change. Many tools (including the MBTI™ and measures of learning styles) offer helpful frameworks for thinking about those differences. No matter how effectively we prepare for resistance to change, some people will simply resist more than others – and take more time than others – to engage with change.

Summary

This section has summarized ideas about the process of change for individuals. It has described a range of perspectives on human motivation and considered how these relate to support for a change effort. Discussion of the way different people think and feel (the way they are 'wired') has highlighted some important considerations when designing and communicating change, and has offered insights into why people embrace or resist change.

Further reading

Bridges, W (2009) *Managing Transitions*

Briggs Myers, I and Mayers, PB (1995) *Gifts Differing: Understanding personality type*

Cameron, E and Green, M (2009) *Making Sense of Change Management*

Huczinsky, AA and Buchanan, DA (2007) *Organizational Behaviour* – an academic reference on a range of OB topics

Pink, DH (2011) *Drive: The surprising truth about what motivates us*

Questions to think about

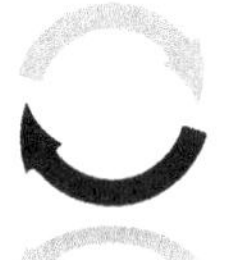

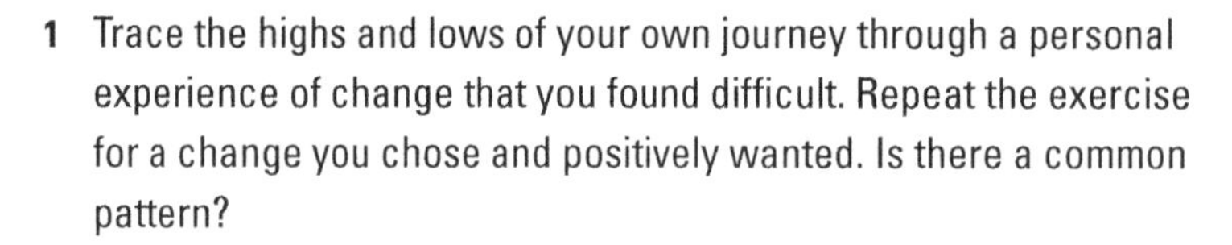

1. Trace the highs and lows of your own journey through a personal experience of change that you found difficult. Repeat the exercise for a change you chose and positively wanted. Is there a common pattern?
2. For a change you have undergone, identify the specific 'losses' you experienced and the personal learning you gained from the change process.
3. Try to identify the main features of your own personality 'type' – if possible arrange to complete a suitable questionnaire and discuss it with the person who administers it for you. How does this affect your approach to changes in your working life?

Section C: Change and the organization

Introduction

Organizations seldom change without some external reason or pressure to do so. Changes may be wide, affecting many of the organization's functions, or narrow, having limited impact outside one department. They may be large, requiring major investment, or small, costing relatively little in finance and people.

This section introduces some metaphors that people use when describing organizations and change. It then focuses on three particular models of the change process. This provides a foundation for us to think about how change initiatives vary and require different approaches, before we conclude with a brief discussion of some factors that help or hinder change.

1. How we think about organizations

In his book *Images of Organization* Gareth Morgan (2006) describes how the way that we think about organizations – the metaphors we hold in our minds – affects our behaviour. In particular the way we approach change is affected by the mental models we use. He lists eight metaphors but acknowledges that there could be others (Table 1.4); one interesting additional metaphor – architecture (Mumford and Beekman, 1994) – is added to the table.

TABLE 1.4 Metaphors of organizations (based on Morgan, 2006)

Metaphor: Organizations as...	What it Means: Organizations...	How it Affects Attitudes to Leadership	Implications for the Way Change is Approached
Machines 	... can be designed and controlled. They can be re-engineered, and components can be changed. They behave in predictable ways.	The principles of scientific management are seen as paramount. Leaders forecast, plan, organize, communicate, coordinate and control.	Change can be planned and managed. People are seen as 'units of production' and can be trained to fit into a new way of working or be replaced by those that can.
Organisms 	... are 'open systems' that adapt and respond to their environment. Different species of organization will flourish in different environments. They have a definite life cycle.	Leaders need to ensure the organization is nourished and the various parts of it are well connected to each other. They address factors that inhibit the organization's growth and health.	The whole 'ecosystem' of the organization has to be considered when implementing change. There will always be different ways to achieve a given end state.
Brains 	... are intelligence-led and resemble a library and memory bank. They have a language system that allows them to process information, reassembling it into new ways of operating.	Leadership is more diffused and knowledge-based; intelligence and ability to connect ideas is valued. Self-organization through 'quality circles' and similar approaches is expected.	Change is seen as a learning process using 'double loop' learning – processing feedback on the organization's control systems as well as the end operations.
Cultures 	... are like an ethnic group with 'shared systems of meaning' and norms, shared beliefs and expectations, which bind people together. Symbols that reinforce these beliefs are very important.	Leadership focus is on the shared frames of reference that make organization possible. People are appreciated for what they stand for in the network of relationships.	Change is achieved through symbolic actions that create, communicate and sustain new expectations. Storytelling and a focus on different aspects of the organization's history can help generate change.

TABLE 1.4 *continued*

Metaphor: Organizations as...	What it Means: Organizations...	How it Affects Attitudes to Leadership	Implications for the Way Change is Approached
Political systems 	... are systems of government managing the common and conflicting needs of various interest groups. Coalitions of interests form, and power is used to get things done.	Power is a key issue. Stakeholders are identified and, through negotiation, alliances are formed. Control of boundaries, information and technology give leverage. Powerful oratory is valued.	Conflict is expected and managed. Attention is paid to aligning various sources of power (formal authority, knowledge/ information, control of resources) to support the change.
Psychic prisons 	... reflect the unconscious 'shadows' we carry over from family and other relationships, so that structures, rules, beliefs and behaviours are not corporate but personal. They can become like cults, seeking to 'tie people in'.	Leaders must be aware of unconscious assumptions they experience or that others project on to them, avoiding 'thought control'. Their awareness of these issues leads them to focus on ethical dimensions of organization, life and purpose.	The personal symbolism of change for individuals and groups needs to be considered. Superficial assumptions of rationality are avoided and care is taken to avoid 'vision' being seen as a cheap promise of a solution to problems.
Flux and transformation 	... are seen as examples of chaos and complexity, where hierarchy and control have limited relevance. Order emerges naturally from a process of continuous transformation.	Leaders must let go of the idea that they truly control outcomes. They can decide on a desired outcome, protect key values and use small changes to create large effects in the right general direction, adjusting emphasis as the future unfolds.	Managing change in the strict sense is impossible! We can understand the flux around us and 'nudge' it where possible, helping desirable outcomes to emerge. Awareness of competing desirable outcomes, and of potential 'feedback loops' to amplify small changes, support positive movement.

TABLE 1.4 *continued*

Metaphor: Organizations as...	What it Means: Organizations...	How it Affects Attitudes to Leadership	Implications for the Way Change is Approached
Instruments of domination 	... are intrinsically systems of control. They harness resources (including people, seen as 'resources') to achieve their purposes, using charisma, tradition, economic power and legal or structural power to gain compliance.	Leaders in organizations may be challenged by this critique, but benefit by seeking to understand it. They can respond by reviewing the social role of their organizations (external), and the needs of organization members (internal) – work–life balance, stress, health and safety etc.	This metaphor implies that change will be an extension of the ongoing bureaucratic power of the organization. Morgan accepts that this is an extension of the political systems metaphor, so similar approaches to change can be expected.
Architecture (Mumford and Beekman, 1994) 	... provide a designed, fit-for-purpose environment for effective work. Organization design exists to support and enable the organization's purpose, providing a context that makes work easier, but without exerting control. Ideally the elegance of the design enriches work.	Leaders take account of the social organization (formal and informal) and of its patterns of communication and behaviour. They consider the activities of the organization and design its processes to meet the needs of both activities and people. Stronger processes are used where they must bear heavier weight.	Changes in activities, social structure or the wider environment are a cause for revising the architecture of the organization's processes. These issues must be kept under review so that processes can be reconfigured to meet the evolving needs of the organization.

Morgan writes:

> my aim is not to present an exhaustive account of every conceivable metaphor that can be used to understand and shape organizational life. Rather it is to reveal, through illustration, the power of metaphor in shaping organizational management and how the ultimate challenge is not to be seduced by the power or attractiveness of a single metaphor – old or new – so much as to develop an ability to integrate the contributions of different points of view. (Morgan, 2006: xii)

Thinking about these (and other) metaphors can make a profound difference to the way we manage change, in a number of ways:

1. It is important to listen to the words used by those leading change, and to identify the patterns of metaphor that lie behind them. This helps to build effective communication with those concerned, using language they will understand and appreciate. It also helps us to recognize where those leaders may have mental models (probably unconsciously) that risk limiting their thinking about change.
2. It provides a framework for thinking about a particular change. Which metaphor(s) provide the best insights into the issues involved? How might we look at the change from other perspectives? This process is like looking through different lenses to understand change more deeply. It helps with defining the change and with understanding its likely impacts.
3. It offers a way to consider different approaches to change offered by different authors and consultants, helping us to evaluate the likely strengths and weaknesses of particular approaches.

2. Models of the change process

There is a sense in which any project or programme methodology implicitly contains a 'change process' (Chapter 8). However, such methodologies need a complementary understanding of the change processes involved. I have chosen to focus on three models that offer insights into these:

1. Lewin's three-stage model – showing how collective mindsets are broken down to enable change.
2. Kotter's eight-step model – showing a road map for change based on common errors made by organizations.
3. Senge's systems thinking model – showing how profound change can be achieved through learning.

A fourth model that explores 'emergent change' is discussed in Section F.

2.1 Change and group processes: Kurt Lewin's three-stage model

In the mid-20th century, social psychologist Kurt Lewin first described the process of individual change as:

- *unfreezing* (when inertia is overcome, and existing habits and mindsets are broken down);
- *change* (a period of confusion as old ways of being are challenged but as yet the future way of being is not clear);
- *refreezing* (when new mindsets and habits are formed and become established, and a degree of psychological comfort is restored).

FIGURE 1.8 Lewin's three-step approach

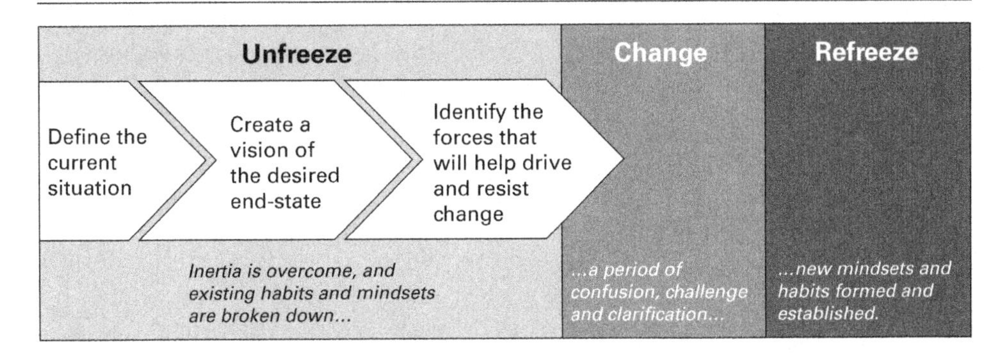

Lewin (1951) extended this deceptively simple model (Figure 1.8) to describe groups in change. He recognized that the collective mindsets and practices of a group must be broken down before a change can occur – and that subsequently effort is needed to consolidate the group's new mindset and practices.

Unfreeze – breaking inertia

Lewin sees three activities in this 'unfreeze' stage:

1. Clearly define the current situation. The more collaborative this process can be, the more effective it is. This is both because people will be more committed to a picture they have defined and because the involvement of more people will make it a richer, fuller picture.

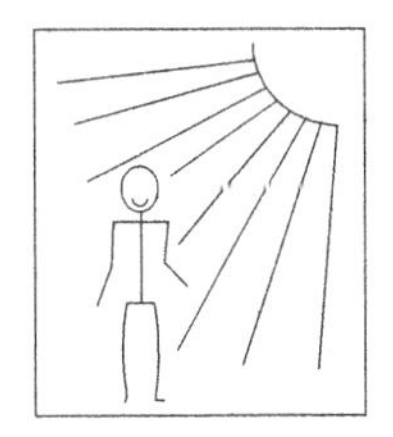

2. Create a vision of the desired end state. Again, the richer, fuller and more attractive this can be – and the more people who contribute – the better.

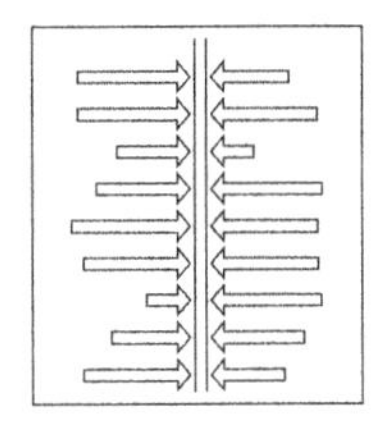

3. Identify the forces that will help to drive and resist the change, increasing the driving forces identified and decreasing the resisting forces. Once again, this is best carried out by a group of those leading and affected by the change. Chapter 2, Section B2.2 describes Lewin's 'force field analysis' and suggests a way to conduct this activity.

In Section B3.6 we have already seen how Schein (1993) built upon Lewin's 'unfreeze' stage with a prescription for those seeking to create change in a group that involves three apparently conflicting activities:

- disconfirmation;
- creation of guilt or anxiety;
- creation of psychological safety.

How can the third of these be compatible with the first two? The first two relate to 'survival' anxiety, which is needed to 'unfreeze'; the third is about reducing learning anxiety, creating safety to learn.

Change – taking people through change

In this stage a plan is followed to implement the intended change(s). Involve people and maintain the safe learning environment that Schein prescribes for the unfreeze stage, allowing experimentation over solutions to problems. Provide great role models with whom people in change can identify.

Refreeze

This is the stage at which new work practices become new work habits, and when new ways of thinking become the conventional wisdom. It is a time for vigilance on the part of change leaders, who must address any tendency for people to talk, think or act in line with the old ways. At this stage it is appropriate to reward behaviours and results that are aligned with the changed environment.

2.2 Planning and leading organizational change: Kotter's eight-step model

A number of prescriptions have been proposed for strategic, organization-level change. The best known of these is the work of John Kotter. His ideas, based on analysis of many change efforts over a 15-year period, were set out in a *Harvard Business Review* seminal article in (Kotter, 1995). The article identified eight common errors that organizations make when trying to undertake major changes. This was followed by his book *Leading Change* (2012a [1996]), in which he elaborated his 'eight-stage process' (Table 1.5). Each stage was an antidote to one of the errors he identified. The whole process offers a roadmap for undertaking major organizational change,

TABLE 1.5 Kotter's eight-stage approach to strategic change

Kotter's Eight Stages	
1 Establishing a sense of urgency	Kotter identifies sources of complacency and ways to raise the sense of urgency, but is clear that this stage is not complete until 'a majority of employees, perhaps 75% of managers overall, and virtually all of the top executives... believe that change is absolutely essential' (Kotter 2012a, p 51). This is a high bar to achieve, but Kotter sees it as essential.
2 Creating the guiding coalition	The change-leading coalition needs to be characterized by trust and a common goal, and must contain people with strong positional power, appropriate and varied expertise, credibility across the organization and effective leadership.

TABLE 1.5 *continued*

Kotter's Eight Stages	
3 Developing a vision and a strategy	Kotter sees vision as: 'a picture of the future with some implicit or explicit commentary on why people should strive to create that future'. The vision needs to be something that people can really imagine, and should offer positive outcomes for the organization's key stakeholders. Combining both head and heart, vision is created by teams, a time-consuming process.
4 Communicating the change vision	The vision needs to be communicated in clear, direct language, using verbal images and analogies. It needs to be repeated frequently through many channels, including opportunities for discussion and feedback. It must be lived out by leaders.
5 Empowering employees for broad-based action	Major change needs the willing effort of a wide range of employees, who really feel that they can make a difference (Section B3.3). Employees can be set free to make that difference by ensuring that the organization's systems and structures support employee action, providing appropriate training to encourage it and removing or sidelining managers who might get in the way.
6 Generating short-term wins	Short-term wins provide a boost to the change initiative. They help minimize negativity and promote support for the change. They also provide opportunities to recognize individuals who deserve credit for contributing to the change thus far. Don't just 'hope' for them to happen; make sure short-term wins are a significant element of the change plan.
7 Consolidating gains and producing more change	There is always a pressure to revert to the old ways. Sustaining and embedding change requires ongoing effort over a long period. Kotter encourages the guiding coalition to 'press on' and deliver more change, increasing resources not reassigning them away from the change effort. He also emphasizes the importance of continued clear leadership and direction from the top, and of good project and programme management disciplines throughout.
8 Anchoring new approaches in the culture	It has been said that 'culture eats strategy for breakfast' – and it sometimes eats change as a second course! It is the nature of culture to be mostly unconscious and deeply embedded over a long period. Kotter points out that even apparently successful change programmes can be 'eaten' over the years if the organization's culture is not aligned with them. It is vital to identify aspects of 'old' culture that threaten the change and to address them through highlighting the positive outcomes of the change, through talking about the old culture, valuing it for its time, and where necessary through using changes of staff (especially visible promotions) to strengthen the new culture that is needed. For more on culture see Section E.

placing a strong focus on the role of effective leadership. It is 'required reading' for those leading or supporting change programmes, not least because many senior organization leaders will also have read it! The delightful fable *Our Iceberg Is Melting* (Kotter and Rathgeber, 2006) is also based on (and teaches) these eight stages.

There is an underlying assumption in Kotter's writing that, given the right process and the right leadership, change can be planned and managed. He acknowledges at a number of points the 'messiness' of change and offers prescriptions for dealing with this. In his seventh and eighth stages Kotter does engage with the complexity of organization systems and how one thing affects another. However, he appears to see organizations and change primarily through the machine, architecture and political systems metaphors described above, and does not engage strongly with the less deterministic metaphors.

2.3 Nurturing and growing organizational change: a systems thinking model

Peter Senge became known for his work on the 'learning organization', particularly through his book *The Fifth Discipline* (Senge, 1993) upon which his further writings have been built. The 'fifth discipline' to which the book title refers is systems thinking, which addresses some of the difficult-to-explain phenomena we see in organizations and in change processes. Senge writes about what he terms 'profound change' in organizations (Senge *et al*, 1999). He uses biological and ecological metaphors to describe the processes that limit organizational growth – and the implementation of proposed changes.

> To understand why sustaining significant change is so elusive, we need to think less like managers and more like biologists... All growth processes in nature arise out of the interplay between reinforcing growth processes and limiting processes. The seed contains the possibility for a tree, but it realizes that possibility through an emergent reinforcing growth process. The seed sends out small feelers. These primitive roots draw in water and nutrients, leading to further expansion – more water, nutrients and so on. The initial growth process is under way. But how far it progresses depends on a host of limits: water, nutrients in the soil, space for the roots to expand, warmth. Eventually, as the tree begins to extend beyond the surface, other limits will come into play: sunlight, space for the tree's branches to spread, insects that destroy the tree's leaves.
>
> When growth stops prematurely, before the organism reaches its potential, it is because the growth has encountered constraints that could be avoided, that are not inevitable. Other members of the same species will grow more because they do not encounter the same constraints. Any particular limit mentioned above – not enough water, nutrients or space for the root system – could potentially keep the seed from growing.
>
> Senge *et al* (1999)

Senge points out that the kinds of systems thinking that explain why different tree seeds grow to different heights, shapes and states of health – or not at all – can be applied to change. To understand how profound change can be nurtured and sustained requires us to understand the many self-reinforcing growth processes that will support and enable change, and the limiting processes that, if not addressed, will stunt or kill it.

A 'self-reinforcing process' is a positive feedback loop or 'virtuous circle'. A 'limiting process' is a negative feedback loop or 'vicious circle'. Chapter 11, Section A2 illustrates these in the context of sustaining change. Understanding the various reinforcing and balancing 'feedback loops' that will affect a change process allows us to look for ways to strengthen the reinforcing processes and to mitigate those that would work against progress. Perhaps some of the constraints can be lifted, too. For example, limited working hours (time available is often a constraint in organization change) could be overcome with more people committed to the change programme.

Senge and his co-authors describe with great clarity the challenges of initiating change, of sustaining the transformation and of redesigning and rethinking the organization:

- Initiating change:
  - people feeling they do not have enough time;
  - people finding insufficient coaching and support;
  - people unable to see the relevance of the change;
  - problems with leaders not 'walking the talk'.
- Sustaining the transformation:
  - anxieties about job security, learning, trusting others in new situations and loss of control;
  - how to measure change, the tension between measurement as learning and as assessment;
  - using culture so that change in a pilot group is not seen as a 'cult' activity.
- Redesign and rethinking:
  - governance (for change programme and organization) as control – or as direction-setting;
  - spreading new practices effectively;
  - giving meaning to strategy and vision.

Throughout they demonstrate some of the typical feedback loops that occur as these challenges are faced. They provide many practical examples from a range of organizations and offer suggestions as to how to nurture and grow change through to maturity.

Kotter's approach to changing organizations is based on highly visible, large-scale transformative change, driven primarily by the senior leadership of the organization through the 'guiding coalition'. By contrast Senge suggests that profound change occurs when small-scale initiatives are skilfully nurtured by well-aligned leadership at all levels of the organization, and then spread. His thinking is closest to the 'organism', 'culture' and 'flux and transformation' metaphors discussed in Section C1 above.

The 'flux and transformation' metaphor helps to explain how change can occur in very large and complex organizational systems, where the nature and extent of the forces involved are not easy to map. We do the best we can with systems thinking, notice the effects on the systems of any interventions we make and adjust our behaviour accordingly. Sometimes the best we can do is to decide on the most important outcomes we wish to achieve and try to intervene in ways that direct the organization's energy accordingly. Both Kotter's and Senge's views contain significant truths and different change situations, and organizational cultures may call for emphasis on one or the other approach. Sections C3, E and F below say more about this.

3. Types of organization change

Different change initiatives vary on a number of dimensions, including:

- how widely they affect the organization;
- how deeply they are designed to change the organization (or part of it);
- the focus of change (structure, technology etc);
- the nature of the change (tightly managed and programme-driven or more 'emergent');
- the extent to which they impact – or will be impacted by – organization culture;
- the time available.

The 'change kaleidoscope' described in Section A2.3 highlights these issues. As well as affecting the extent of the challenge posed to effective change management, these and other similar issues will help decide the appropriate use of change management resources.

3.1 Transforming 'the way we do business'

Long-term change that needs to transform culture requires significant sponsorship from the top of the organization, a high level of change management support and considerable resources. These need to be sustained over a long period (typically one to three years). Further key elements will be:

- commitment to the transformation from members of the governing body (board or similar);
- significant time for selected credible and respected people across the organization to act as agents of change;
- appropriate skills training in change and facilitation for these change agents;
- widespread, sustained and engaging learning events for all staff;
- visible involvement of change sponsors in all such learning events (sustained over time);

- empowerment for individuals and groups to take initiatives in line with the change;
- wide and sustained communication of the importance of the change, and of successes.

The model used will be closest to Senge's systems thinking, with a considerable effort used to create 'growing conditions' favourable to the kinds of change being sought.

CASE STUDY

The IT department of a major banking institution was seen by its business community as unresponsive. The culture was bureaucratic and hierarchical, so it was difficult for the organization's bright, creative people to get things done through the management systems.

A transformation process was put in place, championed by the divisional CEO and led by the board member responsible for quality, with strong support from the Organizational Development (OD) department. Board members identified credible, well-respected staff members to act as continuous improvement facilitators. A major programme of experiential learning was initiated, using the facilitators to help groups to learn and apply continuous improvement tools. All attendees began to identify real work improvements they could make and were encouraged to work with colleagues, using a facilitator, to carry their ideas forward.

3.2 Changing structures

A major restructuring of an organization is usually run as a carefully managed project. A clear vision for the new structure must be sponsored effectively at senior level. The machine metaphor fits this type of change well and the process can be managed using Kotter's 'eight steps'. Typical key requirements are:

- building a partnership between the sponsor and project and change management teams;
- careful selection and training of those who will lead within the new structure;
- ongoing support for the new leaders as the new structure settles in;
- strong communication and training to support all whose working environment will change;
- effective coordinated support and advice from Human Resources (HR), Organizational Development (OD) and Learning and Development (L&D).

CASE STUDY

A product and service development organization moved from a traditional departmental structure to a single, large 'resource pool' of almost 600 people. The disruption for staff members was considerable. They were anxious about the change in their reporting arrangements, and about their skill levels to achieve the flexibility likely to be required.

Change management, HR and the project manager jointly selected new 'resource managers' who were carefully trained in a range of staff management issues. Workshops were run for all staff, using Bridges' work on personal transitions (Section B2). The organization leader attended every session and held a 'clinic' there to address people's concerns. The structure was implemented successfully, with additional HR and L&D support for resource managers in the early months.

3.3 Forming a new team

Provided it has little impact on other areas of the business, the formation of a new team is usually a tactical change that has only minimal need for change management support. It is a case where the 'machine metaphor' fits well, but the strategically oriented approach of Kotter may be excessive. Sponsorship is likely to be at local rather than organizational level. Typical change management issues include:

- liaising with organization design colleagues to ensure the new function has appropriate reporting lines and working relationships with other groups;
- helping the leadership of the new team to identify key transition issues;
- facilitating members of the new team as they meet to negotiate their roles and use of their skills.

It is worth noting that this is a case in which a comparatively small change could create what Senge calls a 'pilot group' – a 'worked example' of a structure that could be replicated more widely in the organization. In this case the 'organism' metaphor would be more appropriate, and a greater change management effort would be justified from an early stage. This 'replicating structure' approach would focus particularly on identifying the factors forming reinforcing and limiting loops, and on how to create conditions in which this and other such teams can develop successfully.

CASE STUDY

The customers of a business providing traditional computer services were requesting rapidly developed, tactical IT solutions to business problems. A few high-performing employees were selected, offering a range of technical skills in building desktop solutions. These were formed into a new 'tactical IT' team, led by a senior manager who was creative, unconventional and understood the business well. OD staff worked with the senior manager to develop a strategy for bringing the team together. The team engaged quickly in sharing individual knowledge, skills and work styles with each other, and negotiated how they could best work together and support one another.

4. Factors that help/hinder change

Of many factors that can help or hinder change in organizations, two in particular stand out: culture and structure.

4.1 Organizational culture

Reference has already been made in discussion of Senge's work (Section C2.3) of the importance of cultural alignment in order for profound change to take hold. This refers to the alignment of culture with a particular change that may be a better or worse 'fit' with it. A relatively 'political' culture with a strong 'command and control' ethic would not easily accept the introduction of a coaching initiative.

However, over time an organization's culture may become so firmly established that it will resist any change. We explore the nature of culture more fully in Section E: for now it is appropriate to say that the capacity to accept change depends on having positive experiences of change. Since the most basic form of change is individual learning, one way to maintain a capacity for change is to ensure the continued personal and professional growth of all staff. Leaders who have a long-term commitment to an organization will foster an openness to change by encouraging and supporting learning activity through which staff continually acquire new skills and knowledge. They also provide opportunities for people to use their growing competence to benefit the organization – which leads to changes.

4.2 Organizational structure

There are many forms of organization and some are more change-friendly than others. A tall, traditional 'family tree' hierarchy is, as Kotter (2014) points out, optimized to deliver business as usual. However, it frequently makes any change more difficult. Managers at many levels all want to be involved and 'have their say'. A change initiative can easily run out of energy before it gets final approval at the right level.

By contrast, a part of the organization that is composed of largely autonomous, self-directed teams is likely to generate a great deal of change. In this case, the risk is not of smothering change but of too many, possibly incompatible, changes taking place around that part of the organization – of a sort of anarchy that may not be in the best interests of the organization.

The challenge is to keep an organization 'change-ready' whilst retaining the stability to do its business effectively. Kotter recognizes that an organization's traditional structure and processes are designed to achieve best results for its day-to-day work. They are not designed to deal with the constant stream of changes that large organizations need in order to deal with increasing complexity (Kotter, 2012b). He proposes a second, strategic 'operating system' to work alongside the 'business as usual' one. This second system is designed to be agile, making use of a network structure to monitor every aspect of the organization's internal and external world. It identifies, initiates and implements changes, constantly reviewing and maintaining the organization's strategy and direction. This is not a freeze–unfreeze–refreeze concept, because there is no strategic steady state to 'refreeze'!

In this kind of organization, Kotter's 'guiding coalition' is reconceived as the owners of this strategic operating system, identifying big opportunities for the organization (Figure 1.9). For each such opportunity the strategic coalition creates a sense of urgency around it. They apply his other seven steps, which are reconceived as 'accelerator processes', engaging volunteer change agents from around the organization to make the initiative happen. The guiding coalition becomes the strategic sun with multiple change initiatives (each with its own mini-guiding coalition) as planets around it. The volunteers who run these initiatives bring to them their daily experience of the 'business as usual' hierarchy. This minimizes the risk that the changes are disconnected from the organization's day-to-day work.

This bold concept deliberately builds into the organization structure a set of processes that can act as reinforcing loops for any change that may be needed. It shows one way in which the organization structure can be configured to create agility and change readiness. Of course to implement such an approach will itself entail a significant change process!

Summary

This section has sought to encourage depth in the way that organizations and their leaders think about change. It has presented a range of metaphors that may unconsciously influence such thought. It has explored examples of both tightly and loosely structured approaches to change and has illustrated situations where each might be most useful. The challenge for change managers is to use these insights to encourage their busy colleagues towards a more reflective approach to future change initiatives. Such reflection enables leaders to become more intentional about the

FIGURE 1.9 Kotter's 'dual operating system' (Kotter, 2012b)

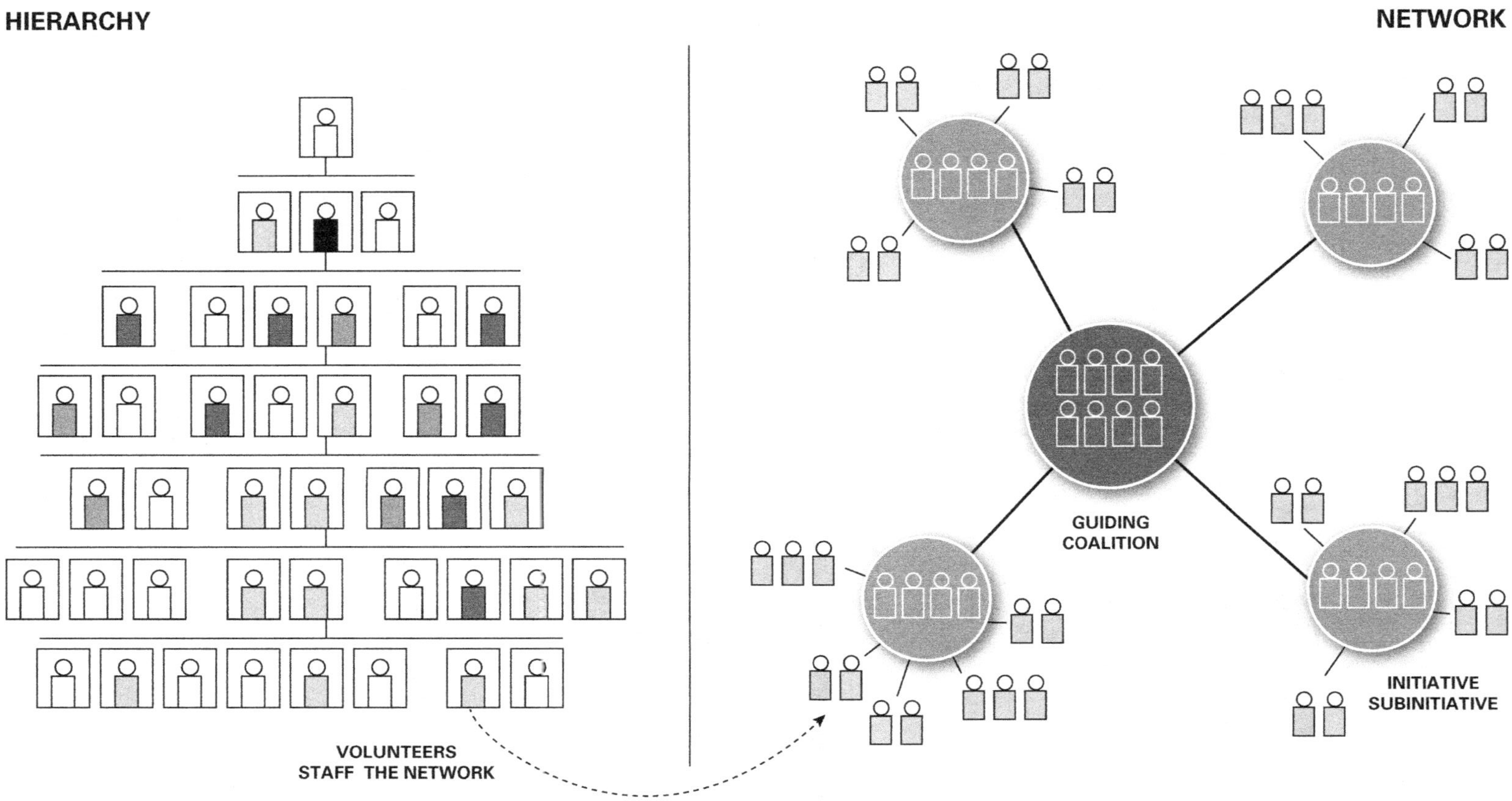

SOURCE: Reproduced by kind permission of Harvard Business School Publishing.

approach adopted to change and the images used. In turn this stimulates organizational and individual learning, and builds change capability.

Questions to think about

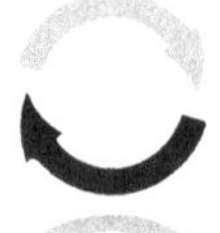

1. What metaphors do you hear from leaders in your organization? What practical impacts do they have?
2. For a recent change initiative, consider which metaphors were most influential.
3. What changes have you experienced that needed a highly structured approach? ... and a more organic approach?
4. How well did the approaches actually applied fit with what was needed?

Further reading

Kotter, JP (2012a) *Leading Change*
Kotter, JP and Rathgeber, H (2006) *Our Iceberg is Melting* (a fable)
Morgan, G (2006) *Images of Organization*
Senge, PM (1993) *The Fifth Discipline*
Senge, PM *et al* (1999) *The Dance of Change*

Section D: Key roles in organizational change

Introduction

In this section I focus on the roles and functions performed by people engaged in change initiatives. These are not 'job descriptions' or 'job titles' in an organizational sense. They are archetypes – 'typical pictures' of these roles and functions – and are not linked (here) to the organizational roles (job titles) used to deliver change, such as change management, project and programme management. Some applications of these roles in organizational settings and related governance processes are discussed in Chapter 7, Section A4 and Chapter 8, Section A.

1. Lifecycle of a successful change

All change begins with an idea. An individual, or sometimes a group, conceives of a way in which things could be different. For organizational change to occur, that original idea must spread, be formed into a proposal and find sponsorship. It must compete with the pressures of 'business as usual' in the line management structure and become accepted by those whose jobs and lives it will affect. This is a perilous journey. And it involves people, each of whom will leave his or her mark on the success of the original idea.

See slide 87 for Diagram

In Figure 1.10 an additional role is added to those mentioned above: 'change agent'. This is not the same as a change manager (although change managers may fulfil this role). It is the role of anyone who, through intentional contact with all those engaged in the change process, provides an objective and supportive communication channel, facilitating the development and implementation of the change.

Various authors have proposed role definitions for the various actors in a change process. Senge *et al* (1999) in particular stress that no 'hero leader' can create profound organizational change. Significant research has been undertaken to identify effective behaviours associated with each role (especially the role of sponsor). The best chance for a change initiative to succeed comes when all roles are fulfilled effectively. Table 1.6 summarizes three such descriptions, showing approximate equivalence of the roles.

Of course, as O'Neill (2007) points out, it is possible for an individual to function in more than one role. However, it is important for anyone involved in change to know what their role is *at a particular time and in a particular situation*, and to perform it well. Change managers are often called upon to provide informal commentary or coaching for others involved in change. They can help people in all these roles to develop a clear picture of how best to fulfil these functions and so to help change succeed.

FIGURE 1.10 Roles in change

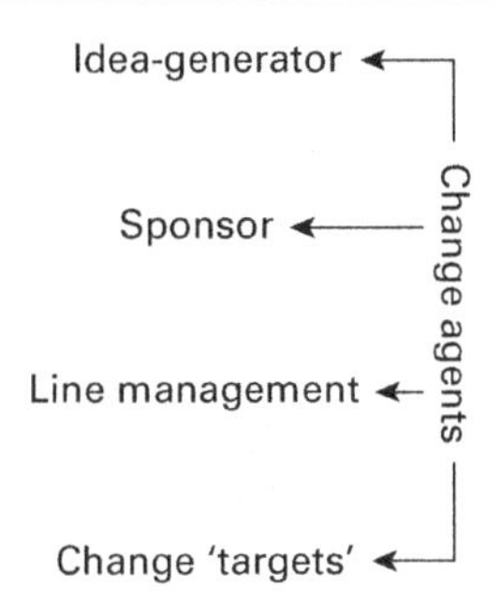

TABLE 1.6 Comparison of roles in change

Our Term	O'Neill (2007, referencing Conner, 1993)	Kotter (2012a)	Senge (1999)
Idea-Generator	Advocate • Develops idea for change • Promote ideas to potential sponsors	(Generally assumed to be a result of senior strategic intent)	(Emerges from 'learning organization')
Sponsor	Sponsor • Has overall line authority • Legitimizes and approves change • Control over necessary people and resources • Clear vision for change • Identifies objectives, outcomes and measures	Executive leadership • Creates a sensible and appealing vision • Designs a strategy • Maintains clarity and urgency • Act as a role model • Address structural barriers to change • Communicate – a lot! • Reduce unnecessary interdependencies • Provide resources for training • Confront those who are blocking change	Executive leader • Creates environment to inspire and support new approaches • Designs supportive systems of performance measurement, reward and governance • Establishes new norms • Learns actively and supports learning • Poses questions • Teaches, mentors and coaches line managers • Role models behaviour
Line Management	Sustaining sponsor • Facilitates in own area a change initiated at executive level	Local leaders and managers • Create and implement plans to deliver strategy • Convert plans into financial budgets • Act as a role model • Ensure effective two-way communication • Provide local leadership and project management • Confront those who are blocking change	Local line leaders • Accountable for results at local level • Authority to make changes in own area • Committed local team • Test practicality of changes

TABLE 1.6 *continued*

Our Term	O'Neill (2007, referencing Conner, 1993)	Kotter (2012a)	Senge (1999)
Targets	Implementers (Conner's 'Targets') • The people who must actually change! • 'Listen, enquire, clarify concerns with sponsor' • Provide feedback to sponsor on how things are working out		
Change Agents	Change agent • No direct line authority • Works with sponsor and implementers • Facilitates change • Acts as 'data gatherer, educator, adviser, meeting facilitator or coach' • Helps sponsors to sponsor, implementers to implement		Internal networkers • No formal authority • Builds broad connections across the organization • Fosters collaboration between line leaders • Carries ideas, support, stories and learning • Act as helpers, advisers and guides • Helps groups identify and access resources

2. What makes a good sponsor?

Continuing research by Prosci (2012) with 650 participants from 62 countries identifies the greatest contributor to overall change management success as 'active and visible executive sponsorship'. The greatest obstacle was said by the respondents to be 'ineffective change management sponsorship from senior leaders'.

The Prosci research supports many of the observations described in Section D1 about the behaviour that defines effective sponsorship of change. Our synthesis of all this wisdom suggests 10 key activities that make a change sponsor effective:

1. Maintaining and articulating a clear and attractive vision for the change, showing how it links to the organization's strategy.

2. Gaining the commitment and involvement of senior and line management, using influence and interactions to advocate the project consistently.
3. Championing the change, building and maintaining a sense of urgency and priority for it throughout.
4. Confronting those who are blocking the change and clearing a path for it to succeed.
5. Genuinely acting as a role model for new behaviours and 'walking the talk', establishing new norms firmly in own immediate team.
6. Communicating about the change consistently, using a variety of media and providing good channels for effective two-way communication.
7. Training, mentoring and coaching line management, remaining accessible to them throughout.
8. Ensuring that resources for the change, especially people and training, are provided; this specifically includes funding for dedicated change management resources.
9. Aligning the organization's infrastructure, environment and reward systems with the change initiative, especially the way performance is measured and managed.
10. Ensuring ongoing alignment of the particular initiative with other organizational initiatives and with the organization's wider strategic goals.

3. What makes a good change agent?

3.1 Change managers and change agents

The terms 'change manager' and 'change agent' are not synonymous. A change agent is anyone who acts intentionally but without formal line authority to facilitate change in the organization. Change agents may be coaches or consultants (internal or external), HR, OD specialists, trainers or other support people. But they may also be supervisors, front-line staff, line managers or others. Whoever they are, when they are functioning as change agents they do so without direct line authority.

This means that change managers, whose organizational role is defined by their knowledge of and competence in change management, may act as change agents some of the time. At other times their role may require them to act with authority in a role relating to their own function.

The comments of O'Neill and Senge (Section D1) allow us to summarize the functions of a change agent as follows:

- to build strong networks across the organization;
- to connect line managers engaged in change with others in similar positions;
- to ensure effective communication takes place up as well as down the hierarchy;
- to observe and spread ideas, information and initiatives;

- to advise sponsors, line managers and targets when they see opportunities to add value;
- to smooth access to resources needed by various groups, knowing where to go for help;
- to help sponsors, line management and targets to fulfil their own roles well and to avoid 'taking over' others' roles.

3.2 Change agents and line managers

Many of these activities require the change agent to act in a consulting role, getting their expertise and insights used by other people over whom they have no authority. Change managers frequently face the same issue, even when they are not acting as change agents. The single most important skill required to be effective in this situation is that of establishing really effective working relationships with line management colleagues and others. The term often used for this is 'contracting'. This does not mean entering a legal agreement. It refers to the process of getting real clarity with the line manager about what each expects from the other in the work they will do together. Notice the importance of mutuality; the line manager has needs, of course, but the change agent also has needs in order to be effective. Peter Block (2000) describes the contracting process like this: 'The business of... contracting... is to negotiate wants, cope with mixed motivation, surface concerns about exposure and loss of control, and clarify all parties to the contract' (p 58).

In addition to getting clarity about what each wants or expects of the other in a social contract like this, it is important to pay attention to the four aspects addressed by Block:

- *Mixed motivation*: there will always be some degree of mixed motivation for line managers in a change situation. They too have investment in the way things have been. Having their own doubts and questions clear at this stage – and change agents being authentic about their own feelings – both builds mutual trust and saves either the line manager or the change agent from being surprised later by unexpected comments or actions from the other.
- *Concerns about exposure*: line managers (and change agents!) operate in organizations where there is a complex and political web of relationships. For line managers, to engage in working with a change agent risks disturbing the position they have. Listen carefully for any such concerns the line manager may feel. Discuss them directly and honestly.
- *Concerns about loss of control*: this is a similar issue to exposure. Organizations work (in part at least) by systems of control. A line manager's reputation and position has been built through this system. To receive help or support from outside may feel like a loss of control. Block suggests asking: 'Do you feel you have enough control over how this project is going to proceed?' In that way, concerns in this area can be addressed openly.
- *Clarity about who is involved*: sometimes change agents experience reluctance from line managers regarding a change process, even though the manager concerned says that (s)he is committed to it. Try through sensitive questioning

to understand any pressures (for example from more senior management) that the line manager is under. It is important to be clear about the power issues around the work.

3.3 *Change agents and sources of power*

Although the ability to establish great relationships with line management colleagues is part of the picture, it is wise for change agents and those working with them to recognize the various sources of power and influence in organizational life. These are discussed in Chapter 4, Section B3 and Chapter 12, Section D.

The key thing to note here, however, is that change agents (when operating as such) do not have access to positional sources of power. In any case, positional power tends to generate compliance rather than commitment. Change agents have to rely instead on personal power, which flows from two sources. One source lies in the distinctive insights and expertise they can offer. The other is fundamentally relational. It is seen in people who are authentic, who are clear about their own thoughts, needs and wants, yet who are genuinely able to engage with the ideas, needs and wants of others. Personal power, when well used, can generate the commitment needed to energize people around a change initiative. Whatever the particular source of power, the outcome tends to be compliance where people feel compelled to accept influence from others, and commitment where people receive it willingly.

3.4 *Other issues for change agents*

The most effective change agents are those who are sensitive to the culture within which they operate. This is important because the culture is often changing, and they need to be clear about the values and expectations of both the old and new cultures. Section E discusses culture and behaviour.

Section D1 describes how change agents can be in a position to offer very effective coaching. Developing skill in this area can considerably enhance the role of any change agent, whether they operate in a formal, designated role or more informally. Some notes on coaching are included in Chapter 9, Section C.

4. Change management and job titles

In organizational life there are formal job titles as well as job roles.

In an increasing number of organizations, change managers are used to stand alongside project sponsors and project/programme managers, helping them to achieve effective change (Figure 1.11). According to Prosci research (2012) over 75 per cent of projects in companies they surveyed have a dedicated change management resource. This practice is strongly associated with the overall effectiveness of projects. In the majority of these cases (62 per cent) the assigned change manager actually sits within the project team for a change. In a further 28 per cent of cases the change manager reports to the project sponsor independently of the project manager and project team. The remainder have other reporting relationships.

FIGURE 1.11 Project structures

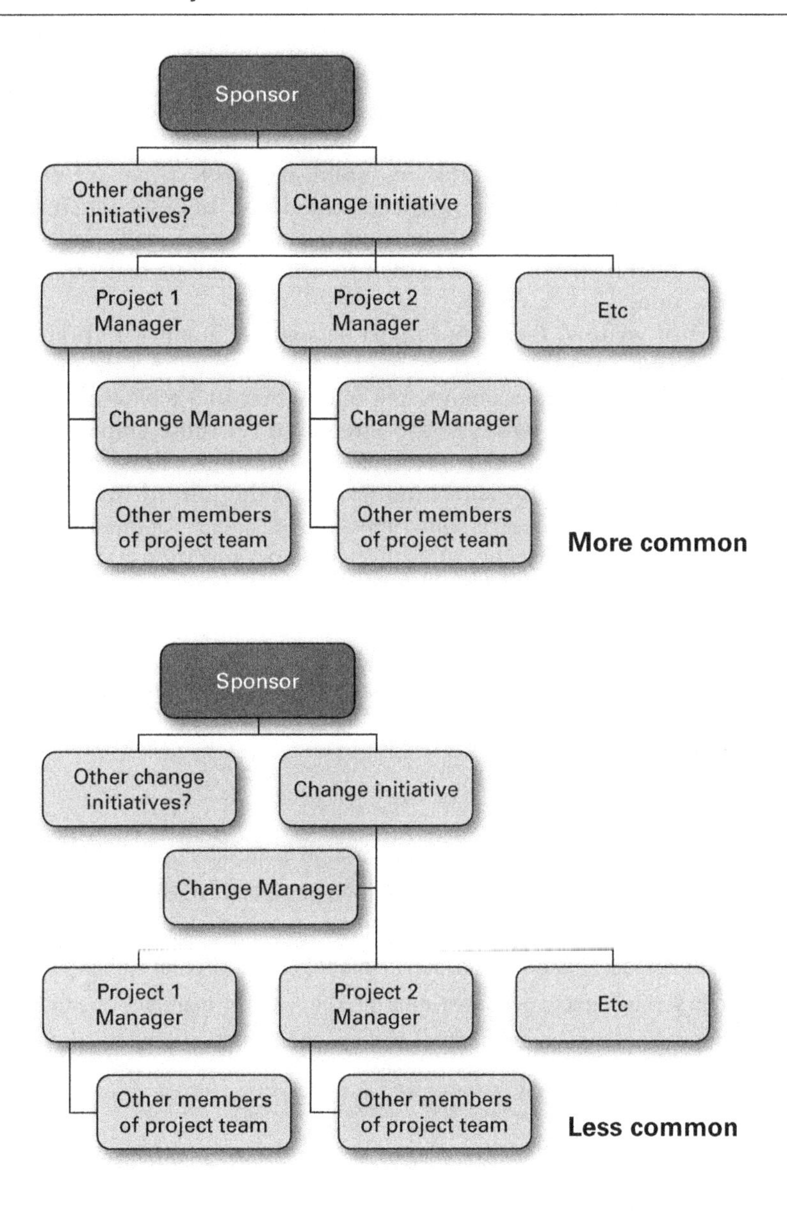

Some commonly adopted programme management approaches (such as Managing Successful Programmes, MSP®), specify the role of a 'business change manager' and accord it equal status to the programme manager in the programme organization structure. The nature of the change management role and its reporting relationship is linked to the organizational change management maturity, with more 'mature' organizations using change managers to support sponsors directly (typically a more strategic role involving high levels of expertise and leadership). Organizations whose change management thinking is still developing embed tactical expertise in projects, focusing on bringing change management insights and change agent skills to this level.

However, this does not deal with the question about who these 'change managers' are. More and more organizations are appointing people with the job title 'change manager'. These may be based within an established project management office or sometimes in a dedicated change management office. In some organizations the Organizational Development (OD) function (usually associated with, but slightly separate from, the HR department) is the provider of change management services to the organization.

At the time of writing, there appears to be some regional variation around the world in how titles are used. For example, a common job title in Australia is 'change analyst', which (confusingly) may refer either to a technical role analysing changing technologies, but which is also often used for those employed to support the 'people' side of change management. This responsibility for contributing to the 'people' side of change is also sometimes assigned the job title 'change advocate'. Networks of change advocates (or sometimes 'change agents' or 'field change agents') are sometimes established by geographically spread organizations. These are designed to provide resources through a period of significant change.

CASE STUDY

A large local government organization going through major change established a network of over 40 volunteer 'change advocates' to fill the gap between the process of delivering change and the people on front-line services who needed to change. Operating as a network, the change advocates engaged with senior managers to promote change and provide feedback from staff. These advocates can be seen as an example of Kotter's 'guiding coalition of the willing' that come together to make the change work.

Our conclusion is that there is a growing consensus about the need for and value of change management at a local infrastructure level, within projects and increasingly at a more strategic level. However, there is as yet little agreement about job titles. People with the job titles 'change manager' and 'OD specialist' sometimes have remarkably similar accountabilities. Tentatively, though, we do see job titles such as these (or similar ones using the term 'director') emerging as the more strategic or policy roles, leading or overseeing those with job titles such as 'change analyst', 'change advocate' and 'change agent'.

5. The key role of line management

CASE STUDY

One CEO was seeking to generate fundamental change across his organization. He believed the executive management was committed, and that much of the 'shop floor' level was committed – yet communications seemed to get lost in the middle, in what he termed 'the blotting paper layer'!

This case-study description highlights the key importance of engaging the middle management – in many ways the heart of the organization – in the change process. At best this level provides excellent, credible local advocacy for the change, acting as visible role models. They can pilot ideas and give feedback on the practicalities of implementing change. They can develop the plans that will make change effective. Failing to engage and envision this core group does indeed create an inert and highly absorbent blockage to the change process.

We describe middle management as 'the heart of the organization' because they are typically people with some years invested in its success and its people, and who in general will want it to succeed. Involve middle management early. Create a sense of urgency – and of the need for change – by giving privileged access to the thinking that has led to the change. Invite help in making proposed changes practical. Show willingness to respond to their concerns and critiques. Above all, communicate copiously with this key layer. Doing so enables them to ensure great communication to their people.

This ability of middle management to communicate credibly and directly to their people is critical. Reflecting on Hyatt and Creasey's (2003) summary of factors contributing to change management success, Cameron and Green comment:

> One of the most striking conclusions to draw is that employees need to hear about change from two people – the most senior person involved in the change and also their line manager. The senior manager is best suited to communicating business messages around the change, whereas the employee's line manager is best suited to communicating more personal messages. This ties in with the notion that the overarching vision and strategic direction once communicated needs to be translated into a local context.
> (2009: 334–35)

The role of middle management in change is discussed further in Chapter 7, Section A4.2 and in Chapter 11, Section A3.3. However, the active support of a critical mass of line managers throughout the initiative is one of the factors that most predisposes change efforts to succeed. It is worthy of considerable investment.

6. Team structures and change

Cameron and Green (2012) list a variety of types of team found in organizations, including those shown in Table 1.7. They highlight how these different, overlapping team structures all affect the implementation of change.

Parallel teams such as quality circles may be key 'ideas-generators' for change. Work teams have to implement change as 'targets', and therefore need appropriate training and support. Project teams will be required to take the strategies and plans of a change initiative and implement them, as part of the overall change plan. Network teams can be used effectively to diffuse change ideas across the organization, supporting the formal communication structures.

However, these various team structures can also become barriers to change. Network teams can become a resistance network. Work teams can reject new operating procedures. Project teams can become bureaucratic and detached from their purpose within the change initiative. Sometimes the very concept of the change is to change the team structure, as illustrated in the case study opposite.

TABLE 1.7 Types of team (after Cameron and Green, 2012)

Management teams	These lead and operate the organization or significant departments within it.
Work teams	Traditional work teams within a function.
Project teams	Teams assembled to deliver a specific, time-bound set of outcomes.
Change teams	A term usually used to describe the governing team leading a particular change initiative.
Matrix teams	These may be a result of formal organization structure or may operate in a more informal, coordination role between different dimensions of the organization.
Parallel teams	Teams working across traditional organizational boundaries on particular issues (such as quality).
Network teams	These are usually based on communities of interest; similar to parallel teams but typically larger, less structured and without formal boundaries.
Virtual teams	This is not strictly a type of team, but rather a way of working when members of any team type are geographically dispersed.

CASE STUDY

One country group within a global organization deliberately created a formal matrix structure. This overlaid work groups designed to address the needs of particular customer groups (large supermarket chains, wholesale distributors, local shops etc) on a structure based on traditional functional expertise (marketing, sales, finance, HR, distribution etc). The nature of leadership changed; all managers and staff had to work by influence and agreement rather than command and control. However, the initiative delivered sustained business benefits.

Kotter's approach to continuous change in organizations (Kotter, 2012b) is referred to in Section C4.2 above. It is based on innovative team structures that link the organization's ongoing operations with a process of continuous change.

When considering a change initiative it is important to consider the variety of teams and team structures that exist in organizational life. Those structures can be harnessed to provide energy and direction for the change, or they can become obstacles. Team structures beyond the 'work team' provide different loyalty groups, which may be important to many people. If these are disrupted by a proposed change, and no adequate attention is given, the commitment and willingness of people to make the change work may be compromised. Teams and team structures are discussed in Chapter 11, Section A3.4 as an Organizational Development (OD) 'lever' for sustaining change.

Summary

In this section we have discussed archetypal roles and functions in change. These offer change managers a framework for reviewing the way their own organizations engage different individuals and groups in support of change. No matter how these roles are allocated in a particular organizational context, they will be needed. The section has also acknowledged the significance of team structures in supporting change, and the risk that they might undermine it if not given appropriate attention.

Further reading

Block, P (2000) *Flawless Consulting: A guide to getting your expertise used*

Kotter, J P (2014) *Accelerate: Building strategic agility for a faster-moving world*

Questions to think about

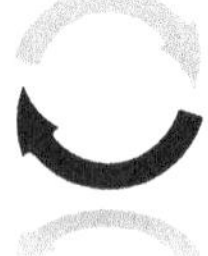

Consider a recent organizational change you have experienced or led. How (and by whom) were the following roles fulfilled:

- Idea-generator?
- Sponsor?
- Change agent(s)?

– How effectively did these roles function?

– How effectively were line management and change 'targets' engaged?

Section E: Organizational culture and change

Introduction

In this section I discuss 'organizational culture'. By this I mean the established system of accepted behaviours, values, beliefs and assumptions that is widely shared within the organization, and which as a result no one notices. In this sense culture is 'what everyone knows' or 'the way things are done around here'. The key is that because 'everyone knows', no one questions – or if they do they are felt to be rocking the boat.

1. What we mean by 'organizational culture'

1.1 Towards a description of organizational culture

Trompenaars and Hampden-Turner (2012) describe cultures of all kinds as having three levels (they describe them as layers, like an onion):

- *Level one (surface): visible artefacts and products.* In organizational terms this will be things like office layout and furnishings (who gets the corner offices, are some chairs bigger and more luxurious than others etc).
- *Level two (deeper): norms and values.* Norms are the shared and accepted sense in an organization of what is 'right' or 'wrong'. They are expressed in formal ways through the company rulebook, and in less formal ways by social control. Values are the basis on which something is seen as 'good' or

'bad', based on the shared ideals and aspirations of those in the organization, and as a result guide how people want to behave 'at their best'. A 'work hard to succeed' ethic, or a strong value about 'work–life balance' are potentially contrasting examples of values. Although they may occasionally be put into words, norms and values are most often noticed when they are violated. The rest of the time they are simply assumed.

- *Level three (deepest): basic assumptions*. In national culture, Trompenaars and Hampden-Turner give as an example the assumption that 'all people are equal'. Basic assumptions are seldom articulated (except as political slogans!) but underpin many of the norms and values of some societies.

CASE STUDY

One example of a 'basic assumption' in operation occurred in a retail pharmacy chain. The assumption was that patient health care, medical ethics and the practitioner–patient relationship were supremely important. The pharmacy chain was bought by a major consumer goods retailer with a strong and aggressive sales culture. The merger failed, largely because the retail branch managers, mostly strongly ethical pharmacists, could not adapt and operate effectively in the sales culture of the new parent company.

1.2 How culture develops and how to identify it

Organizational culture develops for good reasons. At a particular period in the organization's history particular assumptions, values and norms will have led to its success. These are often the assumptions of the founder or of leaders who have been influential during a critical period. As a result, the lessons about 'what really matters' sink deeply into the organizational unconscious, shaping future behaviour from beneath. When change occurs it may threaten this unconscious system and suffer rejection, just as the body's immune system rejects unrecognized invaders.

To manage change in an organization requires sensitivity to these processes and the ability to bring culture to organizational consciousness. There it can be discussed and evaluated for its relevance to current needs. It is then possible to manage key messages across the organization in a way that supports change. But understanding a culture is not a trivial task. Schein (1985) argues that it is not possible for either an external person or an internal person, working alone, to identify the strands of organizational culture. It requires careful collaboration between those inside the organization, well embedded in its culture, and someone external who can see the assumptions that 'insiders' are making – supported by a thoughtful process.

1.3 How culture is shaped

We have already mentioned the importance of managing messages as a means of supporting changes of culture; Carolyn Taylor (2005) describes three mechanisms through which messages are communicated:

- *Behaviours*. Examples she uses to illustrate this include the link between leaders' behaviours and culture produced: humility and willingness to admit mistakes produces openness and learning; asking for commitments and following up produces a culture of accountability; favouritism not based on performance produces politics.
- *Symbols*. 'Any time when one event is seen as part of a larger pattern' (Taylor, 2005), such as patterns in how leaders make choices about use of time or resource allocation. Rituals – also patterns, but this time of expected behaviour – could include a regular informal mid-morning gathering around the coffee machine, which emphasizes a relational culture. Storytelling – again following a pattern, as in the values in fairy stories and national legends – talks about the 'defining moments' of an organization's history, together with its heroes and villains.
- *Systems*. Taylor describes these as: 'those mechanisms of management which control, plan, measure and reward your organization and its people'. Examples include the way HR systems (and especially performance management systems) operate, customer processes and organizational structure (how many levels? how easy is access to senior level people?).

When engaging in any change that touches culture, close attention to all these mechanisms is vital.

CASE STUDY

One company board led the organization towards a personal, consensual, influence-driven leadership culture in place of the previous command-and-control style. After each board meeting they spent 15 minutes reviewing every decision they had made for consistency with the new culture – and on occasions went back and changed a decision that they realized was incompatible with it. The new culture stuck.

1.4 Culture and climate

There is often confusion about how the terms 'culture' and 'climate' are used. We have described above the way we see culture. Organizational climate is somewhat more changeable, reflecting the current feelings and perceptions of key stakeholders. For example, this might include the feelings of staff about the way they are led and resourced, whether they currently experience their workplace as a 'good employer to work for'. Those 'climatic conditions' are influenced in part by underlying culture, just as global climate is influenced by the physical structure of the earth, but are also open to medium-term fluctuations resulting from a variety of non-cultural factors.

2. Key dimensions of culture

2.1 Categorizing culture

There have been many academic and commercial attempts to categorize cultures, and good familiarity with one or two of these can be a helpful shortcut for the change manager trying to understand and interpret the culture of a particular organization. Here I offer two examples of published models.

Taylor (2005) lists five positive cultural focuses that an organization might select:

- Achievement (performance, accountability, delivery).
- Customer-centric (externally focused, service-oriented and sustainable).
- One-team (collaborative and focused on the internal customer).
- Innovative (entrepreneurship, agile, creative and learning).
- People-first (empowerment, development, care).

Blends of these five 'organization types' are certain to exist, and additional focuses are also possible. Taylor stresses the need to obtain clear agreement on the cultural focus that will best serve the organization's future needs, and then to journey towards it. Her emphasis on supporting the journey with effective communication and an appropriate management process is invaluable.

A different approach is offered by Trompenaars and Hampden-Turner (2012). They categorize cultures using two pairs of opposed ideas, each pair forming a bipolar scale:

- A 'task–person' scale provokes thought about the balance between the importance placed on tasks and results, and that placed on people and relationships. Clearly the ideas at both ends of this scale are important, but most cultures tend to value one more than the other.
- An 'egalitarian–hierarchical' scale is mostly about how widely or narrowly power and influence are distributed or controlled.

The authors use these two scales to create four cultural archetypes with very evocative titles: 'incubator', 'guided missile', 'family' and 'Eiffel Tower' (Figure 1.12). They helpfully describe the way that each of these will affect relationships, reward systems,

FIGURE 1.12 Cultural archetypes (adapted from Trompenaars and Hampden-Turner, 2012)

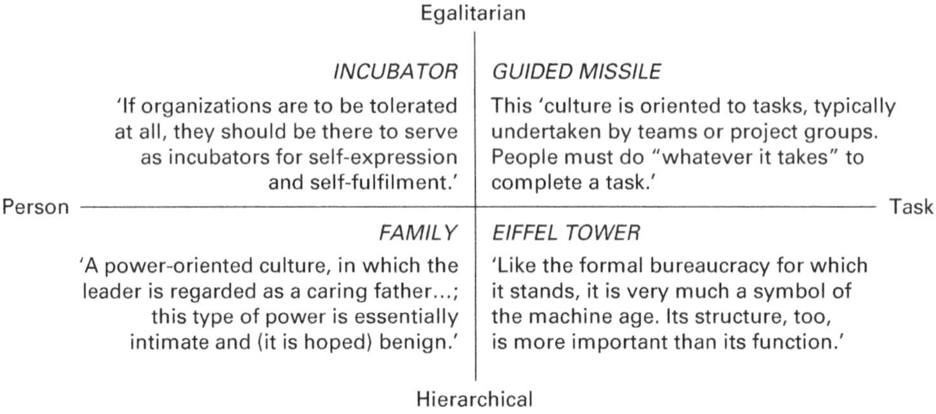

Egalitarian

Person — Task

INCUBATOR	*GUIDED MISSILE*
'If organizations are to be tolerated at all, they should be there to serve as incubators for self-expression and self-fulfilment.'	This 'culture is oriented to tasks, typically undertaken by teams or project groups. People must do "whatever it takes" to complete a task.'
FAMILY	*EIFFEL TOWER*
'A power-oriented culture, in which the leader is regarded as a caring father...; this type of power is essentially intimate and (it is hoped) benign.'	'Like the formal bureaucracy for which it stands, it is very much a symbol of the machine age. Its structure, too, is more important than its function.'

Hierarchical

SOURCE: Trompenaars, F and Hampden-Turner, C (1998) *Riding the Waves of Culture: Understanding diversity in global business*, 2nd edn, McGraw-Hill Education, NY. Copyright © McGraw-Hill Education. (Also published by Nicholas Brealey Publishing, London; 3rd edn in 2012.)

attitudes to authority and people, patterns of thought, change and conflict resolution. Clearly it is possible in principle to 'plot' a particular organization at any point within the space identified by these axes, so that more subtle differences of culture will be reflected here than would be seen in a pure 'type' approach to culture.

Many commercial models and surveys are available. They can be used to measure aspects of culture or climate, and may help to measure changes through a change initiative. In selecting such an approach, consider carefully whether the underlying model focuses clearly on the particular aspects of culture that the organization wishes to modify.

3. Relating 'culture' to types of change

There are too many possible types of change for a complete description to be possible, but we offer some illustrative examples.

The office move (or refurbishment)

A change in the physical location of an office (or school or hospital or factory) usually leads to a change in the use of space. Departments are relocated relative to one another, fewer people have a private workspace, the facilities for social interaction between people change (a small kitchen becomes a coffee machine, or the reverse). The move itself does not have any major cultural implications, but the changes that go with it probably do. People interpret these changes as messages about organizational priorities, about hierarchy and about how people are expected to relate to one another. Careful thought about the cultural impact of proposed changes on those messages will allow undesirable pressures on culture to be foreseen. This is especially true if these 'messages' could be seen as part of a pattern.

The company merger or acquisition

It is wise to assume that every company has its own distinct set of assumptions, values and beliefs, however similar they appear. Efforts to manage integration even-handedly will be overridden by the capabilities of different cultures.

CASE STUDY

One large financial services institution was bureaucratic and stable (but successful) with mostly long-serving employees. It merged with a more entrepreneurial one that had many highly commercial staff used to moving between organizations. Attempts at even-handedness – creating a 'best of both' culture – foundered as staff from the more agile culture of the smaller institution consistently outplayed those from the larger, more traditional one.

The IT implementation

IT implementations range from a simple upgrade of an existing system to a full-scale re-engineering of processes. At the 'simple' end, little cultural effect is likely and change effort can be focused on training and supporting people through transition as the project progresses. As the breadth of the change increases, so does the likelihood that different control mechanisms within the systems will move power around the organization, or that different behaviours will be expected.

Many more such examples could be given, including:

- A consumer products company changes focus from delivering products to delivering service.
- Local government organizations establish partnerships and 'shared services' for 'back office' functions.
- Global finance and trade organizations move to cross-culture and cross-time-zone working.

All these examples indicate the wisdom of assuming that changes of any kind have cultural implications, and of planning accordingly. It is the aspect of change most frequently overlooked when a change appears to be a straightforward one within the 'machine' metaphor. Culture is only one of the lenses through which a change needs to be viewed, but it is profound and pervasive.

4. Leadership and culture

Much has already been said about the importance of leadership behaviour in setting and maintaining culture (Section E1). Schein (1985) goes further. He argues that the primary – possibly the only – function of organizational leadership is to establish, maintain and evolve the organization culture that best allows the organization to perform effectively.

This requires insight and sensitivity at all times, but especially in times of change. Cultural awareness contributes to shaping messages that genuinely reflect their espoused cultures. Those messages are present in the everyday communications engaged in and decisions taken. Change managers have a particular role to play in helping leaders, who are usually more accustomed to addressing operational issues, to identify and manage cultural ones.

Summary

The effects of culture are embedded in every aspect of organizational life. Changes large and small are likely to have cultural implications, whether or not this is intended. It is always wise to consider the possible impacts of change on the organization's outward systems, norms values and underlying assumptions. This helps change managers to consider how to align the culture with the change, so that it does not create an obstacle.

Further reading

Taylor, C (2005) *Walking the Talk: Building a culture for success*

Trompenaars, F and Hampden-Turner, C (2012) *Riding the Waves of Culture: Understanding diversity in global business*

Questions to think about

1. What do you think are the most significant values in your organization (not necessarily the ones that it would advertise!)?
2. How would an outsider be able to see them?
3. What contradictory evidence (if any) might the outsider see?
4. Is the focus of your organization's culture more task or more people? Is it more egalitarian or more hierarchical?
5. What does this mean in practice?
6. What strengths and what weaknesses result from this culture?

Section F: Emergent change

Introduction

The discussion of 'change and the organization' in Section C recognizes that not all change initiatives can be fully planned. Morgan's (2006) 'machine metaphor' provides only one way to look at change. Bernard Burnes (2004), in writing a fascinating case study of organizational change, summarizes the literature about different approaches to organizational change by saying that: 'the two dominant ones are the planned and emergent approaches'.

In this section I offer some comments on the roots of an emergent approach to change, summarize the situations most likely to require such an approach, and make some suggestions on how leadership can be effective in promoting emergent change.

1. The roots of 'emergent change'

1.1 Chaos theory

Links are often made between emergent change in organizations and chaos theory. Chaos theory is a field of mathematics that studies situations where: 'Small differences in initial conditions... yield widely diverging outcomes... rendering long-term prediction impossible in general' (Wikipedia, accessed 15 April 2014). One of the pioneers of this field, Edward Lorenz, is quoted by Danforth (2013) as giving this highly enigmatic summary: 'Chaos: When the present determines the future, but the approximate present does not approximately determine the future.'

A simpler understanding comes from a famous example summarized in the title of a talk given by Lorenz: 'Does the flap of a butterfly's wings in Brazil set off a tornado in Texas?' – the famous 'butterfly effect'. This is not to suggest that any butterfly has the power to create a tornado! However, in principle, the flap of its wings, along with a huge number of other factors, may contribute to the initial conditions for such an event.

In organizational life, it is clear that change depends on a variety of factors ('initial conditions') some of which are difficult to identify. Individuals with no formal power may have a substantial impact on the outcome of a change process. Even the mood of an influential individual on the day that a change is communicated could contribute to initial conditions leading to success or failure. These factors are not strictly random, but are for practical purposes impossible to include in a formal change plan. In this sense it is wise to recognize that even a planned change has elements of unpredictability.

1.2 Complex adaptive systems

Holland (2006) describes complex adaptive systems (CASs) as: 'systems that have a large number of components, often called agents, that interact and adapt or learn'. Some examples quoted by Holland are: financial markets, the internet and the body's immune system. This model also offers a helpful way of looking at organizations and change:

- *Organizations consist of many 'agents'*. These are people and groups of people who work within the same definite, bounded organizational space, and who are interdependent.
- *Organizations are complex*. They are structured around – perhaps even formed by – the many daily interactions between these people and groups. The interactions follow a set of formal rules and systems, together with a range of complex social and cultural conventions.
- *Organizations adapt*. The patterns of behaviour driven by these rules and conventions tend to self-organize and mutate over time. Moreover, the patterns, and the rules and conventions themselves, adapt and change in response to events that occur in the course of the interactions.

From the point of view of organization change, this suggests that organizations will naturally change and adapt over time. It also suggests that all people and groups ('agents') in the organization will contribute to that change, intentionally or otherwise. New approaches emerge best when people are well trained, highly motivated and have the freedom to try things out (empowerment). The tendency to 'self-organization' leads to change that 'bubbles up', often with similar elements emerging in pockets around the organization. Any action that helps to shape such contributions in ways that align them with change objectives will be beneficial. Detailed planning may not be possible, but by working through networks of influence and advocacy emergent change can be encouraged and shaped.

CASE STUDY

In one large IT company in the financial sector the direction of change was set by clear messages from the general manager. He highlighted the unacceptably low service level that threatened the future of the business. Over 12–18 months around 60 per cent of the staff, from board members to junior supervisors and senior technical specialists, were given training to equip them with relevant skills in continuous improvement. They were given time and encouragement to generate improvement ideas, alongside their normal work commitments. Over a period of 18 months there was a very significant change in culture, and the many small changes led to an order of magnitude improvement in service quality performance.

1.3 Complex responsive processes

I have already suggested that the complexity of organizations stems in part from the network of interactions between people and groups. Stacey (2001) emphasizes this process in which one person does or says something ('gesture') and the resonance this creates in another person generates a response. Many of these interactions are programmed by culture or habit, but no particular pattern is inevitable. Small differences in situation will create different gestures and different response.

Stacey writes: 'making sense of organizational life requires attending to the ordinary, everyday communicative interacting between people at their own local level of interacting in the living present. This is because it is in this process that the future is being perpetually constructed as identity and difference.' Across an organization the interaction of these unpredictable gesture-response cycles will create small changes (like waves on a shoreline) or larger ones (like tides and storms).

Stacey identifies three dynamics that affect these interactions and their outcomes:

- How people relate to each other – 'formal' role relationships and 'informal' personal relationships.
- How aware people are of the impacts of their interactions – the degree to which they are 'conscious' or 'unconscious' of these impacts.
- How people define what is and is not acceptable in the 'public space' of the organization – the things that are 'legitimate' (socially accepted) or 'shadow' (less socially acceptable – such as gossip).

Each of these three dichotomies (formal–informal, conscious–unconscious, legitimate–shadow) continually exerts its own 'pull' on the direction of the organization's development, much as the moon's gravitational pull moves the oceans and creates tides. This means that change and development is seldom linear, because these three influences are sometimes aligned, creating large effects, and sometimes opposed, almost cancelling each other.

In managing a change process it is wise to be aware that every conversation, every interaction has the potential to shift the course of that change. It also means that it is unwise to overreact to the ebb and flow of particular events, but to keep clear about the overall direction of travel. It is necessary to be prepared to rebalance communications, and to engage continually with networks of influence across the organization, in order to ensure that change continues to move in a desired direction.

1.4 A VUCA world

The 'VUCA' concept originated in the US military in the late 1990s (Lawrence, 2013). It was an acknowledgement that the 'certainties' of a bipolar, cold war world were over, and that new and unpredictable challenges would follow. The acronym describes an environment characterized by:

Volatility
Uncertainty
Complexity
Ambiguity

VUCA has entered organizational thinking as a description of a world that presents new challenges, new threats and new opportunities. Apart from the notes on chaos and complexity above, a brief survey of most daily newspapers supports such a description of the social, economic and technological forces that shape our lives and organizations (to name but three – the more detailed PESTLE analysis in Chapter 2, Section A2.1 will add to this).

In Lawrence's 2013 paper mentioned above he refers to the work of Bob Johansen, whose response to this VUCA world (Johansen, 2012) is to propose an approach to leadership (described as 'VUCA Prime') characterized by:

Vision – countering *volatility*, enabling the organization to maintain direction.

Understanding – reducing *uncertainty* by being well connected, listening to views from across the organization, from all levels of the organization and from the external world.

Clarity – showing the ability to make sense of *complexity* and offering clear direction.

Agility – responding quickly and in a balanced way to situations as the *ambiguities* unfold.

These leadership characteristics are well aligned with those that enable organizations to address the complexities of emergent change.

2. Change situations that require an emergent approach

An organization change can usually be identified with one of two main archetypes (Burnes, 2004), which as he points out are described (in different ways and using different words) by Kanter, Stein and Jick (1992) and by Beer and Nohria (2000):

- *Swift and sudden* – a short period of turbulent, typically imposed change designed to deliver quick results, often driven by threats to the organization's continued success or survival.
- *Developmental and deliberate* – an extended period of patient work to build the organization's culture and capability.

A change that can readily be seen within Gareth Morgan's machine metaphor – such as the implementation of an IT system update – can generally be implemented in a 'swift and sudden' manner. Changes such as these may contain much detail complexity but are not ambiguous or uncertain. They respond well to a 'planned change' approach. Any change that is necessary for the organization's survival is also likely to be 'swift and sudden' and will similarly be managed as a planned change.

On the other hand it is the nature of culture and capability to build over time, through a 'developmental and deliberate' approach. Although the desired direction may be clear, the precise route is likely to be less so. Deviations and explorations are a common feature of culture change journeys. In such circumstances a more emergent change process should be expected. The CMI CMBoK (2013) puts it like this:

> Where the core of the change is to systems, structures, processes and practices, then planning and scheduling is possible. However, where that core change is in the discretionary decisions people make about their patterns of values and behaviours, no dates can be fixed in advance. People will engage with new patterns of behaviour individually and in their own time.

These two types of change are not mutually exclusive. Elements of both approaches may be seen in any particular phase of a change, though one or the other usually predominates. Moreover, as different phases of change occur over time, the 'developmental and deliberate' may prepare the way for the 'swift and sudden' – or may be used to align culture and capability with a 'swift and sudden' change already made.

CASE STUDY

In a UK construction company a three- to four-year period of patient development (emergent change) created a new pattern of behaviour at all levels, including management behaviour, and a new culture for the organization:

> *[The changes] relied on everyone in the company participating in them and becoming committed to them. The responsibility for their success ultimately rested with those involved rather than being managed or driven by senior managers.*
>
> *(Burnes, 2004)*

This 'developmental and deliberate' change was followed by a rapid restructuring process (six to twelve months) using planned change. The success of the restructuring was built upon the foundations laid during the earlier developmental period.

3. Defining and moving towards a 'future state'

3.1 Describing and defining the future

The complexity described earlier in this section does not mean that change managers and organization leaders are powerless. It is possible to describe and define the direction of change that is required, and to identify indicators which will show that progress is being made.

This can be achieved through a four-step process similar to that pictured in Section C2.1:

Step 1 Start by deciding on the 'big picture' change that would bring great rewards to the organization. The mission statement and strategic goals will help define this (Chapter 2, Section A).

Step 2 Look around the organization as it is now and identify all the current consequences of that change not yet being a reality. List them – what you and others see, hear and feel in the current situation.

Step 3 As an exercise in creative imagination, step into the future organization after the desired change has occurred (perhaps in three or six months, perhaps more). Look around the organization again, and identify all the outcomes of the change, as if it is already a reality. List them – what you and others see, hear and feel in this future reality.

Step 4 Identify the differences between the lists – both in objective, numerical measures and in the more subjective, informal, behavioural indicators where precise measurement is difficult or impossible. The differences will offer clues on how to plan and measure 'steps on the way'.

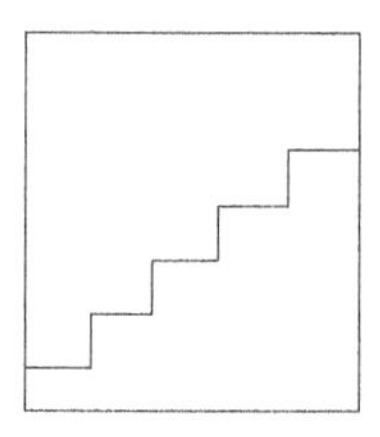

This process – especially if conducted with a group in a facilitated workshop (see Chapter 10) – can yield powerful results. It clarifies and 'makes real' the future state, in terms that can be described effectively to others. It also identifies those leading measures, indicators and markers that will enable all involved to track progress towards the desired state.

3.2 A 'force field' approach to emergent change

In Section C2.1, Kurt Lewin's 'force field analysis' is mentioned as part of a process of planned change. It is also highly relevant for an organization engaged in a more fluid 'emergent change' process. In this context it is helpful to involve as wide a range of constituencies as possible, whether or not they are formally defined as 'stakeholders'. A description of the tool is in Chapter 2, Section B2.2.

The technique encourages those involved to identify all the forces that hold the organization in its current position. It includes the powerful cultural, social and behavioural forces in such an analysis. As a result, all can identify how their own actions, behaviours and interactions with others can be used to weaken opposing forces and to strengthen the forces driving in the desired direction.

Chapter 11, Section A5 refers to the ideas of 'critical mass', 'nudge' and 'tipping points' – and these are all relevant here to help shape emergent change.

3.3 *Kotter's 'dual operating system'*

Reference has already been made in Section C4.2 to John Kotter's (2012b, 2014) increasingly well-developed concept of a 'dual operating system' in organizations. He proposes the traditional hierarchy as the basis for 'business as usual' activity, with a large 'volunteer army' of people gathering around major strategic initiatives to explore and implement them. This latter approach has many powerful features of 'emergent change', even though it is linked to a conventional organization structure.

3.4 *Providing leadership in emergent change*

Leaders cannot succeed in promoting deep, emergent change and transformation simply by more planning. However, leaders can be intentional about their own words, challenging existing paradigms and supporting new ones. They can be sure that their own actions model consistently the new expected behaviours.

Some key guidelines for providing effective leadership in emergent change situations include:

- Accept the limits of what it is possible to direct and control; changes in values and behaviour are seldom linear or fully predictable.
- Notice where the energy of the systems and people is currently focused and the outcomes of this.
- Talk widely throughout the leadership community about any different outcomes that are desired.
- Think in systems terms about the reinforcing and balancing systems you can identify.
- As far as possible, get the leadership community speaking with one voice about the desired outcomes.
- Make changes that you as a leadership community consider likely to shift the current equilibrium, enhancing some positive feedback loops and mitigating some negative ones.
- Maintain a high profile for the desired outcomes; keep discussing them in the organization at every opportunity.
- Observe the effects of the interventions you have made, especially the direction in which the system is moving relative to your desired outcomes.
- Keep repeating the three preceding actions, holding firmly to the 'non-negotiable' outcomes, but negotiating other issues as necessary.
- Celebrate and mark milestones on the journey.
- Remain open to new information that may lead to redefinition of the desired direction.

Summary

Emergent change is best seen as a journey taken in company with others in the organization. A direction is set, and the company of people agree to travel together.

The varied observations, skills and experience of all the fellow travellers may be essential to support the company on its journey, and to identify and deal with hazards and threats that appear along the way. The journey may have an intended – even agreed – destination, but the route must be adapted to suit the company of travellers. Even the destination may need to be reviewed in the light of new information gathered along the way. Safe arrival is a signal for celebrations – and planning the next adventure!

Questions to think about

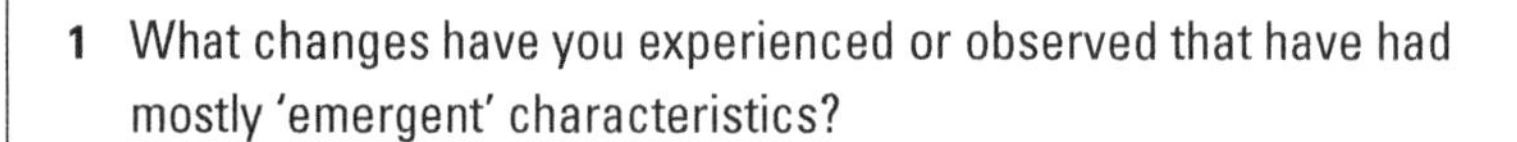

1. What changes have you experienced or observed that have had mostly 'emergent' characteristics?
2. What actions by organizational leaders (or others) helped those changes to happen?

Further reading

Handy, C (1994) *The Empty Raincoat: Making sense of the future*
Johansen, B (2012) *Leaders Make the Future: Ten new leadership skills for an uncertain world*
Senge, PM *et al* (1999) *The Dance of Change*
Stacey, RD (2001) *Complex Responsive Processes in Organizations: Learning and knowledge creation*

References

Adams, J, Hayes, J and Hopson, B (1976) *Transition: Understanding and managing personal change*, Martin Robertson, London
Balogun, J and Hope Hailey, V (2008) *Exploring Strategic Change*, Pearson Education, Harlow
Beer, M and Nohria, N (2000) Cracking the code of change, *Harvard Business Review*, 78 (3), May–June 2000, pp 133–41
Block, P (2000) *Flawless Consulting: A guide to getting your expertise used*, 2nd edn, Jossey-Bass, San Francisco, CA
Bridges, W (2009) *Managing Transitions: Making the most of change*, 3rd edn, Nicholas Brealey, London
Briggs Myers, I and Myers, P B (1995) *Gifts Differing: Understanding personality type*, 2nd edn, CPP Inc, Mountain View, CA

Briggs Myers, I (2000) *Introduction to Type™*, 6th edn, revised by Linda K Kirby and Katharine D Myers, Consulting Psychologists Press Inc/Oxford Psychologists Press Limited, California

Burnes, B (1992) *Managing Change: A strategic approach to organisational development and renewal*, Pitman, London

Burnes, B (2004) Emergent change and planned change – competitors or allies?: The case of XYZ construction, *International Journal of Operations & Production Management*, **24** (9), pp 886–902

Cameron, E and Green, M (2009) *Making Sense of Change Management: A complete guide to the models, tools and techniques of organizational change*, 2nd edn, Kogan Page, London

Cameron, E and Green, M (2012) *Making Sense of Change Management: A complete guide to the models, tools and techniques of organizational change*, 3rd edn, Kogan Page, London

Changefirst (2010) *The ROI for Change Management: How change management makes a substantial difference to project performance*, Changefirst Limited, Haywards Heath (www.changefirst.com)

Change Management Institute (CMI) (2013) *The Effective Change Manager: The change management body of knowledge* (CMBoK) Change Management Institute, Sydney

Conner, D (1993) *Managing at the Speed of Change*, Villard, New York

Danforth, C M (2013) [accessed 16 April 2014] Chaos in an Atmosphere Hanging on a Wall, *Mathematics of Planet Earth 2013* [Online] http://mpe2013.org/2013/03/17/chaos-in-an-atmosphere-hanging-on-a-wall/

Ferris, K (2013) *ITSM Solution Projects Need Organisational Change Management*, Macanta Consulting, Australia

Handy, C (1994) *The Empty Raincoat: Making sense of the future*, Hutchinson, London

Herzberg, F (2003) One more time: how do you motivate employees? *Harvard Business Review*, **81** (1), January 2003, pp 87–96 (reprint of original article from 1968)

Hirsh, S K and Kummerow, J M (1994) *Introduction to Type™ in Organizations*, 2nd edn, Oxford Psychologists Press Limited, UK

Holland, J H (2006) Studying complex adaptive systems, *Journal of Systems Science and Complexity*, **19**, pp 1–8

Honey, P and Mumford, A (1992) *The Manual of Learning Styles*, Peter Honey, Maidenhead

Huczynsky, A A and Buchanan, D A (2007) *Organizational Behaviour*, Pearson Education Ltd, Harlow

Hughes, M (2011) Do 70 per cent of all organizational change initiatives really fail? *Journal of Change Management*, **11** (4), December 2011, pp 451–64

Hyatt, J M and Creasey, T J (2012) *Change Management: The people side of change*, Prosci Inc, Loveland, CO

IBM (2008a) *Global CEO Study Hungry for Change*, IBM, New York

IBM (2008b) *Making Change Work*, IBM, New York

Johansen, B (2012) *Leaders Make the Future: Ten new leadership skills for an uncertain world*, 2nd edn, Berrett-Koehler, San Francisco, CA

Kanter, R M, Stein, B A and Jick, T D (1992) *The Challenge of Organizational Change*, Free Press, New York

King, S and Peterson, L (2007) How effective leaders achieve success in critical change initiatives, part 2: why change leadership must transcend project management for complex initiatives to be successful, *Healthcare Quarterly*, **10** (2), April 2007, pp 70–75

Kotter, J P (1995) Leading change: why transformation efforts fail, *Harvard Business Review*, **73** (2), May/June 1995, pp 59–67

Kotter, J P (2012a) *Leading Change*, Harvard Business Review Press, Boston, MA

Kotter, J P (2012b) Accelerate, *Harvard Business Review*, **90** (11), November 2012, pp 44–58
Kotter, J P (2014) *Accelerate: Building strategic agility for a faster-moving world*, Harvard Business Review Press, Boston, MA
Kotter, J P and Rathgeber, H (2006) *Our Iceberg is Melting*, Macmillan, London
Kübler-Ross, E (1969) *On Death and Dying*, Macmillan, Toronto
Laclair, J A and Rao, R P (2002) Helping employees embrace change, *McKinsey Quarterly*, November 2002
Lawrence, K (2013) [accessed 16 April 2014] Developing Leaders in a VUCA Environment [Online] http://www.growbold.com/2013/developing-leaders-in-a-vuca-environment_UNC.2013.pdf
Lewin, K (1947) Frontiers in group dynamics: concept, method and reality in social science; social equilibria and social change, *Human Relations*, **1** (5), June 1947, available at: http://hum.sagepub.com/content/1/1/5
Lewin, K, in Cartwright, D (ed) (1951) *Field Theory in Social Science*, Tavistock, London
Maslow, A H (1943) A theory of human motivation, *Psychological Review*, **50**, pp 370–96
McClelland, D C (1987) *Human Motivation*, Cambridge University Press, Cambridge
McGregor, D M (1957) The human side of enterprise, quoted in *Management and Motivation*, eds V H Vroom and E L Deci, Penguin, Harmondsworth
McGregor, D M (1960) *The Human Side of Enterprise*, quoted in C Handy, *Understanding Organisations*, 4th edn, Penguin, London, p 36
Moorhouse Consulting (2013) *Barometer on Change 2013: If a change is worth doing, focus on doing it well*, Moorhouse, London
Morgan, G (2006) *Images of Organization*, 2nd edn, Sage, London
Mumford, E and Beekman, G J (1994) *Tools for change and Progress: A socio-technical approach to business process re-engineering*, SCG Publications, Leiden
O'Neill, M B (2007) *Executive Coaching with Backbone and Heart*, 2nd edn, Wiley, San Francisco
Parker, C and Lewis, R (1981) Beyond the Peter Principle – managing successful transitions, *Journal of European Industrial Training*, **5** (6), pp 17–21
Pink, D H (2011) *Drive: The surprising truth about what motivates us*, Canongate, Edinburgh
Pink, D H [undated] [accessed 4 February 2014] *Drive: The surprising truth about what motivates us*, Transcript of Lecture to the Royal Society of Arts, London [Online] http://www.thersa.org/events/rsaanimate/animate/rsa-animate-drive
Prosci (2012) *Best Practices in Change Management*, Loveland, CO
PwC (2004) [accessed 24 September 2013] Boosting Business Performance through Programme and Project Management [Online] http://www.pwc.com/us/en/operations-management/assets/pwc-global-project-management-survey-first-survey-2004.pdf
Ringleb, A H and Rock, D (2008) [accessed 28 April 2014] The emerging field of neuroleadership, *NeuroLeadership Journal*, **1**, 2008 [Online] http://www.davidrock.net/files/IntroNLS.pdf
Rock, D and Schwarz, J (2006) [accessed 28 April 2014] The neuroscience of leadership, *Strategy and Business*, **43**, Summer 2006 [Online] http://www.strategy-business.com/article/06207
Rogers, C R (1957) The necessary and sufficient conditions for therapeutic personality change, *Journal of Consulting Psychology*, **21** (2), pp 95–103, in *The Carl Rogers Reader*, eds H Kirschenbaum and V L Henderson, Constable, London
Schein, E H (1985) *Organizational Culture and Leadership*, Jossey-Bass, San Francisco, CA
Schein, E H (1993) How can organizations learn faster? The challenge of entering the green room, *Sloan Management Review*, **34** (2), Winter 1993, pp 85–92

Senge, P M (1993) *The Fifth Discipline: The art & practice of the learning organization*, Century Business, London
Senge, P M *et al* (1999) *The Dance of Change: The challenges of sustaining momentum in learning organizations*, Nicholas Brealey, London
Smith, M E (2002) Success rates for different types of organizational change, *Performance Improvement Journal*, **41** (1), January 2002, pp 26–33
Stacey, R D (2001) *Complex Responsive Processes in Organizations: Learning and knowledge creation*, Routledge, London
Taylor, C (2005) *Walking the Talk: Building a culture for success*, Random House, London
Trompenaars, F and Hampden-Turner, C (2012) *Riding the Waves of Culture: Understanding diversity in global business*, 3rd edn, Nicholas Brealey, London
Wikipedia contributors [accessed 22 February 2014] Complexity Theory and Organizations, *Wikipedia, The Free Encyclopedia* [Online] http://en.wikipedia.org/w/index.php?title=Complexity_theory_and_organizations&oldid=596690665
Wikipedia contributors [accessed 15 April 2014] Chaos Theory, *Wikipedia, The Free Encyclopedia* [Online] http://en.wikipedia.org/w/index.php?title=Chaos_theory&oldid=604308207

Defining change

02

ROBERT COLE, DAVID KING AND ROD SOWDEN

Introduction

To be successful, change in organizations must first be fully defined and understood. This clarity supports effective engagement with all stakeholders within and outside the organization. It gives a shared foundation on which the differing perspectives of all stakeholders can build a consensus, and a shared commitment to the change. Clear definition also supports a clear assessment of the organization's change capability and capacity: does the organization possess the skills, competences and resources for the change to succeed?

In preparing an organization for change, there are six key questions for organizations to consider:

1 Why is change needed?
2 What change do we need to make?
3 How will the change affect us – both positively or negatively?
4 When do we need to change?
5 Who will lead and facilitate the change?
6 How will we make change a success?

Many people from across the organization, together with expert and specialist advisers, will play a part in answering these key questions. This will involve:

- a diagnosis and analysis of needs, issues, the environment and priorities for change;
- detailed definition and design of the changes that reflects the diverse needs, expectations and aspirations of the organization and its people;
- creation of a viable and achievable change management plan and supporting business case, aligned to the organization's corporate strategic goals.

A clear and concise definition of the change is essential to ensure that the change effort is both focused and sustained. Moreover, change must be benefit driven,

FIGURE 2.1 Unfreezing the present situation (Lewin, 1951)

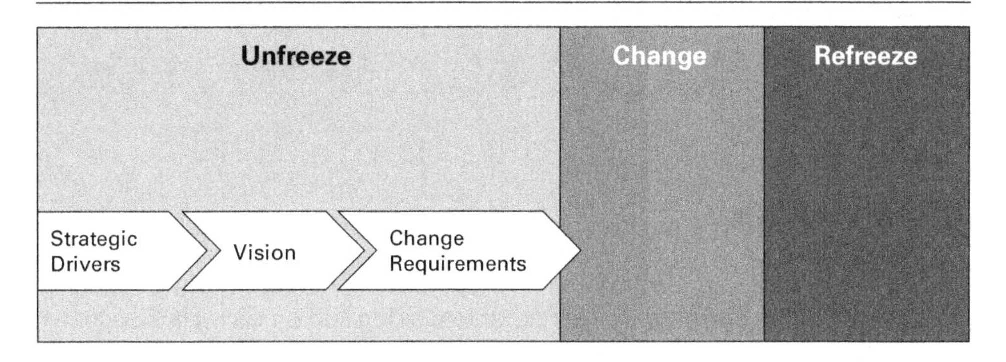

with a clear end-goal – or vision – to work towards. As Stephen Covey suggests in his *The 7 Habits of Highly Effective People* (2011), we should 'begin with the end in mind' (habit 2). Covey says: 'begin each day, task, or project with a clear vision of your desired direction and destination, and then continue by flexing your proactive muscles to make things happen. You create your own destiny and secure the future you envision.' This is as true for organizations as it is for individuals. This chapter explores some of the approaches, tools, techniques and insights that will enable an organization to get started on the change journey towards its desired future.

Kurt Lewin's three-step model (Figure 2.1 and Chapter 1, Section C2.1) provides a useful framework for 'defining change' – and the structure for this chapter. In the 'unfreeze' stage, an organization seeks to:

- reflect new or changed strategy;
- unlock the present way of doing things by establishing a new vision;
- fully define the change requirements.

CHAPTER CONTENTS

Section A: Aligning change with strategy

Robert Cole

Introduction

Strategy defines what an organization is going to do in the future that responds to the changing environment in which it needs to develop and prosper. The reason that most organizations need a good strategy is because with a poor strategy, or in the absence of one, the organization will not survive. The primary purpose of a strategy, therefore, is to show how an organization intends to develop, given the environment in which it operates.

The purpose of this section is to explain some of the principles of strategy development, some thinking tools used to develop strategy in an organization, and the implications for defining change. Nearly all the literature on strategy is based on commercial organizations. However, third sector organizations, central and local government can also use these tools to understand their environment and develop appropriate policies.

1. Background to strategy development

Strategy is a *concept*, a *process* and an *output*. The *concept* is an answer to the question: 'What is our strategy?' The *process* is the thought process required to answer this question. Strategy (expressed as a statement) is an *output* because a particular statement of the strategy is only true at a certain point in time. The concept will evolve and change. Developing a good strategy is difficult. Strategy relies on assumptions about the future: poor prediction leads to a poor strategy.

According to Porter (2009) strategy relies on a combination of a unique proposition to customers and the unique activities needed to deliver that value. Fulfilment of the strategy requires an organization's managers to answer some defining questions that reach to the hearts of both the managers and the organization.

A government organization usually has a unique position built in. Taxpayers do not readily tolerate duplication in government services: although monopoly suppliers, government still needs to deliver value. This why government departments typically have structures that test the value they deliver. This is what encourages the search for improved services and better value for the taxpayer.

For a commercial organization, Porter shows why a strategy that differentiates the organization from the competition is essential. If its business operation is precisely as efficient and effective as its competitors (no more and no less) and is supplying exactly the same value to customers then two things follow: 1) Any small improvement in operations, efficiency or effectiveness is quickly copied by competitors.

Hence there is only *temporary differentiation* as far as customers are concerned; 2) Customers seek out suppliers based on price, so it becomes impossible to sell at anything above cost price. The result is that no business makes a profit to invest in improvement or growth. No economic value is generated and eventually only the business with the lowest cost base will survive.

The purpose of strategy, therefore, is to enable business organizations to survive and prosper by meeting different customers' needs, in different ways, with different activities. Consequently, there is room in the market for many businesses, all creating economic value. It is useful to examine some of the thinking tools for creating a strategy by looking at:

The far environment of an organization. This is the industry structure, the big external drivers and trends (especially technology), and the potential for disruption. This addresses the question: what business are we in?

The near environment of an organization. This concerns competitor organizations, the nature of the value proposition to customers and the business model (the competitive position). This addresses the question: how do we compete?

2. The far environment

It is useful to examine some of the tools frequently used to assess the organization's business environment when creating a good strategy.

2.1 PESTLE

The external drivers in the 'far' environment of an organization are often categorized using the acronym 'PESTLE' (Figure 2.2) as follows:

FIGURE 2.2 PESTLE external drivers

- *Political*: policies and directions of national and local government organizations set some of the conditions for business and for delivery by other government organizations. Political drivers also include the amount of redistribution, the tax ratio, the generosity of benefits, areas of investment (such as renewable energy) and plans for intervention (such as regional development programmes).
- *Economic*: national and global economic circumstances and the ability of different industries and organizations to grow. Drivers may include opportunities for overseas trading and impact of industry-wide trends.
- *Social*: opinions and needs of groups within society. This includes changing trends, the tastes and expectations of societal groups such as for health care. Drivers also reflect changing demographics such as more people living longer and fewer people in the population in work.
- *Technology*: a rapidly moving driver with both major trends and disruptions. Drivers include increasing – and rapidly evolving – use of electronic multimedia communications by individuals and organizations.
- *Legal*: often the implementation of new legislation and policies that place constraints under which organizations must work, as well as opportunities. Some organizations are created through legislation; others see it as a cost.
- *Environmental*: what is happening in the natural world around us, ranging from protecting endangered species to managing weather events. Drivers also include changing attitudes and practices on environmental (green) protection and conservation.

Tip

In practice these 'PESTLE' categories are closely linked and interact with each other. The list provides a useful checklist to help ensure all external drivers are considered. It is critical to obtain information about the drivers seeking trends and early warning signs that might affect strategy. Organizational strategists need to keep abreast of current thinking, events, and analysis.

2.2 Industry

A key concept in the far environment is that of an industry. This is an identifiable group of business organizations doing very similar things in the delivery of value to customers – the food industry, the pharmaceutical industry, the airline industry and so on. Each of these industries has different dynamics and different levels of investment return. An organization must ask: 'What business are we in?' This will identify the value that the managers perceive they are delivering to their customers.

CASE STUDY

Kodak processed camera film into paper images that people can keep. Is Kodak in the chemical business (their processes were all chemical and all the senior managers were chemists)? Or were they in the 'personal memories' business because that was the real value of the photographs they produced? While wrestling with these questions, Kodak missed the revolutionary change to digital images and cameras. They nearly went out of business, even though the digital camera was invented in Kodak and the company held many of the early patents.

2.3 *Porter's five forces*

To understand the level of competition in an industry, and why it makes a particular level of return for its participants, Michael Porter developed an economic model called the 'five forces' model (Porter, 2008). The five forces are:

1. Threat of new entrants.
2. Threat of new substitutes.
3. Bargaining power of new buyers.
4. Bargaining power of new suppliers.
5. Rivalry amongst competitors.

Threat of new entrants

New entrants increase supply in that industry, which tends to drive down prices. A key question therefore is: 'How easy is it for a new company to enter the industry?' Some industries (such as banking) have regulatory 'barriers to entry', making it difficult for new organizations to enter. Others require very high levels of initial investment to set up. Unless profit levels are very high, new entrants will have no incentive to overcome these barriers. On the other hand, industries with low barriers to entry tend to have low profit levels.

CASE STUDY

The airline industry is surprisingly easy to enter. Southwest Airlines started with a flight schedule of six round trips between Dallas and San Antonio, and 12 round trips between

Dallas and Houston. They rented three 737-200s from Boeing, and rented airport gates and other required infrastructure.

Threat of new substitutes

Can the needs of a customer be met by a different industry? For instance, rail travel is a substitute for air travel in some situations. The availability of substitutes limits the price of an offering and differentiation opportunities.

Threat of bargaining power of new buyers

How much can buyers push down prices because of oversupply or poor differentiation? Where two airlines fly the same route, the differentiation is limited to time and convenience. When buying a soft drink most buyers have strong preferences for taste and brand (lifestyle image). This generates differentiation, loyalty and high returns.

Threat of bargaining power of new suppliers

How much value can suppliers in the supply chain claim through their bargaining position? In the airline industry there are only a couple of major aircraft manufacturers, and in each geographic location usually only one airport. Airlines do not have much choice and both aircraft manufacturers and airports make more profit than airlines. By contrast, in the soft drinks industry the main ingredients are sugar, carbon dioxide, water and unskilled labour. These are all commodities, and their suppliers have little power over the soft drinks industry – which makes six times as much return on investment as airlines.

Rivalry amongst competitors

Who are the competition and how fierce is it? What competitive positions are already taken? How differentiated are positions? Are there markets leaders? If so, with how much market share?

A good strategy takes into account all of these five forces. Every business should make sure it is in an industry it can do well in. Changing industry is difficult. However, it is one strategic option, and would result in major changes inside the organization. Approximately half of the economic value of a business comes from its industry situation, so the decision is very important (Bradley, Dawson and Smit, 2013).

Tip

As with external drivers, it is not just the current position of an industry but the *trends* that are really important. The trends help us peer into the future, which is what a strategy is all about. It is often these trends that make staying in an industry a key decision.

3. The near environment

In the near environment the key question is: 'How will we compete?' This translates to the question: 'What is our unique selling proposition (USP)?' This sums up how an organization is delivering distinctive value to its customers, for which they are willing to pay.

A strong competitive position comes from making a distinctive offering to customers relative to your competitors. Competitive analysis in the near environment is essential. Michael Porter (1985) identified three unique positioning strategies:

1. *Overall cost leadership*: usually achieved by becoming the largest business in the industry and exploiting economies of scale.
2. *Differentiation*: achieved by a product or service that offers a feature or capability (or perceived benefit such as luxury or status) that no competitor offers.
3. *Focus*: achieved by establishing an advantageous access to a specific customer segment, geography or product application.

4. Business modelling

A coherent business model is at the heart of an organizational strategy. An organization's business model shows how the strategy is to be implemented. Business activities need to be systemically joined up so that they provide a seamless delivery of the required business value. Typically, organizations will often undertake these activities in different departments or 'silos' (and consequently have problems being joined up). The business model needs to show how the different parts of the organization will work together. Some of these activities just need to be as good as the industry average so they do not become a reason for not buying from you. Others will be your differentiators and need to be superior to the competition. These key activities will be the focus of resources and management attention.

CASE STUDY

In the telecoms industry the big players often have a poor reputation for customer service, with offshore call centres. Some smaller telecoms companies make a feature of their customer service, using onshore call centres, more empowered staff and better response times. They are attracting a market segment of customers who want that type of service and have failed to get it so far.

Systematically joining up an organization's activities to implement a strategic vision is aided by the adoption of 'systems theory'. More is said in Sections C and D about using systems theory and soft systems methods (SSM) to develop an organization's future state vision, and the supporting business models.

5. Strategic delivery processes

Every organization needs a process to deliver and review their strategy. A basic process (Table 2.1) is suggested by Bradley (2012) that includes:

- creativity and searching for innovative ideas to deliver value to customers;
- a method for integrating ideas into options and a coherent story that can be used to explain the concept (a vision);
- a mechanism for making a decision amongst options;
- a process for implementing a strategy by making changes in the business;
- the ability to regularly review all of the above and the effectiveness of the process itself.

TABLE 2.1 Strategic delivery process (Bradley, 2012)

	Idea Generation	Develop and Decide	Execute and Refine
1 Frame objectives and constraints	✓		
2 Baseline performance and capabilities	✓		
3 Forecast what we expect of the future	✓	✓	
4 Search for options to create value		✓	
5 Choose a package of options		✓	✓
6 Commit to deliver the required changes			✓
7 Evolve the strategy over time			✓

5.1 Scenario thinking

Based on some original work in RAND and Royal Dutch Shell, the idea of scenario thinking (Heijden, 2004) is to integrate a range of factors that will contribute to alternative possible futures and to capture them in a story (Figure 2.3). Usually the stories are not that useful outside the group that created them, but participating in the scenario development stimulates thinking in a way that widens horizons and admits new and creative possibilities for a strategy.

This method also identifies the 'preferred future scenario' – where the existing strategy will take the business. This can then be compared with other possible futures and the strategies needed to reach them. Scenarios enable identification of early warning signs that one or another possible future may become more likely so that action can be taken to change or refine the strategy before it is too late.

FIGURE 2.3 Developing possible future scenarios

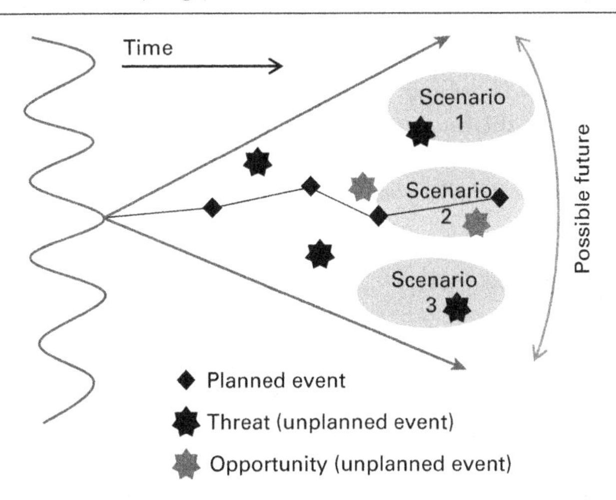

5.2 *'What if' models*

'What if' models are useful to explore possibilities and to test existing ideas for robustness against future events. A series of questions about the actions of players in the industry, competitors and customers can explore potential causes and effects. These can be explored through the use of fishbone (Ishikawa) diagrams (Section D4.2 below). Instead of looking into the past, this technique gets you to position yourself in the future and ask: 'How did we get here?'

Some key questions to ask are:

- What if our main competitor attacked our best market?
- What made that market attractive to them?
- How much might it have cost them to change their business model to deliver the value proposition needed?
- What did we do that made it easier for them to attack our market?
- What was their first move? (This might identify an early warning sign.)

6. Strategy and change

Once the organization has decided on its future strategy, the next challenge is to implement the decisions and align the operation capability to deliver the new business model. This means:

1. Examining where we are now with our current business model.
2. Comparing the current business model against the required business model for the strategy.
3. Determining the differences.

This identifies what needs to change and forms the basis for defining the future vision and change portfolio (programmes, projects and other initiatives) needed to deliver the strategy (Sections C and D).

The delivery of the strategy and the required business performance needs to be reviewed regularly to determine whether the changes have delivered the strategic objectives. Answering this question will demonstrate the clarity and focus of the objectives. The focus for change is to deliver the benefits and thereby achieve the organization's strategic objectives.

Summary

The purpose of a strategy for an organization is to look into the future to seek ways to survive, grow and prosper. The resulting strategy then identifies the changes necessary to the existing organization (its processes, people, assets and information) that will ensure survival, at least, and prosperity, at best. A good strategy will identify a unique competitive position as a value proposition to customers, and the business model needed to sustain that position.

Questions to think about

1. What are the strategic objectives of your organization?
2. Is there a coherent business model that is capable of implementing the strategy?
3. Does the strategy and supporting model provide sufficient information to define the organization's requirements for change?

Section B: Drivers of change

Robert Cole

Introduction

Identifying the drivers of change, the factors driving the need to change, includes the use of this information to maintain strategic focus and energy throughout the change process. It provides the answers to the fundamental questions 'Why change?' and 'Why now?' Section A discussed how strategy can be developed. Following this, the strategic objectives for the organization become the context for all change.

1. The strategic context

1.1 Emergent change

Emergent change arises from within the organization in response to external drivers. These often reflect the emergence of new trends or activities. These drivers are usually the need to keep operations working effectively and efficiently by incorporating new technology and practices from competitors in the industry. Emergent changes do not necessarily change the business model of the organization but may have a significant influence on what needs to be done to maintain the company's products and services to be as least as good as those from competitors and at least as cost-efficient. Changes may also be needed to ensure that the differentiation (USP) that the organization has is maintained, so that the competition are not tempted to emulate it.

A characteristic of emergent change is that it can often be started (almost) simultaneously in different parts of an organization where middle managers have started to solve a problem within their area of control. This can lead to a number of different solutions arising to essentially the same problem, which then need to be aligned with the strategic objectives and a single solution chosen for the whole organization to be efficient and consistent. This can, in turn, lead to the definition of a new vision and business model that lays the foundations for a strategic change initiative. Chapter 1, Section F addresses the wider organizational impacts of emergent change.

1.2 Cascading decisions and designs

The change drivers are part of a strategic process to both create an organization's strategy and implement it through change. This means there are a number of feedback loops and cascading decisions and designs in the process, all of which identify drivers for change. The process (Figure 2.4) moderates the strategy and change design, checks for success and manages failure.

FIGURE 2.4 The change cascade

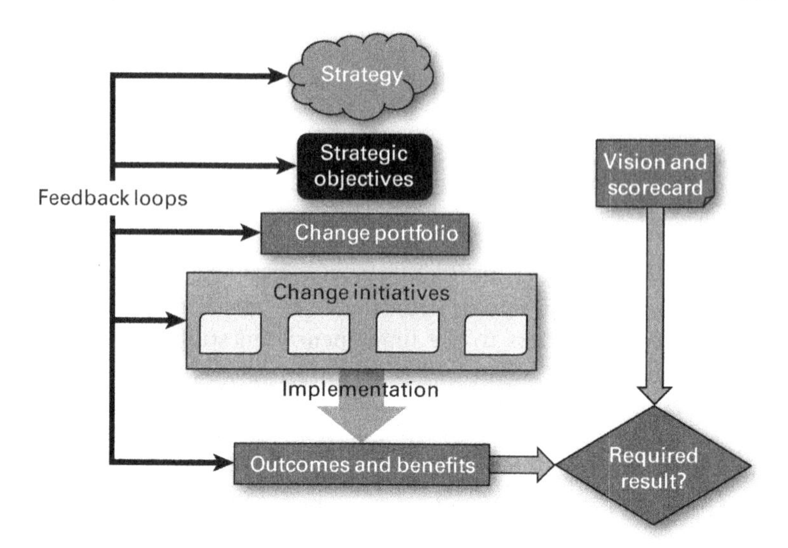

The cascading decisions are strategic decisions about the choice of business model and implementation options, identification of strategic objectives with their vision and performance scorecard (if used).

The change cascade works as follows:

- portfolio decisions about how to achieve the strategic objectives within the capability and capacity of the organization result in a portfolio level plan;
- a number of change initiatives are created;
- implementation of the initiatives includes further cascading decisions leading to delivery of outcomes and achievement of benefits;
- delivered outcomes can be matched against the vision and scorecard to measure success.

At each stage there is a feedback loop involving feasibility and design optimization so that strategy development is informed by the ability to deliver it.

1.3 Implementing strategy through portfolios, programmes and projects

We have seen how strategic intent leads to the development of change initiatives within a portfolio structure. These initiatives are typically managed through projects and programmes, which provide the necessary governance structure for the organization (Figure 2.5) (see also Chapter 8). The relationship between portfolios, programmes and projects can be described as follows:

FIGURE 2.5 Governance hierarchy of portfolio, programmes and projects (King, 2014)

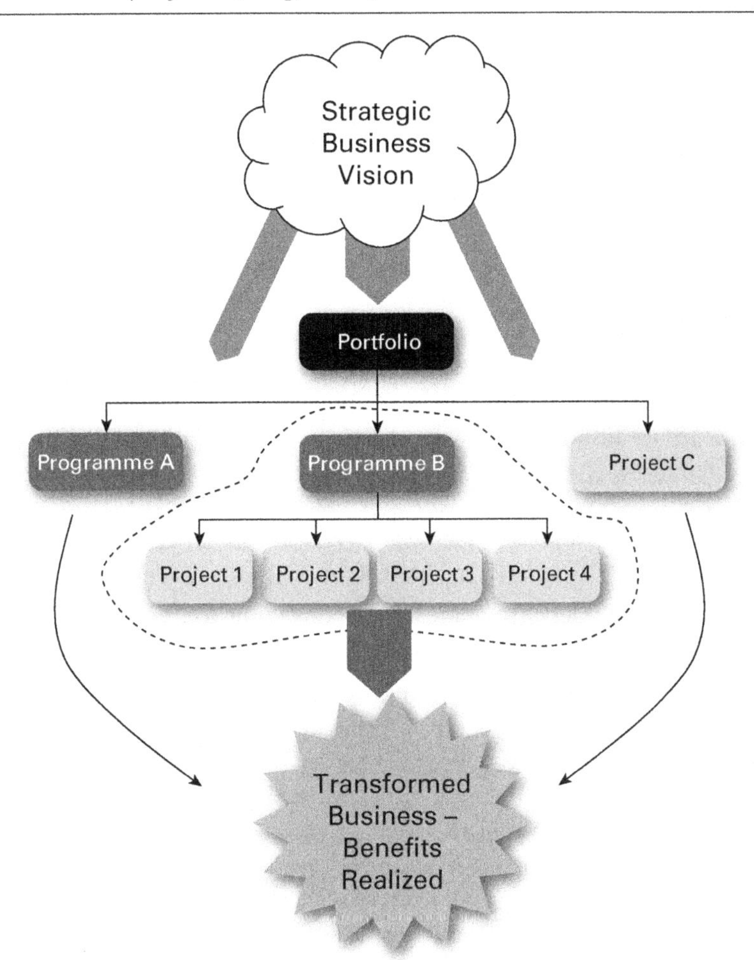

- A portfolio is a group of proposed or current projects and programmes. It may be the whole set of changes being undertaken by an organization or a major subset of these changes. The focus for a portfolio is typically the achievement of strategic business vision and objectives within the constraints of available resources. Timescales are usually open-ended and operate on a rolling basis with new programmes and projects being added, and completed programmes and projects rolling off continuously. Section A explores the role of strategy in defining change.
- A programme is a temporary organization used to manage a group of interrelated changes, each of which may be structured as a project. A programme's focus is on achievement of a strategic outcome, usually encapsulated in a 'vision statement', with a clear articulation of both the

business changes needed and the benefits to be realized. Timescales are usually longer than for a stand-alone project. Sections C and D address the development of strategic vision and definition of change; Chapter 3 discusses the management and realization of benefits.

- A project is also a temporary organization and is used to take forward a specific, well-defined and time-bound piece of work that sits outside 'business as usual'. Projects focus on delivery of fit-for-purpose deliverables that the organization needs, against time, cost and quality criteria. They typically have shorter timescales than programmes.

2. Change analysis

The basis of all change analysis is three questions:

1. Where are we now?
2. Where do we want to go?
3. How do we get there?

Three tools for examining the present situation are:

- the five forces model at the industry level (Section A2.3);
- SWOT analysis for comparison with competitors;
- Lewin's force-field analysis tool for analysing driving and resisting forces.

2.1 SWOT tool

The SWOT tool (Figure 2.6) is used to compare our business model against those of the competition; or in a government organization a comparison with best practice or similar organization. Strengths and weaknesses are typically viewed as 'internal' to the organization, whereas threats and opportunities are 'external':

- *Strengths* are those parts of the business model the organization has now that give a competitive advantage. These should be very clear following the strategic analysis. The organization must defend these strengths from threats.
- *Weaknesses* are those parts of the business model where competitors are better. They are a weakness in comparison to a competitor's strength. The organization must manage these relative weaknesses.
- *Opportunities* are things in the future that the organization may be able to take up, which will lead to either a new or improved strength or a new competitive position. The organization may have to change to be able to seize opportunities.
- *Threats* are things in the future that might affect the organization's ability to maintain its competitive position (strengths) or will enhance a competitor's position. The organization may need to change to avoid or reduce the impact of these threats.

FIGURE 2.6 The SWOT tool

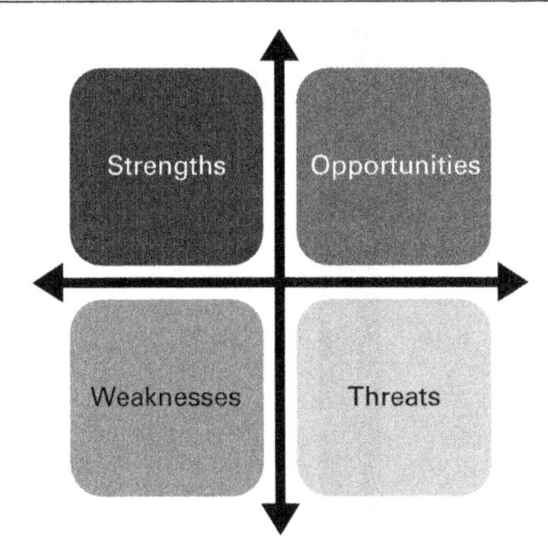

SWOT is a useful tool for aligning strategic analysis with the current operational capability and identifying required changes. It can help identify strategic objectives and priorities and develop a vision at the competitive advantage level.

2.2 Force field analysis

Force field analysis is a very useful tool when considering the case for change. The technique was developed by Kurt Lewin (1951) and is based on his insight that any particular set of circumstances is sustained by a network of forces that are currently in equilibrium. Lewin says: 'An issue is held in balance by the interaction of two opposing sets of forces: those seeking to promote change (driving forces) and those attempting to maintain the status quo (restraining or resisting forces).'

Lewin observed that in many human situations an increase in one force (to promote change) creates a reaction in other forces, seeking to maintain the current equilibrium. He used the term 'homeostasis' for this tendency of systems to maintain their current state.

Lewin developed the use of a diagram (Figure 2.7) in which the 'current state' (down the middle of the diagram) is being maintained by a range of driving and restraining (resisting) forces. As this diagram is drawn, a desired 'end state' of a change process is to the right of the diagram, with all the driving forces pushing that way currently being balanced by restraining forces.

If an organization desires to make change more quickly, then either the driving forces need to be augmented or the restraining forces decreased. Ideally, both of these must happen. This could, for example, involve highlighting the benefits of making a particular change (augmenting the driving force) while at the same time addressing staff concerns about the new processes (reducing the resisting force).

FIGURE 2.7 Force field analysis (after Lewin, 1951)

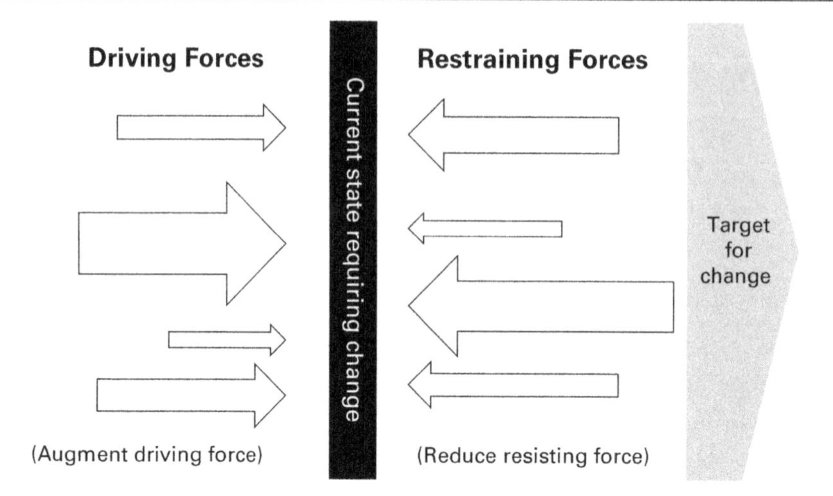

Force field analysis steps

Follow these steps to create a force field diagram in a group setting:

1. On a flipchart or whiteboard, briefly describe the current situation requiring change.
2. Briefly state the desired end state (the target for change).
3. List the driving and resisting forces at work in your change situation. Write one per 'sticky note'.
4. Place the sticky notes on either side of the 'current state' as appropriate.
5. Discuss the results and share ideas and thoughts about how to augment the driving forces and reduce the resisting forces.
6. Capture the results and use them to inform the change process and priorities for change.

Tip

It is advisable to create a force field diagram collaboratively with key stakeholders to ensure a variety of viewpoints and perspectives are considered. Use different size/length of arrows or assign a number to each arrow to indicate its strength to drive or restrain the change.

3. Strategic change plan

Bringing together the strategic vision, strategic objectives and priorities can help to answer the question: 'How do we get there?' This can be captured in a strategic change plan.

This plan will identify deadlines by which changes to the business model must be completed in order to maintain or enhance the competitive position. It will also reflect the priorities that are driven by the far and near environment analysis. This is a high-level plan and will need much refinement before it becomes a *delivery* plan. Its purpose is to set the boundaries for the required change.

The typical contents of a strategic change plan are:

- description of the strategic change drivers;
- business areas impacted by the change to the business model;
- strategic objectives and associated risk level;
- strategic stakeholders identified so far;
- strategic timescales for delivery of outcomes and benefits (for alignment with other initiatives and external drivers);
- SWOT analysis;
- strategic performance measures.

4. Systems approach to change

A useful approach when developing strategy and in identifying the drivers for a change is to apply systems theory and 'soft' systems methods. These methods are explored in Sections C and D. Such methods are particularly appropriate when considering strategic change where there is a degree of uncertainty in the analysis of the future. Changes in strategic direction frequently require people to work in a different way, including adopting new attitudes and behaviours.

5. Monitoring the external environment

The strategic analysis leading to the change plan is just a snapshot in time. Some consideration will have been given to trends and possible future events (risks). As the change implementation cascades down and implementation gets under way, the external environment needs to be monitored, to see what actually happens and how that deviates from the expectation set out in the earlier strategic analysis.

This can be done at a simple level by looking for things that confirm expectations and things that differ from expectations. A better approach is to look out for trends that differ significantly or new trends that may be more important for the chosen strategy. In looking for trends, an organization will consider Porter's five forces model.

Monitoring the external environment is most effective where scenarios were developed to explore possible futures. As part of the scenario analysis early indicators will have been identified to show if one possible future is becoming more likely than another. As a particular scenario becomes more likely (or less likely) then it may mean some aspects of a change implementation become more important than others.

6. Initial stakeholder engagement

The strategic objectives, vision, and strategic change plan indicate what needs to change in order for the organization to survive and prosper. They do not say how the changes are to be achieved. The first step is to use the change drivers to create the consensus for change amongst the stakeholders (Chapter 4 explores stakeholder strategy; Chapter 5 discusses communication and engagement).

Ideally, the development of the organization's strategy involves the internal stakeholders, so the imperative for the change should be shared already. However, this does not guarantee commitment to support the change or the engagement to participate in change design. Early stakeholder engagement seeking commitment and building a compelling case is the next step (Kotter, 2012; Chapter 1, Section C2.2).

Tip

Methods of engagement could include:

- Visioning workshops with rich pictures (Section C).
- Soft systems workshops exploring viewpoints and perspectives (Section C).
- Information workshops with suppliers and customers (Chapter 5).

Summary

All change in an organization should be in support of the strategy either to maintain a competitive advantage or seek a new advantage. In a government organization the change should improve the efficiency of the organization or provide a new function. In both cases the strategic objectives provide the change drivers.

The culture in an organization is crucial to understanding the drivers for change and the impact of change. It will contribute to the analysis of change as it is included in tools such as five forces, SWOT and force field analysis, together with a soft systems approach. The analysis tools will be used and refined as the change cascades through the organization. Emergent change must also be considered, so that the organization's resources remain focused on achievement of strategic objectives.

Questions to think about

1 What tools do you use to analyse change in the strategic context and understand the drivers (for and against, inside the organization and outside)?

2 Do you understand how change cascades down through your organization? How is that cascade managed and change performance measured (governance)?

3 How extensive is the change in your part of the organization? (Invent your own scale and plot a position.)

4 What are the planning boundaries for your change?

Section C: Developing vision

David King and Rod Sowden

Introduction

A clear vision for change is essential as it enables an organization's leaders, managers and change sponsors to identify and communicate the desired end goal, scope and boundaries of a change initiative. Furthermore, it enables all those engaged in or affected by change to understand its purpose and commit to the steps needed to make change work. A clear vision for change also helps people to focus on the wider organizational implications and opportunities.

There is a clear distinction between an organization's strategic mission, goals, objectives and targets on the one hand, and the creation of a vision and narrative for a change initiative on the other.

In this section we use soft systems methods (SSM) and related methods and techniques to explore:

1 Viewpoints and perspectives of change – capturing and exploring different stakeholder viewpoints of the desired 'future state'.

2 Developing a vision for change – applying systems theory to scope and draft a definition of the desired 'future state' and vision for change.

3 Understanding and validating the vision – using rich pictures and storytelling to support the change narrative.

1. Viewpoints and perspectives of change

1.1 Vision

Vision has been described by Manasse (1986) as: 'the force which moulds meaning for the people of an organization', and by Kotter (2012) as 'a picture of the future with some implicit or explicit commentary on why people should strive to create that future'.

When understanding the role of the vision in defining change, it is important to have some common definitions, as there is often confusion between the terms 'vision' and 'mission'. Wikipedia offers these definitions (Wikipedia, 2014a) to differentiate between the two terms: *vision* outlines what the organization wants to be, or how it wants the world in which it operates to be (an 'idealized' view of the world); *mission* defines the fundamental purpose of an organization or an enterprise, succinctly describing why it exists and what it does to achieve its vision.

Within the context of change both are relevant, but the focus for a change initiative is vision. The vision can be portrayed in many different ways and may trigger images and emotions that can be used to bond a group together. The vision for an organization or group may well be complex and difficult to summarize or even quantify. Therefore, best practice is to try to bring this together into a statement that encompasses the values and direction for an organization. This is generally referred to as the 'vision statement'.

An organization's stakeholders will have many different views and opinions about the vision and priorities for change. Some viewpoints could be in conflict and may have to be resolved before you can proceed. Consequently, there may not be a consensus about the 'target' for change. Meaningful and lasting change is most likely to be achieved if there is a *shared vision* of what the business should be like in its 'future state' (Figure 2.8).

FIGURE 2.8 The desired future state is not always clear

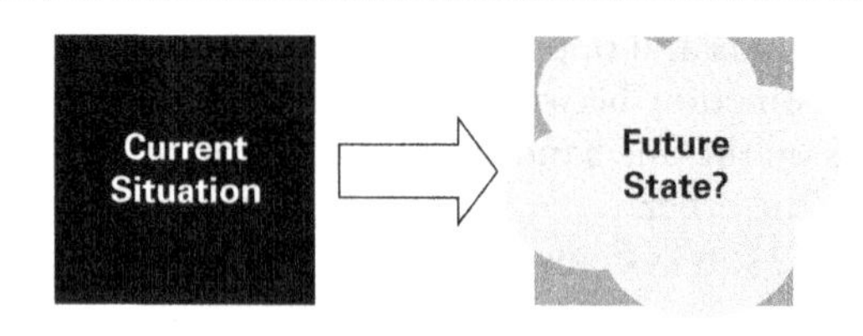

Viewpoints of the desired 'future state' are often influenced by many different drivers. Stakeholders may be responding to symptoms without understanding the root causes of problems or failures. Therefore, the real reasons for change may not always be apparent and need to be established. Soft systems methods (SSM) provide a valuable toolset for capturing, exploring and selecting viewpoints (see box).

Soft systems method (SSM) is an approach for developing a 'vision' for the 'future state' of a given business situation. SSM helps you to explore the different viewpoints of stakeholders, develop models of how things might work and understand the gap between the 'future state' and the 'current state', to identify 'what needs to change'. SSM is based on the work of Peter Checkland (1999) and Brian Wilson (2001) at Lancaster University in the 1960s and 1970s and arose out of attempts to apply systems engineering principles (that is, 'hard' systems theory) to business problems. This form of 'soft' systems analysis recognizes that organizations are essentially 'human activity systems' or 'social systems' and offers a different way of dealing with situations perceived as 'problematic'.

The old adage 'if you know where you are going it is easier to get there' rings particularly true for change programmes in organizations. You would not set off on a journey without first selecting your destination and then planning your route to get there. Business change is no different. Any other approach represents a significant business risk in which time, money and patience will eventually run out.

1.2 Capturing viewpoints

Viewpoints represent possible perspectives on the desired future state, or why the business might exist (its purpose, role or aim). The following steps can be followed to capture viewpoints:

1. Select people from the primary stakeholder group(s).
2. Decide whether to use one-to-one or workshops.
3. Set clear objectives and agendas.
4. Appoint experienced facilitator(s).
5. Use SSM to capture and explore viewpoints and define the target for change:
   - Use listing and mind-mapping approaches to explore all the possible (relevant) future scenarios (ie the 'viewpoints').
   - Test and validate the ideas that best represent the target for change.
   - Compare the target for change with the current state to see what is missing.
   - Use the results to start to describe the changes needed to get you to your target (ie destination) in the most cost-effective and productive way possible.
   - Don't worry if you don't get it right first time – you can always backtrack and try another scenario that works better.
   - Continue until you reach a genuine consensus.

CASE STUDY

A research organization undergoing change assembled a small team of subject matter experts, business analysts and consultants and, using soft systems methods, developed multiple possible future state scenarios over several days. The change leader finally announced: 'Now I feel I understand what we are trying to achieve and can begin to explain it to others in the organization.'

1.3 Using mind maps

Mind maps (first popularized by Tony Buzan (2003)) can be used individually or in groups to visually capture information (Figure 2.9) and are an ideal tool for capturing stakeholder viewpoints:

- The subject of the mind maps can be labelled (or pictured) at the centre.
- Record thoughts as they occur on 'branches from the centre' (like the spokes of a wheel); keep annotations as brief as possible.
- Use images, symbols and diagrams to create a 'rich' picture that brings people's ideas to life.
- Big themes qualify for a main branch; additional or related thoughts on the same theme can be added as 'twigs' from the main branch.
- It doesn't matter too much if you don't differentiate clearly between main themes and secondary thoughts when first building the mind map, as these can be clarified and sorted afterwards.
- The key point is to record all thoughts first, and evaluate them later, as your brain works faster than you can write!

1.4 Selecting viewpoints

Viewpoints generated during the vision-setting process tend to fall into one of three categories:

1. Primary-task viewpoints (the main reasons for its existence, which will be quite specific to the organization).
2. Secondary-task viewpoints (such as 'a system to provide employment' or 'a system to consume resources', which could apply to almost any business system).
3. Issue-based viewpoints (such as 'a system to demotivate staff' or 'a system to slow down progress'); these are often negative but provide some insight into possible problems inside the organization.

FIGURE 2.9 Mind maps help capture viewpoints

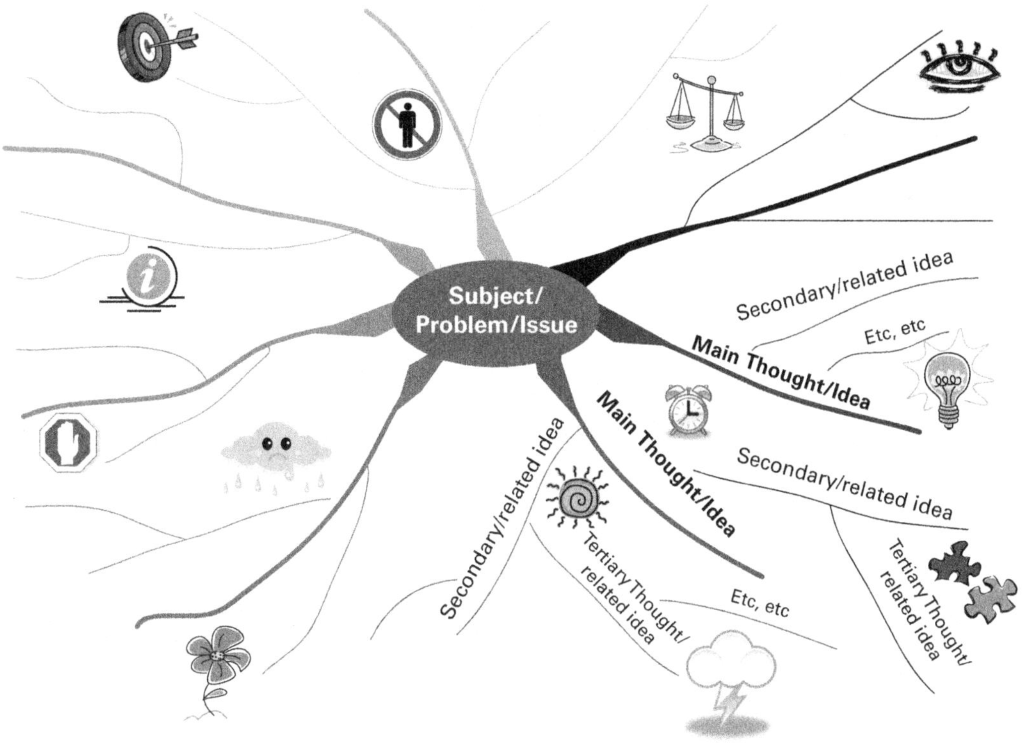

Develop the primary-task viewpoints into business systems ('future state') definitions (BSDs) first – see Section C2.

1.5 Whys, whats and hows

'Why–what–how' is a technique for establishing an appropriate hierarchy for the viewpoints expressed by stakeholders. For each primary viewpoint (ie what you want the business or organization to do) you should identify one or more reasons why you want to do it. Additionally, for each viewpoint you should be able to identify possible ways that this might be achieved (ie how). Viewpoints could be a 'why', a 'what' or a 'how'. Note that more than one 'what' can exist for each 'why', and more than one 'how' can exist for each 'what' (Figure 2.10).

Experimenting with 'why–what–how' enables a clearer understanding to be developed of the 'level' at which change needs to be defined. Is our focus for change at too high a level ('keep people active for longer' is a goal but could be achieved in many different ways) or too low a level ('getting people fit by sponsoring sporting achievement' is too prescriptive and may limit more creative or novel solutions)? Focus on the appropriate level – the 'what' (our primary viewpoint) – ensures the context for the change is understood and the possible options for achieving it are understood as well as self-validating.

FIGURE 2.10 Example of a why-what-how hierarchy

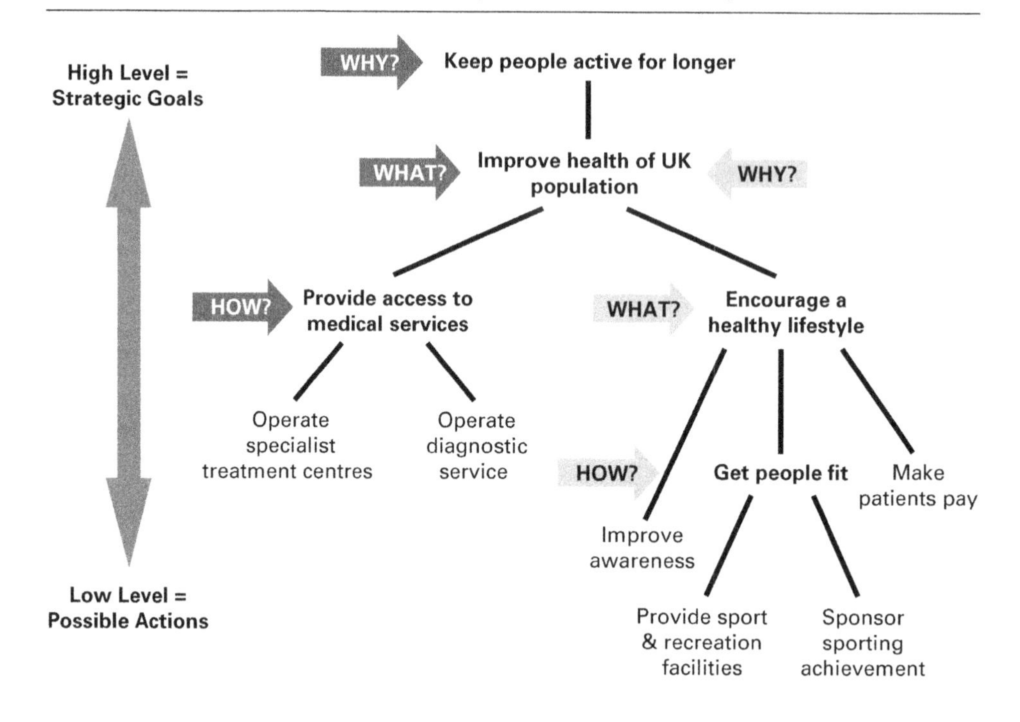

Tip

When creating a 'why–what–how' hierarchy:

- Avoid viewpoints that are too general and could apply to any business system.
- Avoid negative viewpoints that focus on a current problem rather than describing the desired 'future state'.
- Multiple 'whys', 'whats' and 'hows' can exist at each level but ideally there should be one primary 'why' that is the overriding purpose of the change programme.
- You may need to generate several why–what–how hierarchies before arriving at the final programme scope.

2. Developing a vision for change

By applying systems theory you can define a vision statement for the system you want, building on the viewpoints explored and identified as most relevant to the interests and future needs of the organization. In addition, the why–what–how hierarchy helps 'position' the most attractive viewpoints in relation to the transformation needed to achieve or realize it.

2.1 Business system (or root) definition (BSD)

Systems theory identifies six key elements – expressed in an easy-to-remember 'VOCATE' mnemonic (Figure 2.11). In some versions of SSM, this is referred to as 'CATWOE', with 'Weltanschauung' (German for 'worldview') replacing 'viewpoint'. These six elements must be considered when defining the new (desired) business system and highlights the 'human (or "soft") factors', expressed in terms of the people components (owner, customer(s), actors).

According to Peter Checkland and Jim Scholes (1999) a business system is 'a set of activities so connected as to make a purposeful whole'.

Using the VOCATE structure, as shown in Figure 2.11, enables ideas about the desired future state to be captured in a structured business system definition (BSD) (Figure 2.12). Use this template as a guide only, to ensure that all systems components are present. Careful drafting will enhance the clarity and impact of the statement.

FIGURE 2.11 Use 'VOCATE' to structure a definition for the desired future state

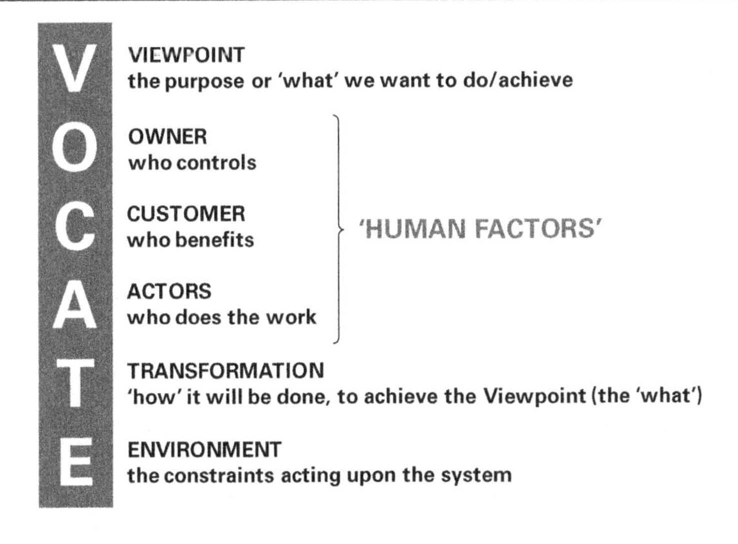

FIGURE 2.12 Example of a BSD with VOCATE components

'Healthy Lifestyle' Business System Definition:

A chief medical officer-owned programme to encourage a healthy lifestyle and improve fitness across the UK population through the provision of accessible and affordable sports and recreation facilities and sponsorship by central government departments, local authorities and health and leisure services, within the limitations of available funding, planning constraints and local demographics.

CASE STUDY

When working with a management team developing a vision for a major change, we finally arrived at a business system definition that everyone was enthused about and committed to. I knew we had reached the point of consensus when they started to criticize my grammar and punctuation!

It may be necessary to develop several BSDs before selecting one that achieves the greatest consensus and provides an agreed basis on which to explore further ideas about the changes needed in the organization to achieve it. A good BSD lays the foundations for a vision for change and drafting of a full 'vision statement'.

To assist leaders in developing an appropriate vision, Nanus (1992) maintains that the 'right vision' has five characteristics:

- attracts commitment and energizes people;
- creates meaning in workers' lives;
- establishes a standard of excellence;
- bridges the present to the future;
- transcends the status quo.

As well as providing a picture of the future, a clear vision inspires people to want to work to achieve it. A leader's efforts to develop a shared vision have been described as 'bonding' by Sergiovanni (1990): leader and followers with a shared set of values and commitment 'that bond them together in a common cause' in order to meet a common goal.

2.2 Writing a vision statement

The challenge when writing a vision statement is to create a set of words that:

- are consumable by a variety of stakeholders and audiences;
- uses terms that are culturally relevant;
- is inspirational to the audience;
- is verifiable, so its achievement can be recognized;
- provides the basis for developing the blueprint or target operating model;
- recognizes constraints and obstacles;
- is appropriate in size and length for its purpose.

To reflect all these characteristics is quite a challenge for one statement, so it is wise to consider having a core statement, which is short and to the point, and then create different representations of it for different audiences, so that it is applied to their frame of reference. For example, the version for shareholders may well have a different focus to that for the workforce.

When creating a vision statement, the output is often the result of where the process starts, so if the starting point is abstracting a future state, then the result will undoubtedly be vague. Consider working on the target operating model or blueprint (at least at a high level initially – see Section D) before defining the vision statement. This may sound as though things are happening in reverse, but having some level of detail will help. Gather together the following information on which to build the vision statement:

- The BSD (if created) – see Section C2.1.
- Drivers and justification for the change, and what type of change it is going to be:
  - compliance (eg driven by a change in legislation);
  - vision led (eg major transformation or innovation);
  - evolving (eg a combination of existing initiatives and projects).
- 'Must do' outcomes and any deadlines.
- Services that will be changed, stopped or started.
- Structural changes to the organization and the supply chain.
- What technology, manufacturing or property changes are anticipated.
- What values are needed to be included that are close to the organization's heart, eg environmental sustainability.

Creating the statement will depend on the organization, but don't be scared to make a few strong statements that stand alone: this is often easier than crafting a page of words. Perhaps create one for each selected viewpoint, setting a positive, ambitious position before reaching a consensus on the vision statement that best captures the desired 'future state'.

Although it is generally accepted that it should be short and to the point, there is no reason why it shouldn't be expanded to aid understanding.

Tip

Avoid these pitfalls for vision statements:

- *The to-do list*: a list of things that need to happen to achieve something, which tend to focus on the obvious and often lack longevity and run out of steam in the first year.
- *Mission statement*: some blunt statements that sound good but are not a foundation for a change initiative.
- *Management waffle*: a few sentences that are vague enough so that key stakeholders can agree, but have little relevance to what needs to happen, or no one is really sure what they mean.
- *Sermons*: goes on for quite a long time, makes lots of promises that cannot be achieved or measured, but excites some people for some of the time, something for everyone, but very little for most.

Finally, a key requirement is to communicate the change vision effectively, at all levels throughout the organization (see Chapter 5).

3. Understanding and validating the vision

3.1 Rich pictures

Rich pictures are an extension of the soft systems approach that allows you to create pictorial representations of a desired future state. Checkland (1999) defines a rich picture as 'the expression of a *problem situation* compiled by an investigator, often by examining elements of *structure*, elements of *process*, and the situation *climate*'.

The resulting visual 'story' enables a wide spectrum of stakeholders to contribute their ideas and experiences and so build a shared understanding of both the structure and purpose underlying the vision. Mind maps can provide a useful starting point for developing rich pictures. By adding a variety of meaningful images, symbols and arrows, the characteristics of the desired future state can be richly illustrated.

Drawing rich pictures (Burke, 2014):

1. To help interpret a situation, choose symbols, scenes or images that represent the situation. Use as many colours as necessary and draw the symbols on a large piece of paper. Try not to get too carried away with the fun and challenge to your ingenuity in finding pictorial symbols.

2. Put in whatever connections you see between your pictorial symbols: avoid producing merely an unconnected set. Places where connections are lacking may later prove significant.
3. Avoid too much writing, either as commentary or as word bubbles coming from people's mouths (but a brief summary can help explain the diagram to other people).
4. Don't include systems boundaries or specific references to systems in any way.

Figures 2.13 shows examples of useful symbols for creating a rich picture and an illustration of a simple rich picture (Figure 2.14), based on the BSD example in Section C2 above.

FIGURE 2.13 Some rich picture symbols

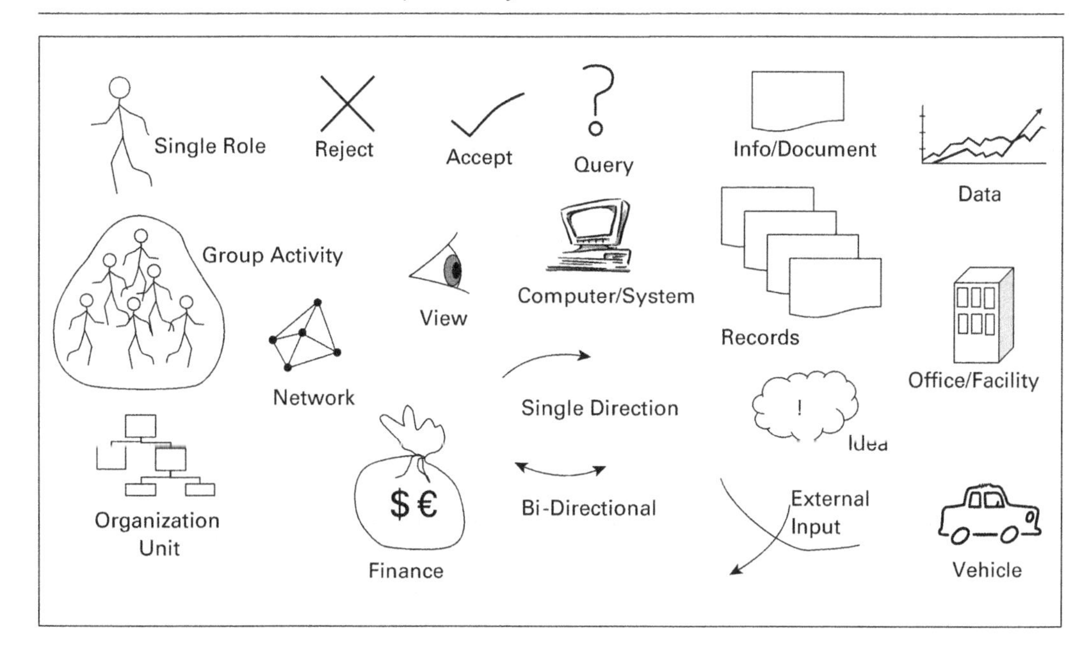

FIGURE 2.14 Rich picture for improving health and fitness

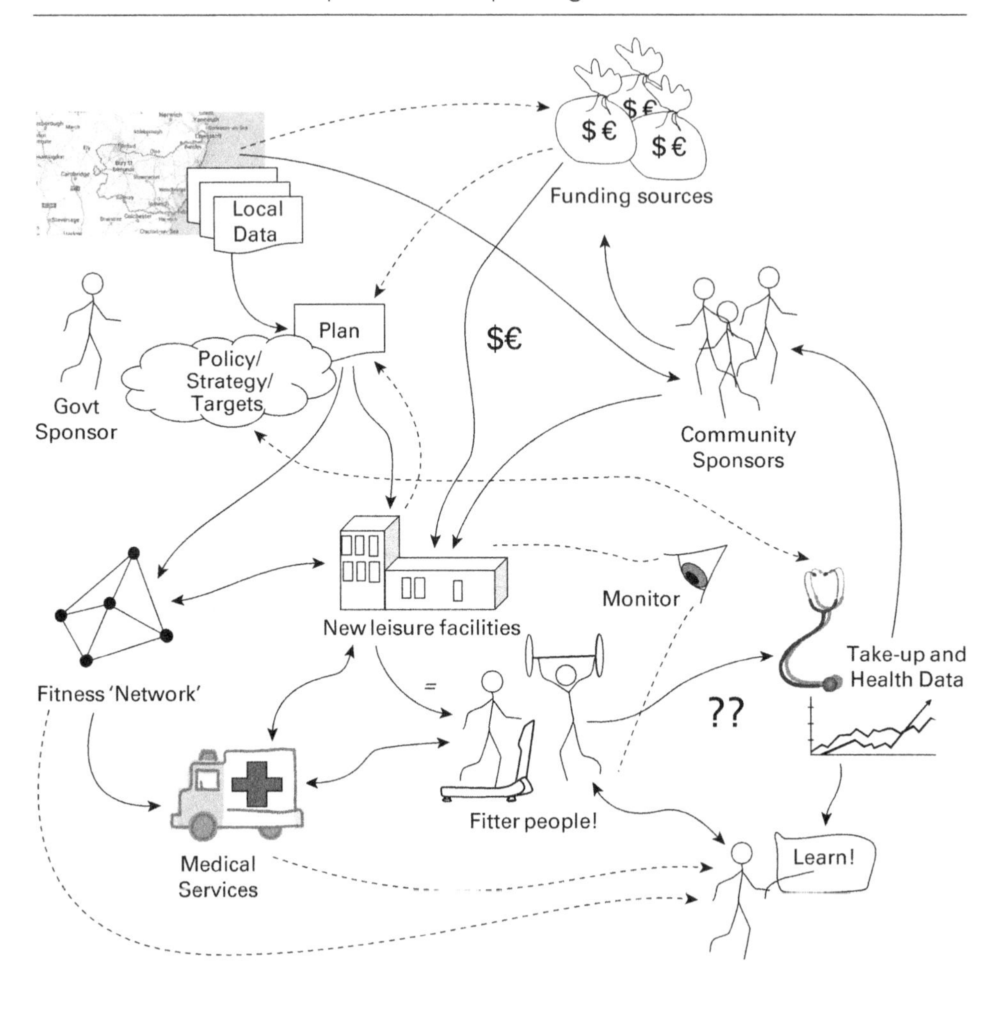

CASE STUDY

There are many examples of rich pictures, the illustration in Figure 2.15 is from a UK government agency outlining their 15-year journey, including the challenges and opportunities that they will face along the way. The journey describes a future where drivers, operators, vehicles, MOT garages and maintainers are fully compliant with regulations. Producing this sort of image using professional artists (this example was produced by a commercial graphic designer) can be expensive, but if the final product is iconic, as this one is, the investment may well be good value.

FIGURE 2.15 Rich picture created for a UK government agency (reproduced by kind permission of Scriberia)

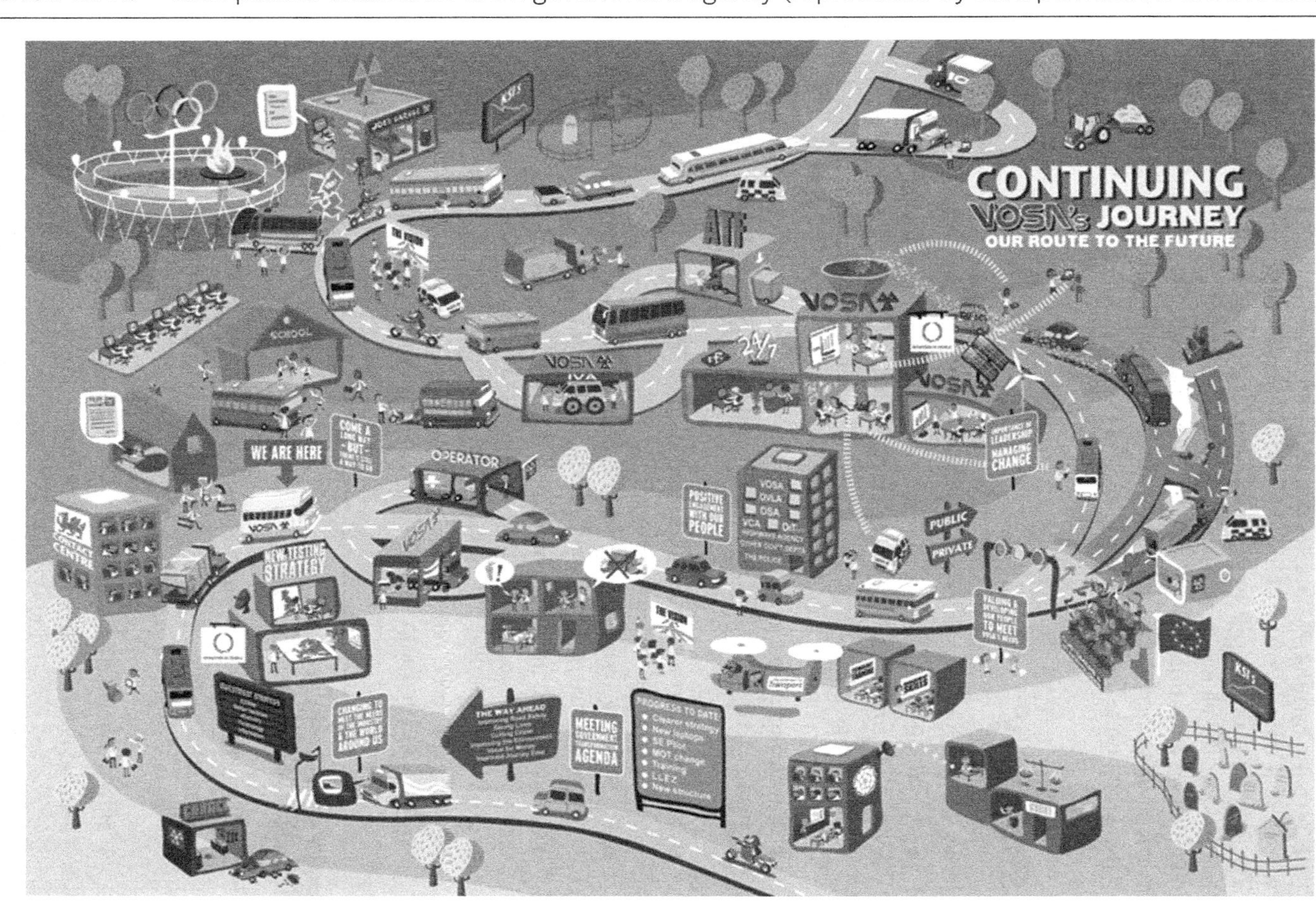

3.2 Storytelling

Rich pictures are a type of storytelling. Storytelling dates back through the ages and long predates writing. Wikipedia defines storytelling as 'the conveying of events in words, and images, often by improvisation or embellishment' (Wikipedia, 2014b). The technique of rich pictures focuses on telling the story about what the world will be like once the change has been delivered, what it will look and feel like to be in the changed organization. For people who have a strong audio preference, this will be a particularly powerful medium. Chapter 5, Section B5.3 discusses the use of storytelling when communicating change.

Summary

- Within the context of change the focus for a change initiative is vision.
- Meaningful and lasting change is most likely to be achieved if there is a *shared vision* of what the business should be like in its 'future state'.
- The old adage of 'if you know where you are going it is easier to get there' rings particularly true for change programmes in organizations.
- Capturing, and selecting from, a wide range of stakeholder viewpoints and perspectives helps build consensus. Mind maps and other creative techniques are useful.
- Select the most relevant and interesting viewpoints as the basis for defining vision using a 'why–what–how' hierarchy.
- By applying systems theory you can define a vision statement (expressed as a 'business system definition') for the system you want.
- It is wise to consider having a core vision statement, which is short and to the point, and then create different representations of it for different audiences. Avoid the pitfalls of creating 'to-do' lists or 'mission statements'.
- Create pictorial representations ('rich pictures') of a desired future state to help validate the vision with a wide variety of stakeholders.

Questions to think about

1 When developing a vision statement for a change programme in your organization what stakeholder viewpoints and perspectives did you consider?

2 How did you use the vision statement to communicate the need and focus for change across the organization?

3 What would be the effects of undertaking a change initiative without an agreed vision?

Section D: Change definition

David King

Introduction

Change definition is the process of developing clear and complete definitions of how the organization will be changed, the nature of the impact on stakeholders and business areas, and the specific changes that will be seen across the organization in behaviour, outputs and outcomes.

Not everyone in an organization will view change in the same way. There will be a wide mix of positive, negative and neutral responses to change. Nor will the path to change be smooth and problem-free. It is important to understand and communicate the 'big picture' of change and help people to view change in its wider context. It will be equally important to draw out the key issues and concerns that people have about change. The objective is to build and share understanding about the change and how obstacles, when discovered, can be overcome or resolved.

This section explores methods and approaches for building, sharing and validating the desired 'future state'; how to use these models to define and analyse the required new 'capability'; determining how this compares to the 'current state' through conducting a 'gap' analysis; and, how to identify problems and concerns that may arise.

1. Conceptual models of the future state

The business system definition (BSD) and vision statements only get us so far. Building models helps to visualize how the business will operate in its 'future state' (building on the BSDs, vision statements and rich pictures discussed in Section C). Models enable more direct comparisons to be made with the current situation – why and how is it different? Models aid learning and ensure a common understanding of what we want, ie our shared 'blueprint' for change. If we have a clear picture of where we want to be, it will be easier to work out how to get there.

1.1 Business activity models

A definition of 'activity model' is 'a structure of distinguishable parts which operate together to achieve some common objective' (King, 2006). Business activity models (BAMs) are 'soft' models that represent diagrammatic prototypes of a viable and complete 'business system' that shows how the future state envisaged in the BSD will operate. Other terms often used to describe such models are 'target operating model' and 'blueprint'.

BAMs comprise the minimum number of activities that would be expected to take place for BSD to function. According to systems theory, features that are common to all systems are:

- *purpose or objective*: why the system exists and what it must achieve;
- *environmental constraints*: factors that will inhibit or constrain achievement;
- *plan or programme*: specific plans and targets against which achievement will be measured;
- *resources*: the specific resources (people, finance, physical, technological) required by the system;
- *working activities*: the primary tasks to be undertaken, what the system exists to 'do';
- *monitoring*: the measurement of achievement against plans and targets;
- *control*: the actions taken in response to the results of monitoring.

These can be described as *generic activities* that must be present in all viable business systems. They have logical interdependencies and can be shown as a generic activity model (Figure 2.16).

The generic model shows that before we can 'do the work', we must have 'devised a plan' for which 'objectives' and 'constraints' have been defined, and 'resources acquired and deployed'. Monitoring of 'effectiveness' of 'doing the work' is set against the 'defined objective(s)' and the 'defined plan'. 'Control action' can be incorporated in any generic activity but is usually seen as a single control activity that generates responsive actions to correct any shortfalls or deficiencies in the system

FIGURE 2.16 Generic activity model (King, 2006; after Checkland, 1999)

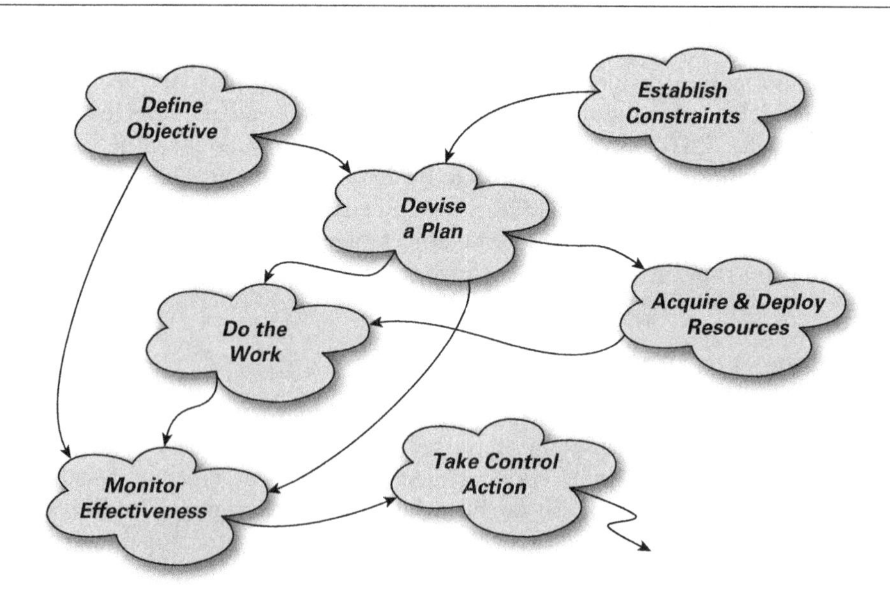

(the 'lightning-strike' arrow depicts a universal/multiple dependency to all other activities in the model).

BAMs show connected activities and indicate dependencies both internal and external to the business system. These models enable business managers and change teams to develop and explore ideas visually, including radical alternatives.

There can be different types of BAM:

- representations of the organization operating in its 'desired future state' (state B);
- the organization operating as it is now (A);
- a plan of how to get from (A) to (B).

Tip

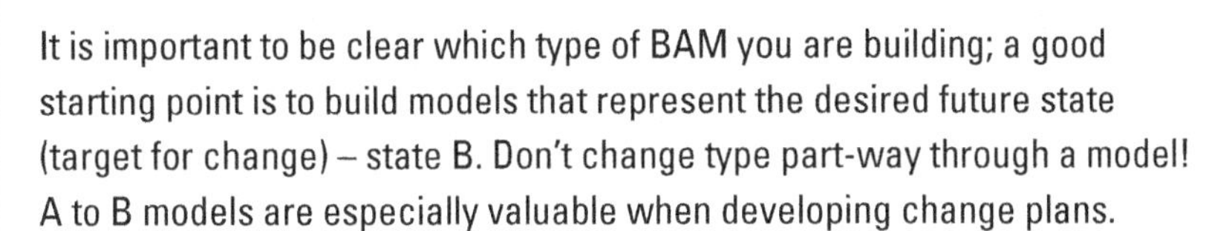

It is important to be clear which type of BAM you are building; a good starting point is to build models that represent the desired future state (target for change) – state B. Don't change type part-way through a model! A to B models are especially valuable when developing change plans.

1.2 Validating the BAM

The BAM must be fully validated with all key stakeholders, to get their buy-in and commitment. Using this checklist:

1. Does the BAM fully reflect the business system definition? *If not you may need to revisit the definition.* Consider writing a new definition or even start again and draw a new BAM.
2. Is the BAM clear and explicit – does it communicate your ideas about the 'future state'?
3. Does the BAM help to identify business critical activities? (This is indicated by the number of dependencies that exist with other activities in the BAM.)
4. Has the BAM enabled you to generate additional or new insights into how the organization could operate in the future?
5. Has the process of building the BAM enabled the key stakeholders to share a common understanding about what is needed?

1.3 Creating business activity models

Follow these steps when creating BAMs:

1. Select a BSD to model.
2. List the activities that would need to take place for the system described to function – try listing first, before starting to draw the BAM.

FIGURE 2.17 Suggested BAM Notations (King, 2006)

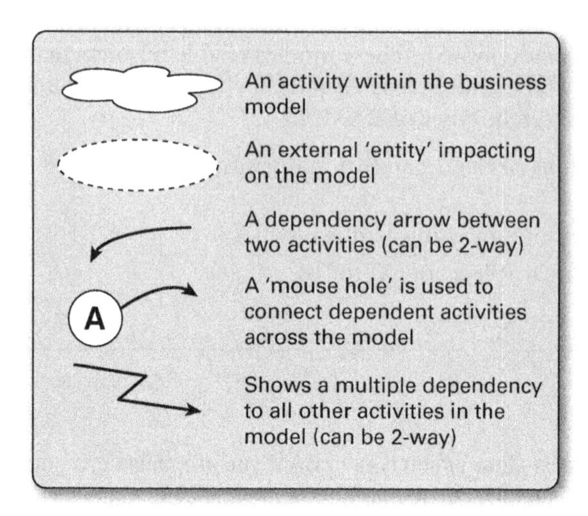

3. Using the suggested notations (Figure 2.17), place each activity in a 'cloud' shape (Figure 2.18) – each activity must contain a verb (eg 'know', 'understand', 'manage' etc). Always use plain, descriptive language.
4. Connect the cloud shapes containing activities with arrows, to show the direction of dependencies between them (ie what needs to happen before and what needs to happen after each activity is undertaken?). Every activity should have at least one input and one output.
5. Show dependencies to activities or processes that are external to the business system being modelled (called 'external entities').
6. Check to ensure you have included the systemic components of the generic model (Figure 2.16).

Tip

The BAM is a model for the 'future state' and is therefore used to model your ideas. Beware of 'reality seepage' whereby you start to model the current situation (although the same technique can be used for different types of models – see above).

FIGURE 2.18 Illustration of a business activity model for 'improving health' (King, 2006)

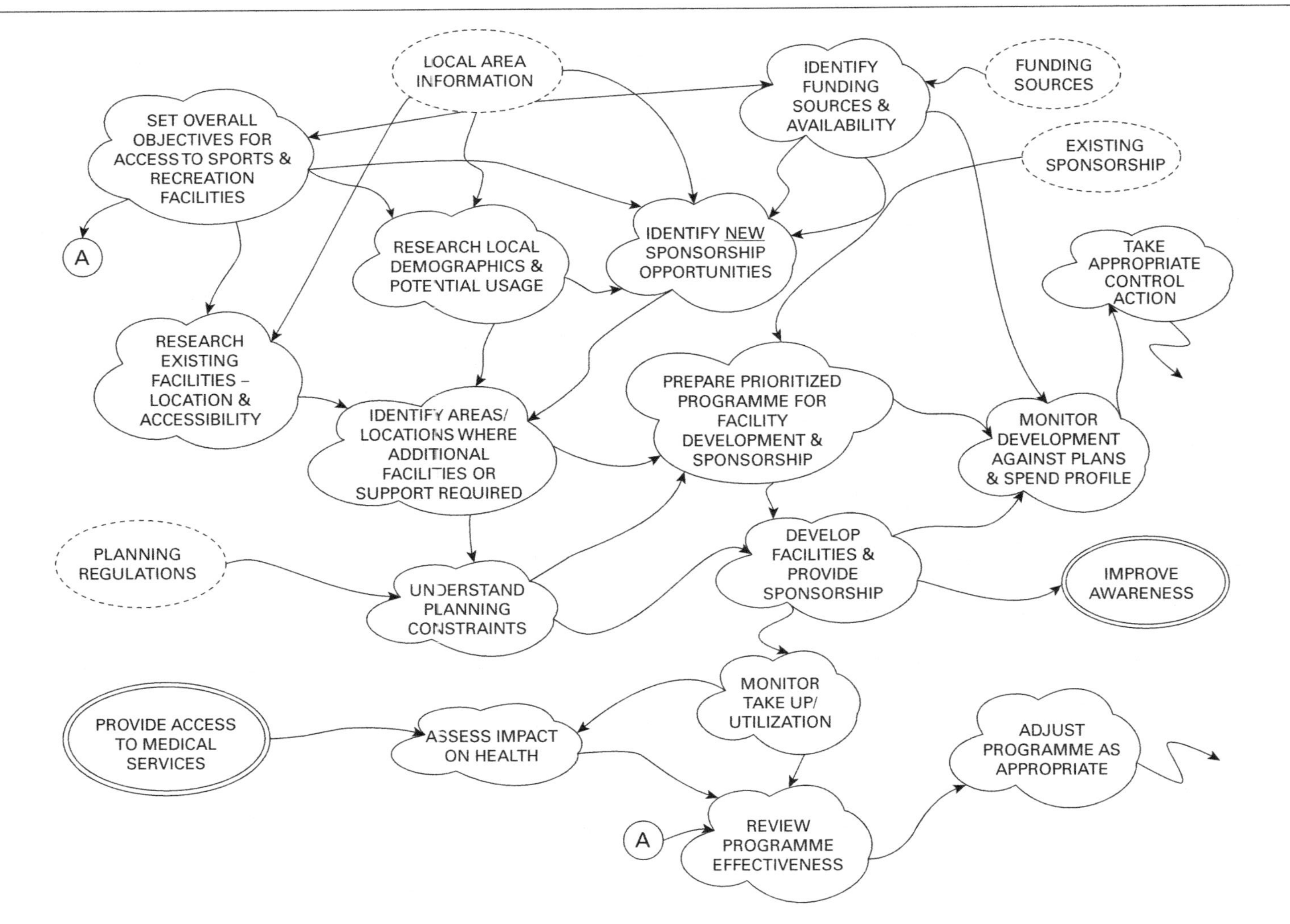

CASE STUDY

Three government agencies involved in funding distribution merged. They used soft systems methods to define and model the required future state business systems for both operational management and delivery of the new organization's services. Over several sessions, the entire operations management team participated in a workshop to create, first, a business system definition (BSD) and then a set of business activity models (BAMs). Together these described how operations would work after the merger. The resulting BAMs provided the foundation for detailed process mapping, organizational and information systems design. They also supported a 'gap analysis' to determine the scope of the changes required.

2. Change requirements – capability analysis

For any change programme to succeed, just having a business model is not enough. The business needs to understand the full implications of the changes it has to make, in terms of the full range of 'capability' required in the future state. A full 'KOPE capability analysis' (King, 2006) provides the basis for analysis of all activities in the BAM:

- Knowledge and information: what do we need to know or understand and what data or information is needed to carry out this activity well?
- Organization and people: what organization structure, people skills and experience is necessary to perform the required task(s)?
- Process and procedure: what processes and procedures need to be followed and what standards, criteria or rules govern its execution?
- Environment and infrastructure: what physical and environmental requirements need to be satisfied for the activity to be performed safely and productively?

Each activity in the BAM must have (without exception) both an input and an output – the activity represents the 'transformation' that converts one into the other. If either input or output is missing, you should query what the activity is for. The combined 'capability' of all the activities in the BAM represents the basis for defining the change programme. The defined 'new capability' forms part of the overall target for change (or blueprint) and lays the foundation for developing the detailed change specification and change plan.

Understanding the full implications of change enables a fully informed decision process about where developments or investment are needed.

FIGURE 2.19 The scope of KOPE capability analysis (King, 2006)

Knowledge & Information
- information needs
- inputs, outputs & data flows
- records and data stores
- data sources and destinations
- management & operational information
- volumes, timeliness, update frequency

Organization & People
- nature of the work
- knowledge & 'know-how'
- skills and competencies
- specialization
- discretion
- staffing levels
- organization structures

Processes & Procedures
- business processes/work flows
- regulations or rules
- working principles
- critical success factors
- performance & quality measures
- delegations

Environment & Infrastructure
- infrastructure and facilities
- working environment & ergonomics
- work style eg interaction, location/movement, time, communications etc
- Flexible/alternative working
- Home/remote access

This KOPE capability analysis also provides the baseline against which specified improvements and benefits can be measured. KOPE capability analysis steps:

1. Select each activity in the BAM in turn (or closely related activities may be grouped).
2. Analyse the required capability in terms of the four KOPE categories (see Figure 2.19).
3. Use a capability summary table (Table 2.2) to capture the required capability for each activity.
4. Remember: you are defining 'future state' capability, not what you currently do (the process of comparison and gap analysis will come later).
5. Use the capability summary table to summarize the total 'new capability', highlighting recurring requirements, themes and priorities.

Tip

When summarizing the required capability for the BAM as a whole, make any reasonable assumptions to enable you to complete the analysis. Consider whether any changes to the BAM are needed, to reflect the more in-depth understanding gained. Remember to record any other emerging issues and risks.

TABLE 2.2 KOPE capability analysis summary table illustration (King, 2006)

Blueprint Model Activities	Knowledge & Information	Organization & People	Process & Procedures	Environment & Infrastructure
1 Set overall objectives for access to sports & recreation facilities	• Strategy and policy • Funding sources • Management information systems	• Policy lead/ director • Research team • Health & fitness sector expertise	• Government goals and targets • Strategic framework • Decision processes	• Communications network
2 Research local demographics & potential usage	• Local area information • Statistical data on access usage	• Data gathering and analysis skills • Commercial awareness • Intelligence gathering	• Commercial sensitivity/ security • Regular reporting cycle • Complete/ accurate data	• Communications network • Intelligence network
3 Research existing facilities – location and accessibility	• Existing facilities per population • Analytical models and tools/ benchmarks	• Research team • Research and analysis	• Criteria and definitions of 'facilities' • Analysis models and process	• Research network – intelligence gathering
4 Identify funding sources and availability	• Existing funding sources/value • Current funding – results/ projections	• Funding sector knowledge • Creativity and problem solving	• Financial criteria and rules • Funding models and procedures	• Field research and sector interaction
5 Identify new sponsorship opportunities	• Health and fitness sector knowledge • Sponsorship 'capacity' and values	• Networking and communications skills • Sponsorship team	• Sponsor selection criteria • Diligence rules and procedures	• Field research/ mobile • Partnership working
6 Identify areas/locations where additional facilities or support required	• Local area information • Statistical data on access usage • Local development initiatives	• Sponsorship programme team • Health & fitness sector expertise	• Criteria and definitions of 'facilities' • Evaluation criteria	• Field research/ mobile • Partnership working

TABLE 2.2 *continued*

Blueprint Model Activities	Knowledge & Information	Organization & People	Process & Procedures	Environment & Infrastructure
7 Prepare prioritized programme for facility development and sponsorship	• Prioritized initiatives • Financial costs and benefits, risks	• Sponsorship programme team • Programme/ project management skills	• Prioritization criteria and rules • Financial appraisal	• Collaborative working • Consultation and consensus
8 Understand planning constraints	• Local development plans • Planning regulations	• Planning and development 'know-how'	• Evaluation criteria • Test and viability assessment	• Research network – intelligence gathering
9 Develop facilities and provide sponsorship	• Sponsorship programme • Objectives and targets	• Sponsorship programme team • Programme/ project management skills	• Programme management • Financial management	• Partnership working • Mobile/field working
10 Monitor development against plans and spend profile	• Performance reports • Sponsorship Programme/plans • Action plans	• Sponsorship programme team • Data gathering, analysis and reporting skills	• Monitoring and reporting procedures • Measurement criteria • Decision process	• Mobile/field working • Analytical – desk-based study
11 Monitor take-up/ utilization	• As 10	• As 10	• As 10	• Analytical – desk-based study
12 Assess impact on health	• Statistical data – trends and effects • Programme data	• Research team • Research and analysis	• Analysis models and process	• Research network – intelligence gathering
13 Review programme effectiveness and adjust programme as appropriate	• As 10 • Specific gaps and shortfalls • Achievements!	• Policy lead/ director • All roles	• As 10	• Collaborative working • Consultation and consensus

This initial capability analysis lays the foundations for more detailed (and frequently specialized) requirements analysis, including process design (Chapter 13, Section C), data and systems analysis, organizational design and infrastructure development.

3. Assessing the impact of change

3.1 Gap analysis

Understanding where you want to be (ie your 'future state' business activity model (BAM) and KOPE capability analysis) does not answer the questions about *how* you get there. You must define precisely what needs to be changed or modified in the current organization and what needs to be retained.

This may include developing new business components and solutions that simply do not exist in the current state. Analysing the gap between the 'future state' defined by the BAM and the 'current state' enables the required change programme to be defined in full:

- Are the activities being undertaken effectively (if at all) and efficiently, and if not what problems have been identified?
- Are there explicit performance measures that enable you to determine the actual shortfall or deficiency?
- Can you clearly identify the specific benefits that would accrue if new activities (ie those not in the 'current state') were undertaken?

Understanding what is different between the 'current state' and 'future state' is the objective of 'gap analysis' and absolutely critical to definition of the change programme (Figure 2.20). However, in reality, key stakeholders in a business may not necessarily share a common understanding of what even constitutes the *current* situation! Each divisional manager and team may understand their own part of the process extremely well but have little idea – or interest – in what happens elsewhere. Vertical channels are very common in organizations and invariably result in poor internal communications and ultimately in poor customer service, when dependent processes don't link up properly.

FIGURE 2.20 Assessing the 'gap' (King, 2006)

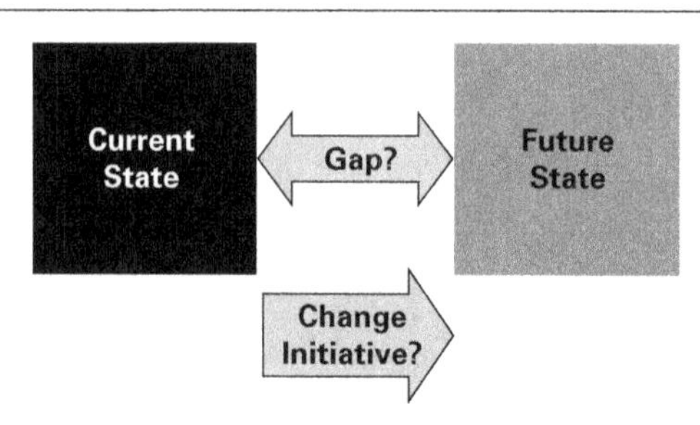

Consequently, you may need to spend some time at this point mapping the current business processes, relationships and dependencies before you can commence a full gap analysis. You can use the BAM technique described above, process mapping (Chapter 13, Section C) or a combination of both to describe the current state.

3.2 The shortfall in 'capability'

The required change programme is all about implementing a new capability across the business. Not everything done now will be the same in the 'future state' and some activities will be completely new or radically different. This may have implications for existing knowledge and data systems, current management and team structures, skills and competencies, present working methods, workflows, quality management and performance controls. You should question whether the whole set-up of the organization is adequately attuned to the needs of owners, management, staff and customers.

3.3 Steps in conducting a gap analysis

- Use interactive, facilitated workshops (Chapter 10), focus groups or one-to-ones to identify the key differences between the defined 'future state' and the 'current state'.
- Map the shortfalls and deficiencies on the BAM using a simple 'RAG analysis' (see Figure 2.22).
- Capture the results of the gap analysis in a simple 'differences' table (see Table 2.3).
- Identify the specific changes required to current business activities. Use the KOPE capability analysis categories to organize your results: Knowledge, Organization, Process and Environment (see Figure 2.21).
- Prioritize the change requirements.
- Capture and record issues and risks as they arise and decide how they will be resolved or addressed.

The BAM can be used to map the differences using a simple 'RAG' analysis approach, as in Figure 2.22.

Tip

Things to look out for...

- *'Non-Starters'* (eg activities 1 and 5 in Figure 2.22): activities that are not done now or that have significant problems and are critical dependencies of two or more activities in the BAM. If this activity is an objective-setting or performance-target-setting activity, then the business system (ie the 'new capability') is doomed to failure if this is not addressed as a priority.

- '*Poor Relations*' (eg activities 4 and 10): these are activities that are done now and appear to be satisfactory but have dependent activities that are not undertaken or have significant problems. By definition this must mean that these activities, whilst giving the appearance of being okay, are in fact being seriously undermined. The old adage of '*rubbish in – rubbish out*' springs to mind here!
- '*Blockers*' (eg activities 7 and 8): beware of activities that have dependent activities that are done well (ie green, or at least amber) but which are themselves either not done or done very badly. This will inevitably cause the business system to break down at these points, seriously impacting on delivery of the required 'new capability'.

FIGURE 2.21 Using the business activity model and KOPE capability analysis to conduct a gap analysis (King, 2006)

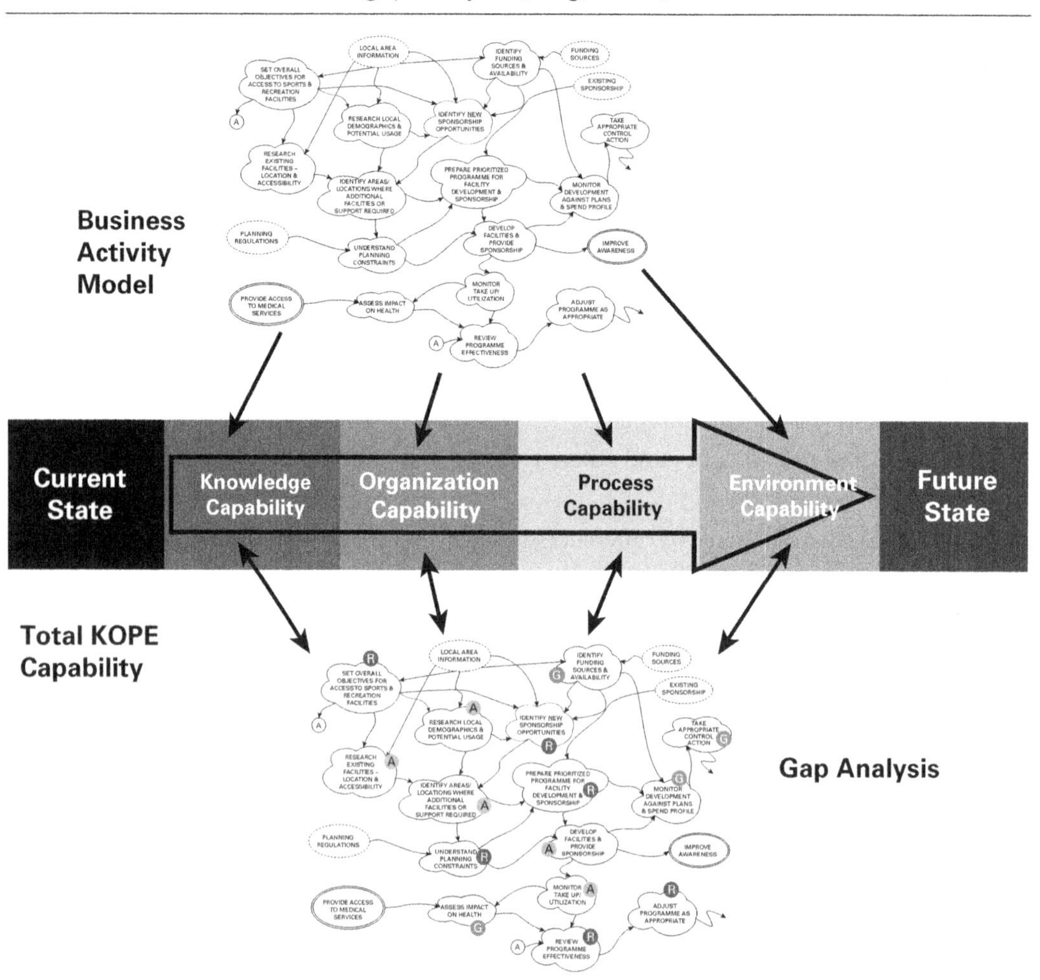

FIGURE 2.22 RAG analysis illustration using the business activity model (King, 2006)

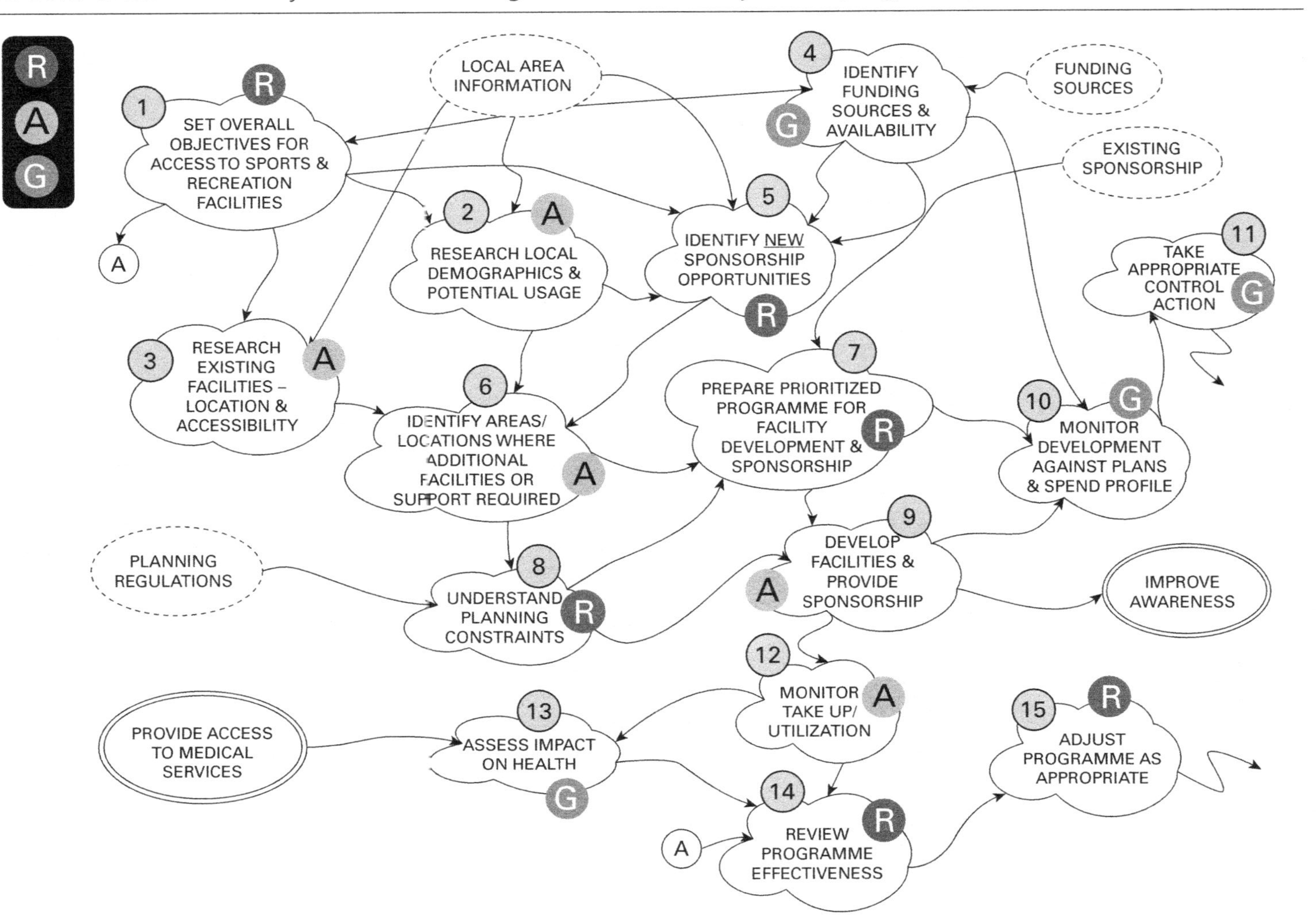

3.4 *Identifying what needs to change*

What needs to change (and what will be included in the change programme) is the result of the 'gap' or comparison between where we want to be and where we are now. This is the minimum required to achieve the 'total capability' defined by the KOPE analysis. RAG analysis offers a graphic method of capturing the results of the gap analysis.

Capture the results of the gap analysis in a 'difference and change requirements' table (Table 2.3) to show the full set of change requirements.

TABLE 2.3 Difference and change requirements table (King, 2006)

	Total Capability	Current State	Change Requirements	Priority
K	eg stakeholder and customer information is needed throughout the development programme	eg stakeholder and customer information is of poor quality and incomplete	eg specify and develop new stakeholder and customer information systems	eg Med
O	eg specialist skills are required for assessing the health values of proposed recreation projects	eg specialisms not defined and skills/ expertise sharing is often restricted within individuals and teams	eg establish a competency and specialist skills register	eg High
P	eg objectives and performance measures must drive programme design and effectiveness (outcomes)	eg objectives and measures are not adequately defined and performance not monitored in a structured way	eg set clear objectives and measures for all programmes – devise new management and monitoring procedures	eg High
E	eg the need for local knowledge and links suggest appropriate proximity to local projects and communities	eg programme development often undertaken centrally, remote from local communities	eg establish a network of 'regional outposts' to liaise with the local community	eg Med

CASE STUDY

In an assignment for a large local government organization, a new authority-wide asset management function was designed using products from a business analysis based on soft systems methods and capability analysis. This included the development of the business systems definition (and supporting vision statement), business activity models, process models and flow diagrams, together with detailed descriptions of information, technology, process and environmental needs. This enabled the authority to create a 'Statement of Requirements' for the successful procurement of a new asset management solution.

The results of the gap analysis also lay the foundations for more in-depth specification of change requirements, an assessment of the full impact of change (Chapter 6) and the development of the detailed delivery plan.

4. Problems and concerns arising from change

As already discussed, stakeholders will view change from a variety of different perspectives and will inevitably raise problems and concerns about the change definition that will need to be properly explored and evaluated.

The interactive nature of development and use of BAMs provides many opportunities for individuals and groups of stakeholders to contribute their needs, ideas and concerns. The whole process of defining change described in this chapter establishes a clear context for identifying and addressing problems that may arise and may affect the plans for and the viability and achievability of change. When evaluating the scope, requirements and priorities for change, problem-solving techniques can be invaluable in unravelling complexity and isolating the causes (as opposed to symptoms) of change.

The BAMs (and any more detailed lower-level models, including process maps) can provide a useful starting point for 'what-if' scenario testing and identification of potential problem areas or 'hotspots'. This approach also helps to identify and document potential risks before they occur, so that the impact of a change programme or project can be understood. Appropriate impact and risk management strategies can then be developed to ensure risks are at best averted and, at worst, the impact on the programme/project minimized. (Chapter 6 has more detailed information on assessing the impact of change and risks.)

4.1 Hotspot analysis

Use the BAMs to identify and map potential impact and 'hotspots' (Figure 2.23). A hotspot can relate to:

- a risk or perceived problem area;
- an issue with an activity or process within the model;
- a dependency between linked activities or processes;
- an external entity or another dependent model (at the same or a lower level);
- an activity or process that has multiple dependencies in the model.

Follow these four steps to conduct a simple hotspot analysis:

1. Use the BAM (and, where developed, process maps) to pinpoint potential hotspots or areas of concern.
2. Characterize each hotspot and determine the level of threat and responsive actions needed.
3. Capture any risks or issues in the appropriate log for the change programme/ project.
4. Review the emerging change definition and update as needed.

In Figure 2.23, the identified hotspots signify potential problem areas with the operation of the future state model, for example in this illustration showing the 'hotspots':

1. Some financial sources may be deemed controversial or related to vested interests.
2. Lack of reliable data and effect of political bias may pose problems.
3. Multi-stakeholder involvement in decision making could cause delays.
4. Variability of local development plans and priorities create added complexity.
5. Agreement on a standard set of health criteria may be difficult.

For more detailed information about assessing the severity of change impacts using a 'change heat map' see Chapter 6.

4.2 Cause and effect diagrams

Another useful technique for exploring identified problems (or a hotspot) is the use of cause and effect diagrams (Ishikawa, 1990), also called Ishikawa diagrams, fish-bone diagrams and herringbone diagrams.

Cause and effect diagrams were popularized by Ishikawa in the 1960s, to support quality control, and can be used to:

- discover the root cause of a problem;
- uncover hotspots or bottlenecks in a process;
- identify where and why a process isn't working;
- refine and update the change definition.

FIGURE 2.23 Mapping change 'hotspots' on the BAM

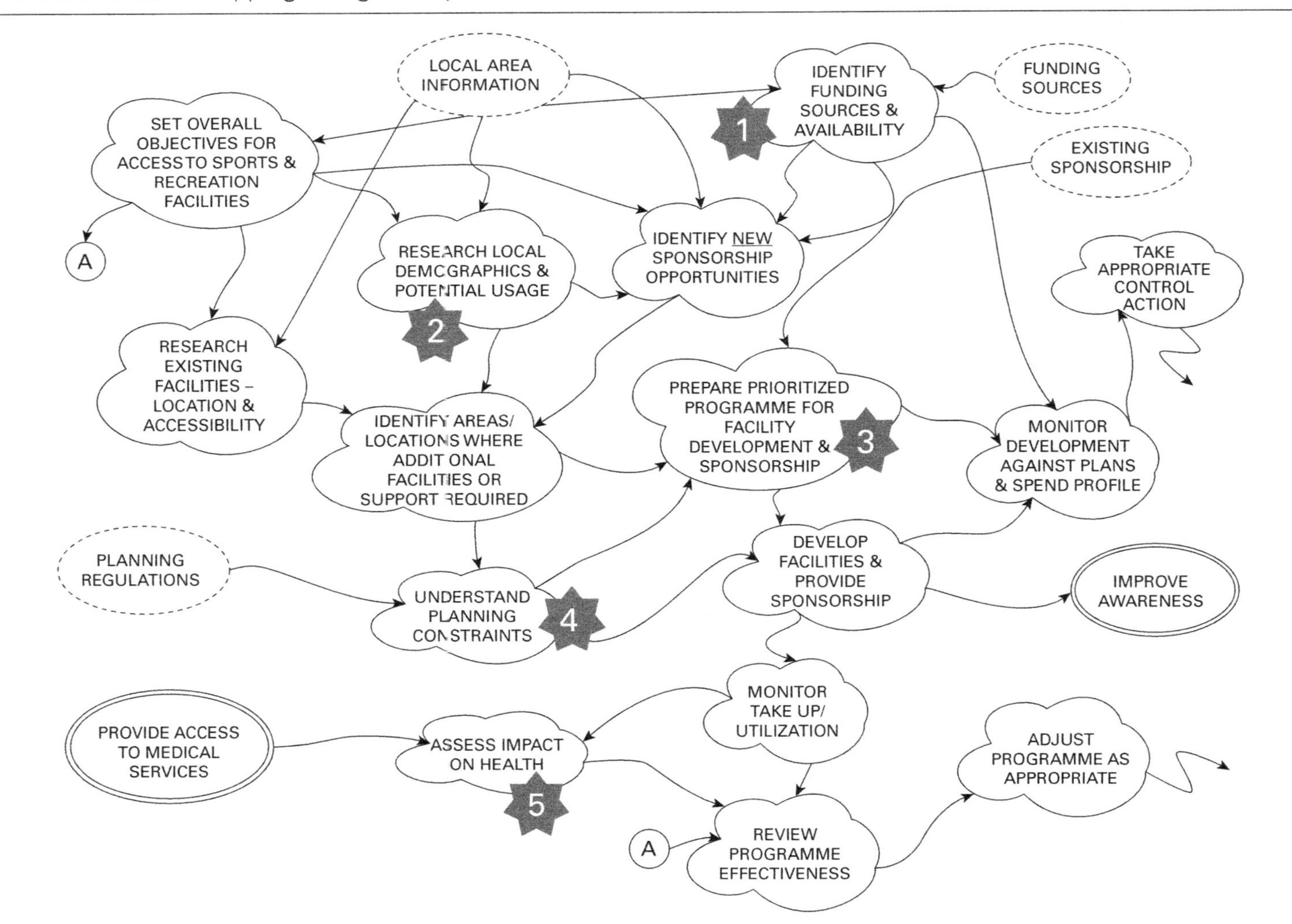

FIGURE 2.24 Generic Ishikawa (fishbone) diagram

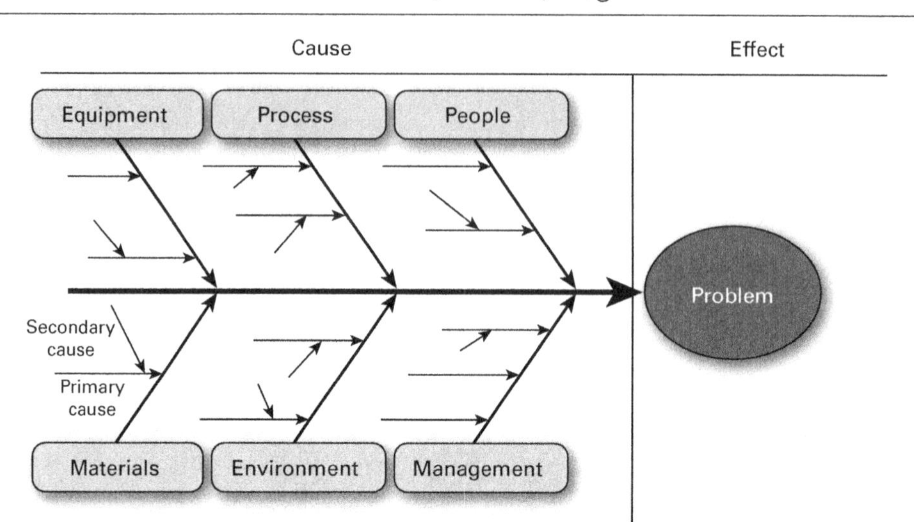

How to create a fishbone diagram (Figure 2.24)

1. In a group, agree on a problem statement (effect). Write it at the right of the flipchart or whiteboard. Draw a box around it and draw a horizontal arrow running to it.
2. Brainstorm the major categories or causes of the problem, or you can use these generic headings:
   - People: those who may be involved with the activity or process.
   - Process: how the activity or process is performed and the specific requirements for doing it, such as policies, procedures, rules, regulations and laws.
   - Equipment/technology: any equipment, computers, tools and so on required to carry out the activity or process.
   - Materials: the needed raw materials, parts, pens, paper and so on.
   - Management/measurements: data and information generated from the process that are used to evaluate its quality.
   - Environment: the conditions – such as location, time, physical environment and culture – in which the activity or process is undertaken.
3. Write the categories of causes as branches from the main arrow.
4. Brainstorm all the possible causes of the problem. Ask: 'Why does this happen?' As each idea is given, write it as a sub-branch from the appropriate category. Causes can be written in several places if they relate to several categories.
5. Again ask 'why does this happen?' about each cause. Write sub-causes branching off the causes. Continue to ask 'why?' and generate deeper levels of causes. Layers of branches indicate causal relationships.
6. When the group runs out of ideas, focus attention to places on the chart where ideas are less well-developed.

Summary

- Building models helps to visualize the business in its 'future state'. According to systems theory, a minimum set of *generic activities* must be present in all viable business systems and are represented in a generic activity model.
- Business activity models (BAMs) show connected activities and indicate dependencies both internal and external to the business system. These 'future state' models enable business managers and change teams to develop and explore ideas visually, including radical alternatives.
- For any change programme to succeed, just having a business model is not enough. A full 'KOPE capability analysis' provides the basis for analysis of all required future state activities described in the BAM – knowledge and information, organization and people, process and procedure, and environment and infrastructure – and provides the baseline against which specified improvements and benefits can be measured.
- A 'gap analysis' identifies what is different between the 'current state' and 'future state' and the BAM can be used to map the differences using a simple 'RAG' analysis approach.
- The results of the gap analysis lay the foundations for more in-depth specification of change requirements, an assessment of the full impact of change and the development of the detailed change plan.
- When evaluating the scope, requirements and priorities for change, problem-solving techniques can be invaluable in unravelling complexity and isolating the causes (as opposed to symptoms) of change. Useful techniques include 'hotspot' analysis and 'cause and effect' analysis.

Questions to think about

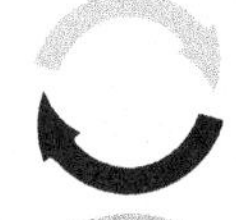

1. When preparing and planning a change initiative in your organization did you use conceptual models to describe how the future state will look and what were the benefits?
2. What relevant knowledge and skills are needed when creating 'future' state business activity models and change requirements and who from the organization should be involved?
3. What techniques did you use to evaluate the 'gap' between the current and future state and how were stakeholder issues and concerns addressed?

Further reading

For more information on strategy:

A text book on strategy: Johnson, G, Whittington, R and Scholes, K (2010) *Exploring Strategy*, Prentice Hall

A collection of the most definitive papers (including some references above): *On Strategy* (2011) Harvard Business Review Press

Also look at the websites of:
Harvard Business Review, www.hbr.org
MIT Sloan Management Review, sloanreview.mit.edu
McKinsey Quarterly, www.mckinsey.com/insights/mckinsey_quarterly
Other websites at major business schools such as London Business School and INSEAD, and other leading consultancies such as Ernst & Young, and PwC

For more on using soft systems methods in practice, when defining vision and change requirements: David King (2006) *Think, Learn, Improve! Turn your business vision into reality* is a useful source of practitioner tools, including some used in this chapter.

For more information on soft systems methods: Brian Wilson (2001) *Soft Systems Methodology: Conceptual model building and its contribution*; and the book by Checkland and Scholes, *Soft Systems Methodology in Action*, are particularly informative.

References

Bradley, C, Bryan, L and Smit, S (2012) Managing the strategy journey, *McKinsey Quarterly*, July 2012

Bradley, C, Dawson, A and Smit, S (2013) The strategic yardstick you can't afford to ignore, *McKinsey Quarterly*, October 2013

Burke, A (nd) [accessed 24 February 2014] T552 Diagramming [Online] http://systems.open.ac.uk/materials/T552/pages/rich/richAppendix.html

Buzan, T (2003) *The Mind Map Book: Radiant Thinking – Major Evolution in Human Thought (Mind Set)*, BBC Active, London

Checkland, P (1999) *Systems Thinking, Systems Practice: Includes a 30 year retrospective*, John Wiley & Sons, New York

Checkland, P and Scholes, P C (1999) *Soft Systems Methodology in Action*, John Wiley & Sons, Chichester

Coase, R (1937) The nature of the firm, *Economica*, **4** (16), pp 386–405

Covey, S R (2011) *The 7 Habits of Highly Effective People*, Simon & Schuster, New York

Heijden, K van der (2004) *Scenarios: The art of strategic conversation*, 2nd edn, John Wiley & Sons, Chichester

Ishikawa, K (1990) *Introduction to Quality Control*, Productivity Press, India
Johnson, G, Scholes, K and Whittington, R (2008) *Exploring Corporate Strategy*, 8th edn, Prentice-Hall, Europe
King, D (2006) *Think, Learn, Improve! Turn your business vision into reality*, Management Books 2000 Ltd, Cirencester
Kotter, J P (2012) *Leading Change with a New Preface*, Harvard Business Review Press, Boston: MA
Manasse, A L (1986) Vision and leadership: paying attention to intention, *Peabody Journal of Education*, **63** (1), pp 150–73
Nanus, B (1992) *Visionary Leadership: Creating a compelling sense of direction for your organization*, Jossey-Bass, San Francisco
Porter, M E (1985) *Competitive Strategy*, Free Press, New York
Porter, M E (2008) The five competing forces that shape strategy, *Harvard Business Review*, January 2008
Porter, M E (2009) What is strategy?, *Harvard Business Review*, November 1996
Sergiovanni, T J (1990) Adding value to leadership gets extraordinary results, *Educational Leadership*, **47** (8), pp 23–27
Wikipedia (2014a) [accessed 25 February 2014] Strategic Planning [Online] http://en.wikipedia.org/wiki/Strategic_planning
Wikipedia (2014b) [accessed 25 February 2014] Storytelling [Online] http://en.wikipedia.org/wiki/Storytelling
Wilson, B (2001) *Soft Systems Methodology: Conceptual model building and its contribution*, Wiley & Sons Ltd, Chichester

Managing benefits Ensuring change delivers value

03

STEPHEN JENNER

Introduction

Benefits are the reason that an organization invests its time, management attention and resources in change initiatives. Benefits are defined as the measurable improvement from change, which is perceived as positive by one or more stakeholders, and which contributes to organizational (including strategic) objectives.

They typically include: increasing revenue; reducing costs; meeting a legal/regulatory requirement or maintaining current systems; and making a measurable contribution to achieving strategic/organizational objectives or reducing risks to their achievement.

While some benefits are automatic (such as where a new contract provides the same service but at lower cost), benefits realization is often dependent on deliberate management action. For example, the outcome of a change initiative might be a reduction in required headcount. The ultimate or end benefits then depend on what management action is taken to redeploy the resulting spare capacity – in reduced budgets, lower unit costs, or being able to undertake some other value-adding activity.

As well as realizing intended benefits, change initiatives can result in dis-benefits. These are defined as the measurable result of a change, perceived as negative by one or more stakeholders, which detracts from one or more strategic or organizational objectives.

Note also that not all positive benefits are planned from the outset – some are unanticipated and emerge as the initiative is developed, deployed or implemented. These are termed emergent benefits.

Whilst benefits represent the rationale for investment in change initiatives (whether established informally, or formally as projects or programmes), research suggests that many change initiatives struggle to demonstrate the benefits they were established to realize – and this applies across the globe, in both private and public sectors, and to many types of initiative. Beer and Nohria (2000), for example, state: 'change remains difficult to pull off, and few companies manage the process as well as they would like. Most of their initiatives – installing new technology, downsizing, restructuring, or trying to change corporate culture – have had low success rates. The brutal fact is that about 70 per cent of all change initiatives fail.' More recently a study by Moorhouse Consulting (2009) reported that only 20 per cent of respondents believed their organizations succeed in consistently delivering the planned benefits of change. More information about this and other research is in Chapter 1, Section A.

So, the fundamental driver for benefits management is the regularly reported poor track record of change initiatives in realizing the benefits they were established to deliver.

CHAPTER CONTENTS

This chapter describes the principles, processes and techniques for effective benefits management and realization in a change initiative:

Section A: Benefits management principles and processes

Section B: Benefits identification, mapping and analysis

Section C: Planning benefits realization

Section D: Supporting benefits realization

Section A: Benefits management principles and processes

Introduction

We should start by asking: what is benefits management? It is defined as the identification, quantification, analysis, planning, tracking, realization and optimization of benefits. Note the objective is to optimize not maximize benefits realization, ie optimization is about doing the best that can be achieved within constraints (most usually costs) and potential other uses of the available funds. Thus, realizing 80 per cent of the potential benefits for only 60 per cent of the cost may be preferred where the savings can be used to fund other initiatives.

Benefits management seeks to optimize benefits realization by ensuring:

1. Forecast benefits are complete (ie all sources of potential value are identified) and realizable – so managing benefits is built on the solid foundations of realistic forecasts.
2. Forecast benefits are realized in practice by ensuring that the required enabling, business and behavioural change takes place.
3. Benefits are realized as early as possible and are sustained for as long as possible.

4. Emergent benefits are captured and leveraged (and any dis-benefits are minimized).
5. The above can be demonstrated – not just as part of the framework of accountability, but also so that the organization learns what works as a basis for continuous improvement.

The value of benefits management can be significant. A study by Ward, Daniel and Peppard (2008) found that while the adoption of more structured approaches to initiative delivery had not resulted in increased benefits realization, the adoption of key benefits management-related practices was associated with greater benefits realization from change initiatives. Recommended practices included robust benefits-based business cases; planning of organizational change and benefits delivery; and evaluation and review of organizational change and benefits realization.

In practice, however, the potential value of benefits management often proves elusive. Common mistakes include:

- an over-focus on tracking forecast benefits and ignoring emergent benefits;
- 'box ticking' approaches where the emphasis is on filling out forms rather than facilitating benefits realization;
- placing too much emphasis on having someone to hold to account should things not work out as intended.

The answer lies in the following key success characteristics of effective benefits management:

- *Active*: rather than passive tracking against forecast, the focus is on an active search for benefits, with ongoing participative stakeholder engagement. As Thorp (2003) says: 'Benefits realization is a continuous process of envisioning results, implementing, checking intermediate results and dynamically adjusting the path leading from investments to business results.'
- *Evidence-based*: forecasts and processes are driven by evidence about what works rather than assumptions and advocacy.
- *Transparent*: based on open and honest forecasting and reporting, and a 'clear line of sight' from strategic objectives to benefits forecast and realized.
- *Benefits-led*: focusing less on the activities undertaken to realize benefits and more on the actual realization of those benefits, ie just as we expect change initiatives to be benefits-led, so too should benefits management be focused on what difference it is making.
- *Forward-looking*: with an emphasis on learning and continuous improvement, rather than backward-looking attribution of blame.
- *Managed across the full business change life cycle*: extending from benefits identification and quantification, through planning, to realization and capturing and applying lessons learned.

Change managers have a key role to play in achieving this, helping to identify and quantify the benefits from a change initiative. It is important to ensure that benefits are aligned with the strategic aims of the organization, and to help business managers and staff to identify any possible negative effects of change. Change managers, especially, act as a bridge between the change initiative and the business areas impacted by change, and liaise with business and operational areas throughout the change process to ensure a continued focus on benefits. This includes ensuring that benefits are 'owned' by the appropriate business managers, who also accept their accountability for benefits realization. They provide input to the development of benefits realization plans and support the business in capturing relevant measurement data for tracking benefit achievement. Chapter 8 says more about the role of the change manager.

1. Benefits management processes

The benefits management processes are as shown in the 'roof' of the model of Figure 3.1:

- *Identify and quantify*: laying the basis for informed options analysis, investment appraisal, and portfolio prioritization; and the management of benefits realization in due course.
- *Value and appraise*: ensuring resources are allocated to those change initiatives that individually and collectively represent best value for money.
- *Plan:* ensuring accountability and transparency for the realization of identified benefits, the changes on which they are dependent, mitigation of dis-benefits (both expected and unexpected), and identification and leveraging of emergent benefits.

FIGURE 3.1 The benefits management model (Jenner, 2013)

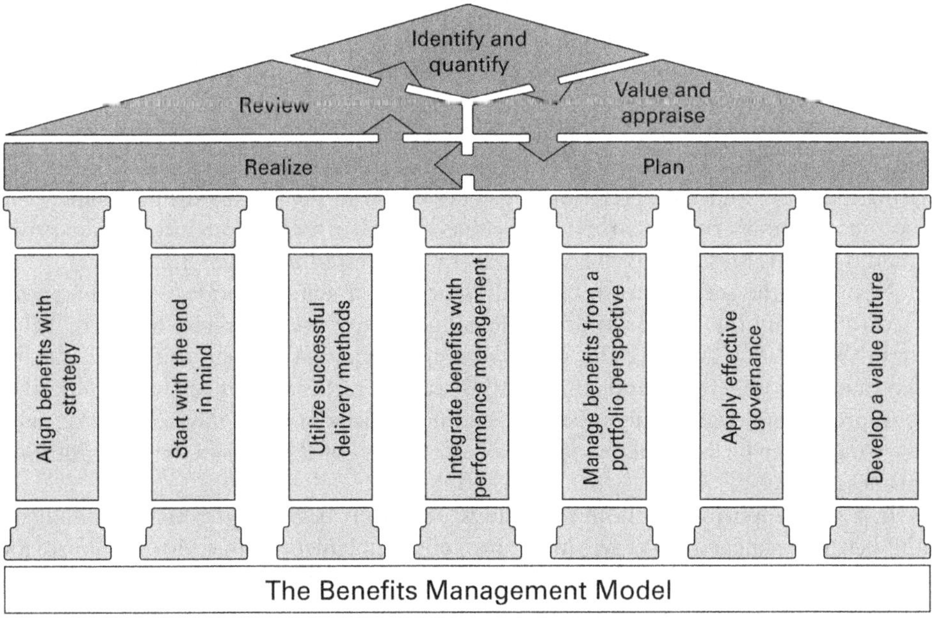

- *Realize*: optimizing benefits realization by actively managing planned benefits through to their realization; capturing and leveraging emergent benefits; and minimizing and mitigating any dis-benefits.
- *Review*: ensuring and assuring that:
  - The benefits to be realized are achievable and continue to represent value for money.
  - Appropriate arrangements have been made for benefits monitoring, management and evaluation.
  - Benefits realization is being effectively managed.
  - Lessons are learned for both the current initiative and as a basis for more effective benefits management practices generally.

While these processes are broadly sequential, their effective operation requires iterative feedback loops throughout. More detail on these processes is provided in Sections B–D.

Defined processes are, however, no 'silver bullet' solution. Their effectiveness depends on a series of principles that represent the foundations upon which successful benefits management processes are built – as shown in the columns of the model of Figure 3.1.

2. Benefits management principles

2.1 Principle 1 – align benefits with strategy

Understanding the contribution of change initiatives to organizational objectives is crucial to effective benefits management. Yet in practice, strategy is often set at too high a level and without meaningful measures, so limiting attempts to consistently determine the strategic contribution of individual initiatives, and indeed the change portfolio as a whole.

One solution is the technique of driver-based analysis. Here, the implicit logic underpinning the achievement of the strategic objectives is made explicit – by articulating the cause-and-effect relationships between (and the drivers of) the elements in the organization's business model or value chain. An example is the service profit chain (Heskett, Sasser and Schlesinger, 1997) illustrated in Figure 3.2.

Note that the service profit chain illustrated is a generic model – organizations need to identify the drivers and key elements in their own business model or value chain. Where this is done, the strategic contribution of change initiatives can be determined more reliably and consistently – and so, rather than investing in initiatives to improve employee engagement or customer satisfaction for their own sake, such investments can be targeted to address specific drivers of elements in the organization's business model.

It is also important to note that the relationship between driver-based analysis and benefits management is two-way, since post-implementation reviews will provide information on whether intended benefits were realized and so help validate and refine the organization's business model.

FIGURE 3.2 The service profit chain

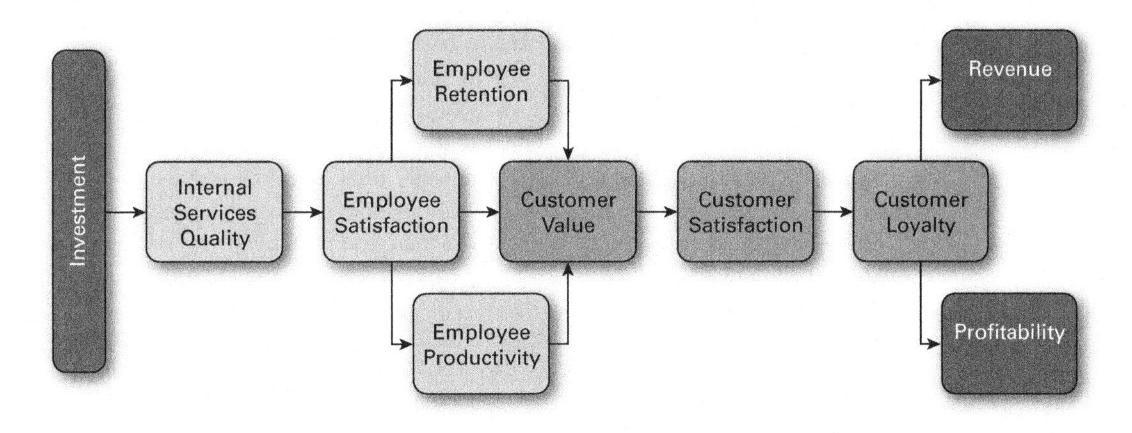

Further information about aligning change to an organization's strategic drivers is in Chapter 2, Section A.

2.2 *Principle 2 – start with the end in mind*

A common mistake is to start with a given change initiative and then identify the benefits that will result from that initiative. This is what Bradley (2010) refers to as a 'cart before the horse' mentality, and Simms (2012) as 'upside down thinking'. Schaffer and Thomson (1992) argue that one cause is that organizations 'confuse ends with means, processes with outcomes', and pursue 'activities that sound good, look good, and allow managers to feel good – but in fact contribute little or nothing to bottom-line performance'.

The solution is to adopt benefits-led change initiatives that 'start with the end in mind', where the scope of the initiative is determined by the benefits required. Based on the analysis by Schaffer and Thomson (1992), six key differences between activity-centred and benefits-led initiatives can be identified – see Table 3.1.

Tip

When completing a benefits map (see Section B.1) start with the problem you are trying to solve or the opportunity to be exploited. Then ask what benefits would be realized if the problem was solved. Only then consider what the scope of the initiative should be.

TABLE 3.1 Activity-centred and benefits-led change initiatives compared

Activity-Centred Change Initiatives	Benefits-Led Change Initiatives
1 The initiative is adopted because it is 'the right thing to do' or a 'no-brainer'. Where objectives are set, they are defined mainly in long-term, non-specific or process-based terms, with no clear linkage from the activity to strategic contribution.	**1** Benefits are identified and the contribution to organizational objectives is clear; and there are measurable, specific, short-term performance improvement goals even when the change effort is long term.
2 The initiative's sponsor urges managers and employees to be patient, take a long-term perspective, and 'keep the faith' as the approach will come good in the end.	**2** The atmosphere is one of impatience for benefits even when the initiative is a long-term change initiative.
3 Progress is measured in terms of measures of activity – people trained, surveys completed etc.	**3** Progress is measured in terms of benefits realized using both leading and lagging indicators.
4 Staff experts and consultants drive the initiative.	**4** Business managers take the lead with staff experts and consultants helping them to realize benefits.
5 Substantial investment is required up-front before any significant benefits are seen.	**5** Incremental and modular approaches are adopted with 'quick wins' being used to generate enthusiasm for the initiative.
6 The approach is based on advocacy rather than evidence. There is no real learning from experience since the solution promoted is accepted as orthodoxy.	**6** The approach is driven by evidence about what works – learnings are fed back to provide insight into the design and prioritization of the next phase of the initiative.

Further information about developing vision and requirements for the desired future state is in Chapter 2, Sections C and D.

2.3 Principle 3 – utilize successful delivery methods

If change initiatives are not delivered effectively, or if they are delivered late, there will inevitably be adverse impacts on benefits realization. Consequently, disciplined and repeatable project and programme delivery methods, as well as the application of guidance contained in the bodies of knowledge (BoKs) from relevant professional bodies such as the Project Management Institute (PMI) and Association for Project Management (APM), as well as the Chartered Management Institute (CMI), are enablers for the realization of benefits. Chapter 8 has more information on project and programme management.

We live in an increasingly complex environment, however, characterized by uncertainty, ambiguity, cross-initiative dependencies, a multitude of often conflicting stakeholder interests, emergent strategy and requirements, and transformational rather than incremental change. The consequence of this increased complexity, ambiguity and uncertainty is that as well as disciplined delivery methods, attention also needs to be given to strategies such as:

- Adapting traditional delivery methods by applying a 'dolphins not whales' (Cross, 2002) approach: ie applying agile, modular and incremental development approaches, and breaking down large initiatives into smaller ones of shorter duration.
- Combining a rigorous start gate to set things up right from the beginning, with regular review throughout the life of the initiative.
- Incremental rather than one-off investment decisions, based on the technique of 'staged release of funding', with continued funding being linked more closely to confidence in benefits realization.
- Ongoing participative stakeholder engagement, including bringing the 'voice of the customer' into the design and delivery of change initiatives.
- Applying a consistent approach to change management such as those discussed throughout this book.
- Adopting a forward-looking perspective based on learning, feedback and insight throughout the business change life cycle. The focus should be less on holding people to account for forecast benefits, than a continuous search for emergent benefits and capturing learnings.

2.4 Principle 4 – integrate benefits with performance management

Wherever possible, benefits and their measures should be integrated into the organization's operational and Human Resources (HR) performance management systems. This includes:

- *Operational performance management*
  - Linking benefits measures to the organization's key performance indicators (KPIs) and making use of data available from the management information system – this minimizes the additional costs of new measurement systems to track and report on benefits realization.
  - Building benefits into business plans and budgets. This is the technique of 'booking the benefits' where benefits are reflected in revised budgets, headcount targets, unit costs and performance targets.

- *HR performance management*
  - Aligning responsibilities for benefits management with individuals' performance objectives – so there is clarity about what people are responsible and accountable for, including implementing the changes upon which benefits realization depends.
  - Aligning responsibilities for benefits management with the reward and recognition processes. Financial rewards are not always the best way to motivate people, but inconsistencies between desired behaviours and the organization's reward and recognition systems can be a real obstacle to progress because they send mixed messages about what is regarded as important. So, wherever possible, link incentives (both financial and non-financial) to realization of benefits.

It should be noted that integration of benefits with the performance management systems does not represent a complete solution to the issue of managing benefits realization. Benefits tracking and reporting is still required as a basis for: confirming that the desired improvements actually materialize (rather than, for example, cutting budgets but only creating an unfunded pressure as planned efficiencies are not realized); understanding what actually causes changes in performance; and for identifying emergent benefits and mitigating dis-benefits. But the cost of such activity and its effectiveness is aided where benefits are integrated, as far as possible, with the performance management systems.

Further information about performance management is in Chapter 13, Section A.

2.5 Principle 5 – manage benefits from a portfolio perspective

The change portfolio represents the total investment by an organization in its change initiatives. That said, benefits are derived from change initiatives so it might be wondered why a portfolio-based approach to benefits management is necessary. The reasons why this is important are because it helps to ensure:

- Consistent alignment of change initiatives with the organization's strategic objectives and performance management systems.
- Good practice is repeatable across all initiatives within the change portfolio – with consequent efficiency savings and enhanced effectiveness in terms of benefits realization.
- Double counting (ie where the same benefits are claimed by, and used to justify, more than one initiative) is minimized.
- Lessons are learned and applied more widely.
- Benefits realization and value for money are optimized.

A portfolio-based approach to benefits management encompasses six main elements, as listed below.

Element 1 – consistent benefits eligibility rules

These rules define how benefits are categorized, quantified, valued and validated in the preparation of change initiative documentation, including business cases. Benefits eligibility rules serve several purposes. They enable consistent appraisal of change and the contribution made to achievement of strategy, they prevent double-counting of benefits and they facilitate benefits realization tracking and reporting.

A consistent approach to benefits categorization is central to the benefits eligibility rules. Common approaches to categorization include splitting benefits into: financial and non-financial categories; by strategic objective; and analysing them into economy (doing things more cheaply), efficiency (doing things right) and effectiveness (doing the right things) groupings.

Tip

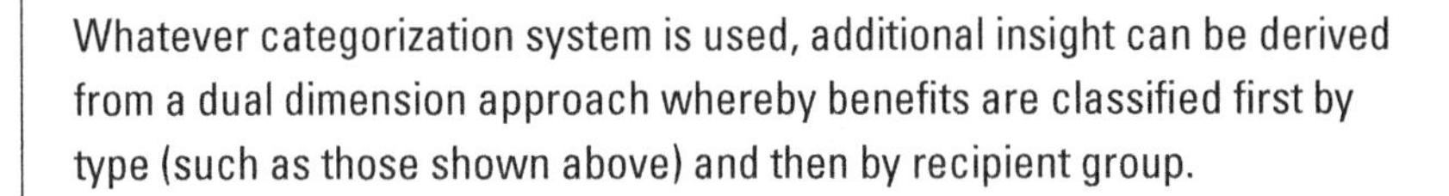

Whatever categorization system is used, additional insight can be derived from a dual dimension approach whereby benefits are classified first by type (such as those shown above) and then by recipient group.

Element 2 – a portfolio-level benefits realization plan

This includes an analysis of the benefits to be realized over the coming planning period (typically a year) analysed by: benefit category; from which change initiative(s); the stakeholders/business unit who will receive them; and impact analysed by time period, eg by month or by quarter. Thus we can see, for example, how much cost reduction will be realized over the coming year, from which initiatives, and which parts of the business will be affected (and when).

Element 3 – reappraisal of the benefits from change initiatives at stage/phase gates and portfolio-level reviews

Good practice is to apply the technique of 'staged release of funding', whereby funding for each phase of a change initiative is only confirmed when the relevant gate review is successfully completed – and funding is limited to that required to take the initiative to the next review. Thus investment of limited resources is linked to regular reappraisal to ensure that the benefits will be realized, and at a price that represents value for money.

Element 4 – effective arrangements to manage benefits post-initiative closure

In practice, many change initiatives are closed down before benefits are fully realized. A portfolio approach can help to address this by ensuring appropriate handover of responsibility for benefits at initiative closure, and by including benefits from closed initiatives in the portfolio benefits realization plan and dashboard report (see Element 5).

Element 5 – clear arrangements for benefits tracking and reporting at a portfolio level

This is facilitated by the use of a portfolio benefits realization dashboard report, which enables effective management oversight of benefits realization against plan and determining when remedial action is required. Typical contents of a dashboard report are realization outturn data compared with plan for each benefit category and business area, updated forecast, and performance of benefits KPIs.

Element 6 – regular and robust post-implementation reviews

These enable lessons learned to be captured and fed back into forecasting on new initiatives and revisions to the benefits management processes that are applied across the change portfolio.

2.6 Principle 6 – apply effective governance

The importance of governance in relation to benefits has been highlighted by the UK National Audit Office (NAO), who report (NAO, 2011) that 'weak governance structures and poor performance management systems have resulted in missed benefits'. In relation to benefits management, four key characteristics of effective governance can be identified, as shown below.

Clear governance

There should be clarity/transparency about who is responsible for what and to whom. This establishes clear business accountability for the change initiative and for the business changes on which benefits realization depends. It also establishes decision making and lines of authority, including regular review, and how benefits are categorized and managed.

This is aided by documenting the governance structures, including key roles and decision rules, and benefits management processes in a portfolio benefits management framework.

Aligned governance

Responsibilities and accountabilities for benefits management should be aligned top-down and bottom-up (from portfolio level to individual change initiative), as well as with the organization's wider governance framework. This provides for eventual realization of individual benefits by clearly identified benefit owners.

Consistent governance

This does not mean that benefits management practices should be applied inflexibly, rather that variations from agreed processes should be subject to approval by the appropriate authority, and the rationale for such decisions should be recorded and communicated to all those involved.

Consistent governance is aided by the agreement of an escalations process and application of the technique of 'management by exception', whereby variances from plan that exceed a preset control limit (eg where the benefits forecast or benefits realization varies from approved plan by +/–10 per cent) are escalated to the next governance level for consideration as to what action is appropriate.

Active governance

Effective governance depends upon an active approach based on planning for success and an emphasis on a searching for emergent benefits. It creates value by leveraging existing capability, rather than passive tracking to check that planned benefits have been realized. The business takes real ownership of change initiatives and realization of the anticipated benefits.

John Thorp (2003) calls this 'activist accountability', 'which goes beyond traditional notions of passive accountability. It includes the concept of "ownership" – meaning active, continuous involvement in managing a program and, most importantly, clear ownership of each measurable outcome and the associated benefits'.

Chapter 8 has more information on change governance.

2.7 Principle 7 – develop a value culture

Managing benefits effectively requires a shift from a delivery-centric culture, where the focus is on delivering capability to time, cost and quality standards, to a value-centric culture, where the primary focus is on realizing benefits. Unfortunately, research finds that there is often room for improvement in this regard. Ward (2006), for example, found that, 'organisations have undue faith in the business cases and that the deployment of formal methodologies gives managers a false sense of security, and perhaps an excuse for not becoming sufficiently involved'.

This can be addressed by first recognizing that successful implementation of benefits management is a business change programme in its own right. Second, don't be too impatient. New behaviour won't happen overnight, but if benefits management processes are applied consistently, and for all change initiatives, then behavioural change will follow.

Tip

Establish a benefits management forum – meeting delivery and change management colleagues on a regular basis helps to break down barriers and disseminate lessons learned.

Summary

The benefits management processes run across the business change life cycle and are discussed in detail in the sections that follow. They are: identify and quantify; value and appraise; plan; realize; and review.

The effectiveness of these processes is dependent on seven principles:

1. Align benefits with strategy: via, for example, driver-based analysis, so that the strategic contribution of individual change initiatives can be assessed in a meaningful and consistent manner.
2. Start with the end in mind: with benefits-led rather than activity-centred change. Benefits should determine the solution rather than vice versa.
3. Utilize successful delivery methods: to implement the enabling and business changes on which benefits realization is dependent.
4. Integrate benefits with performance management: including 'booking' benefits into budgets, headcount targets, unit costs and performance targets; and aligning responsibilities for benefits management with individuals' performance objectives.
5. Manage benefits from a portfolio perspective: so ensuring consistent approaches to assessing strategic contribution; good practice is repeatable across all initiatives within the change portfolio; double counting is minimized; and lessons are learned and applied more widely.
6. Apply effective governance: the characteristics of which are that it is clear, aligned, consistent and active.
7. Develop a value culture: by managing the development of benefits management as a business change programme; and building commitment via techniques such as the 'champion-challenger model' and 'decision conferencing'.

Questions to think about

1. In your present change role you may not have direct control over portfolio-level benefits management – but consider, how can you extend your influence beyond your initiative to add value to other change initiatives? How can you be an 'apostle' for benefits management?
2. Have your organization's strategic objectives been defined in a sufficient degree of granularity so that the strategic contribution of your change initiative can be measured? If not, who could you work with to address this issue?
3. Assess your change initiative against Table 3.1 – is it more benefits-led than activity-centred?

Section B: Benefits identification, mapping and analysis

Introduction

This section encompasses:

- Identification of benefits: focusing primarily on benefits discovery workshops and benefits mapping.
- Quantification of benefits: answering the 'how much?' question by accurately forecasting the scale of benefits anticipated.
- Documenting benefits in the form of a benefit profile.
- The role of benefits in relation to the business case.

The importance of the above cannot be overstated, because the work undertaken here provides the basis for all that follows. If we start off with unreliable benefits forecasts, then subsequent management of these benefits is severely compromised.

Ideally, the focus should be less on identifying the benefits from an established initiative than, as was highlighted in our consideration of Principle 2, (see Section A), on identifying the benefits required and then ensuring the solution is designed to realize these benefits, ie 'starting with the end in mind' with benefits-led change. That said, in many cases the initiative will have been established before detailed work on benefits commences – but this only emphasizes the importance of starting work on benefits identification and quantification as early as possible in the business change life cycle.

1. Benefits identification

Approaches to benefits identification include techniques such as process mapping and value-stream analysis that identify areas that offer potential benefits to stakeholders from process redesign. Process optimization is covered in more detail in Chapter 13, Section C.

The most commonly used approach to benefits identification is the benefits discovery workshop, the output of which will typically be an agreed benefits map. Change managers have a key role to play here in facilitating the workshop (Chapter 10) and in preparing the benefits map.

Various approaches to benefits mapping are in use, but one of the most common is the Benefits Dependency Network (Ward and Daniel, 2006), shown in Figure 3.3 – here the workshop focuses on:

- Identifying the strategic drivers, investment objectives and benefits from an initiative. Drivers represent senior management's views as to what is important and where change must occur within a given timescale, eg the need to increase market share, reduce costs or improve services provided. They exist independently of any initiative. Investment objectives are an organizational target for achievement agreed for an initiative in relation to the drivers.
- Identifying the enabling and business changes required to achieve the benefits desired. Enabling changes are the prerequisites for a business change to happen and are usually one-off, such as the implementation of a new IT system. Business changes, in contrast, are new ways of working that are needed in order that benefits will be realized – for example, adoption of revised processes. They are usually ongoing and can take time to embed themselves as 'business as usual'.

FIGURE 3.3 The Benefits Dependency Network (Ward and Daniel, 2006)

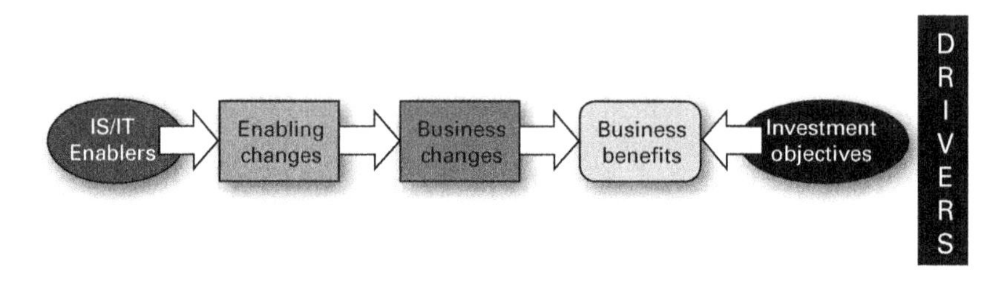

Benefits identification is aided where standard portfolio benefits categories have been identified, as the focus is then on exploring what contribution the change initiative will make to each benefit category.

CASE STUDY

A variation on the benefits dependency network is provided by the example of a benefits logic map from *Managing Benefits* (Jenner, 2013) shown in Figure 3.4 – this example is from the cross-government Tell Us Once programme that encompassed both central government and local authorities (LAs).

Note that the benefits logic map:

- Starts by identifying the strategic drivers and investment objectives for the change (so applying the 'start with the end in mind' principle discussed in the last section).

FIGURE 3.4 Benefits logic map (by kind agreement of Matthew Briggs, Programme Manager, Tell Us Once)

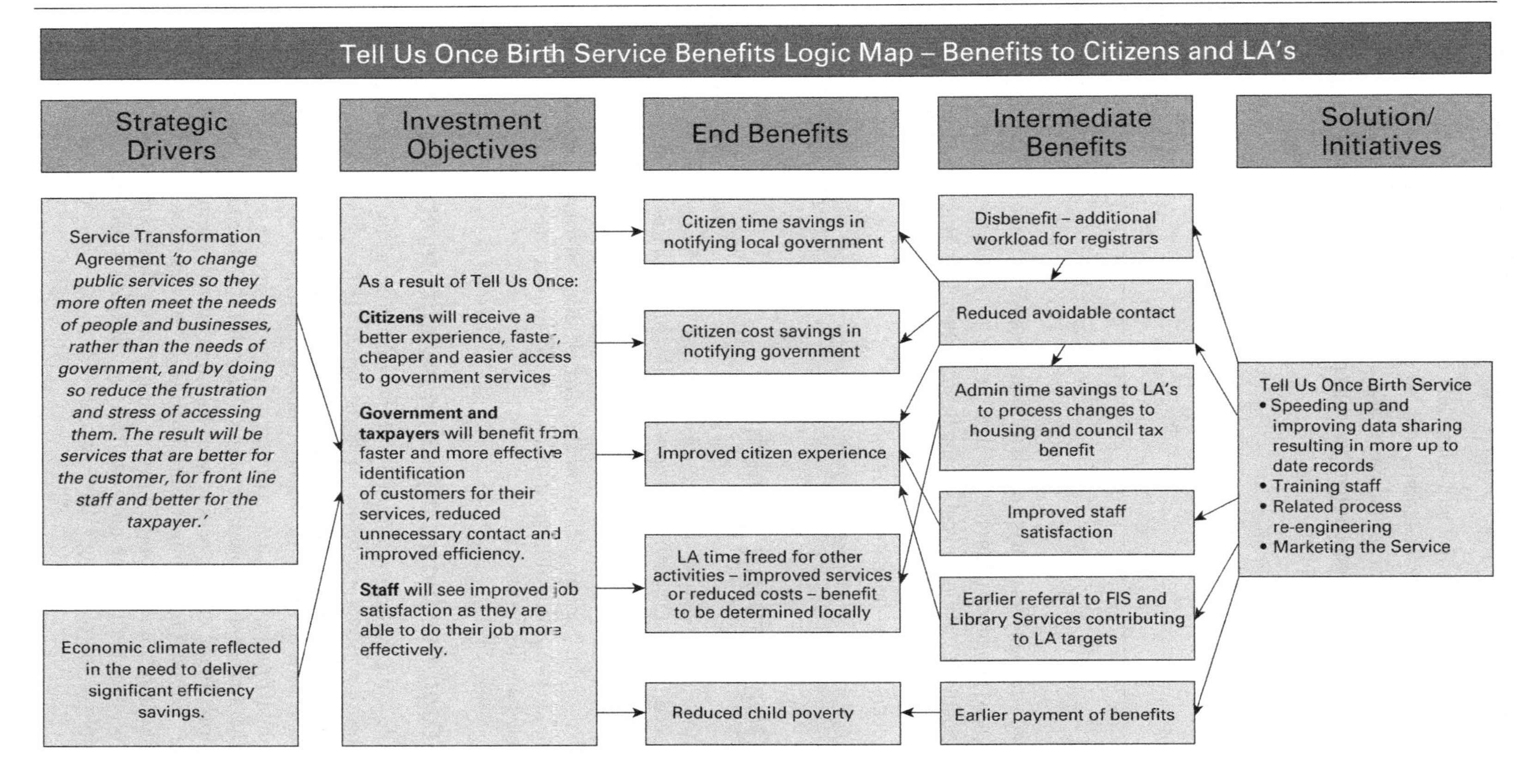

- Distinguishes between intermediate and end benefits – this can be achieved by asking a series of 'so what?' questions, such as: staff time will be saved – so what?; the time saved can be used to reduce caseload backlogs – so what? This results in the organization meeting its targets for case processing and enhancing customer satisfaction (the end benefits).
- Also identifies dis-benefits.

Tip

When the benefits map is complete, undertake a check that all enabling and business changes under the 'solution' heading are both necessary and collectively sufficient to deliver the benefits identified. This should be confirmed by the senior responsible owner (SRO)/sponsor as they are accountable for benefits realization.

2. Quantifying benefits

Research indicates that in many cases the cause of the failure to realize benefits can be traced back to their overstatement in the business case – for example, a research study in Australia by Capability Management (2006) found that: 'Of the business cases reviewed, over 65 per cent misrepresented the benefits.' This is due to two main factors – first, cognitive bias on the part of those involved in forecasting benefits; second, organizational factors that adversely impact the production of accurate and reliable benefits forecasts.

2.1 Cognitive biases affecting benefits forecasting

Lovallo and Kahneman (2003) argue that forecasters suffer from: 'Delusional optimism: we overemphasise projects' potential benefits and underestimate likely costs, spinning success scenarios while ignoring the possibility of mistakes.' Table 3.2 identifies four of the main cognitive biases (sources of optimism bias) and how they can impact on benefits forecasting.

What makes such cognitive biases so powerful is that first, despite the evidence of past forecasting errors, people are often unaware of them. Research by Moorhouse (2011) found: 'Only 10 per cent of SROs feel business cases and benefits realization are adequately understood on programmes across Government and industry, however over 60 per cent feel the understanding on their own programmes is adequate' – an example of the planning fallacy in action. Second, many cognitive biases are linked

TABLE 3.2 Common cognitive biases

Cognitive Bias	Impact on Benefits Forecasting
Expectation or confirmation bias	The tendency for forecasters to select evidence that confirms existing beliefs and assumptions, and discount or ignore evidence that conflicts with these beliefs.
The planning fallacy	The belief that, whilst being aware that many similar initiatives have failed to realize the forecast benefits in the past, this won't affect the current initiative.
The framing effect and loss aversion	The tendency to value losses avoided more than equivalent gains. Hastie and Dawes (2001) note that, 'most empirical estimates conclude that losses are about twice as painful as gains are pleasurable'. Thus, business cases that are framed in terms of what might go wrong if the initiative were not to proceed (lives lost, for example), appear more compelling than if the same initiative's business case is prepared on the basis of the positive outcomes obtained (such as lives saved).
Anchoring and adjustment	In preparing forecasts there is a tendency to 'anchor' on, and give disproportionate weight to the first estimate (no matter how reliable or relevant) and then make insufficient adjustment to reflect changed circumstances.

and reinforcing; and third, they affect experts as well as the general population. For more information on cognitive bias see also Chapter 5, Section A2 (exploring how we process information) and Chapter 10, Section C2.1 (for consideration of another cognitive bias, groupthink).

But there is another explanation for forecasts differing so widely from the benefits actually realized – and it is one where the cause lies less in the cognitive biases that affect us as individuals, and more in organizational factors that mitigate against accurate and reliable forecasting.

2.2 Organizational pressures affecting benefits forecasting

Professor Bent Flyvbjerg (2005) at Oxford University has undertaken extensive research of transportation infrastructure projects – research with a global reach. He concludes that forecasts are, 'highly, systematically and significantly misleading (inflated). The result is large benefit shortfalls.' The cause is what he terms 'strategic misrepresentation', which is defined as, 'the planned, systematic, deliberate misstatement of costs and benefits to get projects approved'. In short, 'that is lying'. This is not restricted to transportation initiatives – comparative research finds that the same issues apply to a wide range of initiatives (Flyvbjerg, 2006).

The cause, according to Flyvbjerg, is either because it is in the economic interests of those making the case, or because it is expected by the initiative's sponsor in support of 'pet' projects. In short, benefits are used to make the case for investment in a preferred solution – and so the emphasis is on identifying benefits, not as a basis for managing their realization, but in order to justify the costs required. The results include:

- Ignoring risks and assumptions, and using best case benefit and cost estimates to calculate the return on investment.
- Deliberate double counting of benefits, ie including in the forecast, benefits that will be realized from other initiatives.
- Forecasting benefits to stakeholders without validating them with those stakeholders – the benefits are the measurable improvement from change, which is perceived as positive by one or more stakeholders – consequently validating benefits with the relevant stakeholder is essential.
- Claiming staff time-savings in full, but with no indication as to how the time saved will be redeployed to value-adding activity.
- Overvaluing benefits – by, for example, including overhead costs (eg accommodation, lighting and heating) even when there will be no realizable reduction in those overheads.
- Failing to account for dis-benefits.
- Ignoring some of the costs required to realize the benefits, eg counting the salary costs saved from staff redundancies, but not including the costs of the redundancy payments.

Whether the cause is cognitive bias or strategic misrepresentation (or indeed both in combination – the so-called 'conspiracy of optimism') the result is benefits forecasts that are unlikely to ever be realized in practice.

2.3 Solutions to more reliable benefits forecasting

Being aware of the psychological and organizational traps that can compromise forecasting accuracy is important, but addressing them is also aided by the strategies outlined below:

- 'Start with the end in mind' with benefits-led change initiatives, ie initiatives where the solution is designed to deliver the required benefits. Thus there is less incentive to overstate benefits as they are the rationale for the investment, rather than being used to justify a preferred solution.
- Stronger leadership. The UK National Audit Office (NAO, 2011) highlight the importance of senior management: 'setting the tone by encouraging honesty in estimates, challenging optimism bias and assumptions and being willing to stop projects which no longer make sense'.
- Effective accountability frameworks that hold people to account for results, by tracking performance through to benefits realization. If forecasters know that robust post-implementation reviews will compare forecast with actual

performance, then there is more of an incentive for them to ensure their forecasts are realistic.

- Requiring benefits forecasts to be validated prior to investment, and wherever possible, 'booked' in budgets, business plans, performance targets etc.
- Regular and robust review – ensure regular stage/phase gates are held at which benefits are subject to independent review, and apply the technique of 'staged release of funding' with continued investment subject to recommitment to the benefits.
- Reference class forecasting – where benefits forecasts are derived from what actually occurred in a reference class of similar projects. Taking such an 'outside view' (as opposed to the 'inside view' where forecasts are built up by considering the initiative in detail) has been found to produce more accurate forecasts, by avoiding both the cognitive biases and organizational pressures identified above.
- Using probability-based rather than single-point forecasts.
- The Delphi technique – Surowiecki (2004) has demonstrated that groups often make better estimates than individuals, the 'wisdom of crowds' effect. The Delphi technique makes use of this by seeking consensus from a panel of subject-matter experts over several rounds of questioning, with the results of the previous round being fed back to the panel anonymously. In this way, the members of the panel are able to revise their conclusions in the light of the views of others. But what is crucial is that the group making the forecasts are diverse and independent – as Surowiecki says: 'the best collective decisions are the product of disagreement and contest, not consensus and compromise'.

Tip

Always seek out a fresh pair of eyes to review and challenge the benefits forecast – identify assumptions masquerading as facts.

3. Completing the benefit profile

Once benefits have been identified and quantified, the next step is to complete a benefit profile. This is the document that records the key details associated with each benefit (or dis-benefit). The typical contents of a benefit profile are shown in the example in Table 3.3.

TABLE 3.3 Benefit profile template

BENEFIT PROFILE FOR [*Insert name of change initiative*]	
No.	Benefit Owner
Profile Agreement Date	Last Reviewed
Benefit category/type	
Benefit Description:	
Scale of Impact	*Scale of impact compared with baseline performance*
Ramp Up	*Trajectory from implementation of the change to full realization of the benefit*
Lifespan	*Assumed lifespan of the benefit and any tail off*
Benefits Valuation	*Monetary value if relevant and state whether cashable or non-cashable*
Measures	*Measures/indicators to be used to assess benefits realization*
Measurement Frequency	*Of each measure/indicator identified above*
Measurement Source	*Source of measurement data*
Stakeholders	*Major individuals or groups affected*
Enabling Changes	*One-off changes on which benefits realization is dependent*
Business Changes	*Ongoing changes on which benefits realization is dependent*
Behavioural Changes	*Behavioural changes on which benefits realization is dependent*
Key Assumptions	*Assumptions affecting benefits realization scale and timing*
Threats to Realization of the Benefit	*Identify any specific threats to benefits realization and include x-ref to relevant risk-register entry*
Costs	*Costs associated with measurement or realization*
Benefits History	*Record any revision to the benefit forecast with dates and body authorizing the change*
Agreement by Benefit Owner	*Sign and date (indicates acceptance of accountability for realization of the benefit)*

Tip

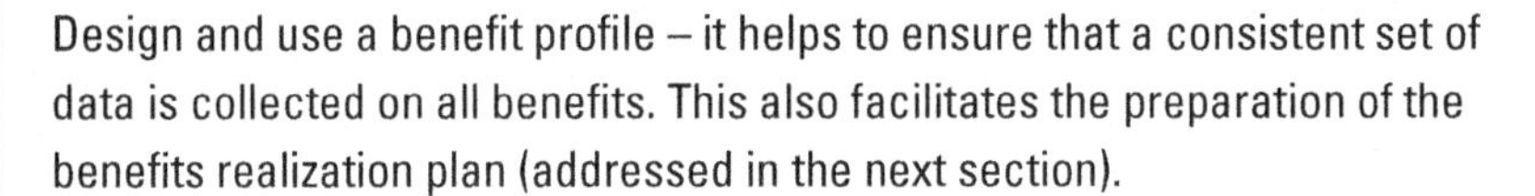

Design and use a benefit profile – it helps to ensure that a consistent set of data is collected on all benefits. This also facilitates the preparation of the benefits realization plan (addressed in the next section).

Rather than completing a single form for each benefit, an alternative is to use a spreadsheet with columns for the key information and rows for each benefit. In this way, a single summary overview of the benefits from a change initiative can be prepared. This can then form the basis for the benefits realization plan discussed in the next section (see Figure 3.6 in the next section).

4. Benefits and the business case

The business case is the document that will be used to record the options analysis and that will, in turn, be used to inform investment appraisal and portfolio prioritization.

The contribution of benefits to the business case can be illustrated by the 'Better Business Cases' initiative being promoted by, among others, the Welsh and New Zealand governments and HM Treasury. This is based on the 'five-case' framework, as shown in Table 3.4.

Summary

Benefits identification is aided by completion of a benefits map that shows how enabling and business changes combine to realize benefits that address the investment objectives/problem to be solved.

Producing reliable benefits forecasts can be compromised by a series of cognitive biases and organizational factors. Overcoming this issue is helped by strategies and techniques such as reference-class forecasting, 'booking the benefits' and the Delphi technique.

Information on a benefit is recorded on the benefit profile – which should be agreed with the benefit owner.

Questions to think about

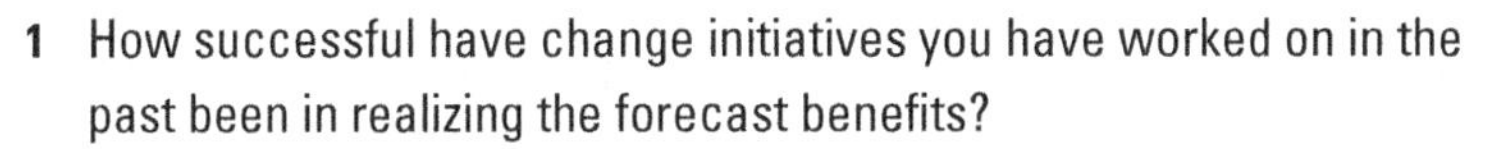

1. How successful have change initiatives you have worked on in the past been in realizing the forecast benefits?
2. Which is the bigger issue facing forecasters in your organization – cognitive bias or strategic misrepresentation?
3. What mechanisms could you apply to your current change initiative(s) to ensure benefits forecasts are reliable?

TABLE 3.4 Benefits and the 'five-case' business case

Case – Focus	Key Benefits Perspective
1 Strategic case – is the initiative supported by a robust case for change?	• Do the benefits clearly contribute to the strategic objectives? • Is the planned strategic contribution quantified?
2 Economic case – does the preferred way forward optimize value for money?	• Do the identified benefits exceed the costs and dis-benefits of the initiative and the results of not investing? • Does the preferred option optimize value for money (demonstrated via an options analysis)?
3 Financial case – is the initiative affordable?	• Are there any cashable benefits that can be recycled to help fund the initiative?
4 Commercial case – is the initiative commercially viable?	• Can supplier payments be linked to benefits realization in some form of gain-sharing or reward-sharing arrangement?
5 Management case – can the initiative be delivered successfully?	• Have adequate arrangements been made for benefits management and evaluation? • Have lessons learned from previous initiatives been applied throughout the business case? • Has a benefits realization plan, with supporting benefit profiles and map(s), been completed?

Section C: Planning benefits realization

Introduction

This section encompasses:

- Awareness of approaches, techniques and mechanisms for:
  - financial analysis and appraisal of benefits;
  - validation of benefits;
  - prioritization of benefits;
  - baselining benefits.
- Assessing change readiness.

- Identifying risks to benefits optimization.
- Completing the benefits realization plan.
- The role of change managers with regard to benefits management.

Effective planning for benefits realization depends on:

- Incorporating iterative feedback loops so that planning documents are regularly updated as new information becomes available.
- A focus on planning as an activity rather than plans as documents.
- Planning extending beyond the forecast benefits to encompass:
  - Emergent benefits: the challenge is to identify, disseminate and leverage these benefits. But this will only happen if dedicated steps are taken in establishing feedback mechanisms, actively seeking out emergent benefits, and including provision in benefits reports for regular updates on the type and scale of emergent benefits identified.
  - Dis-benefits: with the objective of mitigating them wherever possible.
- Achieving transparency and accountability:
  - Transparency: it should be clear what benefits are planned, when they will be realized, how they will be measured/evidenced, and who is responsible for their realization.
  - Accountability: for the business and enabling changes (as identified on the benefits map) on which the realization of benefits depends, and for benefits realization (both intermediate and end benefits) at the initiative and portfolio levels.

1. Financial analysis

Benefits are often expressed in monetary terms as this provides a 'level playing field' for:

- Options analysis: to compare the various options for achieving the desired outcomes and benefits.
- Investment appraisal: to assess whether the benefits justify the costs required on an initiative.
- Portfolio prioritization: to rank initiatives in priority order where resources are limited.

Assigning monetary values to non-financial benefits is not without issue, although economists have developed techniques to determine end users' or customers' 'willingness to pay' or 'willingness to accept' the outcomes of an initiative. Such techniques include:

- Revealed preferences: where values are inferred from observed behaviour in a similar or related situation – for example, by comparing house prices close to an airport with those in similar areas not on the flight path.
- Stated preferences: here questionnaires are used to elicit estimates of people's willingness to pay or accept something.

There are various approaches to options analysis, investment appraisal and portfolio prioritization, each with its own advantages and disadvantages. The three main approaches are outlined below.

1.1 Cost-benefit analysis (CBA)

CBA quantifies in monetary terms as many of the costs and benefits of an initiative as possible to determine whether the benefits exceed the costs and hence whether investment is justified. This approach is most appropriate when the primary investment objective relates to increasing revenue or reducing costs.

1.2 Cost-effectiveness analysis

Here the costs of alternative ways of realizing the desired outcomes and benefits are compared. The decision rule is, all other things being equal, to accept the option with the lowest net present cost (NPC). This approach is most appropriate when the primary investment objective relates to meeting a legal or regulatory requirement or to maintain business as usual.

1.3 Multi-criteria analysis (MCA)

This approach seeks to overcome the problems of unreliable forecasts and difficulties in expressing non-financial benefits in monetary terms, by examining an option or initiative from more than one perspective. It does this by:

- Identifying the factors to consider in making a decision. Typically these factors will be listed under the headings of 'attractiveness' and 'achievability'.
- Weighting these factors to reflect their relative importance.
- Scoring options and initiatives against the weighted factors to calculate an overall score for 'attractiveness' and 'achievability'. These scores can then be combined and divided by the cost to provide a relative strategic 'bang for your buck' assessment.

An example of a MCA template is shown in Figure 3.5.

2. Benefits validation

Validation is a crucial stage in ensuring that forecast benefits are both realistic and realizable. Validation encompasses the following aspects:

- Checks to ensure that benefits claimed are consistent with the organization's benefits eligibility rules – including whether forecasts have been adjusted for optimism bias, or to reflect the organization's track record in benefits realization. This is more than a test for technical compliance – test the

FIGURE 3.5 Multi-criteria analysis template

Factor	Factor Weight	Low	Medium – Low	Medium	Medium – High	High	Weighted Score
Attractiveness		1	2	3	4	5	
Financial Return							
Strategic Fit							
Exploits Capacity & Capability							
Flexibility							
Meets Specified User Needs							
Attractiveness Score							
Achievability		1	2	3	4	5	
Simplicity							
Planning Quality							
Capacity to Drive Progress							
Achievability Score							

assumptions underpinning the benefits forecast by asking whether they are reasonable and reflective of the benefits likely to be realized.

- Research shows that up to 25 per cent of potential benefits are ignored or not identified in the business case.

Tip

Undertake a 'dog that didn't bark' test to avoid what Kahneman (2011) calls the WYSIATI effect ('What You See Is All There Is') by asking are there any additional benefits that have not been included. The use of standard benefits categories can assist in this regard by prompting questions about whether benefits in all the categories have been identified.

- Checks for dependencies with initiatives elsewhere in the organization's change portfolio. This will usually be undertaken by change managers, working with the portfolio benefits manager, and will include checking whether there are any planned or current initiatives that might impact on the benefits claimed.
- Validation of each benefit with the recipient or benefit owner – most usually, operational managers in the relevant business unit, but also strategic planners or policy leads in relation to non-financial benefits that contribute to a strategic objective; and also with end users/customers. This step, more than any other, helps to ensure that benefits are realizable by ensuring they are agreed with those who will be responsible for their realization. This agreement should be evidenced by signing the benefit profile.

Tip

Seek agreement with the relevant benefit owners *prior* to significant investment. Experience shows that asking people to agree to benefits once implementation is under way is a problematic task!

- By, wherever possible and appropriate, 'booking the benefits':
  - Cashable efficiency savings: 'booked' in unit budgets, headcount targets or unit costs. Such savings should be validated by agreeing them with the finance department and the relevant budget holder.
  - Non-cashable efficiency improvements: 'booked' in terms of planned performance improvements to be enabled by the time savings released.
  - Non-financial strategic contributions and performance improvements: 'booked' by updating strategic and business delivery plans (and relevant organizational, business unit and functional performance targets) to reflect the agreed impact of the initiative.
  - Benefits generally (both intermediate and end benefits): 'booked' in individual's personal performance targets.

3. Benefits prioritization

Ultimately, resources are constrained and benefits realization activity therefore needs to focus on those benefits that are judged to be most significant. A relatively simple approach to identifying the relative importance of each benefit is to allocate percentage ratings to each investment objective (so they total to 100 per cent) on the benefits map. The contribution of each benefit to each investment objective is then assessed again by allocating percentages out of 100. In this way, the relative importance of each benefit can be determined.

4. Baselining

A key challenge in planning benefits realization is to understand the 'as is' (or 'current state') performance so that we have a baseline against which to measure the improvement achieved. Factors to consider in baselining current performance include:

- Wherever possible relate baseline measures to existing data from the organization's management information system – this minimizes the cost associated with benefits measurement and helps to demonstrate strategic contribution.
- Start benefits tracking as early as possible during development and delivery, so that data against which to measure benefits realization is available. Provision for the costs of this activity should be included in the initiative's budget (and the 'management case' in the business case).
- Watch out for seasonal trends and normal variation in data – trend analysis should be used to help ensure that reliable baseline measurements are taken.
- Also take into account the impact on operational performance of change initiatives delivered or due to be delivered, ie use forecast baselines where relevant rather than historical ones. This can be achieved by reviewing the organization's business plan, forecast performance targets and future year budgets.

Baseline performance should be recorded as part of the 'as is' information in the business case, along with the 'to be' (or 'future') state, which should include the planned improvement and the performance measures that will be used to determine whether the benefits have been achieved.

5. Assessing change readiness

Poorly scheduled change is a common cause of failure to realize anticipated benefits. Change managers therefore need to assess the readiness of the business to transition to the new ways of working (Chapter 7, Section B).

6. Identifying threats to benefits optimization

Risks will vary from initiative to initiative, but one way in which their identification can be facilitated is by considering threats to benefits optimization in relation to five sources of failure – see Table 3.5. Risk assessment more generally is covered in detail in Chapter 6, Section A.

TABLE 3.5 Threats to benefits realization

Source of Failure	Explanation
Forecasting failure	Benefits are not identified (and therefore are not monitored) or are overestimated.
Delivery failure	So impacting on the scale and timing of benefits realization.
Business and behavioural change failure	The business and behavioural changes on which benefits realization is dependent don't occur, or are poorly scheduled, so causing delay to benefits realization.
Benefits management failure	In relation to capturing and leveraging emergent benefits and mitigating dis-benefits.
Value-for-money failure	The benefits are realized but at excessive cost.

7. The benefits realization plan

This should follow the format used for the portfolio-level benefits realization plan to facilitate consolidation of data and drill down analysis. It summarizes the information included on the benefit profiles and will include an analysis of the benefits to be realized over the coming planning period (typically a year) analysed by, for example: benefit category/type; stakeholder/business areas affected; time period, eg by month or by quarter. It may also include details of the benefits reporting schedule, planned benefits reviews, the budget for costs associated with managing benefits realization, and arrangements for monitoring benefits realization after initiative closure.

Note that where benefit profiles are summarized into a single document (see Section B3) this format can be converted to a benefits realization plan by adding a final column for the benefits to be realized in the following planning period – see Figure 3.6.

This, then, provides the baseline against which progress is monitored via the benefits realization dashboard report. The benefits realization plan will be reviewed on a regular basis alongside the business case at initiative-level reviews, as well as portfolio stage/phase gate reviews.

8. The role of the change manager with regard to benefits management

The responsibilities of the change manager will vary from organization to organization, but as the APM BoK (2012) says, the business change manager is 'responsible for

FIGURE 3.6 Benefits realization plan template

Benefits Realization Plan for [*Insert name of Project/Programme*]

Version: Date:

Benefit category	Benefit Description and Rationale (cross ref to Benefits Map)	Key Assumptions & Dependencies	Benefit Quantification				Benefit owner (shade box if benefit not agreed with owner or owner not identified)	Is the benefit 'booked' in any performance targets/budgets etc? State where.	Benefit to be realized this year			
			Scale of impact anticipated over baseline – if unknown state 'unknown'	Period over which realization will last inc ramp up and tail off	Measures & Indicators to be used – one row for each metric – and specify type ie measures, indicators, evidence events, case studies & surveys	Frequency of measurement			Quarter 1	Quarter 2	Quarter 3	Quarter 4
Intermediate benefits												
Dis-benefits												

benefits management from identification through to realisation'. As such, the change manager's responsibilities extend beyond the life of the initiative. Responsibilities include:

- Reviewing and providing input to the benefits management strategy and benefits realization plan prepared by the programme manager.
- Identifying and quantifying benefits with the support of business managers and programme and project management (PPM) staff.
- Developing and maintaining the benefit profiles in consultation with the benefit owners – including agreeing the scale and timing of benefits realization and measures to be used.
- Ensuring adequate preparation is made for transition and advising the SRO/ sponsor on business readiness for transition.
- Engaging stakeholders to ensure the change is implemented smoothly.
- Monitoring successful transition and that all required project outputs/ deliverables and business changes occur so that benefits are realized.
- Monitoring and reporting on benefits realization throughout the initiative's life, including emergent benefits and dis-benefits.
- Monitoring and reporting on benefits realization post-initiative closure.
- Initiating benefits reviews after closure of the initiative.

It can be seen that much of the detailed work undertaken as part of benefits management will fall to the change manager. But they do not work alone. First, there may well be more than one change manager (for example, one for each part of the business affected). Second, they will also be assisted by the Programme/Project Office in:

- facilitating agreement of the benefit profiles and realization plan;
- tracking benefits realization against plan;
- collating benefits data for reporting purposes; gathering information for the benefits reviews;
- maintaining benefits information under change control.

Third, many organizations have a portfolio benefits manager (reporting to the head of the Portfolio Office) who ensures that a consistent and effective approach to benefits management is applied across the portfolio and that benefits realization is optimized from the organization's investment in change. The portfolio benefits manager's activities include: contributing to benefits identification/mapping and working with change managers to identify additional opportunities for benefits realization, and to minimize dis-benefits.

Further information about change roles and the role of the change manager is in Chapter 1, Section D.

Summary

Planning for benefits realization includes: baselining performance; validating benefits with the recipients/owners; prioritizing benefits, for example on the basis of contribution to the investment objectives; identifying threats to benefits realization; and completing a benefits realization plan, which acts as the baseline against which progress can be tracked. But note – the emphasis is on planning as an activity rather than on producing documents. As such, the objective is to ensure:

- *Transparency*: it should be clear what benefits are planned, when they will be realized, how they will be measured/evidenced, and who is responsible for their realization.
- *Accountability*: for the business and enabling changes (as identified on the benefits map) on which the realization of benefits depends, and for benefits realization (both intermediate and end benefits).

Questions to think about

1. Does your change initiative(s) have a benefits realization plan and how confident are you that benefits will be realized to the scale and timing forecast?
2. Think about the top five benefits of your current change initiative – what are the main threats to their realization and are there adequate mitigating actions in place?
3. On your current change initiative(s), has accountability for all required enabling and business changes been agreed with named individuals and do they have the necessary authority and information?

Section D: Supporting benefits realization

Introduction

This section encompasses:

1. Transition management: ensuring that initiative outputs are fit for purpose and can be integrated into business operations.

2 Measuring and reporting benefits realization at an initiative level: including identifying emergent benefits and dis-benefits. Regarding measurement more generally, see Chapter 7.
3 Identifying when intervention action is required.

FIGURE 3.7 Transition and benefits realization

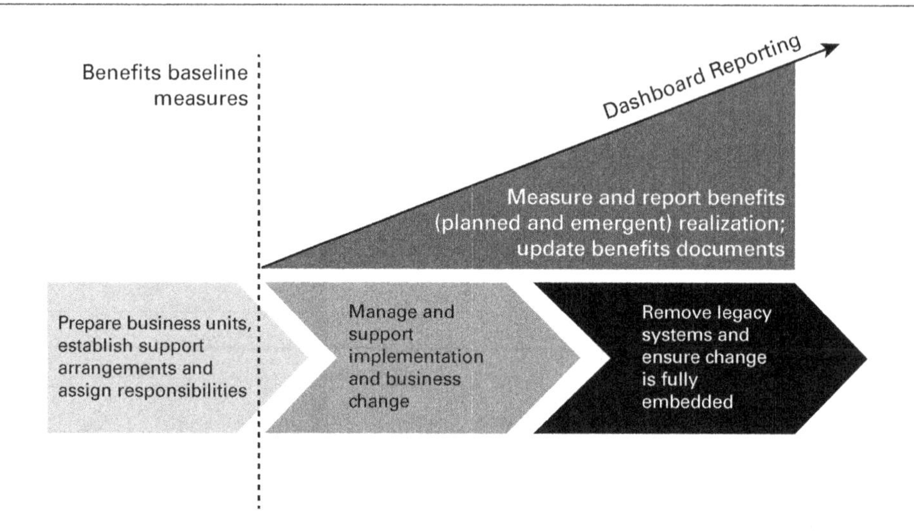

The objective here is to optimize benefits realization (Figure 3.7) by: actively managing planned benefits through to their realization; capturing and leveraging emergent benefits; and minimizing and mitigating any dis-benefits.

While the focus in investment decision making should be on realism (to overcome the twin risks of strategic misrepresentation and optimism bias) the approach to benefits realization should be based on enthusiasm. As Lovallo and Kahneman (2003) argue:

> Draw a clear distinction between those functions and positions that involve or support decision making and those that promote or guide action. The former should be imbued with a realistic outlook, while the latter will often benefit from a sense of optimism.

We also need to distinguish between forecasts and targets. The former – as part of the options analysis, investment appraisal and portfolio prioritization processes – should be realistic; the latter should be motivational and aspirational – and that requires that they be used less as a means of backward-looking accountability, and more as a basis of forward-looking insight and learning. What happens too often is that benefits management focuses on holding people to account for targets as originally forecast, but which are now out of date. A 'blame culture' emerges in which people's attention shifts to appearance-manipulation to make it seem that the initiative is succeeding even if the opposite is the case – and if people's attention is on appearance-manipulation, there is less focus on optimizing benefits realization.

1. Transition management

Here we are concerned with managing the transition from the old to new ways of working and embedding change in the operational business. The responsibilities of change managers include:

- Preparing business units to implement the relevant outputs delivered by the change initiative, while minimizing any disruption to 'business as usual' performance – the project/programme plan should address coordination of the delivery of outputs and business changes.
- Ensuring that responsibility for realization of each benefit/dis-benefit is clearly assigned to named benefit owners.
- Establishing appropriate support arrangements, eg a help desk and FAQs.
- Confirming that outputs are ready for operational use and that staff have been trained – and advising the initiative sponsor on readiness for transition.
- Removing access to legacy working practices and systems – so there is no going back to the old ways of working.
- Managing implementation and ensuring all enabling and business changes occur, but beware declaring victory too early – ensure that the change is fully embedded.
- Working closely with the individual benefit owners in assessing benefits realization (more on this below).

As part of initiative closure, the relevant benefits documentation (profiles and realization plan) should be updated and the 'reference point' for future benefits activity should be agreed – this will often be the change manager. Benefits realization will also continue to be monitored at the portfolio level. Further information on sustaining change is in Chapter 11.

2. Measuring and reporting on benefits realization

At least one measure should be identified for each benefit, although several measures may be selected to provide evidence of realization from multiple perspectives. In this way a 'rich picture' of benefits realization can be obtained from measures that include:

- Leading and lagging measures: selected to evidence benefits realization across the chain identified in the benefits map encompassing:
  - leading measures of enabling changes, business changes and intermediate benefits (see Tip on p 166);
  - lagging measures of end benefits.
- Proxy indicators: especially where direct measures are difficult to obtain. For example, per capita gross domestic product (GDP) is often used as a *proxy measure* for the standard of living.

- Evidence events: ie events that can be observed and which provide evidence that the benefit has been realized. These can be stated in the form of a 'date with destiny', for example, 'Three months from today, the sponsor will visit a front-line office and discuss the improvements seen with staff and customers.'
- Case studies and stories: capturing both good and bad news, as well as lessons learned and illustrating the potential benefits from the change.
- Surveys: of users, staff and management.

Tip

There is often a chain of benefits with intermediate benefits linked to final or end benefits. For example, we might have an initiative that enables earlier invoicing (an intermediate benefit), which results in earlier receipt of income (the end benefit) and so contributes to the objective of reducing working capital. Other intermediate benefits include improved employee morale, more accurate management information and space/accommodation savings. From the perspective of tracking benefits realization, the point to note is that monitoring leading measures of intermediate benefit achievement provides evidence to confirm that end benefit realization can be attributed to a specific change initiative.

More information on measurement is in Chapter 7, Section D.

2.1 Identifying emergent benefits and dis-benefits

As emphasized already, managing benefits extends beyond tracking planned benefits to identifying, disseminating and leveraging emergent benefits and mitigating any dis-benefits. Achieving this is less about the completion of a written plan, and more about establishing a culture in which opportunities are expected and anticipated. This includes:

- Adoption of modular or agile approaches to project design and development, where lessons learned are captured and applied on a regular basis. At a minimum, opportunities should be assessed at each stage/phase gate review.
- Applying what Andrew and Sirkin (2006) refer to as a 'scout and beacon' approach in which:
  - 'Scouts' scan the environment for potential opportunities.
  - 'Beacons' are 'lit' clearly communicating that ideas are welcomed (a change manager is often the nominated 'beacon').
- Ongoing participative engagement with users – a real and ongoing dialogue with users can help identify dis-benefits, emergent benefits and opportunities to create additional value.

- Taking a portfolio approach by asking, on a regular basis, whether emergent benefits are being identified and dis-benefits are being effectively mitigated.

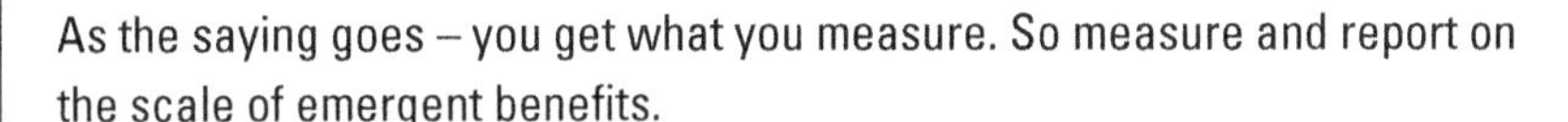

Tip

As the saying goes – you get what you measure. So measure and report on the scale of emergent benefits.

2.2 *Reporting benefits realization*

Effective management of benefits realization is aided by the adoption of reports that convey the salient points succinctly. Options include the following (note that each of these are not exclusive, ie they can be combined):

Dashboard reporting

Following the format and KPIs used at the portfolio level. This aids consolidation of the portfolio-level picture and 'drill down' from the portfolio benefits realization dashboard report to initiative/function/divisional level.

Reporting on a normalized scale

One issue is how to present benefits realization information in a succinct form when different types of benefit have different measures. One approach is to use a normalized scale where a value of 1 is assigned if the actual value matches plan – with values of > 1 where realization exceeds plan and < 1 where it is below plan, and with the values proportionate to the level of realization (for example, if realization is half that planned, a value of .5 would be recorded).

This approach is particularly suited to non-financial benefits, although it can be extended to encompass all categories of benefit. The points allocation can also be expressed as a percentage, which some managers find easier to understand. Either way, this approach enables benefits to be reported on a common scale, the overall position to be consolidated, and reports to be provided in graphical as well as tabular format (Figure 3.8).

For benefits that are regarded as more significant, weightings can be applied to the points scores to reflect their relative contribution to the initiative's investment objectives. In this way, a single figure, the sum of the points, can be used to assess benefits realization progress for the initiative as a whole.

Utilize the benefits map for reporting

Red/amber/green (RAG) ratings can be applied to the enabling and business changes recorded on the benefits map. This provides an early warning signal where failure to complete enabling and business changes will have a consequent impact on benefits realization.

FIGURE 3.8 Reporting using a normalized scale

Quality Improvement Programme

Programme Manager	Sponsor	Report Period	Report Date	Distribution
James Jordan	KateTennant	August 2012	13/09/2012	Programme Board, Investment Committee, Board of Directors

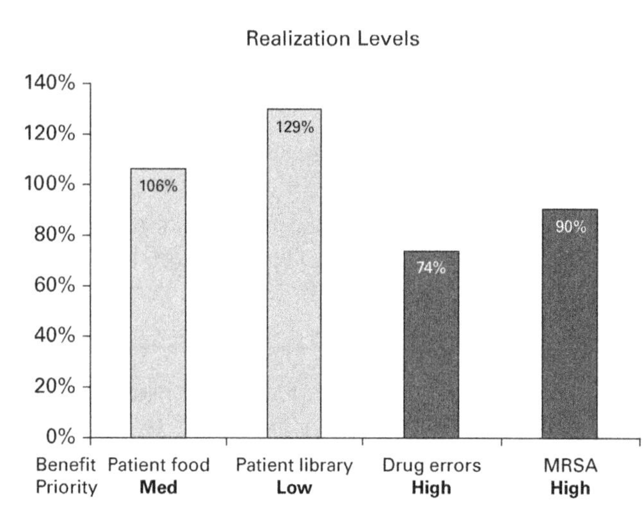

92%
Overall*
programme
performance

Commentary

Drug errors: delayed rollout in A&E → system had smaller impact on errors

MRSA: outbreak in Ward 5, deep clean initiated, all staff repeated IC training

* Average of scores when weighting applied according to priority

SOURCE: Dellar Limited

3. Identifying when intervention action is required

Determining when intervention is required to address emerging benefit shortfalls is facilitated by the following techniques:

- *'One version of the truth'*: the position on benefits realized to date is derived from an agreed source and reported according to an agreed schedule. This is then recognized as the authoritative source of information used for monitoring, reporting and management decision making.
- *'Clear line of sight' reporting*: a technique that ensures the strategic contribution of an initiative can be determined by ensuring the measures used to track benefits realization clearly demonstrate achievement of the investment objectives.
- *The Pareto (80:20) rule*: focus on the benefits that deliver the greatest contribution to the initiative's investment objectives (as identified on the benefits map) and, in turn, the organization's strategic objectives.
- *'Management by exception'*: by which only variances from plan (both in relation to benefits forecast and benefits realization) that exceed a preset control limit are escalated for management attention.

Tip

Combine the technique of 'management by exception' with earned autonomy, ie those parts of the business that consistently deliver on their promises should be rewarded with higher control limits before variances are escalated.

Summary

Benefits represent the rationale for investment in change initiatives. It is therefore crucial that benefits are managed efficiently and effectively. Achieving this requires repeatable processes operating in an environment in which the principles outlined in Section A are fully evident. The change manager has a crucial role in all of this – from identifying, quantifying and agreeing benefits, through effective planning, to their realization, reporting, capturing and disseminating lessons learned.

Questions to think about

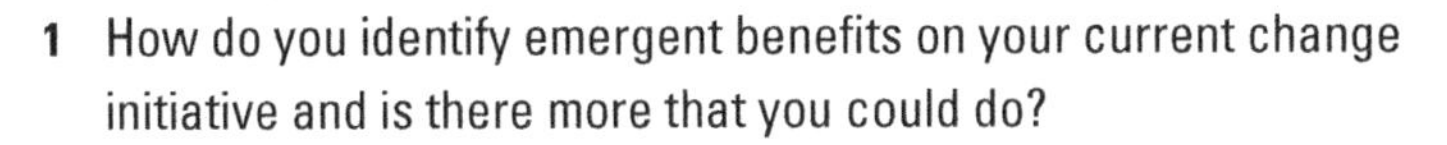

1. How do you identify emergent benefits on your current change initiative and is there more that you could do?
2. Do your progress reports on benefits realization clearly demonstrate the scale of strategic contribution?
3. Could you utilize the normalized scale in reporting benefits realized on your change initiative(s)?

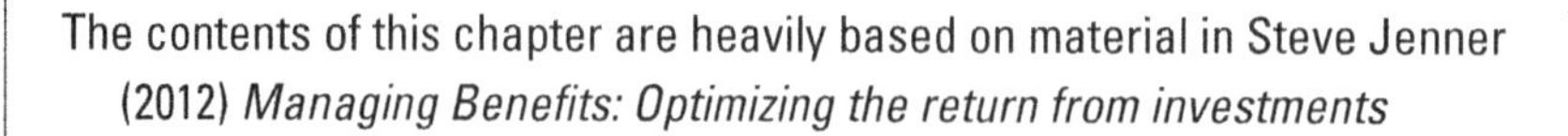

Further reading

The contents of this chapter are heavily based on material in Steve Jenner (2012) *Managing Benefits: Optimizing the return from investments*

Other relevant sources include:

Bradley, G (2010) *Benefits Realisation Management: A practical guide to achieving benefits through change*, 2nd edn, Gower
Jenner, S (2013) *A Senior Manager's Guide to Managing Benefits*, APMG-International, TSO
Thorp, J and Fujitsu Consulting Center for Strategic Leadership (2003) *The Information Paradox: Realizing the business benefits of information technology*, McGraw-Hill
Ward, J and Daniel, E (2012) *Benefits Management: How to increase the business value of your IT projects*, 2nd edn, Wiley

References

Andrew, J P and Sirkin, H L (2006) *Payback*, Harvard Business School Press, Boston, MA
Beer, M, Eisenstat, R A and Spector, B (1990) Why change programs don't produce change, *Harvard Business Review*, **68** (6), pp 158–66
Beer, M and Nohria, N (2000) [accessed 8 May 2014] Cracking the code of change, *Harvard Business Review*, Abstract [Online] http://hbr.org/2000/05/cracking-the-code-of-change/ar/1
Bradley, G (2010) *Fundamentals of Benefits Realization*, The Stationery Office, London
Capability Management (2006) *Research into the Management of Project Benefits, Findings Report 2004–06*, Capability Management
Cross, M (2002) Why government IT projects go wrong, *Computing*, 11 September, pp 37–40
Flyvbjerg, B (2006) From Nobel prize to project management: getting risks right, *Project Management Journal*, August 2006, pp 5–15
Flyvbjerg, B *et al* (2005) How (in)accurate are demand forecasts in public works projects?, *Journal of the American Planning Association*, **71** (2), Spring, pp 131–46
Hastie, R and Dawes, R M (2001) *Rational Choice in an Uncertain World*, Sage, California
Heskett, J L, Sasser, E W Jr and Schlesinger, L A (1997) *The Service Profit Chain: How leading companies link profit and growth to loyalty, satisfaction, and value*, Free Press, New York
Jenner, S (2013) *Managing Benefits*, APMG International, The Stationery Office, London
Kahneman, D (2011) *Thinking, Fast and Slow*, Allen Lane, London
Lovallo, D and Kahneman, D (2003) Delusions of success: how optimism undermines executives' decisions, *Harvard Business Review*, **81** (7), July 2003
Moorhouse (2009) *The Benefits of Organisational Change*, Moorhouse Consulting, London

Moorhouse (2011) [accessed 8 May 2014] Benchmarking SROs Attitudes: The Quandary of the SRO [Online] http://www.moorhouseconsulting.com/news-and-views/publications-and-articles/benchmarking-sros-attitudes-the-quandary-of-the-sro

National Audit Office (NAO) (2011) [accessed 2 September 2014] Initiating Successful Projects [Online] http://www.nao.org.uk/wp-content/uploads/2011/12/NAO_Guide_Initiating_successful_projects.pdf

Simms, J (2012) *The 'Capital Crime'*, Kindle, Amazon

Schaffer, R H and Thomson, H A (1992) Successful change programs begin with results, *Harvard Business Review*, January–February, pp 80–9

Surowiecki, J (2004) *The Wisdom of Crowds*, Abacus, London

Thorp, J and Fujitsu Consulting Center for Strategic Leadership (2003) *The Information Paradox: Realizing the business benefits of information technology*, McGraw-Hill, New York

UK Cabinet Office (2011) *Managing Successful Programmes*, The Stationery Office, London

Ward, J (2006) *Delivering Value from Information Systems and Technology Investments: Learning from success*, A report of the results of an international survey of Benefits Management Practices in 2006

Ward, J and Daniel, E (2006) *Benefits Management: Delivering value from IS & IT investments*, Wiley, Chichester

Ward, J and Daniel, E (2012) *Benefits Management: How to increase the business value of your IT projects*, 2nd edn, Wiley, Chichester

Ward, J, Daniel, E and Peppard, J (2008) Building better business cases for IT investments, *MIS Quarterly Executive*, 7 (1), pp 1–15

Stakeholder strategy

04

PATRICK MAYFIELD

Introduction

Stakeholder engagement is pivotal to the whole process of effective change. It is the essence of leading through influence. Through understanding stakeholders, prioritizing and mobilizing them, change managers begin to gain and sustain the momentum for change.

Given the emphasis of management literature on 'things' – tasks, documents and processes – it is easy to underestimate the importance of engaging people as people. Humans are relational creatures. We make sense of the world through tribes and social units. We find meaning and purpose through those around us.

So it is not surprising that research indicates that an ability to engage with people, and to engage with them often, is correlated with more effective change leadership. It seems that time spent in leading change through relationships with and among stakeholders begins to discriminate the performance of practitioners. Change managers are more focused on their stakeholders and measured in the time they spend in leaning towards people. They achieve better results in the end than those who focus rather more on the technical and process aspects of change. We could conclude from this that people engagement is the 'pull' competence through which much else is contextualized and framed in change management. Conversely, take away engagement in relationships and there is nothing left in change management that really gains any true traction, other than just the mechanical process of change.

If we make an analogy to the brain, relationships are like the synapses in the brain's architecture, and individuals or groups are like brain cells. Neurologists now maintain that functions of memory and understanding are located in traces through the synapses rather than within the cells themselves, as originally supposed. In the same way, we can overemphasize the importance of an individual change agent, instead of valuing the true momentum that happens through the network of relationships within a change.

FIGURE 4.1 The task perspective and the change manager's perspective (Mayfield, 2013)

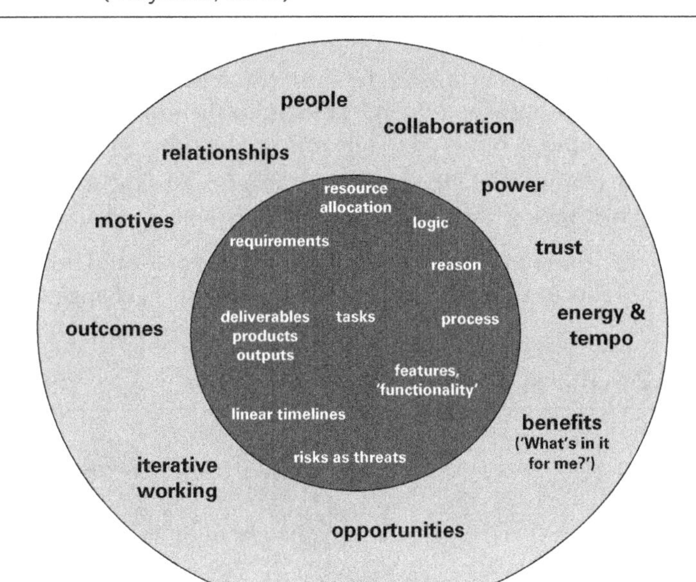

Leadership behaviours

Compare this to the atomized, reductionist worldview of management as a purely technical, task-focused exercise. The inner circle of the diagram in Figure 4.1 shows some of the elements that have been traditionally important to managers. The outer circle adds essential elements within a more progressive view of engagement.

As the change manager enlarges their focus to include the outer circle, they treat people not as fungible resources – things that can be replaced with like for like – nor as objects to be processed, to broadcast at, but rather as unique human beings, irrational at times, emotional, forgetful, with their own agendas, power and fears. These are people with whom change managers can, and sometimes should, have conversations – and may be pleasantly surprised by their responses and ideas. This aligns more with perspectives generally associated with leadership – change managers need to enlarge their perspective to think and observe as a leader.

Some of the terms included in the outer circle might make traditional managers uneasy. It might seem rather unfamiliar territory. However, the pay-off in performance is considerable. With this larger view, change managers become aware of some critically important aspects of change in which people are involved. They will notice more. Again and again leaders with this larger view of things get better results. Consider the value ladder, as shown in Figure 4.2.

Common to any change are various stages:

- The 'new' that is delivered.
- Using the 'new' whilst going through conscious incompetence to conscious competence.

- Embedding the change so that living with it and using it becomes unconscious competence, the 'new normal'.

The ladder is supported by two vital leadership behaviours:

- A leaning to people, as evidenced by the effort a leader makes in reaching out to stakeholders, as measured by the amount of their discretionary time spent in engaging people as opposed to task-oriented work.
- A leaning to action, where the change manager 'pokes the system' in a considered risk-taking manner, observes the response, and adapts.

This illustrates the continuous nature of a 'leaning to people' and 'leaning to action' throughout key events in the journey to realizing value from change.

FIGURE 4.2 The value ladder (Mayfield, 2013)

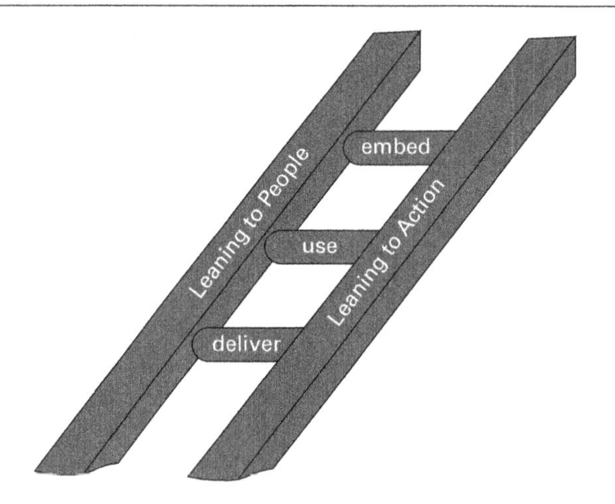

Tip

Set yourself a target to visit or call at least one person a day seeking out their views and opinions. Consciously seek to shift the balance of your discretionary time to be more purposefully people-oriented, rather than task-focused. Note: sorry, e-mailing doesn't count: it is a transactional task-oriented medium.

Principles

In this chapter you will find seven principles of stakeholder engagement. A principle, in our terms, follows Stephen Covey's (1999) criteria. It is:

- *universal*: it will work anywhere;

- *empowering*: it offers change managers some kind of leverage;
- *self-validating*: it may not be obvious to a novice, but it demonstrates its value in practice.

Principles are useful practical orienting statements in ever-changing contexts, which sometimes appear chaotic. Observe these seven principles of stakeholder engagement and you will get better results. The seven principles are covered as follows:

- Section A – Identifying and segmenting stakeholders:
  - Principle 1: You can forget important stakeholders, but they won't forget you.
  - Principle 2: Identification is a continuous practice – new stakeholders emerge during a change, old ones can fade away.
  - Principle 3: Prioritizing and segmenting stakeholders is in a moment in time. Regularly re-prioritize.
- Section C – Managing relationships and mobilizing stakeholders:
  - Principle 4: Some stakeholders are best engaged by others.
  - Principle 5: Seek first to understand, and then be understood.
  - Principle 6: Emotion trumps reason.
  - Principle 7: Demonstration trumps argument.

CHAPTER CONTENTS

Section A: Identifying and segmenting stakeholders

Introduction

For change to be successful, change managers need to know who is involved. Further, being able to categorize a frequently large population of stakeholders is crucial for prioritizing and identifying appropriately different influencing strategies.

PRINCIPLE 1: You can forget important stakeholders, but they won't forget you.

Definition of stakeholder

We should first agree what we mean by the term 'stakeholder': any individual or group with an interest in the change or its outcomes.

Using this definition, change managers begin to identify, analyse and strategize the engagement of their stakeholders. This broad, inclusive definition immediately presents the change manager with a risk: that of missing, ignoring or forgetting important stakeholders. At worst, this can cause irreparable damage. However, by approaching individuals and groups proactively this can, on the contrary, have a persuasive and motivating effect on those parties.

1. Identifying stakeholders

The first step is to recognize and include all stakeholders.

There are a number of methods to identify stakeholders, from rapid listing, group brainstorming to mind mapping. Usually, deciding the categories or segments of stakeholders goes hand-in-glove with identification.

1.1 Identification workshops

Facilitated workshops, with different representatives of the change, can significantly improve the identification and analysis of stakeholders. Invariably the workshop will identify a richer set of stakeholders than by any one individual.

CASE STUDY

When advising a new team that had a particular innovation it wanted to market, each member of the team generated a short list of individuals and groups they felt they needed to engage. The team were led through a process of segmenting and identifying further stakeholders, with the result that they had identified a list more than five times their combined list at the start.

One of the reasons that group workshops generate this kind of outcome is because who is or is not a 'stakeholder' is very much a matter of perception. A well-run workshop begins to open up discussions around whether a particular individual or group qualifies as a stakeholder for this change. These discussions sow the seeds of better stakeholder analysis later on.

The process of identifying stakeholders can be inhibited by a fear that the enormity of communicating with all these people would swamp the team. Engaging with all these people implies exhausting vast amounts of time. This fear is best brought out into the open and compared with the risk of forgetting an important stakeholder. Also, identifying stakeholders is not the same as agreeing to engage them in a certain way at a certain time, or through the same individual. This is the real business of the stakeholder strategy, as we will see below. Further information about facilitation and workshops is given in Chapter 10.

Questions to think about

1. Whom could you invite to such a workshop on your change?
2. Are there representatives of the major segments? (See below.)
3. What fresh perspectives might they bring?
4. Would the workshop actually serve to engage them better in the process?

PRINCIPLE 2: Identification is a continuous practice – new stakeholders emerge during a change, old ones can fade away.

As a change progresses, as its scope alters some stakeholders become less relevant, they lose interest or involvement. The inclusion of stakeholders is therefore dynamic.

Tip

Consider on long changes re-convening an identification workshop. Use it to validate current understanding of known stakeholders.

1.2 Other identification methods

Rapid listing

One of the quickest and most robust techniques for identifying stakeholders at the start is to:

- Gather the core team together.
- Clarify the meaning of 'stakeholder' on the change and why it is important that the team does not miss anyone.
- Get each individual to make a rapid personal list of everyone they can think of, giving them about three minutes to do this.
- Pair people off and ask them to compare their lists, adding new stakeholders as they occur to them.
- Move these pairs into groups of four and repeat the last step.
- Finally ask the whole team to make a joint list.

This works well as a technique because it exploits the creativity of groups and word association.

Group mind maps

Group mind maps are sometimes used as an alternative to lists within workshops. The main branches of the mind map can be the agreed segments. See Chapter 2, Section C1.3 for how mind mapping is used to capture and select different viewpoints.

Conversations

Engagement is not linear. Once we begin purposeful conversations with stakeholders, these yield further insights into other stakeholders. So further stakeholders can be discovered or disqualified as we engage. (See Chapter 5 on communication and engagement.)

Tip

Keep a running list of stakeholders. I use Evernote when doing this as an individual. When working with a team, consider using a wiki or some other collaboration tool. The list of stakeholders then becomes a key source document for stakeholder profiles (see below).

2. Segmenting stakeholders

Segmenting is common practice in marketing. Segments represent a broad group of a type of stakeholder. So by using segments marketers gain a better understanding of their different customers and what propositions are more likely to appeal to each customer segment.

> PRINCIPLE 3: Prioritizing and segmenting stakeholders is in a moment in time. Regularly re-prioritize.

Segmenting helps:

- To prioritize stakeholders. As the change continues, these priorities will change. Some stakeholders will increase in importance to the change, while others may disappear altogether. For example, in an urban development, the mayor begins as a key stakeholder, but during the change, independently, city boundaries are re-zoned, and the mayor is less interested in the outcome. Alternatively, a supplier is initially invited to tender. In time they win the tender as the key supplier. Over this period, their priority as a stakeholder rises.
- Further analysis. By segmenting a subgroup of stakeholders, certain analysis techniques are more appropriate. For example, personas and empathy maps are more appropriate for large, broadly homogeneous groups, whereas power maps are more appropriate for small key groups of individuals.
- To identify particular engagement strategies appropriate for each segment.

One common classification or set of segments is CPIG (Figure 4.3):

FIGURE 4.3 CPIG segmentation

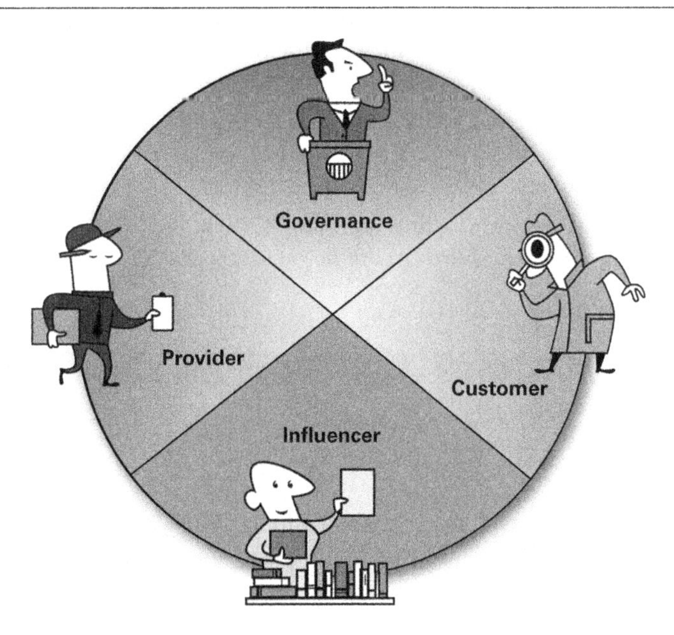

- our customers (C);
- our providers or suppliers (P);
- our influencers (I) – those possibly outside our change but who could inform or influence our change;
- those in governance of the change (G), the decision makers and the regulators, internal or external to our organization.

Having established our segments, these trigger the recognition of all kinds of stakeholders that we might otherwise omit.

3. Scoping engagement

So how far should we throw the net in considering whom to include as a stakeholder? There are a number of factors that help to scope appropriate engagement:

- The *impact* of the change and its *duration* over time. Formal change impact assessments may exist. These will indicate multiple stakeholders. Who are affected? Who might be subsequently affected? (See Chapters 2 and 6.) Sometimes the change will impact well beyond the organization. Public sector programmes, for example, frequently effect social transformation.
- How *power* is distributed. Power is rarely distributed as might be represented in an organization chart. Key process and regulatory 'gatekeepers' have power disproportionate to where they are placed in the organization's hierarchy.
- *Vision* and *visionary stories*. (See also Chapter 2, Section C.) Often change happens in the context of vision, but not always. If a vision for the end game of the change is written or drawn, or explained as narrative with protagonists, this will help to identify the people impacted by the outcomes.
- The organizational *culture*, and how it sees itself working, and how it sees change as legitimate or otherwise. The way the organization works (see Chapters 1 and 2 on this) might be collaborative, so the style of decision making might involve more parties who would consider themselves stakeholders.
- Organizational *reputation*, and who might see it, enhance it, commend it, threaten it, gossip it and leak it. Public relations are affected by major changes.

CASE STUDY

In one global foods business, a major change affected public perception of the company as well as visibly impacting share prices. As a result, we consulted closely with the PR department, who also contributed to who and how we would engage.

- The likely *winners* and *losers* of the change. If a business case exists and if any kind of benefits are identified from the change, these should indicate who benefits. Any kind of risk analysis will also indicate who might lose. (See also Chapter 3 on benefits management and Chapter 6 on change impact.)
- Who is in the temporary organization (*project*) driving the change? Whom do they represent?

Tip

Use the bullet list given above as an agenda in a stakeholder identification workshop.

Summary

An early and continuous step is to ensure that no stakeholder is forgotten. Omitting a stakeholder from our consideration can be a major risk to the success of the change initiative.

There are a number of identification techniques, such as rapid listing and mind mapping. These work well within a workshop attended by the change team and key stakeholders.

Identification continues throughout the change, particularly as stakeholders mention others in conversation.

Segmentation helps prioritize and leads change managers to consider appropriately different influencing strategies, as well as alerting to other hitherto ignored stakeholders. The CPIG segmentation is a simple and established means of beginning the process of segmentation.

Questions to think about

1. Are you aware of all individuals and groups who will be impacted by the change or its outcome? How can you be sure? What might be the risk of missing someone?
2. Whom could you invite to a stakeholder identification workshop? Do you need someone else to facilitate it?
3. How are you recording all the stakeholders? How current is it?
4. When reviewing the list of stakeholders, what segments of like stakeholders are emerging?
5. How extensively do you scope engagement on this change? Have you considered all the factors above in 3. Scoping engagement?

Section B: Stakeholder mapping and strategy

Introduction

Change managers need a sense of who, among the population of stakeholders, are key. Stakeholder mapping takes those stakeholders identified and begins to analyse them, often in comparison to others, frequently using 2×2 matrices. By analysing the characteristics of stakeholders, a number of techniques have emerged. This analysis needs to be assembled into some overarching strategy, particularly where a team or teams are involved, so that everyone stays aligned and 'on message'.

Optimizing relationships with key stakeholders is a critical success factor for a change initiative. But how do we determine which stakeholders are key? What are the relative priorities for us among stakeholders?

1. Stakeholder characteristics

Change managers will seek to position stakeholders in terms of some key characteristics, for example:

- formal position or role towards the change;
- nature of their interests;
- level of their interest;
- level of influence and power;
- energy/emotional attitude to the change initiative;
- likely wins and losses from the change/perceived benefits and dis-benefits;
- likely readiness for change;
- likely resistance to change and likelihood to adopt the innovation;
- level of trust by the stakeholder in the change/change team;
- ability to navigate the change and live in the outcomes;
- relationships between stakeholders, including support and proximity of relationships;
- busyness/cycles of busyness that might distract or displace attention.

It is useful to agree measures and target positions for each stakeholder, using these characteristics, as well as where we suppose each stakeholder is positioned currently. The tension between current and target helps to identify necessary influencing strategies to move the stakeholder to the target position. Of course, these characteristics are not independent of each other as the mind map in Figure 4.4 shows. Below are some methods to analyse these different characteristics.

FIGURE 4.4 The interrelationship of stakeholder characteristics (Mayfield, 2013)

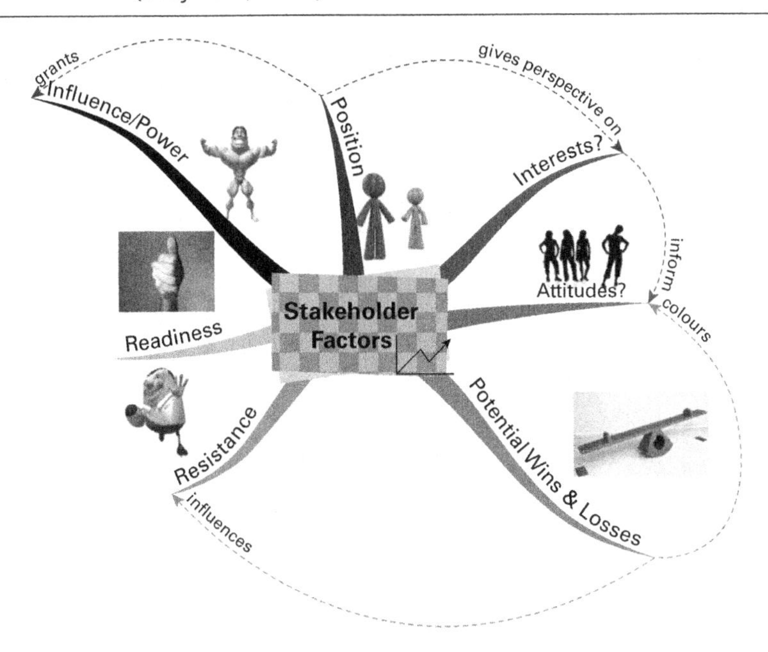

2. Stakeholder interests

Think about what interests each stakeholder in and around the change, or as a consequence of the change. Ask, 'Is this interest shared by other stakeholders also?' The stakeholders and their interests can be captured on a spreadsheet (Figure 4.5).

The stakeholders are listed down the left-hand column and their interests are listed across the top. Often there will be a stakeholder within a stakeholder. In this example there is 'the Board' but within it three directors have been separately identified, within their own variance from the group interests. Since this chart is generated with a spreadsheet, stakeholders can be nested within stakeholders (eg an individual within a group), as shown in the Excel® spreadsheet along the left-hand margin. The finance director, as an individual, may have a different or more specific agenda than his or her other colleagues on the board, so the team needs to identify this director separately for special analysis.

> People are often more comfortable with talking in broad terms about groups and bodies: the board, the executive team, the HR function or the IT group, but it is often the individuals within these that we need to influence. For influential stakeholders it is essential that we identify the key individuals within them.

FIGURE 4.5 Stakeholder interests mapped onto a spreadsheet

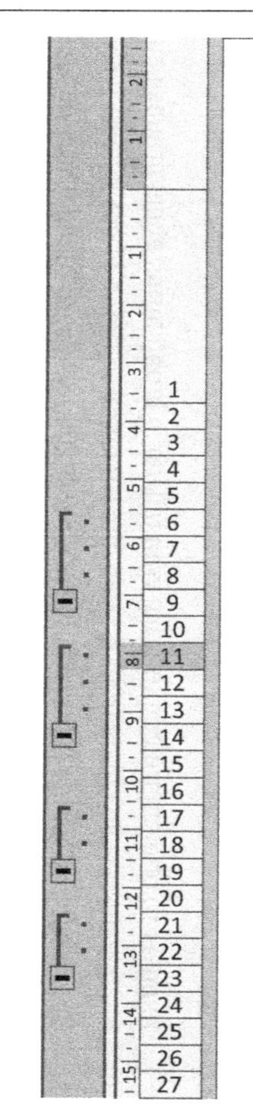

Stakeholder Map

Stakeholder Interests:	Reduced Costs	Improved Performance	Greater Flexibility	Reduced Risk	Shorter Time to Market	Strategic Alignment	Public Image	Competitive Threat	Job Security
Stakeholders									
Board	+6	+5	+4	+4	+5	+4	+4	–1	+1
Chief Executive	+5	+6	+4	+7	+7	+5	+4	–1	+1
Marketing Director	+3		+7	+2	+8	+4	+7	–2	+3
Finance Director	+7	+6		+5	+4	+4		–1	+1
Middles		+4	+4	+3	+3	+1	+3	–1	+3
Senior Managers		+5	+4	+3	+4	+3	+3	–2	+2
Managers		+4	+5	+3	+3	+2	+2	–1	+2
Staff		+2	+3	+1	+3	+1	+4		+3
Customers									
External		+3	+4				+3	+1	
Internal	–2	+4	+5	+3	+2		+2	–2	+2
Influencers									
Union	–4		–1						+4
Press and Media							+1	+2	
Providers									
Main supplier	–3			+2			+1		+1

This type of stakeholder map includes positive and negative attitudes as noted by the shade of the cells. Also the number indicates the strength of the interest by each stakeholder. These values and their scale have been agreed by the team and are documented in the stakeholder engagement strategy. This is just one of a number of variations of these sorts of tables or maps.

We can use this as a checklist in communications planning, checking whether we are covering everything of interest with each stakeholder. As we go through mobilizing engagement with the stakeholders, we can validate our understanding and change the entries as required.

3. Power mapping

Where real power lies is not always immediately obvious. In some organizations, some people wield influence and power disproportionate to their formal position. There may be formal authority vested in someone's role in an organization, but often people lower down in the authority hierarchy 'punch above their weight'; they are more powerful than might first appear from an organization chart. For example, someone in a junior position has power because they are the spouse of the sales director. Chapter 12, Section D has more on sources of power and influence in organizations.

Power maps (Figure 4.6) are useful when you want to identify the key influencers among a small group. This technique is used by some sales people for identifying the key influencer in a buying decision in a target organization.

FIGURE 4.6 An example power map

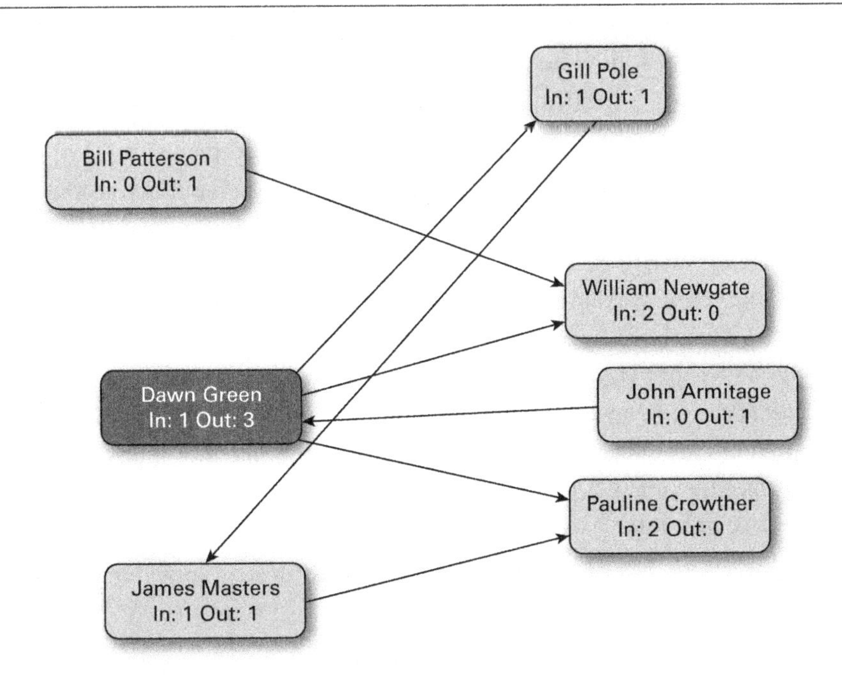

Here's how to use this technique:

1. Agree on, and gain, a common understanding of the context that the group of people is to be studied under, eg subject area, project team.
2. Summarize the context in a short sentence.
3. List all the people involved.
4. Arrange their names in a circle on a flipchart or whiteboard. Leave plenty of space between the names for adding arrows later.
5. Look for cause/influence relationships between each of the people and connect them with arrows. If there is no influence relationship between the people, omit the arrow. If there is a relationship, the point of the arrow needs to go to the person that is most influenced. Do not draw two-headed arrows. Base your decision on observed behaviours.
6. Check the diagram is complete and accurate.
7. Tally the number of ingoing and outgoing arrows for each person.
8. Redraw the diagram, including the number of ingoing and outgoing arrows for each person. Highlight the person with the most outgoings as the likely key influencer in the context.
9. Initially focus on the key influencer; this is likely to be your point of maximum leverage in the context.

4. Attitude to the change/to you

'Attitude' is a broad qualitative term, so adding some working classification is helpful. In his book *Working the Shadow Side*, Gerard Egan (1994) suggests putting all stakeholders into the following categories:

- *Partners* are those who support your agenda.
- *Allies* are those who will support you given encouragement.
- *Fellow travellers* are passive supporters who may be committed to the agenda but not to you personally.
- *Fence sitters* are those whose allegiances are not clear.
- *Loose cannons* are dangerous because they can vote against agendas in which they have no direct interest.
- *Opponents* are players who oppose your agenda but not you personally.
- *Adversaries* are players who oppose both you and your agenda.
- *Bedfellows* are those who support the agenda but may not know or trust you.
- *Voiceless* are stakeholders who will be affected by the agenda but have little power to promote or oppose and who lack advocates.

Working through these categories helps you to think more deeply about the motives and interests of each stakeholder.

The Kübler-Ross model (see detailed explanation in Chapter 1, Section B1) helps track the emotional states of individuals and groups as they navigate a non-negotiable change. Often managers and leaders will have gone through the curve and be going up the other side. They cannot understand why everyone else is not as optimistic as they are, the reason being that other people are still going down! When people are experiencing 'shock, denial, anger, bargaining and depression' (all internally focused) it is difficult for them to hear any communication from those who are further along their personal change journey and are experiencing 'acceptance, discovery and integration'. This is a known problem that medical consultants have to deal with when advising patients on the best course of treatment: shock often means that the patient simply cannot take it all in at that appointment.

Now, overlaying this curve we can see four broad attitudinal states in relation to engagement:

- denial;
- resistant;
- exploring;
- champion.

Where there is a non-negotiable change – where people have to deal with it as there is no alternative – then we can map individual stakeholders on their emotional journey in a grid (Figure 4.7).

FIGURE 4.7 Mapping emotional states

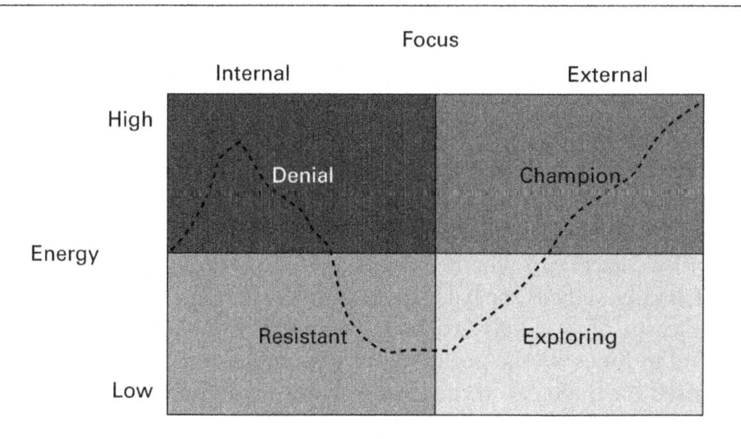

CASE STUDY

One organization used this attitudinal mapping approach in centralizing its geographically dispersed workforce of around 2,000 office workers into one central building. In terms of personal impact on each of these people, this was sometimes traumatic: moving home and schools, lengthening commute, etc. It was clear from the evidence that, despite communications well in advance, many had ignored this and were in the denial zone. As the day approached, resistance surfaced and people realized this was a real threat.

Moving people to 'exploring' was helped by personal stories and research from people who had already moved to the new location and found out about housing, schooling and other local services. Some had found real added personal benefit from improved lifestyle and this was also communicated.

The move was considered by this client to have been a success. About 200 people did not move; they either resigned, took voluntary redundancy or early retirement. It was recognized that for a change on this scale we will never bring around everyone to the change.

5. Wins and losses

A hot topic that runs through most engagements is discussing outcomes and benefits; stakeholders will ask 'What will happen?', 'What's in it for me?' (WIIFM). Even if they don't ask these questions, it is usually helpful to raise these with them at the right moment.

No stakeholder analysis is complete without thinking of such benefits for each stakeholder concerned. Frequently, change creates outcomes that are perceived as negative by some: a so-called dis-benefit. For example, 'reducing headcount' might be a benefit to senior management, but is a dis-benefit to the stakeholder who will lose their job because of it.

Using the benefits distribution grid (Table 4.1) helps to identify all the perceived benefits and dis-benefits for each stakeholder. The key benefits and dis-benefits are listed down the left-hand columns. Each stakeholder is a column to the right, and using the grid we ascertain whether that stakeholder will gain from the benefits or lose. Overall, it gives sight of the balance between benefits and dis-benefits. This balance is a good indicator of the likely attitudinal response from that stakeholder.

People tend to focus on the negative more than the positive when it comes to any change imposed on them, so in the example shown in Table 4.1 we can expect the business users to be fairly resistant. This is an example of a type of cognitive bias called 'loss aversion' (for more on common cognitive biases in communication see Chapter 5, Section A2).

The benefits distribution grid could be regarded as a stakeholder profit-and-loss account. It helps focus on ways to move towards an 'everybody becomes a net gainer/winner'. Whilst rarely possible, this approach can help to identify risks across the mix of stakeholders and identify those who might believe they stand to lose overall. For more on benefits identification see Chapter 3, Section B.

TABLE 4.1 Benefits distribution table (illustration)

Key benefits and dis-benefits by stakeholder	Executive management	Business management	Business users	IS function	Programme team	Finance function
Key benefits						
More effective project portfolio						
Earlier recognition of ineffective projects						
More financial benefits realized						
More non-financial benefits realized						
Improved management of risk						
Reduced IS/IT costs						
Improved image of IS/IT						
Key dis-benefits						
Extra effort by business						
Slower start to programme						
IS project targets threatened						

6. Readiness and resistance

The Beckhard and Harris change formula (details of which are given in Chapter 7, Section A3.1) is often used as a diagnostic of change readiness rather than a route map. For example, one manager used the change formula to gauge the most receptive (least resistant) business units as the best candidates for the next tranche of rollout of a change they were introducing. It is effective when engaging with senior managers, both at the outset of a change and at intervals throughout the change. Such notional measures using the change formula can become part of a change 'dashboard' presented to such managers.

7. Measuring ability

The DREAM© Model (Figure 4.8) tracks some broad states of stakeholders. This is a scale of engagement measuring people through degrees of engagement. It can be used effectively to position, target and track the degree of engagement of different stakeholders throughout the change.

FIGURE 4.8 The DREAM© Model (Mayfield, 2013)

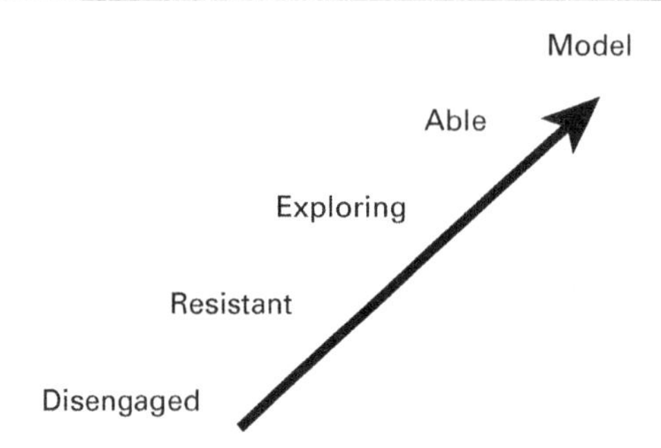

Depending on the type of change, different measures or indicators can be agreed in advance to validate whether a stakeholder has reached a new position on the scale, as shown below:

- *Disengaged*: there is no evidence that the stakeholder is aware of the change or of its outcomes.
- *Resistant*: there is evidence of resistance – objections, obstructive behaviours, non-participation or non-attendance at meetings.
- *Exploring*: is cooperating with the change leaders, but is showing some confusion and desire to understand the full implications of the change.
- *Able*: is evidencing competence in participating, although this still may be conscious and an effort for them.
- *Model*: has adopted and owned the changes, is now at ease with them, and is able to coach others, as well as advocate the benefits.

Not all stakeholders begin at 'Disengaged', nor do all need to achieve the target position of being able to model and explain new practices and behaviours. Nor do stakeholders have to traverse all the intermediate stages; for example, a stakeholder can go straight from 'Disengaged' to 'Exploring'. Moreover, stakeholders can regress to lower stages. An alternative but complementary perspective on achieving stakeholder commitment in a project environment is covered in Chapter 8, Section A3.2.

8. Profiling stakeholders

The results of the stakeholder mapping and analysis of perspectives can be gathered together into a stakeholder profile. The profile can then be used to track a stakeholder through the change. An internal customer relationship management (CRM) system can be used to record these profiles.

An alternative is to chart each stakeholder profile as part of a simple spreadsheet that can then generate charts on any two attributes for all the stakeholders. Figure 4.9 gives an example of this sort of profile, which is a worksheet within a larger Excel file.

In the example in Figure 4.9, the position and ability rows have current ('C') and target ('T') positions. Also, the benefits and dis-benefits have unique identifiers (BN034..., DB004...) that allows cross-referencing with benefits profiling and modelling. Overall, this kind of record allows the change team to see at a glance the current assessment of a stakeholder and the related issues. It begins to help inform an approach to that stakeholder, and perhaps other stakeholders.

9. Personas and empathy maps

9.1 Personas

The word 'persona' is defined as 'the social role or character played by an actor', from the Latin word meaning 'mask'. In marketing, though, it is typically used as a summary for a customer segment, but written as if it were an individual.

The change manager can better empathize with a stakeholder that represents a group by creating a persona. It can offer a deeper understanding of the group's goals and needs, and so help shape particular engagement strategies and messages in a way that is more likely to influence them. It easier for the team to focus on a manageable set of personas, knowing they represent the needs of many.

With this technique, the persona has a fictitious name. It is important to remain relevant and serious; humour usually is not appropriate. Generally, a persona has a human image associated with it (see Tip box).

Tip

For the persona image, use stock photography, although people often find a more casual photo resonates with them. Avoid using a picture of someone you know! A good test of the photo or picture will be when someone in the team feels that the persona reminds them of someone in the group, but it is not an actual photo of them.

FIGURE 4.9 A stakeholder profile

Data of Assessment	dd/mm/yyy					
Unique Stakeholder ID	SM027					
Stakeholder Name	HR Managers					
Impact on Stakeholder	High					
Influence/Power of Stakeholder	Medium					
		Anti	Neutral	Allow	Help	Lead
Position towards change		C →	→	→	T	
	Unaware	Aware	Informed	Equipped	Practised	Exemplary
Ability to change		C →	→	→	T	
Benefits to Stakeholder	BN034	Enhanced Skills				
	BN012	Less time in administration				
	BN016	Greater likelihood of a role in the future business model				
	BN007	Increased productivity				
	BN037	Expanded CV/Resume				
Dis-benefits to Stakeholder	DB004	Loss of job security				
	DB003	Perceived loss of competence				
	DB005	Reduced importance of existing role in the organization				
Perceived Resistance	There is a lot of anger towards the change that could express itself in denial, passive resistance.					
Change Readiness	Low	See separate assessment				
Risks to Stakeholder	Job loss					
	Less sense of expertise/mastery in the new organization; a self-perception of being de-skilled					
	Loss of power and importance					
Date last contacted	dd/mm/yy					
Note:	At follow-up one-hour discussion forum. See notes attached.					
Changes Required from Stakeholder	– contributions to their transition plan – agreements on timings of transition					
Satisfaction Rating	None taken yet. Deemed inappropriate at this time with this stakeholder.					
Next Steps	Consultation meeting with Programme Director and HR Director with this stakeholder, facilitated by HR					

By using the challenging question: 'Would Bill do this?', where 'Bill' is a persona (see below), the team can avoid the common error of providing what people ask for rather than what they would actually use.

Engaging with groups can be constantly evaluated against the personas. If there is disagreement about how best to engage with a particular group, then this can often be resolved by referring back to the persona.

> Caution: there is a danger that we all reinforce social stereotypes. Be careful with this when using personas, and have someone in the group who challenges caricatures of the people represented.

Cooper (1999) summarized the benefits of using personas:

- They help team members share a specific, consistent understanding of various audience groups. Data about the groups can be put in a proper context and can be understood and remembered in coherent stories.
- Proposed solutions can be guided by how well they meet the needs of individual personas. Features can be prioritized based on how well they address the needs of one or more personas.
- They provide a human 'face' so as to focus empathy on the persons represented by the demographics.

CASE STUDY

An example persona

The stakeholder group illustrated here is plant managers within a utility business. The persona of Bill has been created to represent a typical member of this group.

Bill is 42 and has worked in the company since leaving school. He started as an apprentice and has worked his way to this role through being promoted internally. He has an HNC in water mechanics. He has a wife and three children, two of them pre-school. He is a member of a trade union and used to be shop steward for another plant until he was promoted to plant manager.

At the moment he is struggling to make ends meet as his mortgage repayments have increased. His wife is considering working evenings in a restaurant. He feels he is underpaid for the extra responsibilities of being the plant manager.

9.2 Empathy mapping

The empathy map is a supporting technique to the persona that has been used to some effect with a range of organizations. The map helps devise stronger strategies for engaging with such groups.

The map radiates out from the image of the persona (Figure 4.10).

Radiating out of the top of the head is the question: 'What does Bill really *think* and *feel*?' This is where the team attempts to describe what is on Bill's mind. There might be matters really important to Bill that he might not disclose. This is the area to speculate about his motivations and emotions; about what concerns him, makes him anxious; and about his dreams and aspirations.

The sector to the left radiates out from one of his ears, and answers the question: 'What does Bill really *hear*?' We need to look for evidence in conversations with him. What are his colleagues, his co-workers saying? What rumours are reaching his ears? Which media are likely to reach him?

The sector to the right radiates out of Bill's eyes, and answers the question: 'What does he *see*?' It describes what he observes in his environment. What do his surroundings look like? Who are his friends and the people who influence his opinions?

FIGURE 4.10 An empathy map

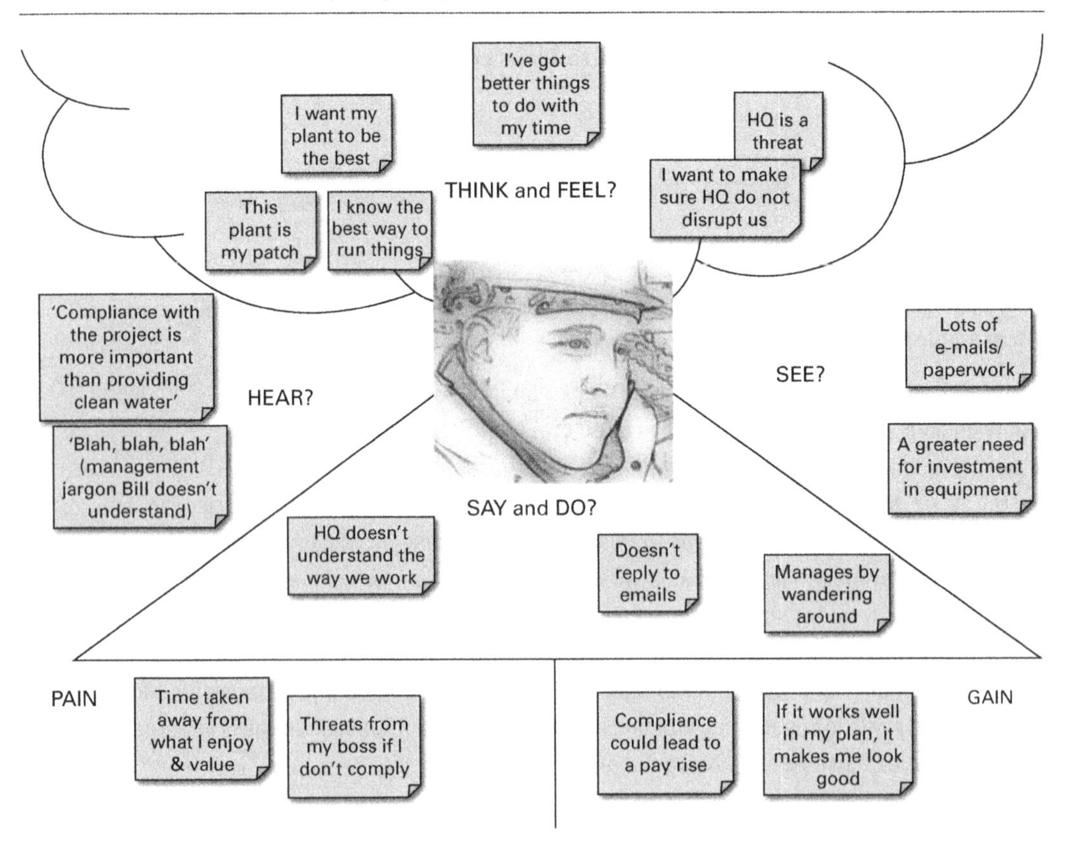

What are the propositions put to him each day? What are the problems Bill has to grapple with?

The lower sector is about what Bill *says* and *does*. It is about his words and actions. What is his attitude? What could he be telling others about your initiative? Look for potential conflicts with what Bill says and what he truly feels. This has consequences when one leaves the conversation. To what behaviour does he revert?

The final two sections at the bottom of the map are pain and gain: what is Bill's *pain*? What are his biggest frustrations? Have you asked him? What are the perceived obstacles standing between Bill and what he wants to achieve? Are there any risks he might fear taking? Is there additional pain that you bring to him with your change? What does Bill stand to *gain*? What does he truly want or need to achieve? How does he measure success? What ways might he use the change to achieve his own goals?

Here are some simple steps to generating a useful empathy map:

1. Start by giving the group an individual persona.
2. Refer to the diagram and draft this face and sectors on to a flipchart or whiteboard.
3. Build a profile with your team for the persona/stakeholder using the questions above.

10. Stakeholder radar

The segmenting used above can be mapped on to a stakeholder radar (Figure 4.11). In two dimensions, this shows not only the individual stakeholders, but also the view

FIGURE 4.11 The stakeholder radar

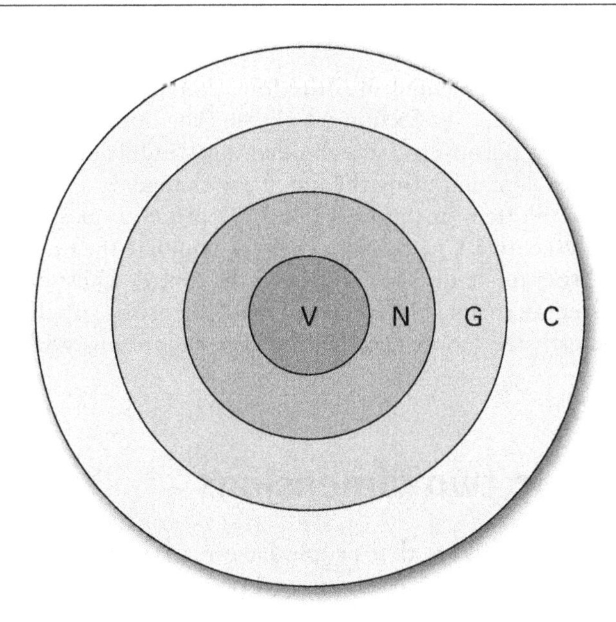

FIGURE 4.12 Segmenting and populating the stakeholder radar (Mayfield, 2013)

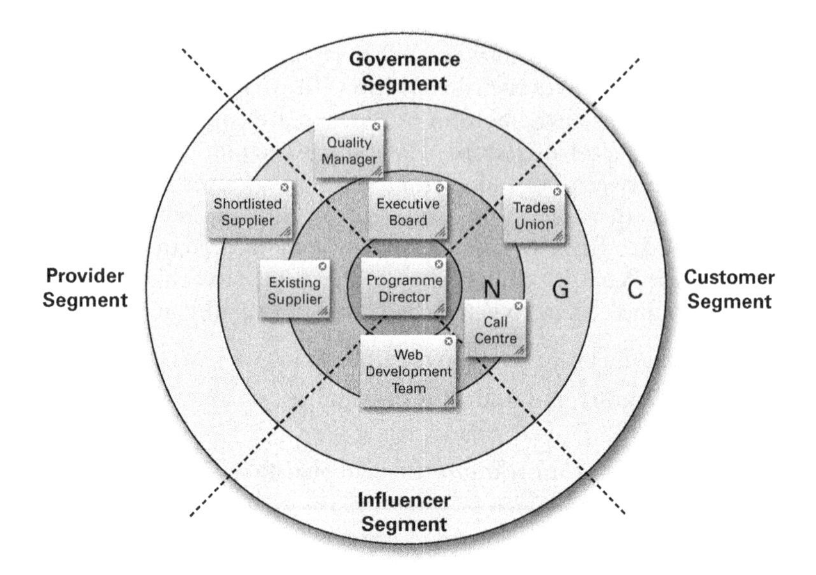

on the level of engagement needed with each of them. From the centre, the different levels of engagement are labelled:

- V for vital to engage.
- N for necessary to engage.
- G for good to have engaged.
- C for courtesy to inform.

The radar can then be segmented into the four domains of customers, providers, influencers and governance (see Section A2 above). The boundaries of the segmented radar (Figure 4.12) are porous; ie a stakeholder may straddle more than one domain, and cross to another domain during the life of the change.

Stakeholders are plotted on the radar, and the primary question becomes: how close are they to the centre? You can then begin to populate the radar. In the example shown here, the programme director is right in the centre, whilst other stakeholders fan out into different domains. Note as well how the existing supplier is closer to the centre than the shortlisted supplier, as they are rather more engaged with the changes taking place.

11. Mapping in two dimensions

There are many different ways that people have mapped stakeholders across two characteristics. One of the most enduring and popular ways is by looking at each

FIGURE 4.13 An example 2x2 power/influence–interest matrix

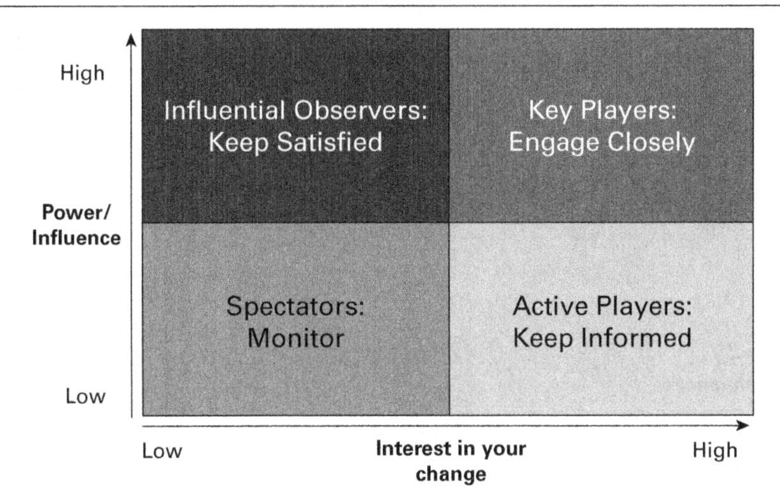

stakeholder in terms of their power/influence over the change against their actual interest in it (Figure 4.13).

Stakeholders (groups and individuals) can then be plotted on this grid. Sometimes, the grids can be used for targeting. For example, a powerful stakeholder in 'Influential Observers' needs to move to 'Key Players'; that is to say, we need them to buy in and to be engaged more actively. It is just as important to ensure we keep certain 'Key Players' in that quadrant and not drift into disinterest. Further, the 'Spectators' need monitoring, as they might move into other quadrants if a new interest or power base emerges.

Figure 4.14 shows how stakeholders can be plotted on to such a graph and another characteristic (attitude to the change, ie 'Allies/Partners', 'Neutrals', 'Opponents/Adversaries') added using a RAG (red/amber/green) legend.

Other common combinations of grid axes are:

- trust versus alignment/consensus;
- impact of the change on the stakeholder versus influence;
- power versus commitment to the change;
- energy versus commitment to the change;
- change readiness versus commitment to the change.

Tip

The number of ways of measuring and mapping stakeholders are considerable. Choose the three or four key ways that you and your team feel are vital to analysing overall stakeholder issues and the consequent strategy. Then keep these analyses current.

FIGURE 4.14 Power/influence–interest matrix with stakeholders and their attitudes mapped

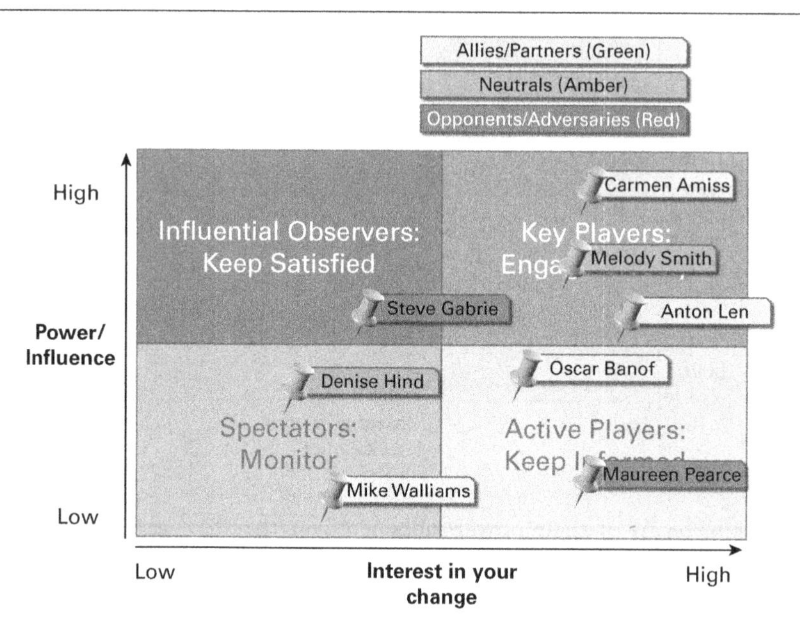

CASE STUDY

In one project, the marketing director of New Media was someone of high influence, and the performance of his line of business was going to be directly affected by the project's outcome (high interest). So he was a key player and needed on board every step of the way.

Consequently, frequent 'face time' was sought with him, usually on a one-to-one basis. Whereas, another stakeholder on the same project was the IT network manager, and his influence was marginal and neither the project nor its outcome would change his working life much; most of the time he was kept informed as a matter of courtesy.

12. Determining engagement roles and responsibilities

Any team works better with a certain level of clarity about individual and shared responsibilities for engagement and communications within a change initiative. With the change team, this clarity helps reduce confusion and the risk of missing steps in

TABLE 4.2 Example of a RACI-X chart

Stakeholder / Team Role	Director	Dept Manager	Super Users	HR	Finance	IT Account Manager	Operatives	Programme Board	Customers	Press Office
Programme Manager	C	C	I	I	C	C	I	C	C	C
Business Division Change Champion	X	A	I	A	A	A	I	A	A	X
Business Unit Change Champions	C	R	A	R	R	R	A	C	R	C
Change Agents	I	I	R		I	C	R	C	C	I
Super Users			C		I	C	C	C	C	I
Comms Analyst, PMO	C	C	I	C	C	C	I	R	C	C
Benefits Manager	C	C			C	I	I	C		C

engagement or unnecessarily creating 'noise' in engagement with duplication of effort. Like all teams, change teams work better where roles are clear, and there are clear operating processes.

A 'RACI-X' chart (Table 4.2) is a simple way of developing a solution. This is an example from a major change across an organization that had grown historically by acquisition, and thus had grown a fairly federal culture.

In this Table the 'RACI-X' stands for:

- **R** Responsible for leading the engagement with that stakeholder (top axis); also known as the relationship manager.
- **A** Approves, authorizes formal communications.
- **C** Consulted on key engagement transactions where appropriate.
- **I** Kept informed.
- **X** Where this team role exclusively manages the relationship.

13. Stakeholder strategy document

When leading a large engagement collaboratively, certain agreements must be written to prevent ambiguity and clarify decisions later. In pulling all thinking together into a stakeholder strategy, this expresses the broad 'how' of engagement.

Items in such a strategy might cover:

- A list of all the stakeholders.
- Analyses of stakeholders, such as the power/influence–interest matrix and empathy maps.
- Prioritization of stakeholders to be engaged.
- The approaches and mechanisms of engagement, possibly broken down by particular segments or categories of stakeholder.
- The roles in engagement. Who in the change team does what in proactive engagement? (See the RACI-X matrix in Table 4.2.)
- Measures of effectiveness, both in terms of communications and positions of the stakeholders.

Establishing a written strategy has a number of benefits to engagement, for example:

- It encourages consistency of message, and so confidence in the change leadership.
- Consistency of who engages whom.
- Ability to decide on re-prioritization stakeholders, for example in a technology system rollout, on an informed basis.
- Defining different engagement strategies with different segments or groups of stakeholders. For example, in the RACI-X matrix in Table 4.2, there was a distinctly different engagement strategy with the media, through the press office.

The roles within the change team are particularly important within the strategy. A classic novice error is to attempt all engagement on their own or directly:

- Engagement needs to be shared within the team as it would exhaust the individual change manager. The team gives bandwidth to the significant effort required to manage all the relationships well.
- Some members of the team are better positioned to engage and influence than others. This may be for reasons of authority, expertise, shared history or personal affinity.
- Engagement needs to happen also with those outside the team, particularly in engaging those in authority. We need to enlist the help and cooperation of other stakeholders in order to engage well.

Segmenting, for example, might reveal that a certain segment or subsegment is best engaged with the primary leadership of one particular person. They take the lead role for agreements with this individual or group, and all others working on the engagement must keep this lead posted of any interactions with that group.

Summary

Analysing a stakeholder is important for identifying the key stakeholders, and towards assembling and maintaining a good engagement strategy, particularly when working with a change team.

There are some standard stakeholder characteristics that we can map, sometimes using techniques specific to a characteristic, such as power. A complete description of these characteristics can be assembled into a stakeholder profile. Some characteristics lend themselves to mapping the current position and the target position. These stakeholder characteristics are not independent of each other, and so the change manager might focus on influencing to change one characteristic (eg perceived wins) so that it changes another (eg attitude to the change or its outcomes).

Often mapping compares stakeholders with each other, and this can be done across two or more characteristics. The most common of such analyses is the power/influence–interest matrix, where each quadrant in the 2×2 matrix lends itself to a different description, and therefore to a different engagement strategy.

When working within a change team or with other stakeholders influencing third parties, defining the engagement roles in a RACI-X matrix and assembling a written stakeholder strategy document is advisable. This helps coordinate everyone proactively influencing others so that they are aligned, do not 'interfere' or undermine another key relationship, and kept 'on message' when communicating about the change initiative.

Questions to think about

1. What are the key characteristics you need to measure and track on this change? Are the measures agreed and defined in the strategy?
2. How are you going to monitor the stakeholders throughout the change? How will you know if they move positions? How will you validate stakeholder assessments?
3. How are you going to record stakeholder assessments? What are the privacy implications? Who will have access to them?
4. Is it clear what the current and target gaps are for stakeholders? Is there an effective engagement strategy to help bridge that gap?
5. What is the balance of wins and losses telling you across the benefits distribution grid?
6. Have you and your team got a manageable and usable set of personas for groups?
7. Is everyone in the change team, and among your key influencers aware of their particular engagement role, know how to do it, and have bought into it?
8. How will the team update itself on what individuals are discovering?

Section C: Managing relationships and mobilizing stakeholders

Introduction

Gaining and maintaining the momentum of change is the challenge of change leadership. Change managers need to consider and execute a range of approaches to managing this momentum. Change often falters after the first flush of enthusiasm. The ability to re-energize and mobilize stakeholders is a key success factor.

This is achieved by:

- Seeking stakeholder opinions on the change and its outcomes, and how it will affect them, their experience, their team, building trust and confidence.
- Listening carefully to stakeholder needs and concerns, responding openly and honestly to questions.
- Exploiting communications technologies to encourage dialogue, collaboration, and the sharing of ideas and information.
- Identifying and engaging the 'bright spots', the opinion leaders, the potential champions, making them advocates, whilst reducing the influence of those who do not support the change.
- Using appropriate tools to 'mobilize' the stakeholders through stimulating interest and desire to take positive action.

1. Influencing strategies

Many influencing strategies that address the issue of momentum in change consider who, among the stakeholder mix, are themselves influencers of others. Frequently, change managers are not the most effective people to influence particular stakeholders. This may be due to a lack of personal chemistry with that stakeholder, a lack of position, a lack of shared history or lack of recognized credentials in the eyes of the stakeholder.

PRINCIPLE 4: Some stakeholders are best engaged by others.

Everett Rogers's (2004) innovation adoption model (Figure 4.15: the model is explained fully in Chapter 7, Section A4.3) is relevant if there is a large population of stakeholders who all seem to have more or less the same power. The strategy is to

FIGURE 4.15 The innovation adoption curve (after Rogers, 1962)

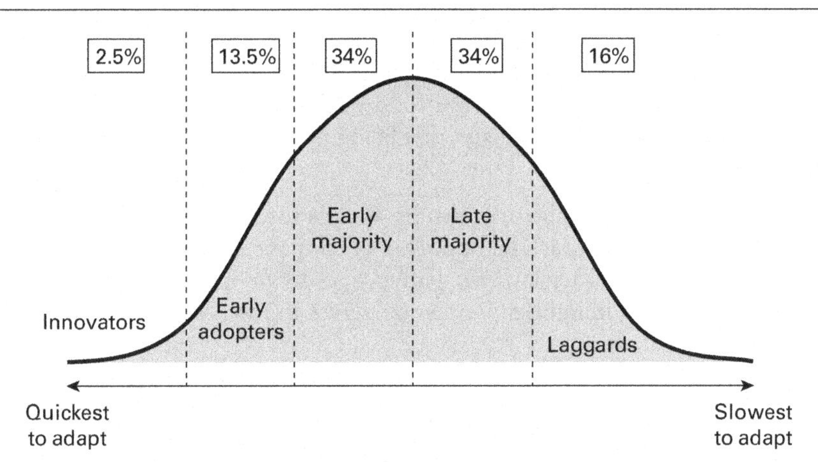

identify and target the early adopters and seek to recruit some of these opinion leaders to the role of champion. For example, you could include some of these people in your stakeholder workshops, as well as asking them to take on key communication events.

Also target and track the early majority, not allowing the change team to be distracted by the apparent apathy or resistance of the late majority. Using this model in this way can give an overall shape to the engagement strategy, build momentum, and reassure key stakeholders that buy-in is proceeding in a predictable manner.

Others have described the value of those stakeholders who already exhibit positive behaviours, modelling the change in what they already do. Pascale, Sternin and Sternin (2010) calls these 'positive deviants' and the Heath brothers (2011) call them the 'bright spots'.

2. Listening as a means of mobilization

PRINCIPLE 5: Seek first to understand, and then be understood (Covey, 1999).

One of the most powerful influencing strategies is first to ask the other person for their interests, their needs and their fears – to be interested genuinely in them and their struggles. The simple courtesy of being interested first in them, of being fully present with them in conversations about them, breaks down more hostility and barriers than anything else I can think of. Listening to others first almost earns us the right to be heard ourselves.

However, this is more than a matter of mere politeness. This principle recognizes that no single person, or even a small group, has a full view of what is actually happening in the organizational system. Understanding how others see a problem is essential if we are to make the right calls. Also, it fits well with an axiom well known among change leaders: *Never start the engagement with your solution.*

You should focus on the need for change. In fact, beginning this way could open the conversation for the other party to propose a better way to meet the change than you had first considered. So why isn't this being done more often? There could be a number of reasons:

- There is the general issue of *busyness*. People forget in the heat of the moment, seeking to grab the opportunity to make their pitch, get agreement and move on. Often we lack the patience to invite opinions, but also we may have an unwillingness to open ourselves to the risk that they might lecture us.
- There is also the matter of *pride*. Can we humble ourselves and sit with these people and listen to their complaints? This can prevent many from getting better at people engagement. We lack the attitude of the servant leader, someone who can lead by serving. If we are willing to stoop to serve, we will make better leaders, and so others will be more inclined to follow us.
- Then there is the desire to exert *power* and *control*. This usually comes from an underlying belief that we know best and that all we need to do is drive the solution through. Best practice is fundamentally different – working with people through a process of change that seeks to bring people on board. This is much more collaborative.

Engaging people in this way uses powerful techniques such as active listening (see Chapter 9, Section C1). This goes some way to practising what Daniel Goleman describes as 'social awareness' (Chapter 12, Section C1), as one of the key competences of an emotionally intelligent leader.

The other half of this principle is that of knowing the right moment to make our position and needs clear. Going in with what we want first is not a particularly persuasive approach, but knowing when to use a pause and then state our position is also vital. We have not seen many leaders progress far without living this principle to some extent.

3. The power of empathy and the other-perspective

The other-perspective is the ability to 'read' a person, to track their thinking, to discern their underlying motives. Other-perspective is more empathy than sympathy. With sympathy, you take on the feelings of another, even to the extent of adopting their feelings and owning their point of view for yourself. That is not always appropriate or helpful. Empathy, however, is the ability to put oneself in another's shoes.

This is part of what Goleman (1999) means by social awareness. He brings some compelling data to the argument that all great leaders, people who operate at a high level of influence and persuasion, have high emotional intelligence in this respect.

Daniel Pink (2014) describes this as a combination of perspective taking and empathy. In order to influence a person to 'buy' your idea or proposal you need to reduce your power and move to humility. He suggests attention to feelings as well as to rational thinking.

4. Inertia and disconfirmation

Several models begin with 'unfreezing' (Lewin, 1951), whilst others argue that inertia to change must be overcome by 'creating a sense of urgency' (Kotter, 1996). All of these admit that the power of habit in individuals creates inertia to change. Yet new habits are the goal, and are energy-consuming to develop. (See Chapter 1, Section A2 for more on both Lewin's and Kotter's models of change in organizations.)

5. Conversation in mobilization

It is easy to overlook the power of the simple, but purposeful, conversation. As a tool of analysis, it is also extremely effective in influencing, particularly if used with techniques like active listening (Chapter 9, Section C1).

When compared with other modes of engagement, such as giving presentations or facilitating a meeting, the conversation is extremely versatile. It spans engagement across the spectrum, from where we know the outcome we want to where the outcome is far from certain, as the diagram in Figure 4.16 shows.

FIGURE 4.16 Engagement modes

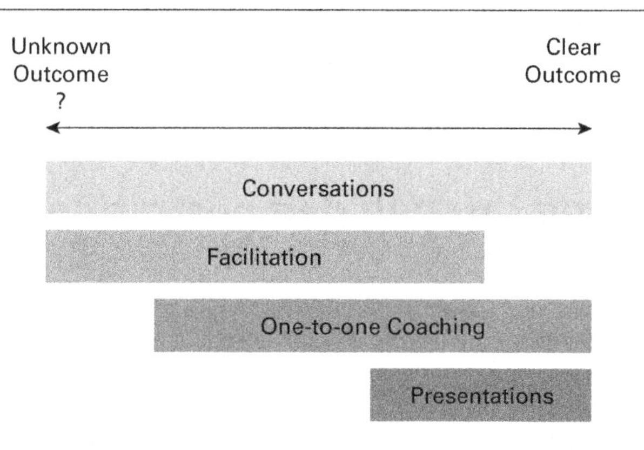

6. Lead with meaning and emotion

PRINCIPLE 6: Emotion trumps reason.

Influencing beyond authority is one definition of leadership (Bennis, 1994). Further, leaders use meaning as key collateral when seeking to influence others. They take care to explain the 'why' of the change, and connect stakeholders with the larger purpose of the change. Kotter and Cohen (2002), Pink (2014) and others have stressed the vitality of connecting stakeholders with the meaning of a change as key to motivating stakeholders sufficiently to change. Engagement with stakeholders should be tailored to making emotional connection (Kotter, 1996; Heath and Heath, 2011). People justify rationally after an emotional response.

7. Resistance to change as a key focus

Overcoming resistance to change is asymmetrical, in that Lewin (1951) and Schein (1985) recognize that coercing some stakeholders to change often merely increases resistance proportionally. Rather, the need is not so much to meet resistance head-on but to seek ways of weakening resistance, with supportive help from the change. More information on resistance to change is given in Chapter 1, Section B6 and Chapter 7, Section C.

8. Collaboration

Collaboration within the team and with key stakeholders remains one of the most enduring themes of all successful influencing strategies. The degree to which a change leader can recruit stakeholders to help with and model the change, the more likely they are to see the change succeed.

9. Influencing through demonstration

PRINCIPLE 7: Demonstration trumps argument.

A powerful means to gaining understanding and credibility towards a change initiative is to be able to demonstrate the change working to some degree. For example, the power of Agile approaches has much to do with demonstrating something working as a means to clarifying vision, requirements and commitment. Initially the working element might be a prototype or an approximation of what the change intends. In this sense, what a team delivers, however imperfect or partial, becomes visionary or at least a stimulus to a visionary future. In this way, conversations can henceforth be based on something tangible.

Early wins have huge value in stakeholder engagement. Early demonstration of progress or success can be powerfully persuasive in convincing other sceptical stakeholders. In marketing, this is described as the 'reason to believe', and empirically has been shown to improve the performance of advertising in generating sales (Hall, 2005).

CASE STUDY

Oxford-based Unipart has a demonstration building where customers can walk around an exhibit and see how RFID (radio frequency identification technology) based logistics systems might work in storing, distributing and fulfilling orders. The exhibit allows customers to play out different scenarios, showing how RFID technology can save time and waste by comparing these with existing practices.

Tip

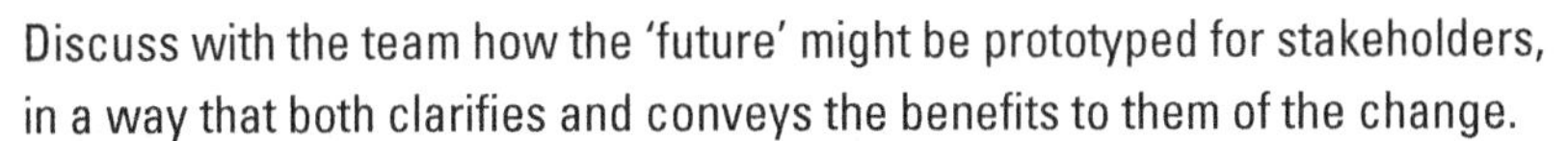

Discuss with the team how the 'future' might be prototyped for stakeholders, in a way that both clarifies and conveys the benefits to them of the change.

Summary

Change managers need to maintain the momentum of change and re-energize engagement throughout the change initiative. A number of influencing strategies can help here:

- Remember that some stakeholders are best engaged by others. Rogers's innovation model suggests that the early adopters are disproportionately influential. Identify and mobilize these people. Collaboration is therefore a key component of engagement.

- Listening is powerfully persuasive. It creates a culture of respect within the change initiative, respect for the stakeholders themselves.
- Empathy and rapport go hand-in-hand with listening. In the urgency of our lives it is tempting to forgo this, but demonstrating good social awareness is the foundation of successful influencing.
- Disconfirmation and urgency do have their place in overcoming inertia. Consider the change resistance: where is it, and what is causing it? Then seek to weaken that resistance rather than push against it.
- The common medium of conversations should not be underestimated in mobilizing change.
- Leading with meaning and emotion is central to effective engagement.
- Demonstrating early successes, early wins, is powerful.

Questions to think about

1. Are you clear about the reasons behind the change?
2. How could you explain or summarize these?
3. What if a stakeholder asked, 'So what?' What response would you have?
4. Is there sufficient urgency to overcome the inertia to change?

Further reading

Cialdini, R (2007) *Influence: The psychology of persuasion*, Harper Business

Duhigg, C (2013) *The Power of Habit: Why we do what we do, and how to change*, Random House

Lee, B (1997) *The Power Principle: Influence with honor*, Covey Leadership Center Inc.

Mayfield, P (2013) *Practical People Engagement: Leading change through the power of relationships*, Elbereth – for a specific treatment of stakeholder engagement for project-based change

Sowden, R *et al* (2007) *Managing Successful Programmes*, The Stationery Office – particularly the chapter 'Leadership and stakeholder engagement'

References

Bennis, W (1994) *Authentic Leadership: Rediscovering the secrets to creating lasting value*, Jossey-Bass, San Francisco, CA

Cooper, A (1999) *The Inmates are Running the Asylum*, Sams Publishing, Indianapolis

Covey, S R (1999) *Principle-Centred Leadership*, Simon and Schuster, London

Egan, G (1994) *Working the Shadow Side: A guide to positive behind-the-scenes management*, Jossey-Bass, San Francisco, CA

Goleman, D (1999) *Working with Emotional Intelligence*, Bloomsbury, London

Hall, D (2005) *Jump Start your Business Brain: The scientific way to make more money*, Clerisy Press, Ohio

Heath, C and Heath, D (2011) *Switch: How to change things when change is hard*, Random House Business, London

Kotter, J P (1996) *Leading Change*, Harvard Business School Press, Boston, MA

Kotter, J P and Cohen, D S (2002) *The Heart of Change*, Harvard Business School Press, Boston, MA

Lewin, K (ed) (1951) *Field Theory in Social Science: Selected from theoretical papers*, Harper & Row, New York

Lewin, K (1997) *Resolving Social Conflicts/Field Theory in Social Science*, American Psychological Press, Washington, DC

Mayfield, P (2013) *Practical People Engagement: Leading change through the power of relationships*, Elbereth, UK

Pascale, R, Sternin, J and Sternin, M (2010) *The Power of Positive Deviance: How unlikely innovators solve the world's toughest problems*, Harvard Business School Press, Boston, MA

Pink, D (2014) *To Sell is Human: The surprising truth about persuading, convincing, and influencing others*, Cannongate Books, Edinburgh

Rogers, E M (2004) *The Diffusion of Innovations*, Simon and Schuster, New York

Schein, E (1985) *Organizational Culture and Leadership*, Jossey-Bass, San Francisco, CA

Communication and engagement

05

RANJIT SIDHU

Introduction

Communication and engagement are at the heart of any successful change initiative. Thorough plans for implementing change may well be in place, but ultimately it is the people impacted by change who need to be prepared to accept it and adopt new ways of doing things. If they have not received sufficient communications or had opportunities to be actively engaged in the process, there will be much greater resistance and change will not occur.

Many potential barriers can get in the way of successful communication. Organizations include diverse groups of people with different perceptions, interests and expectations. Add into the mix high levels of anxiety due to fear of the unknown, which is inevitable during change, and it is easy to see how any meaningful exchange of information and ideas can be hindered.

Different levels of engagement and commitment are required depending where people are along the change journey. This calls for a mix of approaches and levels of communication along the way. A well-thought-out and structured approach to communication and engagement ensures that the right level of interaction occurs with the right people, at the right time, in an efficient way. The illustration below shows an overview of the topics covered in this chapter.

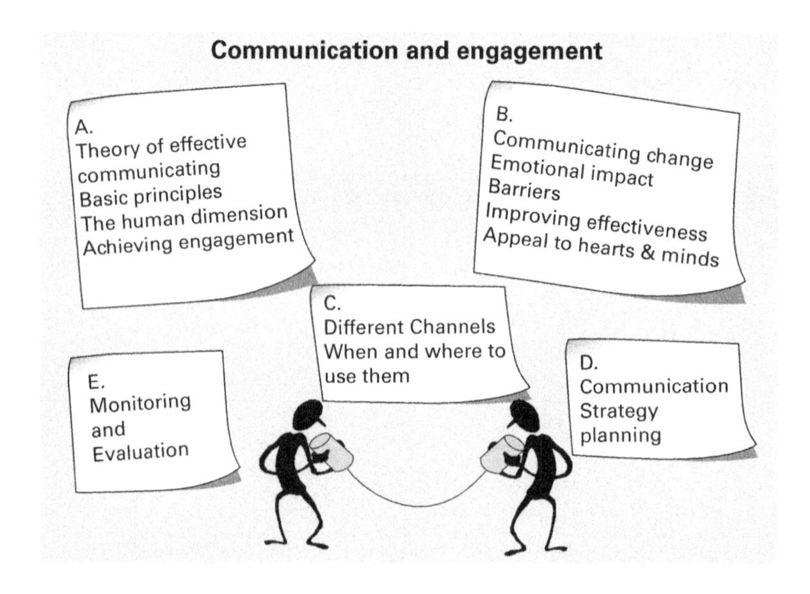

'The organization that can't communicate can't change, and the corporation that can't change is dead.' Nido Qubein, author and chairman of McNeill Lehman

CHAPTER CONTENTS

Section A: Theory of effective communicating

Introduction

Ever since human interaction began, ways of communicating have evolved from making sounds, such as grunting and using body language, into using symbols to record stories, which developed into language, writing, printing, telecommunications and the more sophisticated multimedia that we have today. Through the years, the aims of communication have always been to share information, to allow an exchange of ideas, and to influence the behaviour or actions of others. To achieve successful communication, we need to understand the complexities of what is involved in communicating.

1. Basics of communication theory

An early model of communication, and possibly the most widely referenced, is that of Shannon and Weaver (1949). Their research was carried out whilst working for Bell Telephone Laboratories and is based on how communication worked using the telephone. They wanted to find out how this channel of communication could be used more efficiently. The Shannon and Weaver model depicted a simple linear process for communication, which is a useful starting point for introducing the elements that play a key part in the communication process (see Figure 5.1).

FIGURE 5.1 Transmission model (adapted from Shannon and Weaver, 1949)

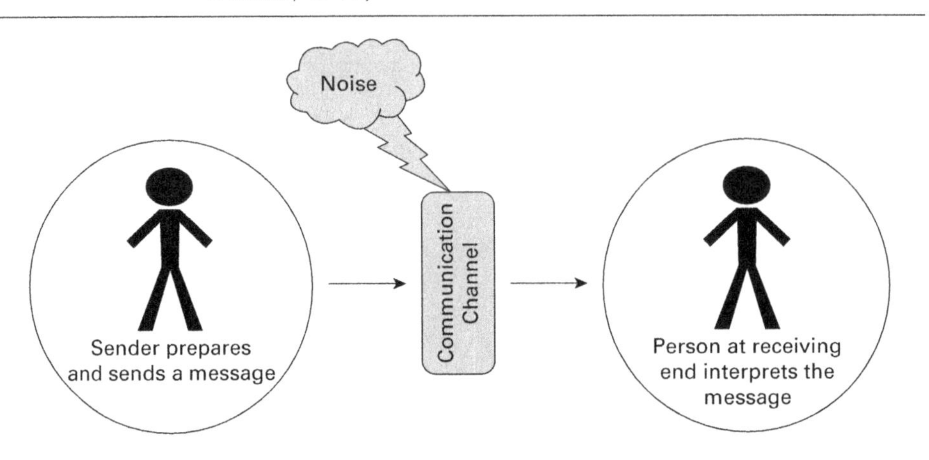

A person decides on what message to send and constructs the message, which is transmitted through a communication channel; the person at the receiving end decodes the message to give it their interpretation of the message that was sent.

The person sending the message needs to translate thoughts into words, symbols, diagrams and so on in order to formulate the message. The person at the receiving end then works the other way around; to interpret the message that has been received in a way they can relate to and take meaning from.

The term 'noise' refers to anything that interferes with the message, from the time when it is sent to when it is received. For example, with a landline telephone, this could be crackling that is heard during a call or, in the case of a mobile phone, it could be a call cutting out due to a weak signal. It was this sort of interference, at a technical level, that was Shannon and Weaver's main concern at the time of their research.

The advantage of Shannon and Weaver's model is that it is relatively simple to understand and generic enough to be applied to most types of communication. However, their model treats communication as a one-way, purely mechanical, process. They considered meaning to be contained within the actual message transmitted, rather than considering how the receiver would interpret the message and give the information their own meaning. Nor did they consider a feedback loop back to the sender of the information. With this model, the only way that the sender can check if the message was received as intended, is to request feedback from the recipient of the message.

Modern communication theory has extended the concept of noise (from Shannon and Weaver's model) to include any interference that makes it harder for the receiver to interpret the message and its original intention. This can involve anything from an uncomfortable chair that the person may be sitting on, to the thoughts, knowledge, experiences and assumptions a person holds at the time of sending or receiving the message. For example, a presentation delivered by a technology expert using very specific technical terms and jargon will fail to deliver anything of real value to a non-technical audience. In this case, using technical terminology creates noise, which

FIGURE 5.2 Noise hinders communication

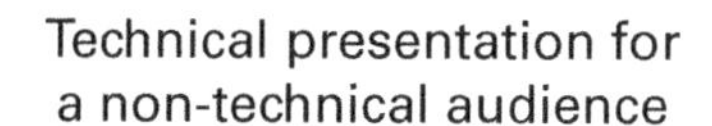

acts as a barrier to effective communication taking place (Figure 5.2). Unless the receiver is able to understand and interpret the information the sender wishes to communicate, the message is of no use.

Tip

Keep the audience in mind when planning any communication.
Put yourself in their position to see things from their perspective and think about their needs, before designing any communication.

2. Cognitive biases – the human dimension in communication

Human beings do not behave as robots, and the complexity of human interaction means that it is impossible to simply send and process factual information alone. Senders and receivers overlay their own experience and meaning at every stage of an interaction, so any message being communicated will contain more than just facts and raw data. This adds to the noise that can get in the way of effective communication.

An individual's interpretation of the world is entirely unique, and is affected by the way they process information. The brain can only absorb a limited amount of detail through the senses in any one moment. To avoid becoming overwhelmed, the brain 'filters' information, in effect taking mental shortcuts to process information.

Examples of this include using a 'rule of thumb' or an 'educated guess'. This helps with problem solving, making decisions, learning and discovery. However, shortcut processing can easily lead to misunderstandings, incorrect assumptions and biased thinking.

Behavioural psychologists have identified many cognitive biases (Kahneman, 2012). Table 5.1 lists four biases that can occur during change, with suggested communication approaches to deal with them.

Cognitive biases relating to benefits forecasting are discussed in Chapter 3. It is inevitable that biases occur and we cannot avoid filtering information that we process. This adds to the 'noise' associated with messages being communicated and leads to possible misinterpretations and incorrect assumptions. This concept is often referred to as the 'arc of distortion' (Chapter 9, Section C2.1). The aim of any communication effort is to minimize the 'noise' as much as possible. One way of doing this is to incorporate opportunities for feedback wherever possible.

3. The need for feedback mechanisms

Feedback is essential for letting the sender know how the message has been received and to turn communication into a two-way process (Figure 5.3). This allows a more meaningful exchange to take place and enables the receiver to be equally involved in the process.

FIGURE 5.3 Feedback is valuable

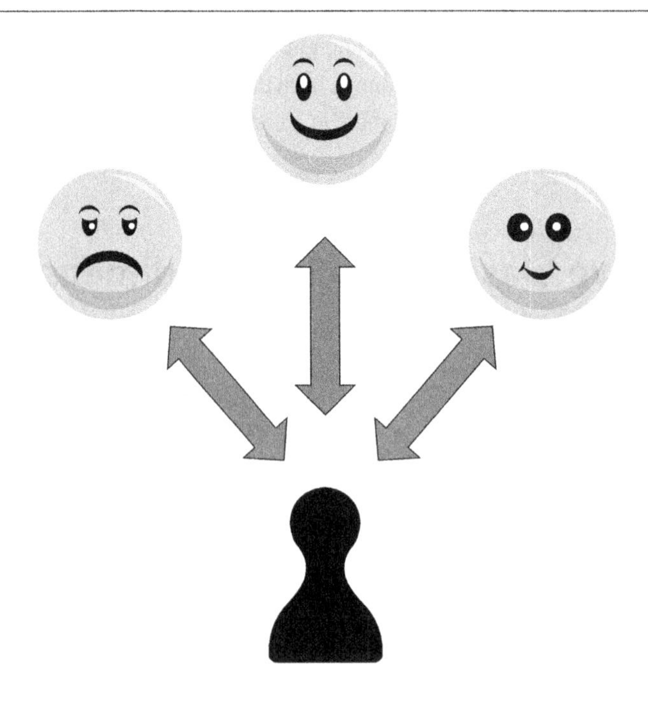

TABLE 5.1 Four common biases and communication approaches to deal with them

Cognitive Bias	Symptoms of this Bias Occurring	Communications Approach to Help Overcome the Problem
Confirmation bias A tendency for people to pay attention only to information that confirms their beliefs and ignore evidence that indicates otherwise.	People argue against the need for any change. For example, a company that has been a successful market leader in the past but is now struggling to remain competitive, may have people who continue to believe they are the best and ignore market data that indicates otherwise.	Communicate reasons for the change and show objective evidence to back this up. Include the losses and problems that will be avoided by changing. Engage people in discussions, so they have an opportunity to develop new insights about the situation. Repeatedly communicate a compelling vision that engages hearts and minds.
Status quo bias A preference for people to keep things the way they are and avoid change.	People not agreeing that change is needed, or they may say that they agree but there is inertia and little action is taken to make change happen.	Ensure communication messages include what will continue and remain the same, as well as what will be changing. Indicate practical next steps and continue to communicate a compelling vision.
Availability bias Tendency to perceive the more memorable or easily available information as the most significant.	A few instances of something not going so well, eg aspects of a new system not working, which lead to people complaining and being negative about planned changes as a whole.	Communicate when and how specific issues raised are being dealt with. Frequently highlight and share success stories, making them visible and easily accessible.
Bandwagon effect The more people come to believe something, the more others want to 'hop on the bandwagon'.	Groups who are resistant to change start to influence others, and resistance spreads. It can of course work the other way, as momentum builds people actively start to adopt changes.	Start to communicate success stories early, eg how successful a pilot was, and continue throughout the change process. Get others involved in communicating these messages.

The concept of feedback originates from the field of cybernetics, which is the science of control systems (Fiske, 1996). A very simple feedback mechanism is, for example, the oil-light indicator in a car – if this lights up, it is a message for the driver that the oil needs topping up. As a result of that information, action can be taken to address the situation. Similarly, during communication, feedback provides valuable information about whether a message has been understood as it was intended. A critical element to make this work is that the sender must be prepared to listen to the incoming feedback and respond accordingly, rather than just be focused on sending messages out. Further information on active listening is in Chapter 9, Section C1.

CASE STUDY

An organization that was suffering the after-effects of a poorly managed, large-scale change initiative, decided to set up an employee satisfaction survey to get a better feel for people's concerns and issues and how they perceived working for the organization. They looked at many different factors such as: what people thought about the way change is managed, working within their teams, how often their managers and leaders communicated with them, the quality of communication and any major issues or challenges that affected their performance. The survey was made available online, but with the option of a printed version. The questions were linked to areas of the senior management team's performance objectives.

Processes were put in place to ensure there was regular feedback for people on the decisions and actions that resulted from the employee surveys. Many positive changes resulted in a short time frame. It changed the way senior management interacted with their people and improved morale considerably. This organization now sees feedback from employee satisfaction surveys as an important and ongoing driver of change.

Gathering feedback from people throughout a change initiative, both individually and collectively, is an essential activity to monitor the effectiveness of communication efforts. This is covered in more detail in Section E.

4. Interpersonal and mass communication

A typical example of *interpersonal communication* would be a meeting where individuals are involved in direct face-to-face interactions within a small group.

Mass communication refers to communicating with large numbers of people, for example sending organization-wide announcements about change within a newsletter, or a video on an intranet. Mass communication tends to be a one-way flow of information and works on the assumption that communication is primarily a mechanical process and all people receiving the message will give it the same meaning in a rational way.

Within organizations both interpersonal and mass communications are taking place. If you consider the intricacies involved in communication between individuals, when this is scaled up to organizations, the task of clear and effective communication becomes even more challenging. The potential for misunderstandings and confusion is vastly multiplied as the volume of people and communications increases, and people will inevitably influence each other with their own interpretations of what the communication means.

5. One-way versus two-way communication approaches

During one-way communication, as the name suggests, the focus is on how to get the message sent. It is useful for imparting information to large numbers of people at the same time and is achieved more quickly than two-way communication. So where there are urgent issues to address and time is a critical factor, one-way communication may be more appropriate. However, this approach can leave people feeling as if change is being 'done to them' as it does not provide them with an opportunity to clarify misunderstandings or voice their concerns.

Using one-way communication works well when the purpose is simply to inform and share information. The problem comes when this approach is used alone, with an expectation that it will get people involved and enthusiastic about a change initiative. There is a big difference between informing people, and getting them fully engaged and committed to change.

Two-way communication on the other hand incorporates a flow of information between the sender and receiver, so that there is an opportunity to have a dialogue and gain feedback (Figure 5.4). Genuine two-way communication allows for more than just checking that messages have been received as intended; it encourages fuller participation in decision making and enables people to shape the approach to change. This goes a long way to gaining fuller participation and buy-in from people, which is fundamental for ensuring changes can be sustained.

Different communication channels and methods allow for varying levels of interaction (Table 5.2). Some channels limit the opportunity for feedback, for example television broadcasting, video messages, or large-scale seminars, where people in the audience may feel inhibited in speaking up. On the other hand, face-to-face interaction between smaller numbers of people encourages feedback and exchange, so that a meaningful dialogue can occur. See Section 5.C for more on communication channels.

FIGURE 5.4 Balancing communication approaches

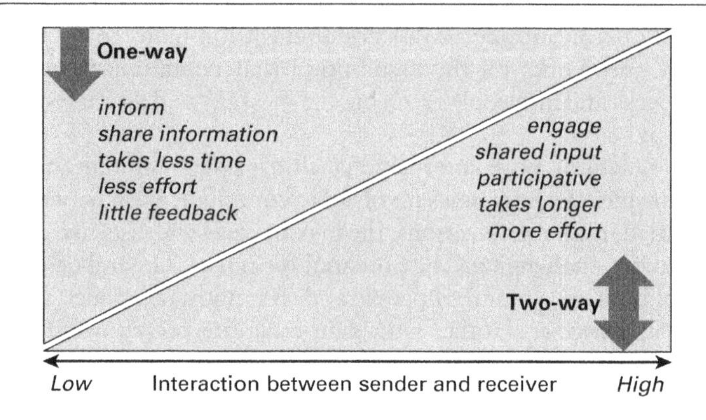

TABLE 5.2 Different communication methods

One-way Communication Methods	Two-way Communication Methods
Presentations;	Open discussion forums (large and small);
Seminars and large-scale meetings;	Smaller meetings, informal interactions;
Newsletters, e-mails;	Workshops;
Websites and intranets;	Surveys;
Bulletin boards, banners, posters;	Instant messaging tools;
Video messages;	Social media platforms;
These favour a one-way flow of information.	These encourage a two-way flow of information.

Tip

Consider what you are aiming to achieve from each communication and the level of interaction that this will require, before deciding on the approach to use.

6. Role of communication to achieve engagement

The marketing discipline has been a driving influence within the field of employee communications. Most people impacted by change are unlikely to be enthusiastic supporters straight away. A relationship marketing approach to communications helps people to move along the change journey. It recognizes that people first need to become aware of the change, and to understand what it means to them, before making the necessary emotional commitment needed to play a role in making change happen. The AIDA (Attention, Interest, Desire, Action) model is one way of representing the steps along people's journey:

- *Attention*: this step is about capturing attention to increase awareness of the change and to highlight its importance. Communication at this point needs to focus on explaining what the change is about, the reasons for the change and to create a sense of urgency if necessary. This step is about informing people and can use a 'tell' one-way approach to get the information to people quickly.
- *Interest*: people become more interested when they understand what the change entails. Communications should provide more specific information that is relevant for this audience, and should focus on the benefits and how it will help them. To aid their understanding of the change, they must have the opportunity to ask questions and have these answered, in a way that is credible. So it is important to think about who does this communicating – and the messages must be consistent across the people involved in communications. Two-way forms of communication are more appropriate at this stage, such as forums and discussion groups.
- *Desire*: at this point people move beyond waiting to be told about the change, to engaging in thinking about it for themselves. They are more open to the idea of this change and the possibilities it could bring from them. Communication messages should be clear about where they can find out more information and how they can become involved. Make it easy for people to get involved. For example: if people have been asked to provide feedback and ideas about proposed changes – do they know how they can do so and is this method accessible for them? There is no point in saying 'log on to the intranet to send us your comments', if they do not have easy access to the intranet.
- *Action*: by this stage they are committed to taking action. They move beyond thinking about the possibilities for them and want to have a meaningful role to play in change. Their active engagement should be encouraged through more participative, two-way forms of communication, such as workshops, and they can be asked to play an active role in making change happen.

The advantage of a marketing approach to communication is that it focuses on the people at the receiving end. Designing communications in this way will help people to travel along the change journey, and make shifts in their attitudes and ultimately behaviours (Fill and Jamieson, 2006). A possible disadvantage is that it can be used in a mechanical way, with insufficient opportunity provided for feedback. In this situation, the audience can become 'targets' to be persuaded, rather than people who can genuinely contribute to the change effort by providing valuable input and helping to shape change.

Smythe (2007: 15) explains that: 'real engagement means asking people to think the business issue through for themselves'. In other words, *telling* people information will not result in engagement. Smythe goes on to say: 'employee engagement is not an end in itself; it is a platform from which to engage everyone in change so that people move beyond "feeling a part of it" to having a meaningful role in it'.

Visible support from the sponsor and involvement from leaders at the top is critical for any change initiative. Using a top-down, one-way approach to convey information, such as the reasons and vision for change, are very useful in getting the information out quickly to large numbers of people. However, to achieve fuller engagement, this should then be balanced by a genuine invitation for people to participate in discussions and offer their feedback. If people are given these opportunities within an environment of trust and openness, they will feel more involved and committed and become more engaged with the change initiative.

CASE STUDY

An organization wanted to introduce flexible working hours to a workforce who were used to working in set shift patterns. This was a big change for a traditional organization, where nothing like this had been attempted before. The leadership agreed that a final decision on how to implement this change would not be made until everyone had an opportunity to understand the full consequences and give their opinions on the proposed changes. Forums were held for people to participate in discussions and voice their opinions. Change agents were nominated in different sections, so people had a point of contact to get their questions answered and share any additional thoughts. The feedback gathered led to some changes to what had originally been proposed, and as a result a more phased approach was used to implement this change. People were more willing to participate because they knew they had an opportunity to influence the outcome, and the result was that these changes were accepted willingly.

Summary

We cannot avoid communicating: we do it instinctively. There are many different ways of communicating and an understanding of the basic principles of communication opens up the opportunity to make considered choices that can make communication more focused and effective. People communicating need to keep in sight the perspectives of those receiving their messages, remembering how the timing and structure of a message can affect how it is received. Understanding different approaches for communication, and when they are appropriate to use, can make the critical difference between the success or failure of communication efforts and ultimately the change initiative.

Questions to think about

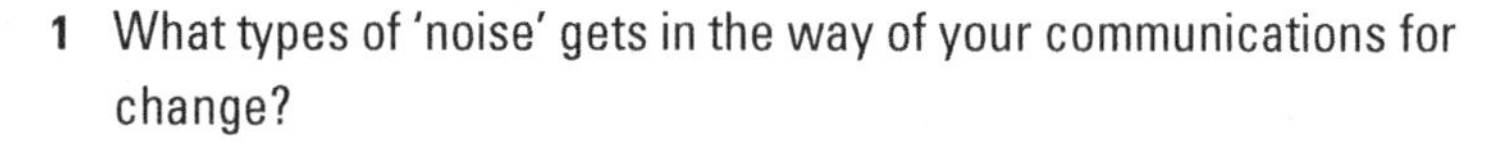

1. What types of 'noise' gets in the way of your communications for change?
2. What biases might be occurring in your environment?
3. What is the balance between one-way and two-way communication for your current initiative?

Section B: Communicating change

Introduction

A consistent and thorough approach to communicating change is essential to:

- build an awareness of the need for change;
- achieve a shared understanding of what is required across stakeholder groups;
- gain people's commitment and get them actively engaged in making change happen.

To accommodate the needs of diverse groups, different types of communication activities and interventions should be considered. People have different preferences for the way they process information, so the same messages need to be conveyed using different formats and styles. Equally it is important to appeal to 'hearts and minds', as making this emotional connection helps achieve fuller engagement during change.

1. The emotional impact of change

During times of change, an emotional journey is taking place, and all communication needs to be sensitive to this. It is important to consider the emotional impact that messages may have on people. If a change initiative is announced using words like 'efficiency drive' or 'rationalization', in a way that implies jobs could be at risk but does not actually state that, people will make their own interpretations of what this means. Trust is of paramount importance: where leaders are less than transparent about the reasons for change, this can be very clear to employees, and they will lose trust.

1.1 Threat versus reward

The human brain still functions as it did in prehistoric times and has two core drivers: to avoid threat, and seek reward (Figure 5.5). Under a perceived threat, people feel anxious, think less clearly and are not as productive. The opposite applies when they are moving towards reward; they are more motivated, more focused, willing to learn new things and get involved – and are much more engaged.

Uncertainty and lack of control over a situation will naturally cause anxiety and stress. People need to be given as much information as possible and be engaged in the change process, so they can regain a sense of control. A leading trigger for the stress caused by a threat response is a lack of control and autonomy (Rock, 2009). Engaging people in the change process early, so they have an opportunity to shape how it is carried out, helps them feel more in control of a situation. Even just a small amount of control goes a long way in reducing anxiety and keeping people from feeling that they are 'under threat'.

When change is highly complex, with many unknowns, there will be much less information available to communicate. This naturally causes greater discomfort and anxiety, but it also offers a greater opportunity to allow people to be involved in shaping the change from the beginning. In the case of more directive change, communication is likely to be top-down with more detail being available, but people still need to know how they can get involved and what part they will play in making change happen. See Chapter 1, Section B.3 for further information about motivation.

FIGURE 5.5 Threat versus reward

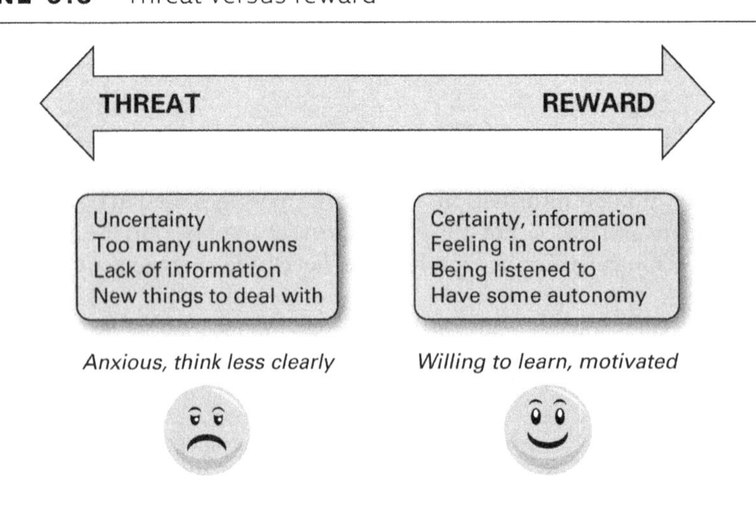

1.2 *Where people are on the change journey*

The change curve described in Chapter 1, Section B1 is a useful framework for describing the cycle of change. Communication and engagement efforts need to be appropriate to where people are along the change curve and help to support them through the change journey. Leaders and managers are often unaware of this, and so their messages are not appropriately aligned with the thinking of their teams. In their enthusiasm to progress with their plans, managers often try to 'sell and push' the idea of change, causing even more resistance and anxiety. Instead they need to support people through the journey that they themselves have been through. People need to understand the bigger picture, the wider context, so they can understand the 'why' behind the change. They need to make sense of this, before they can engage in the process of change.

2. Maintaining a people-focused approach to communication

To develop communication in a way that reduces anxiety and encourages willing engagement, there are six factors that change managers should keep in mind. These are summarized in Figure 5.6 and described below more fully.

2.1 *Don't wait until full information is available*

In the early stages of any initiative, there is a lot of uncertainty, and a lack of clear solutions to give people. So there is a temptation for managers to hold back communications until there is further information to give. Often there are early and enthusiastic big announcements about a proposed change initiative coming down from senior management, which are then followed by long silences. These gaps inevitably get filled by gossip and rumours, which always seem to be negative and gravitate towards the worst possible scenarios.

FIGURE 5.6 Factors to encourage engagement

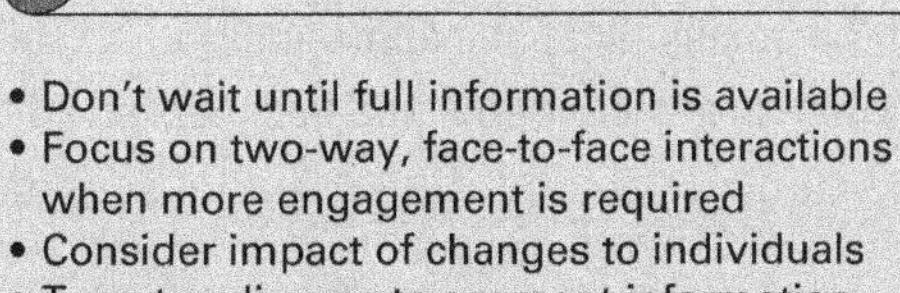

Factors to encourage engagement
• Don't wait until full information is available
• Focus on two-way, face-to-face interactions when more engagement is required
• Consider impact of changes to individuals
• Target audiences to segment information and avoid overload
• Allow plenty of time
• Encourage feedback and act on it

Tip

It is better to say 'we do not know yet and here is what we are doing to find out'. Regular communication keeps people updated on progress and helps to manage the rumour grapevine.

2.2 Focus on two-way face-to-face communication when more engagement is required

Maintain a two-way communication stream that allows people to voice their opinions and concerns. There will be a lot of anxiety and stress, especially if the change involves inevitable endings such as the closure of a division and job losses. People need a trusting and supportive environment where they feel it is acceptable to air their views openly and share how they feel. Communications planning needs to incorporate suitable ways of enabling this, to support people through the change. When emotions are running high, people are less likely to process all the information they receive, so ensure core messages are repeated (Kanter, 2005). It is best to do this by providing the same information but by different means. This repetition helps to generate a feeling of familiarity and eventually more ease about the proposed changes.

It is easier to demonstrate support and empathy in face-to-face situations. People prefer to receive news of changes verbally from another person. Ideally, that person should be a known and trusted source, such as a line manager, so that there is an opportunity for discussion and enquiry (Larkin and Larkin, 1994). An effective approach for communicating widespread organizational change is to follow up announcements from senior management with personal meetings with line managers, who have been well briefed in advance.

Tip

Find multiple ways to communicate the key messages, so these can be repeated and have a better chance of being received. Including face-to-face discussions as part of the communications approach is an excellent way to gather feedback and address any concerns and misunderstandings.

2.3 Consider the impact of change to individuals

As well as explaining the wider context, individuals need to understand how any change relates to them at an individual level. Maslow's hierarchy shows that people's basic needs must be met first (Chapter 1, Section B3.1). This means people's key questions at this point will be: 'How will the change impact me?'; 'What does this mean for my role and position in the organization?' Messages need to connect with people's interests and concerns. This provides a more meaningful and relevant context, so they can understand what the change means for them and are more motivated to take the required actions. This approach helps people translate what could be treated as the 'management agenda' into how it relates to them.

Tip

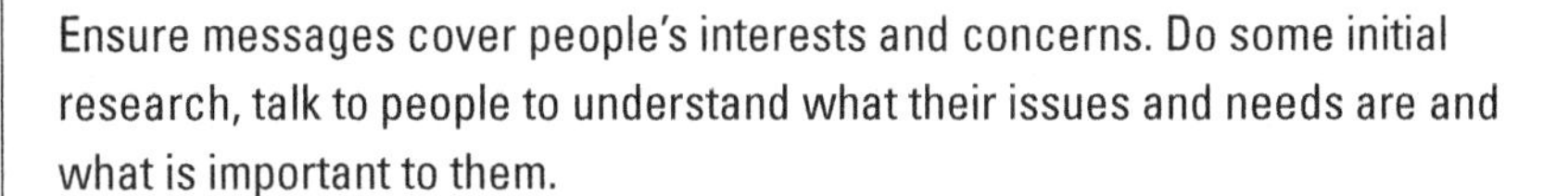

Ensure messages cover people's interests and concerns. Do some initial research, talk to people to understand what their issues and needs are and what is important to them.

2.4 *Target audiences to segment information and avoid overload*

Rather than overwhelming people with all the information available, change managers should take the time to segment their audience and identify the information that each of these needs. Each group may need a different level of detail on the background to the initiative, its goals, timescales, why change is needed, and the impact it will have on them. By segmenting in this way, messages can focus on each group's perspective, be written in terms that they will most easily understand, and clarify 'what's in it for them?'

Tip

Consider the most appropriate people to communicate the information for the target audiences. They should have credibility in the eyes of the audience.

2.5 *Allow plenty of time*

The process of communicating change cannot be rushed. People are not robots that can be programmed to digest information and then be immediately ready for change. The interactions and dialogues needed to build a shared understanding, and make sense of change, require time and patience. Getting people's commitment to change does not happen in one step or one meeting. At the early stages, people are gaining awareness and assessing how the change and suggested actions broadly fit with their lives. Next they move on to evaluate how feasible the actions are. Only at this stage can they begin to absorb, and become engaged with, the detail. This is when the capacity for commitment begins to form. The full journey will cover gaining awareness of the change, understanding its implications, becoming involved with decisions, and becoming committed to its success.

Tip

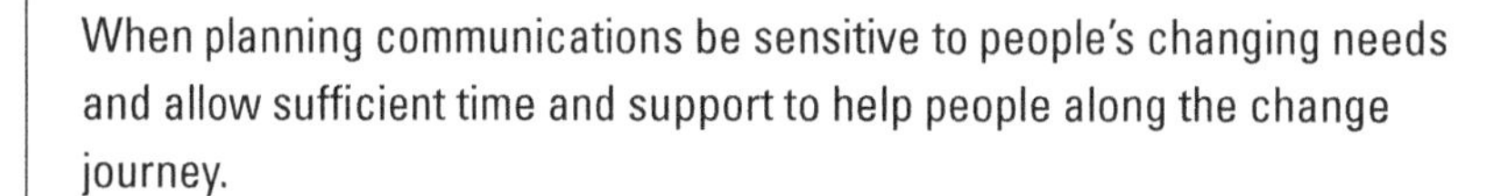

When planning communications be sensitive to people's changing needs and allow sufficient time and support to help people along the change journey.

2.6 Encourage feedback and act on it

It is important that suitable feedback mechanisms are in place to understand people's views and concerns. Feedback is a two-way process and so action should be taken on the feedback received. A timely response to feedback is critical as people will quickly disengage if they feel they are not being listened to, especially if they have gone to the trouble of giving feedback. The response should be as comprehensive as possible, explaining why certain actions have, or have not, been taken.

Tip

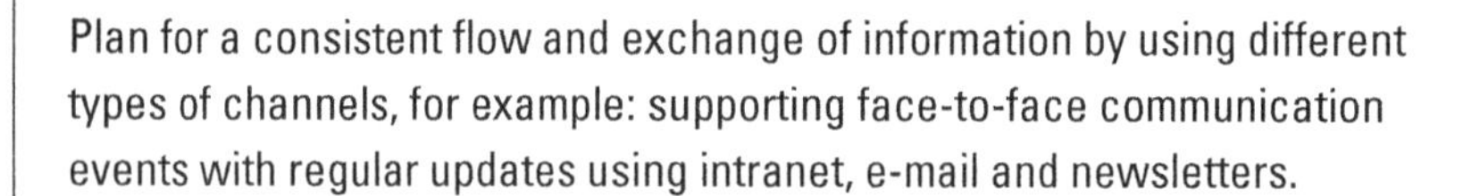

Plan for a consistent flow and exchange of information by using different types of channels, for example: supporting face-to-face communication events with regular updates using intranet, e-mail and newsletters.

3. Barriers to effective communication

There are many potential barriers to communication: the 'noise' that gets in the way of effective communication across the organization (Figure 5.7) (see Blundel, Ippolito and Donnarumma, 2013). Change managers need to maintain continued focus on minimizing this 'noise' throughout the change initiative.

FIGURE 5.7 Barriers to effective communication

3.1 *Emotions, attitudes and perceptions*

The way people interpret information, and the way they feel, affects what they pay attention to and the meaning they attach to any communication. There can also be issues around credibility – if the organization has a history of managing change badly, there will be more cynicism and negative feelings towards any change proposed. This can prevent people from hearing the key messages being communicated and processing that information.

3.2 *Type and amount of information*

If change communications include too little information, the result will be that people have insufficient context to understand the drivers for change or see how it affects them. Information overload is not helpful either. If people have too much information, they may find it difficult to absorb all the detail and simply not have time to read it all. The language used can also be an obstacle, in that it could be overly technical, too high-level and full of abstract concepts without anything concrete and meaningful, or includes an inappropriate amount of jargon or 'management-speak'. The level of information and the way it is expressed should match the needs of the audience.

3.3 *Cultural, social and organizational*

Where the workforce is very diverse, big divides can exist between management and employees, or between different divisions. This creates a 'them and us' culture that inhibits exchange of ideas and sharing of information.

A very hierarchical organization, with rigid and bureaucratic reporting structures, will make the free flow of information between teams and business divisions much more difficult. It also potentially delays important communication being filtered through the different levels. Organizational cultures with a very directive approach rely on senior management making the necessary decisions and telling people what needs to be done. This can also lead to unnecessary delays and a potential communication vacuum. For more information about 'change and the organization' see Chapter 1, Section C.

4. Improving communication effectiveness

Communication is very often designed from the viewpoint of the person sending it, rather than from the perspective of the audience. This is usually because insufficient time has been spent on understanding the audience and how the proposed changes will actually impact them (see Chapter 4 for information on identifying and analysing stakeholders). Below are five best practice guidelines to keep in mind when developing communications messages.

4.1 Identify clear messages appropriate for the audience

Communication needs to remain focused on the main objective and key messages, rather than diverting into too many directions. Uncertainty and confusion arise from an abundance of information that is difficult to interpret, or appears disorganized or paradoxical (Lewis, 2011). The language used should be relevant for the audience. High-level strategic, business-speak is fine for management levels, but may not mean anything to people lower down in the organization. Similarly, too much technical jargon may be appropriate for a very technical audience but will be meaningless to non-technical people.

4.2 Make information simple, clear and easy to navigate

Make it easy for the audience by sticking to simple and clear messages. With written communication, ensure it is easy to navigate and consider the layout, legibility and use of visuals to make the information clearer and easier to digest. Legible messages are more credible and more likely to be taken seriously (Smith and Mounter, 2008).

4.3 Use an appropriate tone and style

Choosing the right tone and style is important as it reflects your attitude towards the audience. It indicates whether the relationship with the audience is intended to be more formal or more friendly and personal. Generally, this reflects the culture of the organization, but it should take into account the type of change you are aiming to bring about.

4.4 Cater for different personality preferences

People have different preferences for the way they process information (see Chapter 1, Section B4). For example, some people prefer general, big-picture ideas whereas others are looking for specific detail. Some people prefer to have options and knowing there is flexibility in the plans and choices available, whereas others need to know there is a clear step-by-step plan to follow and will be concerned if this is not the case (Charvet, 1997). Communications need to cater for these different preferences, by covering all these perspectives. A description of the bigger picture will provide the overall context, and even if all the specific details are not available yet, let people know when they will be available or where they can go to get more detailed information. This helps to reassure them and gives them confidence in the approach being proposed.

4.5 Include the actions required from people and where they can get support

Communications should include actions that people are required to take, and where they can get more information and support from. To set and manage expectations, a schedule of when new information or detail will be available, and how that will be communicated, is also helpful.

Tip

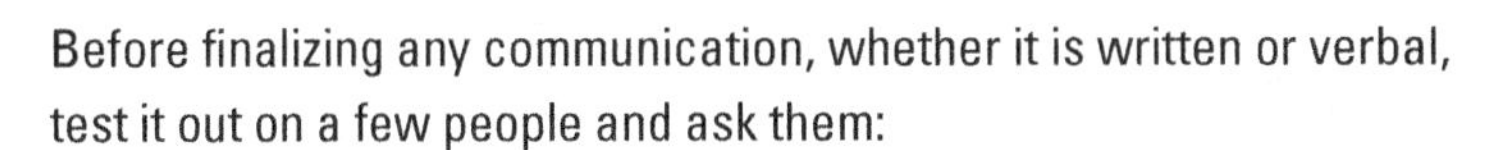

Before finalizing any communication, whether it is written or verbal, test it out on a few people and ask them:

- What do they understand as the key points? Are these clear?
- Is there anything that is vague or that could be misinterpreted?
- Is the overall flow logical?
- Is it easy to follow?
- What can be left out?

CASE STUDY

An organization transformed their culture by focusing on changing the language and tone of their communication from being traditional and overly bureaucratic to much more friendly and approachable. They focused on simplifying all of their communications and adopting a much more personal and friendly style, even for internal, automatically generated e-mail responses.

5. Encouraging engagement by appealing to hearts and minds

Successful communication and engagement approaches appeal to people's hearts as well as minds. This means not only using logical reasoning to explain the drivers and approach to change, but also appealing to their emotions. This emotional connection is necessary to achieve fuller engagement. Three effective ways in which this can be done are:

- symbolic actions and symbolism;
- use of metaphors;
- use of narrative and storytelling.

5.1 *Symbolic actions and symbolism*

It is said that actions speak louder than words. The actions and behaviours of those leading change have a bigger impact on people's level of engagement than any formal presentation. All involved in leading and managing change need to be consistent in demonstrating their commitment through their actions, and become role models for others. For example, if the change initiative requires a shift to working in an open-plan office, then leaders also need to be prepared to give up their offices and make that change.

Consider when Nelson Mandela walked out on the field in the 1995 Rugby World Cup wearing the South African Springbok team's rugby shirt. Following decades of apartheid rule, rugby had been the sport solely for the elite in a racially segregated and deeply divided nation. Yet, in that moment, the act of Nelson Mandela wearing the green and gold rugby shirt was a powerful symbol of a nation uniting as 'one team, one country'.

The way leaders and managers interact with people on a day-to-day basis conveys information about the organizational culture. How responses to people's feedback are managed also sends an important message. It symbolizes the extent to which individual contributions are valued, and this will affect their levels of engagement. The impact of this type of activity should not be underestimated, as it provides a powerful context for the way people interpret things. They will be quick to notice any inconsistencies and this will undermine other communication efforts.

Visual symbols are also extremely powerful and can be used to reinforce important messages. When two organizations merge, the logo of the newly formed company can become a powerful symbol of a new beginning and a new sense of identity. Uniforms, company branding and the type of offices all send messages about what is considered important within the organization. Using a visual image or symbol to represent the vision for change can also be a powerful way of reinforcing the message (Rose, 2010).

5.2 Use of metaphors

Metaphors encourage visual thinking and can be a very powerful way of explaining a situation, in terms that people can more easily understand and connect with emotionally. Examples of metaphors are: 'We'll leave no stone unturned', 'Our bank account is not a bottomless pit'.

A CEO of a technology company wanted to get the message across to the board that they should accept the offer of a buyout by another company. He explained the situation as: 'We are standing on the deck of a burning ship and it's time to act!' This grabbed people's attention and they could appreciate the reasons for this difficult decision.

People are unlikely to understand or remember all the facts and figures about why change is needed, but they will remember if it is explained in simple terms and using imagery that they can connect with. This makes the messages much more memorable and likely to be repeated. However, they need to be chosen wisely. If they do not represent the situation or are not easily understood across the audience, they can cause confusion and have a negative impact.

5.3 Use of narrative and storytelling

In general, organizations and the people within them tend to focus on analytical thinking. This approach may help with appealing to people's minds at a rational level, but it does not engage them at a deeper emotional level. Using stories and narrative is a useful way to do this, because our brains need to be actively involved in making sense of stories. Two things are happening when people hear stories: they are imagining what is happening within the story and analysing the content for information. This satisfies the needs of both the left side (focusing on logic) and the right side (focusing on creativity) of the brain.

Stories are helpful in preparing people for change, as they are a way to describe the future and imply a route for how to get there, without going into specifics or too much detail (Dietz and Silverman, 2014). In fact, stories work best without too much detail, as there needs to be room left for the listener to add their own meaning in order to connect with the story. The most important thing is that the audience is able

TABLE 5.3 Getting people to engage with change

Essential Key Characteristics of a Story that can be Used for Change	Example
Reach a resolution that addresses a problem	*'The merger was successful and went smoothly.'*
Overcome a challenge successfully	*'The two companies had very different cultures.'*
Have a clear key message that is the main point of the story	*'Each company has their speciality and strengths, but together they are much stronger, offer a better service and have more opportunities'*
Use rich sensory language to make it come alive	*Describe some of the characters involved, the angst they felt, their thoughts and concerns.*
Move people to action	*Be clear on what they should do next – eg 'Get involved in the forums to offer your ideas.'*

to relate to the story. Table 5.3 lists the characteristics of stories that can be used for getting people engaged with change.

Tip

It is imperative for the success of any change initiative for the leadership and change teams to be aligned and agree on the key messages around change and the stories to communicate. In this way, even though the different people involved in communicating these stories will be telling stories in their own way, the key points and messages will remain consistent.

As well as using stories to get people ready for change, they can also be used to reinforce change and help counteract negative views during change. For example, sharing people's success stories of how adopting changes has led to better and improved results for them. Stories have a power to influence that is difficult to match through any other type of communication. They can describe the journey through change in a relevant and non-threatening way without the danger of seeming to 'attack the current situation', because there is no right or wrong with stories.

> Denning (2011) describes use of different kinds of stories for different purposes and how they can be used to counteract negativity. He refers to these types of stories as 'taming the grapevine'. He tells the story of a computer manufacturing company, 'where stories circulated about managers not doing any real work, being overpaid, and having no idea what it was like on the manufacturing line. But an additional story was injected into the mix: One day, a new site director turned up in a white coat, unannounced and unaccompanied and sat on the line making laptops for a day. During the day, a person asked him "Why do you earn so much more than me?" His simple reply: "If you screw up badly, you lose your job. If I screw up badly, three thousand people lose their jobs."' While not a story in the traditional sense, the manager's words and actions served as a seed for the story that eventually circulated in opposition to the one about managers being lazy and overpaid. The atmosphere at the facility began to improve within weeks.

Summary

There are many factors to consider when planning communications, from how best to engage people emotionally to the mechanics of how best to structure messages so they can be easily understood. Change managers should work closely with other members of the change team and, if available, specialists from internal communications, to plan and implement robust communication approaches.

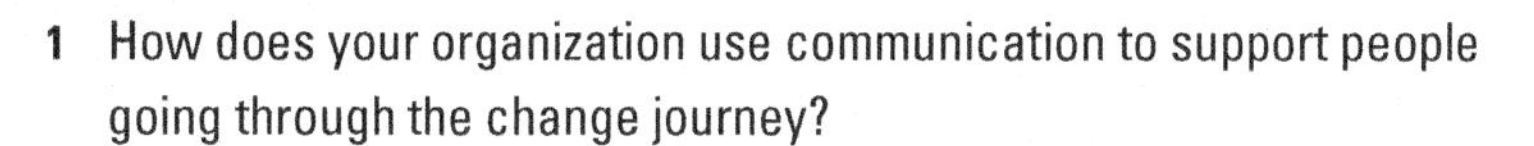

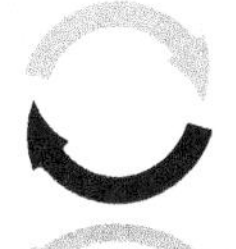

1. How does your organization use communication to support people going through the change journey?
2. In which ways do you segment communication to meet the needs of different audiences?
3. What styles and approaches have you used to engage people's hearts as well as minds?

Section C: Communication channels

Introduction

During any change initiative there will be a diverse range of people with differing communication needs. Change managers need to understand the many different means by which communication can take place, so they can use the most appropriate mechanisms to achieve their communication objectives. These mechanisms are referred to as communication channels.

An effective communications approach recognizes the strengths and weaknesses of different channels and uses them appropriately (Quirke, 2008) to ensure effective communication occurs during change, whether that is top-down, bottom-up or across the organization. Different types of change initiatives need differing levels of communication and engagement. For example, the announcement of a redundancy programme will need a more sensitive approach than the announcement of a new software upgrade for employees' computers.

Decisions about communication channels to be used are often made on the basis of convenience for the sender. This can lead to communication failure. Better choices will be made by focusing on the needs and perspectives of those receiving the messages. Two main communication channels are typically employed during change: push channels and pull channels.

Push channels

Push channels allow information to be sent out to people in a one-way direction. These are useful for making announcements in a timely way, or passing on information to keep people updated. They do not allow for feedback to be given easily, nor do they provide the opportunity for people to get involved: examples of push channels are physical notice boards, printed newsletters, instruction manuals. With push channels, the sender's control over the message ends once it has been released; there is no further influence over how the information will be interpreted.

Pull channels

These are channels that allow people to access or 'pull' information when they want it, and when it is convenient for them: a traditional library is an example of a pull channel. This caters for many different interests and information needs, and people use it when they want to, going to the specific areas that they are interested in. Intranets, information portals and podcasts serve the same purpose. Pull channels are valuable during times of change, and enable people to access information at the point where they need it, and when they are ready to absorb its content. This will vary according to different personality preferences. Some people may need time to reflect on announcements that have been made about change, before they are ready to start digesting that information further.

1. Lean and rich communication channels

There are many means of communicating; the challenge is in choosing appropriately from all the options available. A useful way to select suitable channels is to think in terms of the 'richness' that they offer. A channel is termed 'rich' or 'lean' depending on the following factors:

- *Interactivity*: does it allow quick response, conversation and the chance for interaction? Examples of richly interactive media are those that allow conversation in real time, such as face-to-face meetings, workshops, video conferencing, instant messaging, social media tools and even the regular telephone.
- *Multiple cues*: does it provide multiple layers of feedback signals to help people understand both the literal content of the message and the underlying meanings? Does the channel convey non-verbal cues, such as emotion and feelings, tone or gestures? A large proportion of what is communicated comes from non-verbal content, which influences how the information is received. Face-to-face communication, including video options, is richer as it includes tone of voice and body language. Written text is leaner as there is nothing beyond the words, and the word combinations.

According to research (Mehrabian, 1981), when it comes to communicating feelings and attitude, especially in situations where the words do not seem to match the tone and body language, 55 per cent of the meaning of the message will be taken from the body language, 38 per cent from tone of voice and 7 per cent from the words.

- *Variety and format of information*: does it allow for a variety of different formats and styles of information – for example, visual, numerical? Different people respond to and process information in different ways (Chapter 9, Section A3.2). Rows of data in a spreadsheet can provide a good source for analysis but will not be as compelling as the same information presented visually. A spreadsheet is lean on variety and format of information, while video-conferencing is much richer.

  Decisions around which channel to use for a communication have to be made carefully. A lean medium may provide too little information and result in misunderstanding and confusion. By contrast, a rich medium for a very simple message could distract from the key points. For example, alerting people that the car park will be closed over the weekend does not need a face-to-face meeting. Equally, relying on e-mail to communicate major organizational change would be completely ineffective.

Tip

Where there is least opportunity for misunderstanding, leaner channels are best. Where there is greater uncertainty, significant impact on people or opposing views, then rich channels will be needed from the outset.

2. Three of the most essential channels

These are verbal, listening and visual. When there is so much choice, with new technology advancing almost on a daily basis, it can be easy to overlook the power of these three essential means of communicating. See also Chapter 9, Section A, for more information on learner preferences and presenting information.

Verbal

This includes both spoken and written communication. During any change initiative information will be shared by speaking to people both informally and through more formal presentations. There are also likely to be a vast amount of written messages through update reports, e-mails, bulletins, newsletters, intranet pages, blogs and so on. If available, the internal communications department can advise on corporate style to use for both internal and external communications. The words used are important; they can be used to influence and persuade, equally they can demotivate and make people switch off. See Section 5.2 on appealing to hearts and minds through using metaphors and storytelling.

Listening

This is quite likely the most underrated form of communication and yet it can be the most powerful way of connecting and building rapport with people. See Chapter 9, Section C on active listening. When people are experiencing change and the emotional journey that goes with it, they need to know that their concerns have been heard, before they can move to participating and engaging with change. The only way to assess whether your efforts in implementing change are going according to plan, is by listening to others' opinions and views. This feedback gives you the vital information needed to make change happen.

CASE STUDY

An organization that was struggling after a merger and had been drifting strategically, with the help of a new CEO wanted to change its culture to a more open and trusting environment, where people felt they could have their say. They set up an initiative for all managers and leaders to arrange open forums, to allow people to talk about whatever was on their mind. There was no set agenda. The only rule stipulated was that the managers and leaders in these sessions were not to speak, only listen! After each session, the topics of discussion, and how people felt about these, were recorded via an online portal, so that the information could be reported back to the board. Thousands of people participated in these sessions and, even though it was clearly out of many people's comfort zone, the results led to a major transformation in the organization. Senior management had to start addressing the issues that actually mattered to people. It also helped to create a more open and trusting environment where people felt more comfortable speaking up about the matters that concerned them.

Visual

The saying 'a picture speaks a thousand words' is very apt, as the brain is capable of subconsciously absorbing very large amounts of information almost instantly, whereas it is much slower at processing words. Visuals can act as a mental shortcut for the brain and the simplest image can quickly communicate an important message as well as emotion (Figure 5.8).

FIGURE 5.8 Visual communication

Using visual diagrams and images can make communication more effective and help to reinforce important messages. I say 'can' rather than 'will' as the visuals need to support the intended message and be appropriate for the audience.

An icon is a classic example of a symbol that is representative of a message (Figure 5.9). Airports the world over use the same easily and universally recognized icons to help direct people to where they need to go. Company logos, brand names, type of office and location, the pictures and posters on the wall, are also visual symbols that send out a message. Visual forms of communicating are non-verbal and include use of signals, gestures and body language.

FIGURE 5.9 Iconic symbols

> *'You cannot not communicate.'*
>
> Watzlawick
>
> Meaning that we cannot help but communicate something, even when we are not saying anything. Communication occurs anyway, non-verbally through our facial expressions and gestures.

CASE STUDY

One organization chose to use posters to launch a major change initiative around health and safety. Posters were chosen, as they work well both in digital form and print, and they wanted to cater for a diverse, international population, some of whom were comfortable with the digital world whereas others were not or did not have easy access to the internet. The change team met with communications experts to share the key themes and messages to be portrayed. Other channels were used with posters to promote the change initiative, such as blogs and newsletter updates. People were encouraged to vote for their favourite posters and share their feedback on them, either online or via suggestion boxes. The result was that it created more conversation and people engaged with the change initiative more readily.

3. Fostering collaboration

During any change initiative there is a need to bring groups of people together, to share information, exchange ideas and generate solutions to challenging issues. These groups can be brought together in larger numbers or in smaller, more informal settings.

3.1 *Larger group gatherings*

A traditional view of a large-scale gathering may be that of a big conference, with spotlights pointed towards the speakers standing on the stage talking from PowerPoint slides, whilst the audience sits under dimmed lights, listening passively. That is one way of 'pushing' information to large numbers of people. However, there are no guarantees that the information is understood and this limits a rich exchange of ideas.

Fortunately, there are other ways to bring larger groups together that enable fuller participation and exchange of ideas. Examples include World Café events and Open Space Technology (Chapter 10, Section E5).

3.2 *Smaller face-to-face interpersonal communication channels*

Effective communication and engagement requires two-way interaction (Frahm and Brown, 2006). The effectiveness of face-to-face communication is easily overlooked, but this remains highly valued by employees across all sectors.

This type of interaction can take place in different ways: for example, as one-to-one meetings, group meetings or around the 'water cooler'. Especially during the early stages of change, people need opportunities for conversation to share their thoughts, be listened to, ask questions and exchange ideas. Holding sessions like this provides valuable feedback about what people's concerns are, and allows misunderstandings to be addressed.

Keep in mind that cultural differences will have an effect: for example, in some cultures a strong respect for hierarchy and position may inhibit junior and younger members of staff asking questions or challenging their superiors. Effective facilitation skills and creating a safe and comfortable environment can help to overcome this (see Chapter 10 for more on facilitation and Chapter 7, Section C1 for more on creating a psychological contract). Change managers have a key role to play in supporting and preparing leaders and managers for getting the most from these sessions and creating opportunities for meaningful conversations.

Tip

Keep group sizes for these types of discussions small. This helps create a comfortable and trusting environment where people feel safe to speak out. It encourages the kind of interaction that will build relationships and encourage respect for conflicting views.

3.3 Social media and community-building channels

The emergence of a wide range of social media technologies allows for faster, richer exchanges and wider levels of collaboration than were previously possible. The first era of social enterprise platforms was about facilitating a sharing of knowledge and increasing transparency. The technological developments that have followed add the 'social' dimension, allowing people to connect in a more meaningful way, to help build communities and deliver results (CIPR, 2012). These communities cut across functional and geographic divisions, allowing people to share the issues that really matter to them, but on a much wider scale. They are an effective way to increase interaction across diverse groups, share and exchange ideas and increase collaboration.

Social media includes a wealth of options, including systems such as Facebook, Skype and LinkedIn, and enterprise social networks, which can be controlled to limit access to an organization's employees only, such as Tibbr, Jive and Yammer. New channels are becoming available at an increasingly rapid pace. The extent to which these can meet the objectives of the organization should remain the primary driver for deciding which channels to adopt.

It is important to stress that communication strategies cannot rely on real-time social media interactions alone. More traditional channels, such as intranets, printed documents, and interpersonal interactions with people at all levels, will continue to be important. Each channel serves a different purpose, so a wide range of options should be planned for in order to meet the communication challenges during any change initiative.

CASE STUDY

In one organization, a 'Rumour Buster' group was set up online and they chose to use a number of different channels to support this. Employees were encouraged to post online anything they had heard, and to ask about it. Members of the executive and senior team responded personally. Alongside this, physical post-boxes were placed across the organization, providing the option for people to physically post their rumours anonymously. A champion of the scheme would then post it online on their behalf, so that both the query and the answer could be viewed more widely.

This scheme helped to increase the visibility of the senior executive team, and allowed front-line employees to engage directly with them on their priority issues. The company also organized live question-and-answer sessions between senior teams and staff. It proved to be a great way for them to ask any strategic questions and opened up lines of communication that had not been available before.

Potential strengths of social media

It allows for:

- quick feedback and response to questions;
- increased levels of interaction and engagement;
- connectivity across diverse groups in different geographic locations;
- access to senior management;
- mass communication to spread updates about progress quickly and in an informal way;
- rich communication through use of multiple formats such as images and video;
- people to generate content by adding their own stories and examples;
- building a sense of community and belonging during the uncertainties of change.

Potential pitfalls of social media

These are:

- Increased risk of leaks of confidential information to the wider public, where open platforms are used, ie they are not restricted access.
- Negative comments about the organization, if not managed well, can lead to reputational damage.
- Additional resource is required to help build and sustain social media interaction.
- Lack of strategic purpose and focus in directing how it should be used, so it fails to achieve tangible results.
- Data protection issues on personal data that is collected and used on social media.
- Legal grey areas around personal privacy for comments posted on personal accounts, but which can be seen by the wider public.

Best practice guidelines

These guidelines are helpful for getting the most from social media channels:

- Link social media objectives clearly to the communications strategy for change.
- Train people in social media use so they are comfortable using it.

- Put best practice guidelines in place about what is acceptable and what is not.
- Establish governance to monitor adherence to a clear social media policy.
- Have dedicated resource to generate content and interaction to help build momentum.
- Seek commitment from all levels of management for use of social media.
- Put monitoring systems and processes in place to measure its effectiveness.

Guidelines are essential, especially in those professions where there may be legal restrictions around the information that can be shared; for instance, in the health-care industry where patient confidentiality is key. Social media enables unmediated, quick, peer-to-peer communication without any control from above. This can be challenging within a traditional top-down hierarchical organization with a culture of controlling communication in a top-down fashion. Leaders will also need to demonstrate its use, and be seen to be fully involved with social media, if they are expecting their people to engage with it. It can take time for social communications to become embedded in an organization, so be patient and plan for this.

CASE STUDY

In one company where a social network had been implemented, the uptake had been low. The HR director stopped sending company updates by e-mail, and only made them available on their enterprise social media network. It became obvious that some people seemed much better informed and 'in the know' about company updates than their colleagues. These were the people who had been the early adopters of the social network. People soon changed their behaviour and started accessing the network, as they had no other option and they did not want to be left out. Training sessions were offered about how to use the new tools. They now have four times the industry average rate of participation.

Timmerman (2003) suggests that a pre-planned, top-down programmatic approach to implementation is likely to be associated with 'official' media that emphasize one-way communication. An adaptive approach – one that is more emergent and responsive to stakeholders as conditions and reactions are altered during the course of an implementation effort – will involve use of both formal and informal media, as well as channels that are more interactive and that will accommodate feedback about the implementation effort.

Summary

An effective communications strategy will include a balanced portfolio of communication channels, which meets the needs of the different audience members, is convenient for them and suits their preferences. There are many different types of channels that can be used within organizations. They can be very simple, such as the use of the visual emoticons to represent emotional involvement and use of posters. Or they can take the form of enterprise-wide social media platforms or large-scale, face-to-face events, which encourage greater sharing of ideas and collaboration amongst wider groups.

All those involved in communicating change should look for opportunities to use different types and combinations of channels to support their communication efforts. This will ensure they achieve the appropriate levels of understanding and engagement from people during change.

Questions to think about

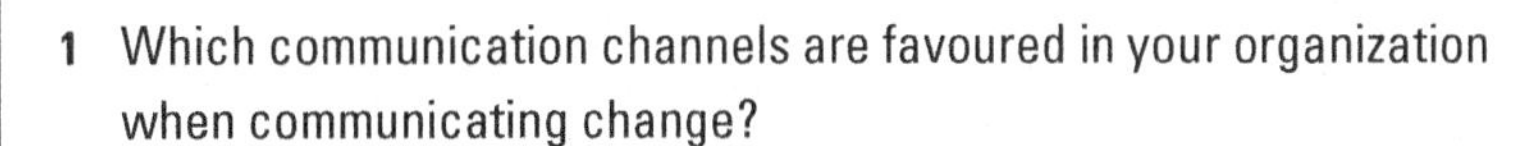

1. Which communication channels are favoured in your organization when communicating change?
2. Which channels have you found to be the most effective in recent change situations?
3. What needs to be done to make better use of the range of channels available to you?

Section D: Communication planning

Introduction

During any change initiative, people need to understand:

- why change is necessary;
- what is involved;
- how it will impact them;
- what role they can play in making change happen;
- what happens next.

Effective communication aims to get the answers to people in a timely way and get them engaged with the process. To do this, communication planning needs to find ways to:

- *Provide information*: to keep people updated with relevant and timely information, ideas and concepts.
- *Provide the context for change*: people need to understand the bigger picture surrounding the changes and be able to relate it to their own situations. This provides a map that helps them navigate through what may otherwise be seen as chaos.
- *Engage people*: allowing them to develop a shared understanding, exchange ideas, relay concerns and contribute to making change happen.
- *Evaluate and gather feedback*: to check how communication is being received and whether it has been effective.

Planning for effective communication

Consistent communication that is impactful and effective in supporting a change initiative requires thorough planning and focus all the way through (Quirke, 2008). Figure 5.10 shows a framework for communication planning. It starts with defining and agreeing an overall communication strategy that clearly outlines the objectives and approach required to support the change initiative. This is used as a basis for a communication plan, which sets out how the strategy will be achieved, in terms of who will deliver, what, when, how and to whom. Communication activities then follow in line with the plan and suitable measures are put in place to check that the communication efforts are achieving the desired impact (Pilkington, 2013). See Section E for more on monitoring and evaluation of communication activities.

FIGURE 5.10 Communication planning framework

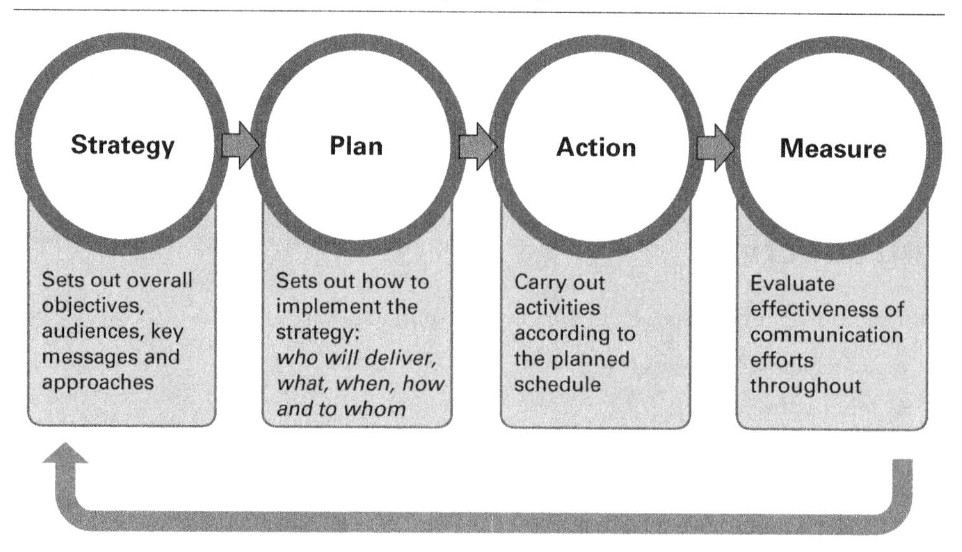

1. Developing a communication strategy for change

A communication strategy outlines how the communication objectives for the change initiative will be met and helps to guide and keep activities focused. The following seven steps can be used to develop a communication strategy.

1.1 *Understand the organizational context* (why *we're doing it)*

What is the nature of the targeted change, and the culture and environment within which this change is taking place? Find out why it is happening, what are the drivers for it, how it links to the wider business strategy and what are the expected benefits (see Chapter 2 on defining change; and Chapter 3 on benefits management). Consider how ready the organization is for change (see also Chapter 7 on change readiness), and what is the priority for this change initiative. Answers to these questions will influence the extent of communication activity required and the approaches and channels to be used.

1.2 *Analyse the audience/stakeholders* (who *we're communicating with)*

Identify the different groups of people/stakeholders who are potentially impacted by the change initiative and need to be communicated with and engaged (see Chapter 4 on stakeholder strategy). Consider where these people are in terms of their awareness, understanding, attitude to change and levels of resistance. This analysis should include what their key concerns are, how the change is likely to impact them, and the issues they face in dealing with change. When there are time pressures, it can be tempting to make assumptions in order to move ahead, but it is essential to take the time to do research and gather as much information as possible. Thoroughly understanding the audience – the receivers of the communication – will ensure that communication efforts are effective.

1.3 *Set communication objectives* (what *we want to happen)*

The analysis from these first two steps gives a better understanding of what is required from people in terms of changed behaviours, attitudes and perceptions. Some groups may just require up-to-date information and reassurance that there is no need to be unduly concerned; others may need details of specific actions required if they are in denial about the change; others may require more support and guidance to help them accept change and become more engaged in shaping it. Consider what each audience needs to know, think, feel and do as a result of the change, before defining specific communication objectives for each of the groups. Objectives should be measurable so that progress can be tracked and any problems in achieving them can be identified early. Objectives should also be linked to key milestones for the change initiative.

1.4 Select communication approaches (how we'll go about it)

Major cultural shifts or large-scale redundancies require a different approach to rolling out a computer system upgrade – because of the differing impacts on people. The need to change behaviours and attitudes requires higher levels of engagement. Simply informing people about change will not be enough, and approaches using richer forms of communication will be more suitable.

In the case of emergent change that will evolve, it needs to involve people in shaping how it comes about. When the change is driven in a programmatic fashion with a clear directive and vision from the top, the emphasis will be on how to inform and 'push' down clear messages through the tiers of management in order to 'sell' the idea to people. At every stage, measure the effectiveness of communication, to track progress and adjust the level of 'push' in messages. The effectiveness measures can be shared, to highlight the benefits of the initiative and prompt information demands, increasing levels of 'pull'.

Tip

A common mistake is to try and 'sell' the change too early, before people are ready to accept that change will happen. Beware of this and pay attention to where people are in terms of their levels of awareness and commitment.

1.5 Develop key messages and themes (what we're going to say)

People need to hear consistent communication messages from multiple sources, which must include their immediate managers and more senior leaders across the organization. This plays a big part in gaining their confidence and overcoming resistance during change. Identifying and documenting the key messages, as a part of the communication strategy, will ensure that the change team, managers and leaders are all delivering consistent information.

Change managers need to bring key stakeholders together to agree what the objectives and messages should be. It is very important for the sponsor and change manager to ensure that everyone agrees on the key messages. This may take longer than expected, but it is worth the effort. Just a few well-timed key messages should focus on the needs of each audience group, so that people are not overwhelmed with information, which could result in as much confusion as offering no information at all.

Messages do not have to be just factual data; they can be put into a narrative form, to develop a story for the change. Different narratives can be used, one at the organization-wide level, and other versions that are more specific to different audience groups.

Use a variety of formats to suit different preferences and have both short and long versions of the messages, ie something that can be stated in less than one minute such as an 'elevator pitch', as well as longer versions. Communication packs with presentation slide packs, frequently asked question sets and so on, all help with providing consistency of messages. Change managers should proactively seek out the right information from the sponsor and other key stakeholders.

Tip

Do the research to find out which issues are important to the audience, and what a good outcome may look like for them. Use this to define the communication objectives for each audience group, and identify what the messages should be and how you will track whether those outcomes have actually been achieved.

1.6 *Identify who will deliver key messages* (who *needs to deliver messages*)

It is helpful to understand the informal communications networks in an organization, and identify the key influencers within different groups (Chapter 4, Section B3). Getting these individuals engaged and involved means that others will follow. Choosing the right champions and ambassadors for change, and using these at the right points during the process, is key for overcoming resistance and moving people along the change journey. It is important to agree clear roles at the outset, around who is saying what to which audience and when. For instance, those impacted by health and safety, financial, or manufacturing changes will have very different perspectives. Each area of change is likely to be introduced by a senior executive, but followed up by a more local representative who can discuss the detailed implications, such as their immediate manager or a 'change agent' (Chapter 1, Section D and Chapter 7, Section A4). Equally, it is helpful for senior executives to be seen explaining the changes and responding adeptly to reactions. At different stages, people have different levels of relevance and credibility. In the early stages of the communication process, more focus can be on leaders to set the vision and direction. As change progresses, the focus will shift to more front-line or direct managers, who can discuss the specific details that are directly relevant for people.

1.7 *Select communication channels* (how *the messages will get there)*

Different communication channels have different characteristics and should be selected to meet the needs of the strategy, the message and the audience. First, decisions need to be made about which channels should be used, and for what purpose. It is then important that channels are used consistently to avoid confusing the audience, as they will get used to expecting a certain type of communication from each different channel. Channels such as newsletters, or e-mail communications, are good for raising awareness, and for bulletin-style updates, but fuller participation and engagement requires face-to-face events such as workshops, round-table discussions and focus groups (Section C discusses communication channels).

2. Developing the communication plan (*when* and *how* we will make it happen)

The information and understanding gained from creating the communication strategy is then used to develop a communication plan (Figure 5.11).

FIGURE 5.11 Communication strategy and plan

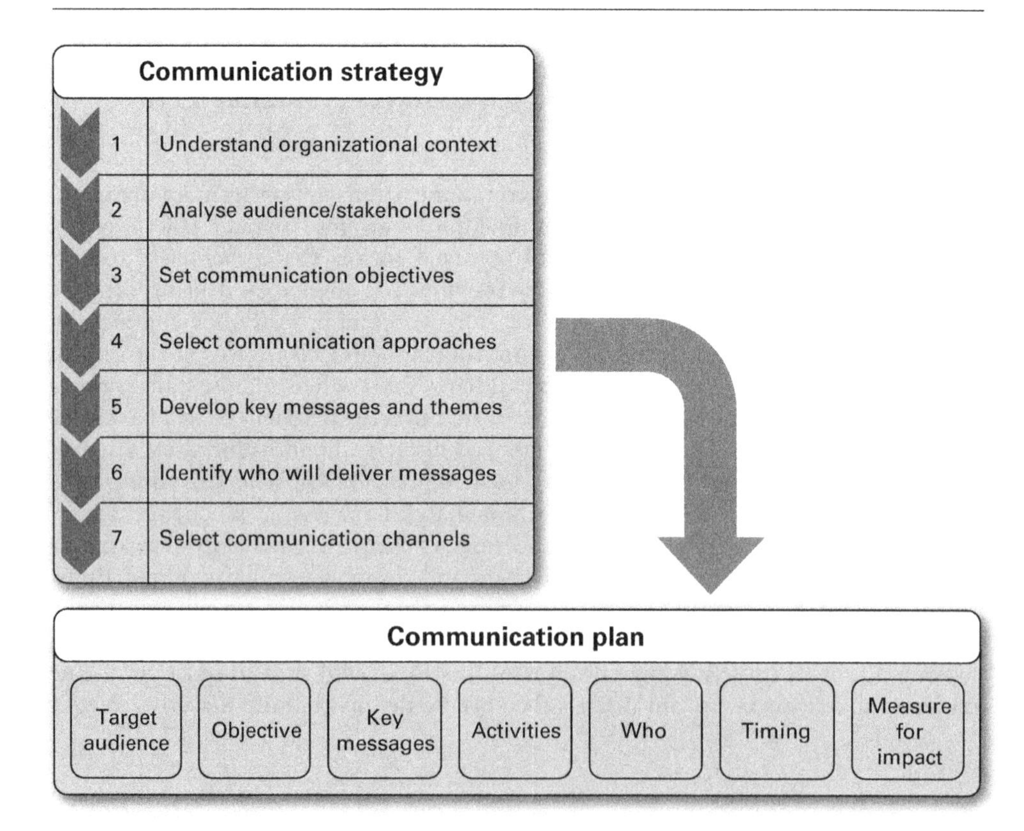

Setting out a well-considered communication plan will ensure that timely, appropriate and consistent activity takes place to deliver all the objectives set out in the communication strategy. It shows who is going to deliver what, when, to whom and how that will be measured, by setting out:

- the target audience;
- the objective that is to be achieved for that audience;
- the key messages to communicate;
- the activity that will deliver those messages and achieve that objective;
- the person(s) responsible for that communication;
- the timing of activities;
- how the activity will be measured.

Figure 5.12 shows an example extract of a communication plan. It can be difficult depicting all the necessary information, especially the detail of the activities and their

FIGURE 5.12 Extract from a communication plan

Audience	Steering Group	Heads of Departments and Managers
Overall objective of communication	They remain committed to supporting this change	They become enthusiastic about the change and actively engaged in change activities with their teams
Key messages	Drivers and benefits for change and clear vision Narrative for why we are doing this and what the benefits will be Progress update	Narrative for why we are doing this and the benefits. What this means for them – impact and new opportunities Actions required of them: Develop key messages and narrative for their areas Conduct briefing sessions with their teams Give their input into content of briefing packs
Activities and timing	Monthly face-to-face meetings Fortnightly progress update reports – first and third Tuesdays of the month	Initial offsite meeting, with external facilitator to explore issues and develop key messages – (by end of next month) Breakfast meeting – with a member of the senior leadership team and the sponsor. 1 day training session on use of social media and writing blogs Newsletter – with updates on progress, and featured stories about individuals' experiences so far, selected from people across different departments – (every two months) Sent via e-mail and placed on intranet Monthly face-to-face meetings
Owner	Change Manager	Change Manager
How activity will be measured	Attendance at meetings Turnaround time on decisions they need to make is within 2 days	Attendance at sessions Feedback gathered in one-to-one discussions

FIGURE 5.13 Extract from a communication schedule

Audience	Activity	Owner	First Quarter															
			Month 1				Month 2				Month 3				Month 4			
			1	2	3	4	1	2	3	4	1	2	3	4	1	2	3	4
Steering Group	Progress report	Programme Manager	x		x		x		x		x		x		x		x	
	Meeting	Change Manager				x				x				x				x
Heads of Departments and Managers	Initial off-site meeting with external facilitator	Change Manager				x												
	Breakfast meeting	Change Manager			x													
	Newsletter									x								x

timing. If this is the case, information from the communication plan about the activities and their timing can be shown separately in a communication schedule. Figure 5.13 shows an example extract of a communication schedule.

Summary

Effective communication is such a critical aspect of managing change that it needs careful consideration from the very start of the change initiative. Those involved in communicating change should understand the aims of the change initiative, consider the terrain and culture within which change is taking place, and use the information gathered from thorough stakeholder analysis to devise appropriate communication strategies and plans for change. The planning process needs to include a careful consideration of the target audiences, the tone and content of the messages, the most effective channels to use, the timing for messages, and how results will be monitored and evaluated. Following a structured approach, as outlined in the steps above, allows you to develop effective plans to maintain a consistent and effective communication effort throughout the change initiative.

Questions to think about

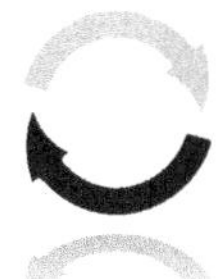

1. How much agreement is there on the communication objectives and key messages amongst your key stakeholders?
2. How did you test whether the key messages were relevant and appropriate for the different stakeholder groups?
3. Do you have regular and varied communication activities scheduled across all the stakeholder groups identified?

Section E: Monitoring and evaluating communication effectiveness

Introduction

Regular monitoring and evaluation of the communications approach is essential to understand if the actions taken are getting the desired results. If they are not, this information will pinpoint the areas where more focus, or a different approach, is needed to ensure the planned benefits can be realized (see also Chapter 3, Sections C and D).

1. Deciding what to measure

Selecting the right things to measure is the critical ingredient for successful monitoring and evaluating. The communications strategy will dictate what needs to be measured and tracked. For example, the strategy will outline:

- What people will be doing differently as a result of the change – are they required to use new processes and systems or interact with customers differently?
- What key messages will they need to have become aware of, understood or acted upon?
- Which channels will be used?

Using this information will guide decisions on what should be measured and tracked as key indicators for success. Initial research can then be conducted to identify the current position of these indicators.

Tip

Always link what you measure to the communication strategy and key objectives.

2. Capturing data

There is no single perfect way to capture information, so a range of different methods will provide better results. Initial research will have to be done to find out the starting position at the beginning of a change initiative, so that improvements can be assessed against this initial baseline. The method selected will depend on what is to be measured. For example, for the communications channels to be used during the change initiative, initial research should identify whether these channels are used currently and how effective they are.

This takes into account both quantity and quality dimensions, which are sometimes referred to as 'reach' and 'richness'. The 'reach' refers to the number of people who, for example, receive a newsletter, and the 'richness' refers to the number who have understood the key messages or taken some action. There are many technology tools available to measure activity, such as how many people read a blog, newsletter or other online content, or whether people click on further links, add comments and so on. These methods are useful for measuring the activity taking place. However, it is more useful to know who is actually reading this content and what impact it has. To understand this, more interaction is required, through the use of methods such as surveys, focus groups, observation and individual interviews (Chapter 7, Section D2).

How well people respond to surveys and requests for feedback depends very much on the way they are asked for this information and how this process is managed:

- Let people know that their feedback is important. If they do not contribute, their voice will not be heard.
- Make it easy and accessible for them to make their contributions.
- Make it clear that the purpose of surveys and questions is to measure the effectiveness of the communication activities and improve them – it is not a test to assess people.
- Follow through with regular updates on how that feedback has been used and the difference it has made.

CASE STUDY

An organization encourages feedback by having senior management team members hold forums for those who responded, to talk about the actions that have been taken directly as a result of their contributions. It is also a question-and-answer session and an opportunity for people to discuss further ideas directly with the senior management team. All actions that have been taken are published online, and stories about these are developed and communicated widely.

3. Monitoring and evaluating data

The data gathered from the activities outlined in the communications plan needs to be analysed, interpreted and evaluated. Decisions can then be made about what actions are required to ensure the communications objectives are met.

For example, if the activities include sending a regular blog and holding team briefings to explain the planned changes, the data captured could include:

- when and how frequently the blog was sent/team briefings were held;
- how many people read the blog/attended the meetings;
- the list of comments added online to the blogs;
- feedback comments about the team briefings;
- responses from surveys or forums that captured additional feedback about how well informed people feel and their levels of understanding about the changes.

The metrics captured are helpful as they show the extent of involvement, ie how many people read the blog and how many comments there are, or how many attended the briefings and the ratings these were given. Evaluation of the data involves taking it further, and analysing the comments as well. This is where the more valuable information can be, which gives a better indication of people's level of understanding and engagement with the change and the types of issues and concerns they may be facing. This level of monitoring and evaluation should take place throughout the change initiative, so the resources required and the processes to make it happen need to be thought through carefully as part of communications planning. Also keep in mind that the level of involvement will vary according to where people are along the change initiative. In the early stages, when people are just becoming aware of the change, do not be surprised by low levels of responses and comments to blogs and articles, for example. However, if this is still the case close to major changes being implemented, then there is more reason to question the effectiveness of the communication.

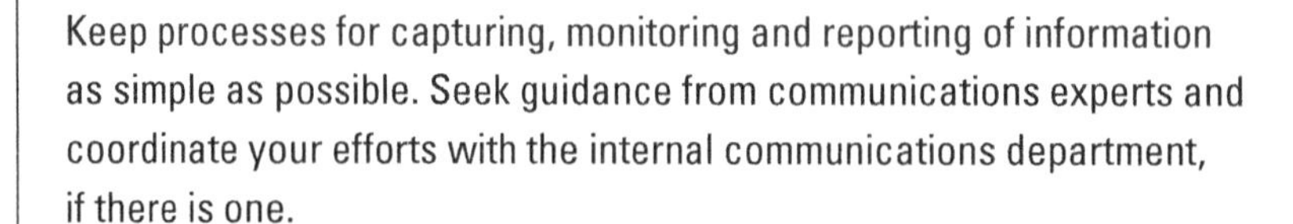

Tip

Keep processes for capturing, monitoring and reporting of information as simple as possible. Seek guidance from communications experts and coordinate your efforts with the internal communications department, if there is one.

4. Reporting results and improving engagement

Feedback works both ways. If people are being asked to take the time and effort to provide their input, in return they need to know what happens to that information and the resulting decisions. Knowing their efforts are making a real difference encourages people to become more engaged and helps to improve the effectiveness of communication. The communications plan should also include the activities for reporting results back to people. Practical considerations for reporting are:

- How will the information be presented to different audiences? Large spreadsheets of endless figures may be meaningless to people. The data has to be translated into a narrative that explains the insights gathered about what is working and what is not. Different audiences require varying degrees of detail and are likely to want it in different formats, across different channels.
- How easily can the data be assembled for reporting? If it takes too long and is an overly cumbersome process, it will not be sustainable and enthusiasm to continue this throughout the change initiative will wane. It helps to have responsibilities and processes agreed as part of the initial communications planning.

The outputs from monitoring and evaluation are invaluable for change managers and other key roles involved in the change process. They can share this type of information with the sponsor, the change team and all those who are involved in communicating change. It will highlight where communication activities are effective and where a different approach or more focus is needed. After all, the purpose of the evaluation is so that you can take necessary action and adapt your approach, to get better results from the communication activities.

CASE STUDY

One organization's internal communications department introduced a new evaluation methodology and dashboard for their communications activities, combining data and presenting it in a visual way. At one level it showed performance against the key objectives identified, another level showed more information about the amount of activity and the outcomes achieved in terms of quality. Summary descriptions were added to communicate the story behind the numbers. They chose to produce monthly updates, to encourage an ongoing focus on communication activities, and the early identification of any negative trends. The results were made available to everyone, and the communications team had briefing sessions with managers and leaders linked to the main objectives being monitored. They found an unexpected benefit of this new approach was that everyone involved appreciated the importance of continuous monitoring and evaluation, whereas initially there had been considerable resistance to introducing this level of analysis and rigour to their communication activities.

Summary

The outputs from monitoring and evaluation are invaluable for change managers and the other key roles involved in the change process. This information will highlight where communications have been fully understood, whether those affected are becoming fully engaged in the process, and where collaboration is making the best contribution. By dedicating time and effort to planning the approach and processes for monitoring and evaluating communications throughout a change initiative, improvements can continually be made to future communication plans and activities. The effort involved in doing this should not be underestimated, and yet this area cannot be neglected. The effectiveness of communications leads to the effectiveness of the overall change initiative.

Questions to think about

1. How do you measure the effectiveness of the different communication channels used?
2. How often do you plan to capture feedback during the change initiative?
3. What mechanisms are in place to let people know about the actions that have resulted from the feedback they provided?

Further reading

Blundel, R, Ippolito, K and Donnarumma, D (2008) *Effective Organisational Communication*, 3rd edn, Pearson Education, Harlow

Denning, S (2005) *The Leader's Guide to Storytelling: Mastering the art and discipline of business narrative*, Wiley, San Francisco

Smythe, J (2007) *The CEO, Chief Engagement Officer: Turning hierarchy upside down to drive performance*, Gower Publishing Ltd, Aldershot

References

Blundel, R, Ippolito, K and Donnarumma, D (2013) *Effective Organisational Communication*, 3rd edn, Pearson Education, Harlow

Charvet, R (1997) *Words That Change Minds: Mastering the language of influence*, 2nd rev. edn, Kendall/Hunt Publishing, US

CIPR (Chartered Institute of Public Relations) (2012) *Share This: The social media handbook for PR professionals*, Kindle edn, Wiley, Chichester

Deitz, K and Silverman, L (2014) *Business Storytelling for Dummies*, Kindle edn, Wiley & Sons, New Jersey

Denning, S (2011) *The Leader's Guide to Storytelling: Mastering the art and discipline of business narrative*, Kindle edn, Josey-Bass, San Francisco, CA

Fill, C and Jamieson, B (2006) [accessed 15 July 2013] *Marketing Communications*, e-book, Edinburgh Business School, Heriot-Watt University library [Online] http://coursewebsites.ebsglobal.net

Fiske, J (1996) *Introduction to Communication Studies*, 2nd edn, Routledge, London

Frahm, J and Brown, K (2006) [accessed 19 July 2013] Developing communicative competencies for a learning organization, *Journal of Management Development*, 25 (3), pp 201–12 [Online] www.emeraldinsight.com

Kahneman, D (2012) *Thinking Fast and Slow*, Penguin, London

Kanter, R M (2005) [accessed 20 July 2013] Leadership for change: enduring skills for change masters, *Harvard Business Review* [Online] http://www.hbsp.harvard.edu
Larkin, T J and Larkin, S (1994) *Communicating Change*, McGraw Hill, New York
Lewis, L K (2011) *Organisational Change: Creating change through strategic communication*, Wiley-Blackwell, Chichester
Mehrabian, A (1981) *Silent Messages: Implicit communication of emotions and attitudes*, Wadsworth Publishing Company, Belmont CA
Pilkington, A (2013) *Communicating Projects*, Gower Publishing, Surrey
Quirke, B (2008) *Making the Connections: Using internal communication to turn strategy into action*, Kindle edn, Gower, Surrey
Rock, D (2009) *Your Brain at Work*, HarperCollins, New York
Rose, C (2010) *How to Win Campaigns: Communications for change*, Kindle Edn, Earthscan, London
Shannon, C E and Weaver, W (1949) *The Mathematical Theory of Communication*, University of Illinois Press
Smith, L and Mounter, P (2008) *Effective Internal Communication (PR in Practice)*, Kindle edn, Kogan Page, London
Smythe, J (2007) *The CEO, Chief Engagement Officer: Turning hierarchy upside down to drive performance*, Gower Publishing Ltd, Aldershot
Timmerman, C E (2003) Media selection during the implementation of planned organizational change, *Management Communication Quarterly*, **16** (3), pp 301–40

Change impact

06

CAROLINE PERKINS

Introduction

Planned organizational change intends to impact the 'business as usual' aspects of the organization in some way or another. These impacts can be both positive and negative, and can affect individuals, teams, business units, the organization as a whole, customers and other external groups. Change can create great disturbance and turbulence in an organization and care is needed to balance 'managing the change' and the ongoing task of 'managing the business'.

Pascale (1999) highlights the difficulty of gaining order in chaotic, uncertain times. His research explains that living systems are difficult to direct due to a weak understanding of cause-and-effect linkages and, as such, our best laid efforts to intervene in a system – to change it or even to replicate it artificially – almost always miss the mark. The best-laid plans are often perverted through self-interest, misinterpretation, or lack of the necessary skills to reach the intended goal.

Identifying and analysing the impact of change is one of the keys to effective change management planning and helps to avoid, or at least minimize, the disruptive effects and support the positive aspects of the change. When assessing the impacts it is important to bear in mind that there is often an organizational 'Pollyanna' effect (when someone thinks only good things will happen or finds something good in everything, after the heroine of the novel *Pollyanna* by Eleanor Porter, 1913). This leads to a tendency to downplay the change, thinking it is easier than it is, and downplaying the impacts.

Tip

As a rough rule of thumb, the more it costs, or the bigger the benefits, then the more potential to disrupt business as usual (BAU) operations. Ask the question, 'Why spend all this money if there is no change?'

FIGURE 6.1 Change impact, risk and continuity interplay

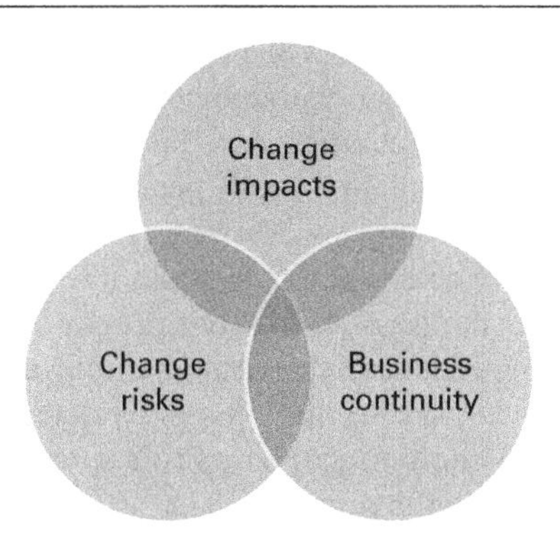

Viewing change management as an important risk management strategy is useful. A comprehensive change plan manages the interplay between the planned change impacts, the risks of the organization *not* gaining the required benefits from change, and business-as-usual continuity (Figure 6.1).

Those leading and participating in change, including people in key change roles, business managers and stakeholders must work together to fully identify the full implications and potential impacts of change. This includes assessing the risks and opportunities associated with change, and bridging the gap between the current and future business environment. The following sections outline how this interplay between impact, risk and business continuity can be assessed and managed.

CHAPTER CONTENTS

Section A: Assessing the impact of change

Introduction

Change impact assessment is the process that analyses the impacts and implications of a change initiative on all aspects of the business, the operations and its people and customers, as a basis for decision making and planning for a change initiative.

Once the change has been properly defined it is important to conduct a full assessment of the impact. The results and insights gained from this activity will have a bearing on how and if the change will proceed. This places the change impact assessment at the heart of the change management process.

Assessing the impacts of the change can be a complex exercise as it brings together all the elements of the change itself, personal responses to the change, the environment within which the change is occurring and other competing demands on people's time, whether at work or in their personal lives.

Assessing the impact of change is a two-step process. The first step is to identify the impacts, from the perspective of the organization, implementation and stakeholder. Once this is complete, the second step is to determine the severity of these impacts for each of the stakeholder groups, taking into account the environmental and change maturity of the organization.

This section covers:

- Methods and techniques for conducting a change impact analysis (including heat maps and process mapping) to gather relevant data and information that addresses the wider implications of change for the organization, its structure, processes, people and stakeholders.
- Methods for evaluating and quantifying the effects and costs of managing the positive effects (benefits) on the one hand, and the unexpected negative consequences (dis-benefits or ripple effect) of change on the other.

1. Identifying change impacts

1.1 Categorizing change impacts

Change impacts can be categorized in three ways:

- *The intended change:* the vision of the new world, the removal of barriers to get there and the disruption to productivity while absorbing the change.

  This is the most important to understand and to plan for. Not only should we examine what is in scope but also what is out of scope for the change initiative, as often this is in scope for the change plan. For example, there is a need to communicate to a business area that they will not be using a new system or receiving a process fix when they were expecting to.
- *The unintended/unplanned outcome:* system outages, process workarounds and misdiagnosed behavioural responses are a few of these.

  This is the category that can have the most long-term impact. It is important to understand that as the change initiative progresses the unintended consequences grow. Constantly reviewing the unintended impacts with key stakeholders, and ensuring that decisions are being made with full understanding of them, is a key change management activity.
- *The change management activities:* the involvement of subject matter experts (SMEs) impacts business as usual, time spent in scheduled training, or in leadership change coaching.

This is the easiest to assess and often how the 'change impact' is articulated to a business area, as they are tangible and have an immediate effect. It is important that these are also explained in context of the planned and unplanned impacts.

It is important to fully examine all impact areas, and to ensure that business leaders gain understanding and sign off on this understanding. As introduced earlier, it is common for businesses to underestimate the impacts of a change (often overstating the benefits at the same time), and the earlier they are understood the less risk for the organization.

CASE STUDY

A manufacturing organization is introducing a new enterprise resource planning (ERP) system in order to gain cost reduction benefits by fewer people being required to run the system. This requires redundancies, centralization of the function, new jobs, new processes and training. A complex change, with a number of organizational dependencies and risks that will need to be managed successfully to ensure the ultimate cost reduction is realized.

Key inputs

When starting to identify the impacts of any change initiative there are a number of key inputs, the most important of which are:

- *The detailed proposal and plans for the change initiative*: these will have identified the change, the deliverables, and the benefits of and the risks to the change happening. For the sake of completeness the change plans should also identify high level impacts, and activities to manage those impacts, as a basis for the change management budget. If this level of analysis was not completed as part of the planning phase, it should be done as part of the impact assessment phase.
- *The gap analysis* (also covered in Chapter 2, Section D3): this forms a high-level view of the starting point (current state) and the ending point (future state) of the organization and therefore the gap that needs to be managed.
- *The stakeholder assessment*: this will help you to identify the key business areas and whether external stakeholders (ie customers) will be impacted. Chapter 4 explores this in more detail.

There are a number of useful models that can be used as a guide to identify change impacts as they relate to the organizational and the implementation aspects of the initiative, as shown below.

FIGURE 6.2 The McKinsey 7-S model (McKinsey & Company)

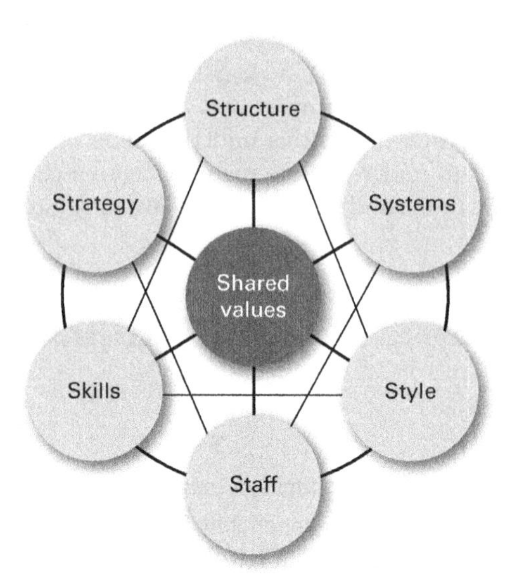

1.2 Organizational impacts

To aid the assessment of the intended change the McKinsey 7-S model (Figure 6.2), developed by Tom Peters and Robert Waterman (1982), identified seven internal aspects of an organization that need to be aligned and mutually re-enforcing if it is to be successful:

1. *Strategy*: the plan devised to maintain and build competitive advantage over the competition.
2. *Structure*: the way the organization is structured and who reports to whom.
3. *Systems*: the daily activities and procedures that staff members engage in to get the job done.
4. *Shared values*: called 'superordinate goals' when the model was first developed, these are the core values of the organization that are evidenced in the corporate culture and the general work ethic.
5. *Style*: the style of leadership adopted.
6. *Staff*: the employees and their general capabilities.
7. *Skills*: the actual skills and competencies of the employees working for the organization.

Regardless of the type of change initiative, this model can be used to understand how a change made in one area can impact the others, and what sort of realignment may be required to keep all elements of the organization productive.

The gap analysis process forms a high-level change view of the starting point (current or 'as is' state) and the ending point (future or 'to be' state) of the organization. Using the McKinsey model to assess the gap will help to determine the impact and the project or programme activities that are involved in realizing the organizational strategy of the initiative.

CASE STUDY

Table 6.1 provides an illustration of a gap analysis for a project to implement a shared services model for an organization. This shows how the McKinsey model can guide the assessment of the intended change of the organization and the project activities that are required to embed the change.

The change activities need to support and address both the 'gap' and the barriers to change. Using a formal approach such as this will help to identify impacts that may have been missed without looking at the organizational interconnectivities. For instance, examining the shared values element identifies that a cultural awareness and collaboration programme will be required across internal and external teams.

TABLE 6.1 Change 'gap' analysis using the McKinsey model 7-S

7-S	Current State	Future State	Change Gap	Issues/ Barriers to Change	Project Change Activities
Strategy	Decentralized approach to HR services, some centralization of finance functions	Finance/HR – shared services strategy to provide value-added services and automate/ outsource transactional work	Agreement to the vision of the organization and the success measures to be employed	Business areas that previously had embedded resources are not willing to give them up, causing build back	Engagement and awareness programme for executive leadership
Structure	Multiple execs and decentralized structures	Single exec of shared services, reduced management layers	New structure, & reinforcing financial and HR system enablers	IR implications for more junior staff Staff freeze may hinder redeployment opportunities	Organizational redesign programme Billing system training

TABLE 6.1 *continued*

7-S	Current State	Future State	Change Gap	Issues/ Barriers to Change	Project Change Activities
System	Multiple finance and HR systems used across the organization	Single ERP system used for finance and HR activities	Knowledge and ability to use the new system and processes	Staff do not like the one-size-fits-all approach of the system	ERP training, coaching and support programmes available to staff in three centres (locations)
Shared Values	Values differ depending on organizational 'silo'	Collaborative ways of working will be emphasized – to support concept of virtual teaming	Collaboration platform across the business, including the outsourced teams	SharePoint™ platform available, not actively used by the organization, some cynicism of value	Collaborative ways of working and cultural awareness programmes
Style	Clear ownership of teams and resources	The introduction of a consulting model requires a change in leadership style and matrix management	Processes and RACI	Lack of clarity around role requirements, loss of productivity and motivation	Leadership training, coaching and support programme
Staff	Combination of transactional and relationship management capabilities	Combination of relationship management and consulting capabilities (due to outsourcing)	Internal consulting capability	May need to 'buy in' capability in the short term to meet immediate needs	Assessment centre and potential redundancy programme New job roles
Skills	Skills built over a number of years to incorporate workarounds	New consulting skills	Upskilling to value-add roles	Business areas may not understand the new model and not value the new skills	Consulting training, coaching and support programme

It is important to test the assumptions that have been made in deciding on the initiative strategy, as Chip and Dan Heath (2010) discovered in their recent research, what looks like a people problem is often a situation problem, and the simpler the solution the more realistic the change. Be very clear about the interventions that are required. For example, they explain that changing people's habits from drinking full fat to skimmed milk is a behavioural change in purchasing habits rather than a change in drinking habits, as families will drink whatever happens to be in the house!

Be wary of the concept of intuitive design and underestimating the difficulties for many people in coming to terms with new ways of working. The design itself is not automatically intuitive; designs are only intuitive if the user already has enough knowledge about the design to understand it and operate it, or the user has enough knowledge to work out how to operate it. The change manager has a role to help the designers ensure that the user has the required amount of knowledge to enable them to use their 'intuition'.

1.3 Implementation approach impacts

There are a number of key elements that should be documented within the change plans to help you understand the change impacts. Nohria and Khurana (1993) developed their own 7-S model, which can be a useful tool to assess the nature of the change, providing a complementary view to determine impacts.

Analysing each of the elements using the questions in Table 6.2 provides an alternative view of the change, which can help to further identify the impacts of the implementation approach used.

TABLE 6.2 Key change plan elements (adapted from Nohria and Khurana, 1993)

Element	Description	Questions to Aid the Change Impact Assessment
Strategic Intent	What is the vision? Is it specific (increase product by x) or is it broad and goals less defined (become more collaborative)?	What would be the employee attitude to the reasons for the change? Is this something they can buy in to and believe? Is it straightforward or confusing?
Substance	Is the change hard (systems, structure, strategy) or soft (skills, style, shared values)?	What does this mean for the type of interventions that are needed (capability gap assessment)?
Sequence	Is the change staggered or big bang?	Can the approach be used to trial outcomes and learn from initial approaches?

TABLE 6.2 *continued*

Element	Description	Questions to Aid the Change Impact Assessment
Style	Is the leadership style top-down (directive) or bottom-up (collaborative)? What are the norms for the organization?	Who will be involved in communication and engagement (selling the message)?
Scale	How many people will be impacted and what is the cost involved? Is this incremental or transformational change?	What options are available to logistically manage the change? Is there a history of this sort of change in the business, how well did it go?
Scope	Is the change organizational/ industry wide or specific to a business unit?	Are there multiple dependencies both internal and external to the organization?
Speed	What speed of change is required for success, immediate results or longer-term benefits?	How quickly and what effort is required to gain behavioural change and realize benefits?

The aforementioned *detailed* proposal and plans can provide the information required to assess the implementation approach impacts. Reviewing the stated business benefits or success measures can give a sense of the scale, scope and speed of the change. Benefits and the business case are addressed in Chapter 3, Section B4. Further information on financial aspects of change is available at Chapter 13, Section D.

CASE STUDY

For a change initiative where increased sales are the main benefit it is important to understand which customer segments and which distribution channels are key to realizing them, and therefore where the scale impacts will fall. The difference in segmentation approach, and therefore impacts, is shown in Table 6.3; the two options have very different impacts.

TABLE 6.3 Impacts of different segmentation approaches

Stated Business Benefit: Financial planners will be selling 5% more business using the new assessment system		
	Option 1	Option 2
Segmentation approach	All planners selling 5% more	20% of planners that do not currently sell high volumes selling 25% more
Change Management – Training Implications	All planners receive online training in the new process	Targeted planners receive face-to-face training and coaching

As previously stated, the *detailed* proposal and plans should also provide an insight into the assumptions that are made in determining the scope of the change initiative. It is important to look at what is in scope and also what is explicitly out of scope for the programme. Often it is the out-of-scope items that cause the most problems for the change programme as the new world butts up against the old world, with incompatible culture, systems, processes etc.

An example of this can be the methodology used to implement the change. Agile methodologies are becoming more and more prevalent as organizations respond to the constantly changing competitive environment (Chapter 8, Section A1.2). Not only does this bring challenges when assessing impacts – as the change may not be fully formed at the beginning of the project and 'emerge' as the design iterations complete – the move to agile methodology may be a change that needs to be managed in itself.

Tip

Introducing agile development methodologies impacts the business as follows:

- The vision may be unclear and difficult to communicate.
- Businesses are not used to or equipped for the new collaborative ways of working, sprints and stand ups.
- The pace of development and implementation may allow less time for training preparation and rollout.

FIGURE 6.3 Impact assessment steps

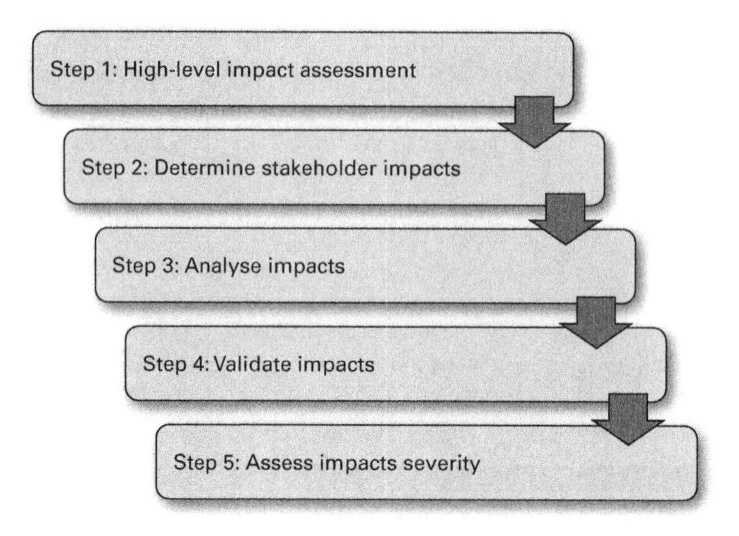

1.4 Stakeholder impact assessment

The stakeholder assessment looks at the scope of the change and identifies the key people and areas that need to be engaged to make the change happen (Chapter 4, Section A). This assessment helps to gauge the impacts at the next level of detail, the stakeholder impact assessment. Stakeholders can be both internal and external to the organization, and impacts can often extend further than initial assessment as more information becomes known.

The following stakeholder impact assessment steps should be followed (Figure 6.3):

Step 1: conduct a high-level impact assessment.

Step 2: determine the specific impacts on each stakeholder/group.

Step 3: analyse impacts in more detail for each business area.

Step 4: validate stakeholder impacts.

Step 5: assess the severity of change impacts.

Tip

When looking to understand stakeholder impacts, it is often useful to work back from the end receiver of the change. Ask: 'Who is the end receiver of the change, who supports them, and who supports this level?' All of these have a role in the change and impacts that will need to be managed. If the scope is organizational-wide it is often useful to look at the whole organizational structure and identify groups that are not impacted.

Step 1: conduct a high-level impact assessment

Start by conducting a high-level assessment of the change to determine the likely level of complexity for each stakeholder/group. This assessment also provides early insight into the required level of investment in the change effort.

CASE STUDY

An example stakeholder impact assessment for the introduction of a new website is shown in Table 6.4. In this instance it was more a case of taking the organizational structure and working out their role in setting up and managing the new website. As can be seen, although the initial assessment seemed to indicate a smooth and easy transition, further analysis identified quite a complex impact picture across a large number of stakeholder groups. The resulting high-level assessment helped to ensure the correct level of investment into change management activities.

TABLE 6.4 Stakeholder high-level impact assessment

Stakeholder Group	Nature of Change Impact
Media, Partners, Unions etc	Interested parties who may see the changes on the new website and misconstrue the nature of them without adequate communication and engagement.
Customer	The customers will experience a change to the website and may find it difficult to locate what they are looking for. This may lead to increased calls to the contact centre or complaints.
Distribution Channels	Third-party organizations use the existing website structures to automatically source quotes, these will no longer work. Financial advisers will be using the websites to find information for their customers and may find it difficult to locate what they are looking for. The content management processes need to be adjusted to support the new website, this includes sign-off responsibilities and writing/brand guidelines.
PR, Marketing & Sales	Sales teams need to play a role in making external parties aware of the website changes. Media play on the new brand and design, indicating a transformed organization.

TABLE 6.4 *continued*

Stakeholder Group	Nature of Change Impact
Customer Support	Call centres will be taking calls from the customers to help them navigate the new site.
Operational Support	The operational areas will provide second-level support to the call centres when they are not able to answer the customers' problems.
Product Development	Will need to understand the new processes for uploading their product information to the new website.
Technology	Develop the system and provide final support if there are problems with the new website.
Finance, HR, Legal	Legal will need to provide sign-off for the disclaimers across the new website. HR need to adjust the approach to recruitment through the use of the new website.
Executive Leadership	Be involved in providing support and energy to the teams that are getting used to the navigation of the new site and helping customers through the change process.

Step 2: determine the specific impacts on each stakeholder/group

Once the role that each stakeholder group plays in supporting the change has been determined, the next step is to work through what this means for them. Table 6.5 leverages the McKinsey 7-S model and can be used as a checklist for assessing the impacts for each stakeholder group. Impacts will differ for each group and it is common for areas to experience multiple impacts.

Step 3: analyse impacts in more detail for each business area

Building on the previous step, we need to analyse and understand the specific impacts that change will have on each business area and what needs to happen for the change to be deemed successful.

TABLE 6.5 Stakeholder impact checklist

Area of Impact	Type	Example
Organizational Changes	Restructure, downsizing, mergers, acquisitions, offshoring.	Due to a change in leadership and strategy the structure of the organization is changing.
System Changes	New systems, system upgrades or replacements. Software or infrastructure.	New hand-held tablets are being used to take orders at tables.
Process Changes	Operational, finance, compliance, reporting policies and processes.	New government legislation requires new compliance processes regarding privacy.
Job Changes	Performance measures, operational to knowledge worker, full to part time, shift work, relocation.	Offshoring an operational function has changed the available roles to be knowledge-based – workers are required to apply for new jobs – trade union involvement.
Behavioural Changes	Compliance, values, beliefs, motivation and rewards.	Changes to the way customers are greeted due to a 'customer first' cultural initiative.
Capability Changes	Increased skill in relation to process, system or behaviour.	Change to the ongoing knowledge required to make the organization compliant after a health and safety legislative change.
Financial Changes	Remuneration, operational budgets, recharges, tax increases.	Change in sales-commissions' structure for a new product.

CASE STUDY

Continuing the example of the new website, we can examine in more detail the impacts to the e-business group, part of the distribution area. The impact as documented in the stakeholder analysis is: 'the content management processes need to be adjusted to support the new website, this includes sign-off responsibilities and writing/brand guidelines'.

Using the stakeholder impact checklist (Table 6.5), to examine the impacts in more detail, it is clear that this high-level impact translates to detailed impacts in all areas (Table 6.6).

TABLE 6.6 Example impacts

Area of Impact	Requirement to Support the Change
Organizational Changes	Creation of a new e-business group within the organization to control and manage the design and style of the new website. Two redundancies in the marketing group due to a redistribution of the work.
System Changes	New content management system (CMS) was introduced to support the new process and provide a workflow capability.
Process Changes	New processes to decentralize content development into product, operational and marketing areas and centralize content publishing and final sign-off in the e-business group.
Job Changes	New job roles, objectives and performance measures introduced for people in the new team.
Behavioural Changes	Change of behaviour for those people who had been used to publishing their own content, requiring them to respect the views and changes that the new process was introducing.
Capability Changes	Training in the new CMS system and training in the correct way to write customer communications in the correct 'voice'.
Financial Changes	New operational budgets to support the new e-business group. Redistribution of budget from marketing areas to support this.

Step 4: validate stakeholder impacts

Once a view of the detailed impacts has been developed it is important to assess and validate the stakeholder impact assessment with the involved groups. This process often identifies any unintended consequences of the change, potentially in time to do something about them.

Validation of impacts can be done in a number of ways:

- *Project documentation*
  - Business requirements: these often have an organizational change-impact section that is developed between the business analyst and the business subject matter expert (SME). These are a good source of information on both the intended change and also where there are out-of-scope areas that may cause problems later and will need to be addressed.

- Use cases: these are an invaluable source of information when they have been developed; they will provide both a 'happy' path and an 'unhappy' path, explaining how a process will work for different scenarios. User acceptance testing often leverages these use cases and can double-check assumptions.

- *Scenario testing*
  - Business workshops: bringing together key subject-matter experts to walk through scenarios is a great way to test impacts, often this will identify key issues that can be solved much earlier than if they had been found in testing – or worse, in a live situation. For example, testing the customer identification paper process against an actual driving licence highlighted that an issue date that is a mandatory piece of information does not actually exist!
  - Customer experience: there are a number of customer experience specialists around that can do everything from record the movement of your eyes to providing role-play opportunities. But if these are not available, simple techniques such as videoing a planned experience – for example, a call-centre operative playing out the new behaviours on the phone with an imaginary customer – can elicit great feedback.

- *Pilots*

  Pilots can provide great feedback and input to a change programme, not only can you test new software, it is possible to trial new support models, the training that is planned and make adjustments as required. Make sure that participants from different segments are involved; include both detractors and early movers to make sure the feedback is well rounded.

Step 5: assess the severity of change impacts

Once the change role and the impacts have been developed for each stakeholder group it is important to determine the severity of the impact to the group, as this will determine the approach to be taken to support them.

In determining their severity, impacts can be assessed as high (red), medium (amber) and low (green). Each organization and potential business stakeholder group within the organization will define these differently so it is important to follow guidelines if they are set.

Impacts are determined in terms of complexity and coverage for each specific stakeholder group. It is important to make sure that each of the stakeholder groups have reviewed the classification impacts to their area and have signed off on them, particularly if they impact operationally, such as resourcing levels or service level agreements:

- *Complexity of impact*: an assessment of the impact of the change, the change activity and the unintended consequences.
- *Coverage of impact*: the percentage of people in this stakeholder group that are impacted by the change.

- *Overall impact*: this is a combination of the complexity and the coverage of the change. This could simply look at the complexity and coverage and take the higher, or often a more subjective analysis can be done that also takes into account what else is going on in the organization.

CASE STUDY

An example impact severity assessment for a project that is changing customer communication processes can be seen in Table 6.7. The combination of complexity and coverage determines the overall rating.

TABLE 6.7 Severity impact assessment

Stakeholder	Number	Type of Impact	Complexity	Coverage	Overall
Customer Contact Centre	200	Off phones for one hour face-to-face training to understand new customer processes. 5% increase in customer calls expected with no compensating resourcing increase for three months as letters are sent out – may impact service levels.	Medium	High (100%)	High
Customers	200,000	Letters sent to explain changes to processes that require them to call if they don't want to accept extra cover/costs. May cause increase in customer complaints.	High	Low (5%)	Medium
Back Office Staff	500	15 minute awareness in team meeting. May receive extra work if customers decide to close their accounts as a result of the change.	Low	Medium (30%)	Medium

2. Change severity assessment

The severity of the impacts will depend on a number of things:

- *The environment*: ie external factors, the culture of the organization, the strategy/vision and what else is going on (organizational heat maps).
- *The change ability of the organization*: does the organization have the leadership, structures and frameworks in place to aid this specific change?
- *The history of change in the organization*: how well change has been managed previously, and how much cynicism or buy-in to the change is observable.
- *The individual responses to change*: each of the people within the change will be at different stages and will respond in different ways to the change.

2.1 Assessing the environment

Organizational heat maps provide an overview of the 'other' change and business-as-usual activities (such as conferences, holiday periods and business year-end) happening across the organization. They provide great context and an idea of the external dependencies for the change. If these are not available, it is important to perform a manual assessment of some sort to understand what else is going on in the organization, and how much stress the organization is under due to competing priorities.

Organizational heat maps or road maps differ by organization; however, for each key business area they should provide:

- a time-based view, monthly or quarterly is usual;
- impacts for the teams within specific business areas;
- both capital projects and business-as-usual initiatives.

An illustration of a divisional-change heat map for a particular quarter (quarter two) can be seen in Table 6.8. This heat map also shows the previous and two consecutive impacts for the same teams. Analysis of the heat map highlights the following insights that will be useful for assessment of any project delivering into this environment:

- Six initiatives are already impacting this business area and should be assessed for dependencies and whether impacts can be reduced by leveraging change activities already scheduled.
- There is an overall high impact for the second quarter, with two of the five teams having a high impact; this should be examined for sequencing in order to alleviate cumulative change impact.
- The previous and following two quarters are also high impact; this is a change-weary business unit that will require additional change activity to support them during this period.

TABLE 6.8 Organizational heat map

Change Initiative	Q1	Team 1	Team 2	Team 3	Team 4	Team 5	Q2	Q3	Q4
One	H	H	L	L	L	M	H	N/A	N/A
Two	M	L	H	L	L	L	H	H	H
Three	H	M	L	L	L	L	M	M	M
Four	M	N/A	M	M	H	M	H	H	H
Five	L	L	H	L	L	L	L	L	L
Six	N/A	L	M	M	H	L	M	L	L
Overall Impact	H	M	H	M	H	M	H	H	H

2.2 Assessing organizational change ability

Assessing how well an organization manages change will provide a good understanding of the effort that will be required to manage the change. The more mature the organization is at managing change, the more likely that there will be a standard framework to discuss change and change support at the senior levels, and standard processes for communication, training and engagement, amongst other capabilities.

The Change Management Institute (CMI) in their white paper (2011) provide an organizational change maturity model (Figure 6.4), that can be used to assess the change ability of the organization and provide valuable insight about the way change will 'land'.

The more mature the organization the better they will be at managing change, the more capable the people will be at absorbing change impacts, and therefore the less severe the change impacts are likely to be. A more detailed description for 'building organizational change readiness' is in Chapter 7, Section B.

2.3 Assessing the history of change

Understanding how well a change will land, and therefore the extent of the impact, will also depend on the history of change in the organization. Many changes will have been tried before, and the amount of cynicism that is experienced within the organization is often a result of previous perceived failures. More information on individual and organizational change can be found in Chapter 1, Sections B and C.

The more entrenched this cynicism is, the more difficult it will be to manage the change effectively and the more severe the impact. Conversely, where the change is brand new to the organization, and is seen as an interesting and valuable step forward, the change will be easier to manage and less severe. Gaining an idea of how well previous change has been managed will provide valuable information to assess the impact.

FIGURE 6.4 CMI organizational change maturity model (OCMM)

1 Initial	2 Repeatable	3 Defined	4 Managed	5 Optimized	OCMM
		Project sponsorship executives are tracking change; KPIs and prioritization processes in place	Organizational change leadership; accurate feedback; constant assessment to change targets	Executive change office, board reporting, agile project governance	Strategic change leadership **Driving** (Should/Why?)
	Repeatable communication and training processes available for business	Business units have view of project change (Heat Map) and ability to influence approach	Standards are in place to roll out change quickly and consistently. Feedback to adjust & manage effectiveness	Business areas comfortable with constant change. Leaders and managers effectively driving	Business change readiness **Receiving** (How/When?)
Ad hoc project change management (focus on comms and training)	Change managers on project, change methodology in place, most projects using	Change and project methodologies linked; change training for project managers	Projects designed and assessed around change management vision and inputs	Smaller initiatives, constant assessment of an ongoing change portfolio	Project change management **Implementing** (What/Who?)

2.4 Assessing individual responses

Cameron and Green (2012) offer an individual change perspective in their 'Five factors that influence individual responses to change' (Chapter 1, Section B6.1) that can help to explain what is going on for various individuals, particularly those who are key influencers or have very particular roles in the change. The model expresses a number of key questions that help to assess the impact of change on individuals and the organization.

Individual responses are important when the change relies on specific stakeholders to communicate and direct the change, and should be taken into account when assessing impacts.

Summary

With the business environment becoming more chaotic and uncertain, understanding change impacts has become equally more complex. The approaches to identify and assess the severity of impacts examined in this section provide some guidance and frameworks to analyse the interconnecting aspects of implementing change. The impact assessment process often provides clarity on risks and business continuity requirements that were not previously understood.

However, change management is not a linear process and it is important to constantly assess impacts as the project or initiative becomes clearer, or as the environment changes (Chapter 2, Section A explores how strategy influences organizational change). No two changes are ever the same and, as such, this is an important aspect of the change process that should not be taken lightly.

Questions to think about

1. Have you linked the planned business benefits with all the stakeholder groups that will be required to deliver and support the changes?
2. Have you assessed the cumulative effects of other changes on the business and the ability of the organization to absorb change?
3. Have you aligned the impacts with the risk assessment and the business continuity planning?

Section B: Assessing and managing the risks of change

Introduction

Risk assessment and management is an essential component of successful change. It can be very useful to position change management as an integral part of a corporate or an initiative's risk management strategy, particularly to senior stakeholders or programme/project managers that see limited value. Clearly, if there was no risk to the organization either in realizing expected benefits or in disrupting the business-as-usual activities, then there would be no need to specifically manage the change.

Heath and Heath (2010) argue that it is important to highlight the possibility of failure as a corollary to the norm of taking the 'rosiest possible interpretation of the facts'. Assessing the risks of the change effectively will help you do this.

A key priority is to work with programme/project managers and business representatives to establish effective governance arrangements that reflect the need to manage the risks of the change. Risks can be hard to identify, and being hit by an unexpected consequence often has a business impact and, in some circumstances, reputational damage. Performing a risk analysis is an essential step in the change management process, and provides a useful communication tool for sharing concerns and communicating vision.

Change risk should be looked at from three perspectives (see Figure 6.5):

- *Strategic*: the risk that the business benefits (or the change) are not realized or sustainable.
- *Business*: the amount, or type, or order of change negatively impacts the productivity of the business or their readiness to receive the change (change fatigue).
- *Programme/project*: the solution development and delivery, and the associated change management activities, are not sufficient to meet the needs of the strategy or the business areas.

FIGURE 6.5 Three risk perspectives

Understanding change risks first requires an analysis of the potential risks and then agreement on the actions that will manage, or mitigate the risk effectively. As with any activity and process within the change management arena, constant feedback and monitoring is required to assess progress and incorporate learnings.

This section covers:

- the terms definition and characteristics of a change risk (threat or opportunity);
- effective risk management governance structure (roles, responsibilities and processes);
- methods and techniques for identifying, capturing, analysing and mitigating/ resolving risks;
- content and use of a risk register for a change initiative, programme or project as basis for management or risks and for compiling reports for decision makers.

1. Organizational risk management

Risk is made up of two parts: the consequences of something happening/going wrong, and the likelihood of it happening. As defined by ISO 31000 (standards relating to risk management), risk is the effect of uncertainty on objectives. An effect is a deviation from the expected (positive or negative). Risk is often expressed in terms of a combination of the consequences of an event and the associated likelihood of occurrence.

The risk management process has a formal and multi-level governance process. An organization's risk management governance structure is designed to cover the whole process of all businesses and ensure various risks are properly managed and controlled in the course of business. This will cover risk management policies and procedures to identify, measure, monitor and control various risks across the organization. Various groups of risk takers assume that their respective responsibilities for risk management, projects and other change initiatives share these responsibilities.

Change managers are responsible for assessing change-specific risks, particularly those affecting business operations and services. They also work closely with the project/programme managers and business leaders to manage and report on their status.

2. Change risk register

The risk management process is standard for most change initiatives. Projects or programmes will normally have a formal risk register (Table 6.9) and often classify change management impacts separately within them.

It is important to make sure that the key risks identified during the change programme are formally monitored and updated through this process. The risk register is updated frequently and reported to senior stakeholders; it is their 'litmus test' of how well the project and the change are progressing.

The risk management process includes a number of activities – identify, assess, plan, implement and communicate – to explain the activity that the risk register supports.

TABLE 6.9 Example change risk-register entry

Description of Risk	Assessment		Mitigating Actions	Owner	Target Date	Status
	Likelihood/ Probability (1–5)	Consequence/ Impact (1–5)				
Contact-centre change fatigue causes attrition due to the number of changes due to competing projects.	4	5	Prepare a road map detailing the different cross-product changes. Determine amount and sequencing of change for each contact centre and identify areas of concern.	Change lead	16 Mar	Not started

Tip

Some organizations find it helpful to use numerical values (eg a scale of 1–5, 5 being high) and multipliers for assessing overall risk assessment. In the example shown in Table 6.9, where the likelihood of the risk occurring is 4 and the impact is 5, the overall risk score is 20 (the maximum would be 25). This scoring system is often accompanied by a simple 'RAG' (traffic lights) indicator to show low–medium–high risk status. The risk register can also include 'proximity' (how soon a risk may occur) as well as information on 'residual risk' after mitigating actions have been taken.

3. Risk analysis

The purpose of a risk analysis is to identify the possible barriers to successful organizational change and then estimate (assess) the likelihood that they will materialize. Identifying risks to benefits realization and optimization is also a key area of focus (covered in detail in Chapter 3, Section C).

The risk analysis leverages the information gathered through the impact assessment process, and particularly the feedback received while validating impacts with stakeholder groups. Use the activities to identify the corresponding issues/barriers/risk, such as those seen in Table 6.10.

TABLE 6.10 Example change risk areas

Change Risk Area	Example Change Issues/Risks
Strategic	Delay/reduction in strategic benefits Reputational risk Negative customer impacts
Business	Decreases to business productivity Inadequate business leadership Operating budget increases post-project Loss of organizational knowledge Inadequate training and communication Low business readiness confidence
Project/Programme	Inadequate change management budget Inadequate impact assessment Inadequate business process analysis System defects

The risk analysis needs to cover the strategic, business and project/programme aspects of the change, but do not need to be IT- or project management-related risks; these may be identified but should be supported more fully in other responsibility areas (see Chapter 8 for more information about using risk management tools in projects).

Specific workshops can be held to gain insights to the change risks of the initiative. A good starter for these sessions is to start with a failure, and ask people to think through how this may have happened.

CASE STUDY

An online business is implementing a new online system for their accounts payable process, where invoices will be entered via a web-based system by their pre-approved suppliers.

The workshop was introduced with the following positioning:

It is two weeks after the implementation of the system, suppliers are not able to enter their invoices into the system, some are starting to experience financial stress due to the previous 'hold' on invoice payments due to the system conversion process, the newspapers are reporting the issues, which is impacting the brand of the business. Why did this happen?

The risk assessment extract shown in Table 6.11 was developed as a result of a change risk workshop.

TABLE 6.11 Risk assessment extract

Change	Issues/Barriers/Risk	Likelihood	Consequence	Overall	Enablers/Actions
Strategic	The reputation of the organization is impacted due to inadequate Public Relations involvement and management	Low	High	Medium	Ensure that the PR group are fully informed and have prepared for potential issues
Business	Invoices cannot be paid for a long period, causing supplier stress and impacting deliveries	Medium	High	High	Develop alternative manual processes for invoice payment if required
	Call centres are not able to support the numbers of calls that are being received following the implementation, affecting all customers	High	Medium	High	Ensure that temporary resourcing and support options are available for the contact centres post-go-live
Project	System upgrades that are not required for the new system impact the performance of the system	Low	Medium	Low	Ensure that the go-live weekend is quarantined from non-essential system upgrades

Once the risk has been identified, the likelihood and consequence of the risk happening need to be determined. This is often subjective and will need to be validated by the involved stakeholders.

4. Mitigating actions

Once the risks have been identified and validated the actions that are required to effectively manage the risk need to be planned and implemented. It is standard process to update and report on the progress of risk management at least monthly. The mitigation activities need to be able to be actionable by the person assigned to own them. Risk responses can include:

- *Acceptance*: effectively the 'do-nothing' option: 'If the risk occurs then we will deal with it.'
- *Reduction*: actions that will change the likelihood and/or consequences of the risk.
- *Transfer*: where some or all of the risk is transferred to a third party, eg insurance.
- *Share*: where a risk is shared by multiple parties using the 'pain/gain' principle.
- *Contingency*: planning ahead for suitable responsive actions should the situation change.

5. Communicating change risks

When presenting change management plans to project steering committees/senior leadership, it is important to provide the status of the key risk and issues that you are managing as context for the activities and to gain leadership support where this is needed. Risk management is a key capability for all senior leaders and they are better able to relate to change management if presented in this way.

Presenting risks as part of business area presentations can help people who are involved in and impacted by the change to understand the importance of the change to the organization, and help to sell why they need to come on board. For compliance projects this is extremely important.

However, be careful that the change is articulated well, taking a too generic or high-level approach does not work; these may be considered 'Black Swan' risks (Taleb, 2007), too generic, outside the scope of the project and better managed at board level. Change risks must be specific and actionable; care needs to be taken about the likelihood and impact of them happening.

Summary

It is important for organizational leaders to adopt a solid and formalized change management strategy to achieve their strategic objectives (Chapter 2, Section A). In Prosci's 2012 benchmarking report, the top obstacle identified by study participants was inefficient change management sponsorship from senior leaders, followed by inefficient change management resourcing.

The change strategy provides activities for mitigating both internal and external risk factors of failure and poor user acceptance and adoption. Presenting change management as a risk management strategy to key stakeholders helps to explain and gain support for change management activities from senior leaders of the organization to reverse this trend.

Questions to think about

1 Have you involved key stakeholders in the risk assessment process?
2 Have you aligned your planned change management activities with the key change risks?
3 Are you effectively communicating the change risks to senior leaders of the organization?

Section C: Business continuity and contingency during change

Introduction

Change can be disruptive and care needs to be taken to balance 'managing the change' with the ongoing task of 'managing the business' (Figure 6.6). The most important risk during change is to business continuity, ensuring that during and after change the business continues to work effectively. Identifying and analysing the impact of change enables effective initial planning and preparation, and helps to minimize the effects of non-controlled change.

The change manager and corporate business continuity roles work together to identify the potential impacts of a change initiative on business as usual. This includes reviewing plans to identify core business processes, confirming impacts, providing input for changes to the process and advising managers of these changes as required.

FIGURE 6.6 Balancing the competing demands and tensions of change

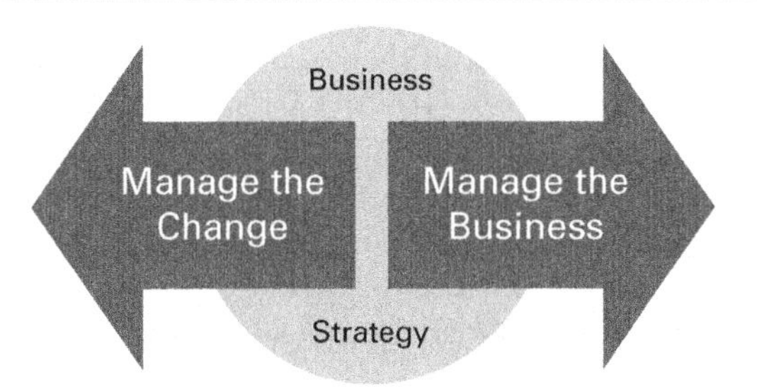

Tip

If the organization does not already have an established process for business continuity, it is important that this is raised as a key risk.

This section covers:

- the principles of business continuity planning and contingency planning methods and techniques;
- awareness of methods and techniques for conducting a business impact analysis to gather information about business functions, processes and systems, including organizational relationships, links and dependencies, using appropriate methods, tools and techniques;
- using the results of a business impact analysis to identify impact 'hotspots' where risks and issues need to be addressed as part of the change initiative, including identification of specific contingency requirements and plans to minimize disturbance to business as usual (BAU).

1. Business continuity planning

Business continuity plans (BCP) minimize the risk of disruption to business and should be developed to:

- gain a good understanding of the risks their business faces, and the consequences if these events happen;
- ensure business continuity plans match the business, fitting in with what the organization does, its size, its resources, where it is based, and how it works;
- making sure that everyone gets involved, at all levels, so they all buy into the idea of business continuity, know what their role would be, and how disruption would affect those outside the organization too.

The entire concept of business continuity is based on the identification of all business functions within an organization, and then assigning a level of importance to each business function. Kenneth Myers (1996) has built a good model for BCP and contingency/disaster recovery if further support is required in this area.

Most standards require that a business impact analysis should be reviewed at defined intervals appropriate for each organization and whenever any of the following occur: 1) significant changes in the internal business process, location or technology; 2) significant changes in the external business environment – such as market or regulatory change.

2. BCP and the change process

Examining the existing BCP for the area can also be a great way to understand the business and existing risks, but it is also important to understand that even the most robust BCP can be impacted during a change initiative.

The following list provides some key areas that can impact a business continuity plan and should be examined in light of the intended change:

- Demotivated staff during downsizing, mergers and acquisition, which affects productivity or the customer experience in a major way without triggering a continuity event.
- Loss of key knowledge or person dependency, as the old is replaced with the new.
- Broken process where systems or people have changed without thinking about or planning for the resulting process changes.
- System outages caused by a new or revised software release are not communicated correctly, leading to lost data or impacted customers.
- New buildings, new contact names, new systems are not factored into the business continuity plans, and they are not tested as part of the change process.

CASE STUDY

A website case study provides a great example of why this is important.

Four weeks after the new site went live, the telephony system crashed at one of the contact centres. As part of the business continuity plan, information was to be placed on the website to alert customers. With the change in website and process they were not able to contact the right person to make the change, as such the customers could not be informed on the status of the issue.

To aid the BCP process it is important to include the following as part of the project or change planning:

- Adequate activity modelling and process mapping (Chapter 2, Section D and Chapter 13, Section C) and assessment of the change impact has been done.
- Cutover processes are tested effectively, pilots and parallel runs work well.
- Business continuity plans are adjusted and tested.
- Business readiness is measured for all impacted groups, and included the changes to BCP plans.

Summary

Change managers are not usually expert in business continuity; however, it is important to understand the concepts and work with key stakeholders to ensure business continuity plans meet the needs of the changed organization.

Questions to think about

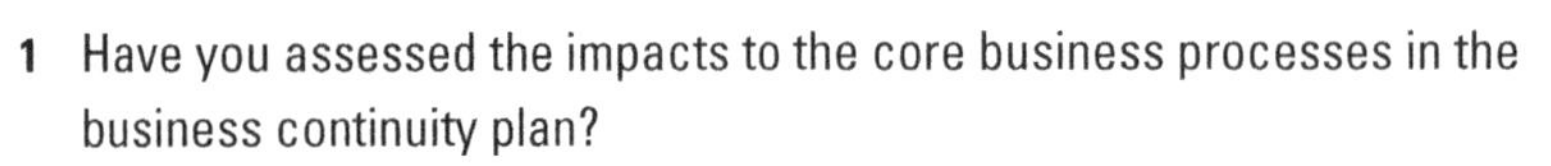

1. Have you assessed the impacts to the core business processes in the business continuity plan?
2. Have you assessed other changes to the business continuity plan in relation to other changes that are impacting the key processes?
3. Have you assessed the business continuity risks and included them in your change risk register?

Further reading

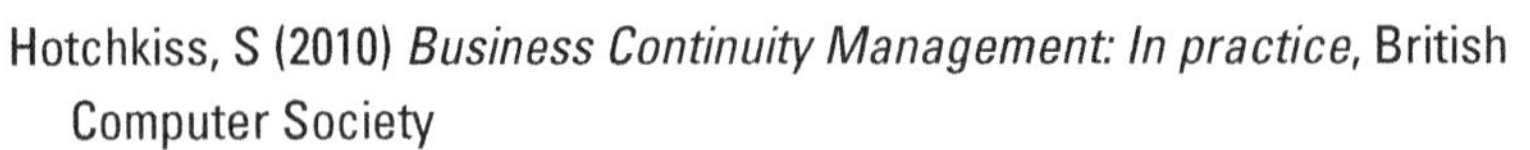

Hotchkiss, S (2010) *Business Continuity Management: In practice*, British Computer Society

Office of Government Commerce (now part of the Cabinet Office of the UK government) (2011) *Management of Risk: Guidance for practitioners*, The Stationery Office

Sterling, S *et al* (2012) *Business Continuity for Dummies*, John Wiley & Sons

References

AS/NZS ISO 31000 (2009) [accessed 2 September 2014] *Risk Management: Principles and guidelines* [Online] http://www.standards.co.nz/news/standards-information/risk-managment/

Cameron, E and Green, M (2012) *Making Sense of Change Management*, Kogan Page, London

Change Management Institute (2011) Organisational Change Management Maturity, White Paper [Online] https://www.change-management-institute.com

Heath, C and D (2010) *Switch: How to change when change is hard*, Broadway Books, New York

Myers, K (1996) *Total Contingency Planning for Disasters: Managing risk, minimizing loss, ensuring business continuity*, John Wiley & Sons, Chichester

Nohria, N and Khurana, R (1993) Executing change: seven key considerations, *Harvard Business School*, Background Note 494–038

Pascale, R (1999) Surfing the edge of chaos, *MIT Sloan Management Review*, Spring, pp 83–94

Peters, T and Waterman, R (1982) *In Search of Excellence: Lessons from America's best-run companies*, Harper and Row, New York

Porter, E H (1913) *Pollyanna*, LC Page, Boston

Prosci® (2012) *Best Practices in Change Management*, Loveland, CO

Taleb, N (2007) *Fooled by Randomness: The hidden role of chance in life and in the markets*, and the follow-up, *The Black Swan: The impact of the highly improbable*, Random House, New York

Change readiness, planning and measurement

07

NICOLA BUSBY

Introduction

Change readiness is concerned with preparing the organization for the changes it is facing. An organization that is ready for change will find it easier to implement and sustain the new ways of working, and therefore reap the benefits of the change.

It is much easier to identify the tangible and practical things that are needed (such as new IT systems or organizational structures) than ensuring the cultural conditions are in place to support the change. This means equipping people with the motivations and attitudes to engage with the change and make it work. However, if this aspect is neglected, there is a vastly increased risk that people will resist the change, fail to adopt new ways of working and that the change will therefore be unsuccessful.

This chapter focuses on the people and cultural aspects – why they matter, how to identify the issues and increase change readiness, how to prepare for resistance to the change and how to measure the impact of any change interventions.

CHAPTER CONTENTS

Section A: Building individual motivation to change

Introduction: building and sustaining commitment to change

Change initiatives need the commitment and motivation of the people who are receiving the change. Unless 'hearts and minds' are won over, people will not make the effort to engage and the change will struggle to be successful.

1. Why work with individuals during change?

Change is a very personal thing. If an organization introduces a change to a team, no two individuals will share exactly the same thoughts and feelings about the change, and no two individuals will react in the same way to the change. However, one certainty is that every individual will have some reaction to the change, ranging on a spectrum between embracing it wholeheartedly to resisting it with every bone in their body.

Chapter 1, Section B explores some of the main theories around individuals and change. For example, Bridges (2009) describes an individual's journey through change as a transition – letting go of existing patterns of behaviours and engaging with new ones. The choice to make this transition is up to each individual, and building individual motivation to change can influence whether this choice is made or not. When working with individuals during change it is crucial to know these theories in order to understand how the proposed changes may affect people's motivation.

2. Expectancy theory and change

The theories of motivation in Chapter 1, Section B3 all attempt to explain specific factors that motivate staff, such as reward, fulfilment and recognition. Expectancy theory says that: 'people will be motivated if they believe that strong effort will lead to good performance and good performance will lead to desired rewards' (Lunenburg, 2011).

In expectancy theory, there are three ways to enhance the motivation of employees, which can be used to keep motivation high during a change initiative. These are:

- Increasing belief that employees can perform their jobs successfully. People may be concerned that they will struggle to undertake the new tasks that a change will bring. Increasing training and support will help them to gain confidence in new ways of working.

- Increasing belief that good performance will result in valued rewards. It is important to be clear what a good performance looks like after a change, and how this will be rewarded. Make sure you carry through on any promises you make about rewards, and remember that reward does not have to be monetary.
- Increasing the expected value of rewards resulting from desired performance. This can be done by making sure that the rewards offered are really valued by employees and, where possible, individualizing rewards to make sure they give the maximum value to those concerned. For example, some employees may value time off in lieu after an intense period of work on a change, whereas others may prefer a cash adjustment to their salary.

3. Increasing motivation for change

3.1 The change formula

The change formula (Beckhard and Harris, 1987) can help to explain the forces that are acting for and against the change for individuals, and therefore pinpoint areas to focus on to increase motivation. It takes the form of a mathematical formula but the explanation is very straightforward:

$C = [ABD] > X$

C = change

A = level of dissatisfaction with the status quo

B = desirability of the proposed change or end state

D = practicality of the change (knowledge of the next practical steps, minimal risk and disruption)

X = perceived 'cost' of the change

Basically, an individual will decide to make the transition if they perceive that the effort or 'cost' of changing is worth it. In order for this to happen, they have to be unhappy with the way things currently are, happy with the proposed solution, and not face too many unknowns or too much risk and disruption during the change. Implied in the formula is the assumption that if either A, B or D are zero then the change initiative will never overcome the 'cost' of the change, people will resist and the change will fail. In this case, the formula can be a very useful way of beginning difficult discussions with the change sponsor and senior management about the wisdom of continuing with the change initiative.

Focusing on raising levels of A, B and D will lower resistance, increase motivation and therefore increase the chances of the individual engaging in the change. Some ideas of how to do this are listed below:

- *A: level of dissatisfaction with the status quo.* Communicating the 'burning platform' (Section B2.1) can help to increase dissatisfaction with the status quo. For example, if the change is being made for regulatory purposes, dissatisfaction with the status quo can be easily generated by making staff aware that they or the organization could face the consequences of acting outside of regulations. For changes that aim to increase efficiency, talking to people about how much time they are currently spending on a task, and exploring what they could do with that time instead (taking a lunch break, leaving on time in the evening), will again soon raise levels of dissatisfaction. Be careful to keep the dissatisfaction within the scope of your change, otherwise people may start to focus on other workplace issues in need of improvement – and which are out of your control.

- *B: desirability of the proposed change or end state.* This can be increased by focusing on the benefits of the change – both corporate and, more importantly, individual. For example, an office move may mean that people are closer to better shops and cafés; a move to electronic filing may result in an environmental benefit of less printing. However small these benefits may be, if well communicated they can increase the desirability of the change significantly.
- *D: practicality of the change.* Being clear on what steps you need users to undertake will help to reduce the fear of the unknown and allow them to plan their time during the change. Users are often concerned that the disruption of the change will affect their performance and reduce their ability to undertake their day-to-day work. This is often the case in the short term whilst a change is being implemented and embedded. It is important to put mitigations in place to reduce risk and disruption as much as possible, and then communicate these mitigations to users. For example, amending performance targets whilst users get used to new software, or planning office moves for a weekend, will show users that the practicalities of the change are being thought about and effort is being put into minimizing risk and disruption.

3.2 Appreciative enquiry

When working in organizational change, it is easy to always focus on the negatives – the high percentages of changes that fail, creating burning platforms to convince people why they cannot continue as they are, expecting and planning for resistance. Appreciative enquiry focuses much more on a positive identification of what is currently working well and explores how this can be built on and strengthened to move the organization to a desired future state. Focusing on the positive helps to increase motivation to change, because all aspects of the change are spoken about in positive terms and because the change is seen as a logical journey. It enhances and develops the positives that already exist rather than focusing on fixing something that is currently broken.

Appreciative enquiry involves asking structured questions around the following four areas, known as the '4-D' cycle:

- *Discovery*: looking at what currently works well in the organization.
- *Dream*: exploring how these successes can be built on and expanded.

- *Design*: creating a plan to implement the dream.
- *Destiny*: moving the organization towards the dream.

Central to the cycle is the 'affirmative topic choice'. Based on the premise that 'human systems grow in the direction of what they persistently ask questions about' (Cooperrider and Whitney, 2005), it is important to make sure the topic is positive. For example, an organization could focus on building a first-class customer experience rather than trying to mend a culture that puts convenience of employees before customer satisfaction.

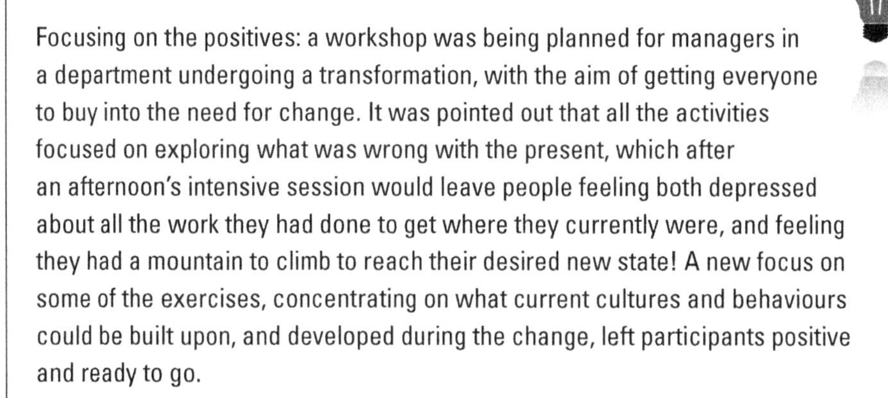

Tip

Focusing on the positives: a workshop was being planned for managers in a department undergoing a transformation, with the aim of getting everyone to buy into the need for change. It was pointed out that all the activities focused on exploring what was wrong with the present, which after an afternoon's intensive session would leave people feeling both depressed about all the work they had done to get where they currently were, and feeling they had a mountain to climb to reach their desired new state! A new focus on some of the exercises, concentrating on what current cultures and behaviours could be built upon, and developed during the change, left participants positive and ready to go.

4. How to work with individuals in large changes

As we have seen, the success of a change initiative is dependent on individuals having the necessary motivation to make a transition from old ways of working to new. Most changes affect large numbers of individuals and it is not possible for one change manager to support each individual through their individual change journey. Therefore, support must be spread out over a larger group of people. This is often done either through setting up a dedicated change agent network, or through using the established network of line managers and supervisors. Each approach has advantages and disadvantages, as discussed below.

4.1 Change agent networks

The role of the change agent is explored in depth in Chapter 1, Section D, where it is defined as 'anyone who acts intentionally but without formal line authority to facilitate change in the organization'.

When going through a change of any significant size, many organizations decide to establish a specific network of change agents, or champions, to support the change. Membership of this network consists of 'on the ground' internal staff, usually one representative for each area, department or team affected by the change. The change agents are nominated by their area to work on the change alongside their 'day job'.

Change agent networks can offer the following benefits:

- One dedicated person to assist in the information flow from the change team to each specific business area and back.
- A network of people across the organization who have the ability to break down silos and look at the effects of the change and possible solutions across different departments.
- A manageable-sized group with which to develop and test ideas, approaches and solutions.
- A source of information and a feedback mechanism for affected staff that is trusted and 'one of us'.
- A group of users with in-depth knowledge about the change, who can challenge, constructively criticize and suggest best ways to approach the change for their particular areas.
- Expert users for new processes or systems brought about by the change.

Recruiting a change agent network

It is important to recruit the right people into the network, and this requires some effort. As the agents will be representing their colleagues for a lot of the change planning, they need to be established and respected enough within their areas for people to trust them with the tasks. However, recruit someone too high up in the organization (team manager, head of department) and they probably won't have the time to dedicate to the role.

One way to get around this is to use the change agent role as a development activity for a team member who can carry out the role supported by their manager and team leader. They will then have the legitimacy for the role amongst the team, and access to the team leaders when necessary.

Some change agents can be successfully recruited by asking for volunteers. This works best when the change is high profile, a priority for the organization or will affect teams significantly. More low-profile changes, or those not seen as core work for teams (eg an IT upgrade), may not attract the same level of interest. A word of caution about asking for volunteers for your network: the role is intended to represent a team or specific area of the business and sometimes people volunteer because they have a personal interest in the change. This may happen especially with changes to employee terms and conditions, and you may find your network focuses more on their own personal issues rather than those of their teams.

It is useful to be clear about what you require from your change agents, outlining what they are expected to do, the type of skills and knowledge you are looking for and especially the amount of time the role will take. As the role will be undertaken on top of a day job, it is important to get agreement from the manager of your agents, otherwise you may find that they cannot give the time to the role as they are

FIGURE 7.1 Change agent job advertisement

Are you excited about the possibility of doing things differently?
Do you always look for ways to make things better?
Would you like to make a difference?

If so, the Change Programme needs you!

This major change initiative is looking for representatives across the organization to:

- Be the link between the change programme and your area.
- Be a local presence with knowledge of what is going on 'inside' the programme.
- Influence the design of the key features.
- Test the new system and processes.
- Support your colleagues during the implementation of the change.

If you have excellent communication skills, the ability to influence and support your colleagues, are happy to offer constructive challenge, and possess the capability to remain positive and enthusiastic under pressure, we want to hear from you.

The role will be in addition to your day job and take approximately 4 hours per week – more during busy periods.

This is an excellent opportunity to be involved with an exciting new initiative that will change the way the organization works. In addition we will offer training and development opportunities and the chance to gain new skills and work with new people.

not being released from other obligations. Figure 7.1 shows an example of an internal advertisement for a change agent.

Developing your network

Once your network is established, your change agents need to be inducted into the change programme with activities including:

- understanding what changes are being planned and the expected benefits;
- getting to know the change team, including the sponsor, and other colleagues in the network;
- being exposed to any proposed solutions, including new IT systems, target operating models, new processes, in order to give early feedback and begin to think about how the changes will impact their area;
- being trained on how to support their colleagues through change, including some of the change models outlined in Chapter 1 of this book, and also in how to undertake basic coaching (Chapter 9, Section C). This is especially useful in maturing the organization to deal with change, as the knowledge and skill can be transferred to other changes once your change has been completed.

Tip

What's in a name? Be careful with the name you choose for your network. The author once struggled to recruit 'Change Champions' as potential recruits did not want to be seen to be passively championing the change. Whilst you want people who widely support what you are trying to do, you don't want mindless support with no challenge. Therefore, choose a name to accurately reflect the role, for example 'Change Pioneer' or 'Change Partner'.

4.2 The use of middle managers

Some organizations choose not to establish specific change agent networks, and use their middle managers as change agents instead. This works well in organizations that are more mature in their change management approach and where line managers are used to taking ownership of change. It is also a good way to implement change, as it is often the middle managers who are key in making the changes work – they need to translate policy into action for the front-line staff, and if they are not engaged they have the potential to jeopardize the success of the change.

The biggest challenge with this approach is the amount of time that middle managers can dedicate to the change. This often depends on the type of change. If it is a major transformational change for the organization then senior managers will be more willing for their middle managers to invest the time. If the change is one of many organizational initiatives, it may be harder for the middle managers to prioritize it over their many other tasks. Building work on the change into middle managers' objectives, targets or work plans is a good way to ensure they are able to dedicate the time needed, and also ensures they have the support of their managers to invest in the change.

Middle managers may not all be supportive for the change, especially in the early stages. Don't forget that they are individuals affected by the change as much as anyone else. You may need to win their hearts and minds before they will be able to support their staff through the change. An induction programme, similar to the one described above for a change agent network, is vital to ensure they are informed and equipped to support their teams properly.

The use of change agent networks or middle managers, as well as all other resources you need for your change (discussed further in Section B2.4), will need to be scaled up or down to match the size, scope and speed of the change. The following considerations are important when planning the size of the network:

- the impact of the change on everyday work;
- the complexity of the change and the amount of training and support that will be required;
- the number and variety of stakeholders who will be affected by the change;
- the geographical spread of the stakeholders;

- the organization's previous experience with changes of this nature;
- the time allowed to complete and absorb the change.

4.3 Working with innovators, majority and laggards

In any change, there will be a range of reactions from people. Some will be very enthusiastic and want to lead the way, some will be very resistant and lag behind. The majority will be somewhere in the middle. In 1962 Rogers (2003) coined the term 'diffusion of innovations' for this effect.

Rogers developed his diffusion of innovations by undertaking an historical study of how innovations took hold in societies. He segmented the society into five categories, depending on how quickly or otherwise they adopted the innovation. Figure 7.2 shows the percentage of people in each category.

This theory can be applied for change initiatives, or innovations, in organizations. Each segment needs to be engaged in a different way to ensure complete adoption of the change. Some ideas of how to do this are listed below:

- *Innovators and early adopters*: these are the pioneers for your change. They are a very powerful group and can be utilized to give out positive messages to their colleagues, lead by example and raise enthusiasm and buy-in for the change initiative. Their enthusiasm and buy-in also make them a good group to use for testing, piloting and early case studies. A word of caution though: expectation management is vital for this group as organizational constraints may mean you cannot move fast enough or be innovative enough to satisfy them. Their enthusiasm can easily turn to disappointment if their expectations are not being met.

FIGURE 7.2 Diffusion of innovation showing percentage of people in each segment

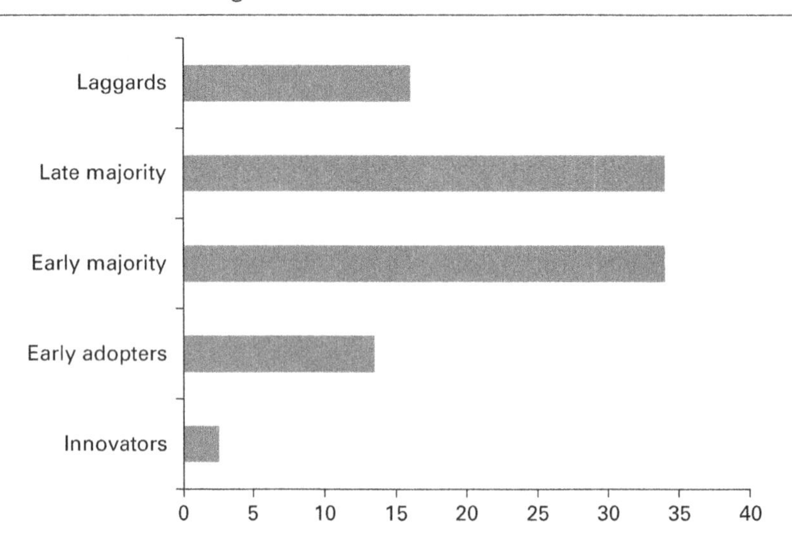

- *The majorities*: these make up the largest percentage of your users (hence the name). They are a vital group to work with as they can be persuaded to support the change, but can also easily resist the change dependent on the information they are given and the behaviours they observe from the early adopters. Messages about benefits, opportunities derived from the change and explanations about what the change will entail will help to swing them over to your side.
- *Laggards*: these will often resist change. It is important to find out whether they are doing this because they generally find change difficult, or because they have genuine concerns about your specific change. If the former, try to keep them from 'poisoning' others and ensure they are given extra support during the change. If the latter, it can be invaluable to the success of your change to engage them and explore their concerns. You may find that they have got ideas or insights that no one else has thought of and which, if addressed, could significantly improve the change.

Tip

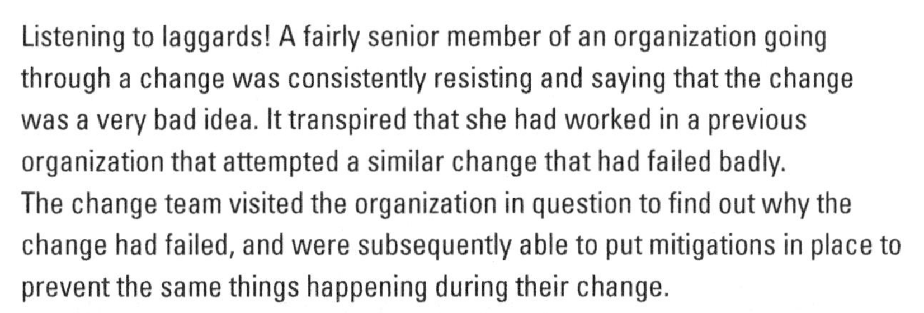

Listening to laggards! A fairly senior member of an organization going through a change was consistently resisting and saying that the change was a very bad idea. It transpired that she had worked in a previous organization that attempted a similar change that had failed badly. The change team visited the organization in question to find out why the change had failed, and were subsequently able to put mitigations in place to prevent the same things happening during their change.

Summary

Change is very personal and each individual will have a diverse reaction to your change. In order for the change to be successful, each affected individual will have to decide to transition from old ways of working to the new.

The following may help to increase individual motivation to change:

- motivational theories (Chapter 1, Section B3), including expectancy theory;
- appreciative enquiry;
- Beckhard and Harris's (1987) change formula.

It is important to set up a structure to support individuals, either a network of change agents or middle managers. There are also different models of engagement for individuals in adopting change, depending on whether they are early adopters, in the majority or laggards.

Questions to think about

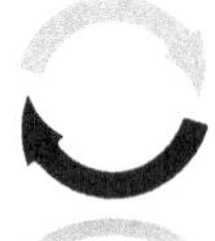

1. How could you use Beckhard and Harris's change formula (1987) to help increase motivation for your change?
2. Would a change agent network or middle managers work best to implement a change in your organization? Why?
3. How could you effectively engage with innovations, the majorities and laggards during your change?

Further reading

Beckhard, R F and Harris, R T (1987) *Organizational Transitions: Managing complex change*, Addison-Wesley, Reading, MA

Cameron, E and Green, M (2012) *Making Sense of Change Management: A complete guide to the models, tools and techniques of organizational change*, 3rd edn, Kogan Page, London

Rogers, E M (2003) *Diffusion of Innovations*, 5th edn, Free Press, New York

Section B: Building organizational readiness for change

Introduction: the capability, capacity and belief to see change through

Successfully implementing change in organizations is tough and failure rates are high. In order to increase the chance of successful implementation, it is important to spend time assessing how ready the organization is to undertake the change, and improving areas that may negatively impact on the change. The organization can also be prepared for the change by understanding what change is happening and why and the key benefits expected. This will help to win 'hearts and minds' and garner support for the effort needed to successfully implement and embed your change initiative.

1. Factors that influence readiness for change and how to assess them

1.1 Environmental factors

A key aspect of change readiness is to thoroughly understand the culture of the organization. Morgan's (2006) *Images of Organization* (see Chapter 1, Section C1) shows that there are many different ways to think of and manage organizational life. In order to prepare successfully for change, it is important to really 'get under the skin' of the organization and understand how it works and why. All organizations have a unique set of factors that will influence its readiness for change, as follows:

- *Culture*: individual organizational cultures vary widely across and within different industries. Whilst organizations within similar fields may share some similarities – for example, non-profit service organizations may be extremely focused on serving their customers – no organization has exactly the same culture (Chapter 1, Section E explores organizational cultures in depth).
- *Values*: company values are often written down. However, it is important to check that these are actually the values that the company operates by, as they don't always translate into practice. Different areas within the organization also may operate with different values – this is more prevalent in large organizations with distinct departments or when organizations are spread over a large geographical area.
- *Management styles*: these can vary widely between organizations and, again, need to be understood in order to prepare the organization for change. Styles can vary from a very autocratic 'tell' style of leadership to a far more participatory style where teams take maximum responsibility for their work (Tannenbaum and Schmidt, 1973).

Taking time to observe the organization at work will tell you a lot about its cultural factors and will help you tailor your preparation for the change. Table 7.1 analyses some organizational observations.

1.2 Competencies in change-related disciplines

Organizational changes need to call on a wide variety of skills and competencies, including:

- HR for any changes to employment contracts, job roles and policies;
- Learning and Development for any new training and development needs;
- internal communications to help with staff engagement;
- project management for the discipline of implementing the change;
- IT for any technological and system changes.

Part of change readiness involves building positive relationships with these departments and teams, and working together to define the scope of where they can help you.

TABLE 7.1 A cultural assessment of some organizational observations

Observation	Could Be an Indicator Of	How This May Impact Change Readiness
What are the seating arrangements and where do managers sit (do they sit with their teams in open plan areas or do they have separate offices with closed doors)?	Organizational culture, management style.	Staff engagement and buy-in is vital for a successful change. A collaborative culture and informal hierarchy means that greater levels of staff may have influence over the change. Greater levels of involvement and buy-in will be needed here than in a culture where staff are more used to doing what they are told.
How available are managers – are they visible within the organization? Can you access their calendars to book meetings? Will they make time to see you or are their diaries crammed with far more important meetings?	Culture, management style.	Leadership of change is vital. Managers need to really focus on and engage with the change in order for it to be successful. If they are too busy to prioritize the change, you will struggle to plan, implement and embed your change successfully.
How do people address each other – formally or informally? Are there breakout coffee areas where people stand and chat? Do teams go out for lunch together? If so, are the managers invited?	Culture.	This may be an indicator of how the organization communicates. If there are lots of opportunities for informal communication, then news may spread quicker than if only formal communication channels are used. There is a greater chance for truthful feedback through informal communication, but be careful as the rumour mill may be very efficient!

TABLE 7.1 *continued*

Observation	Could Be an Indicator Of	How This May Impact Change Readiness
What is the décor of the office? Is it well decorated and tidy and do people take pride in their workplace?	Culture, values.	Pride in the physical workplace may be an indicator of how people feel about their jobs and their motivation levels. If people are motivated to do their jobs well, they will be concerned about the impact that the changes may have and feelings about the change will run high. They may either want to get very involved and own the change, or there may be high levels of resistance.
What hours do people work? Are they heads down all day, working late into the evening? Do they dress formally or informally?	Culture, values.	Like the availability of managers above, staff must also have the time to engage in the change and transition to new ways of working. If there is no slack in the working day, engagement may be more of a challenge and some negotiation with managers about prioritization may be necessary.
What language do people use? Is there a common language with accepted terminology or do people use different words to explain and identify organizational items and activities?	Values.	If people use the same language to describe things across the organization, it could be an indicator that values and shared perspectives are uniform, understood and bought into. Aligning the change to these values could increase buy-in and support.

You may be given resource, eg a communications expert to write your communications, a project manager to run your change, a business analyst to gather the requirements of the new IT system. This is dependent on other pressures and priorities as well as on budgets and resource constraints. Building your change into the annual budget and planning round can help to secure resources from other departments in the business.

There are a few things that can help you when working with other departments during a change, including:

- Be very clear about who is doing what, and how the work is to be managed, quality checked and prioritized. It is important to document what is agreed in order to avoid confusion during the change, even if you just summarize outcomes of a meeting in an e-mail.
- Regular meetings with the people doing the work, and their managers, can help to keep things on track and deal with any issues that arise. This is especially helpful if you are matrix managing the work, or if the person doing the work cannot come and physically sit near you.
- Different departments may have their own ways of working, which you will have to factor into your change plan. For example, tweaks to a new system may have to go through a formal IT change process, or changes to job roles may have to go through a formal consultation with unions or internal staff representative groups. Make sure you are aware of all of these potential processes, both to ensure you factor the time and resources required into your planning, and also so you stay on the right side of organizational policies – and even the law!

You may find that you are planning a change initiative in an organization that does not have well-established support functions. In this case it is important to seek advice, especially on employment issues, through established bodies. Education may be needed within the organization if you are introducing new disciplines. For example, there may be initial frustration with the added bureaucracy and governance of project management methodologies if people have not experienced the benefits of using them in the past.

1.3 Organizational policy

It is often necessary to amend policies to support organizational changes. The policies should be amended after the change has been put in place, as changes don't always end up exactly as planned, and this prevents rework if policies are changed too early.

As part of planning for your change initiative, check the organization's written policies and identify those that may be affected. Also, engage with whoever owns the policies to ensure there are no legal or other constraints to amending them before you introduce your change. Some organizations review their policies at set intervals, so timing your change to coincide with these reviews can be helpful.

Tip

A call centre invested a great deal of time and resource on a change initiative to become more customer focused. A big part of this was training staff to take the time on the phone to put customers at ease, build trust and make sure all issues were discussed fully. However, they failed to update their policy, which stated the minimum number of calls that should be answered within a certain time. The staff were unable to implement their new ways of working as they simply didn't have enough time with each call to cover the extended amount of information.

1.4 Lessons learnt from past initiatives

Organizational changes are never implemented with a blank sheet. Affected users will always remember other changes they have experienced in the past, both in their present and former organizations, and this will set their expectation for your change.

A useful exercise during your preparation is to hold a workshop or focus group with relevant people to find out what has gone well and badly with previous changes. This can be cathartic for the users and gives you an opportunity to understand why people may react in certain ways to your change.

Once you have listed the good and bad elements of previous changes, create a pledge document for your users on how you will work with them during your change. Challenge your users to hold you to account when you don't do this. An exercise like this will go a long way to building trust and transparency with users during your change. Table 7.2 shows a pledge document developed for a real-life change initiative.

2. Laying the foundations for a successful change

2.1 Building awareness of the need for change

It is important to build awareness for the need for change so that people understand why the organization is investing time and resources in the initiative and begin to support the change. Change can put huge pressure on an organization. So ensuring everyone understands why it has to happen is vital for both initial engagement and buy-in, and to support people as things get tough during implementation and embedding.

It is quite common to communicate the need for change through the concept of the 'burning platform' – painting a picture of why the organization cannot stay in the position it is currently in. The 'burning platform' can be effective in getting people's

TABLE 7.2 Example of a pledge document

When Change Has Gone Badly:	When Change Has Gone Well:	Therefore We Pledge To:
It was change for change's sake.	There was a recognition that change needed to happen.	Make sure the need for change is clear.
Decision points took a long time to get to, then change was rushed through.	People listened to our questions and concerns.	Ensure there is enough time to plan properly for the change.
There was a lack of engagement.	There was early engagement.	Engage early and frequently throughout the change.
There was ambiguity, which caused anxiety of the unknown.	Our concerns were acknowledged and understood.	Be clear about what is happening and what is expected from you.
We were consulted but there was no action or feedback as a result.	There was learning from previous mistakes.	Consult, listen to concerns and be clear on how we will deal with ideas, suggestions and issues.
There was a lack of training and support.	Our expectations about the change were managed.	Ensure there is enough training and support for everyone.
We felt defensive, resistant, critical, hostile, sceptical, demotivated.	The change led to a more unified service.	Check frequently on how people are feeling about the change.

attention in your change, but be careful how many burning platforms are being described at any one time, as continual messages of panic can be exhausting and give the impression of constant firefighting rather than planned and controlled improvements within the organization.

A more positive way to build awareness of the need for change is through focusing on the benefits that will be realized through the change initiative. The benefits of change are often on two levels – corporate and local. Whilst staff may be interested in the corporate level benefits, it is really the individual benefits – what's in it for me (WIIFM) – that will win hearts and minds for the change. Holding workshops with users (a good exercise for your change agent network) to explore where they think the local benefits will be can help to build good communications to get buy-in for your change. Table 7.3 shows some examples of corporate versus local benefits for a move from paper to electronic case files.

TABLE 7.3 Corporate and local benefits for a change initiative

Corporate Benefits	Local Benefits
Reduced risk of losing files during transportation around the organization.	Easier to work cases remotely leading to more flexible working patterns.
Reduced storage costs.	Quicker to access files to deal with customer queries.
Potential for 'big data' work to help set future organizational strategy.	Easier to search for information within a file.

Be truthful about the benefits of your change, though. Not everyone may benefit, and some aspects of people's jobs may become more cumbersome, repetitive or less appealing. Be honest about what will improve for people – and what will not. Often, if one thing improves, particularly if it is something that people care a lot about, a lot of other dis-benefits will be tolerated.

Be very careful about how you communicate the need for change if there may be job losses. Whilst there may be very strong corporate benefits for this type of change, the individuals involved may not see any benefits at all. Take advice from HR about how to communicate this type of change, but always be truthful about what the potential impact may be.

2.2 Ensuring participation and building support

One of the best ways to build support for a change is by ensuring that people are able to participate at every stage.

Change managers are often brought in to work on change initiatives once the business case has been approved and implementation is about to start, or when it has already started. In order to ensure participation and build support, change management activities should commence well before this stage, by:

- Involving stakeholders in developing the business case for the change initiative.
- Involving affected users when looking at options for the future state: they will be able to tell you what ideas will work on the ground, and how acceptable different ideas may be in their areas.
- If none of the above are possible, at the very least communicate the work that is being done on the change.

Management are often reluctant to communicate at the early stages of a change, let alone allow active participation by users. Often this is because there are many unknowns at the beginning of any change journey and there is a risk that people will become concerned about potential issues before any answers or reassurances can be given. However, if information is not given, people will fill in the gaps with rumour and conjecture, which can be more damaging and very hard to dispel in later stages of the change. Chapter 5 describes how to communicate effectively during the early stages of a change.

Stakeholder engagement, involvement and communications are all activities that need to recur throughout the change preparation process. As discussed in Section A of this chapter, there is an individual change journey for each person affected by the change, and they will need continual engagement to ensure they move towards accepting and supporting the change. Don't make the mistake of assuming that because one article has gone out on the change in the internal newsletter, and key stakeholders have attended one workshop, that the organization is ready for the change.

2.3 Assessing and developing stakeholder skills

Chapter 4 explains how to identify and work with stakeholders during your change. As part of early engagement with your stakeholders, it is worth assessing their skills in change to identify where development needs to be focused.

There are two types of skills that stakeholders need during change: 1) the skills they will need to operate in the new world after the change is implemented; 2) the skills to transition from old to new ways of working during the change. A rough idea of the first set of skills should be identified during the work in order to define the change needed, which is explored in Chapter 2. This will be further refined by applying the techniques for identifying and meeting learning needs (explored in Chapter 9, Section B).

The second set of skills can be identified during activities to ascertain the organizational culture and lessons learnt from previous changes. For example, if lack of communication and consultation has been reported by staff who have been through previous changes in the organization, some tailored work with senior leaders about the need to communicate and involve others in change will help build their skills in these areas and hopefully prevent the same mistakes happening again. Chapter 9, Section C explores behavioural change and coaching needs in more depth.

2.4 Building a change team

Chapter 8, Section B2 describes how to put together a project team to deliver a change initiative. Often a change manager is part of this team and there is no other dedicated resource to concentrate on the people side of the change.

Section A4 explores the need for change agents or middle managers to implement the change successfully in the business. Section B1.2 in this chapter explores the type of resource needed during change initiatives, and how to utilize this from other departments within the organization. You may find, however, that you have the resource to recruit some of these roles into your team. In this case, the choice is either to recruit from inside or outside of the organization. Table 7.4 illustrates the pros and cons of each option.

TABLE 7.4 The pros and cons of internal versus external recruitment for your change team

Internal Recruitment		External Recruitment (Including Consultants)	
Pros	**Cons**	**Pros**	**Cons**
Applicants will already be familiar with the organization's culture and processes.	The appropriate skills and knowledge may not be prevalent within the organization.	You can choose someone who has exactly the specialist knowledge and skills you need.	Staff can be suspicious of 'outsiders', believing that they do not understand the organization.
Staff will generally trust their colleagues more than they will an outsider.	You may not get 100% of people's time – they may have to keep their day job 'ticking over' as well as working on the change initiative.	Senior managers will often listen to and respect the opinion of an outside expert.	Bringing in outside resource to work on change can increase the feeling that change is being done to people, and reduce opportunities for ownership.
Recruitment can be quick as people can be moved into informal secondments rather than going through formal recruitment processes.	Internal recruits may find it difficult to work on tough change initiatives where there is resistance amongst their colleagues, as they don't want to be seen working 'for the other side'.	Knowledge transfer can increase the capacity of the organization to deal with future changes internally.	External recruitment can be a lengthy process – this may not fit with the timelines of your change initiative.
Working on a change initiative can be an excellent career development opportunity for staff.	Internal recruits may be reluctant to go back to their original role after the excitement of working on a change initiative.	External employees will not have any emotional attachment to the way things are, so can be objective about your change initiative.	External employees will need inducting into the organization, including culture, values and accepted language.

3. Developing a change management plan

Throughout the change planning there will be a set of typical recurring actions that contribute to change readiness. A change management plan is a good way to document these actions and ensure they are carried out.

As each organization and change is different, a 'one size fits all' change management plan will not be successful. However, there are some key areas that will need to be covered in all plans. These include:

- *Stakeholders*: who they are, why they are important, how they are going to be engaged with and how often.
- *Communications*: how the communications are going to be targeted to different audiences, what channels will be used and when, how feedback can be obtained.
- *Developing skills*: how sponsors, the change team and change agents or middle managers will be supported and developed to effectively manage the implementation and embedding of the change.
- *Building support*: what activities are planned to communicate the need for the change and increase buy-in.
- *Resistance*: what are the expected types and reasons for resistance and how these will be dealt with (Section C).
- *Feedback*: how key stakeholders (including users) can feedback their thoughts and ideas about the change and approach to implementation, and how this will be fed into the change planning.
- *Measurement*: how you will know that your change interventions are working (Section D).

Summary

Organizational readiness is a key part of preparing to implement change initiatives. There are a number of elements to this, including:

- assessing organizational factors such as culture, values and management style;
- developing the competencies needed to deliver the change, including utilizing skills from other areas of the business, recruiting into your own team and developing stakeholder skills;
- building awareness and support for the change.

Change management should begin as early as possible in the change process, as should communications in order to minimize the risk of the informal grapevine filling in gaps with rumour and conjecture.

Questions to think about

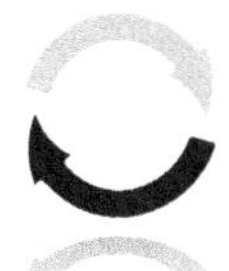

1. What conclusions can you come to about the culture of your organization through observing how it operates?
2. What other teams and departments will you need to work with in order to plan and implement your change?
3. How can you build awareness of the need for your change in a positive manner?

Further reading

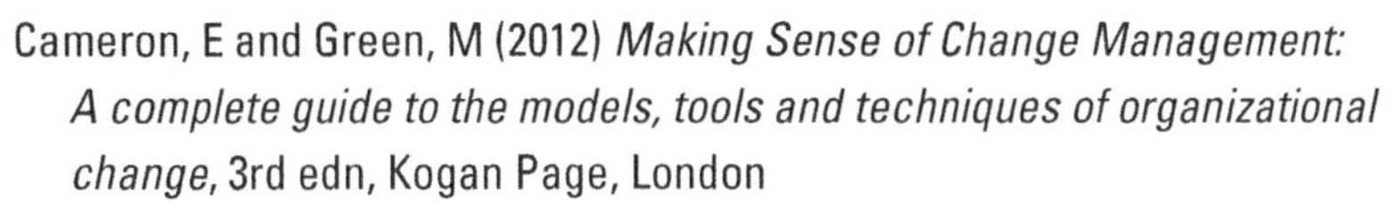

Cameron, E and Green, M (2012) *Making Sense of Change Management: A complete guide to the models, tools and techniques of organizational change*, 3rd edn, Kogan Page, London

Kotter, J P (2012) *Leading Change*, Harvard Business Review Press, Boston, MA

Tannenbaum, R and Schmidt, W H (1973) How to choose a leadership pattern, *Harvard Business Review*, May–June, pp 162–80

Section C: Preparing for resistance

Introduction: understanding that challenges are to be expected

Resistance to change is normal and should be expected and prepared for, no matter how minor or sensible your change initiative may seem. This section looks at the common reasons why people may resist, explores how to identify the types and magnitude of resistance and explains how to build appropriate strategies to deal with this resistance.

1. The 'psychological contract'

One key to understanding why people resist change is to view the world of work through the psychological contract.

FIGURE 7.3 The psychological contract

The CIPD (2013) defines the psychological contract as 'the perceptions of the two parties, employee and employer, on what their mutual obligations are towards each other'. 'Perceptions' is the key word here, as the obligations of a psychological contract are not written down in the formal employment contract, but are the unspoken assumptions and expectations developed through verbal promises and results of past actions.

Organizations that have positive psychological contracts with their staff are rewarded with high levels of employee commitment. This normally translates into a positive impact on performance. If this psychological contract is broken, the results can be a negative impact on job satisfaction, commitment, engagement and, therefore, performance.

It is very important to consider the psychological contract when planning for a change initiative, as alterations to current ways of working can threaten a positive psychological contract. The resulting loss of commitment and engagement may not only mean that the change fails to realize its benefits, but the impacts might be felt a lot wider across the organization and for a long time into the future.

There are various things you can do to help mitigate the threat to the psychological contract during your change:

- Communicate openly and honestly about the change as early as possible.
- Build in lots of opportunities for employees to give feedback and become involved.
- Be realistic about the impacts of the change – don't oversell the benefits, and be honest about dis-benefits.
- Changes that may involve redundancies need extra care and planning. Involve HR very early on and take their advice on how to communicate and handle staff issues. If the organization has a staff consultation group, or is unionized, make sure you talk to everyone you need to and keep them involved from a very early stage.

Tip

Being honest about change. An organization implemented an electronic case-handling system, which was sold as a fantastic opportunity to become more efficient. Senior management was repeatedly asked by concerned staff whether this would mean redundancies, and repeatedly gave assurance that it did not. A few months after the system was implemented it was clear that a large number of staff were no longer needed. The ensuing downsizing exercise broke the psychological contract between the employees and the organization and took years to rebuild.

2. Common causes of resistance

Kanter (2012) lists 10 common causes for resistance during change initiatives, and gives some tips for leaders of change on how to deal with them, as shown in Table 7.5.

3. Identifying likely areas of resistance

In addition to the common causes of resistance listed above, each change initiative is different and it is important to identify which specific aspects of your change people may be unhappy with and therefore resist.

Chapter 2, Section B2.2 describes force field analysis (Lewin, 1951). This is a good tool to use in workshops with affected users to build up a picture of possible areas of resistance. Figure 7.4 shows a force field for an office move, with the arrows illustrating the strength of each of the forces.

TABLE 7.5 Common causes of resistance to change

Reason for Resistance	How to Deal With It
Loss of control over territory	• Leave room for those affected by change to make choices, get involved with planning and take ownership.
Excessive uncertainty during the change	• Create a sense of safety with certainty of process, clear simple steps and timetables.
Change is sprung on people as a surprise	• Don't plan changes in secret – keep people informed of what is happening.
Too many differences at once	• Minimize the number of unrelated differences. • Where possible keep things familiar. • Avoid change for change's sake.
Loss of face from those associated with current state	• Celebrate the elements of the past that are worth honouring.
Concerns about competence	• Provide abundant information, education, mentors and support systems. • Run systems in parallel during transition if possible.
Change is more work	• Allow some people to focus exclusively on the change. • Reward and recognize participants.
Ripple effects – change interferes with the activities of other areas	• Enlarge circle of stakeholders. • Consider all affected parties and work with them to minimize disruption.
Past resentments surface due to the interruption of a steady state	• Consider gestures to heal the past before focusing on the future.
Sometimes the threat is real – change is resisted because it can hurt	• Be honest, transparent, fast and fair. For example, one big layoff with lots of support is better than a series of smaller cuts.

FIGURE 7.4 Force field analysis for an office move

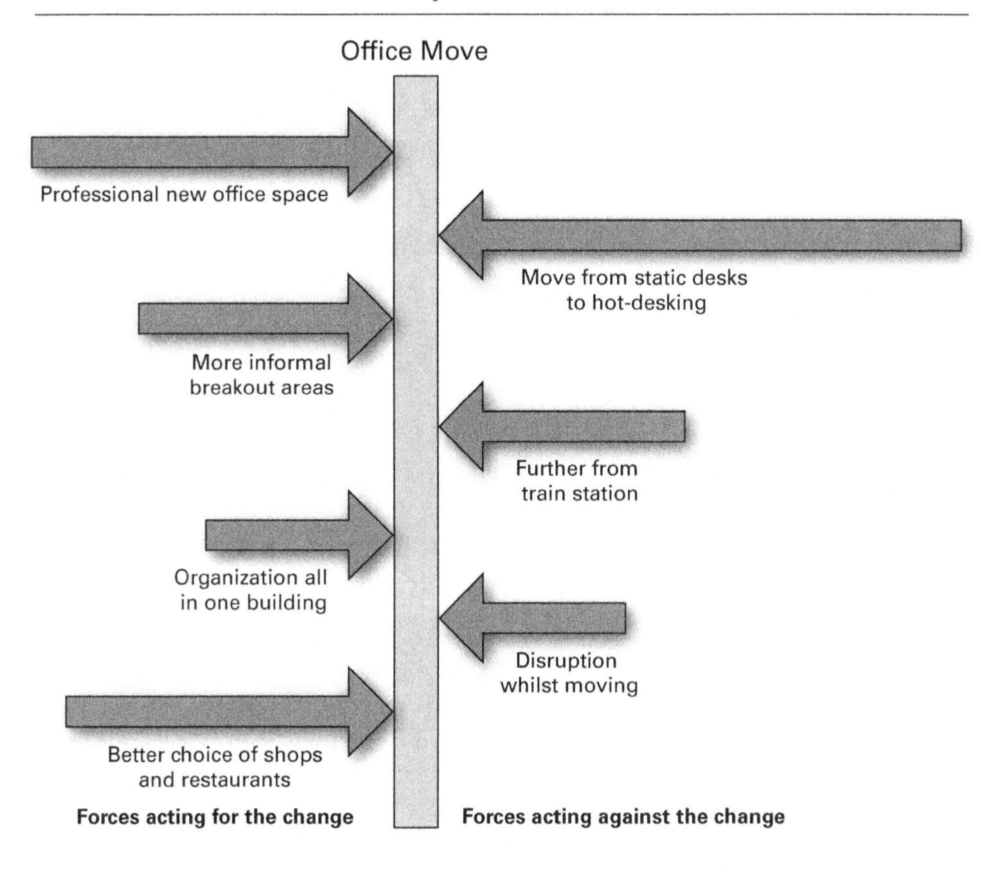

As you can see from Figure 7.4, the forces for and opposing the move are similar in total, but the biggest resisting force is the move from static desks to hot-desking. Focused work with people on accepting the move to hot-desking, and therefore weakening that particular resisting force, will increase the chances of the change being successful.

Tip

The initial reasons given by people for resistance are not always the real reasons. It may be that your change will uncover covert practices or lack of skills that have so far gone undetected and which people will not readily admit. In order to deal with the real issues, dig deep with resistant users to find out what they are truly worried about.

4. Types of resistance and symptoms to look out for

Resistance to change can take on a variety of forms. Table 7.6 explores three of the most common types found during change initiatives.

TABLE 7.6 Common types of resistance to change

Type of Resistance	Symptoms	Things to Be Careful Of	How to Deal With It
Audible unhappiness	Lots of very audible one-way communication to you, senior managers and colleagues about the fact that people are unhappy with the change.	Other people may follow the lead and also become unhappy with the change. Audibly unhappy people can dominate group meetings and workshops. Senior managers may become unsettled about the change if they perceive lots of audible unhappiness.	Engage on a one-to-one basis to ascertain what aspects of the change are making people unhappy. Work with people to identify any benefits they may personally realize through the change. Take feedback on board and, if possible, work with individuals to find solutions to the things they are worried about.
Disengagement	Lack of attendance at events, training and meetings. Lack of participation if forced to attend. Agreeing to proposals and approaches without questioning them.	It is easy to miss these people in the early stages of the change as they keep very quiet. Disengaged managers can negatively affect their teams. People don't get the chance to input into the change planning until it is too late.	Identify reason for disengagement: is it lack of time, denial that the change is happening, latent sabotage? Take the change to them – arrange one-to-one meetings or attend established meetings rather than asking them to attend your organized activities. Increase engagement by involving people where you can, eg in gathering feedback about the change from their colleagues, testing and trying out new ways of working.

TABLE 7.6 *continued*

Type of Resistance	Symptoms	Things to Be Careful Of	How to Deal With It
Sabotage	People bring their own agendas to meetings, workshops and training sessions. Try to 'break' systems and processes. Spread negative rumours about the change to colleagues.	Sabotage is subversive so it is often hard to identify the source. New systems and processes can be fragile in their early stages and quite easily broken if someone really puts their mind to it.	Identify the saboteurs and ensure they know they have been identified. Give people responsibility for aspects of the change in order to increase their buy-in and accountability.

5. Common considerations for building a strategy to manage resistance

Tables 7.5 and 7.6 give some ideas about how to build a strategy to manage resistance. In addition, Kotter and Schlesinger (2008) suggest the following two considerations whilst building your strategy:

- Analyse the following four situational factors:
  - The amount and kind of resistance that is anticipated.
  - How powerful the initiator of the change is in relation to the resisters.
  - Who the people are who have the relevant data to design the change and the energy to implement it.
  - How great the risks are to organizational performance and survival if the change is not made.
- Determine the optimal speed of change: the above analysis will help to decide how quickly or slowly the change should proceed.

In general it is recommended to proceed at a slower pace as this gives time to reduce resistance and ensure all relevant stakeholders are involved in designing and implementing the change. However, if the current risk to organizational performance and survival is very great, it will be necessary to implement the change more quickly, which will involve less buy-in and focus on 'forcing' the change through.

6. Supporting managers and supervisors

Managers and supervisors play a crucial role in the successful implementation of a change. They are the people who translate policy into action and are directly responsible for the teams of people 'on the ground' who have to adapt their ways of working in order to make the change initiative a success. This means they can really influence your change.

Middle management can be a stressful position in which to sit in an organization. Managers have to ensure that directives from senior management are implemented, and also have to deal with resistance and issues from their teams, all whilst maintaining performance standards. If the organization is quite new to change, they also may not have experienced before either going through a change, or managing others through a change. Therefore, it is important to understand that managers and supervisors may need support to buy into and back your change.

Communicate as much as you can with your managers and supervisors. It is important that they are able to answer questions from their staff about the change, and they can be put in an awkward situation if they do not know what is going on. Workshops, briefings and written FAQs can all help managers and supervisors to understand what is going on and also to support their staff.

Managers and supervisors who are struggling with the change may also benefit from some informal coaching or mentoring (Chapter 9, Section C describes coaching). This can help you to support your managers and supervisors to deal with challenges brought about by the change.

7. Building and sustaining momentum

It can take an effort to build momentum for your change initiative and it is even more challenging to sustain that momentum, especially if there is lots of planning needed before implementation, or if the implementation takes a long time.

Momentum can be built through regular communications, engagement with stakeholders and an active change agent network. Timing the build-up of this momentum is crucial. If there is a long lead-in time for the change, it can be detrimental to build momentum for the change too early. People will become frustrated, lose interest and begin to focus on other priorities before the change can actually be implemented.

Building and sustaining momentum during the planning and implementation stages of a change initiative can be supported by four key strategies:

- *Timing of communications*: increasing the frequency of communications will help to build momentum as users hear more about the change as implementation approaches. Chapter 5 explains more about the type and frequency of communications during a change.
- *Phased approach to implementation*: if the nature of your change allows, carry out a pilot or early tranche before rolling out to all users. This gives the opportunity of testing solutions and approaches to the rollout, as well as gathering case studies and 'good news' stories from early adopters. This will increase the interest of users who are waiting to go live, as they hear how their colleagues are getting on. Chapter 8, Section D1, discusses this further.
- *Keep visibility of the change high*: when the change starts, especially if you have built up momentum, it may be the top of everyone's priority list. However, if it is a long rollout, or an extended period of embedding is needed, other things will begin to take people's attention and your change may slip down in people's priorities. In order to keep people focused on the change,

keep the levels of communications and 'good news' stories high. Publish hard data updates, for example '300 more people have gone live with the change this month'.

- *Task managers with the responsibility for delivery*: build successful implementation for their areas into their targets, objectives or reporting. Remember: 'if it isn't measured, it doesn't get done'.

Summary

Resistance to change is to be expected and, therefore, it pays to prepare for it. There are common causes for resistance, for example loss of control or increased uncertainty, but each change will also have specific elements that may also cause resistance.

There are a number of techniques to deal with resistance, depending on the cause and type of resistance you are experiencing and the urgency of the change. Building and sustaining momentum, and supporting managers and supervisors, are both key factors in preparing for resistance.

Questions to think about

1. How might your change threaten the psychological contract? How can you mitigate this?
2. Using Lewin's force field analysis (1951), what are the major forces acting for and against your change?
3. How can you prepare for different types of resistance during your change?
4. What practical activities can you undertake to build and sustain momentum for your change during planning and implementation?

Further reading

Chartered Institute of Personnel and Development (CIPD) (2013) [accessed 12 April 2014] The Psychological Contract [online] http://www.cipd.co.uk/hr-resources/factsheets/psychological-contract.aspx

Kanter, R M (2012) [accessed 12 April 2014] Ten Reasons People Resist Change [Online] http://blogs.hbr.org/2012/09/ten-reasons-people-resist-change/

Kotter, J P and Schlesinger, L A (2008) Choosing strategies for change, *Harvard Business Review*, **86** (7–8), July–August, pp 130–39

Section D: Measuring change effectiveness

Introduction: 'taking the temperature' and tracking progress

Measuring the effectiveness of your change activities can be challenging, as a lot of work in change management is concerned with people's feelings and behaviours rather than producing 'hard' outputs. It is easier to measure activities (eg number of surveys sent out, training sessions held) than progress (eg number of people who are now not so resistant to the change). However, it is important to try and measure progress, not only to check if your interventions are working or need tweaking, but also to reassure your sponsor that they are doing the right thing in investing in change management.

1. Measures of engagement

Change management is all about taking people on a journey. One way to explain this journey is through using the ADKAR® model (Hyatt, 2006). This is a set of five sequential building blocks, all of which are needed to move people through a successful change. The model states that if a change fails to be implemented successfully, one or more of the blocks has usually been missed out. The five building blocks are:

- Awareness of the need for change.
- Desire to participate and support the change.
- Knowledge on how to change.
- Ability to implement required skills and behaviours.
- Reinforcement to sustain the change.

It is important to 'take the temperature' periodically throughout this journey in order to check that people are still with you and have not stalled along the way.

As measuring change is not straightforward, it is worth measuring a number of factors using a variety of methods, both statistical and anecdotal, in order to build a picture of how effective your change interventions are. Measures can include:

- Engagement with the change: do people know what the change is and what it is trying to achieve?
- Feelings about the change: are people generally supportive of what the change is trying to do?
- Readiness for the change: are people prepared and informed about what the change will mean to them?
- Progress with change activities: what and how many activities are being held?

Figure 7.5 shows an example of engagement measures that could be taken during a change journey. They gauge the levels of readiness and commitment to the change by the organization, using the ADKAR® model.

FIGURE 7.5 Example of engagement measures

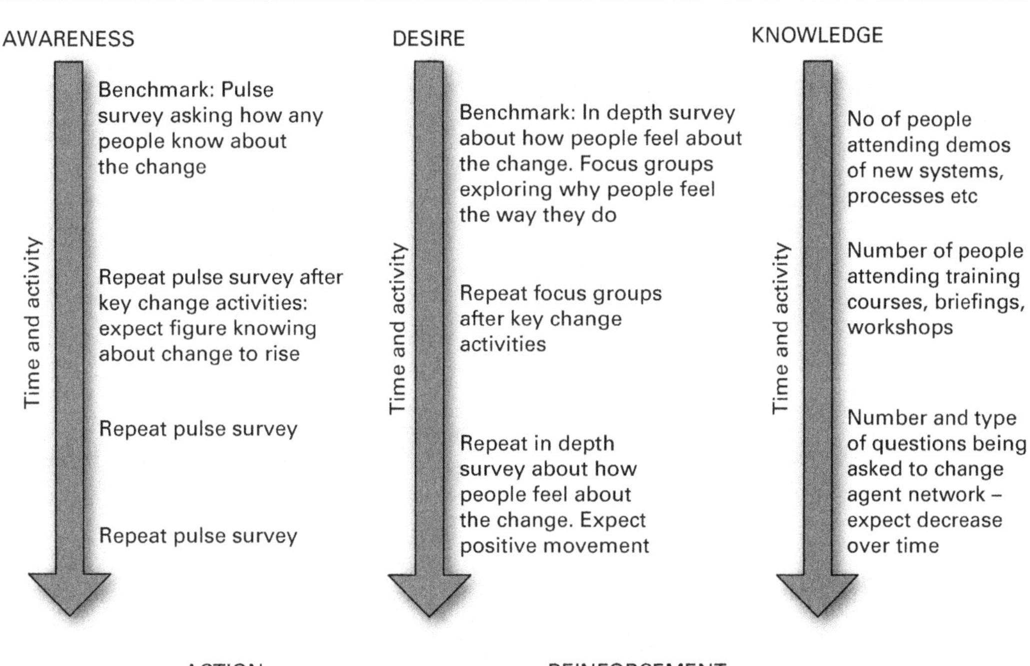

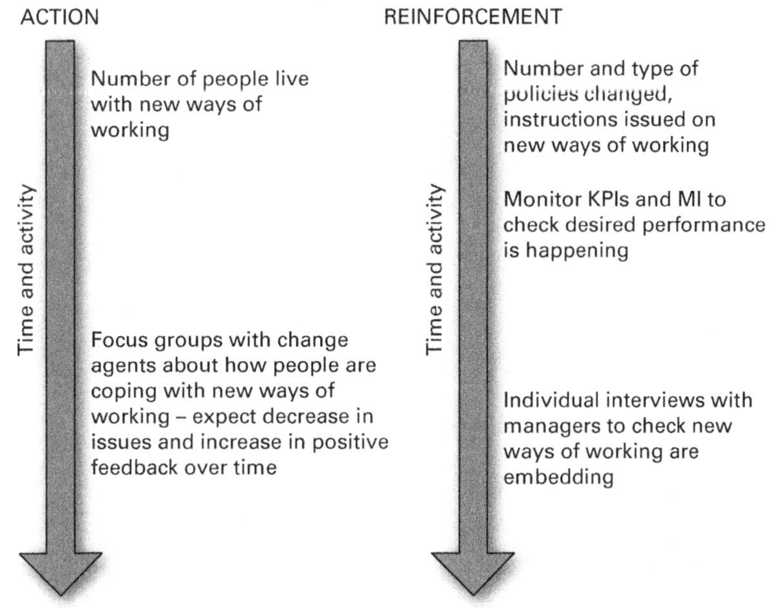

2. Methods of capturing information

There is a range of methods for capturing information about the effectiveness of your change interventions. Table 7.7 outlines the most common. For each of these methods there are some practical considerations, as set out below.

TABLE 7.7 Methods of capturing information

Method	Good For	Data Interpretation	Typical Content
Pulse surveys	Taking a quick temperature check about the change. Can be repeated throughout change journey to measure progress.	Easy to interpret quick yes and no answers.	Are you looking forward to the change? Yes/no.
One-off surveys	Taking a snapshot of opinions and feelings at a period in time from a large group of people. Can be repeated at significant points in the change journey to see if people's readiness and acceptance is changing.	Easy to interpret closed questions such as those with a yes/no answer, on a Likert scale (1–5) or with a tick box selection of answers. Harder to interpret free text answers – best to organize into themes.	On a scale of 1–5, how confident are you in using the new software?
Focus groups	Finding out why something is happening – often used to dig down into the quantitative results of a survey.	Data can be very rich – need to be able to capture it all and pick out themes and salient points.	The survey says that 70% of people are not confident in using the new software. Why do you think that is?
Individual interviews	Sensitive subjects where people may not be happy to discuss their thoughts in public. Senior managers who are too busy to attend focus groups, or who may digress or disagree if put in a group together.	Data can be very rich and personal to individuals. May not reflect the thoughts of the organization as a whole, but can be useful to understand where key stakeholders are coming from.	What are your thoughts on the change? Why do you think that?

2.1 Pulse surveys

A pulse survey is a quick one-question tally to gauge opinion on a specific subject with a yes or no answer. You can carry out your pulse survey in a variety of ways, for example by placing voting tokens and two clear plastic boxes in coffee areas, flipchart tallies on the wall in reception, quick voting buttons on intranet sites. Pulse surveys are very quick for users to do and can be fun, so you can get a big response in a short amount of time, and can repeat them frequently throughout the change without annoying people.

Think carefully about the question you want to ask, as not every question fits neatly into a yes or no answer. For example, asking if people have heard about a change does not give information about what they have heard, how much they have heard, or even if the information they have heard is correct.

2.2 One-off surveys

The internet has made sending out one-off surveys cheap and easy. Check with your internal communications or HR department to see if they have a subscription to any survey software. If not, there are free software packages available that you can use to generate and manage your surveys. The software will also create a variety of graphs and other visuals, which look great for feeding back the results.

Make sure your survey is quick and easy to fill in. Most people will give five minutes of their time to complete a survey but few will spend half an hour. Don't have too many free-text-box answers as they are difficult to interpret, but a free-text comment box in addition to the main questions can be useful if people wish to explain their answer further. Making answers compulsory can annoy your target group, as can overly complicated or leading questions, all of which may increase dropout rates.

Survey results need to be robust in order to be confident in the answers. The sample needs to be large enough, and a high enough percentage of people need to answer. If big decisions are going to be made from the results of your survey, for example approving a business case, it is worth taking expert advice to check that the results are robust. Surveys are self selecting and you may find that only people who are very supportive or very resistant to the change take the time to respond. Beware of survey fatigue if the organization sends out lots of surveys, and try not to interfere with similar initiatives, for example annual staff surveys.

Beware of asking leading questions in your survey and always check the survey with a small group before sending it out, in order to make sure that the questions are clear and unambiguous.

2.3 Focus groups

As these are held face-to-face they can explore issues in a lot more depth than is possible with surveys. They require more time and input from users, so keep them as short as possible – one hour is usually acceptable, more than two is not. Provide refreshments if you can. Even a packet of biscuits from the local supermarket shows that you appreciate people giving up their time to engage in your change.

Between five and ten people is a good number for a focus group. Any larger and it can be difficult for everyone to have their say. Any smaller and you may not get the range of ideas and thoughts that you need. Make sure you invite people who are comfortable in discussing ideas with each other. For example, inviting staff together with their manager may mean that no one feels comfortable about being really honest. Having separate sessions for staff and managers means people may be able to discuss issues and concerns much more openly. Set some ground rules before you begin, including confidentiality, so that people are happy to discuss issues openly. Be aware that focus groups will only give you the ideas and interpretations of that particular group of people, and may not be representative of the wider user group. To mitigate this, it is worth holding a number of focus groups with representatives from different segments of your users in order to get a wider picture of thoughts and concerns.

Take notes on a flipchart about key points raised so that all participants can agree that you are representing their views accurately. You can write up these flipchart notes afterwards and e-mail them to your participants at the same time as thanking them for their time and letting them know what will be done with the information they have given.

2.4 Individual interviews

These are the most time-consuming form of data gathering, but can be very useful to help build relationships and understand issues from key stakeholders who will be influential during your change. Try to meet on neutral territory – not in the interviewee's office. Make the interview as informal as possible in order to put people at their ease and help the conversation flow. Chats in the staff café or local coffee shop work well. Thirty minutes is a good length of time for an interview but they can be done in less if necessary.

The conversation can be more free flowing than in focus groups. You can ask very open questions and see where the conversation goes. However, make sure you keep within scope of your subject. Writing a list of questions and sending them to the interviewee in advance will help them think about their responses in advance and will help you get the conversation back on track if it digresses too far.

Take notes as the conversation is happening, as you won't remember everything afterwards. Repeat your notes back to the participant to check you have captured their views accurately. Check with the interviewee how they would like the information they give you to be managed. Are they happy to be quoted or would they like their thoughts and views to be kept anonymous?

3. Presenting data on employee engagement

As a general rule, when presenting data on employee engagement and change activities it is best to keep it simple and short, especially if presenting to senior managers or your project board. Use diagrams where possible, backed up with data in an appendix, eg a pie chart to show the number of people who have attended training, a bar graph with results from a pulse survey.

Collating and presenting data can show how effective the change management interventions are being, which may not otherwise be picked up. Figure 7.6 is a real-life example of a survey completed by staff attending a training session on a new IT system that was about to be implemented. This shows:

- The vast majority of attendees agreed that the training met its objectives.
- 100 per cent of attendees feel confident they understood the content covered in the training session.
- Most attendees found the session very useful.

However:

- Less than 30 per cent of attendees are confident in using the new system.

The data in Figure 7.6 shows that, even though the staff are pleased with the training session, it does not mean that they are confident in the new ways of working. This means they will struggle to make the transition and, therefore, the success of the change is at risk. Presenting feedback from the training session in this way will build the case for investing in more support to staff throughout the implementation and make sure they are confident in using the new system.

Use a range of qualitative reports to back up your quantitative data, for example quotes from evaluation forms and case studies. Case studies from early adopters of the change are an excellent way of communicating progress to other users, as they will be very interested in seeing how one of their colleagues is getting on with the change. The following short case study offers an example.

CASE STUDY

I am a senior manager in casework and have been using the new technology for about a year. It took a while to get used to working electronically, but the training and support from my local super user really helped when I was getting frustrated.

I have found the new technology has lots of features that are an improvement on paper. Information is more secure; you can search easily for key words; you can increase font size to reduce eye strain; and you can copy and paste text or take snapshots of documents.

I also like that I can be in a different location to one of my colleagues, but still be able to look at the same documents as them. This really comes in handy as I often need to discuss information with people who work in different locations. I also like that I don't have to cart heavy paper files backwards and forwards!

FIGURE 7.6 Training survey

Q1 The session's learning objectives were achieved

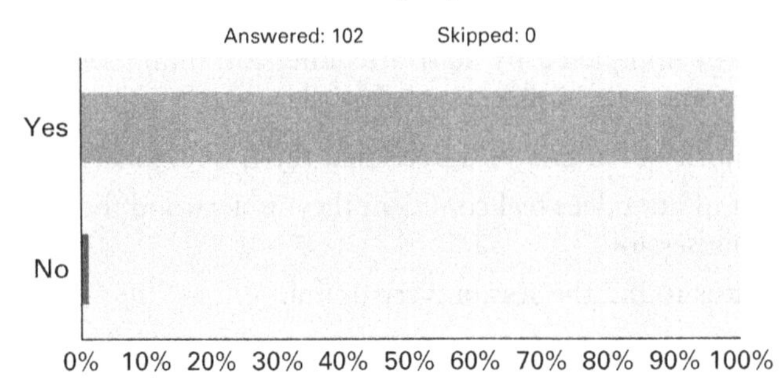

Q2 I feel confident that I have understood the content covered in the training session

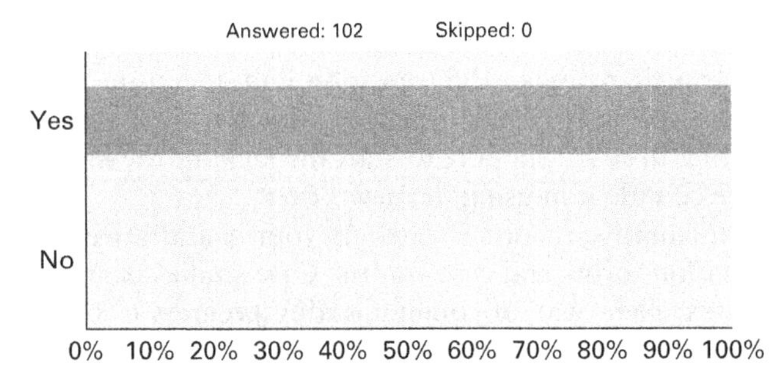

Q5 On a scale of 1 to 10 how useful did you find the training session? (1 being least useful and 10 being very useful)

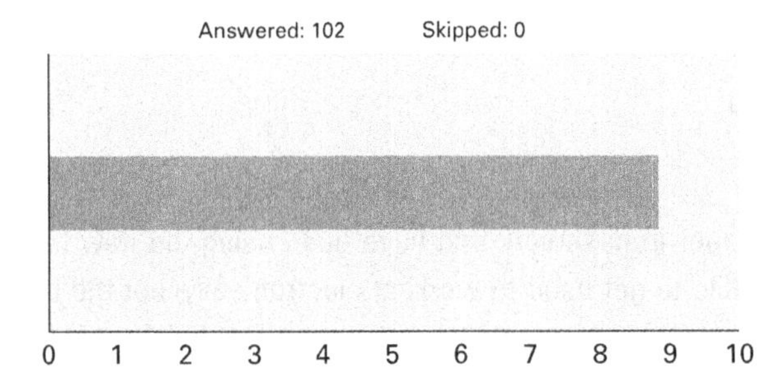

Q6 Having completed training do you think you can now confidently use the new system?

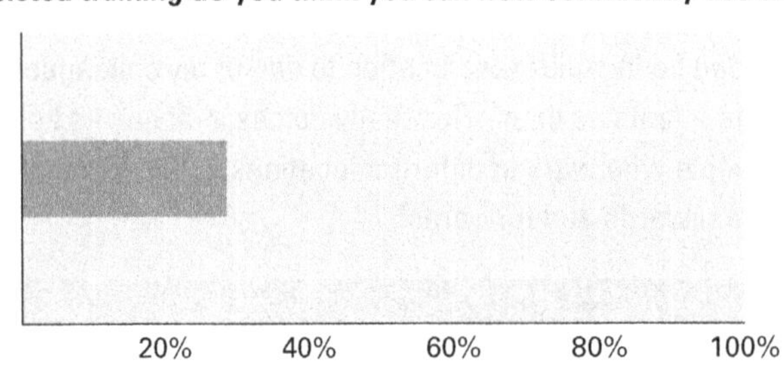

Summary

Measuring change is not simple but there are four factors that could be measured:

- engagement with the change;
- feelings about the change;
- readiness for the change;
- progress with change activities.

Four commonly used techniques for measuring change are pulse surveys, one-off surveys, focus groups and individual interviews, each with their own challenges. Data should be presented to senior managers as simply as possible and in visual form.

Questions to think about

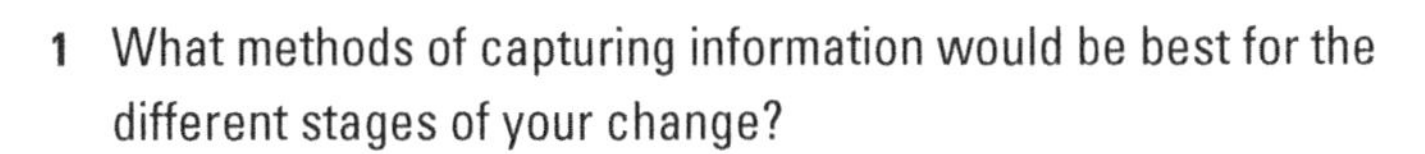

1. What methods of capturing information would be best for the different stages of your change?
2. How can you best present data in order to give your sponsor confidence that the organization is ready for your change?
3. Who from your change could give a good case study for potential resistors?

Further reading

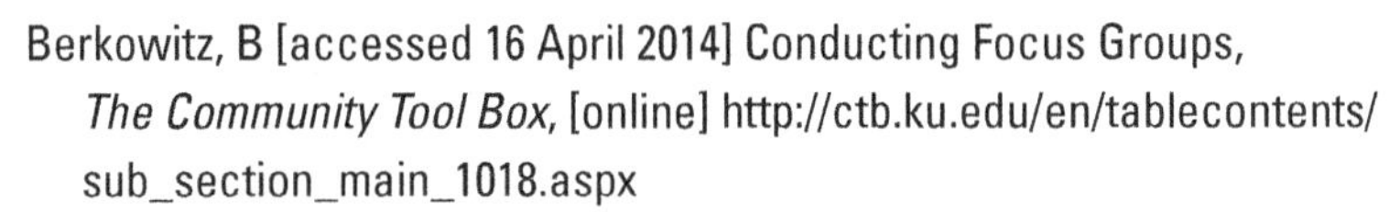

Berkowitz, B [accessed 16 April 2014] Conducting Focus Groups, *The Community Tool Box*, [online] http://ctb.ku.edu/en/tablecontents/sub_section_main_1018.aspx

Hyatt, J M (2006) *ADKAR: A model for change in business, government and our community*, Prosci Learning Center Publications, Loveland, Colorado

Monash University [accessed 16 April 2014] How to Conduct an Interview [online] http://www.monash.edu.au/lls/hdr/develop/4.2.1.html

US General Services Administration [accessed 16 April 2014] Basics of Survey and Question Design [Online] https://www.howto.gov/customer-experience/collecting-feedback/basics-of-survey-and-question-design

References

Beckhard, R F and Harris, R T (1987) *Organizational Transitions: Managing complex change*, Addison-Wesley, Reading, MA

Bridges, W (2009) *Managing Transitions: Making the most of change*, 3rd edn, Nicholas Brealey, London

Cameron, E and Green, M (2012) *Making Sense of Change Management: A complete guide to the models, tools and techniques of organizational change*, 3rd edn, Kogan Page, London

The Chartered Institute of Personnel and Development (CIPD) (2013) [accessed 12 April 2014] The Psychological Contract [Online] http://www.cipd.co.uk/hr-resources/factsheets/psychological-contract.aspx

Cooperrider, D L and Whitney, D (2005) *A Positive Revolution in Change: Appreciative inquiry*, Berrett-Koehler Publishers Inc, California

Herzberg, J F (2003) One more time: how do you motivate employees? *Harvard Business Review*, **81** (1), January 2003, pp 87–96 (reprint of original article from 1968)

Hyatt, J M (2006) *ADKAR: A model for change in business, government and our community*, Prosci Learning Center Publications, Loveland, Colorado

Kanter, R M (2012) [accessed 12 April 2014] Ten Reasons People Resist Change [Online] http://blogs.hbr.org/2012/09/ten-reasons-people-resist-change/

Kotter, J P and Schlesinger, L A (2008) Choosing strategies for change, *Harvard Business Review*, July–August, **86** (7–8), pp 130–39

Kübler-Ross, E (1969) *On Death and Dying*, Macmillan, Toronto

Lewin, K (1964) *Field Theory in Social Science: Selected theoretical papers*, Harper Torchbooks, New York

Lunenberg, F (2011) Expectancy theory of motivation: motivating by altering expectations, *International Journal of Management, Business and Administration*, **15** (1), pp 1–6

Maslow, A H (1943) *A Theory of Human Motivation*, Cambridge University Press, Cambridge

Morgan, G (2006) *Images of Organization*, 2nd edn, Sage, London

Rogers, E M (2003) *Diffusion of Innovations*, 5th edn, Free Press, New York

Tannenbaum, R and Schmidt, W H (1973) How to choose a leadership pattern, *Harvard Business Review*, May–June, pp 162–80

Whitmore, J (2009) *Coaching for Performance: Growing human potential and purpose – the principles and practice of coaching and leadership*, 4th edn, Nicholas Brealey, London

Project management
Change initiatives, projects and programmes

08

IRA BLAKE

Introduction

Project management is chiefly associated with planning and managing change in an organization, yet it can be applied to many situations, such as domestic endeavours. Projects can be various shapes and sizes, from the small and straightforward to the extremely large and highly complex. Chapter 2, Section B1.3 describes the way that projects may fit into the more complex governance structures of programmes and portfolios. The methods, tools and techniques in this chapter are in most cases applicable to programmes and portfolios as well as to projects.

Project management techniques and project planning tools are useful for any tasks in which different outcomes are possible – where risks of problems and failures exist – and so require planning and assessing options, and organizing activities and resources to deliver a successful result.

A task does not necessarily have to be called a 'project' in order for project management methods to be very useful in its planning and implementation. Any task that requires some preparation to achieve a successful outcome can benefit from the application of project management skills and techniques. Even if you never intend to manage a project in your life, it is essential for every manager, and change manager, to at least know and understand what project management is and its purpose.

CHAPTER CONTENTS

Section A: Change within project governance structures

Introduction

Project management is both an established profession in its own right and also a competence that forms a part of many managers' general toolkit. Project management is a specific skill set and the demand for this capability is a reflection of the value placed on project management by organizations in all industry sectors.

All projects result in a change that affects someone. Project managers are focused on defining and delivering the 'what' of change. Managing the impact of change on people requires a specific skill set and a focus on the 'who' and 'application' of change. This is the remit of change management.

1. Understanding the project environment

In any company, there are a number of things that anyone will be working on to be proactive or reactive to the changing environment. Many projects begin as ideas either to fix something that is broken or move the organization towards an aspirational goal or vision.

All projects have at least three phases: set-up, delivery and close down. Commonly, the middle or delivery phase is divided into several chunks, so projects can realistically have four, five or more phases. How projects are broken down into component phases or stages make up the project life cycle. The phases are comprised of project workstream plans (such as change management) that need to be in alignment with the phase timeline. This is fairly common terminology. Sometimes projects form part of a project hierarchy (eg a programme), but in all cases there are standard procedures and documentation that need to be coordinated and produced.

Programmes are made up of groups of interrelated changes that may be delivered through a number of different projects, which require an oversight of the purpose and status of all the moving parts to ensure the overall programme goals are likely to be met – possibly by providing a decision-making capacity that cannot be achieved at project level or by providing a project manager with a contextual perspective when required. For example, a project might deliver a new factory, hospital or IT system. By combining these projects with other changes, the overall programme could deliver better treatment from a new product, shorter waiting lists at the hospital or reduced operating costs due to improved technology.

A portfolio is a group of current and prospective projects and programmes managed to deliver business goals or a strategy, eg business transformation. Portfolios often do not have a specified time frame and operate on a rolling basis, with new projects being added and completed projects rolling off continuously.

1.1 Governance structure

A clearly defined governance hierarchy creates a path of accountability for every project and activity within an organization (Figure 8.1). The governance structure is the mechanism of 'how' the project is managed.

The purpose of a project governance structure is the accountability for:

- ensuring strategic objectives are met/supported by the project;
- ensuring project solutions are acceptable to the business and can be implemented;
- prioritizing project needs with other initiatives and business as usual (BAU);
- decision making and escalation for complex and wider business issues.

FIGURE 8.1 Types of governance bodies (Blake and Bush, 2009)

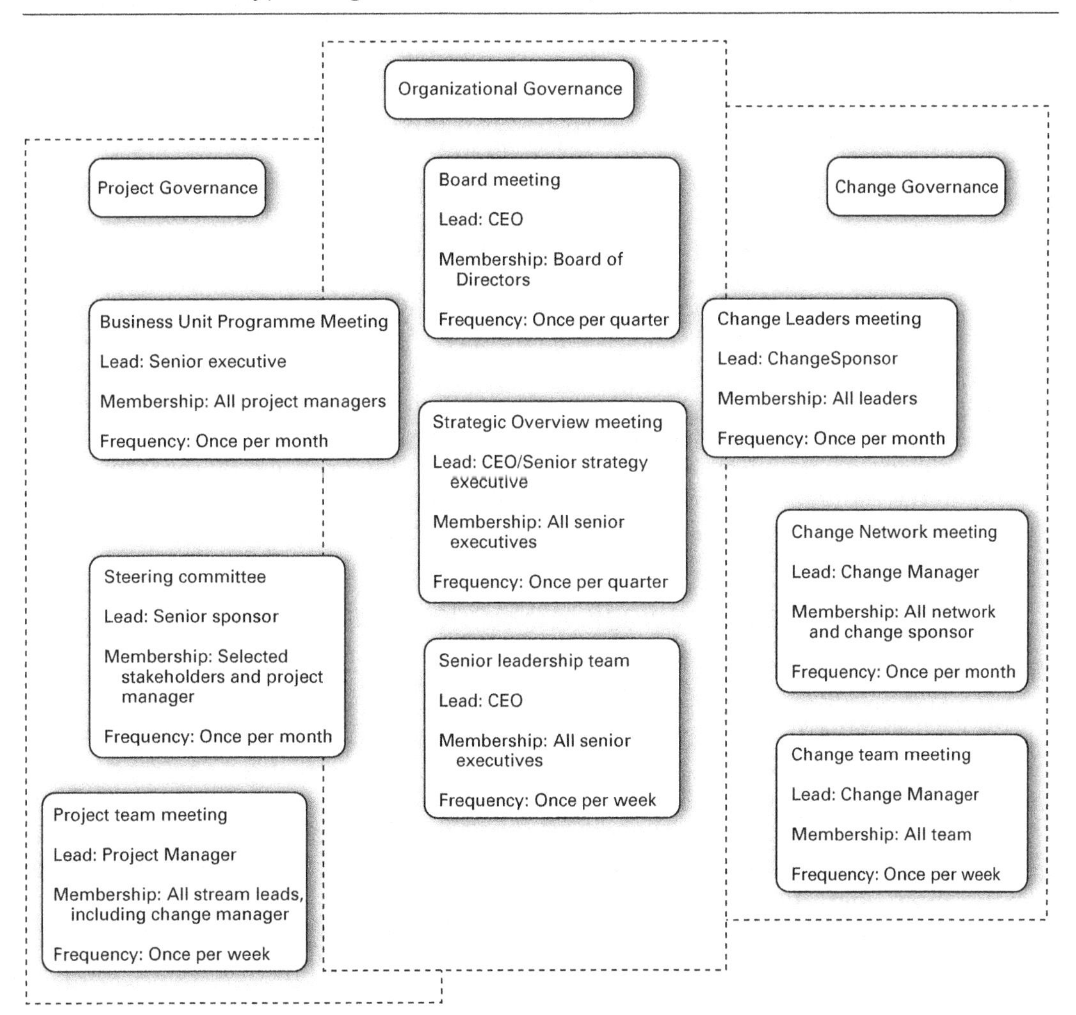

Depending on the scale and complexity of the project, there will be a number of different governance bodies, committees and/or boards. The relationship between these groups will be shown on the project organization chart. Each group will have a defined remit described in its Terms of Reference (ToR) document and also a list of its members and their roles/job title. The ToR document outlines the level of authority and decision making that is delegated to a group, and also the escalation route for issues requiring a greater level of authority.

Levels of authority

Situational leadership theory, developed by Paul Hersey and Ken Blanchard (2012), suggests that delegation of authority depends on the kind of task and the maturity of the people to whom the tasks are delegated.

The authority to make decisions in the context of a project (remit) is defined in the project governance structure. In complex and large-scale projects, there is often a need to distribute controls and for the sponsor and project board to delegate their authority. The hierarchy of authority helps individuals to understand from whom they are to receive guidance and direction, and helps to establish efficient communication paths between individuals, teams and leaders in an organization.

Portfolio/programme management office: purpose and function

Coordination, collation and storage of project standard procedures and documents is the responsibility of the Portfolio or Programme Management Office (PMO). The PMO has accountability to ensure that the project is compliant, required artefacts are produced and quality standards are met. Within these constraints, a change manager assigned to the project will be responsible for certain deliverables, progress reporting and documentation.

The PMO is a valuable resource for change managers and will provide guidance, templates and ensure compliance with the project methodology/approach. The PMO collates inputs and produces reports and essential information on the status of the project to the governance structures, and disseminates decisions and requests from those bodies to the project team(s) in a consistent and timely way.

1.2 Project methodologies: considerations for change management

In many respects, a project is like a separate organization within an organization; set up to exist for a finite time and to achieve a specific outcome. Projects have a defined set of structures, roles and responsibilities and have activities and processes that operate independently to the normal day-to-day work or business as usual (BAU). Formal methods of project management offer a framework to manage this process, providing a series of elements such as templates and procedures to manage the project through its life cycle.

There are many different project management methodologies available, each promoted by its owner as having some special advantage or suitability to your project – and coming with its own unique language. The most popular are PRINCE2®, PMI (PMBOK®) and SCRUM™. Many companies have their own methodology that is often some form or hybrid of these. Most systems are proprietary and are sold as a package of services that will include training sessions and consultancy alongside documentation that will include templates and guidance notes. When you look at all the different systems it becomes apparent that they are variations on one of two major types: 'waterfall' and 'agile'.

Waterfall methodology

The waterfall method is a sequential process in which progress is seen as flowing steadily downwards (like a waterfall) through the phases of initiation, requirements, specification, analysis, design, development, testing, implementation and maintenance. The waterfall method originates in the manufacturing and construction industries that are highly structured environments in which after-the-fact changes are prohibitively costly, if not impossible. The central idea behind the waterfall model is that time spent early on making sure requirements and design are correct saves much time and effort later. Some waterfall proponents prefer the waterfall model for its simple approach and argue that it is more disciplined. The waterfall progresses linearly through discrete, easily recognizable and explainable phases and thus is easy to understand; it also provides easily identifiable milestones in the development process.

The concepts behind the waterfall process are:

- high-level requirements should be concrete before design begins (otherwise work put into a design based on incorrect requirements is wasted);
- design should be complete before people begin to implement the design (otherwise they implement the wrong design and their work is wasted);
- make sure each phase is 100 per cent complete and absolutely correct before proceeding to the next phase.

One argument in favour of the waterfall model is that it places emphasis on documentation (such as requirements documents and design documents). Knowledge can be lost if team members leave before the project is completed, and it may be difficult for a project to recover from the loss. If a fully working design document exists, new team members or even entirely new teams are able to familiarize themselves by reading the documents.

Agile methodology

Agile approaches came about in response to the challenges faced by using more sequential project management methods. For example, for more complex projects with greater uncertainty and within fast-paced change environments, it becomes increasingly difficult to define detailed requirements early on, with any degree of confidence. This is commonly evident in complex technology projects where end users tend to have difficulty defining the long-term requirements without being able to view progressive prototypes. Agile approaches use the idea of iterative and incremental development to allow detailed requirements to be defined later as the solution evolves.

Agile projects manage the design and build of solutions in an incremental, flexible and interactive manner. It requires individuals with specific skills and competencies from the relevant business, with supplier and customer input and there are also links to lean techniques and Six Sigma.

Agile methods were developed in recognition that, during a project, the customers can change their minds about what they want and need (often called requirements churn), and that unpredicted challenges cannot be easily addressed by traditional project methods. Some specific techniques have been developed that support this approach:

Timeboxing

Timeboxing is a technique that sets a fixed period of time to achieve one or more objectives. The timebox is managed by adding or removing elements from the scope of the objective(s). This focuses work on the most important elements and depends on the effective prioritization of these elements. Agile projects are divided into timeboxes, each having its own deliverables and timeline. It is the project stakeholders who determine the priorities.

Sprints

One of the most commonly used agile methods is SCRUM™. An iteration or sprint is the basic unit of progress within this method and each sprint is started by a planning meeting, where the tasks for the sprint are identified and an estimated commitment for the sprint goal is made. A sprint ends in a review-and-retrospective meeting, where the progress is assessed and lessons for the next sprint are identified. Sprints are restricted to a specific duration. The duration is fixed in advance for each sprint and is normally between one week and one month, although two weeks is typical. The SCRUM™ method emphasizes having a working product at the end of the sprint that is really 'done'. In the case of software, this means a system that is integrated, fully tested, end-user documented and deployable.

An advantage of developing solutions iteratively and incrementally is that they can constantly gather feedback to help refine those requirements. The intended result is a project that best meets current customer needs and is delivered with minimal costs, waste and time, enabling companies to achieve business benefit gains earlier than via traditional/waterfall approaches.

1.3 Methodology types in programmes

Project management is supported by a set of processes and methodologies that define how to run a project. The selected methodology will have a profound effect on the project environment and culture, and drive how the workload is organized and managed. It is common that projects in a programme may be applying different methodologies, eg a web-development project could be using agile while the ERP (enterprise resource planning) system it integrates with, such as SAP, could be using waterfall for their project.

2. Project management tools

In addition to formal methodologies, projects adhere to specific processes and techniques. Collectively, managing these define the remit of a project manager. Some of the commonly used tools in project planning and project management, are critical path analysis (CPA) and Gantt charts.

Critical path analysis

Critical path analysis (CPA), also called critical path method (CPM), is a logical and effective method for planning and managing complex projects. A CPA is a diagrammatical representation of what needs to be done and when, and is good for showing interdependent factors whose timings overlap or coincide. A CPA is normally shown as a flow diagram, with a linear (organized in a line) format and to a specified timeline. It also enables a plan to be scheduled according to a timescale. As a simple example – making a fried breakfast (Figure 8.2).

FIGURE 8.2 Simple CPA example

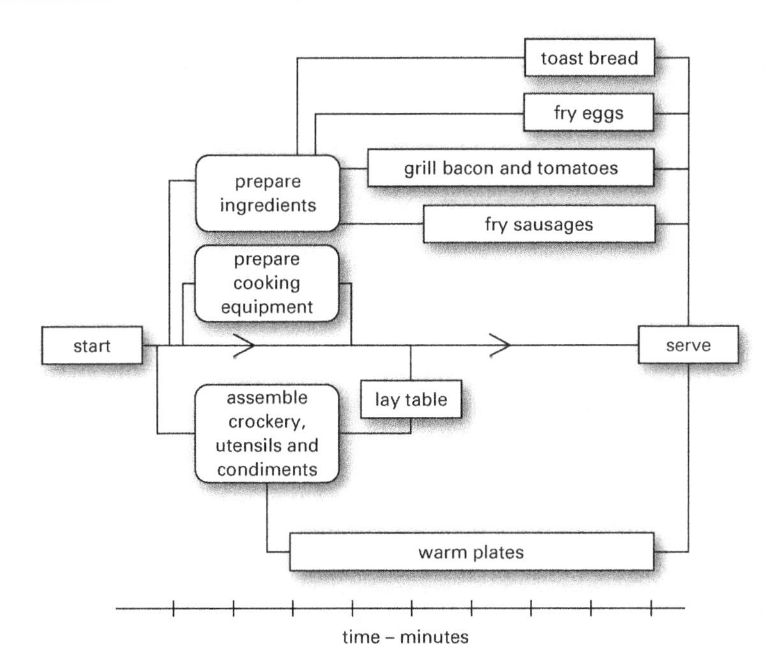

Gantt charts

Gantt charts (Figure 8.3) are excellent models for scheduling, budgeting, reporting, presenting and communicating plans and progress easily and quickly. They are

FIGURE 8.3 Basic Gantt chart example

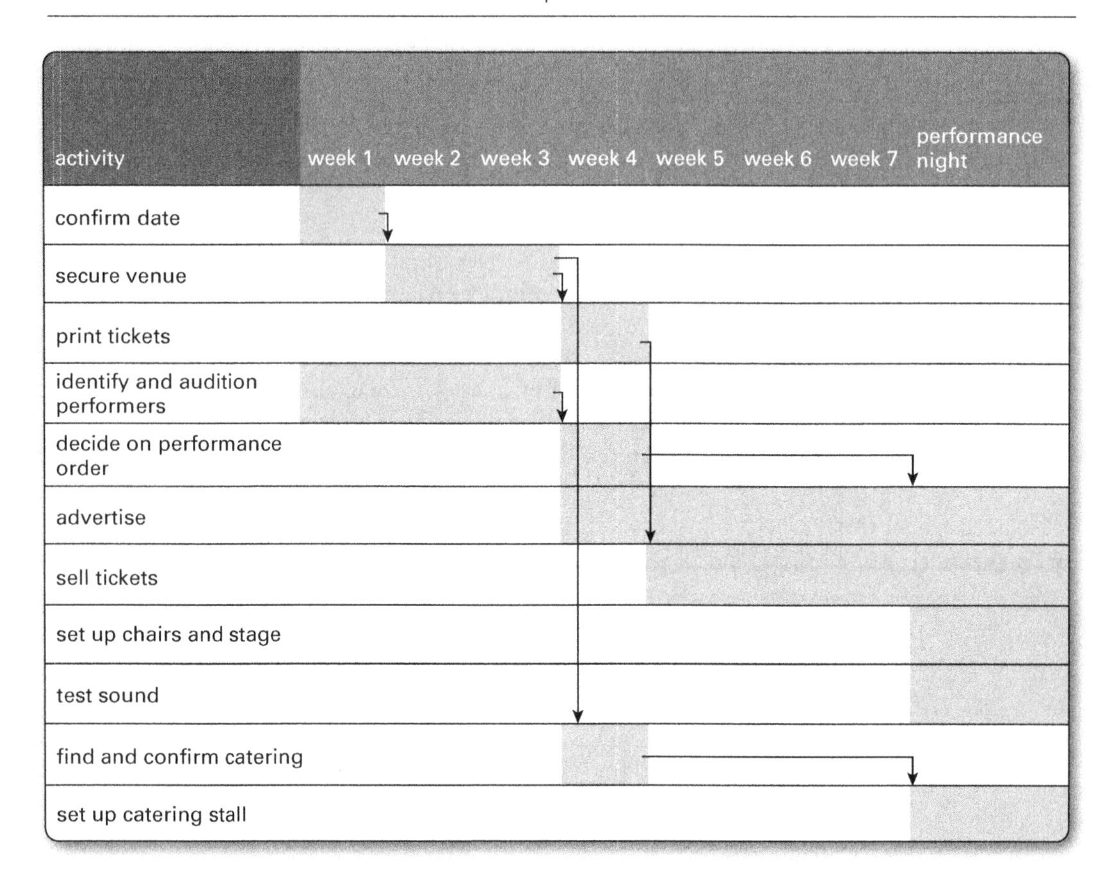

usually constructed using Microsoft Project or a spreadsheet application and every activity and task has a separate line. At the end of each line additional columns can be added for as many factors as you need, eg cost, resource, type, dependencies, task duration and effort required.

When creating a Gantt chart it is important to understand the distinction between effort versus duration. The effort required to complete a task is the actual number of hours needed to spend focused on the task to get the job done. Duration is the elapsed time from when the task was first started to when it is complete.

A Gantt chart can be used to keep track of progress for each activity and how the costs are incurred. Content can be moved around to report on actuals versus planned, to reschedule and to create new plan updates. Costs columns can show plan and actuals and variances, and calculate whatever totals, averages, ratios, etc that you need.

Project software

Project management also extends to the use of some specific tools, eg Microsoft Project, or the use of familiar tools such as Microsoft Excel, but potentially using functionality unfamiliar to general business users of the application. Most projects/ project managers make the decision for mandating software tools to be used as standard in the project, such as:

- collaborative file management;
- version control;
- planning tools;
- analysis and reporting tools;
- shared risk and issue logs;
- business process modelling;
- quality management.

Sometimes no special tools are used.

Tool selection

The tools mentioned above each have their strengths and particular purposes, and traditional project management systems with their checklists and templates, processes and procedures can reek of rigidity and bureaucracy. The challenge for smaller projects is to make use of project management techniques at an appropriate level. It makes little sense to produce copious documentation on a tiny project; the effort has to be justifiable by the result.

Good project practice

Project management tools and techniques represent accumulated best practice and the same basic principles apply whichever system you use. The different systems have much in common and provide a framework, but the success of a project depends on the skills and capability of the people running it.

This is particularly relevant to the management of risks and issues and document control. Logs are documents created at the start of a project and provide templates for recording the concerns, threats and unanswered questions identified by those associated with the project. The PMO usually has the accountability to maintain these records, but it is the shared responsibility of all project team members to contribute, review and provide updates for the logs to remain relevant.

Change managers often have no say in the tools that are being used and need to pay attention and plan for the learning curve inherent in developing their skill, and the change team's skills, in the selected software and tools.

3. Identifying key roles and owners

Successful projects are those that are given direction and support from a high level within the organization. It is important for any major undertaking to have the senior management team ultimately responsible for the project. This means taking ownership on behalf of the client organization and putting their name to or associating their personal reputation with the outcome. In any project you need to get the right team together in order to deliver a successful result. This team is often referred to as the steering committee. In most cases, the steering committee appoints a 'project board' or equivalent to provide operational support to the project sponsor and project manager.

3.1 Project sponsor and project board

A project sponsor is concerned primarily with corporate and CxO (senior executive)-level project justification, funding, liaison, benefits, reporting, leading and decision making about the project's implications for the organization and wider situation, together with vital, specific and pragmatic support for the project manager role. The sponsor is unlikely to play an active part in the day-to-day management of the project, but they set the objectives for the project in line with the strategic plan, ensure that appropriate resources are committed and resolve issues where necessary. It follows that the sponsor must have sufficient authority over all parts of the organization that are impacted by the project. The sponsor normally chairs the project board.

A project board is usually comprised of key business roles representing the different interests in the project. These can be generally classified as:

- *Business lead*: representing all future users of the output of the project (eg a new system, a new or refurbished workspace, a new process and set of related paper forms).
- *Partner/supplier*: representing those sections of the organization (including external suppliers) whose work will generate the outcome (eg IT for a new system implementation).
- *Customer*: representing the stakeholders who expect to get the benefit from the output(s) of the project.

3.2 Project stakeholders and influencers

For a project manager, the priority (eg in event of a resource conflict) is clear. However, change managers must take the wider and longer-term view of the impact to the business and whether project work should be prioritized over business as usual (BAU). These impacts may have considerable consequences for the project: for example, disengagement of stakeholders (see Chapter 4 on stakeholder strategy) and a negative perception of the project or increased costs for BAU that would reduce the expected benefits.

It is the norm in projects for stakeholders to rotate in and out of roles, usually at a much higher rate of turnover than business functions. A key challenge for change managers in projects is continuously maintaining the current stakeholder landscape and onboarding new stakeholders into the project. High levels of stakeholder churn also means managing a wide range of maturity with regards to understanding and commitment in terms of how informed different individuals and groups are about the project.

3.3 Change management governance

Change managers operating in a project environment must often adopt several roles (or may need to establish a team of change managers to fulfil these roles) in the project:

- business change leadership (at programme level);
- project leadership team member (managing trade-offs, dependencies, critical path);
- change workstream manager (reporting, resourcing, compliance to standards – plan, monitor and deliver change management activities in the plan);
- change management subject matter expert/team member (execute change tasks and ensure the development of skills and knowledge transfer to build change management capability in the project team).

Change management structure

Organizations are complex systems in which there is a high degree of interconnectivity between components – and the boundary of ownership, especially of information, can be difficult to establish. An overview of all change initiatives planned and under way ensures that each is delivered effectively through the application of a consistent methodology and performance metrics. The remit of the group or function (sometimes referred to as the Change Management Office or CMO) performing this task must be organization-wide, as change is rarely confined to one area, and even small changes to a seemingly self-contained process can have knock-on effects. The users of this function are a wide cross-section of roles across the organization, including those responsible for strategic planning, project managers and departmental managers and business leads whose work is impacted by the changes.

Change management is usually represented at several hierarchical levels within a project or programme. Usually the role requiring the greatest application of project management knowledge and skills is where change management is a work package or workstream embedded within the project (Section B.3.1). As such, there is an expectation that this will be subject to and compliant with the selected project methodology and tools. This means participating in project activities, completing reports, updating standard documents, and producing plans in the required format and frequency.

This is often challenging as some change managers are either uncomfortable with this level of structure or believe that change is more organic and evolving in nature, making such structural rigour redundant. The ironic thing about change management is that not all change is deliberate or can be predicted. There needs to be a balance between planning what can be planned, and maintaining the flexibility to react to unplanned change when it emerges. Whatever your personal view regarding the nature of change, it is essential that a common understanding of the change management approach is reached and expectations are agreed with the project manager in order to avoid conflict and mitigate any negative impact on the project.

3.4 Understanding the business change landscape

Change managers on projects are either internal resources (ie employees) who are seconded from a central function of another department within the business or external consultants. In both cases, it is likely that the change manager may be unfamiliar with the operations and initiatives in the area of the business impacted by your project. Understanding the change landscape creates a context and identifies relationships between your project and other activities that either your project depends on or that depend on your project.

Context of change initiatives

In today's competitive environment, very little stands still in operations, information technology or processes. As a change manager you cannot assume that your project is the 'only game in town'. To understand what must change for a project to be delivered, a change manager needs to create a baseline or norm against which to compare the future and assess the scope and scale or change required. This can be challenging when there are tens or hundreds of business change initiatives in progress at any point in time. Not all of these initiatives will be relevant to your project, but identifying those that are, or will be, will help a change manager to 'future-proof' their change management plan and build in review points to update information to ensure that no conflict exists with other related projects.

A good place to start building contextual knowledge for your project is the PMO. An essential document for every project is the project definition document. This can be an excellent source of information about other projects' scope, key stakeholders and benefits.

An organization is a complex system and a useful tool for breaking this system into components to facilitate understanding and target opportunities for improvement is the target operating model (TOM) detailed in Chapter 2. The TOM also shows the relationships between the business units in the organization's portfolio and the process by which investments (such as projects) will be determined among them. The TOM road map shows the schedule and timeline of strategic change initiatives that will affect different areas of the business and current projects.

The PMO has access to these important documents, and experienced change managers ensure that they are familiar with and understand the context, as explained in these documents, before undertaking analysis or planning activities for the project.

Managing scope and expectations

Projects are executed quickly, and success is often measured by how much has been done or the number of changes that have been implemented. There is, however, an obvious shortcoming to this approach. A change can be put into place, but in many instances there is then a time lag while the change is fully absorbed by individuals, and their behaviour changed and sustained, before any of the benefits can be realized. For example, when a new IT system is implemented, often users are not confident or proficient in its use despite training being given. It is only with repeated use that user competency increases and productivity or cost-saving targets are reached. Understanding the scope and scale of what is being introduced, before embarking on a change, will help with the management of that time lag between implementation and realization.

The change management workstream has the responsibility to help those leading the project to identify what is likely to change in terms of people, processes, organization capability and culture – as a direct impact of the project. It is critical that there is clarity of scope relating to what the project will 'own' and change that is attributable to other projects or initiatives. Managing the challenge of 'scope-creep' (the absorption of numerous incremental changes to the original project or plan scope that collectively poses a significant risk to the achievability of benefits or outcomes) is essential for the change workstream manager as it will determine the quality of change interventions and the effort/resources available to deliver the work.

Diluting the project change management plan with additional, non-project activities will result in an unsuccessful project outcome and may generate a poor perception of the value, effectiveness and professionalism of change management in the organization.

Balancing business change and project needs

A key challenge for change managers is managing the inevitable tension between the needs of the project and the needs of the business regarding change management. As a member of the project team, there is a duty to meet the delivery targets required such as milestones, date and budget. Often a delay in early deliverables, such as process redesign, may reduce the amount of time available to downstream activities to less than was originally planned.

Change managers will need to decide what can be absorbed (or not) and what the consequences and risks might be for change management deliverables. It may be that the best option for the project overall will be at the expense of the quality of or increased risk to change management deliverables. For example, the project may decide that changes will be rolled out across the business team-by-team, meaning that some teams will have to wait weeks or months until they receive the benefits promised. It may also be that in order for teams to collaborate during the rollout period, some teams may need to take on extra tasks or learn interim or manual processes that will quickly become obsolete.

Change managers, like all project personnel, need to be flexible and adapt to such changes when they happen. The challenge is not about how to avoid the bumps and bruises that come with change (because you can't), but more about how you respond when things do not go as you expected.

Summary

It is essential for every manager, and change manager, to at least know and understand what project management is and its purpose. Throughout the life of a change initiative, change managers and project managers will need to work together to ensure that the two disciplines are in step, and that a consistent language and terminology is used so that stakeholders understand what the initiative will achieve and how.

Questions to think about

1. Why does this project exist and what are the desired outcomes or benefits expected by the business stakeholders?
2. What other change initiatives exist that relate to or have a bearing on the success of this project?
3. What is the methodology being applied and what are the structures and governance that support the project?
4. Do I understand the language and key project terms and tools being used in the project?

Section B: Establishing a project

Introduction

A typical project starts with someone having an idea, which then gains acceptance informally through discussion with colleagues and then through a more formal process involving senior management. A funding model and process must then be agreed before the project can start, staff appointed and work begins. Fundamental to establishing a project is the definition and governance of the benefits case (Chapter 3). Once the benefits case has been approved, the project budget is released to the project sponsor. The project sponsor appoints a project manager and the project then enters the first stage of the project: set-up phase.

1. Project set-up phase

The purpose of this phase is to establish the project and put in place the structures, processes and procedures for managing the project. A high-level project plan is created with an indicative timeline, phases and key milestones that create a framework for determining where cost will be incurred and the resources required to deliver the project.

1.1 Project controls

Once reporting and review mechanisms are defined, control mechanisms are needed to help identify and deal with the things that come from 'left of field' to throw the project off course. These are categorized as risks, issues and changes. Quality should also be the subject of clear control procedures.

Change control refers to suggested or actual changes or amendments to the project itself – not any necessary changes to business processes or ways of working required as part of the project – sometimes termed managing scope.

The documents or 'logs' to help track and monitor risk, issues, scope and quality are established during the set-up phase of the project. The ongoing process of project control is part of the iterative cycle of project management and is a shared responsibility of everyone in the project.

1.2 Project documentation

Sometimes, the importance of having project documentation in place for a project does not always resonate with managers. Writing documentation takes time and money, and the size of the project and the methodology has a bearing on the number of documents needed. For small projects, the emphasis is on the minimum requirements. Medium-size projects require more documentation, and large or complex projects require the most because they require a great deal of communication and coordination. Superfluous documentation can slow down the entire project by requiring team members to create lengthy, repetitive specifications or test plans instead of spending their time on delivering the actual project.

Typical documents that indicate a well-established project include, but are not limited to:

- *Project definition document*: this covers project justification and purpose, objectives/goals, benefits, budget, methodology, governance, controls etc.
- *High-level project schedule/plan*: this captures high-level project phases and key milestones.
- *Work breakdown structure*: this provides a 'who-is-doing-what' view of the project.
- *Scope document*: this states the project requirements, the agreed scope and known exclusions, constraints and assumptions.
- *Detailed project work plan*: this keeps track of the activities, work packages, resources, durations, costs, milestones, critical path, etc.
- *Quality assurance plan*: this tracks the quality standards that your project deliverables will have to align to. These may typically include product-testing approach and tools, quality policies, quality checklists, deviations definitions, quality metrics, product defect severity grades, acceptance criteria, cost of poor quality, etc.
- *Risk plan*: this contains the project risks and the related mitigation plans, as well as the project opportunities and the related exploiting plans.

Developing project documentation becomes even more crucial when working with government-regulated and government-validated systems such as those used in the medical, pharmaceutical or defence industries.

1.3 Gathering business requirements

Many techniques are available for gathering requirements. Each has value in certain circumstances and, in many cases, you may need multiple techniques in order to gain a complete picture from a diverse set of clients and stakeholders. Some of the approaches available are:

- *Interviews or focus groups*: the most common technique for gathering requirements is to sit down with the clients and ask them what they need. The discussion should be planned out ahead of time, based on open-ended questions to get the participants to start talking and then probing questions to uncover requirements.
- *Questionnaires*: more informal, and they are good tools to gather requirements from stakeholders in remote locations or those who will have only minor input into the overall requirements. Questionnaires can also be used when you have to gather input from large numbers of people.
- *Prototyping*: a relatively modern technique for gathering preliminary requirements that you use to build an initial version of the solution – a prototype. Sharing this with the business generates more requirements and a refined prototype is developed. This repetitive process continues until the product meets the critical mass of business needs, or for an agreed number of iterations.
- *Use cases*: basically stories that describe how discrete processes work. The stories include people (actors) and describe how the solution works from a user perspective. Use cases may be easier for the users to articulate, although the use cases may need to be distilled later into the more specific detailed requirements.
- *Day in the life of (DILO)*: is especially helpful when gathering information on current processes. Some people have a hard time explaining what they do or why. Watching people perform their job may be necessary before you can understand the entire picture.
- *Request for proposals (RFPs)*: vendors may receive requirements through an RFP. This list of requirements is there for suppliers to compare against their own capabilities in order to determine how close a match they are to the client's needs.

2. Establishing the project team

A project team works together to execute the tasks necessary to meet customer/ stakeholder requirements. The project manager starts laying the foundation for effective teamwork before a project team meets for the first time (see Chapter 12, Section B1).

Project managers have overall responsibility for delivery of the project against a defined set of outcomes or scope. They will put together a project team with representatives from different workstreams, including change management, whose contributions are essential to successful project delivery. This is the first activity for the project manager in the set-up phase.

The change manager has an important role to play. They need to encourage and support the project manager to invest time in developing the team and working with them to build their change capability. Change managers can also advise project managers how to establish a relationship with their team members before the team begins to meet as a group. Otherwise, they may not feel connected to the rest of the project team or, worse, may feel put upon and lack any commitment to the project.

2.1 Project people

The project manager has to start by choosing the best people for the job. This sounds obvious, but determining the best candidates is not always straightforward. Pulling together a group of strong, results-oriented individuals for a project team is part science, part art. It is important to make sound decisions about who is likely to perform well on the project team and who might be better suited to other opportunities. Sometimes project managers do not have the luxury of choosing team members – and resources may be assigned to the project team.

Change managers can have an influential role in helping the project managers and use their networks and organizational knowledge to make sound choices for the project. Many factors concerning potential members have to be considered, including:

- the skills required of them to complete project tasks;
- their level of influence in the organization;
- their access to a network of other resources;
- their capacity to participate effectively;
- their ability to work well in a team environment;
- willingness of stakeholders to commit resources.

Once the required resources have been identified there will also be decisions on the type of resources, such as:

- knowledge and skills mix: employee secondment, contractors, consultants, supplier partners;
- full-time versus part-time;
- co-located team versus distributed team (including offshore).

Generally the PMO has responsibility for contractual challenges (including the payments schedule), onboarding, recruitment, financial/cost/resource budget etc. The change manager contribution includes role profile and definition of change team roles, CV screening and interviewing, induction and change skills development.

2.2 Procurement and vendor management

Project procurement management is about establishing, maintaining and closing relationships with suppliers of goods and services ('vendors') for the project. The PMBOK®

defines project procurement management as: 'the processes necessary to purchase or acquire the products, services, or results needed from outside the project team'.

There are four major processes:

1. *Plan procurements*: this involves the creation of the project procurement management plan. Decisions are made on which items will be made by the project team and which will be bought. Procurement documents will be prepared and criteria will be developed upon which to base the selection of vendors.
2. *Conduct procurements*: the vendors are selected and the procurement contracts are awarded. Resource calendars are created that will detail when resources will be used, and the project management plan will be updated based on the availability of the resources.
3. *Administer procurements*: this is the management of the relationship with the vendors as the project proceeds. It results in the creation of procurement documents and may result in changes to the project. A system of contract change control will be used to carefully analyse and determine whether changes to contracts are needed. Reviews will be undertaken of procurement performance; inspections and audits may be used; performance reports will be produced; and systems used to ensure payment to contractors when appropriate.
4. *Close procurements*: these are the processes that are needed to end procurement contracts, either after their successful completion or earlier if that is appropriate. Audits might be undertaken on project work, and negotiations may be necessary to resolve contract disputes. Usually a record management system will be needed for contract documentation.

3. Establishing the change management workstream

Enlightened project managers will identify the need for a change management lead early enough for the change management workstream to be operational during the set-up phase. However, this is not always the case, and late onboarding of a change management workstream means that planning is often executed in parallel to activities and delivery.

The key things for a change manager to understand at this stage are:

- how the project's work is being organized, ie usually in several phases;
- planned delivery of work, ie overall timeline and what happens when;
- what constitutes success, ie usually defined by success factors or criteria.

3.1 Change workstream management

Change workstream managers develop and own the plan for delivery of the business change. The plan must also reflect and be aligned to the overall project plan.

The responsibilities of a change workstream manager are similar to those of a project manager, in that a change workstream manager must execute the same tasks, albeit within the limitations of the workstream scope:

- agree, manage and update the plan;
- monitor progress and report against the plan;
- allocate work to individuals within the team;
- manage the work of and utilize resources in an efficient manner;
- maintain a cooperative, motivated and successful team;
- keep records/logs of the risks, issues, dependencies and assumptions.

Project and change workstream accountability

Where the roles of project managers and change managers diverge is in their objectives and key result areas (KRAs). Whereas the project manager is also accountable for those tasks listed above, the change workstream manager has a different set of accountabilities, as illustrated in Table 8.1.

Accountability for the delivery and/or realization of benefits is not covered by Table 8.1 as responsibility and accountability may be split between two or more project roles and this is agreed during set-up phase.

Project change initiative and approach

The project change initiative and approach document(s) is the first deliverable or product that a change manager will be requested to produce. The purpose of the project change initiative and approach is to define and document the scope, and to set expectations of what the change management team are accountable for delivering for the project.

Often included in the project change initiative and approach is an outline of a high-level plan, key activities and deliverables (ie the 'how') for change management to achieve the desired business change outcomes as defined by the project.

This, and all subsequent products, will be reviewed and signed off by key project stakeholders. A well-constructed change initiative document has several benefits in addition to its primary purpose, including that it:

- unifies all people-related activities (change, communication, engagement and training) in one place;
- sets expectations and educates project members about change management;
- defines change governance with broader business engagement;
- identifies success factors meaningful to the organization (ie adoption not delivery);
- provides a reference point to challenge issues of scope-creep;
- sets a context and baseline for resource and planning assumptions.

This acts as a blueprint for the individual working in the role of change workstream manager.

TABLE 8.1 Comparison of project manager and change manager

	Project Manager	Change Manager
Critical Success Criteria	Deliver the deliverables & achieve benefits case to specified scope and quality	Ensure the organization is ready, willing & able to accept change
Purpose/Outcome	Project executed to time, with agreed resources and within budget	Ensure stakeholder & business expectations are met
Customer Satisfaction	Customer requirements must be understood as these are the basis for the project to be delivered against	Customers' views and needs may change through the life of the project and must be respected
Line Reporting	Governance structure (eg programme manager, project/programme board, sponsor etc)	Matrix reporting – project manager & business change leadership/function
Key Responsibilities	• Defining scope • Planning & identifying resources • Task scheduling & prioritization • Identifying & allocating resources • Managing & tracking tasks to completion • Resolving problems and issues • Project delivery & wrap-up	• External project communications • Stakeholder management • Change readiness • Change impact • Capability development • Training needs • Business engagement • Business transition • Sustaining change

SOURCE: Uncommon Expertise Ltd, 2014

Key areas of accountability

During projects, change leaders need to take personal accountability for achieving successful change outcomes and benefits. Change leaders may also need to support business leaders to understand their roles and responsibilities in the change. They may also need to be encouraged and supported to demonstrate their commitment to the project through actions and behaviours.

An essential strategic capability required for successful projects is the leadership for change through people. This includes building a change network or community, the development of behaviours, and alignment of values with the target operating model. Change management also has the accountability for building commitment, cooperation and change capability within the project board, project team and change network.

On a tactical level, change managers also have the following accountabilities:

- compliance to organizations' change management methodology (if one exists) and ensuring standards and common tools across the programme;
- understanding and communicating changes, and consequences from changes, in the external business environment;
- project board representation.

Change management specialists play a key role in ensuring that change initiatives deliver value to the project and to the business by increasing employee adoption and usage. Their primary responsibility is to create and implement change management action plans that maximize employee acceptance and minimize resistance. Ultimately this will accelerate benefits realization, increase value creation, ROI and the achievement of results and outcomes.

Change team ways of working

Part of the role of every workstream manager is to manage the expectations and assumptions of their team. This begins with recording assumptions and expectations from the start with agreement from all team members. Some team members may push to shortcut this process in order to save time, thinking that the team can figure it out as they go along. However, discussing the rules of engagement up-front will be time well spent when the team is in the thick of executing the change management plan – when resources are stretched, timelines are truncated and when conflicts can arise.

An effective way for a team to discuss and establish how they will work together is to use a team operating agreement (TOA). The TOA serves as the guidelines and ground rules to help the team work productively together over the course of the project. It is a living document and may be updated as the need arises throughout the course of the project. The TOA can be constructed to include anything that the team would like to have worked out and documented, and it usually includes:

- Team communications:
  - how information will be shared;
  - where documents will be stored;
  - confidentiality.
- Decision making:
  - how the team defines 'consensus';
  - how voting is conducted;
  - what happens when the team cannot come to an agreement.
- Meetings:
  - who will lead meetings;
  - how the time will be used;
  - where they will be held and who should attend.

- Roles and responsibilities:
  - what is expected of each team member and each member's role in the project team.
- Personal courtesies:
  - mobile device use during meetings;
  - reminders about 'overtalking' and interrupting.

Team members draft the TOA together, and the document should be signed by all members of the team.

Summary

Many key decisions are made during the period when a project or programme is being established. Gathering business requirements is a critical activity and is typically the first time the project will engage with many of its stakeholders to determine the business needs that the project should satisfy. Requirements refine the scope and shape understanding of many aspects of the project, including the business case, plans, budgets, standards and operating processes for the project.

Questions to think about

1. How will business requirements be gathered, reviewed and shared with stakeholders? Who will be required, what will they do and for how long?
2. Who are the groups of people collaborating and making up the project team? What are their roles and responsibilities?
3. What processes and practices will be followed and what is the role of change management in these?

Section C: Delivering a project

Introduction

The delivery or 'run' phase of a project is often broken down into several phases. The number of phases depends on the scope and complexity of the project. Different organizations and methodologies may use a naming convention, but often the number of phases and what they are called is decided by the project manager. Commonly, project delivery phases include the following as a minimum: definition, delivery and implementation.

1. Definition phase

Following on from the project set-up phase (Section B1), project definition is the first phase in project delivery and consists of three modules: determining purposes (stakeholder needs and values), translating those purposes into criteria for both product and process design, and generating design concepts against which requirements and criteria can be tested and developed.

As the definition phase progresses, focus shifts from analysis to defining the solution to get the organization to its post-change state. There is no magic formula or cookbook that will automatically lead to the best solution, so it is important to generate and explore possible opportunities and solution options before going into designing the solution.

1.1 Solution definition

The purpose of solution definition is to facilitate discussion, collaboration and develop clarity of vision between the business and technology communities. Additionally, the deliverables promote a common understanding of gaps, opportunities, constraints and critical dependencies associated with the programme of work that must be carried out.

This is usually done through a series of workshops with key stakeholders and subject matter experts (SMEs). The purpose of these workshops is to validate the changes identified by the project's customer needs assessment, or requirements gathering process, and to assess the suitability of different solutions to deliver those requirements and the strategy. The project may be associated with a change in technology and it is important to understand what business requirements will be met – and what will not be delivered by the new system – so that expectations can be managed.

1.2 Delivery planning and scheduling

The production of an overall project delivery plan is a key part in the development of any project. There are many ways to produce such a plan; it might be done with pencil and paper, be a word-processed table or a spreadsheet, or be held in a dedicated application such as MS Project or Clarity.

These plans are generally organized in phases, with the number of phases dependent on the complexity and scale of the project. The delivery plan sets out the work or 'work packages' to be completed during the project, with their start and finish dates, the resources required and a cash-flow profile or budget that will show at what stages of the project money will be spent.

Contingency

Thorough project planning and involving the right people in the development of the change management plan will ensure that it is achievable and will reduce the risk of any serious oversight. However robust and future-proofed the plan is, it is pragmatic to leave some room for manoeuvre (aka contingency) so that the project can be flexible enough to deal with potential areas of ambiguity and additional or reprioritized work, if they arise. Documentation can be quite useful as an historical record and a way to share information to a wide audience, and judgement will need to be applied to what is appropriate and useful.

For a change manager, the objectives of the definition phase are to confirm or create a shared view about the future: change vision, fit with strategic objectives, scope of the change, and how much resistance the project is likely to encounter.

1.3 Plan integration

A project is like a car engine – all the streams, activities and tasks need to be synchronized with each part performing the tasks it has been designated: IT, Business Processes, PMO, Information Management, Governance, Communications, Finance, HR, etc. Planning project-delivery tasks in a structured, integrated way promotes the coordination of critical and essential project tasks and identifies synergies and opportunities for collaboration or sharing of resources across projects and programmes.

The phases in the project plan are broken down into activities and deliverables, which are allocated to teams (project streams) who define and own the tasks (Figure 8.4). In reality, what often happens is that each stream will define their own activities, requirements and resource needs and then the project manager or PMO will splice them all together with a common timeline.

FIGURE 8.4 Illustration of hierarchy of plans in a programme

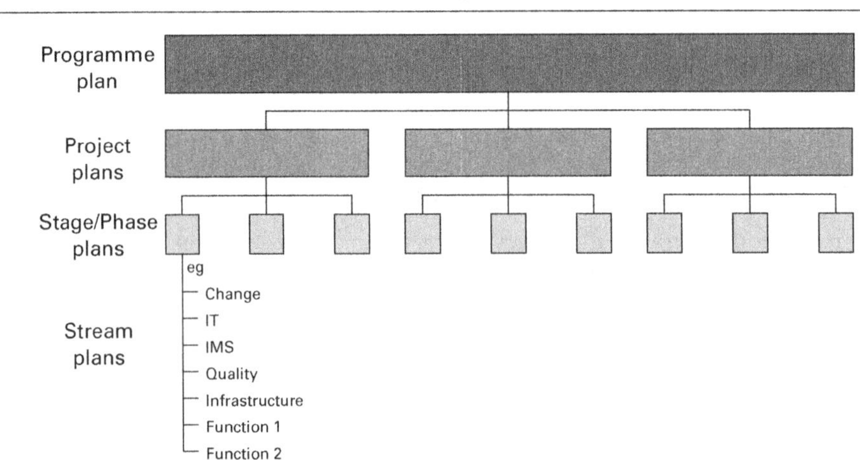

Stream plans identify the activities and tasks at a detailed level, including start and end dates and resource requirements. This level of detail is particularly valuable in reducing duplication and confusion if responsibilities for different activities are shared between different teams or individual roles. Progress is monitored against and reported on for each workstream and phase until the project reaches completion.

2. Implementation phase

Implementation is where the bulk of work defined by the project happens and must both deliver the needs of the project and incorporate local needs and priorities at the business unit level. The implementation phase is concerned with the identification and management of the integrated activities, deliverables and time frame in the delivery plan, and provides an operational framework to prioritize and schedule them. A whole bunch of trade-offs can be made as dependencies, priorities and budgets are decided.

Key activity focus in this phase include:

- milestones;
- dependencies;
- start and end dates for key activities;
- schedule (order, timing and 'float');
- resource allocation;
- budget;
- delivery reviews;
- risk assessment.

2.1 *Milestones and activities*

A milestone is an event that is often used to mark the completion of an activity or deliverable. In addition to signalling the achievement of a key product, a milestone may also signify an important decision or the derivation of a critical piece of information, which defines or affects subsequent activities in the delivery plan. Milestones are frequently used to monitor progress, but there are limitations to their effectiveness. They usually show progress only on a subset of activities, and ignore non-critical activities.

It is common for resources to be moved from non-critical activities to critical activities to ensure that milestones are met. This may give the impression that the project is on schedule when actually some activities are being ignored.

2.2 *Dependencies*

It is common to find that some tasks will be dependent on each other – for example, you can't paint a wall until the bricklayers have finished building it. Reliance on one piece of work finishing before the next can begin (a dependency) becomes visible as the plan is developed, and so a reasonably accurate timescale for the whole project can be set. The detailed stream plans should make these dependencies clear – if the wall is not built on time, or a venue for the event cannot be found, other tasks in the workstream or project may be delayed.

Critical path

Scheduling the earliest and latest date that essential activities can start and finish establishes a project's 'critical path'. This is an important indicator used to track project progress against the delivery timeline. Any delay of an activity on the critical path directly impacts the planned project completion date. Non-critical path activities have 'float' and can be delayed without making the overall project longer.

Float, in a project context, means the flexibility within the schedule between the earliest date a task could be completed and the latest completion date, eg a two-day task that could start on Monday morning and must be complete by the end of Friday has a float of three days.

2.3 Delivery reviews

The end of phases (also known as 'stage-gates') of the project are natural stopping points to stop and look back over what has been accomplished. Stage-gates describe a point in a project or plan at which development can be examined and any important changes or decisions can be made relating to costs, resources, profits, etc. Answers to objective questions at each stage determine if:

- required deliverables are being met and the project can proceed;
- project scope and schedule needs to be adjusted and needs to stop or pause;
- elements of – or all of – the project need(s) to be abandoned;
- a do-over of the previous stage is required (eg due to quality concerns).

The composition of the list of gate review questions is defined by the methodology, stakeholders/sponsor and may include specific change management criteria.

3. Change management delivery

Ideally, the change delivery plan should be developed in parallel with the project plan. In reality, what often happens is that the change delivery plan is created some time after the project plan. This can be a constraint, but in a more positive light it can also be a helpful framework on which to hang change activities and deliverables. If that is the situation, change managers must do what they can within these limitations and negotiate the rest with the project manager. If you can substantiate change requirements and evidence the need to do something, it will be in their interest to listen – and compromise if necessary.

If project delivery plans and reports do not yet exist, change managers may need to make some assumptions to continue developing the change delivery plan. It is essential to capture these assumptions so that they can be reviewed and updated as the project definition gains clarity. Proactively defining a draft change delivery plan will, at the very least, demonstrate an organized approach that can be shared and discussed with others.

3.1 Defining the scope of change management

See Chapter 2 for more detailed information on defining change. During project definition, the project scope can be fairly fluid. Despite this, work will be expected to produce an indicative set of plans and documents in parallel. The simplest way to get an indication of the scope of the change (how big is the change from what we do today) and scale of the change (how many people, processes and other resources will it affect), is to construct simple *from/to* statements: 'What does someone or a group of people do now, and what will they do after the change takes place?', 'What would need to happen in the business areas or teams to make them successful?' Developing from/to statements helps to bring that first bit of clarity to what needs to happen, by whom and by when.

Useful sources of information to help you develop your understanding of the changes include the benefits case, project definition document and the business requirements. As new material becomes available (such as the change impact assessment), statements may need to be refined and validated.

3.2 Managing changes to scope

Transformational and cross-functional projects can offer a unique view of barriers, risks and issues that negatively impact the effectiveness of an organization. Often the project provides a change manager with an opportunity to identify and highlight the need for action in business areas related and unrelated to the project, which will improve the effectiveness or efficiency in teams and functions. An experienced and effective change manager proposes approaches or solutions to these opportunities and always caveats those proposals with an assessment of the resources, costs and timeline required, and where in the business, or programme portfolio, ownership sits.

Increases or changes in scope once a project is under way or 'in-flight' usually results from a change in the business environment (external), or as the result or repercussion of a set of decisions that affect the programme (internal). These unexpected changes can put a drain on resources and also a strain on budgets. For waterfall method projects particularly, it may undermine the change management plan, and can also reduce the value of the project to the business as a whole. Agile projects are better equipped to absorb unexpected changes, and these are generally managed through a reprioritization of requirements.

The work required to address unexpected change is known as 'firefighting'. Firefighting is most often what causes a project to spiral out of control. Constant firefighting consumes project resources, which means that planned work, which provides value to the project, may not get done.

3.3 Developing a change delivery plan

The importance and process of change planning is covered in Chapter 7, Section B3. So if planning is so important, why are so many change managers tempted to skimp on it? There are a number of reasons – first, in today's business culture the emphasis is on the 'doing'. Plus, society (and customers) has developed a 'want it now' mindset so it is sometimes hard to resist the sense of urgency this generates. Planning is also not a 'sexy' activity – it takes time and there are no quick wins or immediate returns. So while life makes short-changing the planning process easy, it also takes away the safety net when you are finally faced with the realities of managing change in a project.

Planning tasks in a structured, hierarchical way promotes the coordination of stakeholder, communication, business readiness and training tasks. The planning process itself can be a very effective tool for communication; from setting objectives to deciding on tasks, you will need to talk to all those people who can bring knowledge to the project or are likely to be involved in its implementation. Objectives and roles must be clear so that people will know where the project is going and what they have to do. If it is handled well, the planning process will set up channels of communication and draw participants into involvement in the project.

Planning brings other more subtle benefits. The 'golden thread' is the backbone of the change delivery plan. It is comprised of the 'must do' change activities essential to deliver the change initiative and project success criteria. As a change manager, having this clarity can help with prioritization of change effort and allocation of resources and budget.

Considerations for change delivery planning

Before leaping into developing the change delivery plan, it is important to understand and decide the project management approach, as there is a shift in emphasis between waterfall and iterative that will require the change manager to ask a different set of questions and deploy a different toolkit (Table 8.2).

A traditional or 'waterfall' project influences the adoption of a change management approach to one that is concerned with informing, anticipating and planning for a defined set of activities that will drive a specific result. For example: 'We are going to plant barley in this field on this date, and here's your step-by-guide to planting barley in this field.'

Agile projects are not conducive to defining a gap or the difference in business processes. In this project environment, the change management approach is about creating favourable conditions for change, so that when the specifics of the change are known, people can embrace and absorb it. For example: 'We don't know if we will plant barley, potatoes or cabbages but we will clear the ground, plough and nourish the soil so that when we do know, we can get on with planting.'

Getting started

Some change management models, such as McKinsey's 7-S, or Johnson's culture web (Johnson *et al*, 2013), can also be a useful starting point for the content of a change management plan. Each of the components can be used as an activity line in the change management plan, to be elaborated into sub-activities and tasks. Once individual

TABLE 8.2 Illustration of different change management approaches for projects

Waterfall Methodology		Agile/Iterative Methodology	
Focus on: closing the gap (defined by)	Approach is: journey from as-is to to-be	Focus on: how do we need to be (defined by)?	Approach is: build the future
What is changing?	Change impact assessment	What are we changing to?	Capability development plan
How prepared are we for the changes?	Change readiness assessment	How receptive to the changes are we?	Organization architecture and road maps
Where are the gaps?	Training needs analysis	What do we need to make change happen?	Resource and skills model

SOURCE: Uncommon Expertise Ltd, 2011

tasks are identified, an assessment on the amount of effort (usually in 'man-days') can be made and this will form an essential input into the resource plan. Once you have created a change delivery plan you can reuse this as a template plan for subsequent projects that can be tailored to purpose.

3.4 Executing the change delivery plan

This phase is about developing the 'how' and the detail of the change management solutions to address the people, process, structure and culture needs of the future organization. It is when the change networks and stakeholders are mobilized, toolkits developed, and deployed implementation and transition plans are put together to ensure the organization is ready to take on the change.

Characteristic change activities for this phase are covered in more detail in other chapters and include:

- building the change network (Chapter 7, Section A4);
- stakeholder management (Chapter 4);
- road map development (sustainability and culture) (Chapter 1, Section E);
- micro (operational) organizational design (Chapter 13, Section A6);
- collaboration with HR with regards to policies and processes (Chapter 13, Section A);
- development of training courses and materials (Chapter 9, Section B).

Refine and update the plan

The change management plan is a formal document that lays down how change management is to be managed, executed and controlled. Throughout the project, it is 'progressively elaborated' as new information is available or new levels of task detail are developed. Put simply, after its creation (ie the baseline plan), it is continually refined, revised and updated to reflect current and expected progress. Comparing a current or updated change management plan to an earlier version of itself identifies changes that may have a bearing on stakeholder expectations and that inform the project communication plan.

It is important to remember that plan revisions and updates must be communicated and agreed with the PMO and project team, as changes you make may impact other workstreams, the critical path and impact the accuracy of project reporting. Well-established projects usually have a formal process for plan revisions.

Measure change effectiveness

In order to demonstrate that change management interventions have been effective, change managers must define and agree a set of measures and indicators relevant to the project objectives – ie a change delivery scorecard. The selection of metrics and specific measures should have input from users and needs strong buy-in from senior stakeholders and project governance.

Considerations when defining a change scorecard include:

- Cadence (rhythm): measurement to take place in a consistent and regular way.
- Actionable: ensure measures are understood and what will happen as a result.
- Need: set and encourage expectations that measures will be available when expected.

Sharing of – or the application of – metrics in practice needs to go beyond simply reporting the numbers. Context is as important as the data – and providing a rationale, root cause analysis and mitigating actions taken is essential for any change management scorecard.

Summary

Change planning is covered in Chapter 7, Section B3, but there are some specific concepts unique to projects. During the process of developing change management plans, it is important to consider concepts such as effort versus duration, critical path, dependencies, milestones and best practice. Change management plans must be integrated with the other workstream plans and reviewed regularly to monitor progress against deliverables and the delivery timeline, and to consult on any amendment or modification to the plan(s).

Questions to think about

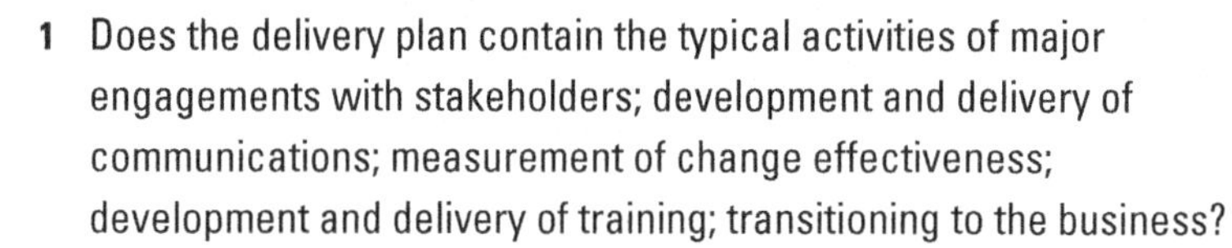

1. Does the delivery plan contain the typical activities of major engagements with stakeholders; development and delivery of communications; measurement of change effectiveness; development and delivery of training; transitioning to the business?
2. Does the change management team have the required skills and knowledge of the project tools and planning software to develop and maintain the delivery plan?
3. Is there a detailed communication plan to share key project information and updates? Who needs to be involved and who will do what?
4. What are the risks, issues and assumptions from a change management perspective? Are they documented and being actively managed?

Section D: Project completion and transition

Introduction

The main concern for the change stream in this phase is on the deployment of tools and interventions, and capability development. Benefits realization (Chapter 3) is also a feature of this phase, as is change sustainability planning (Chapter 11).

1. Project completion

The completion of a project is generally characterized by the deployment of the changes to products, systems and services delivered by the project. Securing adoption of and embedding the change successfully has implications for work done during the project. It is important, therefore, that at the start of the project, planning takes place for what will happen to the outputs at the end.

1.1 Deployment and rollout

This section identifies options for deployment of the solution or changes into the business, and considerations that will need to be addressed by the rollout activities defined in the project delivery plan. When selecting a rollout approach, it is important to identify the advantages and disadvantages, risks, estimated time frames, and estimated resources for each.

These options include:

- gradual deployment or phased approach (including pilots) (Table 8.3);
- parallel running (Table 8.4);
- one-time conversion and switchover ('big bang') (Table 8.5).

TABLE 8.3 Phased approach

Advantages	Disadvantages
Gain knowledge and experience during initial phase/pilot that can be applied to later phases.	Duration of project is longer than 'big bang'.
Possible to introduce modules whilst refining or training for later modules.	Dependencies between modules could be missed, increasing risk that solution functionality and integrity is compromised.
Time available for adjustments.	Increased stakeholder expectations and risk of diluting or diverting effort from main rollout.
Reduces risk of resource constraints as implementation is spaced out.	Increased costs for continuous change over an extended period of time.

TABLE 8.4 Parallel running

Advantages	Disadvantages
Employees can learn the new while performing BAU work.	Increased risk of confusing employees when to use or apply the changes.
Continued operation of old BAU provides built-in backup if the new fails.	Increased costs to run duplicate systems, and inefficient if employees have to repeat tasks (eg duplicate data entry).
Least risk of 'performance dip'.	Risk of increased pressure and expectation of employees to parallel work.
Gradual adoption for employees.	Adaptation might be slower, and old or undesirable behaviours continue.

TABLE 8.5 One-time conversion

Advantages	Disadvantages
Shorter implementation time.	Details may be overlooked in the rush to go live.
Transitioning difficulties and 'pains' are condensed.	More pronounced 'performance dip' and highest impact on productivity.
Employees trained on the new (ie no need for interim or changeover tasks).	Employees have less time to learn new skills, processes etc.
Implementation happens on a single date and everyone is clear when.	A failure in one part of the system could affect others.

The options are assessed by comparing them to the business requirements and selecting the one that is most appropriate for the project. Once a rollout option has been selected and agreed by project governance and stakeholders, the approach will inform key change management activities, eg communications and training. Due to the complexity and number of activities required for deployment and rollout, these activities are sometimes accorded their own phase and managed through a separate rollout plan.

Deployment checklist

The following list provides an example of considerations to be addressed by the deployment and rollout activities:

- Logical work breakdown, key milestones and dependencies during transition and deployment.
- Contingency plans and workaround(s) in the event that problems arise.
- Specific activities related to new and/or existing equipment, facilities and location.
- Specific activities related to user experience changes, including access to available support.
- Systems and data backup(s), planned outages, conversion plans, etc.
- Hand-off(s) between project teams, vendors, operational staff and support staff.
- Communication(s) to client and end users: periodic status updates, and notification of completion/system availability.
- Transition review to assess and document results of the transition, issues found, corrective actions to be taken, workaround(s) to be implemented, etc.

1.2 Support for implementation

After deployment, there are a number of project-related activities to complete if the change is to have a chance of sticking. These include diagnosing bottlenecks, barriers or gaps in processes, systems and resources that will need troubleshooting to resolve. Many of these fall under the category of 'operational support', for example:

- Do people know where to go for more information on the project or the change? (Websites, floorwalkers, super-users, managers, help desks and change networks should be kept up to date on all developments until transfer to business as usual.)
- If the change is technology-based, when the technology breaks (we guarantee something will fall over in the first week) does everyone on the project team know the emergency or backup procedures and any manual workarounds?
- Are the emergency and contingency communications in place to help users?
- How frequently will you gather target/employee feedback about how effective the change is, or the level of employee acceptance?
- Who has the responsibility for acting on the immediate feedback?
- What mop-up training will be available to cover any unintended blind spots?

These areas of 'operational support' are often the first areas to feel the effects of the change and are also good indicators of potential problems further down the system or process.

2. Business ownership of change

Once the project objectives have been delivered and the new systems and processes have stabilized, it is time to transfer ownership into the business. When you are handing over a project to the business, there are two types of activities to consider – those that will cease with the end of the project, and those that will be maintained and enhanced by the business going forward.

2.1 Closing project activities and handover to the business

It is essential to map all the activities that will end, and those that will be passed to the business. To do this, we recommend holding a workshop with representatives from across the project and the impacted business areas. During the workshop, collectively you will need to identify the activity, owner, date of close down and, if applicable, the business owner and date that the handover will be complete.

With the activities that end, choose a close-down date based on final acceptance of last deliverable. Plan for any post-close-down clean-up such as:

- organizing and backup of project's shared drives;
- filing or archiving any project-relevant materials;
- conducting lessons-learned workshops;

- completing final project gateway and audit reviews;
- submitting close-down report to sponsor and steering committee.

Planning for handover to the business

For project activities that are being handed to the business, work with the identified business owner to plan the handover. As you have just implemented the 'to-be', this is the new 'as-is'. Handover should include:

- passing on electronic and paper files of materials and documents;
- meetings scheduled in the future with stakeholders to review and maintain anything related to process/technology/people/performance/benefits measures;
- documented maintenance process for updates and improvements to change (quarterly reviews, etc);
- documented roles, responsibilities and KPIs for maintaining process/technology/performance – this should be done as part of the transition plan, but if that was not completed during the project it should be reviewed now and added to the business owner's job description and performance criteria;
- knowledge transfer or training sessions to up-skill future owners;
- sharing tips and lessons learned from the project owner to the business owner.

2.2 Project close down and recognition

Once the closure and handover activities are complete, it is time for project closure. A closure ritual is important, as during a project the work is very intense, and ownership and team bonding can be very strong. That sense of investment does not dissolve overnight, nor should it. People's efforts should be recognized through an event such as a close-down party, and include rewards and recognition. Some ideas to do so are:

- Hold final lessons-learned session for each group.
- Provide personalized letters/cards of recognition from the executive sponsor.
- Create a slideshow of photographs that chart the journey from beginning to end.
- Distribute small packs of the 'top five' materials created over the course of the project, with 'how to' guides.

As the project closes down, resources will likely leave the project on different days. Schedule all the leaving events, lessons learned and parties well in advance, so that people will be able to attend. Separately to any event, all project team members will need to complete or have interim performance reviews. This is especially true of those who were part of change governance – the change leaders and change network. While it may seem obvious to do performance reviews for the change team and change manager, feedback should be provided at the very least to the change sponsor, change leaders and change network. It is important that they are recognized for their effort not only by the project, but also by the line manager for the role they are returning to post-project.

Dispersal of the change workstream

Most projects are disbanded after implementation and rollout is complete, but change management does not end there. Once the change is live, the change management emphasis shifts from effecting the change to sustaining it. What most organizations and projects fail to recognize, plan and budget for is the time and effort required for the change to become embedded and 'business as usual'.

Characteristically of projects, the teams will disappear over time and the change manager will probably be the last one there to turn off the lights. This means that all the tasks left undone at the end of a project may need to be done by this role. It is good planning to keep at least one team resource to help with the documentation, reporting and closure activities. The amount of effort required is commonly underestimated, and solo change managers can easily get overloaded and overwhelmed by the very end, which can affect the quality of handover to the business.

3. Transition to business as usual

Transition focuses on enabling and supporting behavioural change as a result of the solution that is delivered or released into the organization (Chapter 11).

As well as implementing operational improvements, the change manager needs to take a cross-organizational view and ensure that synergies and barriers are identified, as conflicts will negatively impact productivity during and after transition and long-term effectiveness of the organization. A common misalignment is different performance targets and measures: for example, where one team is measured by customer satisfaction and another on processing time.

3.1 Transition planning

A transition plan is essential to complete the project and get the best value from the work that has been funded and delivered. It is common to not know all the answers at the start of the project, but thinking through the issues and developing a short plan that can be expanded on later will highlight issues such as access, maintenance, continuous improvement, development, performance and ownership (including intellectual property rights) – and may have implications for project delivery work.

A transition plan defines the steps by which the solution will 'go live', including logistics, cutover arrangements (such as interim metrics, parallel processing etc) and the identification of quick wins to build momentum and receptivity to change.

In planning transition activity, you need to decide what you want to gain from it. An evaluation component should be included in order to assess if the original intention has been achieved. For example, if people are invited to visit your website, checking the usage logs indicate if this is actually happening.

3.2 *Sustaining change*

Sustainability is about what happens to project outputs after the project. Some project outputs will be archived at the end of the project, some will live on after the project ends (eg content hosted by a service), and others may be taken up and transformed. A sustainability plan is an assessment of which project outputs should be sustained after the project ends, how, and by whom (Chapter 11).

In developing the sustainability plans, a change manager should be guided by the project manager and any requirements stated in the project definition document. Some projects create a product or service specifically intended to be sustainable, with requirements – about design, service levels, intellectual property, etc – that must be followed.

Summary

There are several options for rolling out the solution to the business, each with different advantages and disadvantages. The business must decide which option best suits its needs, having considered the relative risks, costs and benefits. Transition is where ownership for the changes moves from the project to BAU and, as a result, the project closes down. Effective change managers must pay particular attention to stakeholder reactions during transition, especially where the deliverables are failing to meet expectations or where the training is proving to be ineffective.

Questions to think about

1. Which rollout option offers the best solution for the project, and is this achievable for the business? What possible consequences can be anticipated?
2. Is there a clear and achievable training plan? Has training been developed for all impacted employees and has the content been validated with the respective stakeholders? Who will be required for training and for what duration?
3. What ongoing support is available once the changes go live?
4. Have all the change management deliverables been met? Is it understood what was achieved and lessons identified to be passed on? Have contributors to the success of the project been recognized?

Further reading

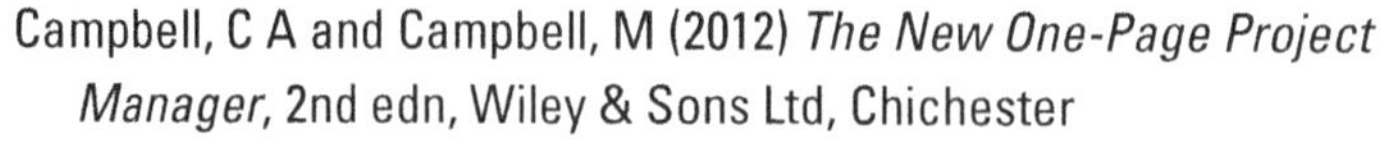

Campbell, C A and Campbell, M (2012) *The New One-Page Project Manager*, 2nd edn, Wiley & Sons Ltd, Chichester

Franklin, M (2014) *Agile Change Management*, Kogan Page, London

Graham, N (2010) *PRINCE2 for Dummies*, Wiley & Sons Ltd, Chichester

Layton, M C (2012) *Agile Project Management for Dummies*, Wiley & Sons Ltd, Chichester

Newton, R (2012) *The Project Manager: Mastering the art of delivery*, 2nd edn, Pearson Education, Harlow

Nokes, S and Kelly, S (2007) *The Definitive Guide to Project Management*, Pearson Education, Harlow

Online resources:

Chapman, A [accessed March 2014] Project Management [Online] http://www.businessballs.com/project.htm#project-management-tools

Neal, H [accessed April 2014] A Guide to ERP Implementation Methodology [Online] http://blog.softwareadvice.com/articles/manufacturing/erp-implementation-strategies-1031101

Suchan, J [accessed March 2014] Build Effective Project Teams [Online] http://office.microsoft.com/en-us/project-help/build-effective-project-teams

User:Ap [accessed March 2014] Project Management [Online] http://en.wikipedia.org/wiki/Project_management

West, R [accessed March 2014] Running a JISC Project [Online] http://www.jisc.ac.uk/fundingopportunities/projectmanagement

References

Blake, I and Bush, C (2008) *Project Managing Change*, Pearson Education, Harlow

Hersey, P and Blanchard, K (2012) *Management of Organizational Behaviour*, 10th edn, Pearson Education, Harlow

Johnson, G *et al* (2013) *Exploring Corporate Strategy: Text and cases*, 10th edn, Pearson Education, Harlow

Project Management Institute (2013) *A Guide to the Project Management Body of Knowledge* (PMBOK® Guide), 5th edn, The Project Management Institute, Newtown Square, PA

Education and learning support

09

RICHARD SMITH

Introduction

Change and learning are very closely linked. Edgar Schein (1995) went so far as to say this:

> My own thinking has evolved from theorizing about 'planned change' to thinking about such processes more as 'managed learning'.

Effective change managers are not expected to be specialists in training, learning and development. In many cases they will be able to work alongside such specialist colleagues, drawing on their expertise, experience and resources. However, the close connection between change and learning means that change managers do benefit greatly from a good working knowledge of learning theory, skills development, training planning and coaching. This enables them personally to address such issues when necessary, and to make the most effective use of specialist colleagues when they are available.

A word about 'training' and 'learning'

These terms are often used quite interchangeably. The organizational 'training departments' of a few years ago are now rebranded as 'learning and development'. However, the difference between these words is (or should be) more than merely semantic. When we speak of training, it focuses attention on the activity of the 'trainer', who is responsible for delivering 'training' to the 'trainee'. 'Learning', on the other hand, approaches the issue from the other side. It focuses on the activity of the 'learner', who is no longer a passive 'trainee' but an active participant in the learning process. The role of the former 'trainer' is now to create and facilitate an environment in which the learner engages effectively with what needs to be learned. Of course, in most real situations elements of both these paradigms operate together. However, this chapter prefers the word 'learning' and focuses on how to help it take place.

CHAPTER CONTENTS

Section A: Learning theory and skills development

Introduction

> Learning is described as 'the process of acquiring knowledge through experience which leads to an enduring change in behaviour' (Huczynski and Buchanan, 2007). However others have offered wider ideas about learning. It is 'a qualitative change in a person's way of seeing, experiencing, understanding, conceptualising something in the real world' (Marton and Ramsden, 1988). Learning includes both the procedural elements required to complete a task and gaining the underpinning or background understanding and attitudes needed to perform the task effectively in its organizational context.
>
> (CMI, *The Effective Change Manager* (CMBoK), 2013)

Although the title of this section refers specifically to 'skills development', this section will address the wider concept of learning referred to in the CMBoK definition above. The section focuses on principles that are applied in later sections. It traces the roots of learning theory, and then considers some key aspects of giving effective instruction. It then discusses the relationship between learning activity and the preferences of individual learners, considers the impact of learning on short-term performance and concludes with discussion of learning and the process of changing attitudes.

The quotation that began this introduction contains a definition of learning that links 'acquiring knowledge' and 'experience' with 'behaviour'. This is a very good starting point for a discussion of learning theory.

1. The roots of learning theory

1.1 Animal magic

Early scientific studies of learning theory used animal models (such as dogs, cats, rats, birds and monkeys). The underlying thinking was a simple input–output one – stimulus–response ('S-R') theory, as shown in Figure 9.1.

FIGURE 9.1 Stimulus–response learning

By using rewards, experimenters in the first half of the 20th century (including IP Pavlov, EL Thorndike and BF Skinner) showed how behaviour could be trained. Selecting some behaviours for 'reinforcement' (usually the reward of food) the desired behaviours could be made to happen more frequently. Where these selected behaviours were trained to respond to a specific stimulus (Pavlov's dogs are a well-known example) the resulting behaviour is known as 'conditioned response'. The key is the close association of the behaviour and the reward. The training of domestic dogs is still often based on this approach.

More sophisticated experiments showed that animals could learn to operate levers or open doors where they believed that there would be food behind them. Rats could learn their way around mazes to a destination where food would be found.

However, in all these cases the trained behaviour reduced when the reward was no longer provided. The conditioned response was said to have suffered 'extinction'. Yet this was not evidence that *learning* had been 'lost': sometimes it recovered spontaneously. Moreover, the time required to re-establish the conditioned response in those animals that had lost it was much shorter than was required for initial conditioning.

A related example of invisible learning was seen in another series of experiments. Rats that had been given free but unrewarded access to a maze, and had explored the maze over a period of time, learnt much quicker than others to find their way to food when that was introduced. Both this situation and that of 'extinction', above, demonstrate that learning is not *always* visible in behaviour. The rats had clearly developed something like a 'mental map' of the maze through their exploration of it, though this learning became visible only when it was useful. This is known as 'latent learning'.

Experiments to reinforce natural but generally unrewarded behaviour (like operating a lever) were extended to see what would happen when reinforcement was not given *every* time that the lever was pressed, but was inconsistent – say every third press. It was found that such intermittent reinforcement could be very effective, especially when the frequency of reward being given for the activity varied (eg not *every* third lever press, but *on average* every third lever press). This kind of reinforcement (known as 'variable ratio reinforcement') led to slower learning but proved very enduring. Many human habits are reinforced in this way, and the implications for the popularity of gambling are not difficult to see.

Animal experiments on learning were also conducted using 'punishment' – a negative 'reward'. Some of these would be abhorrent to a sensitive 21st-century mindset. The outcomes were actually quite ambiguous in their results. Some experiments seemed to demonstrate that selected behaviour was effectively inhibited by punishment, whereas slight changes to the experimental model could demonstrate a neutral response or even the reverse effect. However, where punishment was directly and closely associated with a behaviour, that behaviour was inhibited. In human terms, many of us can think of a major mistake we have made and the way the consequences (embarrassment, loss of face, perhaps even loss of income or job) have a lasting effect. Learning can result from specific instances of 'punishment' – but a generally punitive atmosphere has the effect of inhibiting learning (Wright *et al*, 1970).

In the workplace, rewards are likely to consist of attention from valued colleagues or the boss through feedback, recognition of achievements, acknowledgment of contributions made, opportunities offered, and may be financial or involve promotions. Herzberg's studies (Chapter 1, Section B3.4) suggest that money acts as a positive motivator primarily because it symbolizes recognition and makes it tangible. Workplace 'punishments' are likely to be primarily social and reputational, though in extreme cases formal disciplinary processes may form part of this function.

Even in this brief description of animal experiments we gain some interesting insights into human behavioural learning. But it is clearly not the whole story.

1.2 From animals to humans

Where human learning is concerned we have many layers of complexity overlaid on that encountered in animal studies, especially as regards motivation to learn (Chapter 1B explores this further):

- The cognitive process described by expectancy theory (Chapter 1, Section B3.3) suggests that there is a calculus that people make about the connection between their behaviour and a particular outcome.
- Herzberg's research suggests that once basic needs are fulfilled (so that attention is no longer on policy irritants, working conditions and relationships, and money) positive motivation comes from other things such as a sense of achievement, recognition from others and the intrinsic interest of the work itself.
- It is not always easy to be sure what is actually providing the rewards. Famous experiments at the Hawthorne plant of the Western Electric Company in Chicago in the 1920s changed physical working conditions (lighting etc) a number of times, improving them further and further. Productivity improved each time. Further changes were then made, actually making the same conditions worse – and productivity continued to climb! The reward was not, it appears, so much in the changing physical conditions as in the management attention experienced by the workforce.

But motivation is not the only issue. The human capacities to think, to analyse and to engage in self-aware reflection emphasize cognitive learning processes.

2. Learning and effective instruction

2.1 Learning physical skills

Psychologists have long been interested in the nature of skilled performance. With physical ('psycho-motor') skills such as learning to drive, to play the piano or to use a computer keyboard, the key is of course practice. But the practice needs to be of the right kind. It is often said that 'practice makes perfect', but that is not necessarily true; more accurately, 'practice makes consistent'. To 'make perfect' the learner must pay attention to the right components of feedback, noticing how they relate to an identifiable standard. In this way, successive cycles of repetition can bring the learner ever closer to that standard. The process works as shown in Figure 9.2 (using as an example learning a piano piece). Notice that, in this case, attention is focused on the auditory and kinaesthetic senses – not on sight, watching where fingers are being placed. The aim is to condition the right connections between body and feedback.

FIGURE 9.2 Training example: psycho-motor skills

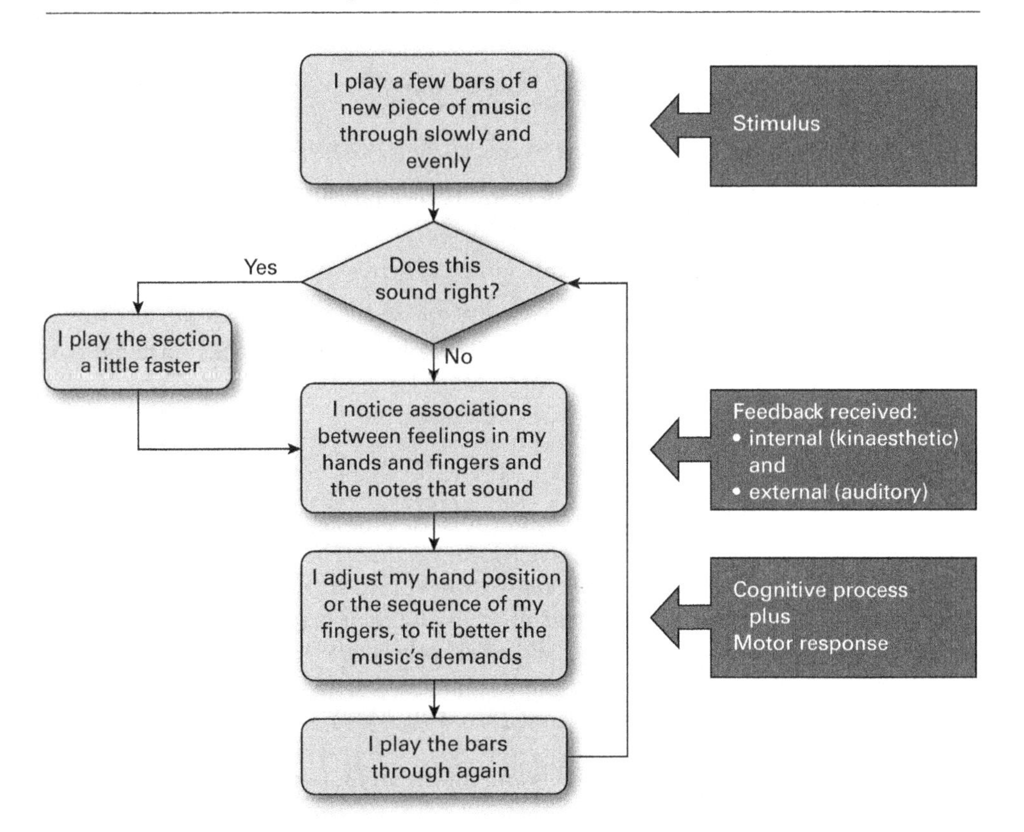

2.2 *Using the senses*

The previous section made much of using the 'right' senses. From the point of view of stimulating learning, it is important to recognize that any new information we wish people to process must come through their senses:

- sight;
- hearing;
- touch;
- taste;
- smell;
- kinaesthetic sense.

Kinaesthetic sense is the 'internal sensory data from receptors in muscles, tendons and joints' (Wright *et al*, 1970). It is how you know where to find the gear lever of your car without looking.

In general, selecting carefully the right senses for what someone needs to learn, and accessing as many of the senses as is practical and appropriate, improves learning:

> I hear and I forget;
> I see and I remember;
> I do and I understand.
>
> Confucius (551–479 BC)

There are some practical implications of this ancient observation:

- Training people simply by 'telling them' is very much less successful than showing them.
- Both together – showing and explaining – is better still.
- Getting the learner to be as active as possible in the process is even better.
- And getting the learner to teach others consolidates and embeds learning best of all.

2.3 *Memory*

Clearly, memory is closely linked to learning. It is used for learning facts and concepts, but also in storing experiences that have learning value. The latter – the experiences – are generally well remembered especially if they have strong emotional 'anchors', either positive or negative. People remember vividly their first kiss, and the occasion when they got something badly wrong and everybody laughed. Learning processes that involve activity, especially activity with other people where there is the strong association of energy and warmth, can be very powerful. Many senior team-development events make use of this.

Where the learning is to do with facts and information, four strategies can be very useful:

- *Repetition*: those of us whose schooling included learning and reciting multiplication tables will recognize the value of this approach.

- *Mnemonics*: these are verbal tricks to provide a structure for remembering. These are most effective if the individuals can develop their own. Some decades on I can still remember the nonsense sentence 'Valerie Will Not See My Pet Rat' – I invented it as a student to help me remember Thurstone's 'seven factor model of intelligence': Verbal comprehension, Word fluency, Numerical, Spatial awareness, Memory, Perceptual speed, Reasoning (Thurstone, 1947).
- *Structure*: For groups who are learning to instruct, I frequently give the task of recalling 20 'random' items presented for just 20 seconds. The number recalled almost doubles when I group the items by meaning instead of presenting them randomly. Use of logical structures or sequences have the same effect as grouping by meaning. Again, if learners structure facts and information in ways that have meaning for themselves, they will remember more effectively.
- *Images*: all the texts on memory include the suggestion of associating things to be remembered with strong visual images – the more humorous and bizarre the better. To remember the name and 5 December birthday of a (fictional) Mary Smith who has striking black hair, I might create a mental image of her as a blacksmith wearing a seasonal hat and holding up a newly made iron number 5.

All these strategies are associated with so-called 'long-term' memory, because that is most relevant in a workplace context. Contemporary research suggests that 'memory' is not really like a recording of things we have experienced through our senses. Rather it is a set of connections that allows us to re-create (more or less accurately) what we 'remember'. Thus 'memory' is in part a creative process, affected by subsequent events and experiences.

2.4 The 'nine events of instruction'

These ideas are seen in a different form in Gagné's 'nine events of instruction' (EduTech; original reference: Gagné and Medsker, 1996). First developed in the 1960s and 1970s, this structure is helpful in designing and reviewing learning activities and training events.

Here are the 'nine events' as described by the online resource EduTech wiki, with my comments in italics:

1. Gain attention: eg present a good problem, a new situation, use a multimedia advertisement, ask questions.

   People learn best when they see the 'big picture' and why such learning matters. In the change context this is the place to link the learning to the change initiative it is supporting, and to stimulate motivation for that overall purpose.

2. Describe the goal: eg state what students will be able to accomplish and how they will be able to use the knowledge, give a demonstration if appropriate.

   Help learners to be clear what they can DO with what they will learn. Again, this aids motivation to learn and creates a picture of the outcome for them personally, both relevant to successful change.

3. Stimulate recall of prior knowledge: eg remind the student of prior knowledge relevant to the current lesson (facts, rules, procedures or skills).
   The value of this step is twofold. One, it reduces learning anxiety, since learners see the new learning as an extension of something they already know. Two, it helps learning directly by preparing a set of mental 'links' that learners can use to establish the new learning in their minds.
4. Present the material to be learned: eg text, graphics, simulations, figures, pictures, sound, etc.
   All the comments above about memory and practice apply here (Sections A1.4 and A2.1).
5. Provide guidance for learning: eg presentation of content is different from instructions on how to learn.
   Helping learners to think about the process of learning in relation to the particular material adds to the quality of learning and varies the focus. There is an opportunity here to relate the learning not only to the process but also to the purpose of it in a wider change initiative.
6. Elicit performance 'practice': let the learner do something with the newly acquired behaviour, practice skills or knowledge.
   Test questions, discussions on how to apply, group work to identify applications and/or difficulties – any of these can be 'applications' for cognitive material.
7. Provide informative feedback: show correctness of the trainee's response, analyse learner's behaviour, maybe present a good (step-by-step) solution of the problem.
   If the 'practice' has involved a physical skill, feedback should have been part of the practice session. If it is more cognitive learning, discussion in full group of possible responses with 'model answers' or debate on the strengths and weaknesses of various ideas fulfils this function.
8. Assess performance, test if the lesson has been learned.
   Find a way to evaluate the learning at the end of training. More is said on this in Section B.
9. Enhance retention and transfer: eg inform the learner about similar problem situations, provide additional practice.
   Prepare the way for immediate application of the learning. If this is not possible, consider rescheduling the training within the change initiative until initial learning can be followed quickly by practical application. This is a fundamental learning principle!

3. Learning and the individual learner

The impact of personality on learning preferences is discussed briefly in Chapter 1, Section B4.1. This section discusses two other approaches that take account of the preferences of individual learners.

FIGURE 9.3 The 'learning loop' (Kolb, 1984)

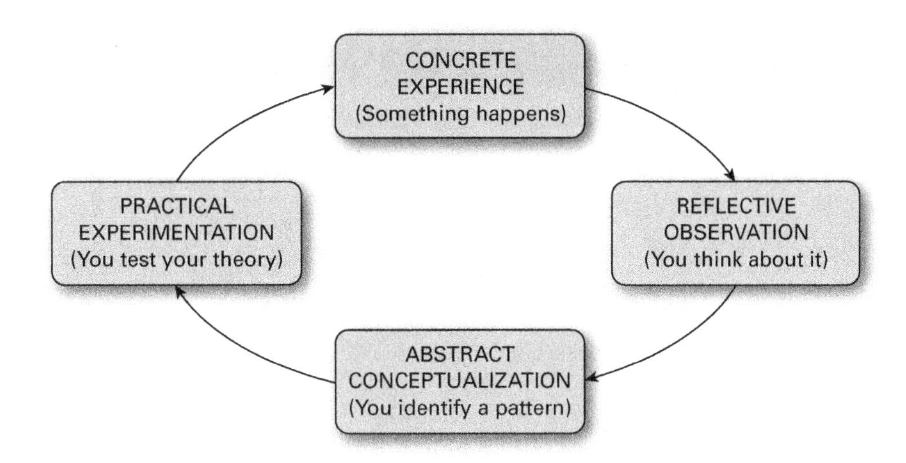

3.1 *The learning process and learning styles*

All personal change involves unlearning old ways of behaving and learning new ones. It is helpful, therefore, to have a way of looking at the learning process and how different people like to learn. David Kolb (1984) described a cyclical process of adult learning. Figure 9.3 shows both the terms he originally used for the various stages and an indication of what he meant by them.

To take a practical example, suppose a sales person has a particularly successful meeting with a customer (concrete experience). For learning to take place, leading to improved effectiveness, the sales person must think back over the meeting and notice what happened (reflective observation). Suppose the observation was that the sales person had, early in the meeting, spent longer listening before making proposals. The sales person then forms a hypothesis: 'Listening carefully to customers before making sales proposals leads to more productive customer interactions' (abstract conceptualization). As a result, the sales person then decides to spend longer listening and exploring the customer's agenda in the next sales meetings (practical experimentation). This creates further experiences and learning continues. Notice that the evidence of learning is that behaviour changes.

It is possible to enter this 'learning cycle' at any point. Another sales person present at the customer interaction could just as easily have been the reflective observer, formed the hypothesis and themselves experimented with new sales behaviours. Or the sales person could read a book making recommendations about listening more (abstract conceptualization) and decide to put this into practice. It is even possible (though less probable) that a sales person would decide to experiment randomly with sales behaviour, though in reality this would probably be based on at least a 'hunch' (abstract conceptualization). Notice that if any of the steps of the learning cycle are not taken, learning is inhibited or lost.

TABLE 9.1 Learning styles (Honey and Mumford, 1992)

Someone with a preference for this stage...	Is described as a...
Concrete experience	Activist
Reflective observation	Reflector
Abstract conceptualization	Theorist
Practical experimentation	Pragmatist

Peter Honey and Alan Mumford (1992) took this thinking a step further with their observation that different individuals possess different 'learning styles'. These represent distinct preferences for one or more steps of the learning cycle, or tendencies to 'skip' one or more steps, which will diminish learning opportunities. As set out in Table 9.1, they label the learning styles like this:

- *Activists*: typically learn most happily from experience, preferably new experiences involving other people. True activists are constantly busy, enjoying the challenge of anything new and always ready to 'have a go'. The risk for activists is that their tendency to move on rapidly from one experience to another may mean that they fail to learn effectively.
- *Reflectors*: like to learn from watching others and from thinking back over their own experiences. Thorough and careful in character, reflectors absorb and consider all possible angles before drawing conclusions. Reflectors lose opportunities to learn because they tend to take too few risks to gain many practical experiences, and may not engage sufficiently with others.
- *Theorists*: prefer learning that proceeds logically from 'first principles' and appreciate clear theoretical models. They are happy to absorb their ideas through reading. They appreciate lectures that offer credible explanation of sound theory, or which systematize and integrate data from experience. They may miss learning opportunities due to their aversion to intuitions and creativity, and their intolerance of ambiguity.
- *Pragmatists*: like to test and apply ideas and theories, especially where they have practical relevance to a current problem. Their realistic and practical approach to problems makes pragmatists open to new techniques and to anyone who can help or coach them as they try them out. Pragmatists lose learning opportunities by rejecting or ignoring ideas for which they can see no obvious and immediate application.

Table 9.2 sets out some examples of activities that might particularly suit the preferences of different learners. Of course, none of the examples in Table 9.2 are uniquely preferred by a single learning style. Pragmatists can learn well from observing others,

TABLE 9.2 Learning activities and learning styles (after Honey and Mumford, 1992)

Activists	Reflectors
On-job learning by trial and error Coaching from a respected practitioner Activity-based learning in groups Well-simulated work environments	Observing others 'live' or on video Action learning sets (see note below) Making notes and keeping learning diary Well-simulated work environments
Pragmatists	**Theorists**
Practical workshops On-job learning by trial and error Applying tools and models to practice situations Well-simulated work environments	Courses and seminars Lectures and presentations Reading and personal research Well-simulated work environments

NOTE: An 'action learning set' is a small group of colleagues, usually from different parts of an organization, who commit to meeting regularly to learn together. The learning comes from actual work experiences of members of the 'set'. Participants each present and discuss their real work challenges, and develop options using one another as a resource. Members of a 'set' hold one another accountable for taking action on their individual challenges, and for learning from the process. The set provides its members with both support and challenge (Revans, 2011).

theorists can learn from coaching and so on. Also, the fact that a learning method is less preferred does not necessarily mean it will be less effective. However, the examples illustrate some of the range of options that may support a learning journey, and the learning styles most likely to appreciate each learning method.

3.2 Learner preferences and presenting information

Fleming and Mills (1992) researching in a higher-education context found that many students had a decided preference for how they received information, as set out in Table 9.3.

Many find the 'VARK' approach (Table 9.3) to considering learning preferences as personally insightful. The most significant practical response to Fleming and Mills's model is to consider in any training activity how it might be received by those with different VARK preferences.

3.3 Adapting learning methods to learner preferences – caution and counsel

The point here is not to suggest that all those involved in change or in learning design must be trained users of the questionnaire 'tools' associated with the models

TABLE 9.3 VARK preferences (after Fleming and Mills, 1992)

Visual	This preference favours images and symbols over other ways to receive information. Charts, diagrams and creative images are used to aid learning.
Aural (or auditory)	People with an aural preference like listening to information, favouring lectures, MP3 files and the radio.
Reading/Writing	Some people find reading and note-taking to be a highly effective means of learning.
Kinaesthetic	Fleming and Mills use this term in their own way, saying that this is a 'perceptual preference related to the use of experience and practice (simulated or real)... it is not a single mode because experience and practice may be expressed or "taken in" using all perceptual modes – sight, touch, taste, smell and hearing.'

discussed in this section. Rather it is to encourage all involved in helping people learn to be observant about what is working for particular individuals. The 'learning styles', VARK and MBTI®, may help to guide these observations. The important thing is then to adapt the learning approach to best meet the needs of different individuals.

Some academics question the evidence that meeting the learning preferences of groups of learners actually improves the effectiveness of learning (Coffield *et al*, 2004; Pashler *et al*, 2008). Nevertheless, designing learning processes to address differing preferences as far as possible, perhaps even allowing flexibility for different people to access the learning in different ways, often improves learning design.

4. The learning process, performance and pressure

4.1 The 'learning dip'

Ramesh Mehay (2010), in a paper associated with the training of medical practitioners in Bradford (UK), helpfully outlines a widely recognized learning process, the origins of which are difficult to identify. Known by a variety of names, Mehay describes it as the 'conscious competence learning model'. It describes the stages that a learner goes through when learning a new skill, as shown in Figure 9.4.

Of course, in a change situation, the process can begin with 'unconscious competence' in the old 'business as usual' world. Learners are precipitated into 'conscious incompetence' as a result of the change. Through training the learner achieves 'conscious competence', and through continued practice moves to achieve 'unconscious competence' once again. The period of focus (conscious incompetence and conscious

FIGURE 9.4 The conscious competence learning model: the way we acquire a new skill

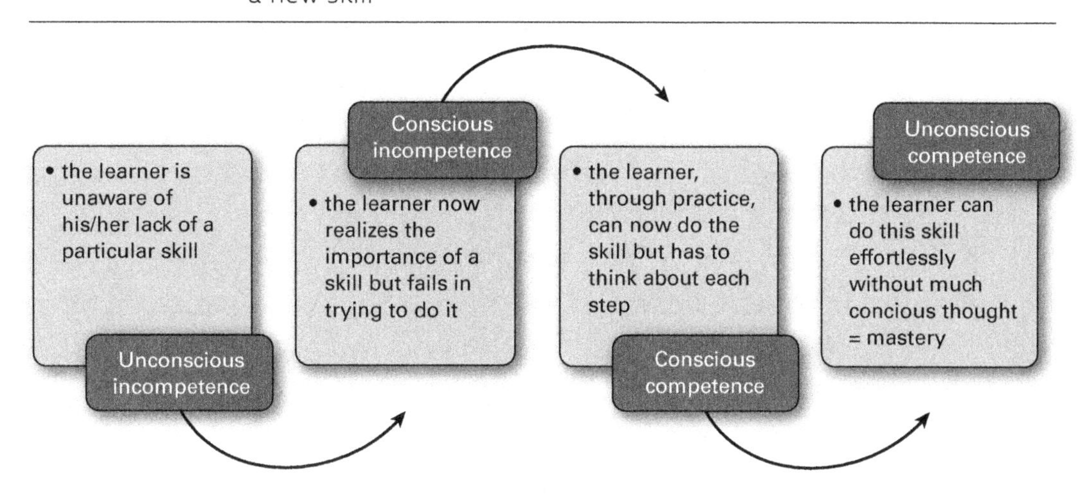

SOURCE: *The Essential Handbook of GP Training and Education*, Ramesh Mehay (ed) (2012)

FIGURE 9.5 The 'learning dip' following a change

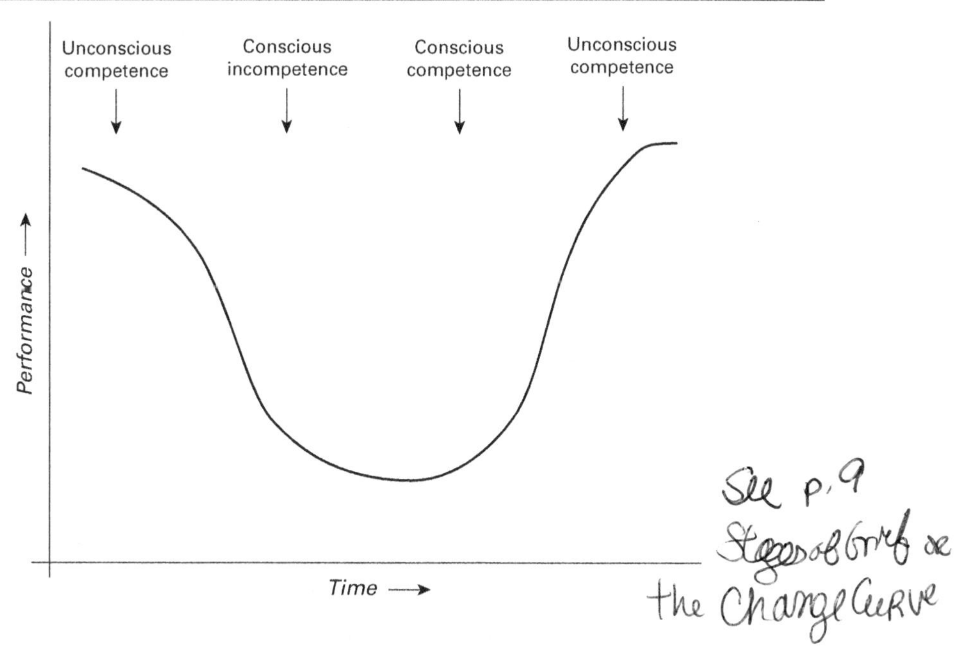

competence) can be a period of anxiety for the learner – the fear of failure is most acute here, and the 'ghosts' of past learning experiences come back to haunt!

This process has implications for job performance, too (Figure 9.5). The skilled performance or mastery associated with unconscious competence is fluent and quick. Errors are infrequent. As soon as the learner has to pay conscious attention to the

FIGURE 9.6 The effect of pressure on performance

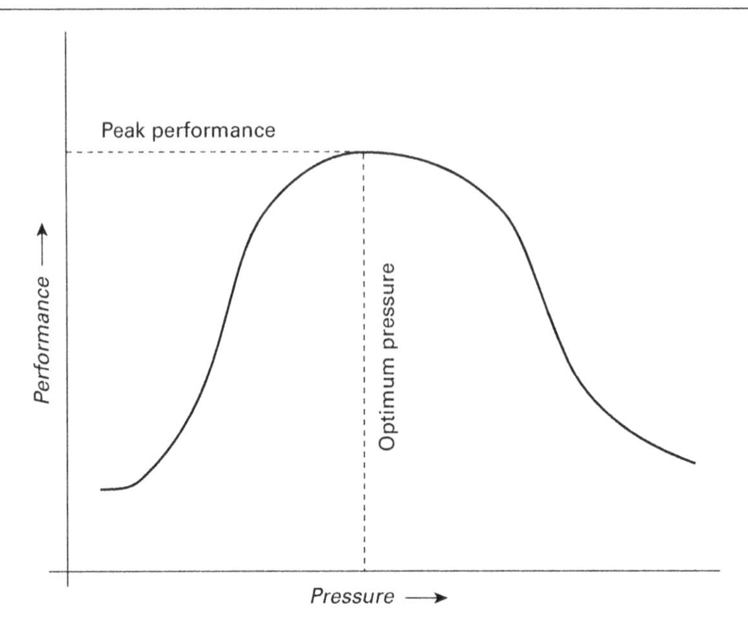

skill – and especially before basic competence is achieved – productivity declines and error rates climb. There is a significant fall in job performance. When planning any change that will involve people in learning new skills where they have previously been highly competent, a learning dip such as this must be expected and planned for. The extent of the dip and the speed with which recovery takes place will be a function of the timeliness and effectiveness of training provision.

4.2 Pressure to learn

One other graph is relevant here. It pictures the relationship between performance and pressure (Figure 9.6). As pressure increases, performance also increases – to a point. A certain level of pressure brings out the best in most people, though the pressure required (and that can be tolerated) varies for different individuals. After that optimum point, the stress associated with the pressure inhibits performance.

The significance of this for the learning process lies in the need to build performance to high levels. If speed of performing a work task is a critical factor in the target behaviour, increasing speed of performance during the training is important. Periodic but controlled 'speed tests' allow the learner and instructor to assess progress. (The same principle applies, of course, to performance characteristics other than speed.)

5. Attitudes – beyond skills and knowledge

5.1 *Attitudinal training?*

Mention has already been made of the processes by which physical (psycho-motor) skills are developed, and by which knowledge is acquired. Both are clearly important in workplace learning generally and in change situations in particular. However, there is a further, potentially sensitive, aspect of learning that affects the way skills and knowledge are applied. It is the question of attitude.

The 'attitude' of a person is their mental and emotional stance towards a person or group, or towards an idea, plan process or change. Changing people's attitudes is not something that can be generally achieved by a simple training session. However, attitudes are learnt, and can be changed or developed, given the appropriate information and influences. This can be crucial in change situations.

The reason that I described this as a 'potentially sensitive' topic is that in most liberal democracies the value of autonomy and 'making up my own mind' is deeply embedded. We abhor the idea of 'brainwashing'. However, our free-thinking is only partially real. All advertising is aimed at influencing our attitudes to products or services, and political communications have a similar goal. Our current set of attitudes is based on the vast number of influences and information we have experienced through our lives to this point. As John Maynard Keynes is reputed to have said: 'When someone persuades me that I am wrong, I change my mind. What do you do?' Two useful approaches to thinking about attitude change are described in the next two sections.

5.2 *The 'attitude spectrum'*

In Figure 9.7 an individual's current attitude on a topic is represented as a position on a spectrum. Around their current views, values and feelings is a 'zone of tolerance' – a range characterized as 'fairly close to my own attitude'. If presented with a new value within their 'zone of tolerance' ('A'), they will tend to assimilate it into their own attitude – and move somewhat towards it (to the right in this diagram). Presented with a value outside their 'zone of tolerance' ('B') they will tend to resist it, and their attitude will change to emphasize the difference – to the left on the diagram.

FIGURE 9.7 An 'attitude spectrum'

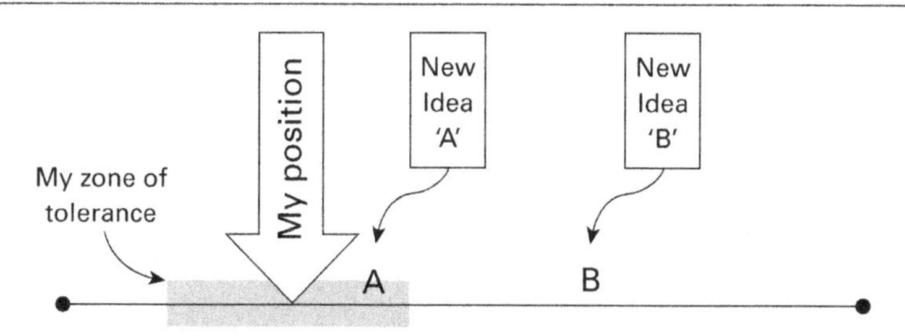

This suggests that one way to help people to respond to new attitudinal requirements in change is to widen their 'zones of tolerance'. Exposing people to a wide range of different views, values and feelings *but without the pressure at that time to make any personal response* can help people to become more open – with wider 'zones of tolerance'. Experiences of learning together with people from other very different workplace settings can help achieve this. As a result, when new ideas associated with change are presented they are more likely to be accepted and assimilated. On the other hand, care needs to be taken when presenting values very different from those in a prevailing culture. Here, attitude change may have to be by small increments.

CASE STUDY

A major UK engineering plant making car bodies was buying new body presses from a Japanese supplier. The employee relations history had been difficult and resistance was expected to the 'new technology'. The 'shop floor' workers who would operate the new machines were asked to visit a Japanese car factory to see the presses in action. Seeing the different work culture and application of the presses in Japanese factories led to the operators returning with the views that: 'they are great machines and we can run them better than our Japanese colleagues do'. When the presses were installed they did in fact deliver higher output than the equivalent factory in Japan.

5.3 The 'attitude triangle'

Another way to think about attitude change is to recognize the (over-simple but useful) concept of the 'attitude triangle' (Figure 9.8). In this model we consider the attitude of a person ('Me') to another person and to an idea. The 'idea' could be a change, a value set, a group norm or any psychological 'object' towards which 'Me' holds an attitude.

The principle is that people seek congruence in their attitudes. As the diagram is drawn 'I' like the 'other person', but dislike the 'idea'. The problem is that the 'other person' I like actually *likes* the 'idea'. This 'dissonance' is uncomfortable for me. The extent of my discomfort will depend on how much I like the 'other person' and how much I dislike the 'idea'. There are two solutions that could minimize my discomfort: like the 'other person' less, or like the 'idea' more – which way I go will depend on which is more important to me.

Of course other permutations of likes and dislikes can be described in this way. For example, if the 'other person' is someone I *dis*like and they *like* the idea, my own dislike of the idea is strengthened.

FIGURE 9.8 An attitude triangle

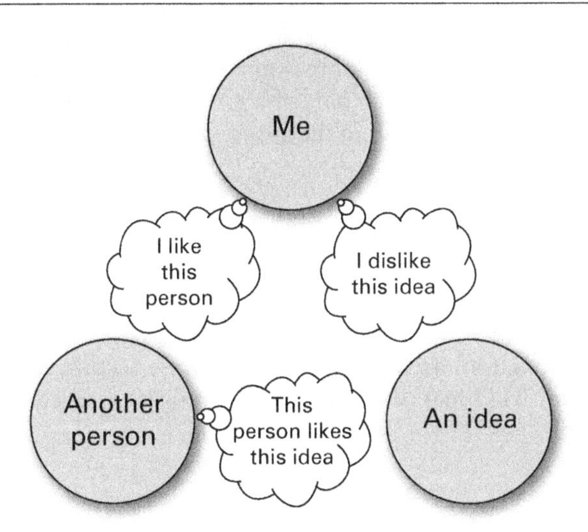

This model suggests that when there is a need to influence people it is important to have credible, respected people who clearly espouse the target attitudes. Role modelling by senior people is important, but the extent to which that genuinely influences attitudes depends on the respect in which those senior people are held. I am much more likely to be influenced by a 'nearby' leader whom I like and respect. It is important in times of change to find 'opinion leaders' who are credible, highly respected and (ideally) well-liked by those whose attitudes you need to influence. It is also important to identify those who may have unhelpful attitudes and decide how their influence can be mitigated.

CASE STUDY

A law firm planned to introduce a new performance management process to improve staff development. The partners feared that if they championed the process there would be suspicion from staff that they were introducing it only for professional compliance reasons. A specialist consultant was invited to meet and discuss performance management issues with all the affected staff, allowing opportunity for concerns and prejudices to be explored with someone who was seen as both expert and more neutral. Staff members with previous negative experiences had the opportunity to discuss their concerns with the accepted expert amongst a group of colleagues. The consultant's discussions with staff influenced the design of the process and it was introduced successfully, with substantial support from staff.

This 'triangle' helps to explain the importance of group approval and disapproval when new norms are being formed during changes of culture. Cameron and Green (2012) make the important point that group reinforcement through social approval and disapproval is essential to establish and reinforce the norms of acceptable behaviour. If I value and want to be part of a group I will want to follow its norms. Discussion and clear agreement within the group undergoing change helps to establish those norms.

5.4 *Planning for attitude change*

When considering using learning processes to effect changes of attitude, it is important to consider all stakeholders. In particular, Gerard Egan's list of stakeholder categories may help to ensure that all are addressed (Chapter 4, Section B4). Some 2×2 grids (Chapter 4, Section B11) may help to identify priorities for changing attitudes in a change situation.

Summary

This section has outlined some key threads in the fabric of learning theory and its application, considering motivation to learn, methods of instructing and memory issues. It has identified the need to think about both the learning required by a change, and the people who need to learn. The tendency for learning to create a temporary 'performance dip' has been highlighted. Finally, the section has introduced the importance of planning for attitudes that may need to change, as well as skills and knowledge.

Questions to think about

Consider a change initiative that you have experienced:

1 How could learning processes for knowledge and skills have been improved?

2 What was done to take account of different learners' individual needs or preferences?

3 What attitudes needed to change? In what ways could those changes have been helped more?

(Now apply the same questions to a current change initiative in which you are involved.)

4 Make an opportunity to use the 'nine events' as a guide for developing and delivering a training session.

Further reading

Harrison, R (2009) *Learning and Development* – offers an excellent foundation for understanding L&D issues and their practical application in an organization

Huczynski, A A and Buchanan, D A (2007) *Organizational Behaviour* – a valuable reference on a range of organizational behaviour issues. Chapter 4 gives a good review of learning theory

Section B: Identifying and meeting learning needs

Introduction

Managing successful change initiatives includes ensuring that the knowledge, skills and attitudes of all involved are developed appropriately. This requires that learning needs are analysed and gaps identified, learning and development plans are developed and implemented and that the effectiveness of the learning is evaluated. Ideally these activities leave a legacy of training designs and materials, which continue to offer value as the change is embedded in the organization.

This section focuses on some practical applications of the learning theory explored in Section A. It offers an introduction to some approaches that learning and development (L&D) professionals might use to identify learning needs, to plan and schedule training, and to design and evaluate learning. It offers a limited selection of basic tools that can be useful in these processes. The aim is to help change managers to make more effective use of the skills of their L&D colleagues, and to provide a basic toolkit for situations where professional L&D support is not available.

1. Identifying and analysing the needs (KSAs)

1.1 What is needed?

The principles of identifying learning requirements are not fundamentally different to other aspects of planned change:

- Identify how things are now (the current **knowledge, skills and attitudes** (KSAs) of different stakeholders and groups of stakeholders).
- Identify what is required during and after the change (what KSAs will be required of each stakeholder and stakeholder group, both in order to get

through the change process successfully and to be effective once the change is complete).

- Identify the gaps (new KSAs that each stakeholder and group must develop).
- Plan to meet them.

Notice the choice above of the word 'stakeholder' rather than 'jobholder'. This emphasizes the importance of considering the learning needs of stakeholders both within and outside the organization. This frequently includes customers, suppliers and other key groups impacted by a change. It may be appropriate for the organization to provide learning opportunities for such stakeholders in order to ensure the success of the change initiative.

Notice also the use of 'KSAs' in the description. Some of the learning that is needed will be simple procedural learning, but some will relate more to the 'soft skills'. Soft skills typically relate to the behavioural and personal effectiveness of people, to group processes and to relationships. Such skills can be developed and formal training activities can help with this. However, developing soft skills takes time, reflection and practice.

1.2 Single- and double-loop learning

In a paper on developing leadership, Reg Revans (1979) offered an equation that underlines an important aspect of learning for change:

$$L = P + Q$$

where L is learning, and P is what Revans called 'programmed knowledge' – the sort of expert knowledge or procedural skill gained from books or traditional courses. Q is the 'questioning insight' that comes from action as a reflective practitioner in any discipline. This process of acting as a reflective practitioner uses what is sometimes called 'double-loop learning'.

All engineers are familiar with single-loop feedback systems (Figure 9.9) in which an action in the system has a result that is measured and a link provides feedback to the activator. The thermostat in a home heating or cooling system is an example of this.

FIGURE 9.9 Single-loop feedback

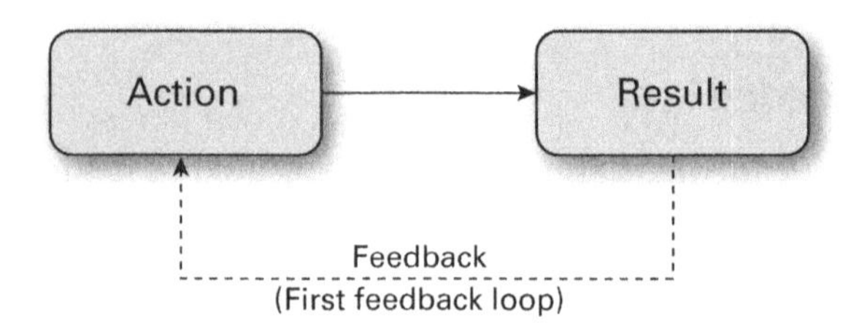

FIGURE 9.10 Double-loop learning

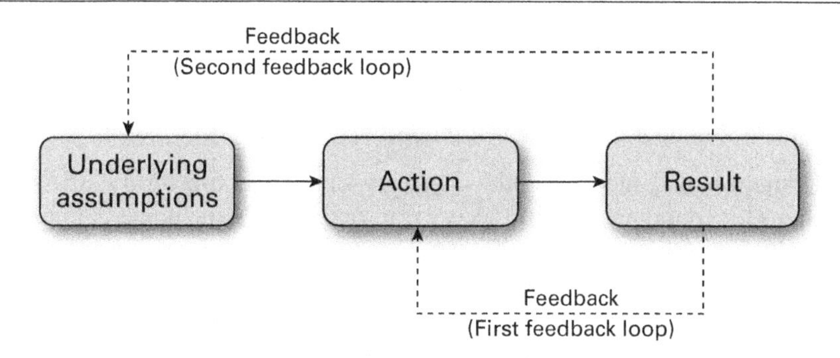

Double-loop learning (Figure 9.10) is more complex and recognizes that as human beings our action decisions are based on paradigms – sets of underlying assumptions – about how things work. This extends well beyond technical systems to social systems, such as business organizations, and to personal and interpersonal transactions. 'Reflective practitioners' (and increasingly some artificial intelligence systems) respond not only to the immediate feedback but also review their own assumptions about how the world operates.

Reg Revans (1979) wrote:

> In conditions of change there is bound to be uncertainty... programmed knowledge (of necessity drawn from the describable certainties of more than one past) may inhibit the exercise of leadership and the freedom to pose fresh questions (Q).

In the paper cited, Revans was particularly addressing the question of leadership development, but the comment extends to any attitudinal change and 'soft skills' learning.

When planning any learning in times of change, this distinction between 'P' and 'Q' is important. If programmed learning is all that is required, simple single-loop learning feedback will be sufficient to develop or test knowledge and skill. However, if learners will need to respond flexibly to a variety of contexts, creating unexpected or unplanned situations, the learning process must be designed to include 'double-loop' feedback. Such feedback develops the 'questioning insight' needed to recognize and, where necessary, to revise the underlying assumptions on which future actions will be based.

1.3 Finding the information – HR records

The process of identifying current knowledge and skill often starts with the Human Resources (HR) function (Chapter 13, Section A). Although seldom perfect and complete, HR systems represent the fullest and most accessible information available. The organization's HR team are typically important allies of those planning for change, and should be involved as early as possible in the process. HR information systems are likely to include information about:

- recruitment and selection (including individual résumés);
- learning and development;
- performance management;
- workforce and talent planning;
- organizational design and development.

This information will help to build a picture of the organization's KSAs. (Note: requirements for confidentiality and security of such records, including data protection rules, usually mean that they must be searched and information compiled by the HR team.)

Where organizations possess a comprehensive file of job descriptions or accountability statements, these too will give insights into the current KSAs expected in the organization. Depending on the format used, the KSAs may be listed and explicit, or may have to be inferred (Figure 9.11).

1.4 Other sources of information

Where completely new knowledge and skills are required, it is unlikely that the HR systems will have captured relevant information. It may be possible to gain the help

FIGURE 9.11 A job description format

Department Corporate Accounts	
Job Title Accounts payable team member	
Main purpose of job To ensure that external invoices are validated, authorized and paid securely and in line with company payment policies.	
Major activities	**Measures of success**
To receive invoices and enter onto Company control system.	All invoices recorded on system by end of day. Complete information in each invoice record.
To obtain and check authority to pay.	No unauthorized payments made.
To manage payment terms for different suppliers.	Corporate payment terms adhered to. No late payment penalties.

of L&D specialists or HR business partners in surveying various key groups in the organization. Pencil-and-paper or online surveys may be used to allow stakeholders to self-rate on key skills, engaging them from an early stage in identifying what new knowledge and skills they may need. The promise of full and appropriate training can reduce learning anxiety and so reduce one source of potential change resistance.

2. Job analysis

2.1 The jobs cover approach

Where simple issues of skills cover arise as a result of change (perhaps due to a reduction in headcount) a simple 'skills cover chart' such as that shown in Figure 9.12 may be useful. In the example shown, a blank cell in the matrix indicates no requirement for the individual to apply a certain skill. The subsequent coding used here is additive, which works well with pen and paper. However, the method of coding can be adapted to circumstances and the use of colour makes spreadsheet versions of such charts easy to read – perhaps using a simple 'RAG' (red–amber–green) code. Another variant would use a scale (perhaps 1 to 5) to indicate levels of proven performance. Using this approach it is also possible to conduct a simple risk analysis, identifying the adequacy of skills cover for holidays or sickness.

FIGURE 9.12 Skills cover chart

Activities / Names	1. Receive invoices	2. Obtain authority	3. Manage terms	4. Issue payment	
Alex	⊗	⦸			
Bernie	⊗	⊗			
Chris	⦸				
Denny	⊗	⊗	⊗	⊗	
Eric	⊗	⊗	⦸	○	

○ = needs to do this   \ = training underway   X = fully competent

FIGURE 9.13 A KSA chart

Department Corporate Accounts		**Job Title** Accounts payable team member	
Major activity	Knowledge	Skills	Attitudes
To receive invoices and enter onto Company control system	1. List of approved suppliers 2. Handling new suppliers 3. Invoice control system (computer)	1. Accessing and using invoice control system 2. Opening new supplier account	1. Vigilance for spurious invoices 2. Care for system security
To obtain and check authority to pay	1. List of authorities by department 2. Policy response times from departments	1. Relationship skills with departments	1. Importance of system reliability 2. Value of good relationships with departments
To manage payment terms for different suppliers	1. Policy payment times for different supplier categories 2. Basis for exceptions, process for these	1. Telephone skills for dealing with suppliers	1. Value of good supplier relationships 2. Fairness to suppliers 3. Care for accuracy
Issue manual payment (cheque)	1. Policy on manual payments	1. Operating cheque printing system	1. Protective towards payment system

2.2 KSA charts

One approach that often proves useful is to develop 'KSA charts' for key stakeholder groups (Figure 9.13). Where there are suitable job descriptions or accountability statements, these can complete the first column of such charts, showing the main activities or key accountabilities of the job concerned. Note: some professionals avoid using the word 'attitudes' in this context; attitudes are hard to define and observe. For those who take this view, 'behaviours' is preferred as a proxy for attitudes, offering equivalent but observable characteristics.

Charts such as these need the insights of those close to the stakeholder role, so engaging the support of jobholders, their managers and HR business partners will be important. For other types of stakeholder, consider who can best help to develop such charts. Field sales staff may have valuable insights into customer groups, and buyers may have comparable links to suppliers.

For jobs within the organization, HR may be helping line managers draft new job descriptions. These will enable 'future state' KSA charts to be developed, so that key differences in knowledge, skill and attitude requirements resulting from the change can be highlighted.

Having identified the categories of KSA required, obtaining ratings of individuals' current status may be obtained by interviews with – or surveys of – jobholders and/or their managers. This is sensitive territory. If it is possible to give categorical and credible reassurance about job security, and the need for a shift in skills and knowledge is accepted, this process may be possible as described. If, on the other hand, people are insecure about their future employment, then they are unlikely to cooperate willingly in such data gathering, and the 'counsel of perfection' for gathering information may have to be moderated.

Charts such as these can be used in a variety of ways. For example, the proportion of the jobholder's time on each activity could be included; this would identify changes to the balance of work in the job, as well as in KSA.

In most change situations it is worth considering the use of KSA charts or an equivalent technique to analyse the key learning issues raised by a change. This is particularly so in jobs and areas of the organization where the change impact is high.

3. Training planning (with L&D – collaboration is ideal)

3.1 *Who needs what?*

The process of planning and scheduling training for a change initiative is best conducted as a joint enterprise involving a change manager and professional L&D colleagues. Once learning needs have been identified and analysed, the challenge is to plan how best to address them.

An early stage of this process is to identify groupings of KSAs that can or should be learned together. It is a key principle of learning that things should be learnt the way they will be used. This means that the grouping of KSAs should reflect the combinations in which they will be applied after the change is complete. Collaboration with training designers and/or other learning specialists will help to identify how much time should be allowed for learners to gain competence in each learning module (group of KSAs).

A practical approach to this is to use a spreadsheet (Figure 9.14) in which the rows are either named individuals or identifiable, coherent groups of people (with the number of people alongside). The columns will be the KSAs identified as needed. This is like the 'skills cover chart' above, but on a large scale. Cells can be coded to show the need for the particular person/group to possess a particular KSA. For individuals, the degree of competence can be shown. As appropriate groups of KSAs are identified to reflect the combinations in which they should be learned, columns can easily be reordered to show the resulting learning modules.

FIGURE 9.14 Example KSA spreadsheet

Cells coded by need:
Light = 'nice to have'
Medium = 'important'
Dark = 'essential'

Current competence of groups assessed in cells as % competent

	① Active listening	② Business skills	③ Customer service	④ Discount policies	⑤ Escalation of calls	⑥ Feedback processes	⑦ Etc.
Account Managers (13)	50	60	50	30	20	70	
Business Specialists (7)	10	80	40	30	10	20	
Call Handlers (54 – 2 shifts)	60	30	40	20	50	0	
Discounts Supervisors (9)	0	20	20	70	60	50	
Etc.							

In this illustration, moving columns 1, 3 and 5 together would suggest a 'customer skills' module offering skills development for call handlers and account managers.

3.2 Scheduling learning activities

Having identified a number of learning modules on which the change initiative will rely, the kind of chart described above will indicate the numbers of people requiring each module. Learning professionals will offer estimates of the learning time to allow for each module, based on ideas about the most appropriate learning design (Section B4). This should allow the learning activities to be added to the plan for the change initiative as a whole – typically added to a Gantt chart. Logistical issues about availability of numbers of people for learning activities may extend the overall time planned. Practical issues such as peak staff holiday periods and peak trading seasons must also be considered.

It is a key principle of learning that it should be followed immediately by its application. This means that the learning activities should ideally be delivered 'just in time', immediately before the change is implemented and the learning will be used. If this is not practical, consider allowing for phased development of relevant KSAs so that the last stage of the learning (or a 'refresher session') occurs immediately before live use. This may increase learning costs but, to adapt Peter Drucker's famous saying: 'If you think [effective] training is expensive, try ignorance!'

3.3 Defining what is to be learned

Writing good learning objectives is a skill set in its own right. However, the heart of the matter is to be clear what the outcomes must be. As Steven Covey's second 'habit' suggests: 'Begin with the end in mind.' Writing good learning objectives means completing the following sentence (or variants of it): At the end of the learning activity, learners will be able to...

This sounds simple, but often requires considerable careful thought. Here are three examples taken from the learning activity 'learning to drive a car':

1. *'At the end of training the driver will be able to identify correctly the meaning of, and correct response to, all road signs within the territory of the licence that affect motor vehicles.'*

   This is a knowledge objective and it is clear how success could be established. Note that it imposes a 100 per cent success rate, which is appropriate in this case as a learning objective. The formal driving test might still allow a margin of error on some less common or less important signs. The objective is appropriate, too, in that the knowledge test it implies reflects the way the driver will need to interpret road signs after training. An alternative would have been '*will be able to describe correctly all road signs...*' – but this requires verbal skills not relevant to driving and is *not* related to how the target knowledge will be applied in practice.

2. *'At the end of training the driver will be able to perform basic safety checks on the condition of the vehicle.'*

   This objective includes some knowledge and some skill components. It also fails to specify what are the 'basic safety checks'. This is not necessarily a problem in a learning objective, provided that there is a separate document that lists what the checks are, how they are performed and the standards to be achieved. Covering all these details with a long series of individual 'micro' learning objectives is tedious and unnecessary.

   Consider the following extreme options and you will see how inappropriate levels of detail undermine the value of learning objectives: '*will be able to maintain a car*' or '*will be able to replace the dust cap correctly after inflating a tyre*'!

3. *'At the end of training the driver will consistently show appropriate caution when performing manoeuvres.'*

   Caution is an attitude. The skilled behaviours to demonstrate that attitude must be documented and (as the objective says) displayed consistently. The target attitude is evidenced not just by the skilful display of target behaviours but by the ingrained, habitual way in which they are applied. The range of manoeuvres included must also be specified in a separate document. The minimum is those required for a national driving test, but learning objectives may include additional items. As a result, the driver will be more effective after training.

   Note that one or more additional learning objectives are required to specify the skilful (not merely cautious) execution of these manoeuvres. This objective is designed to focus attention specifically on attitude.

This 'learning to drive' example illustrates that:

- For one learning activity there are usually a number of specified learning objectives.

- Learning objectives should include all knowledge, skills and attitudes relevant to the work.
- Outcome measures or indicators should relate well to the way the job will actually be done.
- Success standards set in a competence test may be different from those set as learning objectives.
- The level of detail must be appropriate (supplemented by other documents where necessary).
- Attitudinal objectives can be specified through consistent patterns of behaviour.

Finally, supervisors of the work activity must be able to sign a list of learning objectives, confident that anyone who meets those objectives will perform effectively in their role.

3.4 Who will provide the training?

This will of course depend on the design (Section B4 below) – but the design also depends on the provider. Table 9.4 sets out some of the options to consider, with associated advantages and disadvantages. Combinations of these are, of course, possible.

4. Learning design and channels

4.1 Learning objectives and the learning journey

The need to specify learning objectives well has been covered in Section B3.3 above. The process of learning design starts there and works backwards: 'What do we need to do so that a learner can meet those learning objectives?'

A common mistake is to assume that a 'course', 'workshop' or 'briefing' will provide the learning that is needed. In reality most people learn most of their work skills and knowledge in the context of doing the job. The problem with a purely 'on-job' learning approach is that it can be random, slow and difficult to assure quality. All these disadvantages can be mitigated and, if the job exists somewhere *as it will be after a change*, on-job learning may be a valuable part of the learning journey. Notice the caveat: 'as it will be after the change'. Remember the principle that 'things should be learnt the way they will be used'. If the learning situation is too different from the post-change one, there are risks of 'negative learning'. This means developing bad or irrelevant habits, ways of working that may interfere with effective performance in the future.

The concept of a learning journey referred to above is helpful. The metaphor is a reminder that each learner is on a journey from one state of KSA to another. It is unlikely that they can 'teleport' from 'now' to 'then', so understanding and planning their learning as a journey is helpful. Some parts of the journey can be supported and accelerated by formal and structured training 'interventions'. Others can be more

TABLE 9.4 Training provider options

Provider	Advantages	Disadvantages
Change sponsor	High credibility.	Time and availability. Possible distance from actual jobs.
Change manager	Understands and can advocate the change initiative.	Time and availability. Subject matter expertise may be limited.
Internal subject matter experts (SMEs)	Subject matter expertise! Local organizational knowledge.	Training expertise not guaranteed. Time and availability.
Internal trainers	Training expertise high. Local organizational knowledge.	Subject matter expertise may be limited. Time and availability.
Existing jobholders	Really know the job context! Established level of knowledge and skill.	No clear guarantee of support for change (but can select for it). Instructional skills can vary (but can train for these).
External supplier	Greater availability. Can select for subject matter expertise. Learners may see externals as more credible. Learners may feel secure about being open with externals.	Cost. Less aware of local conditions in the organization. Confidentiality concerns.

self-directed if learners are clear what their next destination is and have a clear map to help them get there.

4.2 Learning methods and their applications

There are many possible learning methods: Table 9.5 sets out just a few, with comments on the applications for which each is most suited and how to make them work best.

TABLE 9.5 Learning methods

One-to-one or small group on-job instruction	• Great for skills training on a specific task or series of tasks. • Practical and (relatively) inexpensive. • Requires available jobholders who already possess the skills AND are trained as instructors. • Requires preparation by instructor.
Problem-solving groups	• People learn together as they solve real work problems. • Needs sufficient knowledge of the topic within the group. • Group dynamics can be designed to develop cultural norms. • Relatively inexpensive – apart from salary bill of attendees! • Needs a skilled facilitator.
Small group lecture and discussion	• Good for developing knowledge and understanding. • Build cohesion and shared understanding in a group. • Appropriate for team leaders/managers to convey change messages. • Group dynamics can be designed to develop cultural norms. • Relatively inexpensive – apart from salary bill of attendees! • Needs a suitably skilled instructor/discussion facilitator.
Large presentations and lectures	• Good for conveying consistent information and messages. • Appropriate for change sponsors and senior leadership to convey change messages. • Relatively inexpensive – apart from salary bill of attendees! • Build knowledge in those who can listen well. • Best if presenter is both credible and skilled. • Needs to be kept short for best impact (<30 minutes). • Can be extended for question-and-answer session if there is energy for this and the presenter is sufficiently skilled.
Formal courses – usually small- to medium-sized groups	• Flexible – can be designed to include all sorts of knowledge and skills development. • Must vary learning methods to keep all participants engaged. • Should include experiential elements – knowledge can be conveyed more cost-effectively in other ways. • Require skilled design and delivery.
Computer-aided or computer-based learning	• Good (and very cost-effective) for teaching knowledge, understanding and application consistently to many people. • Testing can easily be built into the module. • Relatively high initial cost – the design needs to be very good. • Needs good help system including accessible support team.

TABLE 9.5 *continued*

Computer simulations – individuals, small groups or larger groups working in teams	• Develop knowledge, understanding and application. • Can build cognitive and analytical skills. • Flexible to use with different sizes of learning group. • Group dynamics can be designed to develop cultural norms. • Need skilled and knowledgeable facilitation. • High initial investment – difficult to design well.
Practical simulations – small groups or larger groups working in teams	• Develop a wide range of knowledge, understanding, application and analytical skill. • Can be designed to build relational and practical skills. • Group dynamics can be designed to develop cultural norms. • Need skilled and knowledgeable facilitation. • High initial investment – difficult to design well.

Some of the learning methods in Table 9.5 can be adapted for delivery using videoconferencing or webinars to create a 'virtual classroom'. This approach offers significant savings in the time and costs of travel, but may risk loss of impact and effectiveness. A 'learning journey' may use a combination of learning methods. 'Blended learning' uses online delivery for parts of a learning programme (allowing learners to select times and places to suit their own needs) combined with a face-to-face element to cover other aspects.

4.3 Learning styles and learning methods

In Section A3, different approaches were outlined to understanding learners' preferred 'learning styles'. The implication was that a variety of methods, selected to appeal to a range of styles, would be of benefit. Examples are offered at the end of Section A3.1. However, all learners can appreciate – and learn effectively – from well-simulated work environments. This is because within a simulated work environment, as in the 'real' work situation, there is space for people to manage their own learning preferences:

- *Simulated environments can be created as full-scale replicas of a real-world environment.* For example, a full-scale retail store was initially used exclusively for training purposes during the change programme for a retail pharmacy chain.
- *Simulated environments can be created in a training situation*, using carefully designed learning resources. For example a fast-moving consumer goods (FMCG) company uses a classroom-simulation to re-create a supply-chain environment, as part of a major relaunch of its global supply chain. Other classroom-type simulations use computers to help teams learn financial management, marketing or strategy.

- *Simulated environments can be created in desktop computers through the internet*, using gaming techniques and 'avatars' to build individuals' knowledge, understanding and even relational skills. Social media can be interfaced with this to integrate real-world collaborative learning. One large financial institution built such a system to help graduates learn how to network and interface with a range of senior leaders around their global business.

Whatever the route, the learning journey must provide everyone with practical opportunities to develop and demonstrate the knowledge, skill and attitudes that fully meet the learning objectives. This is not new wisdom!

> *'One must learn by doing the thing; for although you think you know it you have no certainty, until you try.'*
>
> Sophocles, *Trachiniae*, 415 BC

5. Evaluating learning

5.1 *Why evaluation matters*

There are many approaches to evaluating learning. It is a specialist area within L&D, so where evaluation is important, the expertise of L&D specialists should be sought and used. From what has already been written in this section it will be clear that learning evaluation cannot be retro-fitted to any programme. It depends on proper identification of learning needs and on specifying clear and robust learning objectives.

Evaluation is important because it can provide:

- learning feedback for individual learners;
- developmental feedback for trainers and managers of learning;
- validation information for the learning programme or process;
- guidance on improvements that could be made to the learning programme or process;
- clarity about any remedial learning that may be needed to achieve objectives;
- baseline information about the readiness for a change to 'go live';
- a basis for evaluating learning costs against the benefits;
- a basis for evaluating suppliers of learning.

5.2 Models of evaluation

Two widely respected approaches to evaluation of learning are shown in Table 9.6. Elements of the two approaches that are approximately equivalent are shown alongside each other (the information is nicely summarized in Hogan, 2007).

TABLE 9.6 Learning evaluation models

Kirkpatrick (1967) *('Kirkpatrick evaluation')*	**Warr, Bird and Rackham (1970)** *('CIRO model')*
	Context How needs have been identified and analysed. **Input** How the learning activity has been designed and the delivery methods employed.
Reactions How learners respond to the material taught and the methods by which it is taught.	**Reaction** The learners' reactions to the learning experience.
Learning Evidence of knowledge, skills and attitudes actually acquired by learners (at end of learning process).	**Outcome (immediate)** Changes in learners' knowledge, skills and attitudes assessed at the end of the learning process.
Behaviour Evidence of learners' behaviour change in the workplace (known as 'transfer of learning').	**Outcome (intermediate)** Evidence of learners' behaviour change in the workplace (known as 'transfer of learning').
Results Improved outcomes for the individual and/or the organization.	**Outcome (ultimate)** Improved outcomes for the department, business unit or organization.

It is always difficult to link specific learning activities with wider organizational outcomes – there are too many uncontrolled variables. However, for the reasons given above, evaluation is important; it is worthwhile to gather and analyse the best available information about learning effectiveness.

Tip

One colleague commented: If you apply a mathematical standard of *absolute* proof training, evaluation will always fall short. However, good and systematic data can provide the standard of proof required by criminal law in many legal systems – *'beyond reasonable doubt'*!

5.3 Evaluation methods

Evaluation of *context* and *input* is essentially an analytical process. L&D professionals are the appropriate people to assist with this, and can offer help to improve the design and delivery.

Reactions of learners are often obtained through a 'customer satisfaction survey' approach. There are more detailed suggestions about measurement in Chapter 6. For now it is only necessary to advise clear thought about what reactions you need to gather and why. Many readers will have been presented with end-of-course 'happy sheets' that are ambiguous or ask for irrelevant information. At best they assess 'reactions' rather than learning outcomes. In the right circumstances it is possible simply to ask learners (perhaps as a group) to offer feedback. This can be very effective. Chapter 10 suggests a way of doing this using De Bono's 'six thinking hats'. Whatever the method, it is helpful to understand the learners' perspective on things that should be: a) increased (or emphasized more); b) decreased (or emphasized less); c) done differently.

The purely *learning* or *immediate outcome* effectiveness is best assessed immediately at the end of the learning process, before return to the workplace. This avoids contamination by cultural issues, workplace norms etc. Pencil and paper or on-screen tests of knowledge, practical tests of skills and surveys for attitudes can all be useful. Designing such assessments is best done by those with appropriate specialist training – and the assessment methods themselves should be validated before serious use.

Tip

Many years' experience writing test questions tells me not to underestimate the time and effort required to write even 'simple' multiple choice questions that:

- are not too easy;
- have one unambiguously correct answer;
- have wrong answers that are all clearly wrong;
- can be interpreted only in the way intended by the question writer.

Before using any such question you design 'for real' it is essential to try them out on a group of people similar to those who will take the test. The results of doing this are always a surprise!

It may be possible to observe directly the workplace *behaviour* or *intermediate outcomes*. Surveying learners' supervisors provides an alternative to independent 'live' observation. Data from such surveys is usually simpler and less expensive to obtain, but may be subject to distortions, based on the relationships between the supervisor and the learners (and those between the supervisor and the person asking for the information!).

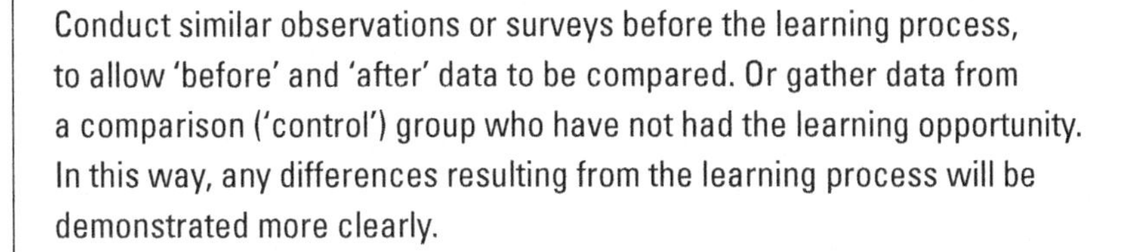

Tip

Conduct similar observations or surveys before the learning process, to allow 'before' and 'after' data to be compared. Or gather data from a comparison ('control') group who have not had the learning opportunity. In this way, any differences resulting from the learning process will be demonstrated more clearly.

Showing the *results* or *ultimate outcomes* of learning is often a challenge. It clearly helps if business purposes for the learning were defined beforehand, and measures of success identified. However, many benefits of learning will be wider than these measures. Measures of productivity, error rates, response times and other 'hard' measures can all be appropriate. 'Soft' measures may also be appropriate: staff turnover, length of stay in job, absence rates and staff attitude surveys can all give additional insights into benefits derived from the learning. Chapter 3 (managing benefits) has a useful contribution to make to the debates about learning evaluation.

Summary

Learning needs may relate to knowledge, skills and attitudes. The current situation and future needs of all stakeholders can be mapped and gaps identified. The appropriate method to address these gaps must be chosen on a case-by-case basis. Learning methods, the 'target audience' and the schedule are elements of a learning plan. The starting point for learning design is a set of carefully considered learning objectives. The crucial step of evaluating the learning is also based on the learning objectives, as well as on wider organizational goals.

Understanding these learning management processes enables change managers to collaborate effectively with L&D colleagues or, in the absence of such support, to produce workable training plans themselves.

Questions to think about

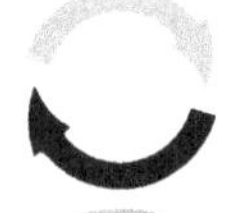

1. Select a job you know well and draft a KSA chart for it.
2. For one 'major activity' in the KSA chart, write learning objectives for someone needing to become fully competent in this activity.
3. Design a suitable 'learning journey' for this 'major activity', using a range of learning methods.
4. How should the results of this learning activity be evaluated?

Further reading

Beevers, K and Rea, A (2013) *Learning and Development Practice* – written for those studying L&D, and contains much practical material that develops the themes of this section

Harrison, R (2009) *Learning and Development* – offers an excellent foundation for understanding L&D issues and their practical application in an organization. Part 4 is especially helpful

The UK's Chartered Institute of Personnel and Development (CIPD) has an excellent website with many useful resources freely available. Some are restricted to CIPD members but many, including the excellent series of 'factsheets', are available to anyone who registers with the site [Online] www.cipd.co.uk

Section C: Behavioural change and coaching

Introduction

To include a section on behavioural change and coaching in a text on change management is both appropriate and dangerous! It is appropriate because the experience around the world of those engaged in change management is that they need to 'coach' others from time to time. In particular, they find value in coaching line management colleagues in behaviours likely to support effective change. However, it is also dangerous to include this section. Coaching at its best is a sophisticated application of interpersonal skills, helping people to develop their effectiveness using work situations as learning opportunities. Change managers are not expected to be professional coaches and, some would say, 'a little learning is a dangerous thing'. Further reading, well-designed coach training, personal experience and reflection should all be used to build on the brief introduction offered here.

I start by describing the core behavioural skills of active listening and managing feedback, then discuss issues in structuring coaching, and end with some further comments about coaching in change situations. This section is not written for professional coaches, and no true 'client' relationships may be involved. However, when referring to the people involved in a coaching encounter I use the words 'coach' and 'client' as a convenient shorthand.

1. Active listening in coaching and change

1.1 Purpose and benefits

The objective of active listening is to understand how another person perceives some aspect of the world. In a change situation this may mean understanding as completely as possible how other people perceive that change. This encompasses their understanding of it, their attitudes to it and their feelings about it. In coaching, active listening enables the coach to 'tune in' to the inner and outer worlds of those being coached, to understand their situations and their goals. This ensures, for example, that discussion of development options is based on the real starting point for an individual.

Active listening is discussed more frequently than it is practised! It can be seen as a cluster of interpersonal behaviours and used as if it were simply a technique. Used merely as a communication technique it can risk being seen as manipulative. At its most effective, active listening reflects an attitude in which a person is prepared to suspend his or her own agenda for a time in order to understand another person more fully. Used with integrity in this way it builds bridges of understanding and relationship.

1.2 Core active listening behaviours

There are several behavioural components of active listening, as set out below.

Clearing the decks (inner preparation)

This is the inner process of choosing to set aside other current preoccupations and any personal agenda in order to focus on building genuine understanding of a situation from another person's perspective.

Giving attention

Body language makes a critical contribution to helping another person to know (s)he is being understood through giving them focused attention. Body language includes posture and gestures (open, receptive, oriented towards the other, and ideally echoing the level of energy displayed by the other person) and eye contact (focused on the other person, noticing his/her responses, but without simply staring). Occasional vocal responses (mmm, hmmm etc) may also form part of demonstrating focused attention.

Reflecting content

This is typically the behaviour of 'playing back' to the other person what (s)he has just said (usually just the last few words) in his/her own words.

Paraphrasing

This is similar to reflecting content, but uses the listener's own words. Done effectively this really does communicate a high level of understanding. The other person hears his/her own meaning accurately captured in the listener's words. However, care must be taken to avoid distorting the intention of the other person, or the opportunity to understand the other person in his or her own terms will be lost.

Reflecting feelings

Understanding is demonstrated very powerfully by reflecting to the other person any feelings (emotions) – either positive or negative – you perceive in what (s)he is saying or how it is being said. Examples would be: 'You sound more and more excited as you describe that meeting'; or 'As you describe that meeting you sound weary'. Be careful not to 'tell' people how they are feeling; simply describe what you see and hear.

Questions

In general, questions (whether open or closed) that remain on and extend the agenda of the other person are experienced as expressing understanding. They often begin with 'So...'. They often extend and apply what the speaker has said: 'So does that mean that you...'. (Note: questions designed to find facts or explore issues are perfectly legitimate. However, since they typically reflect elements of the listener's own agenda or interests, they are not strictly 'active listening'.)

1.3 Connections with conditions for facilitating change

Chapter 1, Section B3.7 contains a brief outline of Rogers's (1957) work on factors enabling personal growth and change. A well-developed skill in active listening enables change practitioners to demonstrate the 'core conditions' described by Rogers.

2. The role of feedback in behavioural change

2.1 Behavioural change

The CMI describes behavioural change like this:

> Behavioural change is the process by which people adjust the way they characteristically operate in the world. It includes the underlying patterns that others might see as their 'personal style', and which critically affect the responses people make to them. (2013: 132)

FIGURE 9.15 Double-loop feedback and behaviour

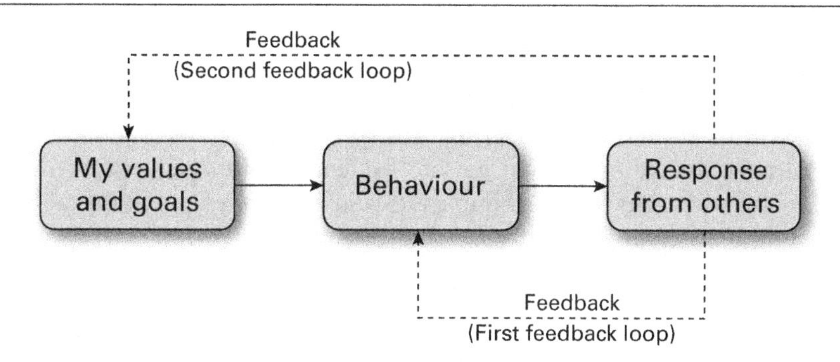

The way that individuals operate in the world, and particularly the way they relate to others, are formed as habits and are deeply embedded through life's experiences. They do not usually change either quickly or easily, and are not very 'trainable' in the short term. Carefully designed behavioural skills training has some value. It can offer tools and techniques to help people adjust their behaviour. However, most change of this kind is a process that relies on a form of 'double-loop feedback' (Section B1.2), as shown in Figure 9.15.

Feedback in this context may be more or less explicit. It may be that people take the time and care to tell me what impact my behaviour has on them, applying good principles of behavioural feedback. More frequently, I may simply observe the impact my behaviour has on others and form my own conclusions. Such conclusions are based on my own interpretations, fears, self-image, biases and personal history, and may not represent very accurately the responses I get from others. Explicit feedback from others helps to avoid misinformation entering the feedback process.

FIGURE 9.16 'Arc of distortion'

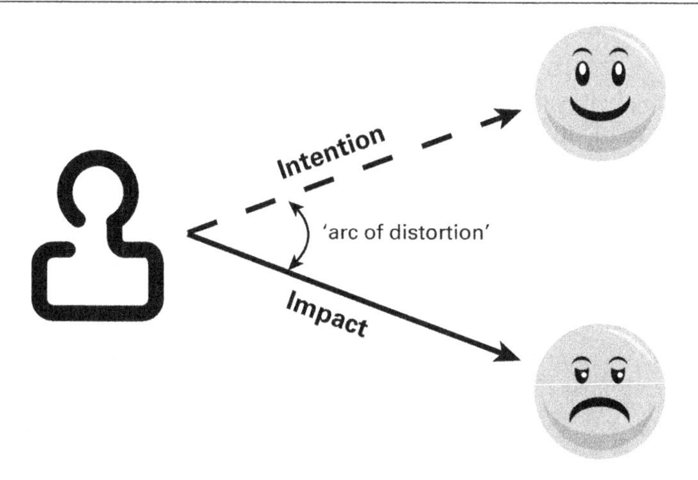

Such feedback helps to minimise what is often referred to as the 'arc of distortion' (Figure 9.16) associated with my behaviour. This term is often used in communication theory (see Chapter 5). In that context, it relates to the factors that cause misunderstandings in my communication. In the broader context of human behaviour, it describes the way in which the impact of my behaviour may be different from the intention that lies behind it. The factors causing this gap are less significant for our present purpose than the fact that getting feedback from others about my actual impact (as opposed to my intended impact) gives me the opportunity to calibrate my behaviours more accurately in future.

2.2 Guidelines for giving effective behavioural feedback

Giving effective developmental feedback is a valuable skill in its own right. In addition to its vital importance in a coaching context, it is used by the most effective leaders, managers and change agents in a variety of contexts. Here are some widely accepted guidelines for giving effective developmental feedback:

- *Helpful intention*
  Feedback tends to be destructive when it is used as a cover for making the giver's own point. It is not an excuse for 'dumping' irritation on someone! True feedback is given in a way that considers the needs of the person receiving it.
- *Given privately*
  Feedback to an individual should in most cases be given in private. This allows both affirming and critical observations to be explored without compromising the dignity of the person receiving the feedback.
- *Descriptive, not evaluative*
  When giving feedback it is better not to give an evaluative judgement of the behaviour observed (Figure 9.17). This tends to promote a defensive response. By describing the behaviour observed and its impact (on oneself or the reaction observed on others) the recipient gains information on which to base future behaviour. The individual remains responsible for the decision to use the feedback or not to do so.
- *Specific*
  Describing behaviour and the reaction in clear and specific terms helps the recipient to identify the particular behaviours that lead to unintended impact. For example, to be told that one is 'dominating' will probably not be as useful as to be told that: 'Just now when we were discussing [the issue] you did not acknowledge what any of us said and kept pushing harder for your own solution. I felt forced to accept your idea or face attack from you.'

  Equally, to be told that a presentation was 'really good' is less useful than to be told, for example: 'In that presentation you clearly outlined at the beginning the points you were going to cover. As a result I could follow your logic very clearly.'

FIGURE 9.17 Descriptive feedback

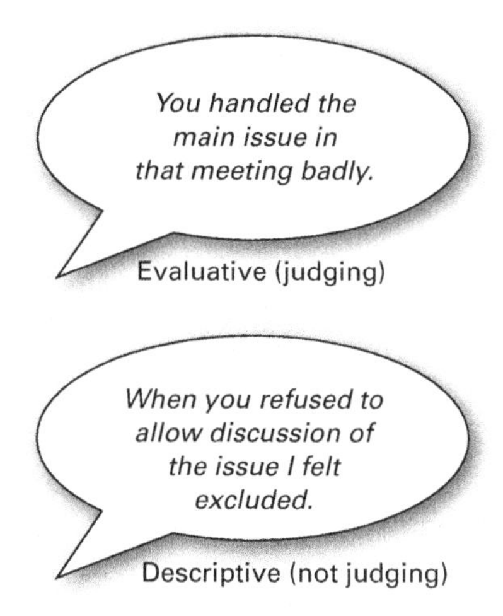

- *Actionable*
  Feedback focuses on behaviour – which the receiver can do something about. Frustration is only increased when people are reminded of some shortcoming over which they have no control.
- *Welcome*
  Feedback is most useful when it is requested by those receiving it. It is especially valuable where receivers have identified the kinds of behaviour on which they would value observations. At the least, when giving feedback, ask the receiver for permission: 'Would you like my feedback on this?'
- *Timely*
  In general, feedback is most useful at the earliest opportunity after the behaviour concerned. The situation and feelings are freshest in the receiver's mind. However, if the situation giving rise to feedback has been particularly difficult or distressing, a little distance in time (and emotional distance) is usually helpful.
- *Balanced*
  In general, it is easier for people to receive and integrate feedback when the negative (critical) aspects do not overwhelm the positive, affirming elements. Aim to offer at least as much affirming comment as critical observation. Feedback that is entirely positive is fine (if this is honest) but feedback that is wholly negative is not usually developmental.
- *Checked and confirmed*
  Some people have a tendency to filter out the positive aspects of feedback and hear only the critical comments. Others have tendencies in the opposite

direction! Check that feedback has been heard the way it was intended, by asking the receiver to repeat or paraphrase it. This makes it possible to check that both the focus and balance of the feedback have been properly understood.

2.3 Some guidelines for receiving feedback

Especially in the context of coaching, it may be necessary to help the person being coached to receive feedback in an appropriate way. This will apply not only to feedback given by the coach, but also to feedback received from others that may relate to the coaching process.

Recipients of feedback need to understand that feedback from others gives them the potential for increased choice about the way they will behave. To take fullest advantage of this opportunity, there are some simple, common sense rules on how to receive feedback appropriately:

- *Listen non-defensively*
  Feedback sometimes touches a raw nerve. Listening does not necessarily mean that the recipient accepts or agrees with what the other person is saying, but by listening carefully the recipient is likely to learn something helpful.
- *Seek clarification*
  The kind of exploratory questions discussed in Section C1.2 are particularly appropriate, remaining on the 'agenda' of the person giving feedback.
- *Ask for examples*
  If the person giving feedback is talking in general terms, it is helpful to ask for specific examples (when, where, with whom, words used etc).
- *Thank the feedback giver*
  Giving feedback is seldom easy and always demands a certain amount of time and effort. Feedback is best seen as a gift, even if in the end the recipient decides not to change anything as a result.
- *Evaluate*
  It is for the person receiving feedback to decide on the value of the feedback and any 'next steps'. This is best done privately and after some reflection, not at the moment the feedback is given. The exception is a coaching setting, where discussion and evaluation of feedback may be helpful.
- *Cross check*
  Feedback from one individual is valuable data about how that one individual is impacted by behaviour. One helpful role of a coach is to help the person being coached to devise appropriate ways to gather feedback more widely.
- *Decide*
  Decisions on what – if any – aspects of behaviour the recipient wishes to modify as a result of feedback are best made when all the above steps are complete. Time to reflect, perhaps with the help of a friend, colleague or coach, is very beneficial. If the receiver does decide to work on an area, continued feedback will be needed to help monitor progress and performance. Ask for it!

FIGURE 9.18 Feedback summary

Giving
developmental feedback
• Helpful intention
• Given privately
• Descriptive, not evaluative
• Specific
• Actionable
• Welcome
• Timely
• Balanced
• Checked and confirmed
Receiving
developmental feedback
• Listen non-defensively
• Seek clarification
• Ask for examples
• Thank the feedback giver
• Evaluate
• Cross check
• Decide

2.4 The purpose and value of feedback

Feedback, then, is a way of giving and receiving help with continuous improvement of personal performance (Figure 9.18). It is a corrective mechanism for people who want to learn how well their behaviour matches their intentions. As one well-known cliché has it: 'Feedback is the breakfast food of champions!' (An anglicized version would probably read: 'Champions eat feedback for breakfast!')

3. Understanding coaching

3.1 What we mean by coaching

The model of elite sports coaching is the one most frequently adapted by advocates of coaching at work. It acknowledges that coaching is not primarily a remedial activity, but can help people of different levels to perform better. It incorporates elements of feedback and direction. It includes the element of diagnosis, analysing current levels of performance, and the reasons for it, as the basis for future development. Critically, it also includes the setting of clear goals for performance improvement.

One element is not explicit in this description, but is critical in the work context (and in fact in the sports context). This is the need to involve the 'client' fully in *joint* diagnosis of the current situation, *joint* goal setting, *joint* analysis of options and in *making real commitment* to the next steps.

3.2 The coaching 'contract'

The term contract is frequently used to describe the relationship between a coach and a client, using the legal concept as a metaphor. The 'contract' here is an explicit agreement between the coach and the client about how they will work together to improve the client's performance. It includes what each can expect of the other for the duration of the coaching arrangement. In an organizational context it is likely to include:

- what outcomes the coaching is designed to achieve ('Why are we doing this?');
- the level of confidentiality the client can expect from the coach ('How open can I afford to be?');
- what the coach is offering the client ('What will I get from this?');
- how the coaching process will work ('What will coaching feel like?');
- what the client will be expected to do ('What will you expect from me?');
- how much one-to-one time the coach is offering the client ('What are you offering me?');
- how long the coaching is expected to last ('How open-ended is your support?');
- when the coaching contract will be reviewed ('For how long am I committed to this?');
- how both parties will evaluate the coaching process ('What will success look like?').

The contract may be a wholly verbal agreement, or may be written down (perhaps in an e-mail or other confirmation of what has been agreed). In organizational life the needs and expectations of the client's manager may be important and become part of the coaching contract.

3.3 An approach to coaching

One of the best-known and widely respected models of the coaching process is that developed by Sir John Whitmore (2009). He uses the acronym GROW™ (Figure 9.19) to set out the key elements around which coaching can be structured:

FIGURE 9.19 The GROW™ model of coaching

Goal	Defining a clear and motivating goal to which the client can be committed
Reality	Analysing and specifying current levels of performance and the reasons for these
Options	Identifying options the client can select to develop from the current reality to the goal
Will	Testing and securing the client's will and determination to take the next steps

This framework can be used to structure a single coaching meeting and as a template for a coaching process. It suggests questions that the coach may helpfully use in discussion with the client, for example:

- *Goal questions*:
  - What is your objective? What are you aiming to achieve?
  - What would that look like? Sound like? Feel like?
  - How would others be able to see the change?
  - What advantage would this give you?
- *Reality questions*:
  - On a scale of 1 to 10, how far are you towards your goal (target performance)?
  - What aspects of your goal (target performance) are already a part of your behaviour (at least some of the time)?
  - How do you achieve this?
  - How does it look/sound/feel when you operate this way?
  - What elements of your goal are most difficult for you? Why?
  - What obstacles prevent you from behaving in line with your goal?
- *Options questions*:
  - What opportunities do you have to practise your goals (apply your target behaviours)?
  - Which elements of your goals will best be developed in these various situations?
  - Whom can you trust to give you feedback (in the various settings identified as opportunities)?
  - How can you gather that feedback?
  - Are there other ways you could track your own performance and behaviour?
  - What sources of objective data are there on your performance?
- *Will questions*:
  - What will you do before we meet again?
  - On a scale of 1 to 10 how certain are you that you will take the development opportunities you have identified?
  - What will be the rewards to you of making the changes you plan?
  - What problems might arise?
  - How can others help you stay on track?
  - How can I help you?
  - When we next meet, what will you be saying to me about your progress and development?

Of course, these questions are only illustrative, and an effective coach does not place too much reliance on asking questions. Listening and exploring the clients' ways of seeing their development are central. Even so, the example questions above should give a practical idea of how a coaching conversation might run in each of the four areas of the model. Closing each conversation with clarity about the next steps and a clear commitment by the client is particularly important.

4. Coaching and the change manager

Most frequently the skills of observing behaviour, giving timely and developmental feedback and listening actively will be sufficient for a change manager to give effective support to people through a change initiative. These opportunities to give this kind of support tend to be episodic and not to form part of a longer-term coaching plan.

There are, however, occasions when a key individual in the change process – perhaps the sponsor – needs to model different behaviours as part of a change process. If a relationship of trust exists between the sponsor and a change management colleague or change agent, more systematic feedback and coaching may be both desirable and possible. In these cases, it is important to consider: 1) whether the change manager or change agent is the best person to coach; and 2) whether the change manager or change agent has the time to act as a coach.

If the answer to both these questions is 'yes', then it may be appropriate to invite the potential client to consider engaging in coaching with the coach concerned. Done well, an intervention of this kind can significantly enhance both the success of a change initiative and the credibility of the coach.

Summary

No short text can turn a reader into a skilled coach. This section has offered practical guidelines on two core skills that are useful to all supervisors, managers and leaders: active listening, and giving and receiving feedback. Neither is likely to be new to the reader, but both are skills that can be improved by consistent application. Moreover, both are core to the discipline of coaching, which has been introduced briefly here as a valuable skill for change managers to develop.

Questions to think about

1 Which situations in your work or personal life would benefit from greater use of active listening?

2 Considering the last time you gave feedback to a colleague (or friend), how could you have used the checklist in this chapter to achieve more with the feedback?

3 Think of a colleague or subordinate for whom you can identify a development opportunity where coaching might help. Write down three questions for each step of the GROW™ model that you could use in a coaching discussion. (Note: this is an exercise. You are not committing to hold this discussion!)

Further reading

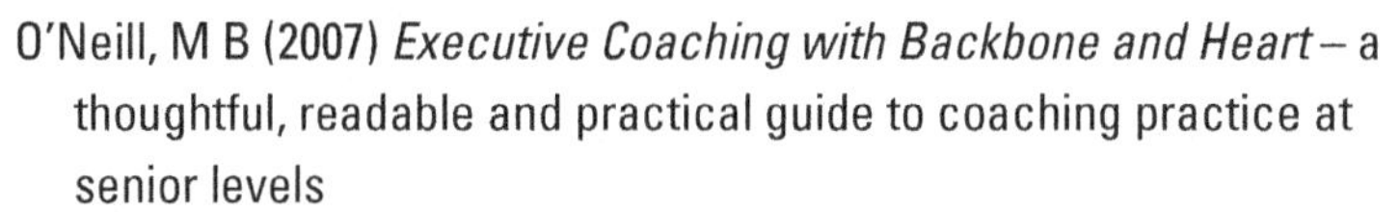

O'Neill, M B (2007) *Executive Coaching with Backbone and Heart* – a thoughtful, readable and practical guide to coaching practice at senior levels

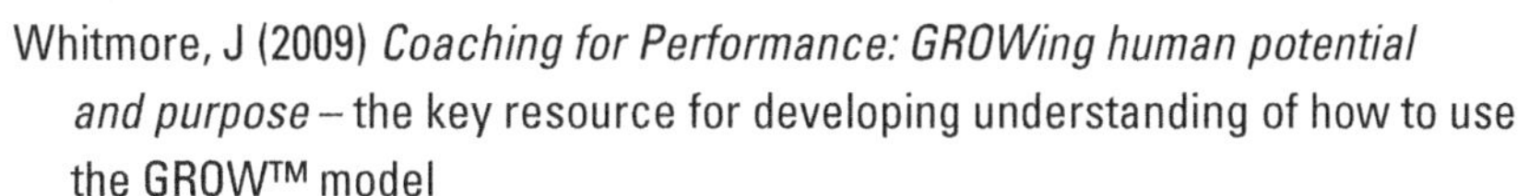

Whitmore, J (2009) *Coaching for Performance: GROWing human potential and purpose* – the key resource for developing understanding of how to use the GROW™ model

References

Beevers, K and Rea, A (2013) *Learning and Development Practice*, 2nd edn, Chartered Institute of Personnel and Development, London

Cameron, E and Green, M (2012) *Making Sense of Change Management: A complete guide to the models, tools and techniques or organizational change*, 3rd edn, Kogan Page, London

Change Management Institute (2013) *The Effective Change Manager: The change management body of knowledge*, (CMBoK) Change Management Institute, Sydney

Coffield, F *et al* (2004) [accessed 30 April 2014] Learning Styles and Pedagogy in Post-16 Learning: A Systematic and Critical Review, *Learning and Skills Network* [Online] www.itslifejimbutnotasweknowit.org.uk/files/LSRC_LearningStyles.pdf

EduTech Wiki contributors [accessed 5 March 2014] Nine Events of Instruction, *EduTech Wiki, A resource kit for educational technology teaching, practice and research* [Online] http://edutechwiki.unige.ch/mediawiki/index.php?title=Nine_events_of_instruction&oldid=11040

Fleming, N D and Mills, C (1992) [accessed 4 March 2014] Not Another Inventory, More a Catalyst for Reflection, *To Improve The Academy*, **11** [Online] http://www.vark-learn.com/documents/not_another_inventory.pdf

Gagne, R M and Medsker, K L (1996) *The Conditions of Learning Training Applications*, 5th edn, Wadsworth, Belmont, CA

Harrison, R (2009) *Learning & Development*, 5th edn, Chartered Institute of Personnel and Development, London

Hogan, R L (2007) [accessed 4 April 2014] The Historical Development of Program Evaluation: Exploring the Past and Present, *Online Journal of Workforce Education and Development*, **2** (4), Fall [Online] http://opensiuc.lib.siu.edu/cgi/viewcontent.cgi?article=1056&context=ojwed

Honey, P and Mumford, A (1992) *The Manual of Learning Styles*, Peter Honey, Maidenhead

Huczynski, A A and Buchanan, D A (2007) *Organizational Behaviour*, 6th edn, Pearson Education, Harlow

Kirkpatrick, D L (1967) *Evaluation of Training*, McGraw-Hill, New York

Kirkpatrick, D L (1996) Revisiting Kirkpatrick's four-level model, *Training and Development*, **50** (1), pp 54–57

Kolb, D (1984) *Experiential Learning*, Prentice Hall, London

Marton, P and Ramsden, P (1988) What does it take to improve learning? in *Improving Learning: New perspectives*, ed P Ramsden, Kogan Page, London, p 271 (cited in Harrison (2009), p 95)

Mehay, R (2010) [accessed 5 March 2014] The Conscious Competence Learning Model [Online] www.essentialgptrainingbook.com

Mehay, R (2012) *The Essential Handbook for GP Training and Education*, Radcliffe Publishing Limited, London

O'Neill, M B (2007) *Executive Coaching with Backbone and Heart*, 2nd edn, Jossey-Bass, San Francisco, CA

Pashler, H *et al* (2008) [accessed 30 April 2014] Learning Styles: Concepts and Evidence, *Psychological Science in the Public interest*, **9** (3), December [Online] http://steinhardtapps.es.its.nyu.edu/create/courses/2174/reading/Pashler_et_al_PSPI_9_3.pdf

Revans, R (1979) [accessed 25 March 2014] Action Learning: Its Terms and Character [Online] http://www.revanscenter.com/files/Download/reg-revans-manuscripts.pdf (a later version of this paper was published in 1983 in *Management Decision*, **21** (1) [Online] http://www.emeraldinsight.com/journals.htm?issn=0025-1747&volume=21&issue=1

Revans, R (2011) *ABC of Action Learning*, Gower, Farnham

Rogers, C R (1957) The necessary and sufficient conditions for therapeutic personality change, *Journal of Consulting Psychology*, **21** (2), pp 95–103, in H Kirschenbaum and V L Henderson eds, *The Carl Rogers Reader*, Constable, London

Schein, E H (1995) [accessed 25 March 2014] Kurt Lewin's Change Theory in the Field and in the Classroom: Notes Toward a Model of Managed Learning [Online] http://www.a2zpsychology.com/articles/kurt_lewin's_change_theory.htm

Thurstone, L L (1947) *Multiple-Factor Analysis: A development and expansion of the vectors of the mind*, University of Chicago Press, Chicago

Warr, P, Bird, M and Rackham, N (1970) *Evaluation of Management Training*, Gower, London

Whitmore, J (2009) *Coaching for Performance: GROWing human potential and purpose*, 4th edn, Nicholas Brealey, London

Wright, D S *et al* (1970) *Introducing Psychology: An experimental approach*, Penguin, Harmondsworth

Facilitation

10

DAN SKELSEY

Introduction

Facilitation is the act of planning and managing a group meeting so that it achieves its objectives in a timely and effective manner. During the meeting, the facilitator focuses on the agenda and group dynamics, allowing the participants to focus on the subject matter of the meeting. Good facilitation enables groups to succeed. A well-facilitated meeting is one where the participants take ownership of the results, and leave with a sense of achievement and a belief that their time has been well spent. There is a need to structure the meetings to ensure that differing views are considered and decisions reached. Recently, technology has opened up more options and, perhaps, also created more problems.

Group meetings are often referred to as conferences, roundtables, forums or workshops. By any name, they are often an effective way to achieve many change management tasks, such as:

- identifying issues, risks or stakeholders;
- defining the change and understanding the implications;
- engaging with stakeholders;
- developing strategies and plans;
- solving problems.

Very often the change manager needs to organize and manage these meetings. Using the tools and techniques of facilitation improves the outcomes and builds ownership and engagement with the participants.

Poorly facilitated meetings do not achieve their outcomes – and thus waste people's time. Many organizations track the cost of people's time – and getting many people in a room for several hours can quickly add up to a substantial cost.

Adding it up

A project manager recalls being asked to a meeting while working for a large organization. He was not told of the purpose of the meeting or given any context. He did not know the people who invited him. He arrived to find that about 25 people had been asked to attend the meeting and, just like him, they had no knowledge of what or why the meeting was called or who the organizers were.

The project manager was working with the HR department and knew that almost all the attendees were contractors charging an average of $1,000 per day. This meeting was costing about $4,000 per hour.

The organizers arrived late, thanked everyone for attending and then proceeded to have a discussion between themselves in front of the audience. The meeting was intended to be an all-day event, although most left by the mid-morning break. The project manager stayed until lunchtime because 'there is an awful fascination in watching a train wreck'. Years later, he still does not know why he was invited.

Aside from the financial implications, poorly facilitated meetings leave problems unsolved or lead to a reduced commitment to follow through on agreed actions. They lower staff engagement and often create cynicism and scepticism around the topic under discussion.

CHAPTER CONTENTS

Section A: The role of the facilitator and the skills required

Introduction

A facilitator is an individual who develops and manages the processes and structure for a workshop or meeting so that it can be effective in achieving its objectives. The facilitator focuses on the agenda, processes and dynamics of the meeting, thereby allowing the participants to focus on the core subject matter and work together effectively.

This section will look at the role of a facilitator, and addresses the important skill of questioning. Good facilitators are also practised in the art of active listening (Chapter 9, Section C1).

1. The role of the facilitator

The role of the facilitator is summarized in Table 10.1.

TABLE 10.1 The role of the facilitator

Preparation (See Section B for more information.)	• Understands the objectives. • Prepares an agenda. • Prepares the participants.
Manages the agenda but not the content (See Section C for more information.)	• Opens and closes the meeting professionally. • Remains independent of the content and does not take sides. • Manages the group process and associated timing. • Looks ahead and predicts how the agenda will unfold or needs to be changed. • Is prepared to change the agenda if required.

continues overleaf

TABLE 10.1 *continued*

Manages the dynamics (See Section C for more information.)	• Creates an atmosphere that encourages open contribution. • Is observant of individual reactions and group dynamics. • Is prepared to intervene when required. • Challenges groupthink.
Professional approach	• Maintains energy. • Presents to the group as being open, fair minded, honest, competent, calm and confident. • Respects the participants. • Values the time of the participants.

Valuing the time of participants

A psychotherapist recalls an international teleconference. The participants came from three time zones. There was nine hours between the furthest time zones and it was quite late at night for some. The meeting was scheduled for one hour but went on for about two hours before an attendee asked when it would end. Half-way through, the organizer took a phone call leaving everyone else with nothing to do but listen to one end of the conversation.

2. Techniques of questioning

2.1 Open and closed questions

Closed questions invite short and generally factual answers. For example 'What type of laptop do you have?' By contrast, open questions invite longer responses and may lead into new areas. For example: 'How do you use your laptop to help you with your work?'

Funnelling is a series of questions that move from open to closed or vice versa. It can be a useful technique for gaining the maximum information. For example:

1. 'How do you use computers in your work?'
2. 'What kind of presentations do you prepare?'

3 'Do you have a standard presentation on facilitation?'
4 'How long does it go on for?'

2.2 *Asking a group*

Is the question for an individual or for the group? This should be made clear at the beginning of the question. If the question is for an individual, then starting with the name makes this clear, such as 'Gabrielle, how do you deal with difficult customers?' If the question is for the group, then the type of response and how the speaker will be selected should be made clear. For example: 'Everyone take five minutes to write down how they deal with difficult customers, and then I will call for volunteers.' Or: 'Hands up if you would like to share your method for dealing with difficult customers.' Then, after hands go up, 'I'll start on the left and work my way around.'

2.3 *The five whys*

The five whys is a problem-solving technique that has its roots in manufacturing. The idea is to keep asking the question 'why' until you get to the root cause of the problem. It is based on empirical evidence that it typically takes five repeats of the question to get to the root cause. For example:

- Why did you get up late? Because my alarm did not go off.
- Why didn't your alarm go off? Because it reset to midnight.
- Why did it reset to midnight? Because there was a power outage.
- Why doesn't it have a battery back up? It does but the battery failed.
- Why did the battery fail? Because I haven't replaced it for years.

2.4 *Kipling's six servants*

Rudyard Kipling described six basic questions that are useful in many situations:

> I keep six honest serving men
> (They taught me all I knew);
> Their names are **What** and **Why** and **When**
> And **How** and **Where** and **Who**.
>
> From 'The Elephant's Child', by Rudyard Kipling (emphasis mine)

2.5 *What would that look like?*

Asking people to describe a future situation is a technique for developing more detail around a vague idea. Variations on the question include 'What would that look like?', 'How would you know that you have succeeded?', or 'How would that look to [someone else such as a customer]?' Frequently these types of questions need to be asked several times in order to drill down into deeper and deeper detail.

2.6 ORID

ORID is a structured questioning technique. Sometimes called the 'focused conversation method', it was developed by the Institute of Cultural Affairs in the United States. It is a sequence of questions in four stages: objective, reflective, interpretive and decisional (Table 10.2).

TABLE 10.2 The four stages of ORID

Stage	Purpose	Typical Questions
Objective	To establish relevant facts.	What did you see? What happened and when?
Reflective	To establish feelings or make connections.	How did it make you feel? What does it remind you of?
Interpretive	To extrapolate to a bigger picture, discover implications, look for a pattern, or find reasons.	What can we learn from this? What does this mean for us? Why did this happen?
Decisional	To decide next steps.	What decision is required? What are the next steps?

Summary

The role of the facilitator is to prepare a solid and well-thought-through agenda, and to manage the meeting by simultaneously managing the agenda and the group dynamics; all the time maintaining a professional approach.

Questions to think about

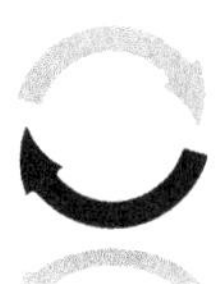

1. How well are you prepared for workshops?
2. How often do you change the agenda in workshops when it becomes apparent that the current agenda is not working?
3. How practised are you in the techniques of active listening and questioning?

Section B: Preparing a group process

Introduction

This is the process of designing a facilitated group event on a solid foundation of understanding the objectives, the constraints and the participants. Good preparation is the cornerstone of good facilitation. This section starts by summarizing the factors to be considered and then addresses each one in detail.

1. Factors to be considered

The factors set out in Table 10.3 need to be fully thought through as part of preparing a group meeting.

TABLE 10.3 Preparing a group process

1. Purpose	This is the objective(s) of the meeting or series of meetings (Section B2).
2. Product	This is the output required from the meeting(s) (Section B3).
3. Participants	Participants in the meeting are sometimes predetermined. Often there is a choice about who will participate (Section B4). It may also be necessary to consider external facilitators (Section B5).
4. Process	Process is the steps required to achieve the objective. Breaking down the objective into steps and choosing techniques for each step is the central part of creating an agenda (see B6) and this is where the process is documented.
5. Place	The place or venue for the meeting must be chosen and prepared (Section B7).
6. Practical tools	The tools required for the process are chosen (Section B8) and it is useful to create a checklist of materials to take.
7. Probable issues	Consideration of the risks may lead to a change in the plans prepared (Section B9).

2. Purpose – setting objectives

It is important to start with the purpose of the meeting or series of meetings. This may require several discussions with the people who want to see the objectives achieved. These would explore why the group process is required, and come to a clear understanding of the objectives. Here are some useful questions to ask during these discussions:

- Is there any relevant history to this objective? For instance, have there been previous failed attempts to reach this objective?
- Is a group process the best way to achieve the objective and why?
- Will all the participants understand the objective?
- Is there a common understanding of what success will look like?
- Can the objective be achieved in the time allowed? (Initially this will be based on rough estimates but as the agenda is developed so will the understanding of the time required.)
- If there are multiple objectives, what are the priorities?

3. Product – techniques for capturing and organizing the information in a session

Facilitators make sure that information is captured while the session is in progress and make it available to the participants. This allows participants to refer back to work completed earlier in the session. A very good starting point is to 'put it on the wall'. Putting flipcharts, whiteboard printouts, and Post it® notes, or other sticky notes, on the available wall space is simple and very effective. Many of the techniques listed in Section E lead directly to information being organized in this way.

Techniques for preparing output after the session will depend on the detail required and the time available after the meeting. Often this takes the form of converting output from the session into formal electronic documents. The type of output required from the meeting – and who will prepare it – should be agreed before the meeting is planned. This includes understanding what the output will be used for.

Output from the session can be captured in a number of ways:

- photographs of the results on whiteboards, flipcharts or sticky notes on a wall;
- printouts from electronic whiteboards;
- video or audio recordings, which, for privacy reasons, would be announced at the beginning of the session;
- information captured by other technologies such as collaborative software or social media;
- notes taken during the session.

If notes are to be taken during the session, this usually requires an assigned note taker. This person often finds it hard to contribute whilst taking notes, and should be selected with that in mind. Except in the smallest of groups, facilitators do not act in the role of the note taker. Presenting back the notes taken during the meeting can help to verify the notes and remind people of progress made so far. The timing of this should be chosen so that it does not interfere with the natural momentum of a successful meeting. There are also technologies that will synchronize an audio recording with the note taken. This can be a useful way to review the notes after the event.

4. Participants – selecting and preparing participants

Smaller groups are easier to manage but are less likely to have all the required information and expertise. Some people may feel they should attend as recognition of their position in the organization, and others may like to attend to increase their status. Selecting participants can be a messy and thankless task, but a good grasp of the stakeholders in the objective will aid considerably (Chapter 4). In the context of a change initiative, workshops can be held as a form of communications, and the communications strategy will provide important pointers as to who should attend (Chapter 5). Questions to consider when selecting participants are:

- Who are the stakeholders in the objective?
- What levels and types of expertise are required?
- What level of authority is required?
- Does the number of people match the venue? If not, then either the venue or the numbers attending must change.
- Is there justification for the additional cost to the organization of large numbers of staff attending?
- Is the additional work required to facilitate extra people manageable?
- What happens if some stakeholders are left out?

It is useful to discuss the list of selected participants with some of the chosen participants. This checks the appropriateness of the list and starts to build engagement in the workshop.

Participants should be as well prepared for the meeting as is reasonable. This includes an invitation to attend that clearly states:

- the venue, including any information about how to get there;
- the timing, especially proposed start and end times;
- the objective;
- a summary of the agenda (perhaps just the major steps) with the proviso that it might change;
- any preparation that they are expected to do before attending.

Prior to the meeting, preparation by participants might take the form of gathering data to present at the workshop. Alternatively, it may be studying material that sets the background or context of the workshop.

5. Participants – external facilitators

External facilitators often cost money, need to be briefed and don't understand the workings of the organization. So why use an external facilitator? Reasons to use external facilitators include:

- The organization lacks sufficient facilitation expertise or the people with facilitation expertise need to participate instead of facilitating.
- Potential conflict within the group will be more easily handled by an outsider who is perceived to be independent.
- Internal politics threaten to disrupt the group process.
- It is necessary to demonstrate that the results of the workshop were achieved with an open, transparent and equitable process.

6. Process – creating an agenda

The basic method for creating an agenda is:

1. Breaking down the objective into component steps.
2. Choosing the techniques and structure appropriate to each step.
3. Allocating time to each step.
4. Adding in time for opening, closing and breaks.

Figure 10.1 shows a sample agenda. Although agendas will vary widely and must be designed to suit the objectives, there is a structure that is frequently used:

1. Present the context.
2. Identify a long list of items such as stakeholders, issues, actions to take or requirements.
3. Putting like with like to remove duplicate items.
4. Ranking, sequencing or prioritizing items.
5. Addressing the items in order.

This structure could be used several times within one meeting. For instance, it could be used to identify stakeholders and who are the most significant; then to identify the stakeholder risks and prioritize them; and then to identify a plan to manage these risks. This structure starts with divergent thinking to generate many items or ideas, and then moves to convergent thinking attempting to narrow down the options to a few actionable solutions.

FIGURE 10.1 Sample agenda

Objective: Identify actionable plans for making work life easier for parents with young children.

Output: Recommendations for further analysis. At least five ideas with simple plans and risks. All ideas that are generated, even if not in top five, should be recorded.

Attendees: Gabby, Ben, Sam, David, Audrey, Philip, Sunila, Achim, Awadh, Carol and Afshin.

Timing: Arrive 8:45 am for a 9:00 am start; day will finish at around 4:30 pm. Morning refreshments and lunch will be provided.

Venue: The Sky room, Conference Centre, 265 Somewhere St. See attached map and instructions.

Step	Start Time	End Time	Activity and structure
Open session	9:00	9:15	Facilitator introduction. Round robin introductions. Facilitator presents a summary of the agenda. Agree ground rules.
Context	9:15	9:45	A presentation by the HR director. Time for questions.
Workplace Issues	9:45	9:55	Everyone working alone writes down every workplace issue affecting parents with young children and sticks them on a wall – one issue per sticky note.
	9:55	10:20	One person goes to the wall and, with others calling out, starts to group like issues with like issues and removes duplicates.
Break	10:20	10:35	Morning break
Actions to address workplace issues	10:35	11:00	Depending on the quantity of data, either address individual issues or groups of issues. Split into three syndicates and give each syndicate a set of issues (or groups) to work on. They should explain possible solutions rather than analyse them.
	11:00	11:30	Each syndicate presents back to the overall group. As they present, one member of the syndicate 'ticks off' issues and the ideas are posted on a new wall. Issues without an idea are placed in a 'sin bin'. Ten minutes per syndicate.
Search for more ideas	11:30	12:00	Brainstorming session – start with round robin and then free for all. 'Any other ideas'. Add these to existing list of ideas.
	12:00	12:15	One person goes to wall and, with others calling out, starts to group like ideas with like ideas and removes duplicates. (This step may be quite simple.)
Lunch	12:15	1:15	Lunch (can be shortened if running late).
Prioritize ideas	1:15	1:35	Ideas are plotted on a XY axis with 'easy to do' versus 'low to high impact'. This is done by one person with others calling out.
	1:35	1:45	Top five ideas (perhaps more) are selected from XY – one person selects with whole group calling out. Should be obvious from the XY axis.
Develop plans and risks	1:45	2:45	Five pairs of two – each take one or two ideas and develop simple action plans. Major steps to be taken. For each step what, who, how and where (if relevant). Also identify risks to the plan. Includes an opportunity for 10-minute break. Note that Awadh is an experienced planner and will float between groups and help them plan.
	2:45	3:45	Each pair presents plans, takes questions and comments. One member of pair records comments. Roughly 10 minutes per pair.
Close session	3:45	4:15	Facilitator summarizes, addresses any outstanding actions, reviews with group using six hats review, and closes session. Note: this is an early finish, which allows some 'slack' time.

The following factors should also be considered when creating the agenda:

- Breaks should occur at regular intervals.
- Time is required for introductions at the beginning, and opening and closing comments.
- Time is required for the participants to move into and out of syndicates, and the inevitable milling about and moving of furniture.
- Time can be saved by sending out background material in advance of the workshop.
- Generally, the more participants, the more time is required. This can be partially managed by the appropriate selection of structure and techniques (see Section E).
- Using 'slack time' (Schwarz *et al*, 2005) in an agenda creates a contingency against problems with time.

Creating an agenda is an iterative process. The time allowed must be matched to the complexity of the objective, the number of participants, the knowledge of the participants, and whether or not the participants work well as a team. Sometimes these factors can only be balanced by increasing the time allowed or reducing the scope of the objectives.

7. Place – selecting and preparing the venue

Very often the choice of venue will be restricted by the constraints of budget and availability. However, a suitable venue will have:

- Sufficient floor and wall space for the techniques suggested in the agenda, including break-out spaces.
- Furniture that can be moved to accommodate the different working arrangements.
- Access to any technology required. This might mean sufficient power outlets, internet access and screens or walls to project onto.
- A comfortable working environment with a well-maintained temperature and low external noise.

Commercial venues such as hotels and conference centres will often inflate the number of people who can be comfortably accommodated in a given room. Personal inspection is always recommended.

The venue will need instructions for preparation in advance of the meeting. The facilitator will need to arrive at the venue earlier than most participants in order to check that the room has been arranged suitably and to set up any equipment that is required.

8. Practical tools – technology in physical meetings

There are some basic principles to apply when choosing technology for physical meetings:

- The technology must be accessible.
  - All participants should have access to the necessary equipment (not everyone has a smartphone or a tablet).
  - All participants need to know how to use the technology, unless it is being reserved for presenters/facilitators – in which case they must know how to use it.
- The technology must be appropriate.
  - Do not choose a technology just because it is new or 'cute'.
  - Use the right technology for the process.
- Simple is good. Complexity has a way of failing and having unknown consequences.
- The technology should be robust and failure should be unlikely.
- It is essential to have a backup plan in case of technology failure.
- Setting up the technology at the beginning of the session takes time and may require technical support.

Many group meetings find that all that is required is simple physical tools such as flipcharts, sticky notes, pens, Blu-Tack®, and whiteboards. Some other tools to consider are:

- Electronic whiteboards.
- Interactive whiteboards.
- Internet access for the facilitator and the participants.
- A projector and a laptop.
- Electronic meeting management systems.
- Still cameras or video cameras can be used to capture information generated by the group. For example, photographing the whiteboard. Modern phones often have cameras of sufficient quality for this.

With the permission of the speakers and in large-scale events, social media – either with access restricted to certain groups or publicly available – can be used to:

- Provide information about venues, timing, and agendas as well as preparatory materials or the content of presentations.
- Post the results of events.
- Provide platforms for comments, questions and voting.

A checklist of tools and materials and how they are set up is a valuable aid for the facilitator. It allows the facilitator to plan when to arrive for the set-up and what support might be required. It can also be used as the basis for instructions to the venue.

9. Probable issues – what if?

Consideration of possible risks to the workshop can lead to stronger preparation. Table 10.4 shows a few possible risks and suggested mitigations.

TABLE 10.4 Common risks and how to manage them

Common Risk	Managing the Risk
Technology failure	• Does the workshop need the technology? • Test the technology. • Have technology support nearby.
Key stakeholders (especially subject matter experts) do not attend	• How important is the stakeholder to a successful event? • Can a substitute be found? • Check availability before scheduling the event. • Confirm attendance a day or two prior to the event.
Participants object to the purpose of the workshop (an example would be when they are asked to discuss the details of a change and this is the first they have heard about it)	• How does this workshop fit with the stakeholder engagement and communications planning? • What prior knowledge do the participants have? • Allow time to discuss the purpose.
Time runs out	• Are the time estimates realistic? • Has slack-time been built in? • Can the breaks be shortened? • What would happen if the meeting ran over time? • Can the scope of the objectives be reduced? Are they prioritized to make this easier? • Can different issues be worked on in parallel by different people?
The room turns out to be unsuitable	• Inspect the venue before booking it. • Send clear instructions for the set-up of the venue. • Arrive with plenty of time to fix issues before the workshop is scheduled to start. • Are there other spare rooms?

Summary

Strong preparation for a workshop event is the foundation of good facilitation. Each of the following factors must be considered (the 'seven Ps'):

1 purpose;
2 product;
3 participants;
4 process;
5 place;
6 practical tools;
7 probable issues.

Getting these factors right will go a long way to ensuring a productive and enjoyable event.

Questions to think about

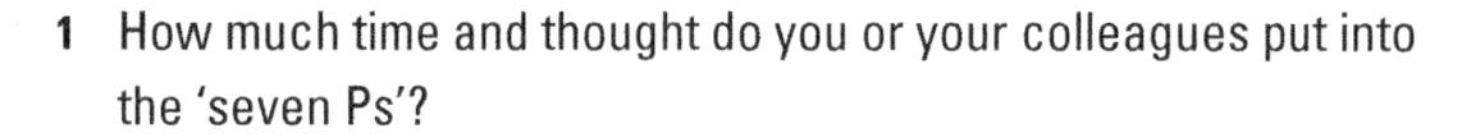

1 How much time and thought do you or your colleagues put into the 'seven Ps'?
2 Can you think of a time when you attended a poorly prepared workshop? Which aspects had not been planned properly?
3 How would your regular team meetings benefit from better preparation?

Section C: Facilitating a group process

Introduction

Facilitating a group is managing the process to help the group to reach the best possible result and take ownership of it.

This section starts with opening a session, and discusses group dynamics and individual reactions as the session progresses. It looks at techniques for intervening and addresses how and when to change the agenda as the session evolves. Finally, we examine the crucial step of closing the session well.

1. Opening a session

Opening a workshop is the opportunity to establish the tone and rules for the meeting. It must be informative, succinct and set an expectation of success. This is the time to:

- Acknowledge the participants individually, or, in large-scale workshops, acknowledge the groups and interests present. In smaller meetings, this can be done by asking each person to introduce themselves.
- State the meeting objective and summarize context. If detailed context is required, this will be a subsequent agenda item.
- State the facilitator's role clearly. This will vary according to the nature of the objective, agenda and participants. If there are supporting roles, such as a note taker, these should also be mentioned.
- Summarize the agenda.
- Establish the ground rules.

Tip

If asking individuals to introduce themselves, it is useful to be specific about the information required, otherwise some will see it as an opportunity to discuss their entire life. For example 'let's introduce ourselves with name, where we work, and how long we have been with the organization'.

Ground rules establish appropriate ways to interact and become a useful basis for intervention by facilitators. Established teams may already have ground rules, but groups that have not met regularly will need these to be established. Asking the group to suggest ground rules first is the best approach. Facilitators can always make tentative suggestions of their own. A typical list of ground rules is:

- Be on time after breaks.
- Listen to others and show respect. Sometimes phrased as 'let others speak'.
- Turn off mobile phones.
- There are no stupid questions.
- If having a side conversation, be expected to have to repeat it to the group.
- An agreement on the required level of confidentiality about what is said in the meeting and the outcomes.

2. Watching for group dynamics

The symptoms of positive and helpful group dynamics include:

- a free flow of ideas;
- a willingness to debate ideas and suggestions without getting personal;
- a willingness to listen without interrupting;
- positive dispositions with people showing interest and acting in a friendly and supportive manner.

However, there are also a number of unhelpful group dynamics that can occur, which might require intervention (Section C4). Good preparation will minimize much of this. Tom Justice and David Jamieson believe that '98% of all problems anticipated by [beginner] facilitators simply don't happen if the group sessions have been carefully designed and planned' (Justice and Jamieson, 2012).

> *'You handle the vast majority of potential group problems through careful design and planning, before the group ever convenes – not during the session by using an arsenal of tricks.'*
>
> *The Facilitator's Fieldbook,* Tom Justice and David W Jamieson

2.1 Groupthink

Groupthink (Janis, 1972) describes a common phenomenon where the desire for consensus leads to poor decision making. The symptoms are:

- complacency: a feeling that the group cannot fail;
- rationalization: not listening to counter arguments;
- high moral ground: the group ignore the ethical consequences of its decisions;
- stereotyping: those who are opposed are described as biased, weak or incompetent;
- peer pressure: dissenters are seen as 'disloyal';
- self-censorship: doubts about the group consensus are not expressed;
- illusion of unanimity: silence is taken as assent;
- mindguards: self-appointed members protect the group from information that contradicts the consensus.

Common techniques for counter-attacking groupthink are:

- encouraging participants to critically evaluate proposals;
- encouraging the opinions of junior participants before calling on the senior participants;

- seeking the views of specialist experts;
- looking at alternative options;
- appointing a 'devil's advocate' whose role is to take and defend the opposite view.

2.2 Negative reactions

Groups or individuals can display a range of negative reactions such as anger, people looking uncomfortable, cynicism, personal attacks or withdrawal. These can have a range of causes such as:

- Speakers not making their point clearly. This often comes about from too much specialist technical language or the use of slang.
- A feeling that the meeting is going nowhere.
- A feeling that some or the entire objective is being ignored or misunderstood.
- Participants perceiving that their point of view is not getting full consideration.
- Discomfort with the way this particular part of the process is being tackled.
- Some people attempting to dominate the conversation.
- Expressions of different and perhaps conflicting personalities (Section C3).

2.3 Endless discussion that goes nowhere

If the discussion is not core to the objective, use of a 'parking lot' (Section E3.5) allows the group to move on. However, endless discussion that goes nowhere can have a range of causes. One simple cause is that everyone is just enjoying agreeing. This is a time to summarize and move on to the next topic.

Sometimes key information is missing. Can the information be discovered easily and quickly? If not, this calls for an action plan to discover and use the information, perhaps in a second meeting.

Sometimes genuine consensus is hard to find. Is consensus required? If so, techniques such as debating teams, described in Section E4.5, can help achieve consensus. Alternatives to consensus are to use some form of voting or prioritization system, such as the range listed in Section E. Results of a voting system or similar can always be reported afterwards, alongside the cases for each major view.

3. Personality types and how they react in group settings

People are varied and facilitators recognize this and do not insist that everyone does the same thing. As long as the participants are not sabotaging the process or withdrawing, they should be allowed to contribute in their own ways.

There is more information on the underlying differences between individuals in Chapter 1, Section B4. However, it is usually not possible to know the personality traits of all participants (or indeed any) in advance of a workshop. Often these traits do not have a material effect on the process. During a group meeting, an individual's preferred way of working can become apparent. When this clashes with the agenda or the majority view, intervention is required.

In a group meeting, it is the observable symptoms that are important. Given below are some of the more common ones.

3.1 The quiet ones and the talkers

In meetings, there are some who naturally talk a lot and some who naturally stay silent. This need not be a problem but it can become an issue when:

- The talkers are dominating and making it hard for others to contribute.
- There is a need to get input from the quiet ones.
- People are quiet because they are withdrawing from the process rather than because it is their natural style.

It is *not* appropriate to tell the talkers to be quiet, and care should be taken when asking the quiet ones to say something. The solution to the problems spelled out here usually lies in changing the group structure (Section E2). Asking everyone to work on their own and list ideas, or giving everyone a chance to vote, will ensure equal input from all.

It may be necessary to confirm that people are withdrawing from the process and why this is. An example may be that if the particular topic under discussion does not interest them, then the situation can be resolved by suggesting they work on the side on an alternative topic, or on preparing for the next step in the agenda. If they are withdrawing because they feel that their concerns are not being heard, then the facilitator may offer them a chance to present their case formally to the group.

3.2 The people who love process and those who do not

Section E offers a variety of tools to use in a group meeting. More tools are available throughout this book. Not everyone is equally comfortable with every tool. Some people feel hemmed in by process and suspicious of the outcomes. This leads to withdrawal and less ownership of the results. There are a number of ways to overcome this problem and often they should be used in combination:

- explaining how the tool works and why it has been chosen;
- offering a variety of tools that will perform the same function and let the group choose;
- allowing some individuals to use different tools.

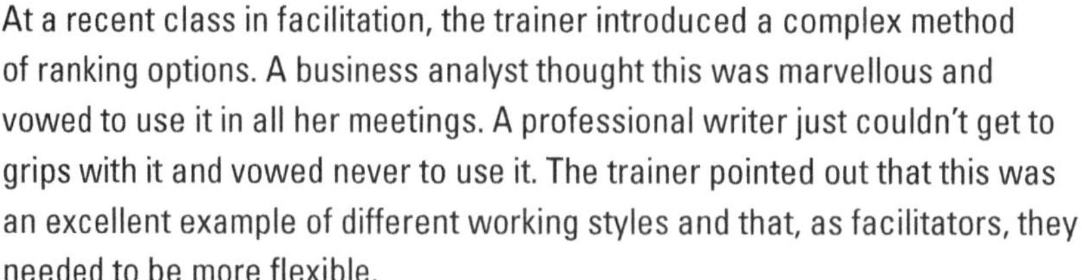

Love the process

At a recent class in facilitation, the trainer introduced a complex method of ranking options. A business analyst thought this was marvellous and vowed to use it in all her meetings. A professional writer just couldn't get to grips with it and vowed never to use it. The trainer pointed out that this was an excellent example of different working styles and that, as facilitators, they needed to be more flexible.

3.3 The optimists and the pessimists

A level of optimism brings energy to a meeting and opens up possibilities. Some mistake pragmatism for pessimism. A level of pragmatism grounds the meeting and ensures that decisions and actions are achievable. However, too much optimism or too much pessimism can derail a meeting and lead to poor outcomes.

Pessimism will often take the form of blanket statements such as 'it won't work', 'we tried that and it didn't work' or 'they will never allow it'. These blanket statements should not be taken as 'gospel'. Simply asking for a list of reasons that can be worked through turns these statements into useful input. If the pessimism takes the form of 'yes, but' closing conversations down, then using 'yes, and...' can be a way of positively building on the conversation.

Over-optimism can be a symptom of groupthink (Section C2.1). It may also take the form of an individual refusing to deal with real issues. In this case, deferring to the rest of the group is effective.

The six hats technique covered in Section E3.6 includes formalized pessimism (black hats) and optimism (yellow hats). This is also a good way to balance the input of the two views.

4. Techniques for intervening

The following is a simplified version of the diagnosis-intervention cycle described by Schwarz (2002):

- *Observe behaviour*: look for patterns or individuals that are reacting differently. For example, one of the participants is clearly getting angry.
- *Deduce meaning*: why is this happening? For example, the participant is angry because, while trying to get across their point of view, they are being continually interrupted by another participant. But why the frequent interruptions? It could be because the speaker is not being clear and may need help to make the point clearly. However, for the purposes of this example, assume it is because the interrupter is trying to get their view to 'win out'.

- *Decide whether to intervene and how to intervene*: not all conflict is unhealthy – however, without intervention, the situation described above will get worse.

Sometimes a simple reminder of the appropriate ground rule is sufficient. This may either be a general reminder or directed towards an individual. For instance: '[Name of participant], one of the ground rules was to let others finish speaking.'

Schwarz (2002) and many others have found it useful to describe the observations. For instance: 'I can see that some are getting disconcerted at the level of interruptions, so...'

The most effective intervention often takes the form of a change or addition to the technique, or how it is being used. In the example above, the intervention might take the form of: '[Name of participant], I can see that you are anxious for your point of view to get a fair hearing. If you take a few minutes to jot down your main points and then present them to the rest of the group, that will ensure your view is given a proper airing.'

Interventions should focus on cause and effect (Schwarz, 2002), rather than make imperatives or ask questions (Mann, 2014). For instance: 'If you had 10 minutes to draft a few points and then made your case to the group that would ensure it had a fair hearing' rather than 'You should...' or 'Would you like to...'.

Schwarz (2002) has some other dos and don'ts for the facilitator:

- *Do* help others to interpret technical language and other poorly phrased points. This is done through the use of questions and feedback.
- *Do* use words that distance from the group such as 'you' or 'the group' rather than 'we'.
- *Do* use proper nouns such as '[Name of participant]' or 'The Executive Committee', rather than pronouns such as 'he/she' or 'they', which can be vague.
- *Don't* use judgemental words such as 'that is an aggressive option'. Aggressive is a judgemental word.

5. Changing the agenda

An agenda is simply a plan made with the best information available at the time. As the meeting unfolds, new information comes to light and it is always necessary to look forward to see if the agenda needs to be changed. Causes for this can include a change in the scope or complexity of the objective. Sometimes it will become clear that the objective is more complex or wider in scope than was originally envisaged. Occasionally, the original agenda will need to be changed because the original estimates for time were wrong.

If the problem is insufficient time, then there may be opportunities to drop or shorten low-priority agenda items. Alternatively, use time-saving techniques such as forming syndicates with each working on a different part of the objective. Time needs to be allowed for the syndicates to report back to each other. If these options do not resolve the problem, then parts of the agenda will need to be deferred to another meeting.

Having designed a change in the agenda, it should be proposed using the cause-and-effect approach (Section C4). For instance: 'You only have 60 minutes left and four issues to address. Split into four syndicates, with each syndicate working on a different issue for 30 minutes and then presenting back to the group. This will give you time to address each issue properly.' The group may suggest alternative arrangements but at least the issue of time is being addressed.

6. Closing a session

Closing a session is a critical step. It is a chance to summarize what was achieved and what was not, agree the follow-on actions and review the session. Ideally, participants should leave a workshop with a sense of pride and achievement. Creating clarity on the next steps and thanking them for their time and their contribution will help to foster this feeling.

Reviewing the session is useful because it helps the facilitator to improve their skills and, more importantly, it allows the participants to voice their feelings. There are many techniques for doing this and each facilitator will have their own preferred method. Suitable for groups of up to about 15 people, here is one using De Bono's six hats (Section E3.6 has more on this method):

1. Remind people what the six hats mean. Perhaps display a graphic of the six hats to remind people of the meaning of each colour.
2. The facilitator will represent the blue or 'process' hat.
3. For each hat, in the order given below, give the participants a short time (one or two minutes each) to write down the main bullet points for a particular hat when thinking about the workshop:
   - red: emotional reactions to the workshop;
   - white: the facts about the workshop;
   - yellow: what was good and positive about the workshop;
   - black: what criticisms they would make about the workshop;
   - green: what ideas they have for improving the workshop if it were run again.

Then start with one person and ask them what they wrote for the red hat. Next, go round the room asking if anyone has anything to add. Repeat this for each hat except blue. The main points could be recorded on a whiteboard.

After the session is completed and closed, facilitators:

- Reflect on their own performance, what went well and what could have been done better.
- Prepare and deliver output as agreed.
- Follow through on any commitments owned by them.

Summary

Strong preparation should be followed by strong execution. This starts with a professional opening to the session and sets the expectations and ground rules. While managing the session, the facilitator is observing group dynamics and individual reactions. The facilitator is also looking ahead to see if the agenda is still a viable plan. If necessary, the facilitator intervenes skilfully to bring the session back on track.

Questions to think about

1. Do your regular team meetings have ground rules? Are they followed all the time?
2. Have you ever been in a workshop where you had wished that the facilitator had intervened earlier?
3. Would your regular team meetings also benefit from a more professional closing?

Section D: Virtual meetings

Introduction

A virtual meeting is one where one or more of the participants are in different locations. This might mean one or more people remotely joining a physical meeting. It might be two or more physical locations joined by communication technology. In this case, there is the possibility of using co-facilitators at the other locations. Finally, it could be that most or all of the participants are in different locations.

This section takes a look at how to select a mix of technologies for virtual meetings. Then it examines the additional problems that plague virtual meetings and how to address them.

1. Selecting the technology

There is a vast array of collaborative technology available, from the simple telephone to the use of multiplayer platforms or virtual worlds. Real-time collaboration tools include videoconferencing, virtual whiteboards, shared screens, and messaging or 'chat' software. Many collaborative technologies introduce only short time lags and can be used in parallel with other more real-time tools. These include e-mail, file-sharing software and shared databases.

The humble telephone is the oldest, most reliable and easiest to use of all the communication technologies. It is often sufficient for virtual meetings. However, there is no visual element to the telephone. The common web browser allows the introduction of visuals, which can be enormously useful.

There are a number of factors to consider when selecting technology:

- Is it appropriate to the task?
- Do the benefits outweigh the cost?
- Is it robust or does it fail frequently?
- How easy is it to use? How will participants learn how to use it?
- Is it readily accessible? Does it require high levels of internet access? Does it require special equipment or software?
- Do all participants have equal access? Can arrangements be made for those with lesser technological access? (Section E2)
- Is it sufficiently secure for the nature of the task? Most web-based communication is inherently insecure.
- What level of technology support is required?

2. Issues in virtual meetings

Good practice for physical meetings is also good practice for virtual meetings. However, virtual meetings bring extra issues. It should also be noted that virtual teams benefit from meeting face-to-face early on (Watkins, 2013). While this may not be possible for a one-off virtual meeting, it is worth exploring the possibility if a series of meetings is planned.

2.1 Small talk

Small talk is important (Mittleman, Briggs and Nunamaker, 2000). It helps to build a relaxed and open atmosphere. Encouraging small talk in the breaks and in the period when participants are joining the meeting is very valuable.

2.2 Who's there?

This is particularly a problem in teleconferences, where it is not always clear who is present and listening in. Some participants, unsure if senior people are present, will be reluctant to speak out (Mittleman, Briggs and Nunamaker, 2000). This can be addressed by listing the roll call at the formal start of the meeting, and periodically checking in with all participants using their names.

2.3 Imbalance of access

Imbalance of access arises when different participants are using different technology to access the meeting. Participants with lesser access can feel at a disadvantage and left out. Examples include situations where some participants are physically together and others are remote, or some participants are using videoconferencing while some only have audio access. In cases of imbalanced access, it is helpful to make a special point of seeking input for each agenda item from the disadvantaged participants and ensuring that they have access to shared documents.

2.4 Time zones

Participants can be in different time zones. Virtual meetings can span the globe, meaning that participants can be at different ends of different days. It might be late Tuesday evening in the UK and early Wednesday morning in Australia. Energy levels will vary enormously. A long meeting starting in the morning for some participants may stretch into normal sleep time for other participants. Planning for this and avoiding, as much as possible, extremes of time is often all that can be done. Often there will need to be compromises from both ends of the time-zone range. Sometimes it is more effective to have several shorter meetings rather than one long one.

2.5 Technology failure

Technology failure is a constant threat. Testing the technology prior to the start of the meeting is helpful. It is useful to maintain alternative communication tools such as texting or e-mail so that other arrangements can be made if required. This might include rescheduling or falling back to simpler technology.

2.6 Body language

The absence of – or reduced – body language cues is an issue. Even videoconferencing is not as good as face-to-face for body language cues. All participants need to compensate by paying more attention to the audio cues. These include raised voices, personal comments or total absence of comment.

2.7 Multitasking

Participants might attempt to 'multitask'. In the absence of videoconferencing, some participants are tempted to do other tasks. During the meeting they might check their e-mail or browse the internet for reasons unrelated to the meeting. This is a form of withdrawal. Discussing this in the ground rules, regularly polling for comment, or using a round-robin style of conversation (Section E2) all help to manage this.

2.8 Background noise

Background noise can be a problem. Some participants may join the meeting from noisy venues such as airports or cafés. It is important to address this as soon as it becomes apparent and suggest solutions such as muting the participant's microphone.

2.9 Who's talking?

Without an element of videoconferencing, it can be quite hard to tell who is talking. Frequently, participants will lose the first part of someone's comment while trying to work out who is talking. This is especially true in larger meetings. A helpful ground rule can be that when a new person starts speaking, they state their name at the beginning. For instance 'Sam here. Have we considered...'.

2.10 Too much talk

Multiple overlapping conversations are even harder to follow in virtual meetings. It is up to the facilitator to manage these using techniques such as:

- appropriate ground rules such as 'no interruptions';
- using round robin to ask for comments and questions;
- a clear agenda;
- tracking the agenda.

2.11 Following the agenda

'It is harder to follow a meeting process from a distance' (Mittleman, Briggs and Nunamaker, 2000). This reinforces the need for a clear agenda that has been distributed in advance. Facilitators reinforce this and explicitly state the transition from step to step. If the agenda needs to be changed mid-meeting, this is also made very explicit.

2.12 Tracking the data

Tracking the data can be harder during virtual meetings. The facilitator arranges for data to be captured but it is helpful if participants can refer to this during the meeting. Technologies such as shared screens and virtual whiteboards are useful for this. If a basic teleconference is being used, then the facilitator periodically recaps the main points.

Summary

The principles of good facilitation for physical meetings apply equally to virtual meetings. However, virtual meetings can bring additional problems, which arise from:

- imperfect technology (technology failure, imbalance of access, too much talk);
- reduced visual cues (reduced body language, multitasking, tracking the agenda and data, 'who's there?');
- the physical locations of the attendees (time zones, background noise).

The lack of small talk seems to arise from an accumulation of all the problems listed above. All this means that care should be taken to choose the appropriate technology and use it well.

Questions to think about

1 How productive are your virtual meetings?

2 Could the technology used in your virtual meetings be used more effectively?

3 Do your virtual meetings experience some of the problems listed in this section? How are they dealt with?

Section E: Facilitation structures and techniques

Introduction

Structures are how people work together, such as on their own or in groups. Techniques are tools for achieving the next part of the objective, such as brainstorming ideas or voting to select a preferred option. The facilitator chooses both the structure and the technique for each part of the agenda.

This section of the chapter lists a variety of structures and techniques that can be used to progress a task. Many of the other chapters in this book also offer tools that are suitable for workshopping. Just a few examples are:

- many of the tools identified in Chapter 2, Defining change;
- the benefits logic map in Chapter 3, Section B1;
- stakeholder identification, mapping, personas and empathy maps in Chapter 4, Sections A and B;
- the process diagrams in Chapter 13, Section C, Process optimization in organizations.

There are many more tools available for the interested researcher; a number of references listed for this chapter are excellent sources for more tools.

1. Basic principles

When selecting the structure and technique to use, there are some basic principles to apply:

- break the objective into steps, each with its own purpose;
- the steps build up into an agenda;
- match the technique to the purpose of the step;
- techniques can often be combined;
- consider the size of the group, the nature of the venue;
- allow for different working styles;
- consider an appropriate structure;
- vary the structures as the workshop progresses.

It is common near the beginning of the workshop to use divergent thinking to generate many items or ideas, and then move to convergent thinking, thus attempting to narrow down the options to a few actionable solutions. Brainstorming and listing known ideas are examples of divergent thinking. Tools for grouping like with like, connecting and prioritizing are forms of convergent thinking.

2. Structures

Structure is how the participants work together. For example, they may work as individuals, syndicates or as a whole group. Different structures have different advantages and disadvantages. Often intervention can take the form of changing the structure. For example; 'There seem to be two opposing views here. You could form a syndicate around each view and ask them to prepare their case to present to the other group. This way both sides will get a chance to clearly state their case.'

2.1 Working as individuals

This is when everyone quietly works on their own. For example, everyone writes a list of issues on their own, with each issue on a different sticky note.

The benefit is that everyone gets an equal opportunity to provide input and it negates the influence of more dominant people. However, it will generate a lot of duplicate ideas and it can take time to remove the duplicates and sort them into groups of similar ideas.

2.2 Working in syndicates

This is when the overall group of participants is divided into smaller syndicates. This can bring one of three benefits. First, different syndicates can work on different tasks or issues, thereby saving time. Second, syndicates can be constructed to offer different views on the same topic, offering constructive debate. The third possible benefit could occur when the workshop is being used to survey opinion. Working in syndicates allows individual opinions to be anonymous and can also have the effect of bringing 'extreme' opinions back towards the centre through group discussion. However, syndicates can be dominated by individuals and the facilitator will need to watch the group dynamics of each syndicate.

Sometimes it can be helpful to have expert individuals floating between syndicates, providing help as needed. When syndicates are preparing to make the cases for different points of views, avowedly neutral individuals may float between syndicates. Similarly it can be very helpful for syndicates to send people to 'spy' on other syndicates, bringing useful information back to their 'home' syndicate. The facilitator will need to expressly state that this is within the rules. Otherwise some will object and others will not think of it.

2.3 *Working all together*

This is when the all the workshop participants work as one group. It could be a general group discussion with everyone able to contribute and no formal process for selecting the next speaker. This is the default structure for most small and informal meetings. It could be everyone calling out ideas to one person who records them on a whiteboard. Both of these allow people to 'bounce' off one another and build on each other's contribution. It reduces duplication and simplifies the next task of sorting. However, some may be reticent to contribute while others may dominate.

2.4 *Round robin*

A variation on working all together is when the facilitator calls on each individual in turn to contribute. A simple example is going round the room and asking participants to introduce themselves. This ensures that everyone gets a chance to contribute. If necessary, duplication can be reduced by specifically asking people if they have anything to add to what has already been said.

However, some people may not like being 'put on the spot' and asked to speak to the whole group, while others may be nervous about publicly disagreeing with others in the room. The order in which people are called can be important. For instance, in an environment where groupthink (Section C2.1) is seen as a risk, the most senior should be asked to talk last.

2.5 *Presentations*

This is when one or a few people present to the wider group. This is frequently used when someone has expert knowledge or when there is a need to make the case for a point of view. It is often used at the beginning of workshops to set the context of the overall workshop. The facilitator may need to intervene if the presentation starts to veer off its brief, or if it starts to threaten the overall timetable.

3. Techniques for building information

3.1 Brainstorming for new ideas

This is a well-known technique for creating new and, perhaps, 'off the wall' ideas. It is useful when a group seems stuck with a few stale ideas or when the task is to actually generate new ideas, such as new product ideas. It is not the same as listing information (see the next technique below) such as identifying all the stakeholders in a change.

Brainstorming often works best when one idea inspires another. Start by setting the brainstorming ground rules. This should start by asking the participants for suggestions. The facilitator may also offer tentative suggestions of their own. Typical ground rules for brainstorming are:

- stick to the question;
- do not criticize other people's contributions or shut them down;
- build on previous ideas if you want to;
- time will be allowed at the end for any explanations or clarifications.

The question needs to be clarified and it must be open-ended. Make sure the generated ideas are recorded in a simple list. They can be grouped and prioritized later.

Ideally this becomes a spontaneous free-for-all, but it may be necessary to get the ball rolling with a round-robin structure (Section E2.4). It is important to keep the momentum and it can be helpful to stimulate the creative thinking with various prompts:

- How would famous people, real or not, look at it? People such as Robin Hood, Walt Disney, Steven Spielberg, Gandhi?
- How would generic professions look at it? Professions such as a lawyer, an architect, a biologist, an engineer or a sales person?
- How would other people see it? Other roles such as a customer, a family member or a child?
- Using analogies. For instance, 'So is it like competing in a Grand Prix formula one race with a 20-year-old family sedan?'
- How would you explain this to someone born 100 years ago?
- Write down 10 ideas that start with 'Wouldn't it be good if...'

When the ideas stop coming, then the brainstorming stops. However, the discussion of the first list may stimulate further ideas and this should be specifically mentioned.

3.2 Listing information

This is a starting point in many workshops. It starts with open questions such as: 'Who are the stakeholders?', 'What are the issues?', or 'Identify all the risks'.

The structure used for this can influence the output. Consideration should be given to the strengths and weaknesses of working individually, in syndicates, as a whole group or using a round robin. In all cases, the means of recording the information must be clearly identified. Once identified, the initial list will often need to be sorted, grouped and duplicates may need to be removed.

Sometimes people will run out of ideas and it can help to stimulate them by asking them to recall a similar situation or to walk through the situation in their head. Alternatively, consider the situation through someone else's eyes, such as the customer.

3.3 *Putting like with like*

After a step that involves brainstorming or listing information, it is often necessary to make sense of a long list of items. Grouping items with other similar items can be very helpful in this process and makes it much easier to spot duplicates. If each item was written on a separate sticky note and stuck on a wall, then it is simply a process of moving the sticky notes around into groups. It can be useful to add headings to each of the groups. Further work in the workshop may focus on the groups of items rather than the individual items. Figure 10.2 shows an example of putting like items with like items and adding an appropriate heading ('Group A' and 'Group B' in Figure 10.2).

FIGURE 10.2 Putting like with like

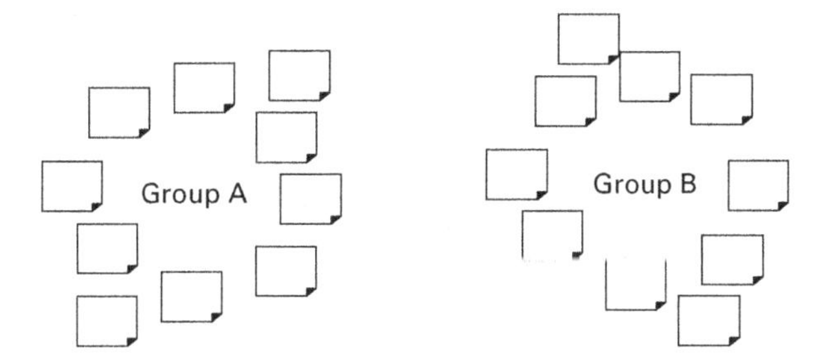

3.4 *Connecting information*

Sometimes there is a relationship between different items of information and this can be shown by placing the items on a board or wall and connecting them by pinning pieces of string. There can be different types of relationship such as:

- sequential or 'this must happen before that';
- hierarchical or 'this is part of that' or 'this person works for that person';
- distance or 'this is a weak/distant link' or 'this is a strong/close link'.

Sequential linking is often used with planning or analysing processes. Hierarchical is often used in organizational topics, and distance could be used to analyse the relationship between stakeholders.

3.5 Parking lot

A 'parking lot' is simply a place to record topics that do not fit the current discussion. It should usually be on public display and always be available to record on. If someone raises a topic that does not fit the present step in the agenda, acknowledge it and use the act of recording it on the 'parking lot' as a visible sign that it will not be forgotten: 'Nothing can make a group lose focus quicker than going off the agenda to some tangent unrelated to the task at hand. A few people will probably want to join in on the tangent, but most will be annoyed' (Justice and Jamieson, 2012).

As the workshop proceeds it may be possible for the facilitator to remove a topic – with the permission of the person who raised it – from the parking lot. If the parking lot has grown extensively then it is probably a sign that the agenda is not dealing with real and relevant concerns and that it will need to be reviewed. It is best to close the session with an empty parking lot, and this may mean private or public discussions with some of the individuals who raised the topics. Options for dealing with topics that remain on the parking lot are:

- Agree that they are no longer relevant.
- Agree that they are relevant but not a priority.
- Agree that they have already been discussed elsewhere in the agenda.
- Agree that they are relevant and a priority and should be discussed before the session ends.
- Agree that they are relevant and a priority but can be discussed at another meeting or elsewhere.

3.6 Six hats

Six different coloured hats represent six different modes of thinking. Many of us can be stuck in just one or two modes of thinking, and the analogy of putting on a different hat encourages us to look at something with a different mindset. The concept was developed by Edward De Bono in his book *Six Thinking Hats* (1999) and, as already briefly covered in Section C, the six different hats or mindsets are:

- White hat: this focuses on data and facts. Also look for gaps in the data.
- Red hat: this focuses on the feelings, emotions and gut reactions of yourself or others.
- Black hat: this takes a negative view. What are the bad points? What won't work?
- Yellow hat: this takes the opposite view of the black hat and takes an optimistic view. What makes this a great idea? What are the good points?
- Green hat: this is the creative mindset. It is similar in its mindset to brainstorming. Often it looks at what could be added to the idea under consideration.
- Blue hat: this is about process control. Frequently, the facilitator will be wearing the blue hat.

The six hats methodology can add structure to a discussion and can be used in many situations. It can be particularly useful when everyone is agreeing all the time or when there is a need to balance optimism and pessimism.

It helps to have a visual aid, such as a poster, to remind people of each hat. It works well when the whole group is wearing the same colour hat at the same time. An example of this is given in Section C6 on closing a session.

3.7 Acts of God

Change will often create negative reactions. Sometimes it is better to surface complaints rather than let them fester and create hidden agendas. This technique allows the group to vent their negative feelings and focus on positive outcomes. Acts of God is based on a common English phrase used in insurance policies about things beyond our control.

Simply generate a list of complaints or issues that affect the group and then categorize them according to this scheme:

1. Acts of God that must be lived with.
2. Acts of lesser gods that probably have to be lived with – but at least it is possible to communicate with the lesser gods and to let them know.
3. Issues that are shared with others (eg another section of same organization) and can be jointly resolved.
4. Issues that can be worked on but help may be required.
5. Issues that can be worked on without help.

It can be too easy to categorize a problem as an Act of God and the facilitator may need to probe to ensure that absolutely nothing can be done about it. Time should be allowed after an Acts of God session to develop plans for tackling those issues that can be dealt with.

3.8 Action planning

Many workshops end with lists of actions to be addressed. Sometimes this is a simple list of things to be done and who will do them. Sometimes a more detailed approach is required. Table 10.5 offers an example of how to allow more detail to be added to each action.

TABLE 10.5 Action plan

Actions	Start Date	End Date	Who	Where	How	Notes
Action 1						
Action 2						
Action 3						
Action 4						

4. Techniques for prioritizing, decision making and reaching a consensus

Often a long list needs to be prioritized, or a few or only one option must be selected.

4.1 Voting

Voting is a way of selecting one or more items from a list. It allows everyone to participate and it is seen as fair and transparent. Voting can be done by a show of hands, giving group members' sticky dots to stick on items on the wall, or one person could write votes on a whiteboard while others call out their decision. If there is a need for a secret ballot, votes could be dropped in a hat or passed to the facilitator.

There are many voting schemes. The simplest approach is to give everyone one vote. However, if the intention is to pick several items from the list, participants may be disgruntled that they can only express an opinion on one item. Alternatively, each participant could be asked to 'like' or 'not like' each item. A simple count of the number of 'likes' for each item will lead to a ranked list. This can be quite quick when combined with a show of hands.

Another approach is to give each person somewhere between three and 10 votes. Often the number of votes each person is given is roughly half the size of the list that is being examined. They can give all their votes to one option or spread them evenly or unevenly amongst several options. This has the advantage of encouraging the participants to consider the relative merits of all options rather than choose a single favourite.

Similarly, but requiring more time, each participant could rate each item on a scale of, say, one to five and the results for each item for each person could then be added up. This is a more detailed approach and takes longer.

These methods can be combined if the voting is done in several rounds, with each round selecting a smaller list for the next round of voting.

4.2 MoSCoW

MoSCoW stands for Must, Should, Could and Won't. It is one way of categorizing a long list of items:

- Must: you absolutely must have these and cannot possibly do without them.
- Should have: you really need them, but if you really had to then a workaround could be found, even though it would be extra effort.
- Could: would be good to have if circumstances allow.
- Won't have: won't have this time but may have it at another time.

This approach could be used to select functionality for software, or requirements for something that must be built or designed.

FIGURE 10.3 Two examples of using an XY axis

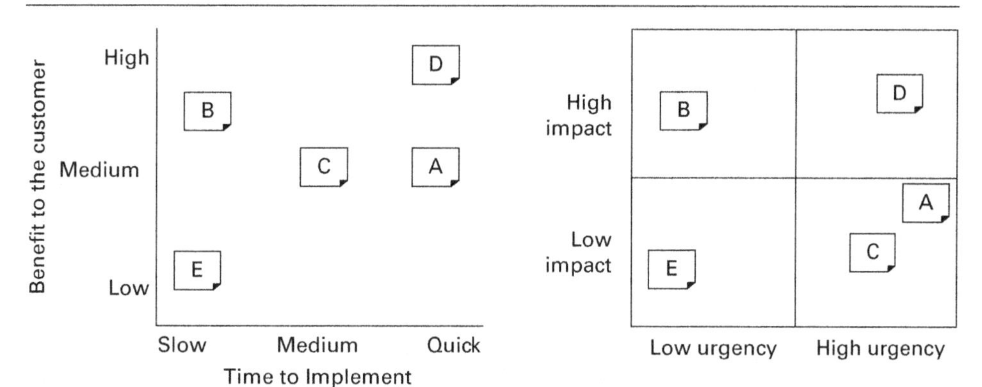

4.3 *XY axis*

Sometimes items need to be rated on two unconnected criteria such as benefits versus time to implement for actions, or impact versus urgency for problems. Obviously, high-impact and high-urgency problems would be tackled first, or priority would be given to high-benefit and quick-to-implement actions. Chapter 4 has a number of examples of how the XY approach can be used for stakeholder mapping.

Items can be plotted on an XY axis with each axis representing different criteria. Figure 10.3 shows examples of this. In practice, this can be done by placing sticky notes on a diagram or numbering a list and then writing the numbers on a diagram. Sometimes the diagram is split into four quadrants, as in the example in Figure 10.3.

4.4 *Matrix comparison*

An XY diagram compares items against two criteria. Sometimes it is necessary to compare items against three or more criteria. Table 10.6 shows a matrix comparing

TABLE 10.6 Matrix comparison

Options	Cost	Quality	Risk	Benefit
Option 1	32	4	Low	1
Option 2	16	3	Medium	2
Option 3	27	2	High	3
Option 4	20	5	Low	4
	Actual figure	Score out of five	Low-medium-high	Sorted in order

options against cost, quality, risk and benefit. Different columns can be rated in different ways. In the case of Table 10.6:

- cost is given as an actual figure;
- quality is rated on a scale of one to five;
- risk is rated as high, medium or low;
- benefit has been ranked top to bottom.

4.5 Debating teams

When there are two or more viewpoints, and consensus is important, the group can be split into debating teams. These are syndicates tasked with the job of making the case for a particular viewpoint. Generally, the debating teams would each present their case to the whole group.

There are a numbers of ways that this can be done. Each team could be made up only of people who support a particular view. Neutral people could float between teams asking questions as the cases are being prepared, or be randomly assigned to a team. Neutral people could also be used to make the actual presentations, forcing the teams to clearly think through their reasons for a viewpoint. Another option is to have teams made up of people who support a viewpoint and people who are against it, acting as 'devil's advocate'.

5. Approaches to larger workshops

5.1 World Café

World Cafés are built around the metaphor of cafés with their relaxed conversation. There are several design principles (**www.worldcafe.com**):

- set the context;
- create a hospitable space;
- explore questions that matter;
- encourage everyone's contributions;
- connect diverse perspectives;
- listen together for insights;
- share collective discoveries.

The process is as follows:

1. Create an environment modelled on a café. Typically this means sitting around tables, with tablecloths and, perhaps, flowers and refreshments. Provide drawing paper and coloured pens. There should be between four to six places at each table.
2. Introduce the session, explaining the process and putting the participants at ease.

3 The process involves rounds of conversation at each table and then people moving to new tables. Each round is between 20 and 30 minutes.
4 At the end of each round, each participant at the table moves to a different new table. They may or may not choose to leave one person as the 'host' for the next round. The host would briefly tell the next set of participants who join the table what happened in the previous round.
5 Each round is prefaced with a question designed for the specific context and desired purpose of the session. The same question can be used for multiple rounds, or the questions can evolve from round to round.
6 After several rounds (three is a number frequently mentioned) start to record the results on a wall or projected picture. This will usually take a person skilled in capturing and summarizing the information and presenting it in an interesting and clear manner.

World Café is a technique that can be used with anywhere from 12 to several hundred people. It is generally a creative process and works best with open-ended questions.

5.2 Open Space Technology

This can be thought of as a structured way to encourage ad hoc conversations. The approach is sometimes called 'self-organizing meetings'. It has been used for groups ranging from five to two thousand people. There is little or no technology involved.

At the beginning of an Open Space, the participants sit in a circle or in concentric circles for larger groups. The facilitator welcomes the participants and briefly states the theme of the session, but there is no place for lengthy speeches. Then the facilitator asks all participants to spend the next short period, perhaps 10 minutes, to think about the theme and identify issues or opportunities. A blank agenda is drawn up on a large wall identifying meeting spaces and time slots.

Participants are then invited to raise topics. Anyone who has a topic to raise walks to the centre of the group, writes a very short description on a sheet of paper and announces it to the group. This topic is then placed in an available slot on the agenda.

Anyone may raise a topic, but they are then expected to host the conversation and keep notes. There will usually be an agreed way to keep notes. For instance, typed into a laptop and collated and shared electronically.

Opening and creating the agenda may take an hour or more. Then the sessions start. Whoever wants to attend a session will attend. This means some sessions may be crowded and some may be completely empty except for the 'host'. Attendees at a session may leave part-way through and join other sessions. Sessions typically last for about 90 minutes and the whole gathering can take from a half-day to two days. When the session is over, the notes are collated and sent to each attendee.

The originator of Open Space Technology, Owen Harrison (2008), has stated that there are three principles and one law. The three principles are:

- Whoever comes to a session are the right people for that session.
- Whatever happens is the only thing that could have.
- Whenever a session starts is the right time for it to start.

The law is called the 'Law of Two Feet'. It simply states that if at any time an attendee is neither learning nor contributing, then they should use their two feet and move on. Open Space Technology works best when tackling complex issues with diverse people, who have diverse ideas and a passion for the problem.

Summary

The structure is how people work together and each structure has its place:

- Everyone working on their own allows people to contribute equally and not be dominated but this can lead to a lot of duplication.
- Working in syndicates can save time by looking at different tasks in parallel or it can be used to form debating teams.
- Working all together allows people to build on each other's contribution, but can lead to a few people dominating the conversation.
- Round robin gives everyone a chance to be heard.
- Presentations allow people to set the context or make a case for their point of view.

Techniques for building information start with divergent techniques such as brainstorming and listing, and are then followed by convergent techniques such as putting like with like. There are various methods for prioritizing or building consensus such as voting, XY axis, matrices or forming a debating structure.

Two innovative approaches to larger groupings are World Café and Open Space Technology. These both allow large groups of people to enter into useful debate. World Café is more structured than Open Space.

Questions to think about

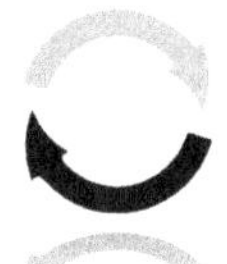

1. Do you think about the structure in your workshops?
2. Do you use the same techniques all the time or do you try to match them to the needs of the objective?
3. Can you think of times when you would use World Café or Open Space Technology?

Further reading

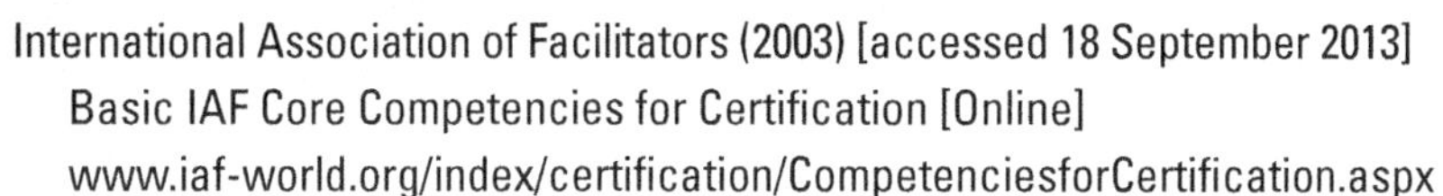

International Association of Facilitators (2003) [accessed 18 September 2013] Basic IAF Core Competencies for Certification [Online] www.iaf-world.org/index/certification/CompetenciesforCertification.aspx

Justice, T and Jamieson, D W (2012) *The Facilitator's Fieldbook*, AMACOM, New York

Mann, T (2014) *Facilitation: Develop your expertise*, Resource Publications, Newbury

Schwarz, R *et al* (2005) *The Skilled Facilitator Fieldbook: Tips, tools, and tested methods for consultants, facilitators, managers, trainers, and coaches*, Jossey-Bass, San Francisco, CA

World Café Community Foundation, *World Café Method* [accessed 13 February 2014] [Online] http://www.theworldcafe.com/method.html

References

De Bono, E (1999) *Six Thinking Hats*, Back Bay Books, New York

Janis, I L (1972) *Victims of Groupthink*, Houghton Mifflin, New York

Justice, T and Jamieson, D W (2012) *The Facilitator's Fieldbook*, AMACOM, New York

Harrison, O (2008) *Open Space Technology: A user's guide*, 3rd edn, Berrett-Koehler, San Francisco, CA

Harrison, O [accessed 13 February 2014] Open Space for Emerging Order [Online] http://www.openspaceworld.com/brief_history.htm

International Association of Facilitators (2003) [accessed 24 April 2013] Basic IAF Core Competencies for Certification [Online] www.iaf-world.org/index/certification/CompetenciesforCertification.aspx

Mann, T (2014) *Facilitation: Develop your expertise*, Resource Publications, Newbury

Mittleman, D D, Briggs, R O and Nunamaker, J F (2000) Best practices in facilitating virtual meetings: some notes from initial experiences, *Group Facilitation: A Research and Applications Journal*, 2 (2), Winter, pp 5–14

Schwarz, R (2002) *The Skilled Facilitator: A comprehensive resource for consultants, facilitators, managers, trainers and coaches*, Jossey-Bass, San Francisco, CA

Schwarz, R *et al* (2005) *The Skilled Facilitator Fieldbook: Tips, tools, and tested methods for consultants, facilitators, managers, trainers, and coaches*, Jossey-Bass, San Francisco, CA

Watkins, M (2013) [accessed 11 February 2014] Making Virtual Teams Work: Ten Basic Principles [Online] http://blogs.hbr.org/2013/06/making-virtual-teams-work-ten/

World Café Community Foundation, *World Café Method* [accessed 13 February 2014] [Online] http://www.theworldcafe.com/method.html

Sustaining change

11

HELEN CAMPBELL

Introduction

Organizations invest time, money and energy in change because they want to do, be or have something different. Not just for a day or a week but as an integrated part of the evolving organization. As we have seen in previous chapters, humans love the status quo and will go to great lengths to get back to it. Despite evidence time and time again telling us that changes are not self-sustaining, we continue to turn a blind eye a week or two after 'go-live' – long before the benefits have been sustainably delivered.

> *'Planting the seed may provide a sense of achievement but only with careful planning beforehand and vigilance afterwards will we produce the food we need.'*

This chapter explains some of the underlying principles, models and tools that a change manager uses to make sure the change sticks and, more importantly, stays stuck! The first part of the chapter covers some of the common concepts used when planning, measuring and sustaining change. Alongside each of these concepts is a clear indication of what it is, why it is useful and how it is applied. A case study is also used to illustrate how a change manager applies each topic. At the end of the chapter are a few practical checklists for each stage of the change, which will help practitioners focus on sustaining change throughout.

Change managers continually look at the big picture and the long term to make sure the change sticks. Chapter 7 shows how they work with the business and the project team to ensure that the change and the environment 'fit' together to enable as easy a transition as possible. They understand the concept of levers and leverage and the full range of levers at their disposal. They have the skill and experience to be able to apply the right one(s) at the right time. They check that levers are having the desired effect, and are ready to change their approach in response to feedback and new information. They understand that every change and every environment is different and that the need to sustain the change and the way in which this manifests itself is different every time. They understand the nature of human behaviour and how this helps and hinders the successful sustaining of change.

Change managers start working on how to sustain the change as soon as they come on board and they don't stop thinking about it until the benefits are delivered. However, sustaining change is a team effort and the change manager needs to build strong relationships with colleagues across the organization. The people impacted by the change (internal and external) provide valuable insights into the environment into which the change will be delivered. The human resources (HR) and organization development (OD) teams offer critical expertise. The business risk management team are constantly on the lookout for strategic, operational, reputational and financial risk. It is not unusual for a change initiative to raise significant risks in all these areas. Within the project team the people developing the change solution have an important role to play and the change manager works with them to make sure the solution and the approach to implementing it enable those on the receiving end to easily adopt and embed it. Finally, the Project Management Office (PMO) ensure all project risks are reported, prioritized and managed, and the change manager makes sure that risks to the adoption and sustainability of the change are on the risk register from the outset (Chapter 6).

Tip

Introducing the topic of sustaining change into change management practice can be tricky – especially if your organization is one of those that believes a change is finished a week or two after implementation or where leaders are reluctant to be held accountable for specific outcomes. Adapt your approach depending on the environment you are working in and do what you can to raise awareness of the risks to benefits realization.

CASE STUDY

Introducing the Captain Engineering case study

Captain Engineering had been experiencing problems with customer orders. They had traced the main cause of the problems back to a lack of communication between functions within the organization. This in turn was resulting in duplication of tasks, conflict and confusion, which in turn was preventing them from meeting customer orders quickly and accurately. One of the barriers to cross-functional communication was the strong hierarchical structure that was forcing people to communicate up and down the chain of command. Carmel had been appointed to the role of Change Manager and, throughout this chapter, you will see how she applies each of the concepts and tools to ensure the change sticks, stays stuck and ultimately enables a better customer experience.

Sustaining different types of change

No matter what type of change it is or what approach is used to develop and implement it the change manager is responsible for making sure it sticks and stays stuck to the extent required to deliver the benefits. Where change is more evolutionary, emergent or iterative, the change manager clearly identifies the critical dependencies for the next stage of the journey. Whilst their toolkit is largely the same, the way they apply it is different, with a focus on the multiple waves of change, which elements need to stick before the next wave comes in and which waves will need to 'unstick' previous changes in order to succeed.

CHAPTER CONTENTS

Section A: Sustaining change concepts

This section provides information and practical examples of how to apply some core concepts that are behind the successful adoption, embedding and sustaining of change.

1. Concept of 'fit'

What is it?

Change will have a smooth transition into operation if it 'fits' the environment into which it is being introduced. A good fit means that adoption is relatively painless, whilst a poor fit results in high levels of angst.

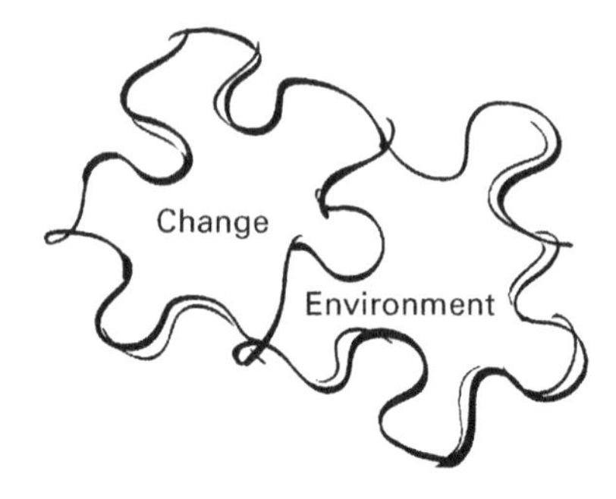

Why is it useful to a change manager?

It guides both the design of the solution and the activities required to prepare or adapt the environment (including the people) for its introduction (Chapter 7). Changes that don't fit their environment when they are introduced can result in unnecessary tension, conflict, poor performance, low productivity, high staff turnover, a legacy of 'bad' change for the future *and* no benefits!

How is it applied?

As we saw in Chapter 7, change managers are closely involved in the design of the solution to make sure it can be adopted and sustained by the recipients as quickly and easily as possible. For example, if a change involves getting 'square pegs' into 'round holes' in the organization, change managers apply the techniques outlined so far in this book to adapt both the square pegs (the solution) and the hole (the human and other aspects of the environment into which the solution is being introduced). They do this just to the extent required to enable the 'square pegs' to be adopted, integrated and sustained as quickly and painlessly as possible and the benefits delivered.

CASE STUDY

Captain Engineering – fit

Carmel used the concept of 'fit' to work out how best to design cross-functional communications channels without any major changes to existing processes, so that they could be introduced without major disruption. She also used it to identify the areas of the change that would clash with existing skills and processes and would therefore need to be adaptod to 'fit' thc new way.

2. Systems thinking

What is it?

Systems thinking is a form of analysis that identifies the positive and negative ripple effects of the change and change management activities. It is arguably one of the most important and powerful processes that a change manager offers. Systems thinking encourages the change manager to look at the organization and its environment as a series of interdependent systems – where a change to one area naturally has ripple effects elsewhere. The 'system' can be internal (for example, the reward system or the financial management system) or external (such as political, social, regulatory or economic). It works on the basis that an action influences something, which influences something else and eventually flows back to the initial element via a positive or negative feedback loop. In a change management context, a positive feedback loop reinforces attempts at change, whereas a negative feedback loop supports the status quo. See Chapter 2, Sections C and D for more on using systems theory and soft systems methods when defining change.

To use a generic example: putting your foot on the accelerator increases fuel flow, which in turn makes the car go faster. When you check the actual versus the desired speed of the car you alter the position of the accelerator and the cycle starts again. Using a systems diagram this would look like the flow in Figure 11.1. To apply this thinking to a change management situation might look like the systems diagram in Figure 11.2.

FIGURE 11.1 Generic system diagram

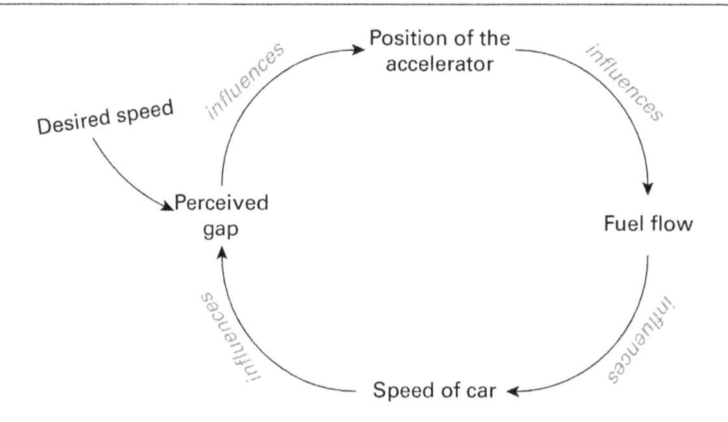

FIGURE 11.2 Example change management systems diagram

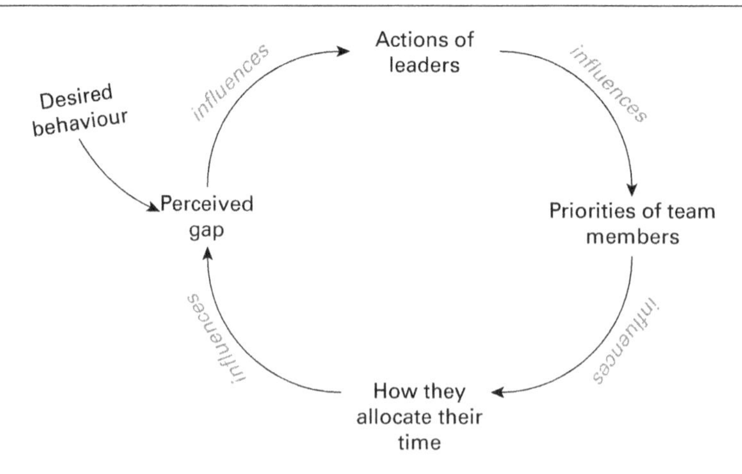

FIGURE 11.3 Expanded change management systems diagram

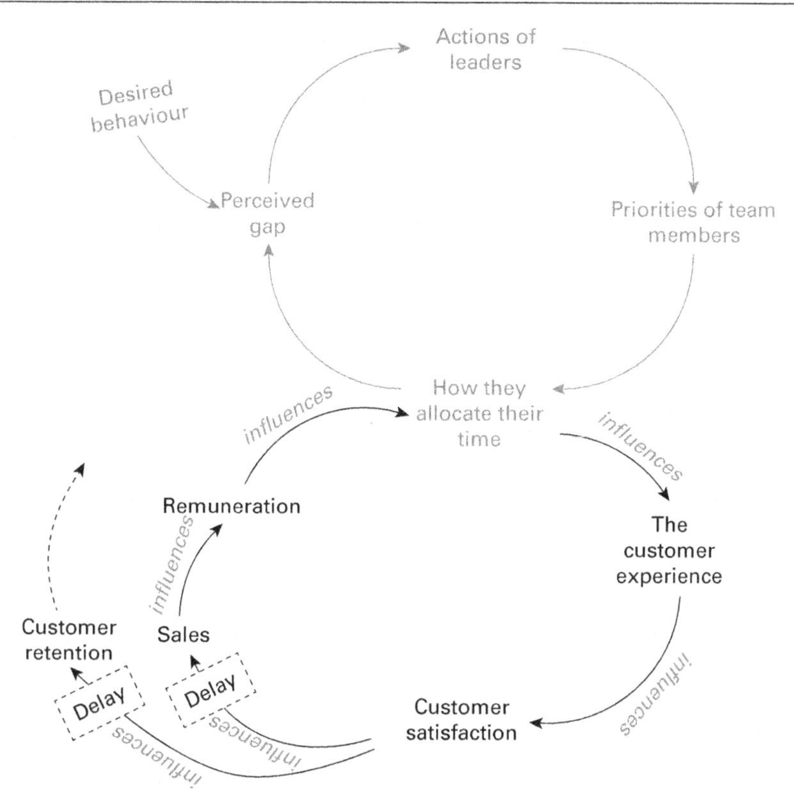

To take this one step further we can expand into another system and identify the influences on the customer system, as shown in Figure 11.3. This example shows how the actions of leaders can have a ripple effect on customer satisfaction, retention and sales results. Note also the concept of 'delay' introduced with this diagram. Not all responses are immediate and it is important to understand the nature and effect of those delays on the change and its benefits.

Why is it useful to a change manager?

Project teams often isolate the solution from the environment in order to reduce complexity and focus delivery. Systems thinking enables change managers to recognize the complex dynamic reality by viewing the whole picture in order to understand the influence that the change will have on its environment and vice versa.

How is it applied?

Change managers use systems thinking in a variety of tasks and, when it comes to sustaining change, the main application of systems thinking is to identify the forces that will help and those that will get in the way of the change sticking and to exploit, remove or minimize their impact as appropriate.

Systems thinking requires a major shift from the linear approach more common in projects. It is based on the ability to see the big picture – both in place and time – and how each element is interdependent on each other. As Peter Senge says: 'cause and effect are not closely related in time and space' (for more on Senge's thinking see Chapter 1, Section C2.3). The change manager takes into account the short-, medium- and long-term effects of the change and any approach to sustaining it. A strategy that looks promising during implementation can sometimes unravel over time and undermine the realization of benefits. Considering a variety of perspectives helps to understand the true effect as well as the influence that change may have on other systems, including any that will derail the change. Systems may exert a different type and level of force at different times, and it is the skill and experience of the change manager that ensures there is more forward motion overall and that the change has the momentum it needs to stick and stay stuck.

CASE STUDY

Captain Engineering – systems thinking

Carmel thought about which systems would be involved in making sure the new communication channels remained effective and delivered the improved customer experience required. She worked with the HR and Communications departments to identify formal and informal systems relating to recruitment, reward, physical environment and decision making to find those that would help the change stick and those that might derail it. Against each of these systems she jotted down some questions that would help her to understand the power of each one (see Figure 11.4).

3. Levers and leverage

> *'Small changes can create big results.'*
>
> Peter M Senge

FIGURE 11.4 Captain Engineering – relevant systems and their influence

1. The recruitment system - do recruiting processes and standards need to be changed to ensure that new management recruits prefer and are skilled in the new way of working?
2. The formal reward system - understand whether the way people are rewarded and promoted will help or hinder the move to a less hierarchical environment and whether making changes to these standards and processes would help reinforce the new approach.
3. The informal reward system - to understand the 'unwritten rules' that can be exploited and those that will need to be modified if the change is to take hold sustainably.
4. The physical environment system - what messages are our buildings and office layout sending and what changes will we need to make to support the new behaviours?
5. The formal communication system - look at the way information flows through the organization. Who communicates, how often, about what and through what channels? What elements may inadvertently reinforce the old ways and prevent us from being successful?
6. The informal communication system - find out who listens to who about what and how I can leverage these channels to reinforce the change.
7. The leadership development system - what is the content of the training our leaders receive and what changes do we need to make so that it sends a clear message about the non-hierarchical approach and equips them to perform well in this environment?
8. The governance and power system - who has authority to make which decisions and does this support a flatter structure?

What is it?

Levers are the elements of a change and its landscape that can be activated in some way to enable or support adoption on a broad scale. Leverage is where a small amount of effort targeted in the right place (ie the right lever) at the right time can have a big effect on the outcome.

Why is it useful to a change manager?

Change managers alone cannot identify and deal with every individual's barriers to adopting the change. By identifying and applying the right levers, the change manager kicks off waves of mutually supporting, self-perpetuating activity that are able to create and maintain the required effect on a large number of people over a long period of time.

How is it applied?

Levers are used to avoid or minimize the harm from forces stopping or inhibiting adoption and encourage the forces that will have a positive effect. Leverage is used to influence individuals sufficiently so that they voluntarily demonstrate and maintain the required new behaviours, where it is often the small things that will have a big effect on the outcome. The nature of systems thinking – seeing our world as a complex array of interdependent systems, all of which can influence each other – leads nicely to the concept of levers and leverage. Imagine flying in a helicopter high above the change. As you look at the landscape from a variety of perspectives the patterns of influence emerge – what influences what and how; how activities, people and outcomes are linked interdependently. From there, the change manager decides where and how to act so that the desired outcome is reached. They play out the various scenarios to see what effect different strategies might have. When they are satisfied they have thought through the rippling consequences of each strategy, they confidently invest their time and energy in the ones that will have the best outcome. These may be avoiding or limiting the damage from a disruptive system, or exploiting the power of a supportive system.

CASE STUDY

Captain Engineering – finding leverage

Carmel had already identified the systems that were relevant to the change. Now she had to work out which of these would provide the greatest leverage to make the change stick. She drafted the list before going to check it with her colleagues in HR (see Figure 11.5).

FIGURE 11.5 Captain Engineering – the power of levers

The change will stick when...	Leverage (High, Medium, Low)	Effect (Short, Medium or Long term)
We recruit people who prefer a collaborative approach	Medium	Long
The informal reward system rewards cross-functional communication	High	Long
Leaders actively and visibly demonstrate communication across functions	High	Long
Leaders actively and visibly encourage communication across functions	Medium	Long
We create activities which require cross-functional communication	Medium	Short
We structure the teams to align to the customer order process	Medium	Medium
We counsel those that continue hierarchical communication	Medium	Short
We publicly recognize those that are communicating in the new way	Medium	Short
...		

3.1 Types of levers

The case study illustrates the wide range of systems and therefore levers that are available. Levers that encourage people to adopt change fall into three broad categories – emotional, procedural and structural:

- *Emotional levers* are those that exert an internal pressure to change such as guilt, pride or feeling part of the 'in-crowd'. For example, the warm glow from being praised by your boss, or the peer pressure when you are the last person in your team to adopt a change. To some extent these levers are always necessary for sustainable change adoption, but in some cases the change cannot succeed unless the people impacted truly *believe* they need to sustain the new behaviour.
- *Procedural levers* are those imposed by the process that a person needs to follow. For example, if the sales person needs to enter the details of their customer's order into the new sales system in order for the customer to receive their goods then they are unlikely to avoid this step.
- *Structural levers* are those that are implicit in the way the organization is controlled – and will exert a force accordingly. For example, the way that elements of the organization are grouped together or managed separately; the messages implicit in the structures about the priorities of elements such as customers, financial management or technology.

We now look at how these categories of levers translate into specific change management strategies.

  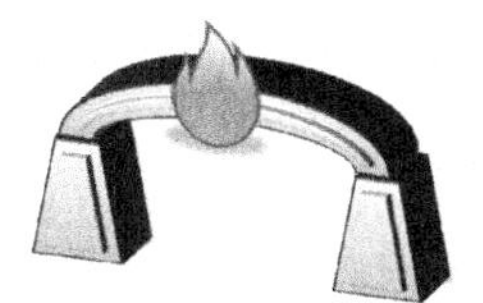

What are they?

The status quo is a comfortable place to be. Change recipients have spent many months and years nestling into their current groove and it is going to take a significant amount of effort to get them, and keep them, out of it. Ultimately, if there are no consequences for not changing, then why expend the energy? Motivation to change what we do and how we do it sustainably varies depending on the individual and the circumstances. There are various theories of motivation (Chapter 1, Section B3). The change manager is aware of these and applies them appropriately to the situation. One of the simplest to apply is incentive theory, which states that people require a combination of *away from* motivation ('if I don't do it there will be negative consequences for me') and *towards* motivation ('there will be a reward for doing the "right" thing'). The key to these strategies working is that the individual must consider the consequences important at the time they are used. The basis of this are three major strategies:

- *Carrot*: reward them for doing the right thing and having the right attitude with something those individuals value. This reward may be financial or non-financial. For example, when the sales team completes the transition to the new system they may prefer a party and public praise. If you need to persuade people with legacy skills to stay in their role for long enough to complete the transition, a bonus or other financial incentive may provide the motivation they need. These are examples of providing effective short-term motivation. An example of a longer-term 'carrot' strategy would be to consistently provide new opportunities to those with a positive attitude towards the change. The process for allocating the rewards must be transparent, as people will be on the lookout for any signs that procedural fairness is compromised.

- *Stick*: inflict a penalty for activities and behaviours that undermine the success of the change. Remembering that in general people are not deliberately doing the wrong thing these penalties should start with minor consequences such as the absence of rewards. For example: 'My colleague Jane won the competition for data accuracy this week. My boss is going to help me understand what I need to do to improve my score.' As further motivation, the change manager makes it clear what will happen to the organization, its customers, divisions and the individual if benefits are not realized.
- *Burning bridges*: carrot-and-stick strategies can lose their effectiveness when used over the long term or repeated frequently. A strong but often neglected strategy is to make it impossible for your people to do things any other way. This requires a focus during the design of the solution. A simple example is in the embedding of a new system that automates a manual process. The design of the system and the associated processes can ensure that it is not possible to complete the transaction unless every worker uses the new system in the way it was intended.

Here's what a team member may encounter when they try to work around such a system:

> Most of my customers don't have their tax details with them when they apply so we used to enter '99999' in the old system and it would let us carry on with the application. I tried putting '99999' in the new system but it is clever! It knows when I have tried to trick it and won't let me complete the application until I have entered the right information. Now we make sure we ask customers to bring their tax details with them so that it doesn't hold up their application.

Sustainable behaviour change

'Behaviour is the best way we know of getting our needs met.'

William Glasser, *Choice Theory: A New Psychology of Personal Freedom* (1999)

One of the best models around for helping to understand how hard it is to change human behaviour – and that also gives the change manager some clues about how to approach this – is Jonathan Haidt's reworking of the Indian classic about the rider and the elephant. The rider represents the logical, rational mind – which needs facts and information about a change and why adoption is critical to success. The elephant represents the emotional and autonomic self – the one with a mind of its own who tends to act without consideration of the consequences. As a simple example, when an individual is placed in front of a piece of chocolate cake it is the rider that reasons 'I should not eat that as I am trying to lose weight'. By contrast, it is the elephant that is saying 'eat the cake... I love cake... eat the cake...'. The elephant is bigger, stronger, has more stamina and is harder to control than the rider. Haidt suggests that sustainable behaviour change requires the appropriate appeals to both the rider (the most powerful facts, figures and rationale) and the elephant (with messages aimed at emotions such as desire and fear). He also suggests 'shaping the path' – in other words, making it impossible (or really troublesome) for the elephant to do anything other than what you need.

How are they applied?

Change managers ensure that consequences are in place to encourage the right behaviour and to deal decisively with behaviour that could undermine the success of the change. They use a combination of carrots, sticks and burning bridges to reward attempts to change and inflict negative consequences for actions that undermine the change. They keep up the pressure required to get people across the line sustainably.

CASE STUDY

Captain Engineering – burning bridges

Carmel had identified that the leaders' offices presented a physical barrier to the desired open communication and also symbolized the hierarchical culture she needed to shift. Several of the leaders had suggested that their offices be turned into meeting rooms but Carmel knew that if the offices remained then the leaders would be tempted to move back in. She could see that in the longer term they may need more meeting rooms, but this need could be met in other ways for the time being. She knew she had to 'burn their bridges' and dismantle the managers' offices. The new open office would force ongoing interaction between managers and their teams, which would be critical to changing to a more egalitarian culture.

Tip

Look out for planned incentives or penalties that are no longer powerful. For example, linking adoption to the size of the staff bonus may have made sense in the planning, but if the poor company performance led to no one getting their bonuses last year then this lever will no longer have the power it once did.

3.2 *Environmental levers*

What are they?

Levers in the environment are the physical elements of the landscape such as the office layout or quality of the training rooms. For example, if a change aims to automate a paper-based process then the physical shelving and storage that was required to accommodate the paper should be removed, as both a symbol of the inevitability of the change and also as a way of 'burning bridges' by preventing people going back to the old paper-based ways. External examples might be the physical location or surroundings within a town or city. For example, if the change aims to encourage more customers to visit a shop, the fact that it is in a centrally located shopping centre is a lever that the change manager can exploit.

How are they applied?

Kurt Lewin told us back in the 1940s that a person's behaviour is a function of both the person and the environment or situation (Lewin, 1947). He did this via his equation $B = f(P \times S)$: B = behaviour is a function of the P = person and the S = situation. Likewise, James Carloppio (2010) pleads with us not to 'put the alcoholic back in the pub' as he tells how expensive rehab services can be wasted if the alcoholic is able to go back into the environment that encouraged the old behaviour.

CASE STUDY

Captain Engineering – environmental levers

Carmel thought about the elements of the physical environment that would support the change and those that would get in the way. She had already identified that the managers' offices would reinforce the old hierarchical ways of working and decided that taking down those walls during the working day would provide a strong symbol to reinforce the shift that was happening. The managers' dining room and their reserved parking spaces would also have to go – both as a strong symbol of the new way of working and to prevent the old ways creeping back in.

3.3 *Leadership levers*

What are they?

Leadership levers are anything that influential leaders do or say before, during and after the change. These may be formal leaders within the hierarchy or informal leaders who influence others without any formal authority (see the explanation of sources of power in Chapter 1). People look at the way their leaders are reacting to a situation to decide how they themselves will behave, so leadership levers can be swift and powerful when applied in the right way consistently. Edgar Schein (2010) uses the concept of primary embedding mechanisms that leaders use to send non-verbal messages about beliefs, values and assumptions to their team. These include how they spend their time, how they react to problems, how they allocate resources and how they reward or penalize team members. Line managers in particular can have one of the biggest influences on a person's decision to adopt a change. Indeed as TJ and Sandar Larkin (2006) point out, research has shown that people are up to nine times more likely to adopt a change if their direct manager discusses it with them, rather than a senior leader or a representative from another area. Ultimately we are driven, consciously or subconsciously, to perform in a way that offers status and security and therefore ensures our survival – and that means pleasing the boss!

Actions speak louder than words

Words make up only around 7 per cent of the message so it is the tone of their voice, body language and ultimately the actions leaders take that send a much stronger signal about the type of behaviour that will be rewarded (see Chapter 5, Section 5.1 on symbolic actions). When a leader *says* that the change is important, but is then unable to answer any questions about it, you can almost hear the change momentum grinding to a halt!

Tip

Recruit, train and reward change leadership as part of a strategy to build change capability in the organization.

How are they applied?

The change manager asks: what message should the leaders send to reinforce the change and what is the most powerful way of sending that message? They identify the formal and informal leaders with the greatest ability to directly or indirectly influence the adoption and integration of the change. They roll out activities and support mechanisms to leverage the leaders' influence appropriately.

CASE STUDY

Captain Engineering – leadership levers

Carmel knew that to kick off the change she needed a powerful demonstration of the new behaviours from the senior leaders, so she got agreement from the CEO and the executive to be the first to relinquish their offices. This would role-model the required change. In addition, she asked them to actively and visibly engage more with the people around them and 'talk up' the change in order to send a clear message to managers that attempts to rebuild barriers will be frowned upon.

Tip

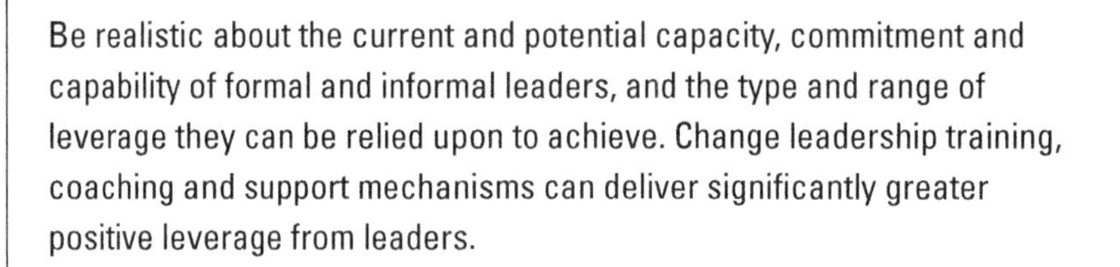
Be realistic about the current and potential capacity, commitment and capability of formal and informal leaders, and the type and range of leverage they can be relied upon to achieve. Change leadership training, coaching and support mechanisms can deliver significantly greater positive leverage from leaders.

3.4 Organization Development (OD) levers

What are they?

The OD toolkit is often one of the most powerful that a change manager can access, as it is a well-established part of the organization's control system. OD ensures that the organization is structured and equipped for maximum effectiveness and efficiency. Working closely with the OD and HR team enables leverage of areas such as organization and team structure, performance management processes and standards, reward systems and job design – in order to encourage those impacted to adopt and sustain a change.

How are they applied?

A key focus will be how current elements of the organization (how people are grouped together, the scope of their role, reporting lines, career paths and performance systems) might inhibit the adoption or sustaining of the change. In parallel, the ideal design of these elements to support the change can be envisaged, enabling negotiation with the relevant functions and leaders to agree a suite of organization changes that deliver as many positive forces as possible. Below are some typical OD levers with some questions that help to identify whether they are a useful way of reinforcing a change.

Job design

If we were starting from scratch how would we design the roles to support the change? Which tasks group together logically into one role? By looking at new processes, work volumes, current and future skill requirements, available talent and professional and personal development paths it is often possible to design roles that make it hard to go back to the old ways and still provide satisfying and stimulating jobs.

Role descriptions

If we were starting from scratch how would we write the role descriptions for the people in these roles? How can role descriptions be changed to highlight the important elements of the change? For example, important stakeholders, new responsibilities, skills and desired behaviours for the person in the role.

Organization structure

How can we change the structure of the organization to make it easier to adopt and sustain the change? For example, if an organization's stated aim is to 'put the customer at the centre of everything we do' it would help to move from a functional structure (Figure 11.6) to a structure that gives more visibility of, and therefore influence to, the customer groups (Figure 11.7).

FIGURE 11.6 Functional organization structure

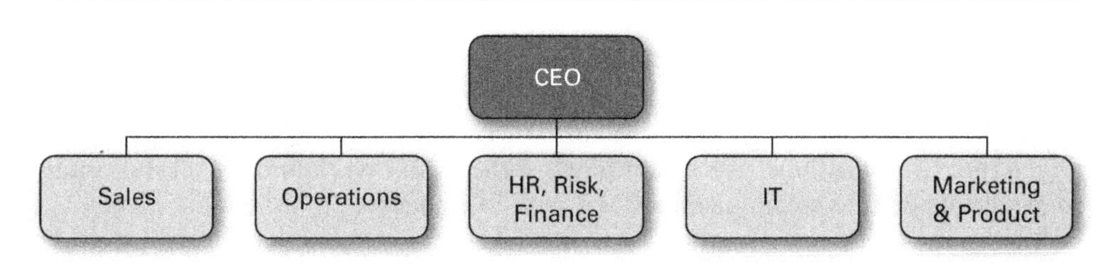

FIGURE 11.7 Customer organization structure

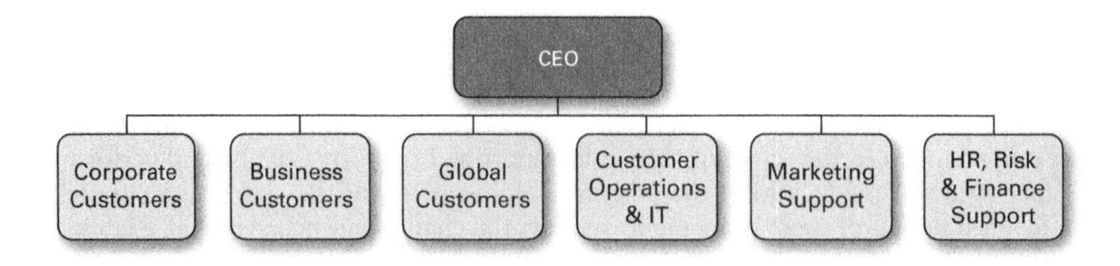

This new structure ensures that workflows and decisions are primarily based on the customers' needs. This also illustrates how a change of name for a department (for example changing from 'Operations' to 'Customer Operations') can help to remind those working in that department about what is important, and therefore reinforce the change when supported by other activities. Other organization structure options might include a regional structure, creating subsidiary companies, a structure based on the core processes of the organization, centralized or decentralized control. See Chapter 13, Section A6 for more information about organization design.

This is a good example of burning bridges. When the team is structured in a way that groups the right people together and designs the interdependency between roles to align to the change, it can be difficult for recalcitrant or fearful recipients to find their way back to the old way.

Tip

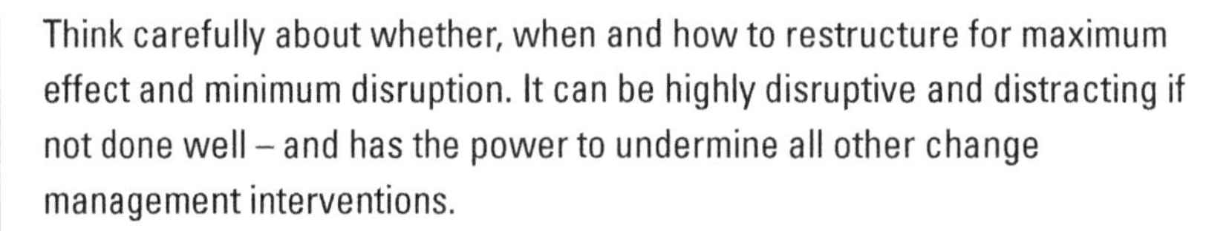

Think carefully about whether, when and how to restructure for maximum effect and minimum disruption. It can be highly disruptive and distracting if not done well – and has the power to undermine all other change management interventions.

Team structure

If we were starting from scratch how would we build the team to support this? How should we change the team structure to accommodate and support the change given the nature, volume, timing and flow of the team's work and the level of interdependency between team members and with other teams?

Performance management systems and standards

Performance measures at the individual, team and organization level can work well together to reinforce a change. Whilst some organizations are moving away from formal annual performance review processes most still work with their employees to identify a set of task- and behaviour-related objectives (sometimes referred to as Key Performance Indicators (KPIs), Key Results Areas (KRAs) or Balanced Scorecards), which are designed to set the organization's, team's or person's priorities. Careful planning of KPIs, and an awareness of the behaviour they will drive and the ripple effects they will have, makes them an influential lever for sustaining change when they are used wisely. When applied without forethought they can have just as strong an effect on undermining the change. For example, measuring customer service by 'number of problems solved' means the customer service area is under pressure to close problems – regardless of whether the customer is happy. Using 'customer satisfaction' as a measure drives more helpful behaviour.

There can be a strong temptation to believe that changing the impacted people's KPIs is enough to make the change stick. However, this will only work if the following criteria are in place:

- Performance targets are few in number so that they can provide effective focus and motivation.
- KPIs drive, not undermine, the behaviour that will support the change.
- Leaders consider this a critical process and give it the appropriate time and effort throughout the year.
- Rewards reflect the level of achievement.
- Rewards are valued.
- Objectives remain relevant and motivating throughout the performance period.
- It is complemented with other levers and strategies.

It is important to remember that OD levers will be met with concern at best and extreme resistance (and industrial action) at worst (see also Chapter 13, Section A). As we saw in Chapter 7, Section C1, the psychological contract implies that people must have a safe environment within which to take their first tentative steps towards the new way of working. A good change manager understands the perceived personal threats that come with changes to people's status, and provides the support required to help those impacted make the transition (see also Chapters 1, 6 and 7).

CASE STUDY

Captain Engineering – OD levers

Carmel needed to make sure that information flowed freely between the functions involved in receiving, processing and building customer orders. After a meeting with the OD manager she jotted down some OD levers that would help to sustain the change (see Figure 11.8).

FIGURE 11.8 Some OD levers

- ✓ *Allocate clear accountability for the end-to-end processing of customer orders within one role.*
- ✓ *Organize teams so that those who need to work closely together on the customer order process are in the same team or at least the same department.*
- ✓ *Align the rewards system to reflect the importance of fulfilling customer orders quickly and accurately.*
- ✓ *Ensure that each of the role descriptions involved clearly articulates the skills, experience and performance standards required of that role.*

Tip

Look for levers among the formal and informal reward mechanisms and apply those with the greatest ability to reinforce the change. In some cases, the reality of how work flows around the organization, how people are promoted and the scope of their role bears little relation to the written documents!

4. Levels of adoption

What is it?

Chapter 4 addresses the different needs and expectations of various stakeholder groups during change. Once the change is implemented the change manager focuses on getting each group to the point required to deliver benefits – and keeping them there. Consider the three levels from the model by Herbert Kelman (1958) outlined in Figure 11.9 – compliance, identification and internalization. Some changes, phases or stakeholders may only need 'compliance': for example, if the change requires only a simple one-off action such as updating your new e-mail signature. If your office is relocating to the other side of town you may need people to 'identify' more strongly with the change. When the change impact is significant, leaders are usually required to reach a level of internalization so that they can be authentic advocates.

Why is it useful to a change manager?

Not all changes require everyone impacted to fully embrace the change. By having a good understanding of the level and type of commitment required by each group at each phase of the change, the approach can be tailored accordingly – focusing resources and measurement on the areas of greatest need. See Chapter 4 for information on stakeholder analysis, and Chapter 7 for strategies to build appropriate levels of adoption.

FIGURE 11.9 Level of adoption required for different types of change

Level	Need	Length of Commitment	Level of Initiative Required	Reinforced by	Level of Commitment Required
1. Compliance	'I need to be able to tell them what to do and they'll do it'	Short term	Low	Rewards and penalties	Accept
2. Identification	'I need them to understand why they need to do this and the consequences of not changing'	Medium term	Medium	A sense of meaning	Willing
3. Internalization	'I need them to be able to make decisions about what, why, when and how things are done'	Long term	High	Alignment to values	Committed

How is it applied?

During the planning phase it is important to create a common understanding of, and commitment to, the level of adoption that is required for the change. This information also forms the basis for measurement after implementation.

CASE STUDY

Captain Engineering – levels of adoption

During the planning stage Carmel thought through what levels of adoption the change would need in order to create and sustain the momentum it needed. This enabled her to focus her time and energy on the most critical areas and, when the new way of working was implemented, this would form the basis of her measurement (Figure 11.10).

FIGURE 11.10 Required levels of adoption

	Before the change	During the transition	Adopting the change
Senior Leaders	Internalization	Internalization	Internalization
Leaders	Identification	Internalization	Internalization
Team members	Compliance	Identification	Internalization

Tip

Laggards... In the latter stages of most changes there will still be laggards, to use Everett Rogers's (2003) terminology – people who cannot or will not adopt the change. Whilst it is sometimes possible to deliver the planned benefits in spite of this, the organization must identify and manage the cumulative effect of this behaviour on the organization's agility. Sometimes if you can't *change* the people you need to change the *people*!

5. Tipping point and critical mass

What is it?

Malcolm Gladwell talks about the tipping point as being 'the moment of critical mass, the threshold, the boiling point'. During planning and transition the change manager feels the full force of resistance in all its forms. When the groundwork for change adoption has been done, however, there comes a point – a week, a month or a year after implementation when it starts to feel easier, the change has a momentum of its own and no longer needs specific attention to make it stick – that it is just happening all on its own! Figure 11.11 provides a simplified illustration of the typical relationship between effort and adoption and the point at which the tipping point occurs.

Chris Meyer (2010) talks about how the concept of critical mass relies on the assumption that behaviour is contagious (good and bad) and gives the definition

FIGURE 11.11 Relationship between effort and adoption

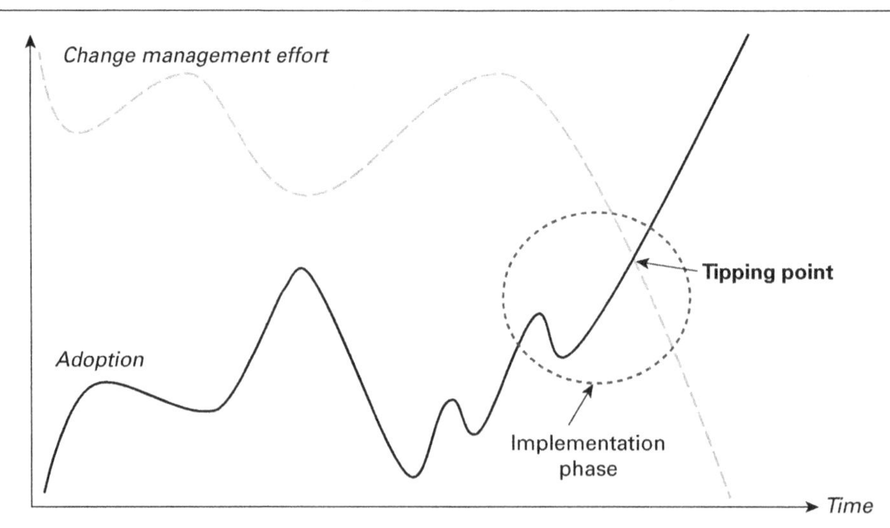

of critical mass as 'when the people and systems operating in the new way achieve unstoppable momentum'. He also points out that this is the point at which we can safely accelerate the elimination of the old way.

Why is it useful to a change manager?

Change managers agree the criteria to be used to describe the tipping point of the change, and the point at which it will reach critical mass using objective and subjective targets and measures to track whether the change is on track to deliver the benefits sustainably.

How is it applied?

In the latter stages of development the change manager is building up to a point where the change needs to progress under its own steam, and the right conditions need to be in place as soon as possible after implementation for this to happen. This may mean targeting new stakeholders or changing the targets and approach to existing ones. For example, early in the development phase one of the line managers impacted may just need to 'help it happen', but in order to sustain the change they need to move to 'make it happen' at implementation.

CASE STUDY

Captain Engineering – tipping point and critical mass

Carmel had a meeting planned with Sue, the programme sponsor, and one of the things she was keen to discuss was her understanding of what critical mass would be required to sustainably deliver the changes they needed. She also wanted to find out what Sue would be looking for to indicate that they were reaching a tipping point. In preparation for the meeting she jotted down some ideas about what she thought people would be doing and saying differently when the change was successful (Figure 11.12).

FIGURE 11.12 Captain Engineering – tipping point and critical mass

- ✓ *Tipping point 70% ???*
- ✓ *Signs of critical mass*
  - ✓ *Customer orders are 99.5% accurate and on time (benefit from business case)*
  - ✓ *People are communicating through a variety of channels directly with the people they need*
  - ✓ *It is unusual to have to channel a communication via your manager to another team*
  - ✓ *Managers are actively encouraging their team members to 'go direct' 'pick up the phone' 'go over and see them'*

6. Reinforcing systems

Having introduced the idea of an 'unstoppable momentum' through the concepts of levers, leverage, tipping point and critical mass, how do you make sure that the momentum stays on the right tracks? Knowing when and how to intervene is a critical skill of the change manager. Here we come back to our systems thinking again, but this time instead of using it to analyse effects we use it to create the effects that we need to reinforce the change.

6.1 Vicious and virtuous cycles

What is it?

Vicious and virtuous cycles are self-driving mechanisms that have feedback loops where each iteration of the cycle reinforces the first – keeping it vicious or keeping it virtuous. The momentum within these cycles is such that they will keep going until there is some sort of interruption from outside the cycle. A vicious cycle that affects most of us happens when we don't exercise. We put on weight; now we've put on weight we don't look good in our gym gear; now we don't look good in our gym gear we don't like going to the gym; now we don't like going to the gym... you get the idea. It is an ever-increasing cycle of negative reinforcement. This cycle breaks when we cannot get into our outfit for a friend's wedding and we are once again motivated to exercise. Systems thinking is behind the identification and setting up of the right cycles.

The typical change vicious cycle (Figure 11.13) shows how an influential group of people reacting negatively to initial teething problems can send the change spiralling off the rails. As they complain, it leads others to doubt the change and their need to engage with it. When they don't engage with it, it starts to unstick. As it unsticks it reinforces their perception that there is something wrong with the change.

On a more positive note, Figure 11.14 shows an example of a virtuous cycle that kicked off when a computer company brought out a new laptop. It was quite different to their other models and the sales team was not confident about explaining it to the customers in the early days after its launch. This virtuous cycle shows how the situation gained momentum and, through several reinforcing steps, delivered a good outcome for everyone. In this case it would only take the return of one or two faulty laptops to interrupt, and potentially reverse, that cycle.

Why is it useful to a change manager?

Once again this relates to the concept of leverage – getting the greatest effect from the least effort. The change manager wants to 'light the blue touch paper', retire and have every aspect of the change self-drive and self-regulate the embedding process.

How is it applied?

Change managers work hard to prevent, spot and intervene with vicious cycles and to create virtuous ones. They think through the ripple effects of alternative strategies

FIGURE 11.13 Typical change 'vicious cycle'

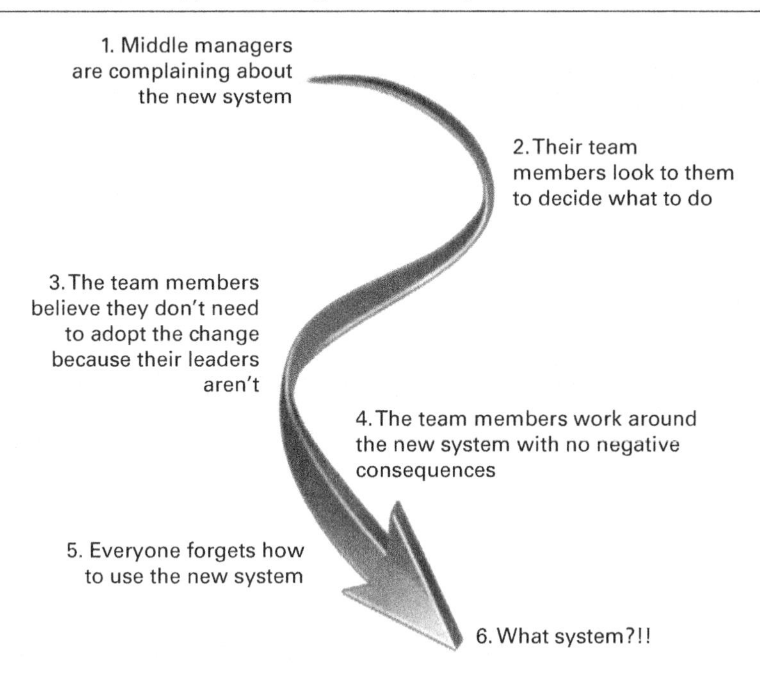
1. Middle managers are complaining about the new system
2. Their team members look to them to decide what to do
3. The team members believe they don't need to adopt the change because their leaders aren't
4. The team members work around the new system with no negative consequences
5. Everyone forgets how to use the new system
6. What system?!!

FIGURE 11.14 Typical change 'virtuous cycle'

1. The sales teams were nervous about selling the new laptop
2. A few customers bought one
3. Customers liked it
4. Customers told their friends
5. Their friends bought the new laptop
6. The sales teams sold more laptops
7. The sales teams became more competent and confident selling the new laptops
8. The organization increased its market share

to find the two or three interventions that will start the ball rolling. Once the momentum takes hold they are on the lookout for external elements that will interrupt it.

Senge and Goodman (1999) suggest targeting three reinforcing systems simultaneously to create a sustainable impetus for change:

R1 – individual personal results: 'I'll change because it matters to me.' Interventions make clear the 'What's in it for me' (or WIIFM) for each stakeholder group.

R2 – networks of committed people: 'I'll change because it matters to my colleagues.' An individual's need to fit in with the tribe can be triggered if we can build a belief that the change matters to their colleagues.

R3 – improved business results: 'I'll change because it works.' Ultimately people want to see that the change has achieved something worthwhile, so the change manager shows how it is having a direct positive effect on the success of the organization. The change manager considers which types of reinforcement strategies will work best for the particular change and nature of stakeholder.

CASE STUDY

Captain Engineering – vicious and virtuous cycles

In her planning Carmel had put together some ideas for creating virtuous cycles. Working back from her desired outcome of delivering customer orders quickly and accurately she identified a series of events that would naturally flow to the outcome being achieved. One such virtuous cycle that she plans to use is outlined in Figure 11.15.

She also jotted down some ideas about the key messages that would need to be in her communications plan for each stakeholder group, checking that she had included the full range of R1, R2 and R3 messages.

7. Measuring change adoption

What is it?

It is not enough to follow your intuition or have a hunch about what is working and what is not.

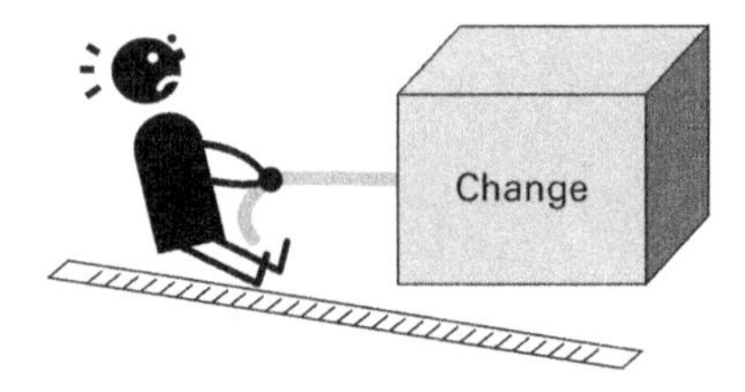

FIGURE 11.15 Captain Engineering – virtuous cycle

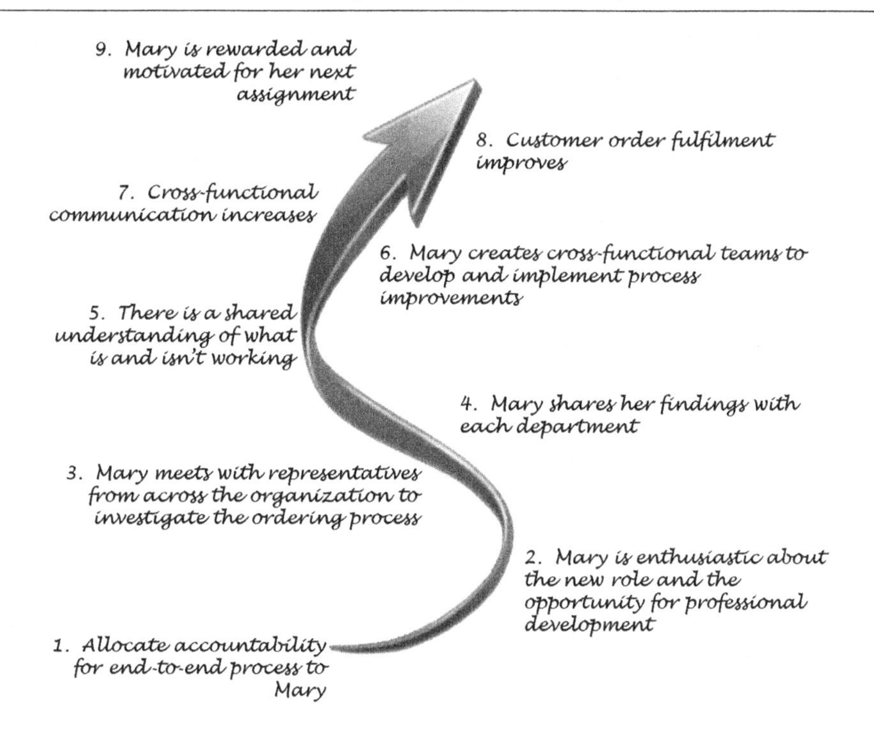
9. Mary is rewarded and motivated for her next assignment
8. Customer order fulfilment improves
7. Cross-functional communication increases
6. Mary creates cross-functional teams to develop and implement process improvements
5. There is a shared understanding of what is and isn't working
4. Mary shares her findings with each department
3. Mary meets with representatives from across the organization to investigate the ordering process
2. Mary is enthusiastic about the new role and the opportunity for professional development
1. Allocate accountability for end-to-end process to Mary

Stakeholders want to see data that backs up the change management strategy and reassures them that time, energy and money are being well spent. Chapter 7 provided some useful information about monitoring and measuring change. There may be a different set of measures for adoption, embedding and sustaining the change, but they should always meet the following criteria.

- no more than three;
- each have a clear link to the desired outcome;
- have no or minimal negative influence on behaviours;
- data is relatively easy to collect;
- uses an established and effective reporting mechanism and forum.

Why is it useful to a change manager?

Having accurate and reliable data to show whether the change is sticking to the extent required to deliver benefits is a key leading indicator for business leaders. They enable the change manager to flag risks and give clear, timely recommendations.

Lapse or relapse?

Relapse is normal, so the change manager expects people to relapse and plans for it. Anyone who has tried to give up smoking or improve their diet can tell you that. The research tells us that to relapse 6–7 times is normal in personal change, and the factors that affect each individual's success vary enormously. So if relapse is normal let's see it as a temporary lapse not a 'relapse' – as this conveys more of a sense of a temporary blockage with an assumption that the journey will continue.

How is it applied?

Working back from the desired benefits (as well as possible dis-benefits mentioned in Chapter 3) change managers identify the indicators they will look for, who will collect the data, how they will analyse and report on it and who will have accountability for acting on the results. This requires systems thinking skills to assess the implications of different options, thinking through the positive and negative ripple effects that can result from measurement, and reporting and tailoring the approach to suit.

CASE STUDY

Captain Engineering – change adoption measures

Carmel knew she would need some data to back up her views if she was going to galvanize the senior leaders into action. She looked at the work she had done so far, particularly on the levels of adoption, critical mass and tipping point. She also went back to the benefits realization plan and used the change and business outcomes as benchmarks for measurement. Next she decided what evidence she would look for to indicate whether the change was sticking. Some of it would be objective data and some would inevitably be based on subjective judgements. She knew that monitoring what people were doing could cause a range of unhelpful behaviours if they felt like they were being 'checked up on', so she tested her ideas on some of the impacted team members and adjusted her approach based on their feedback. She wanted to make sure the measurement and reporting was done in a way that would encourage them to ask questions, provide feedback and raise concerns.

8. Transition management

What is it?

Transition management is arguably the point at which the change is in most jeopardy. It is the high-risk phase during which the change is implemented and it becomes a reality for those impacted. The change manager adapts their approach from one of careful preparation to active vigilance. William Bridges' (2009) transition model outlined in Chapter 1, Section B2 suggests the way in which we need to regard the period of transitioning to a new way of working with endings, a neutral zone and a new beginning.

Tip

Beware stereotypes here, as someone who is an early adopter for one change may be a laggard for another.

Why is it useful to a change manager?

By thinking about transition as a separate phase, and using the knowledge about how people transition, change managers develop strategies and measures dedicated to this delicate and high-risk process.

How is it applied?

During transition the change manager's plan allows for everyone to be at a different stage in their personal transition as well as in the change as a whole. They balance these two elements to create the momentum required to sustain the change long after implementation.

The transition model offers strategies to support people at each phase of the transition. To enable endings, a company that is moving to a new building might have a 'farewell to the building' party where people can reminisce. Alternatively, if a change requires a significant change of skills there may be an opportunity to reflect on the success that the previous skillset has brought to the company. The risk with people in this zone is that often their managers and colleagues, who may already have moved on, try to 'jolly' them out of it, ignore their concerns or move them on before they are ready. Unless they move out of the ending zone under their own steam they will always have a foot in this camp and will not be able to truly embrace the new beginning.

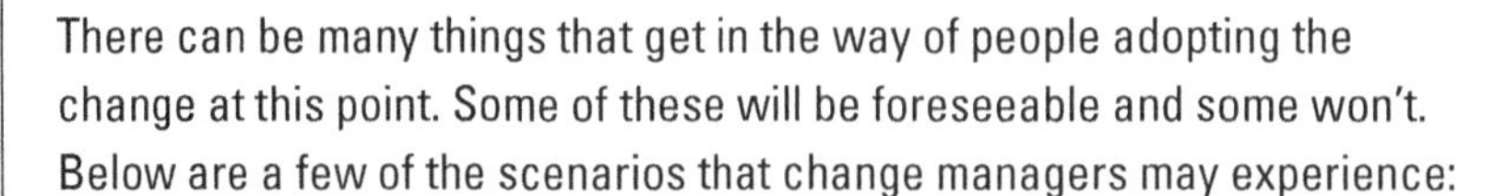

Barriers to adoption

There can be many things that get in the way of people adopting the change at this point. Some of these will be foreseeable and some won't. Below are a few of the scenarios that change managers may experience:

- Our people are 'change fatigued'. Whether they have had too much change or too much bad change they just don't have the energy to focus on this one.
- The recipients are not ready. They thought they were but now the time has arrived they need more support, more training and more time.
- 'You never told me...'. As people struggle to adapt to the new ways they become more fearful and engage in disruptive behaviours aimed at distracting attention away from themselves and, if possible, delaying or derailing the change.
- No one is watching. There do not appear to be any positive or negative consequences for changing the way they do things.
- There is a problem with the measurement. Perhaps we are measuring the wrong thing or measuring in a way that leads recipients to cover up rather than raise problems.
- No one cares. Our measures indicate that some remedial action is required if the benefits are to be realized but no one wants to make it happen. Which leads us on nicely to...
- There is no money or resources. Budgets often cut off shortly after implementation, which means that when the inevitable remediation work is required there is no one to do it and no money left in the budget.
- Humans will be humans! Despite the best efforts of the change manager, human behaviour can be an unstoppable force. If it is working against adoption of the change it can seem like an unwinnable war.
- We expect to return to 'business as usual' after the change. If business is 'as usual' after the change then surely the change has failed!

Adapted from *Managing Organizational Change*, Helen Campbell (2014)

For the people in the neutral zone the change manager's aim is to maintain a sense of momentum and provide a specific path to the future. For example, Jeremy from the sales team has finally accepted that the new ordering system is going to happen next week and is now ready to learn what he needs to do to make it happen. The change manager makes sure he is swept up in the momentum of the implementation by sending him regular progress updates along with the specific information he will need to be successful. They make sure that his focus is kept firmly on the 'here and now' and how this links to future success.

The new beginning is obviously the goal for any transition, and the change manager activates as many levers as they can to move people into this zone quickly and prevent them from slipping back when the change hits its inevitable snags.

Tip

In reality people will move repeatedly between the zones of Bridges' transition model (endings, the neutral zone and new beginnings) throughout the implementation and it is precisely this movement that can undermine the realization of your benefits in the weeks and months following implementation.

Everett Rogers's diffusion of innovations (Chapter 7, Section A4.3) also plays an important part when looking for ways to build and sustain the critical mass. The change manager maintains the momentum created prior to and during the implementation of the change by engaging the different audiences in a way that supports and leads them to adopt the change as quickly as possible. Typically this will involve engagement of the early and late majority segments.

Summary

There are a wide variety of useful concepts to help change managers plan for and monitor the sustainability of the change. Change managers know which ones to use when – and keep an eye on their effectiveness so they can take advantage of new opportunities or change course when required.

Questions to think about

1. How well do our changes 'fit' their environment at implementation?
2. What level of adoption do we need in order to realize our planned benefits?
3. Which levers (carrots, sticks, burning bridges, environmental, organization development and leadership) will provide the greatest leverage for our change?
4. How can we trigger a virtuous cycle for our change?
5. What measurements will support the right behaviour and provide an accurate assessment of whether the change has been adopted?

Section B: Useful checklists and tools

1. Planning to sustain change

The challenge of sustaining change begins during the planning phase, where as soon as change managers come on board, they typically:

- ✓ Ensure that sufficient and appropriate budget and other resources will be available for the period from implementation until the change or business outcome is sustainably delivered.
- ✓ Ensure the solution design actively considers the ease of adoption and is adapted accordingly.
- ✓ Engages with and involves the HR, OD, L&D and Communications departments.
- ✓ Plans the criteria and targets that will indicate the change is sticking (for example: change outcomes, business outcomes, adoption levels, critical mass and tipping point).
- ✓ Plans the measures, how data will be collected, reported and actioned.
- ✓ Analyses the potential positive and negative ripple effects of the change and the proposed change management activities – and adapts approach accordingly.
- ✓ Plans the levers and reinforcing systems that will be applied at each stage of the change.

✓ Lays the groundwork to ensure that everyone is ready to activate the levers and work towards the targets at the right time.

✓ Monitors changes to the desired change outcomes, business outcomes and benefits, and updates plans and measurement systems accordingly.

✓ Plans the most effective transition approach.

✓ Actively monitors the plan to ensure that strategies will still have the intended effect.

Whilst the change does not need to reach its tipping point into critical mass until after implementation, change managers constantly work to create the conditions needed for this to occur. Key questions during the planning phase are:

- What conditions will be in place to tell us we have reached a sustainable tipping point for our change? (To the extent required to deliver the required benefits.)
- What are the lead indicators that we are on track?
- Who are the stakeholders who will be most influential in creating this state? What is in it for them? What information, skills and support do they need to equip them?
- What barriers might there be to creating critical mass quickly? How will we mitigate these?
- What barriers might there be to gaining a sustainable tipping point? How will we mitigate these?
- What or who can we leverage to help us reach a sustainable tipping point and therefore critical mass quickly?
- What do I need to do differently to increase our chances of success?

2. Managing the transition

By the time the change is ready to be implemented some or all of the prerequisites for sustaining it are in place, including:

✓ An up-to-date business case for change, outlining a full range of benefits that must be delivered (quantitative and qualitative, direct and indirect).

✓ Project governance processes and discussions that cover risks related to the adoption and sustainability of the change.

✓ The design of the solution has taken into account the ease of adoption and integration.

✓ Benefits have been continually and visibly monitored, reported and realigned in response to new information.

✓ Evidence of strong recipient ownership of and accountability for the change at implementation.

✓ Resources and governance are available for a period *after* implementation until benefits are realized.

By now the solution is ready to roll out with the people, and the environment carefully prepared so that the change will transition smoothly into operation. But the transition needs a period of intense and specific attention to enable this smooth transition to become a reality. This period requires a fresh perspective and will highlight issues and opportunities that have been missed along the way. Change managers stay vigilant to these and continue to adapt their approach to deliver the outcomes.

During this phase the change manager typically:

- ✓ Implements strategies to help people let go of the old ways, move quickly and confidently through the neutral zone to consolidate and celebrate the new beginning.
- ✓ Monitors the effectiveness of adoption levers.
- ✓ Maintains a forward-looking focus with patience and persistence.
- ✓ Monitors the transition phase of the change recipients at an individual, team and organization level.
- ✓ Looks out for potential slippages and obstacles that may derail the change, and acts quickly to report and remediate them.
- ✓ Represents the views of the change leaders and change recipients when highlighting and discussing teething problems.
- ✓ Measures and reports progress and risks.
- ✓ Alters their approach in the light of new information.

Tip

No matter how well prepared you thought you were there will be surprises – be ready to find them and respond accordingly!

During the transition phase change managers ask:

- Is the situation what we expected?
- Are the planned activities still the right ones?
- Are they having the planned effect?
- Are they having the effect we need? What will get in the way of that effect lasting?
- How quickly and in what direction are people moving through the transition?
- How might it come unstuck?
- Who might be likely to unstick it?
- What do I need to do differently to increase our chances of success?

3. Adopting and embedding change – making it stick and keeping it stuck

Doing everything possible to enable a smooth transition thus far, the success of any change is at its highest risk of failure at the point of adoption. This is because it is new and fragile, full of uncertainties and unknowns; in limbo between the people who built it and the people who will own it – and this phase is full of surprises.

During this phase the change manager typically:

- ✓ Remains vigilant to what is happening over a broad landscape – people and things, short and long term.
- ✓ Uses systems thinking to pre-empt ripple effects of unexpected events on adoption and integration.
- ✓ Differentiates between solution problems, temporary transition tensions and real obstacles.
- ✓ Is on the lookout for any planning assumptions that are no longer valid and strategies that are not having the desired effect.
- ✓ Adapts their approach when required.
- ✓ Monitors delivery of the desired change and business outcomes and benefits.
- ✓ Measures the levels of adoption and integration, reports openly and fixes things that are getting in the way of adoption and integration.
- ✓ Kicks off and monitors reinforcing systems.
- ✓ Reports the most significant risks to the fragile new change and therefore benefits realization.

During the adoption phase change managers ask themselves:

- Does it look like the change is sticking and benefits will be realized?
- Are the leaders talking and acting in a way that will help the change stick?
- Are people doing, thinking and being what the change needs?
- What effect is the measurement and reporting having on our ability to openly discuss teething troubles and ideas for improvement?
- Are the activities I have planned still the right ones?
- Are they having the effect I had planned?
- Are they having the effect we need? What will get in the way of that effect lasting?
- How might it come unstuck?
- Who might be likely to unstick it?
- Where is the critical mass? Have we reached out tipping point yet?
- How are we going towards our stated change and business outcomes?
- What risks to sustainability will still exist after I'm gone – and who will have accountability for these?

Tip

Workarounds are your friend – they are the path of least resistance and should be shared, or they are a human behaviour loophole and need to be closed off! Either way, the recipients must feel confident raising them.

4. Change management tool – sustaining change

Towards the end of the transition and adoption periods there can be overconfidence in what has been achieved (or exhaustion after all the hard work) and attention turns to the next business priority long before benefits are realized. By this time the change manager has already laid the groundwork to ensure that reporting on the success of the adoption and integration of the change is expected, valued and actively discussed. At an appropriate point in the transition (usually after the excitement of implementation and before everyone turns their attention to other priorities) the change manager reports the top three risks or issues that will prevent the change sticking or staying stuck, and therefore prevent return on investment and benefits realization. See Chapter 6 for more information about risk management. Table 11.1 shows a typical sustainability risk assessment that is adapted from the standard risk log.

Summary

Activities required to sustain change start right at the beginning of a change – when it is just an idea. They usually continue long past implementation until benefits are delivered, realigned or abandoned. Change managers play a critical role in enabling a change to be sustained, by applying the concepts of fit, systems thinking, leverage, tipping point, critical mass and reinforcing systems. They work closely with colleagues in the impacted teams, HR, OD and risk teams to develop and implement powerful strategies to make the change stick and keep it stuck.

TABLE 11.1 Sustainability risk assessment

Risk Factor (people, process, system)	The changes may not stick and the benefits may not be delivered if...	Probability at handover (H/M/L)	Probability 3–6 months after implementation (H/M/L)	Corrective action required	Impact on benefits and ROI (H/M/L)	Business-as-usual owner

Questions to think about

1. At every significant phase of the solutions development do we ask ourselves what changes we could make to enable this to be easier for people to adopt, embed and sustain?
2. Do our conversations, reporting and governance have sustaining change as a priority in the run-up to and monitoring of implementation?
3. Is there a culture of accountability in our organization that supports strong business ownership of the work required after implementation?
4. Does our organization provide funding, focus and resources until we have realized the benefits we need?

Further reading

For more on the magic of systems thinking – Senge, P M (1993) *The Fifth Discipline: The art and practice of the learning organization*, Century, London

For more on the business activities required to sustain change and complement the change manager's efforts – Campbell, H (2014) *Managing Organizational Change: A practical toolkit for leaders*, Kogan Page, London

For more about the power of communication in driving successful adoption – Larkin T J & Larkin S (2006) *Communicating Big Change*, Larkin Communication Consulting, 3rd edn

For more on leadership and cultural levers – Schein, E (2010) *Organizational Culture and Leadership*, 4th edn, Jossey-Bass, San Francisco, CA

Bernstein, D A (2011) *Essentials of Psychology*, Wadsworth, Belmont, CA

Cohen, D S (2005) *The Heart of Change Field Guide: Tools and tactics for leading change in your organization*, Harvard Business School Press, Boston

Haight, J (2006) *The Happiness Hypothesis: Finding modern truth in ancient wisdom*, cited in In praise of followers, R Kelley, *Harvard Business Review*, November (1988)

King, J E (2000) White-collar reactions to job insecurity and the role of the psychological contract: implications for human resource management, *Human Resource Management*, 39, pp 79–92

Kotter, J P (1996) *Leading Change*, Harvard Business School Press, Boston

Lawson, E and Price, C (2003) (accessed February 2014) The psychology of change management, *McKinsey Quarterly*, June [Online] http://www.mckinsey.com/insights/organization/the_psychology_of_change_management
Prochaska, J O and DiClemente, C C (1994) *The Transtheoretical Approach: Crossing the traditional boundaries of therapy*, Dow-Jones/Irwin, Homewood, IL
Towers Watson (2012) [accessed February 2014] Clear Direction in a Complex World: Change and Communication ROI Study Report [Online] http://www.towerswatson.com/en-GB/Insights/IC-Types/Survey-Research-Results/2012/03/Clear-direction-in-a-complex-world-2011-2012-change-and-communication-ROI-study-report

References

Bridges, W (2009) *Managing Transitions: Making the most of change*, 3rd edn, Nicholas Brealey, London
Campbell, H (2014) *Managing Organizational Change: A practical toolkit for leaders*, Kogan Page, London
Carloppio, J (2010) Change Management Institute Conference Presentation, Sydney, Australia
Kelman, H (1958) Compliance, identification and internalization: three processes of attitude change, *The Journal of Conflict Resolution*, **2** (1), pp 51–60
Larkin, T J and Larkin, S (2006) *Communicating Big Change*, 3rd edn, Larkin Communication Consulting
Lewin, K (1936) *Principles of Topological Psychology* (republished by Munshi Press in 2007)
Lewin, K (1947) Frontiers in group dynamics: concept, method and reality in social science; social equilibria and social change, *Human Relations*, **1** (1), June, pp 5–41
Meyer, C (2010) The Frontier of Change: Five Strategies to Accelerate Change to Critical Mass [pdf]
Rogers, E M (2003) *Diffusion of Innovations*, 5th edn, Free Press, New York
Senge, P M (1990) *The Fifth Discipline*, Doubleday/Currency, New York
Senge, P and Goodman, M (1999) 'Generating Profound Change', in *The Dance of Change: The challenges to sustaining momentum in learning organizations*, Nicholas Brealey, London
Schein, E (2010) *Organizational Culture and Leadership*, 4th edn, Jossey-Bass, San Francisco, CA

Personal and professional management

12

RAY WICKS

Introduction

A change management role can be extremely demanding. It requires high levels of personal commitment and resilience to remain motivated and perform well consistently through the change initiative. Having the skills to deal with personal emotions and actions, while managing the emotional fallout and challenges of organizational change, requires deep inner resources and self-discipline. Developing skills in areas such as personal leadership and emotional intelligence equips change managers with the resources required to manage themselves more effectively and, importantly, to lead others by example.

Change managers are instrumental in developing high-performing change teams, who have a shared sense of purpose and the motivation needed to deliver successful change. The development of strong interpersonal communication, effective influencing, negotiation and conflict management skills, mean they have a wide range of personal approaches and strategies for dealing with diverse groups of people at all levels of the organization. These skills give them the flexibility and confidence to deal with the tough challenges that arise during any change initiative.

While it is important for change managers to understand the processes of change, this chapter explores the similarly important personal qualities that a change manager brings in delivering successful outcomes. It examines the critical aspect of a change manager's role of engaging with people to exchange information, gain their support, facilitate collaboration and help resolve any tensions that change may create. Using the theories and models of leadership and teamwork provides perspectives on how today's change manager may need to vary style and strategy to deliver the outcomes required.

Tip

Use the chapter to create a checklist of areas to reflect on 'How am I doing?' at regular intervals during the change and to ensure that issues are not overlooked.

CHAPTER CONTENTS

Section A: Leadership principles

Introduction

Change managers provide leadership throughout the change initiative, both for those over whom they have line authority and for those over whom they have no such authority. The ability to build relationships, engage with people and influence them to gain their support for a shared purpose is what helps to drive change initiatives forward. Effectiveness in this role comes from being self-aware and continuing to build appropriate skills.

Understanding personal strengths and weaknesses allied to understanding how and when to use appropriate leadership styles and approaches are important components in delivering successful outcomes.

1. Personal effectiveness

For people who hold influential roles in change, personal effectiveness is both a goal and a responsibility if success is to be achieved. Change managers set an example to others by taking responsibility for being as effective as possible for the delivery of their part of the outcome.

People look to leaders and managers of change to be role models, demonstrating the actions and behaviours for others to follow ('walking the talk'). While change managers will apply their own approach (Section A3), the flexibility needed to meet the demands of change requires personal motivation to acquire the necessary skills and knowledge. The focus in this section will be:

- Knowing *what* to do during change and being able to use the *tools* that will assist. This means using the experience of others and the understanding and research from practitioners who suggest strategies and models that can be used during change. The ability to interpret the knowledge so that it can be applied to the local context is a vital component of understanding.
- Applying appropriate *skills* flexibly during the change. This is the range of skills needed to engage people in their individual and collective roles in delivering change. This also includes the interpersonal skills necessary to overcome blockages, such as influencing, negotiating and overcoming conflict.
- Leaving a positive *legacy* for future change. When the change has been completed, has the learning been captured so that the organization and individuals have an improved understanding and capability to deal with future change?

2. Self-awareness: putting yourself in the picture

It is a useful skill of change managers to be able to see 'themselves' as others see them and to be sensitive to how individuals and teams respond. Individuals and teams respond more readily to change managers who understand themselves and are able to regulate their behaviours and emotions when faced with challenges and setbacks.

> *'He who knows others is wise; he who knows himself is enlightened.'*
>
> Lao-tzu (604 BC–531 BC)

Self-awareness is being conscious of what a person is good at while acknowledging what there still is to learn. On an interpersonal level, self-awareness of strengths and weaknesses can bring the trust of others and increase credibility – both of which will increase effectiveness. At an organizational level this translates to modelling a culture that values learning and development (L&D) as a key attribute for organizations undergoing change.

Self-awareness also includes values and beliefs. They are the source of the attitudes and behaviours that guide what a change manager does, and the energy and focus that are invested. This awareness embraces how a person reacts in normal circumstances and, importantly, also when under pressure – as will undoubtedly be the situation at times during organization life or when managing change (Section C – emotional intelligence).

2.1 *Becoming more self-aware*

Feedback from tests and inventories

Having a framework for self-awareness helps to identify strengths and development areas. Personality tests such as Myers-Briggs (MBTI® – Chapter 1, Section B4.1) and Emotional Intelligence inventories all help to add to the understanding. Often the tests are self-assessments, so what can be particularly useful are 360-degree instruments that allow bosses, colleagues and team members to provide feedback.

Learning from reflection

Peter Drucker in 'Managing Oneself' wrote: 'Whenever you make a decision or take a key decision, write down what you expect will happen. Nine or twelve months later compare the results with what you expected.' Drucker called this self-reflection process 'feedback analysis' and said it was the 'only way to discover your strengths'.

Exploring values and beliefs

Stephen Covey in his book *The 7 Habits of Highly Effective People* believes that before we can really understand the seven habits that make a person more effective they have to work from the 'inside-out' to understand their 'paradigms' and how to make a 'paradigm shift'. The more aware we are of our basic paradigms, maps or assumptions, and the extent to which we have been influenced by our experience, the more we can take responsibility for them. We can examine them, test them against reality, listen to others and be open to their perceptions, thereby getting a larger and more objective view. The way we see the problem *is* the problem.

Self-awareness is an active and ongoing process. As the context changes and the challenges of change management become more complex so a change manager will be exposed to an increasing range of demands on their capabilities. Regular reflection and feedback will help maintain currency and provide data that builds confidence or provides an agenda for further development. Self-development workshops, shadowing change practitioners, research, networking events and so on will all help to expand understanding and skills.

3. Leadership and authenticity

There have been many studies attempting to determine the definitive styles, characteristics or personality traits of effective leaders. No study has produced a clear profile of the ideal leader. What has been identified is that while a change manager with leadership responsibilities can learn from other leaders' experiences, trying to be like them is unlikely to bring guaranteed success. Rather, people trust leaders who are genuine and authentic not a replica of someone else.

In 2003 Bill George published *Authentic Leadership: Rediscovering the secrets to creating lasting value*. He stated that 'authentic leaders demonstrate a passion for their purpose, practice their values consistently and lead with their hearts as well as their heads. They establish long-term meaningful relationships and have self-discipline to get results. They know who they are.' An authentic style is therefore highly individual, emerging from a person's life stories of experiences, whether these are positive or negative.

Whether responsibility for change is as a sponsor, change manager or project manager, leadership is likely to feature. While there can be a tendency to focus on inspirational qualities, Goffee and Jones (2000) provided research showing that in addition to a range of characteristics of inspirational leaders there were four unexpected qualities required to win the hearts and minds of followers:

- *Reveal your weaknesses*: this means being authentic, including not hiding or denying any weaknesses (although not weaknesses seen as vital). For a change manager this 'honesty' of approach will help to build trust and collaboration with stakeholders and enhance their approachability.
- *Become a sensor*: this requires developing an ability to collect and interpret subtle interpersonal cues, detecting what is going on without others spelling it out. This 'intuition' helps to gauge the responses necessary to connect with others. There will be many individuals and teams to connect with during the stages of change, each with their own agenda and challenges. Many change initiatives have high-level sponsorship, and local leaders and managers will make supportive statements. In practice, levels of support may vary and a change manager who understands the challenges and can sense a need to look beyond the words of support to deal with the reality is likely to achieve a more positive response.
- *Practice tough empathy*: effective leaders empathize fiercely with their people and care intensely about their people's work. They are also realistic and understand when to be empathetically 'tough'. This means giving people not necessarily what they *want*, but what they *need* to achieve their best. Change managers will often be responsible for delivering solutions that have longer-term benefits but that create short-term 'pain'. While understanding and empathy is important to show an awareness of the issues, it is vital that decisions and actions reflect what is needed for a successful outcome to be achieved.
- *Dare to be different*: this means capitalizing on unique qualities that a leader may have such as imagination, creativity, innovation etc in order to inspire and motivate others. Care needs to be taken that these are applied in a way that is not perceived to be arrogant. Change leaders and managers cannot deliver change alone. They need followers. It can be inspirational and developmental to work with managers who look at challenges in a different way in order to generate ideas and a range of solutions. The refreshing characteristic of doing things differently and achieving a positive outcome can be energizing when faced with the challenges of change.

The learning for change leaders is that the qualities that leaders have that make them successful is that they inspire people by appealing to their hearts and minds. A change manager would therefore benefit from developing a personal (and authentic) style that works for them, including, where appropriate, acknowledging the qualities listed above rather than attempting to copy superstar qualities attributed to a few high-profile leaders.

4. Leadership approaches

Delivering change outcomes will be influenced by the way that managers motivate, gather and use information, make decisions and handle the obstacles and challenges that come their way. The 'style' of leadership used to create the climate for change is a factor that will influence how followers respond and, hence, eventual success. The following are some views as to what effective leadership comprises.

4.1 Visionary leadership

Warren Bennis (1994): 'The first basic ingredient of leadership is a *guiding vision*. The leader has a clear idea of what they need to do – professionally and personally – and the strength to persist in the face of setbacks and failures. Unless you know where you are going, and why, you cannot possibly get there.' The change vision will typically come from the sponsors of change, with the change manager translating the vision while engaging others with components of effective 'management' that align people to the challenges of change.

4.2 Transformational leadership

Bryman's (1992) transformational leadership involves the leader raising the follower's *sense of purpose and levels of motivation*. In this style of leadership the aim is to create a common sense of purpose between the leader and followers, whereby the leader raises the follower's confidence and expectations of themselves. Transformational leadership comprises:

- charisma;
- inspiration;
- intellectual stimulation;
- individualized consideration.

Bryman distinguishes between '*transformational*' and '*transactional*' leadership, where the followers meet expectations on a task-by-task basis.

CASE STUDY

The CEO of a European food manufacturing and distribution organization gave an inspirational speech at a conference that provided a clear context for the changes that were needed, a motivating vision for the future and confidence in an ability to deliver. The whole management team in attendance were energized by what the CEO had said and left the conference determined to play a positive part in the initiative.

Six months later, progress was considered 'disappointing', staff engagement was low and business as usual was back as the priority. More was needed to engage people at all levels in order to deliver sustainable change.

The turning point came when the change team worked with local managers to help them communicate and translate organizational strategy into meaningful and actionable steps for the workforce – real progress was made.

The learning for the organization was that while inspirational speeches are important to initiate change, and at various points during the change, they must be quickly supplemented by 'management' tasks of translating vision into practical realities at a local level.

4.3 Adaptive leadership

Heifetz and Laurie (1997) suggest that adaptive leadership is what is required of 21st-century organizations. Adaptive leadership is about 'taking people out of their comfort zones and letting them feel the pressure and conflict' that comes from change. Leaders set the challenges that the organization needs to address and empower the people to adapt and resolve. This thinking contrasts with the call for vision and inspiration as in other theories, which Heifetz and Laurie consider is counterproductive as it encourages dependency from employees.

4.4 Connective leadership

Jean Lipman-Blumen (2002) points to the context of leadership as being increasingly global and distributed. In these environments the key to the ways of thinking and working is to confront and deal constructively with both *interdependence* (overlapping visions, common problems) and diversity (distinctive character of individuals, groups and organizations). It is important for sponsors of change and change managers to reach out and encourage *collaboration* among stakeholders, even where relationships have not been positive in the past. Leaders also need to help others make good *connections* and to develop *a common purpose across boundaries* thus building commitment across a distributed organization. Six important strengths have been identified for connective leaders:

- ethical political know-how;
- authenticity and accountability;
- a politics of commonality;
- thinking long-term, acting short-term;
- leadership through expectation (setting high expectations, trusting people and avoiding micro-managing);
- a quest for meaning.

4.5 *Emotionally intelligent leadership*

Daniel Goleman (1998, 2000) states that the 'best' leaders as defined in his research base their success on emotional intelligence competencies. He uses six basic styles of leadership and says that the best leaders are skilled at several and have the *ability to switch between styles* as the circumstances dictate. These styles are shown in Table 12.1.

TABLE 12.1 Leadership styles

Coercive	This 'do what I say' approach can be very effective in challenging situations or where working with difficult employees. But in most situations, coercive leadership inhibits the organization's flexibility and dampens employees motivation.
Authoritative	This is a 'come with me' approach. The leader states the overall goal but gives people the freedom to choose their own means of achieving it. This style works well when the change is drifting. It is less effective when working with people who are more experienced than the leader.
Affiliative	The leader here has a 'people come first' attitude. This style is particularly useful for building team harmony or increasing morale. Caution here is where poor performance is allowed to go uncorrected.
Democratic	This gives people a voice in decisions and hence builds organizational flexibility and helps to generate ideas. This style can lead to time spent in debate and meetings, with decisions taking longer and employees potentially feeling 'leaderless'.
Pacesetting	A leader who sets high performance standards and exemplifies them has a very positive impact on employees who are self-motivated and highly competent. But other employees can be overwhelmed by the leader's demands for excellence.
Coaching	This style focuses more on personal development than on immediate work-related tasks. It works well when employees are aware of their weaknesses and want to improve, but not when they are resistant to changing their ways.

4.6 *Flexibility in leadership approach and style*

Cameron and Green (2012) identify different skills or activities that the leader needs to perform according to the different phases of the change process: 'Phasing enables a leader to see the need for flexibility in leadership approach and style, as the change moves from one phase into another phase.' Cameron and Green identify the *inner leadership* (what goes on inside the leader) and *outer leadership* (observable actions of the leader) requirements of a leader for each phase. Examples would be:

- When establishing the need for change with stakeholders: *inner leadership* relates to managing emotions, courage, energy, integrity; *outer leadership* could include researching, presenting, influencing and negotiating.
- Building the change team: *inner leadership* could include organizational awareness, adaptability, taking initiative, drive and energy; *outer leadership* on the other hand is likely to involve facilitating discussion, establishing relationships, team building, problem solving and dealing with politics.
- Communicating and engaging: *inner leadership* includes patience, analysis of how to present to different audiences, managing emotions particularly when dealing with resistance, adaptability and empathy; *outer leadership* could involve persuading and engaging, presenting, listening, being assertive and networking.
- Consolidating progress: *inner leadership* involves social awareness, taking time to reflect, steadiness of purpose; *outer leadership* involves reviewing objectively, celebrating success and giving feedback.

In a diverse and distributed workforce there is a need to adapt approaches as the needs of individuals and teams are modified. The same will apply as the phases and progress of the change dictates. Change managers therefore have the challenge of combining authenticity with approaches and styles that connect with the needs of the individual, and with the evolving needs of the change itself.

Tip

Keep these points in mind for leadership success:

- Know what you want from any situation.

- Notice and keep aware of what you are getting.

- Remain flexible to keep changing what you do until you get what you want.

5. Problem solving and creative thinking

All change will involve varying degrees of problem solving and creativity as challenges arise or options need consideration. The change manager will at intervals be faced with issues where a different/creative approach to thinking through both the problem and potential solutions will be required. One of the key parts of a change leader's role is to generate the environment and opportunities that provide a flow of ideas to overcome blockages and move change forward.

Change managers should harness the creativity of others for the diversity of ideas and perspectives, and for the learning that accrues as a result. Exploring some of the more creative approaches to problem solving will expand the range of options/solutions.

The following techniques are some of the most widely used:

- Brainstorming – see Chapter 10, Section E3.1
- Force field analysis – see Chapter 2, Section B2.2
- Mind maps (Tony Buzan) – see Chapter 2, Section C1.3
- Fishbone technique – see Chapter 2, Section D4.2
- Thinking hats (Edward de Bono) – see Chapter 10, Section E3.6

Summary

While 'authority' may carry some weight in leading change, the ability to engage others and overcome resistance requires much more. Winning over people's hearts and minds requires leaders who, while being their authentic self, also have awareness during the various phases of change of the need to operate flexibly. The challenges that change brings will require inner strength and perseverance as well as the application of a range of skills and strategies, which if they do not exist will need to be learned.

Questions to think about

1. What challenges does being 'authentic' bring to a leader?
2. What actions would a leader focus on with the change team in the early stages of a change initiative?
3. What are the advantages and disadvantages of adopting an 'Adaptive' leadership approach to change?

Further reading

Bennis, W and Goldsmith, J (2010) *Learning to Lead*, Basic Books, New York
Blanchard, K (2000) *Leadership and the One Minute Manager*, Harper Collins, New York
Collins, J (2001) *Good to Great*, Random House Business Books, London
Nayar, V (2010) *Employees First, Customers Second*, Harvard Business Books, Boston, MA
Senge, P (2003) *The Fifth Discipline*, Nicholas Brealey Publishing, London
www.themindgym.com (creative problem solving)

Section B: Building team effectiveness

Introduction

Change managers consider how to set up the most appropriate team and combinations of teams during a change initiative, those that will ensure the best chances of success. Many different types of teams can be established during the course of a change initiative. Building team effectiveness means developing teams that have a strong shared sense of purpose, who plan and organize their work around that purpose, and foster an atmosphere of openness and trust, so that they can perform at the optimum level.

You cannot do it alone. Successfully delivering a change initiative requires building a team or teams that have the ability and credibility to influence stakeholders and engage and guide the organization through the change itself. Without strong teams with a clear sense of purpose change initiatives seldom have the support, energy, speed and sense of urgency to succeed.

1. Stages of team development

Tuckman's five-stage team development model explains that as the change initiative progresses, and the team develops maturity and ability, team relationships change (Tuckman and Jensen, 1977). The change manager will be required to adapt responses to create and sustain an effective team. The stages are as follows:

- Stage 1 – *forming*
  When a team is formed there will initially be a high dependence on the change manager for guidance and direction. Team members may ask questions that provide direction, while individual roles and responsibilities may be unclear. Change managers will need to be directive in answering questions about the background to the initiative and the team's purpose, objectives and links to the business units.
- Stage 2 – *storming*
  Typically there follows a period of uncertainty as team members attempt to establish themselves in relation to other team members and the change manager. Team members are likely to want to test and challenge the assumptions made. Team members may come with a variety of experience and status as well as personal styles and approaches, each of which can lead to differences of opinion. In this stage, emotions may dominate over objectivity, particularly where there is no appetite for compromise. The change manager will be sensitive to the situation and, using coaching and team 'workshops', can help to focus the group on its aims and deliverables.
- Stage 3 – *norming*
  In the norming stage the team have established a way of working together that is focused on achievement of outcomes. Storming is replaced by

agreement and consensus among the team. Roles and responsibilities are understood and they have clarified with the change manager the purpose, why certain decisions were made and the assumptions they were based on. The team's energy is focused on the allocated tasks, and significant decisions are made by the group following discussion and debate. Smaller decisions may be delegated to individuals or small teams within the group. Communication across the group is more open, commitment is strong and there is a desire to resolve issues objectively.

- Stage 4 – *performing*
  The team has a sense of unity. They have a shared vision and are able to stand on their own feet, using the change manager to deal with issues of links to the sponsor or significant problems that require focus. The team embodies the way of working collectively to achieve tasks, supporting each other through the peaks, troughs and challenges that arise. They have the desire to improve still further and learn from their experiences. The team has a high degree of autonomy and the change manager feels comfortable to delegate.
- Stage 5 – *adjourning* (also known as *mourning*)
  When the change is successfully completed, its purpose fulfilled, everyone can move on to new things, feeling good about what has been achieved. The change manager will need to be empathetic, recognizing the potential sense of loss of the team dynamic and the insecurity from the change.

The phases of team development described by Tuckman are not discrete, such that once a phase is reached the team moves forward to the next stage. While this may be the usual progression it is not the inevitable progression. In practice, teams may go backwards or oscillate between the stages, or just get stuck, caused by factors such as change in personnel, major differences of opinion, changes in strategy, variation in performance standards or commitment of team members, or failure to meet targets.

Tip

When putting together a new team, as soon as possible arrange a team-building/get-to-know-each-other event. The aim is to 'break the ice', getting to know and understand more about each other and creating a basis on which to build constructive working relationships. The agenda could include: hobbies and interests; likes and dislikes; favourite food/holiday/country/hotel/film; thing most proud of; what people won't know about me, etc. The event will have most impact if it can be held face-to-face.

In the three sections that follow, the change scenario set out in the box below is used to illustrate how three comparable views – Glaser and Glaser, John Adair and Patrick Lencioni – can be applied to provide perspectives and understanding on the creating of a high-performing change team.

Scenario: why the change is necessary: a not-for-profit organization is funded by government and the budget has been reduced by 20 per cent while demand continues to escalate.

The change: the initiative that is sponsored by the executive is to introduce 'commercialism' into the organization. Implementation involves disciplined budgeting, zero cost accounting, business cases for expenditure over an agreed level, centralized procurement, culture change, training and communication programmes.

The change team responsible for implementation will consist of representatives of each of the main business units in the organization together with financial specialists and project managers.

2. Developing an effective team

Glaser and Glaser (1992) identified five elements to be applied to creating an effective change team that would help to deliver an outcome in the above scenario. They are:

- *Team mission, planning and goal setting*
  The team needs to have meetings to gain clarity around the reason for change, the vision and the anticipated problems, risks and issues. The output would be a clear and strongly held sense of purpose and an ability to answer questions from stakeholders. Armed with an understanding, the team can remain focused on delivering outcomes.
- *Team roles*
  The change manager will meet with individual team members regularly to clarify roles so that they are more accountable and understand what they need to do to be successful. The initiative in the above scenario is likely to receive resistance, particularly as it involves a significant culture change towards 'commercialism'. Team members may therefore need training and coaching in dealing with resistance and influencing skills (Section D). It will also be important that the team work collectively to understand each other's roles and accountabilities and where interdependencies exist.

- *Team operating processes*
  The team will need to have certain enabling processes in place for people to carry out their work efficiently together. Both participation in all of the processes of the work group and the development of a collaborative approach are at the heart of effective teamwork. This means that they will agree on frequency of team meetings, how they will make decisions and resolve issues.
- *Team interpersonal relationships*
  Given the challenging nature of the initiative, the change manager will encourage team members to actively engage with and support each other. It also requires open communication and willingness to share information. Successes will vary according to the challenges that each team member faces, and communication will be important to ensure that individuals are supported to balance workloads and overcome problems.
- *Inter-team relations*
  The change manager will consider the team interdependencies and how relationships can be developed to facilitate delivery of the change initiative. Encouragement can also be given to the team to develop relationships and communicate with other teams.

3. Balancing focus on results with effective people management

John Adair (2009) in his action-centred leadership model would suggest that successful implementation of the change initiative in the scenario above would be dependent on the focus that was given to three core management responsibilities – task, team and individual, as set out in Table 12.2. Adair stresses the importance for a manager to focus on all three areas, with the danger of problems occurring if too much emphasis is on one of the three elements at the expense of the others.

4. Overcoming the dysfunctions of a team

An alternative perspective in creating an effective change team comes from the work of Patrick Lencioni. He argues that the true measure of a team is that it accomplishes the results that it sets out to achieve and to do that on a consistent, ongoing basis, a team must overcome five possible interrelated dysfunctions:

- Dysfunction 1: *absence of trust*
  A team that lacks trust will conceal their weaknesses and mistakes from each other, hesitate to provide constructive feedback, and waste time and energy managing their behaviours for effect. A team built on trust will openly admit their weaknesses and mistakes and not be afraid to ask for help. It will accept questions and challenges from other members where it is for the greater good of the team, and take risks in offering feedback and assistance.

TABLE 12.2 Balancing focus on task, team and individual

Task	• Identify vision, purpose and direction. • Identify resources. • Establish responsibilities. • Set standards, quality, time and reporting parameters. • Monitor and maintain performance against plan. • Assess risks and challenges and potential 'derailers'. • Modify resource allocation to provide flexibility when needed.
Team	• Establish and agree standards of performance and behaviour. • Monitor and maintain discipline, ethics, integrity and focus. • Develop teamworking and cooperation. • Motivate and provide a sense of purpose. • Agree roles. • Agree communication protocols. • Ensure training needs are met.
Individual	• Understand the team members as individuals. • Identify individual responsibilities and objectives. • Give recognition and praise. • Develop and utilize individual capabilities and strengths. • Develop individual freedom and authority. • Provide coaching where necessary.

In the scenario above, team members are taken from the various business units. Members of the team are unlikely to know each other and it may take time for trust to be earned. Delivering the initiative requires relationships with each business unit and there is potential for pressure for 'favours'/differential treatment. Any lack of consistency will impact on trust.

- Dysfunction 2: *fear of conflict*
  Without trust people will not have the open and constructive debates that are necessary to arrive at better thought-through decisions. A team that fears conflict will create an environment where politics and personal attacks thrive, and waste time and energy. Teams that have no fear of conflict will discuss openly the most important and difficult issues and actively seek and explore ideas from all team members.
- Dysfunction 3: *lack of commitment*
  If a team has not aligned behind a purpose then the individual members who did not agree with the strategy will ultimately be less committed to that approach. A team that fails to commit will have ambiguity around direction and priorities, lack confidence and fear failure. It will engage in excess analysis and discussions, and lack decisiveness.

An initiative that seeks to bring commercialism against a deeply established culture that currently exists is likely to mean that team members themselves have doubts. The change manager will need to spend time with individuals to ensure the team is totally committed and aligned toward one goal and has clarity around individual and group objectives.

- Dysfunction 4: *avoidance of accountability*
  If the team is not committed to a course of action, then they are less likely to feel accountable (or hold other people accountable). A team that avoids accountability will create resentment among team members who have different standards of performance, and will miss key deadlines and deliverables. It may also place an undue burden on the team leader to provide discipline.
  A team that accepts accountability will identify potential problems quickly and challenge one another about their plans and approaches. It will establish respect among team members who all hold to high standards, pointing out to others any deficiencies or unproductive behaviour.
- Dysfunction 5: *inattention to results*
  Individuals focus on achieving their own goals and are less likely to care about group results.
  A team attentive to results will feel the 'pain' when the team fails to achieve its goals and will willingly make sacrifices for the good of the team. The change manager may choose to use Lencioni's approach to 'test' team dynamics at various stages during the change. Effective teams are built on fundamentals such as trust and commitment and can form a productive if challenging agenda item for team meetings or team-building events.

5. Working with a changing team or context

The composition of teams will inevitably shift during the course of the change effort. This may be because members may be added for their expertise or influence or perhaps because the size may grow as the change initiative grows.

Dan Cohen (2005) suggests that working with a changing team is inevitable but care must be taken to:

- Sustain leadership involvement. Although leadership involvement will evolve care must be taken to ensure commitment through all steps of the change process to sustain respect and influence.
- As teams grow and spread, often at lower, local levels, care must be taken to ensure that a consistent sense of urgency exists and that appropriate measures are in place to monitor individual and team performance.

The context in which change teams operate is also likely to be subject to change becoming more diverse and complex. The change manager building effective teams will need to be very aware of both the skills and experience that individuals bring, as well as being sensitive to the many issues that the relationship brings.

6. Leading virtual teams

One increasingly common team type are 'virtual teams' (Chapter 10, Section D), which are teams that are formed for a purpose but where team members are distributed across an organization, often at considerable distances, as will be the case in global organizations. An additional challenge regularly faced by members of a distributed virtual team is that team members may have pressure of local priorities that cause them to lose focus on the objective and responsibilities of their change team.

Working independently, separated by time and distance, means that people working virtually need a very high degree of clarity if they are to deliver business goals. In a virtual team coordination is therefore particularly important and this can be both explicit and implicit.

Explicit coordination is in the form of agreements, procedures, systems and protocols. These elements should be agreed and adhered to, and ensuring that the team follows them is a key leadership task. Explicit coordination using media such as video/telephone conferencing is vital for complex/interdependent tasks.

Implicit coordination is where team members are proactive, anticipating the needs of other team members. It requires team members to be engaged, aware of the team and what everyone else is doing. Use of e-mail and social media helps with the engagement, but equally important is the encouragement and positive feedback from team managers.

Communication is therefore a key component of an effective virtual team. The biggest challenge is that formal 'task-based' virtual communication often does not provide the opportunities to build relationships. The leader's role here is to encourage team members to focus both on communicating at a social as well as behavioural level. Where possible, face-to-face events will prove useful but also technologies that allow visual communication, such as video conferencing, will ensure connection is made and mean less chance of miscommunication or misunderstanding.

Summary

While change is becoming more complex and demanding, what we observe from the above is that building an effective team to deal with the challenges change brings has broadly consistent requirements. In the scenario used here, it requires a change manager who is able to galvanize a group of diverse individuals into a team, through its various stages of development. It requires adapting leadership style during the team's evolution while remaining focused on providing purpose and direction, both individually and collectively, in order to deliver a successful outcome. It requires managers who can provide clear direction and standards when needed but are able to take a supportive role when team capability matures to a stage where management is more subtle, intervening on an as-needed basis. Of crucial importance where the drive from sponsors for results contrasts with the ability or willingness of the business to accept change is the balance that is achieved between achieving the task and sustaining the energy, morale and capability of the people.

Questions to think about

1. What contribution could a change manager make to help a team through the 'storming' stage (Tuckman) of team development?
2. Lencioni points to trust as a key factor in an effective team. How can a manager create trust in the relationship with the team?
3. What strategies could a change manager responsible for a virtual team use to achieve team unity?

Further reading

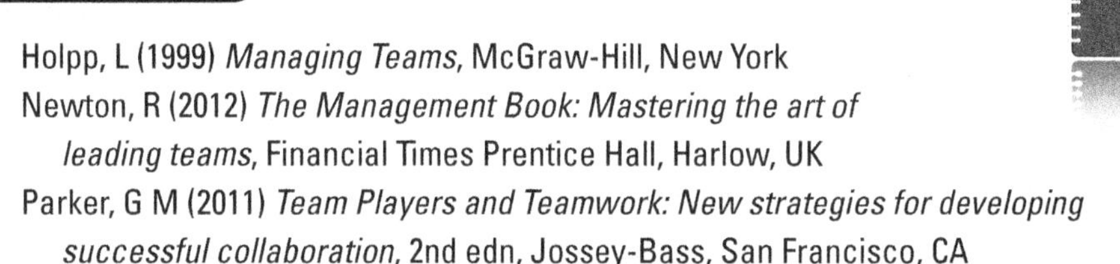

Holpp, L (1999) *Managing Teams*, McGraw-Hill, New York

Newton, R (2012) *The Management Book: Mastering the art of leading teams*, Financial Times Prentice Hall, Harlow, UK

Parker, G M (2011) *Team Players and Teamwork: New strategies for developing successful collaboration*, 2nd edn, Jossey-Bass, San Francisco, CA

Section C: Emotional intelligence

Introduction

Change managers who demonstrate strong emotional intelligence are more effective in dealing with the challenges that are inevitable during any change, particularly the people and emotional aspects of change. They are self-aware, can manage their own emotions and deal with others' emotions so are better placed to influence others using appropriate interpersonal skills. This results in lower levels of anxiety or stress during change, both for themselves and for others around them. They recognize early warning signals of unhelpful emotions and step in to deal with these effectively before issues escalate to a point where progress of the change initiative is hindered.

1. What is emotional intelligence?

Emotional intelligence was raised in 1990 by Peter Salovey and John D Mayer, who published their paper on the subject. Their definition:

> Emotional intelligence is a type of social intelligence that involved the ability to monitor one's own and others' emotions, to discriminate among them and to use the information to guide one's thinking and actions. (Salovey and Mayer, 1990)

The concept was popularized by Daniel Goleman (1998). He considered there to be five components of emotional intelligence in the working environment:

- *Self-awareness*: the ability to recognize and understand your moods, emotions and drives, as well as their effect on others.
- *Self-regulation*: the ability to control or redirect disruptive impulses and moods/the propensity to suspend judgement – to think before acting.
- *Motivation*: a passion to work for reasons that go beyond money or status/ a propensity to pursue goals with energy and persistence.
- *Empathy*: the ability to understand the emotional make-up of other people/ skill in treating people according to their emotional reactions.
- *Social skill*: proficiency in managing relationships and building networks/ an ability to find common ground and build rapport.

Reuven Bar-On (2000) developed an 'Emotional Quotient Inventory' (EQI) that measures emotional quotient in five areas:

- *Intrapersonal*: includes recognition of personal feelings, self regard, self-actualization, independence and assertiveness.
- *Interpersonal*: interpersonal relationships, empathy and ability to be constructive and cooperative.
- *Adaptability*: adjustment of emotions, thoughts and behaviour to changing situations, problem solving.
- *Stress management*: ability to cope with adverse events, stressful situations and the ability to control one's emotions and resist or delay a temptation to act.
- *General mood*: the ability to maintain a positive attitude even in the face of adversity.

The importance of emotional intelligence can be understood in the context of change as it relates to emotional self-awareness (Section A2) and how this awareness can be channelled to regulate personal emotions and to relate to and engage others constructively. Change managers who understand and can demonstrate emotional intelligence greatly enhance their chances of engaging positively with stakeholders.

2. Can I learn emotional intelligence?

The question here is whether emotional intelligence can be developed or whether it is a more enduring personality trait. Daniel Goleman (1998) among others suggests that: 'emotional intelligence can be learned but the process is not easy, it takes time and commitment'. Significantly, Mayer and Salovey (1997) point out that emotional intelligence is not fixed for life and may be improved with suitable training.

The overall approach to be taken is focused on feedback and coaching, possibly aligned with established learning activities such as interpersonal skills training (Chapter 9, Section B). Focusing on emotional capability requires individuals to have the courage to look with an open mind at their capabilities and to accept honest feedback from others. Emotional Intelligence inventories such as those designed by Bar-On (EQI) can help to identify development areas. Managers may also have completed other personality questionnaires – the Myers-Briggs Type Indicator® (MBTI®), the Occupational Personality Inventory (OPQ) – that will help to build an accurate initial picture as a starting point.

To a large extent emotional intelligence is exhibited in interactions with other people and thus needs input from them, perhaps from processes such as 360-degree feedback. This helps in obtaining more accurate feedback and can be a valuable development activity in its own right.

Trusted coaches are required who can use the data obtained to pinpoint where energies should be focused. Coaches need to be skilled at timely, specific feedback that takes account of the needs and sensitivities of the individual.

3. Resilience

Developing emotional intelligence helps to build personal resilience, which is essential for coping with the challenges of bringing about successful change. Resilience is an awareness of one's own feelings and emotions, balanced with an ability to avoid being 'swamped' by them. In other words, even when aware of personal feelings of cynicism or frustration that can accompany change, a manager will continue to make effective decisions and fulfil accountabilities. This needs an ability to maintain focus on results or actions while also being able to express personal feelings effectively. Managers with resilience have the ability to adapt and bounce back when change does not go as planned. Resilient managers do not dwell on failures; they acknowledge the problem and focus on what is needed to get change back on track, while learning from the experience.

Building resilience requires:

- practising an ability to think positively;
- maintaining perspective;
- developing a strong network of supportive relationships;
- ability to cope by taking care of mind and body;
- ability to adapt and bounce back when things do not go as planned.

The work of Martin Seligman (2006) suggests that it is possible to train the mind to think positively and learn from our experiences. With a belief that if we are in control of our minds we can choose the reaction to any given situation then it is possible to remain calm and look objectively at any given situation.

4. The emotionally intelligent change manager

Emotional intelligence has been found through research from authors such as Daniel Goleman to have a significant correlation with performance. Successful change managers can be expected to have the following four competencies that are core components of emotional intelligence:

- *Being centred and grounded*: when successful change managers are centred and grounded the people around them see them as having a stable mood even when things get tough.
- *An ability to take action*: change managers here are decisive. As part of their decision-making process they take into account the views of others.
- *A participative management style*: understanding and connecting with people is a priority. Strategies aim to win the hearts and minds of their people.

Tip

True emotions are difficult to accurately assess. Be cautious about making early judgements or assumptions about others' emotions, as initial reactions or lack of emotion may not be indicative of a person's ongoing feelings. These may vary once the implications of the change have been absorbed and understood. Allow reflection time and then, if you want to know how someone feels, ask them!

- *Being tough-minded*: successful managers are resilient in dealing with obstacles and difficult situations. They manage to persevere in the face of obstacles, overcome challenges and handle pressure well.

Tip

Handling pressure may need a release valve. It can help to have people to turn to who listen, are non-judgemental and can provide suggestions and perspectives. Identify a support group of individuals to whom you can turn when the going gets tough, preferably outside your working environment.

Summary

While emotional intelligence can be included as part of change managers' skills in leadership, its potential impact – both positive and negative – makes it a worthy subject for separate focus. Controlled and positive emotion is an ingredient that can provide excitement and energy to a change. However, where a change manager is insensitive to more negative aspects of emotion that can occur – at any stage during change – and fails to channel them towards successful outcomes, then the change can be compromised. Understanding what emotional intelligence means and taking responsibility to develop personal capability is a useful asset to facilitate change.

Questions to think about

1. Why is self-awareness an important factor in emotional intelligence?
2. How would you describe the difference between 'intrapersonal' and 'interpersonal' skills?
3. What part does resilience play in change management and how can resilience be developed?

Further reading

Balogun, J and Hailey, V H (2008) *Exploring Strategic Change*, 3rd edn, Pearson Education, Harlow

Cameron, E and Green, M (2012) *Making Sense of Change Management: A complete guide to the models, tools and techniques of organizational change*, 3rd edn, Kogan Page, London

Goleman, D (2009) *Working with Emotional Intelligence*, Bantam Books, New York

Section D: Effective influence

Introduction

Change managers recognize the need to adopt different strategies and tactics, depending on the people involved and on the situation. For example, some people need reasoned logic and facts, while others respond better to an approach that appeals to their values or emotions. It could be a simple transactional exchange of favours, which is mutually beneficial to either side, or a more coercive approach demanding full compliance. The ability to influence people in order to facilitate change is a critical skill for change managers.

> Influence is defined as:
>
> *'a force one person (the agent) exerts on someone else (the target) to induce a change in behaviours, opinions, attitudes, goals, needs and values'*
>
> and
>
> *'the ability to affect the behaviour of others in a particular direction'.*
>
> French and Raven (1959)

1. Sources of power

Power is a source of influence and change managers will need to understand the source of their power as part of their ability to deliver effective outcomes. Change managers can have formal power by virtue of their position or perhaps because of being experts in their field, but influence will be well received if accompanied by personal qualities and skills. One of the most notable studies on power was conducted by the social psychologists French and Raven (1959) who identified five bases of power: legitimate, reward and coercive (positional power sources); expert and referent (personal power sources) – as set out in the sections below.

1.1 Positional power sources

These are:

- *Legitimate*: this comes from the belief that a person has a formal right to make demands and to expect compliance and obedience from others. If a change manager, for example, relies on legitimate power in the form of executive sponsorship as the only way to influence, it is unlikely to be enough. To be effective a change leader will need more than this and, in fact, may not need legitimate power at all.
- *Reward*: this results from one person's ability to compensate another for compliance. The challenge here is that the change manager may not have much control over rewards, particularly when managing a project or matrix team. While they will be responsible for providing feedback on performance they may have little direct power to reward.
- *Coercive*: this comes from the belief that a person can punish others for noncompliance. Threats and punishment are rarely appropriate as it can cause unhealthy behaviour and dissatisfaction in those who the change is reliant on.

1.2 Personal power sources

Relying on positional forms of power alone to effect change will result in an autocratic form of management. To be effective, developing expert and referent power will be a more successful combination:

- *Expert*: this is based on a person's superior skill and knowledge. When the people leading and managing the change have the knowledge and skills that enable them to understand a situation, suggest solutions and use solid judgement, people are more likely to listen to them. When expertise is demonstrated, people tend to trust and respect what is said.
- *Referent*: this is the result of a person's charisma, admiration, appeal, worthiness and right to respect from others. A manager with referent power often has a personality that makes people feel good and tends therefore to have influence. Relying on referent power alone is rarely a good strategy for a manager who wants longevity and respect. Combined with expert power, however, it can help in achieving success.

The influential change leader takes care to consider each stakeholder and their relative power and interest in the outcome of the change initiative (Chapter 4). This provides the basis for more objective strategies that reflect the focus that may need to be given to each of them.

The difference between power and influence can be evidenced in the manner that each is used in order to achieve an outcome. Power is the degree to which people will accept decisions without question. Influence is the ability to convince people of the validity of the decision. Using power when influence is needed may be necessary on occasions but enthusiasm is more likely from the person being influenced than it is from the person being 'made' to do something.

2. Influencing styles and approaches

Managers will use different influencing styles in order to persuade others to meet objectives. By understanding the various styles managers can adapt their own style to either match or complement others in order to have a productive and effective influence on an outcome. There are two basic modes of influencing others. Within these modes there are a wide range of approaches, tactics and behaviours that managers can use to accomplish outcomes and persuade others:

- *Push*: this approach is logical and forceful, with quick results. When using this mode, managers make demands on others to achieve their own agenda. When used well this can deliver results and provides a clear and unambiguous message of what is required. There is a danger, however, that this approach if not well received will result in people who are not receptive or cooperative and cause greater resistance.
- *Pull*: this is where the manager focuses on the individual in the decision-making process, working from their point of view and helping them to understand their stake in the outcome. This will lead to more engagement but may take longer to deliver the outcome that both parties want.

3. Influencing models

Building on the push/pull modes of influence the following two models develop the understanding of how strategies can be used to influence others. The influencing strategies to be used will depend upon the situation, the 'natural' style of the change manager together with the anticipated and actual response of the individual or group to be influenced.

3.1 Cialdini's six principles of influence

Also known as the 'Six Weapons of Influence' these are six principles that his research showed (Cialdini, 2006) were effective in convincing and influencing others (Table 12.3).

TABLE 12.3 Using Cialdini's principles of influence

Reciprocity	To use reciprocity to influence others there will be a need to identify objectives and think about what is wanted from the other person. The need then is to identify what can be given in return that will be valued relative to the request. For instance, if help to implement is required from a business unit the change manager may provide resources to train people that will speed implementation and minimize disruption.
Commitment or Consistency	The need here is to get people's commitment early on. Confirmation in writing is valuable as a record of what has been agreed, especially for long or complex programmes of change.
Social Proof	This principle can be used by creating excitement around the change. The aim here is to gain support from influential people in the organization by building a sense of energy that the stakeholders will want to be a part of.
Liking	The aim here is to build good relationships with stakeholders and ensure time and effort is given to build trust and rapport. Care needs to be taken not to try too hard to be liked such that authenticity is lost.
Authority	Here managers can use both their own authority and that of influential and powerful others.
Scarcity	This principle can be challenging for managers to apply as it is based on people missing out if they don't respond quickly. Given that organizational change will take place if a change manager can create a sense of urgency, by getting support for those that are early adopters it can generate enthusiasm based on fear that support will not be so readily available later in the implementation cycle.

3.2 *Musselwhite and Plouffe: when your influence is ineffective*

Musselwhite and Plouffe (2003) identified five influencing styles that they saw as effective (Table 12.4).

TABLE 12.4 Musselwhite and Plouffe's effective influencing styles

Rationalizing	'Using facts, logic and past experience to persuade' Using this approach during change would mean providing stakeholders with reasoning and logical arguments to support the rationale for change, to deal with questions, arguments and 'what-ifs' that arise from discussions on implementation and to articulate what would happen if change were not to take place.
Asserting	'Using a forthright approach and pressure to convince others' This approach ('push') is used to achieve what is on the change manager's agenda while ensuring that a relationship is maintained. Here the message is delivered with conviction, with a clear understanding of demands, requirements, standards and expectations.
Negotiating (see also Section E)	'Using compromise and cooperation to achieve goals' Clearly explaining the benefits and/or consequences of accepting the change manager's approach enables others to understand the implications of compliance or non-compliance. In this approach the change manager may offer rewards to motivate or get agreement and may, if needed, use authority to exert pressure in the negotiating process.
Inspiring	'Using stories and emotional appeals to create cooperation' Change managers using this approach would use their relationship skills and personality to engage with stakeholders to provide optimistic views of the future. Stakeholders often respond best when they have a clear picture of what you are trying to achieve. Using this approach the change manager may help the other party to 'see, hear, feel' the vision, outlining the exciting possibilities and opportunities. Metaphors, analogies or imagery may be used to paint a picture of the desired outcome (Chapter 5, Section B5).
Bridging	'Getting others to work together to achieve the goal' Here change managers help to develop a sense that all stakeholders are standing on common ground and have a complete understanding of what is happening, helping to build rapport and creating an environment of trust. This 'pull' approach requires the change manager to summarize common ground, common areas of agreement and common values as a means of pulling people together to see and move to one common aim, the common picture. It helps others to see the collegiate responsibility to act and seeks compromise from others where a common goal can be established.

CASE STUDY

The change manager of a global engineering organization was given responsibility to implement a best-practice approach to manufacturing. The change, which was considered unpopular at a local level, involved significant 'down time' in order to modify systems and processes. Initially the change manager used an assertive/rational approach to influencing factory directors and their teams, which carried weight via the business logic and level of sponsorship.

Over time local pressures prevailed, which meant that to deliver orders 'down time' to deliver the change would not be possible and, despite the longer-term benefits, change would at best be delayed or even possibly ignored. Faced with resistance, influence strategies needed to be reconsidered. The politics of the situation meant it was unlikely that the sponsor would take punitive action, the change manager therefore decided to work at a level of bridging.

Using respected local practitioners and experiences of success stories, local change agents were selected and trained who were able to negotiate a phased implementation plan. Discussions were held with the local teams who, armed with a vision and an understanding of best practice, developed an implementation plan that delivered the change that was needed while renegotiating contracts that satisfied local customers.

Summary

While change will originate largely from a business opportunity or need, successful implementation relies heavily on people. People need to be persuaded of the need for change and the extent and detail of support that will be required. For those involved in leading and managing change, influencing skills are therefore critical. Reliance on the various forms of power often present in change initiatives will not on its own create the buy-in and enthusiasm needed to achieve success.

The ability of a change manager to identify the difference between resistance, superficial compliance and real commitment is a key component of influencing. The flexibility to respond to those differences by applying a range of strategies such as those identified above will be a significant contributor to a successful outcome.

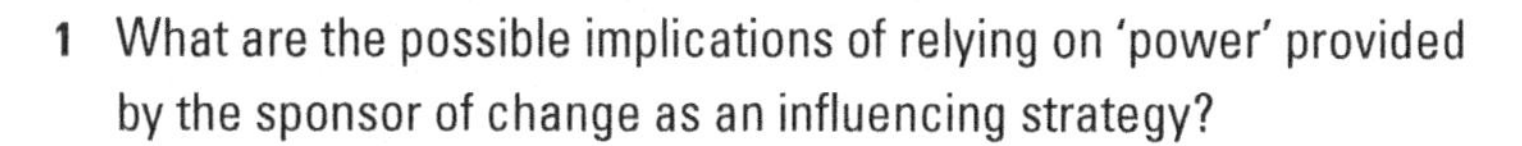

Questions to think about

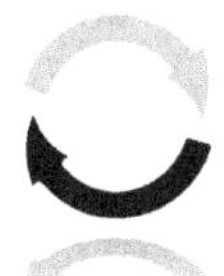

1. What are the possible implications of relying on 'power' provided by the sponsor of change as an influencing strategy?
2. How would you describe the difference between the 'push' and 'pull' approaches to influencing?
3. What are the relative merits and challenges arising from the principles of 'liking' and 'authority' in Cialdini's six principles of influence?

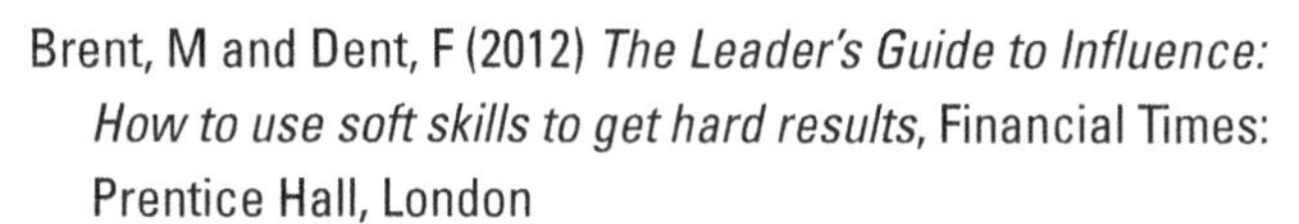

Further reading

Brent, M and Dent, F (2012) *The Leader's Guide to Influence: How to use soft skills to get hard results*, Financial Times: Prentice Hall, London

O'Conner, J and Seymour, J (2011) *Introducing NLP: Psychological skills for understanding and influencing people*, Conari Press, San Francisco

Section E: Negotiating

Introduction

Change managers will over time deal with challenges that arise due to people having differing interests and conflicting needs that require negotiated solutions. Change managers will also need to negotiate levels of support and cooperation, particularly from internal stakeholders, in order to deliver a successful outcome. This is particularly likely where a stakeholder is required to provide time, resources, effort and commitment that could divert attention from their own responsibilities and priorities.

Negotiation will be considered effective when it delivers a positive outcome while maintaining good or enhanced relationships between the negotiating parties. Maintaining a good relationship is particularly important with internal stakeholders from whom ongoing or future support may be required (Chapter 4). This section looks at the different approaches to negotiation, a view on a practical strategy for negotiation and the emotional and cultural implications of negotiation.

1. Defining negotiation

Negotiation is 'a two-way communication to reach an agreement when both parties have a combination of shared and opposed interest' (Fisher and Ury, 1999). Negotiations are a 'vehicle of communication and stakeholder management. As such they play a vital role in assisting to obtain a better grasp of the complex issues, factors and human dynamics behind important issues' (Alfredson and Cungu, 2008).

The change manager may use strategies of both influence and negotiation but there is a difference between the two. Negotiation and influence (Section D), both involve skills and strategy, but negotiation is a two-way process where the possibility exists for both parties to trade/benefit, whereas influence is more one-way in the sense that while the interaction may be two-way the aim is to get another person or people to believe or act in a certain way without necessarily receiving anything in return.

2. Approaches to negotiation

Stephen Covey (2013) suggests that while much of our background may focus on winning or losing, particularly in sporting terms, when it comes to negotiation the aim should be win–win. This approach focuses on cooperation, with all parties feeling respected and committing to subsequent action.

This can be contrasted with change managers who at the first sign of challenge revert to an authoritarian approach, perhaps based on the power of sponsorship to get their way and face the danger of creating a win–lose situation. They may achieve what they want and thus 'win' but the approach can leave the other party feeling they have 'lost'. In such cases the 'losing' party may comply but the level of cooperation, trust and whole-hearted commitment will be diminished. Successful outcomes require give and take between people or teams, and negotiation to resolve any issues or tensions.

2.1 Achieving win–win

Change managers should be careful not to focus exclusively on their own agenda. This is likely to create a defensive response and could bring unwelcome resistance. Covey (2013) suggests that win–win embraces five interdependent dimensions:

- *Character*
  Character is seen as a foundation of achieving a win–win situation. It involves integrity built on a platform of keeping commitments and achieving mutual trust. It means having the 'maturity' to engage in open and honest dialogue together with a consideration for the views and feelings of others. It incorporates a belief system that win–win will ultimately create better outcomes.

- *Relationships*
  Relationships are created and sustained through a genuine respect for the other person and their point of view. In practice this may mean sustaining conversations to achieve a real understanding of the issues involved.
- *Agreements*
  Agreements help to clarify expectations between the parties involved in the negotiation. They provide a mutual understanding of what is required in terms of: results, parameters, resources, accountability and consequences. The agreement represents win–win with the change manager and other parties to the negotiation working to support achievement of its elements.
- *Systems*
  Win–win solutions require systems that are consistent with the aims of the change. Where cooperation is required then systems should measure and reward its achievement.

CASE STUDY

A joint project seeking to combine engineering expertise with medical experience to solve health problems found difficulties in negotiating operating protocols and procedures. What was rewarded and valued varied greatly between the two populations and this interfered with cooperation and trust. Time invested in understanding the respective values and needs of each group unlocked the impasse and enabled them to find measurement and reward systems that satisfied their respective needs.

- *Processes* (Section E4)
  Covey recommends that the key to 'win–win' negotiations is to have a process or strategy that starts with seeing the problem from the other person's point of view, separating the person from the problem. Subsequent steps identify the key issues and concerns, the potential outcomes that would be acceptable and the range of options that would generate the results.

3. Phases of negotiation

Fisher and Ury (1999) suggest that successful negotiation has four phases: preparation; exchange information and disclose necessary details; bargaining; and closure. These are set out below.

3.1 Preparation

This is where data and information are acquired that may prove necessary to bring a situation to agreement. During preparation, it helps to look for win–win agreements that focus on shared interests. This opens the door to finding positive solutions acceptable to all stakeholders to the negotiation.

Tip

The win for a change manager may consist of delivering an outcome in the short term where the benefit to the other party may be longer term and/or potentially organizational rather than local. The change manager should therefore be armed and familiar with the data that supports a win that the other party can engage with, both logically and emotionally.

As change can result in resistance, a change manager should also prepare a fall-back position before entering into bargaining. A good fall-back position would include details on the following:

- A 'best alternative to a negotiated agreement'.
- A 'worst alternative to a negotiated agreement'.
- A 'walk away point'. This is the point at which parties agree to step away from the issue to regroup later to consider the options – or end the negotiations because the options are unacceptable.
- A 'zone of possible agreement' where interests overlap with the other negotiating parties.

3.2 Exchange information and disclose necessary details

This phase aids efficiency and reduces frustration by ensuring relevant information is available to all and appropriate considerations are made prior to meeting.

3.3 Bargaining

It is at this stage that most of the interaction between parties takes place and individuals display a range of negotiating styles and tactics to make their case (Section E4). It is during bargaining that the risk of unsuccessful or troublesome negotiations is highest.

3.4 Closure

This phase formally seals and binds parties into the outcomes of the agreement.

4. Conducting negotiations

Looking at the negotiation itself, a further subdivision of four steps (Fisher and Ury) offers a useful process for change managers who may be conducting negotiations in a challenging business climate.

4.1 Separate the people from the problem

Fisher and Ury suggest that every person involved in the negotiation has two separate kinds of interest. The first is their own respective agenda while the second is the interpersonal relationship between the two parties. The main problem occurs when the relationship becomes confused with the agenda issues being addressed. Change managers will be most successful when stepping back and focusing on the issues and challenges that the other person faces, instead of reacting to emotions that may be in evidence.

4.2 Focus on interests not positions

The issue here is where change managers focus on respective positions rather than issues and concerns. What change managers need to understand and determine are the key issues that concern both parties. The question often asked is: *what do you want?* The more important question that is rarely asked is: *why do you want this?*

4.3 Mutual options for mutual gain

Even though both parties may be successful in recognizing the problem there can be a tendency for each party to want to impose their own solution, particularly where the relationship is not strong. The obstacles to overcome are:

- jumping to conclusions or solutions too quickly;
- searching for the single answer;
- thinking that solving the problem is their problem.

Successful negotiation occurs when change managers first identify their possible options and then cooperate to decide on the best mutual course of action.

4.4 Insisting on objective criteria

In the final phase Fisher and Ury stress that 'the pitfall of getting into a battle of wills must be avoided'. They say that the aim should be to negotiate on the basis of objective criteria. Objective criteria consist of value, costs, standards, efficiency or any principle agreed as fair and reasonable. Three basic points need to be remembered:

- discussions on each issue to be a mutual search for objective criteria;
- be both reasonable and open to reason as to which standards should be used and how they should be applied;
- never bend to pressure, only to principle.

5. Emotionally intelligent negotiating

> Being an effective negotiator requires attunement to one's own emotions and the ability to relate affirmatively to the emotions of others.
>
> David Ryback, *Putting Emotional Intelligence to Work*

Specifically, emotionally intelligent negotiators have the capacity to:

- identify the emotions they and others are experiencing;
- understand how those affect their thinking;
- use that knowledge to achieve better outcomes;
- productively manage emotions, tempering or intensifying them to achieve a successful outcome.

Negotiating often creates varying degrees of anxiety based on reasons such as *lack of control*, *unpredictability* and *absence of feedback* (Leary, Pillemer and Wheeler, 2013). It can also depend on an individual's *beliefs and attitude about negotiating*, which influence feelings and behaviour at the negotiating table.

Effective negotiators understand that managing emotions means more than identifying them and setting them aside. They prepare emotionally as well as substantively for any negotiation needed to create necessary outcomes.

6. Cultural impacts on negotiation strategies

The philosophy behind negotiating while accounting for culture is the same as for influencing, conflict and any other interventions that involve persuading others – and that is the need to understand who you are interacting with. Culture, which is generally a term for 'how we do things around here', can relate to numerous situations (Chapter 1, Section E). Organizations may have cultures within departments where, for instance, 'Sales' are very different from 'Finance' or 'HR'. There can be generational cultures; there can be religious, social as well as geographical cultures – each will have characteristics that will be a factor in deciding on negotiation strategies.

CASE STUDY

A financial services organization found that change originating from HR was perceived by other business units as being 'soft' and as a result negotiating implementation agreements was difficult. By focusing on the business benefits of the change, and using business units as sponsors of the change, HR strategies were seen as more acceptable and implementation significantly improved.

Reflecting on the cultural implications must be a factor that the change manager takes into account when negotiating. Whether the differences are in terminology used, social etiquette or beliefs and attitudes, these could become barriers to successful negotiation if they are not recognized and addressed. Frequently checking to ensure there is shared understanding becomes even more important when the cultural differences are sensitive or deeply embedded.

Summary

Negotiating is a process that can be approached in many ways. No matter what strategy a change manager chooses, success lies in preparation. The key to negotiating a beneficial outcome is the negotiator's ability to consider all elements of the situation carefully and identify and think through the options. At the same time, negotiators must be able to keep events in perspective and be as fair and honest as circumstances allow. By looking at the other party as a 'partner' rather than as an opponent, and by working together, negotiators have an opportunity to create the win–win solutions that benefit both sides.

Questions to think about

1. What is the difference between negotiation and influence?
2. Why might it be challenging to achieve win–win solutions in change situations?
3. What factors would you typically include during the 'preparation' stage of negotiations?

Further reading

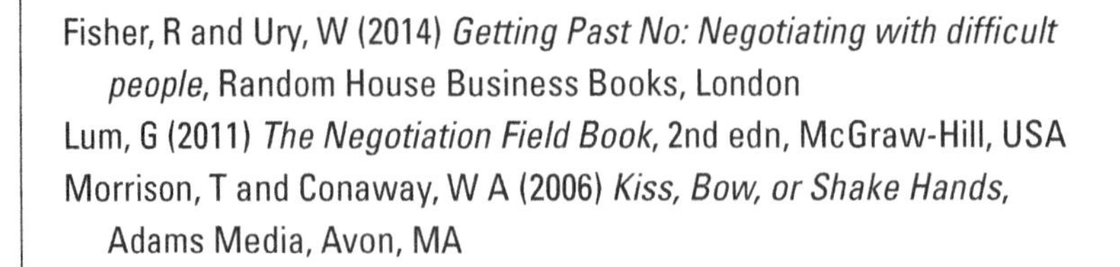

Fisher, R and Ury, W (2014) *Getting Past No: Negotiating with difficult people*, Random House Business Books, London
Lum, G (2011) *The Negotiation Field Book*, 2nd edn, McGraw-Hill, USA
Morrison, T and Conaway, W A (2006) *Kiss, Bow, or Shake Hands*, Adams Media, Avon, MA

Section F: Conflict management

Introduction

Change managers are frequently faced with conflict situations that need resolving in order to avoid unnecessary delays to the change initiative. There is likely to be more conflict in environments with higher levels of uncertainty and ambiguity, more diverse groups of stakeholders, unclear priorities and tight resource constraints.

Change managers can anticipate disruptive conflict, and find timely resolutions to deal with it. However, conflict is not always negative – it can be used for generating more creativity and improving the quality of decisions. All those responsible for change, from the sponsor to those responsible for local implementation, face change scenarios involving tensions that could result in conflict. Handled sensitively, but with an understanding of the needs of the initiative, conflict can be a creative force and can highlight problems and possibilities. Conflict not dealt with or handled badly leaves fractured relationships and reduces the potential for a successful outcome to the change.

1. What does conflict mean?

Managing conflict involves 'designing effective strategies to minimize the dysfunctions of conflict and enhance the constructive functions of conflict in order to enhance learning and effectiveness in organizations' (Rahmin, 2002).

Conflict can relate to incompatible preferences and objectives and not just activities. In order for 'conflict' to occur it has to exceed a threshold level of intensity before the parties experience (or become aware of) any conflict. This principle of conflict threshold is consistent with Baron's (1990) contention that opposed interests must be 'recognized' by parties for conflict to exist. In other words, people must care enough that they want to engage in communicating their reasons for disagreement.

2. Sources of conflict

The first logical steps in resolving conflict is to identify the problem and then identify what caused the conflict. Psychologists Art Bell (2002) and Brett Hart (2000) identified eight sources of conflict, as listed below.

Conflicting needs

Change will involve competing for scarce resources, recognition, and power. Since it is likely that these will be needed to meet existing and emerging objectives, any claim that threatens their availability will create conflict.

Conflicting styles

Those seeking to deliver change will differ in their approach to dealing with people and problems. These differences create conflict. Change managers who understand how to accept and deal with conflicting styles can harness the potential of differing perspectives that the conflict creates.

Conflicting perceptions

People see the world through their own lens and differences in perceptions of events can create conflict. Conflict can occur when a change team with a variety of assigned roles perceives that work allocated to a member of the team does not match assigned responsibilities, creating rumour and gossip as to why.

Conflicting goals

Change can create a moving target of deliverables as stakeholders negotiate and renegotiate according to evolving circumstances. The tension of time versus quality is a regular cause of conflict, as is the capability to deliver versus resource availability.

CASE STUDY

A sponsor and business leader initiated a significant change to supply chain arrangements. The early briefings were communicated in 'big-picture' terms to the team. The lack of detail created confusion and a multiplicity of views and opinions. Some members of the team were comfortable working with ambiguity, and others needed greater clarity to be able to operate effectively. The situation was further complicated by a reluctance of some team members to seek clarification from the leader for fear of being considered to lack strategic capability. The situation was resolved when the business leader appointed a deputy, who was more analytical, to be the 'bridge' from the business to the change team.

Conflicting pressures

Change by its nature can create pressure within organizations, and where pressure to deliver business as usual is combined with a demand for change, tensions and conflict can occur. Pressure is further increased where demands to deliver better, cheaper, faster are added.

Conflicting roles

Situations can exist where one team member may view a task as his or her responsibility but where roles are not clear; others may see the task as their own and conflict can result.

Different personal values

Values are meaningful for people and hence when challenged can be a particularly sensitive and emotional cause of conflict. Where, for instance, change generates a need to work longer or different hours this can create conflict for those who value time outside of work. Ethical values can be tested when organizations focus on profitability and sacrifice things such as customer service, product quality or people protocols.

Unpredictable policies

Whenever an organization's policies are changed, inconsistently applied or nonexistent, misunderstandings are likely to occur. People need to understand their organization's rules and policies. The absence of clear policies, or policies that are constantly changing, can create an environment of uncertainty and conflict.

3. Conflict resolution versus conflict management

The difference between resolution and management of conflict is more than semantic (Robbins, 1978). Conflict resolution implies reduction, elimination or termination of conflict. A large number of studies on negotiation, bargaining, mediation and arbitration fall into the conflict resolution category. Resolution, while potentially valuable where conflict has a dysfunctional impact, is seen as less valuable where it reduces the opportunity for a successful outcome.

Rahim (2002) suggests that the need is for conflict management and not conflict resolution. Conflict management does not necessarily imply avoidance, reduction or termination of conflict. It involves designing strategies to minimize the dysfunctions of conflict and enhancing the constructive functions of conflict in order to enhance learning and effectiveness in organizations (Section F4).

It is important for change managers to be able to differentiate between conflict that is having a dysfunctional effect on delivering successful outcomes, which needs to be resolved, and conflict that has a useful purpose that needs to be managed. It is helpful during the stages of change that people are comfortable to highlight potential conflict situations and are proactive in dealing with conflict. Sponsors who want to ensure the initiative launches positively will be proactive in understanding and dealing with conflict that could create blockages.

4. Maximizing the positive aspects of conflict

If managed well, conflict will deliver positive outcomes. Change brings challenges and tensions: effective managers bring these to the surface and encourage debates that will highlight issues that need to be dealt with. By managing conflict successfully a change manager can solve many of the problems that surface during change as well as getting additional benefits (see MindTools.com):

- *Increased understanding*: the discussion needed to resolve conflict expands people's awareness of the change, giving them an insight into how they can achieve personal and collective outcomes.
- *Increased group cohesion*: when conflict is managed effectively team members can develop stronger mutual respect and renewed confidence that they can work together.
- *Improved self-knowledge*: conflict pushes individuals to examine their objectives in close detail, helping them to understand the things that are important to them, sharpening their focus and enhancing their effectiveness.
- *Creativity*: differences of view and opinion can surface ideas and information that add dimensions to strategies that deliver change outcomes.
- *Trust*: trust in a manager and the team members will be enhanced when conflict is dealt with fairly and constructively.

Tip

Change managers must themselves be comfortable with conflict and develop personal strategies for dealing with it. They must also appreciate the limits of their influence and when to seek guidance or involvement of those with appropriate authority (depending on their situation this may include senior managers or the HR function).

5. Knowing your preferred style

While there are models and tools that help understanding and resolution of conflict situations, change managers need to be aware of their own capability and confidence levels. Some managers approach conflict situations differently, depending on the conflict, the people involved and the issues. Other managers tend to respond to conflict in a similar way. Change managers benefit from knowing how they typically approach conflict, as a starting point to finding ways to resolve conflict that will derail change if not dealt with effectively.

In the 1970s Kenneth Thomas and Ralph Kilman identified five main styles of dealing with conflict that vary in their degrees of cooperativeness and assertiveness:

assertiveness is defined as behaviours that are used to meet personal needs; *cooperativeness* is defined as behaviours that are used to meet the needs of others. They argued that people typically have a preferred style for dealing with conflict. However, they also noted that different styles were most useful in different situations. They developed the Thomas-Kilman Conflict Mode Instrument (TKI) which helps to identify the style a person tends towards when conflict arises.

The styles included are:

- *Competitive*: people who tend towards a competitive style take a firm stand and know what they want. They usually operate from a position of power drawn from factors such as position, rank, expertise or persuasive ability. This style can be useful during change when decisions need to be made quickly; when the decision is unpopular; or when defending against someone who is trying to exploit the situation for their own purpose. However, it can leave people feeling bruised, unsatisfied and resentful when used in less urgent situations such as prolonged periods of change.
- *Collaborative*: people tending towards a collaborative style try to meet the needs of all people involved. These people can be highly assertive but, unlike the competitor, they cooperate effectively and acknowledge that everyone is important. This style is useful when a manager needs to bring together a variety of viewpoints to get the best solution; when there have been previous conflicts in the group; or when the situation is too important for a simple trade-off.
- *Compromising*: people who prefer a compromising style try to find a solution that will at least partially satisfy everyone. Everyone is expected to give up something. Compromise is useful when the cost of conflict is higher than the cost of losing ground, when equal strength opponents are at a standstill and change deadlines are approaching.
- *Accommodating*: this style indicates a willingness to meet others' needs at the expense of the person's own needs. The accommodator often knows when to give in to others, but can be persuaded to surrender a position even when it is not warranted. This person is not assertive but is highly cooperative. Accommodation is appropriate when the issues matter more to the other party, when peace is more valuable than winning, or when a manager wants to be in a position to collect on this favour. However, people may not return favours, and overall this approach is unlikely to lead to the best outcome.
- *Avoiding*: people tending towards this style seek to evade the conflict entirely. This style is typified by delegating controversial decisions, accepting default decisions and not wanting to hurt anyone's feelings. It can be appropriate when the controversy is trivial, when someone is in a better position to solve the problem or where it is a short-term measure in waiting for a better moment. However, in many situations this is a weak and ineffective approach to take.

6. The effects of each conflict management style

Kilman (2011) identified that the application of each of the styles had to be appropriate for the person and situation. Misreading a situation and applying an inappropriate style will have a negative impact on the situation (Table 12.5).

TABLE 12.5 Kilman's conflict management styles

Style	Positive	Negative
Competing	Achievement of your own objective. Boosts ego and confidence. Tension stimulates interest and creativity. Long-held resentments can be brought out into the open.	People feel defeated ('win–lose'). Increases the distance between people. Fosters a climate of distrust and suspicion. People increasingly look after their own interests.
Accommodating	Maintains a harmonious relationship. Avoids 'losing face'. Establishes trust by your cooperative behaviour. Reduces tension.	Giving up on your own objectives. Possible loss of credibility and self-confidence. Resentments are suppressed. Creativity and interest are not stimulated.
Avoiding	Reduces the tension associated with a conflict. Temporarily avoids negative effects. Allows delay in order to be better prepared. Conflict may resolve itself if left alone.	The issue is not resolved. The communication system breaks down. Unspoken resentment or hostility can damage future relationships. No opportunity to develop new or better ideas. Conflict can get harder to handle because the situation worsens.
Collaborating	Achieves a 'win–win' outcome for both parties Provides recognition and acceptance of the other's needs, abilities and expertise. Better ideas are produced and tested. Improves communication and relationships. Promotes learning.	Time-consuming. Possible exposure of confidential business information. A collaborative resolution may not be possible.
Compromising	Each party achieves some of its objectives. Reduces the tension of a 'win–lose' battle. Facilitates teamwork. Maintains a harmonious relationship with the other party involved.	Neither party fully achieves its own objective. The solution may be weakened to the point of being ineffective. A lack of real commitment on either side.

Summary

This section has highlighted the tensions, positive and negative, that create a need for conflict management. As has already been seen, the wide variety of stakeholders – many with emotional investment in its outcome – will mean tensions and differences of opinion. Lencioni (2002) (Section B4) argued about the vital importance of conflict as evidence that a team is functioning openly and effectively. What is clear is that in change of any significance with a team of engaged people, change managers will have to deal with conflict situations. The option of avoidance, unless temporary, is not one that will feature in the options of an effective change manager. Conflict will happen and the emotionally intelligent, skilled change practitioner will face the challenge, reflect, devise an appropriate strategy and deal with it!

Questions to think about

1. Why does change tend to create conflict?
2. How can a change manager benefit from conflict?
3. What factors influence the style used to resolve conflict?
4. What are the dangers of adopting a single preferred style when dealing with conflict?

Further reading

Cloke, K and Goldsmith, J (2011) *Resolving Conflict at Work: Ten strategies for everyone on the job*, 3rd edn, Jossey-Bass, San Francisco, CA

McConnon, S and McConnon, M (2010) *Managing Conflict in the Workplace*, 4th edn, How To Books, Oxford

References

Adair, J (2009) *Effective Team Building: How to make a winning team*, Pan Books, London

Alfredson, T and Cungu, A (2008) [accessed 20 February 2014] Negotiation Theory and Practice: A Review of the Literature [Online] http://www.fao.org/docs/up/easypol/550/4-5_negotiation_background_paper_179en.pdf

Baron, R A (1990) Conflict in organizations, in *Psychology in Organizations: Integrating science and practice* (pp 197–216), eds K R Murphy and F E Saal, Hillsdale, NJ

Bar-On, R (2000) Emotional and social intelligence: insights from the emotional quotient inventory, in *Handbook of Emotional Intelligence*, eds R Bar-On and J D A Parker, Jossey-Bass, San Francisco, CA

Bell, A (2002) [accessed 11 March 2002] Six Ways to Resolve Workplace Conflicts, McLaren School of Business, University of San Francisco [Online] http://www.usfca.edu/fac-staff/bell/article15.html

Bennis, W (1994) *On Becoming a Leader*, Addison-Wesley, Reading, MA

Bryman, A (1992) *Charisma and Leadership in Organizations*, Sage, London

Cameron, E and Green, M (2012) *Making Sense of Change Management: A complete guide to the models, tools and techniques of organisational change*, 3rd edn, Kogan Page, London

Cialdini, R B (2006) *Influence: The Psychology of Persuasion*, Harper Business, New York

Cohen, D S (2005) Building guiding teams: creating a climate for change, in *The Heart of Change Field Guide: Tools and tactics for leading change in your organisation*, Harvard Business Press, Boston MA

Covey, S R (2013) *The 7 Habits of Highly Effective People*, Simon and Schuster, London

Drucker, P (2005) [accessed 20 April 2014] Managing Oneself [Online] http://hbr.org/2005/01managing-oneself/ar/1

Fisher, R and Ury, W (1999) *Getting to Yes: Negotiating an agreement without giving in*, 2nd edn, Random House, London

French, J P R and Raven, B (1959) The Bases of Social Power, in *Studies in Social Power*, ed D Cartwright, pp 150–67, MI Institute for Social Research, Ann Arbor, MI

George, B (2003) *Authentic Leadership: Rediscovering the secrets to creating lasting value*, Jossey-Bass, San Francisco, CA

Glaser, R and Glaser, C (1992) *Team Effectiveness Profile, Organizational Design and Development*, King of Prussia, PA

Goffee, R and Jones, G (2000) (accessed February 2012) Why should anyone be led by you, *Harvard Business Review*, September–October [Online] http://hbr.org/2000/09/why-should-anyone-be-led-by-you/ar/1

Goleman, D (1998) [accessed 7 April 2014] What makes a Leader?, *Harvard Business Review*, Nov–Dec [Online] http://hbr.org/best of hbr1998/

Goleman, D (2000) [accessed 10 May 2014] Leadership that gets results, *Harvard Business Review*, Mar–Apr [Online] http://hbr.org/product/leadership-that-gets-results/an/R00204-PDF-ENG

Hart, B (2000) [accessed 14 April 2014] Conflict in the Workplace, *Behavioral Consultants, PC* [Online] http://www.excelatlife.com/articles/conflict_at_work.htm

Heifetz, R and Laurie, D (1997) The work of leadership, *Harvard Business Review*, 75 (1), Jan–Feb, pp 124–34

Kilman, R H (2011) Celebrating 40 Years With the TKI Assessment: A Summary of My Favorite Insights [Online] https://www.cpp.com/PDFs?Author_Insights_April_2011.pdf

Leary, K, Pillemer, J and Wheeler, M (2013) [accessed 19 February 2014] [Online] http://hbr.org/2013/01/negotiating-with-emotion/ar/2

Lencioni, P (2002) *The Five Dysfunctions of a Team: A leadership fable*, Jossey-Bass, San Francisco, CA

Lipman-Blumen, J (2002) The age of connective leadership, in *On Leading Change*, eds F Hesselbein and R Johnston, pp 89–101, Jossey-Bass, New York

Mayer, J D and Salovey, P (1997) [accessed 26 March 2014] What is Emotional Intelligence? [Online] http://www.unh.edu/emotional_intelligence/EI%20Assets/Reprints...EI%20Proper/EI1997MSWhatIsEI.pdf

MindTools.com [accessed 15 February 2014] Conflict Resolution – Resolving Conflict Rationally and Effectively [Online] http://www.mindtools.com/pages/article/newLDR_81.htm

Musselwhite and Plouffe [accessed 20 April 2014] When Your Influence is Ineffective, *HBR Blog Network*

Rahim, M A (2002) Towards a Theory of Managing Organisational Conflict, *International Journal of Conflict Management*, **13** (3), pp 206–35
Robbins, S P (1978) 'Conflict management' and 'conflict resolution' are not synonymous terms, *Californian Management Review*, **21** (2), pp 67–75
Ryback, D (1998) *Putting Emotional Intelligence to Work*, Butterworth Heinemann, Boston, MA
Salovey, P and Mayer, J D (1990) [accessed 27 July 2013] Emotional Intelligence, University of New Hampshire (pdf) [Online] http://www.unh.edu/emotional_intelligence/EIAssets/
Seligman, M E P (2006) *Learned Optimism: How to change your mind and your life*, Vintage Books, Random House Inc, New York
Tuckman, B W and Jensen, M A (1977) Stages of small-group development revisited, *Group and Organisational Studies*, **2** (4), pp 419–27

Organizational considerations

13

TIM COLE, MARTIN LUNN, UNA MCGARVIE AND ERIC ROUHOF

Introduction

The four sections in this chapter reflect decisions made to include these topics in the CMI CMBoK. None of these topics is the particular responsibility of a change manager (more than any other manager), and no specialist knowledge is expected. However, a 'blind spot' regarding any of them, and failure to seek appropriate specialist support at the right time, could derail a change initiative. The authors who have contributed to this chapter are specialists in their own fields. They have been asked to offer here a brief introduction to their subjects. These are intended to: 1) equip change managers with an understanding of key concepts; and 2) enable change managers to work effectively with relevant specialists in their own situations.

CHAPTER CONTENTS

Section A: The change manager and Human Resources (HR)

Una McGarvie

Introduction

Human Resources (HR), or Human Resource Management (HRM), refers to how an organization effectively harnesses and maximizes the value of its people to achieve its strategic goals. Organizations can be viewed as systems. HR understands the people elements of the system and how changes to one part of the system can have repercussions for other areas across the organization. In particular, HR understands how the organization engages with, incentivizes, develops and manages its people. Crucially, it has the management information required to understand the totality of the workforce, its demographics and capabilities, the current baseline and future projections of workforce composition.

Change is about people; all change affects someone. In order to plan and manage change effectively it is important to understand who is affected, when, where, how and why. HR understands which people elements within the organizational system need to align not only to overcome resistance to change, but also to embed and reinforce change.

1. Engaging with HR

At the start of the change process an analysis is undertaken of the proposed change, its impact and the readiness for change of those affected. This involves looking at a range of factors that affect people, including the existing processes, technology, organizational structure, organizational culture, values and skills. Early involvement of HR enables a timely assessment of the people factors affected and solutions identified that are most likely to succeed (Table 13.1).

At the end of the change process HR can help to embed and sustain change. This is covered in more detail at the end of this section.

2. Understanding how HR is organized

The way HR is organized can have a significant impact on the change management approach and introduce complexity to the change manager role. Failure to understand this can impact on cost, timescales and resourcing. Consider the following examples of HR structures:

TABLE 13.1 Key areas of HR expertise and their importance to change managers

HR Area	What it Covers	Importance to Change Managers
Pay and Reward	How individuals are remunerated, rewarded and incentivized, including non-financial incentives such as improved holiday entitlement.	It is important that the new 'right' behaviours are rewarded and the old 'wrong' behaviours are not, also that the incentives chosen are relevant, fair and cost-effective.
Pensions	Money paid to a person on their retirement from work. Company pension schemes can be costly to maintain and to the organizations inheriting them, for example, during outsourcing.	Changing an individual's employer may affect pension entitlements, which are protected by legislation. HR ensures that these rights are not inadvertently violated and the cost of maintaining them is not overlooked.
Recruitment and Selection	The process and approach an organization takes to recruiting new people. It also covers placing people in roles within an organization, either on level transfer or promotion (or occasionally downgrading).	Change often involves redefining, eliminating or creating roles and recruiting people to the change team itself. HR can assist with recruitment, arranging temporary contracts and transfer agreements for people. Being seen to be fair, open and non-discriminatory in selecting people to roles is vital to engage people in the change and limit dissatisfaction.
Learning and Development	Ensuring people have the right skills to do their job and establishing a learning culture that supports and enables achievement of strategic goals.	Change requires learning new things and unlearning old habits. Learning encourages people to engage with change. Learning professionals can ensure a suitable learning strategy is developed to support change.
Workforce and Talent Planning	Having the right people, with the right skills, in the right place at the right time. Understanding the workforce's current demographics, skills and experience and those needed to meet future requirements.	Understanding where people work and what skills are available. For example, relocating work may make economic sense but is not viable if the required skills are not available in the new area.

TABLE 13.1 *continued*

HR Area	What it Covers	Importance to Change Managers
HR Policy	How organizations handle people-related activities such as recruitment, diversity, disability, learning and performance management. They form the basis of 'how we do things here'.	It is important to ensure that actions taken during change comply with agreed policies to prevent costly official complaints, appeals and industrial action. If the change involves redundancy, HR can advise on the process to be followed.
Organizational Design and Development	The approach an organization takes to organizing all its constituent components (including people, processes, operations and culture) to achieve its strategic goals.	Changes to structures, reporting lines, process and culture cannot be made in isolation. These elements are interrelated. Success requires strong change management supported by HR expertise.
Industrial Relations/ Employee Relations	Managing the relationship between an organization's management and its employees. Employees may elect worker representatives to negotiate for them in the form of works councils, trade unions or other organized forms of associations of workers.	Worker representatives can help communicate, facilitate and educate workers in times of change. Legislation ensures that effective engagement happens. Ineffective engagement can lead to prolonged and costly industrial action.
HR Metrics	The data organizations need to maximize the value from people. It can include absence rates, turnover, diversity statistics, benchmark comparisons, age and other demographic information.	Outsourcing requires organizations to provide accurate data on the people being transferred. It is important to know what data is available, what reports are possible and how data can be exported to other systems. HR can interpret this data and ensure that valid conclusions are drawn.
HR Transactions/ Service Centres	Many organizations use service centres to handle employee queries. Queries can cover pay, terms and conditions, pension entitlements and so on.	It is important that service centre staff are briefed about changes and what the official response to queries should be. They can also signpost people to existing employee welfare and support services.

- *Devolved versus centralized HR*
  A centralized HR function can make it much easier to identify and access HR expertise. Roles and responsibilities are clear and there is usually one senior role such as a HR director to approve the deployment of HR expertise and resource. Where aspects of HR are devolved to business areas this can add complexity. For example, it may result in different HR practices across the business or different funding models for services such as resourcing and learning. However, a devolved structure may mean that those representing HR in the business, often called HR business partners, have a strong understanding of business areas and are well placed to support the change team in understanding how change will impact that area.
- *Shared HR functions with other organizations*
  Some organizations seek to reduce the cost of HR operations by sharing functions with other organizations. Examples of this can often be seen in government organizations where shared centres of excellence provide HR policy, recruitment and learning services. This can impact on the ability to access support for the change project, as you may be competing with demands from other organizations with different business priorities.
- *Outsourced HR functions*
  Outsourced HR service centres have become common as a means of handling transactional aspects of HR. There may be charges for HR services and the added complexity of dealing with multiple suppliers, contractual constraints over the services available and data protection implications for access to HR data.

3. Employment legislation and change management

Employment legislation sets out the rights of employees and other workers (eg agency or contract workers) in an organization. Individual countries have their own laws and regulations that impact on employment. What relevant legislation exists and how it is applied within a country needs to be understood by the organizations operating there. In addition, some countries are subject to legislative and regulatory policies that emerge from multinational organizations such as the European Union (EU). Where change initiatives cross national boundaries it is possible that organizations must handle employment matters differently in different jurisdictions.

Changes in work patterns, employer, demographics, numbers employed and employment of specific groups of workers may have a legal and regulatory impact (Table 13.2). Employment law is complex. Falling foul of it can be costly in terms of both time and financial penalties. The first source of advice on these issues should be HR. Complex issues may also need referral for legal advice. Involving HR early in discussions about proposed changes that affect people's employment enables potential legal and regulatory implications to be identified and planned for.

TABLE 13.2 Key areas of employment legislation that change may impact

Type of Legislation	Impact on Change Manager Role
Discrimination Ensures people are not treated unfairly on the basis of a 'protected characteristic'. This term means an identifiable characteristic that is prohibited by law as a basis for different treatment. Examples include gender, age, sexuality, race, disability and religion. Such legislation applies to all workers contracted to work for the organization.	Changes to people's tasks, process, working hours, work location, buildings, uniforms and technology all have the potential to breach discrimination legislation. An 'impact statement' will assess if the proposed change will have a more detrimental impact on any particular class or group of workers. Where a potential breach is identified, HR can advise on action to be taken.
Bullying and Harassment Harassment usually refers to sexual advances. Bullying is 'causing a person harassment, alarm or distress by using threatening, abusing or insulting words or behaviour, or disorderly behaviour, or displaying any written sign or other visible representation that is threatening, abusive or insulting' (Martin, 2006).	Bullying can include perceived threats about job security, deliberately overloading competent people and blocking access to promotion or training opportunities. It is important that communications or behaviours of those leading and representing change cannot be construed as bullying and that people are safe from retribution if they speak out.
Redundancy Changes in economic circumstances and operating environments mean employers may need to lose some employees. Redundancy impacts both those who leave and those left behind. It also affects the organization's reputation. Legislation describes how organizations must consult with those affected, including notice periods to be given.	Medium to large organizations may already have redundancy policies in place covering consultation, potential redeployment, notice periods, treatment of outstanding holidays, redundancy pay, support services and time off to search for new work. Failure to comply with these policies during the change process can lead to disputes arising.
Contract of employment It is a legal requirement in most countries for employees to have a contract of employment. This sets out what is expected of each party and their rights. Changes that may impact on contracts of employment include alterations to working times, relocation, outsourcing, takeovers and mergers.	A signed contract is binding on both parties and can only be changed with the agreement of both. Where change impacts on contracts of employment a consultation process will be required. Unilateral changes can lead to disputes and costly legal proceedings.

TABLE 13.2 *continued*

Type of Legislation	Impact on Change Manager Role
Relocation Businesses may need to relocate for a variety of reasons. Before relocating employees it is important to understand if there are any restrictions concerning relocation built into employee's contract of employment.	Relocation must be deemed to be reasonable in terms of timing, distance and impact on the employee. It should not unfairly impact people on grounds of protected characteristics. Relocation packages for employees can be costly. Relocating from an area where an organization was the major employer may also incur political or reputational risk.
Transfer of Employment Rights Designed to maintain and protect the employment rights of workers where there is a change in the legal entity for which they work. Workers may have the right to transfer to the new employer on the same terms and conditions as they had with their previous employer. There is significant complexity and risk associated with this legislation. Legal advice is recommended.	Transferred rights can include a wide range of benefits including early retirement benefits, which can place a long-term liability on the recipient organization. Both the outgoing and incoming employer will need to consult with the affected employees or their elected representatives. The new employer must be provided with full and accurate information on the transferring employees. Failure to disclose could lead to the receiving employer suing the former employer.
Working-time regulations These specify where employers must provide paid statutory holidays, set out the maximum hours employees are able to work and how long they can work without rest breaks. Countries may also have regulations preventing workers being compelled to work on particular days that have religious significance.	The legislation outlines the parameters within which employers can expect employees to work. In some circumstances employees and employers may be allowed to opt out of these regulations. However, putting pressure on people to opt out is illegal.

TABLE 13.2 *continued*

Type of Legislation	Impact on Change Manager Role
Data Protection This typically covers the following: • People have the right to know what information is being collected about them, what it is used for and by whom. • Information must be protected, retained only whilst needed and made available only on a restricted 'need to know' basis. • Information must be accurate, and must be obtained and retained lawfully.	All existing and new information needs to be reviewed and checked for compliance. Employers retaining personal data may also need to be included on a register of data controllers. Employees have the right to request to see information held about them and failure to disclose this could lead to a fine. Change programmes need to understand the data protection legislation in the countries in which data is being obtained from and stored. Where international boundaries are crossed, different data protection requirements may apply.
Constructive Dismissal This allows employees to treat an employer's behaviour towards them as if it was a dismissal, even if their employer had not formally dismissed them. Where the employer's behaviour is so unreasonable as to make it untenable for an employee to continue working for the organization and they leave, the employee could make a successful legal claim against the employer.	As changes are implemented in organizations, it is likely that not everyone will be happy. This does not mean that they can resign and claim constructive dismissal. However, if the changes are seen to be unfair or unreasonable, or are the culmination of a number of 'unfair changes', then a case of constructive dismissal may be upheld.
Board Level Employee Representation Some countries have legislation that requires employee representatives to be included on the supervisory board or similar overseeing bodies. This enables employees to have input into the organization's strategy or provide employee representatives the right to elect members to such boards and influence key strategic decisions.	Change managers need to understand how strategic decisions are made within the organization. Where an organization operates across national boundaries, different approaches to strategic change may be required in different parts of the same organization.

CASE STUDY

An international IT company had a 10-year outsourcing contract coming to an end and had to prepare for a new organization to take it over. Legislation required a consultation period of one month. However, the company operated a three-month notice period to give people the chance to look for other work if they did not want to transfer. This caused conflict, because the recipient of the outsourced service wanted the transfer to be implemented quickly. They focused only on the IT and service aspects, not on the needs of the people.

Consultation with HR ensures not only that legal requirements are met but also that organizational HR policies are adhered to. Proper consultation facilitates the effective and ethical transition of people to new employment arrangements.

4. Change management and HR policy

The website of the Chartered Institute of Personnel and Development, a UK-based international professional association for HR Management, defines HR policies as: 'A written source of guidance on how a wide range of issues should be handled within an employing organization, incorporating a description of principles, rights and responsibilities for managers and employees.'

HR policies ensure people understand how employment issues will be dealt with. Some are designed to ensure that the organization complies with legal requirements. The number and types of policies an organization has will ultimately depend on its size, its business practices and its particular employment needs. Hence the types of policies existing in different organizations can vary widely (Table 13.3).

HR procedures provide practical advice and guidance to employees about how to enact HR policies, giving step-by-step instructions of what needs to be done, by whom and when.

TABLE 13.3 Typical HR policies in organizations and considerations for change managers

HR Policy	Description of Policy	Considerations for Change Managers
Absence Management	Explains the various sorts of absence (illness, maternity, paternity, bereavement, childcare and ongoing medical conditions) and how the organization handles them.	Where change impacts on people's working hours, location or job role then it is important to consider the absence management policy. People may accrue rights that need to be taken into account. For example, a woman currently on maternity leave may be eligible to apply for roles arising out of the change process.
Anti-Bribery	Bribery is the offering of incentives to an individual for the purpose of inciting them to act improperly. Bribery policies explain what the organization considers to be bribery and how employees need to respond to any attempts to use bribery.	When change involves procurement of goods or services there may be offers of hospitality and gifts by those bidding for contracts. Understanding the organization's bribery policy protects the integrity of the procurement process.
Diversity, Equality and Inclusion	Organizations are required to prevent unlawful discrimination of individuals on the grounds of protected characteristics. Such policies explain the organization's approach and what is expected of employees.	Change may cause undue difficulty to a specific group of workers. The use of equality impact assessments will help identify if this is a risk.
Learning and Development	This may cover how many days' learning a person can expect in a year or whether a financial sum is allocated per individual. It could also cover how learning and development is accessed, defining the responsibilities of the individual and the organization.	Understanding people's expectations around learning can help influence how change initiatives approach the development of new skills and expertise in the workforce.

TABLE 13.3 *continued*

HR Policy	Description of Policy	Considerations for Change Managers
Performance Management	This explains how the organization will establish agreed standards of performance with individuals, how performance will be monitored and measured and poor performance addressed.	Change may impact on job roles or headcount. If poor performance becomes a reason to dismiss someone from an organization, it is important that any existing performance policy is followed, in order to reduce appeals and disputes.
Recruitment and Selection	This explains the recruitment process, how eligibility for jobs is determined, how skills or experience are assessed, and the types of assessment that may be used.	Change may require alteration to job roles or recruiting new skills into the organization quickly. Understanding the correct process for filling roles will ensure that people view the process as fair and open.
Reward and Recognition	This covers the types of rewards and benefits individuals might get, including compensation packages, childcare schemes, bonus schemes, performance pay and so on.	It is important to identify ways to incentivize and engage people in the change process. These policies explain which types of incentives are acceptable and, crucially, which are not.
Travel and Subsistence	This describes how the organization refunds and manages payment for workers who are required to travel as part of their job role. It can include mileage allowances, meal allowances and types of travel that are allowed.	Change projects often require people to engage in travel. These policies ensure that expenses incurred are allowable. These costs may need to be factored into the change business case.

CASE STUDY

An organization underwent a series of mergers. As a result there was a legacy of many different types of employment contracts in place. When further change initiatives were undertaken affecting people's terms and conditions, they were not starting from a common position. Significant work was involved in negotiating changes to all these different contracts.

HR policies can have a major impact on how change is undertaken. Time must be included to consult and negotiate effectively. Failure to follow such policies can lead to disputes and escalation to external bodies for resolution.

Tip

Involve HR early in the change process so that the impact on people and timescales can be determined. Key questions HR will ask include:

- Will this change affect a specific group of employees?
- Will it affect work patterns, pay, benefits or location?
- Will it change the numbers or demographics of employees?

5. Employee relations

Employee relations (ER) or industrial relations (IR) is concerned with managing the relationship between an organization's management and representatives of its employees. Such arrangements take various forms in different countries, including trade unions, confederations, federations, councils, alliances, committees, congress and labour unions. The roles of these bodies varies between countries and is influenced by legislation, membership numbers, organizational size, the sector in which they operate and location.

Organizations need to understand the customs, practices and legal requirements at play in the countries in which they operate. They must use this knowledge to engage appropriately with employee representatives, especially during times of change. It cannot be assumed that what works well in one country will also work in another. As labour becomes more mobile and as organizations expand into new global markets there is additional pressure to consider not just how to engage with workers at a local or national level but also at a wider global level.

CASE STUDY

In 2008 Britain's biggest trade union, Unite, merged with North America's largest private sector union, the United Steelworkers Union (USW), to create a global union called Workers Uniting. The global union undertakes collective bargaining and develops common strategies to prevent reductions in members' rights. In addition, Unite is also affiliated to a number of global federations that represent and promote the rights of workers operating in specific industries around the world.

In countries where membership of collective bodies is declining this can impact on how organizations manage relations with their employees, especially during times of change. There has been an increased focus by organizations on employee engagement. Simply put, this is the extent to which employees commit to the organization, its values and its business. It affects their willingness to 'go the extra mile' – sometimes described as 'discretionary effort'. Employee engagement relies on employees having a sense of being treated with fairness and trust by their organization.

Change projects are disruptive and often impact on the elements that underpin employee engagement. Poorly managed change can lead to disengagement and costly disruption. HR understands the appropriate channels to ensure that engagement is effective in each local area. In addition they have the expertise to advise on those aspects of the change that will need to be negotiated with employee representatives. Where there is a lack of collective bodies to negotiate with, HR can act as employee advocates.

Tip

Keeping people informed of the impact of change on them is critical to maintaining engagement. Set out what the business is trying to achieve, what approach will be taken and how you will ensure that what you do is fair and will not discriminate against people. Also remember to communicate what support is available to help people, for example, employee welfare, wellbeing and outplacement services.

There are significant benefits of having employee bodies to work with during the change process. Such bodies can help to communicate information, provide support for learning and identify learning gaps (especially where employees may feel too vulnerable to acknowledge skill deficiencies). These bodies can also support the priority of people and provide an appropriate channel for people issues. This helps to ensure that the focus of the change initiative does not overemphasize task elements at the expense of the people. Identifying who to engage with and the best mechanism for doing so should be considered as part of establishing the governance structure and stakeholder engagement strategy for any change programme (Chapter 4).

CASE STUDY

A public sector organization with over 70,000 employees uses impact assessments as part of all their change programmes. These review the impact of change initiatives on people. The completion of employee impact assessments is confirmed as part of the project review processes.

6. The impact of organizational design

The traditional expectation of a hierarchical organizational design has evolved and organizational structures can now vary significantly. In addition, even within an organization, different business functions operate using different structures, making organizational design (and redesign) a complex area.

Stanford (2007) defines organizational design as 'the outcome of shaping and aligning all the components of an enterprise towards the achievement of an agreed mission'. But what are these 'components' and how do they interact with each other? A helpful model for understanding the different components of an organization is the McKinsey '7-S' framework (Chapter 6, Section A1.2). It describes seven inter-related elements of an organization (all beginning with 'S' in English) that influence an organization's ability to change. To be effective and profitable an organization must ensure that all these elements (including any informal ones) complement and support each other, and are aligned.

When involved in organization design there are some key principles:

- Organizations are systems (Chapter 1, Section C2.3 and Chapter 11, Section A2).
- Changing one element will impact on other parts of the system (Chapter 6, Section A1.2).

- Design organizations around their business strategy and what they are in business to do.
- Organizations do not exist in a vacuum. External changes can affect how they operate, where they operate and potentially their fundamental business strategy (Chapter 2).
- Effective organizational design can be resource intensive and take time.

Organizational design is best undertaken by those with a specialist understanding of organizational behaviour and expertise in applying organizational design techniques. Chapter 11, Section A3.4 describes some Organization Development (OD) levers for sustaining change.

CASE STUDY

An organization was undergoing a significant restructure to align to a new global strategy. Some areas allowed people to volunteer for redundancy without fully considering the impact of this policy. When allowing people to take voluntary redundancy the restructure team failed to consider the skills needed to deliver the future business strategy. Those who remained after the redundancy process were those with less marketable skills, and managers inheriting the new structure found it difficult to make the business profitable.

It is unlikely that there is a single design that can work for an organization. Effective performance may be achieved through a variety of configurations. Organizational design needs to identify a range of alternatives from which the most appropriate option is selected (Table 13.4). Nadler *et al* (1992) suggest four steps to organizational design:

Step 1: determine what is not working well, identify performance gaps and review how current performance relates to the desired strategy.

Step 2: establish a strategic design or 'umbrella structure' focusing on the top layers of the organization, roles, structures and corporate governance.

Step 3: incorporate the detail such as workflows, process, dependencies, relationships and people factors that drive or inhibit change.

Step 4: generate the plan for implementation, how it will be monitored and how issues will be managed.

TABLE 13.4 Common types of organizational design and implications for their use

Type of Organization	Description	Implications for Use
Hierarchical 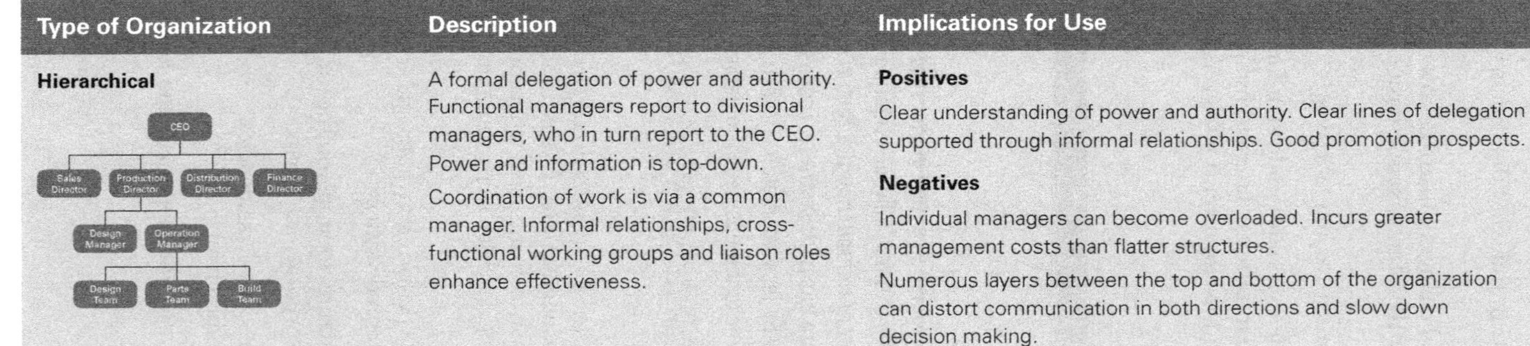	A formal delegation of power and authority. Functional managers report to divisional managers, who in turn report to the CEO. Power and information is top-down. Coordination of work is via a common manager. Informal relationships, cross-functional working groups and liaison roles enhance effectiveness.	**Positives** Clear understanding of power and authority. Clear lines of delegation supported through informal relationships. Good promotion prospects. **Negatives** Individual managers can become overloaded. Incurs greater management costs than flatter structures. Numerous layers between the top and bottom of the organization can distort communication in both directions and slow down decision making.
Centralized 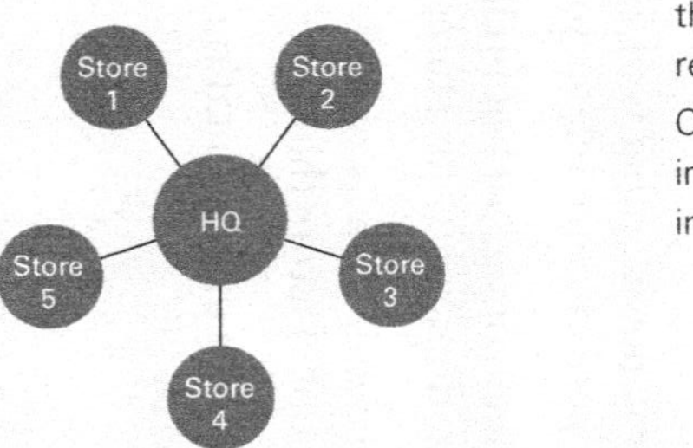	Power and major responsibilities are kept at the centre. The centre sets targets and retains control. Coordination of work and dissemination of information is from the centre out, or from individual business units back to the centre.	**Positives** Clear standards are established for all business units. The centre controls major decisions and strategy. Costs can be controlled and economies of scale achieved. **Negatives** Managers in outlying business units may lack control. Communication between different business units may be limited. It may discourage innovation.
Flat Structures CEO Sales, Production, Distribution, Finance, HR	Very few layers between the CEO and the rest of the organization. Power can be based on relationships and budgets.	**Positives** Speedy decision making with fewer layers for approvals. Enables faster and clearer communications. People at the bottom are closer to and know those at the top (and vice versa). **Negatives** Fewer promotion opportunities. Reward options need to compensate for lack of promotion. Roles and accountabilities can become blurred. May not be sustainable as the organization grows.

TABLE 13.4 *continued*

Type of Organization	Description	Implications for Use
Decentralized	Significant power is devolved to individual business units, which leads to variation in how procedures and processes are undertaken. The centre may establish targets but does not decide how individual business units meet those targets.	**Positives** More autonomy and greater motivation for those in the outlying business units, which can respond quickly to changes or challenges. **Negatives** Duplication of key functions (and resources). The centre may not be aware of day-to-day decisions or challenges. Quality may vary across units, impacting on overall reputation of the organization.
Matrix structures 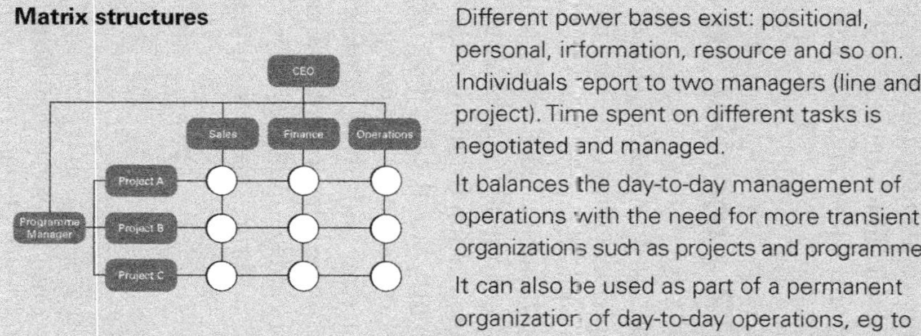 	Different power bases exist: positional, personal, information, resource and so on. Individuals report to two managers (line and project). Time spent on different tasks is negotiated and managed. It balances the day-to-day management of operations with the need for more transient organizations such as projects and programmes. It can also be used as part of a permanent organization of day-to-day operations, eg to provide a matrix of specialist functions across different market segments. To work effectively it requires more autonomy and empowerment for all involved, together with strong leadership skills.	**Positives** More flexibility to resource short-term organizations such as projects. Greater flow of communications and collaboration. Enables the sharing of skills and expertise **Negatives** Needs clear demarcation and agreement on reporting, time management and line management accountabilities. May lead to conflict over allocation of resources. Can be confusing to individuals wanting to arrange leave and personal development as this may need approval from two people.

Tip

Key questions to ask when undertaking organizational design:

- What key elements of the organizational strategy must the design deliver?
- What is happening in the external environment?
- What organizational components, people, factors and behaviours must change?
- How will the proposed design work end-to-end?
- How does the design support the processing, collection and analysis of information?
- Is there sufficient flexibility built into the design?
- How will implementation be undertaken?

In reality organizations will contain varying combinations of these structures. Poor choice of structure can lead to inefficiencies, and it is important to balance expected benefits with possible disadvantages. HR can help with the analysis and redesign of the organization and with transitioning people to the new structure.

7. Using HR expertise to embed change

So far we have focused on the benefits of including HR early in the change process to enable the implementation of change to proceed effectively. To conclude this section it is important to highlight the role HR can also play in embedding and sustaining change. Chapter 1 introduced Lewin's model of change (unfreeze, change, refreeze). In order for change to stick (or refreeze), and to prevent people reverting back to old ways of working, it is important that the organizational culture is aligned with the change and supports it. HR can advise where existing policies and practices can be used to reinforce desired new behaviours. Crucially they can advise where changing policies and practices will avoid reinforcing old and unwanted behaviours. Long after the change process has ended, HR can use people surveys to gauge the impact of the totality of change initiatives across an organization. This information is then available to inform future business strategy.

Summary

This section has outlined some significant aspects of HR in organizations, focusing on its relationship with change management. The level of HR support varies from organization to organization, and the range of expertise described in this chapter may not be available in every situation. Where appropriate expertise is not available internally, change initiatives may need to use external specialists instead. However the resource is provided, change initiatives benefit from early consultation and ongoing alliance with HR colleagues.

The author would like to thank Ann Gaskell, Head of Projects and Programmes at Steria UK, and Chris D Bell, HR Systems Manager at HM Revenue and Customs, UK for their contributions to the case studies, which help bring Section A to life.

Questions to think about

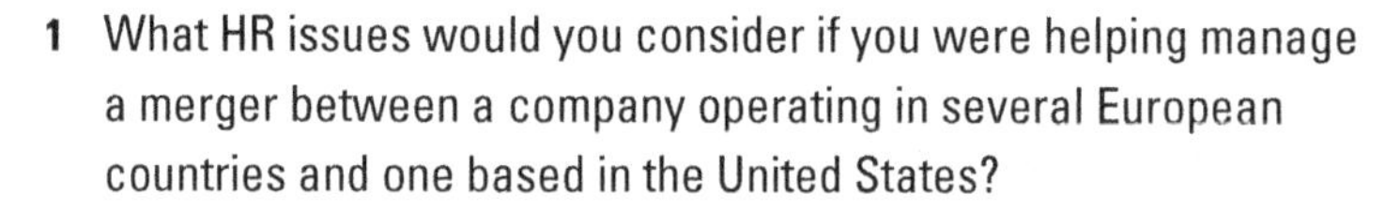

1. What HR issues would you consider if you were helping manage a merger between a company operating in several European countries and one based in the United States?
2. A global manufacturing business is proposing to outsource its production activities, transferring affected employees to an outsourcing company. This may involve relocation of their jobs. What HR implications might the manager of this change need to consider and plan for?
3. A telephone sales and call centre employs a significant number of disabled staff. A change is proposed from the current decentralized structure to a matrix structure, which will involve some changes to job descriptions and possibly relocation of up to 50 per cent of its staff. What HR risks are there?

Further reading

Entrekin, L and Scott-Ladd, BD (2014) *Human Resource Management and Change: A practising manager's guide* – provides a good overview of some of the important HR issues involved in the management of change

Roper, I *et al* (2010) *Critical Issues in Human Resource Management* – gives a clear explanation of some of the key issues around outsourcing and managing employee relations

Nadler, DA and Tushman, ML (1997) *Competing by Design: The power of organizational architecture* – a great introduction to the process of organizational design. The authors make a clear case for the importance of having the right design to maximize organizational performance

References

CIPD (2003) [accessed 24 January 2014] Reorganising for Success in the 21st Century; CEO's and HR Managers' Perceptions [Online] http://www.cipd.co.uk/NR/rdonlyres/C3F16CBB-E53E-4F40-9A5C-2EABB2430941/0/org_success_survey.pdf

CIPD, Definition of HR Policies [accessed 24 January 2014] [Online] http://www.cipd.co.uk/hr-resources/factsheets/hr-policies.aspx

Entrekin, L and Scott-Ladd, B D (2014) *Human Resource Management and Change: A practising managers guide*, Routledge, London

Martin, D (2006) *The A-Z of Employment Practice*, Thorogood, London

Nadler, D A *et al* (1992) *Organizational Architecture: Designs for changing organizations*, Jossey Bass, San Francisco, CA

Nadler, D A and Tushman, M L (1997) *Competing by Design: The power of organizational architecture*, Oxford University Press, Oxford

Roper, I, Prouska, R and Chatrakul Na Ayudhya, U (2010) *Critical Issues in Human Resource Management*, CIPD, London

Stanford, N (2007) *Guide to Organization Design: Creating high-performing and adaptable enterprises*, Profile, London

Section B: Safety, health and environment issues in change

Eric Rouhof

Introduction

This section gives an introduction into SHE (safety, health and environment) management and describes the interaction with change management. (The author acknowledges the variety of terms used around the world for this field: health, safety and environment (HSE), environment, health and safety (EHS), health and safety (H&S) and others.)

The section describes the relationship between a change manager and SHE issues, and indicates some tools to be used. Examples are included to clarify key concepts. Change managers are not expected to possess specialist expertise in SHE issues, but they should be able to identify potential areas of risk. They should also know when to seek and use the expertise of appropriate specialists.

The following topics are discussed:

- What is SHE to an organization?
- SHE management.
- How does change management interact with SHE?
- Managing SHE during change.
- Summary.

1. What is SHE to an organization?

In this section the following definitions are used:

- *Safety:* this term refers to the potential negative effects on the wellbeing of people due to an episode in which they are exposed to harm. Examples could include a trip or fall, a chemical explosion, contact with rotating equipment or acute exposure to toxic vapour.
- *Health:* this term applies to the potential negative effects on the physical and mental status of people resulting from sustained exposure to harmful agents. This can range from a stressful work environment to long-term exposure to harmful chemicals.
- *Environment:* this term covers the burden put on the ecosystem (water, soil, air and all non-human organisms) due to human activity. Examples here include emissions of volatile organic substances (vapours), disposal of chemicals to waste water and waste going to landfill.

For any organization, SHE is at least a boundary condition. Organizations have to operate within the legal framework set by the authorities on safety, health and environment. In most jurisdictions a range of agencies impose a vast set of rules. Such agencies typically include labour inspection, fire departments, health and safety agencies and environment agencies (Table 13.5).

Many organizations develop their own policies and requirements regarding SHE. Typically these go beyond mere compliance to regulations. They define and guide expected SHE behaviour and performance, and shape the desired culture. A well-known model used to classify a safety culture is the Hearts and Minds safety culture ladder, which sets the context for all SHE-related activities (Figure 13.1 – Energy Institute, 2003).

TABLE 13.5 Some examples of legal and other regulatory requirements regarding SHE

Regulations	Safety	Health	Environment
Maximum number of working hours per day	x	x	
Storage of chemical drums	x	x	x
Train people on safety aspects of equipment they use	x		
Number of escape routes	x		
Permitted emissions (substances and volumes)			x
Maximum concentration of a chemical allowed		x	
Permit to operate a plant	x		x

FIGURE 13.1 The Hearts and Minds safety culture ladder

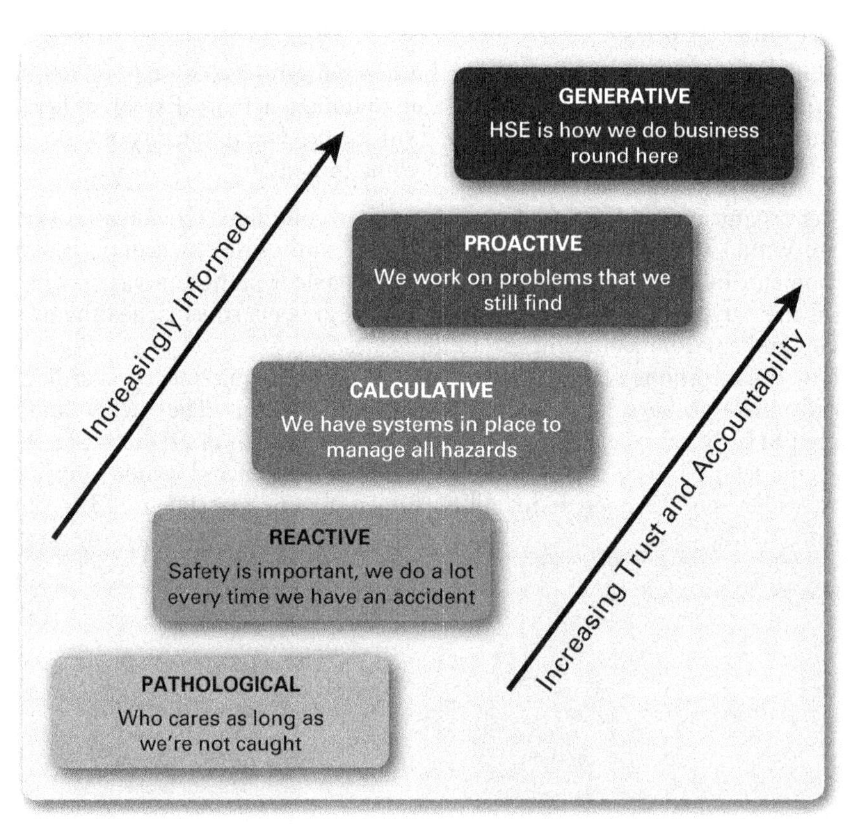

Source: Used by kind permission of the Energy Institute, Hearts and Minds safety culture ladder (www.energyinst.org/heartsandminds)

2. SHE management

SHE management is a particular form of risk management. There is a sense in which all management is about risk. This is especially so if one accepts that risk and opportunity are the same, though differing by mathematical sign – 'opportunities' are seen as positive and 'risks' as negative. The SHE challenge is to manage the risk exposure of the organization regarding safety, health and environment.

However, the situation is complicated by the paradox of SHE management. It is a form of risk management – but there is also a core value attached to it: 'no one gets hurt here'. It is important to recognize, acknowledge and respect this paradox, which helps to understand and guide behaviour.

From a risk perspective, if SHE performance is equal to or better than the standard set (either by external legislative parties, or by organizational policy), risks are deemed sufficiently under control. If not a gap exists, exposing the organization to additional and unacceptable risk.

The concept of 'risk' is widely described as the product of 'impact' and 'probability':

$$Risk = Impact \times Probability$$

When assessing risks, both the impact of a situation or event and its probability must be included. SHE management is not about striving for zero risk: that situation does not exist in the real world. It is about 'acceptable risk'. Risk management for SHE follows some basic steps:

- Assessment of a situation ('What is the risk?').
- Compare the risk to the standard ('Is the risk higher or lower than the "acceptable level"?').
- Define and implement mitigating controls to reduce excessive risk ('How can we manage the risk?')
- Ensure mitigating controls are effective and sustained ('How do we monitor and maintain controls?').

In SHE literature, controls are usually considered in three categories:

- hardware controls (eg equipment, safety devices);
- software controls (eg procedures, standard operating procedures (SOPs), work instructions);
- mindware controls (eg behaviour of people, mindset, culture).

Every organization will have its own sets of controls to address the particular SHE risks it faces. When improving SHE in lower-maturity organizations, it tends to be more effective to focus on hardware controls. In organizations with higher SHE maturity levels, attention will be on all three types of control. Some situations present particular SHE risks that may require that one or two of the controls take priority, but in general it is a good principle to establish a balance of all three.

CASE STUDY

Consider someone whose hobby is to ride a motorbike. It is a great hobby offering a high degree of freedom, steering with your weight, feeling the wind, smelling the environment. It is, however, an activity that has some risks, as traffic accident statistics clearly tell us. In order to make this hobby sufficiently safe (remember the term 'acceptable risk level') we can distinguish examples of the three types of control:

- hardware: a good braking system;
- software: clear traffic rules and procedures (such as who has priority at junctions);
- mindware: the driver's behaviour, controlling his right wrist on the throttle.

If only two out of three controls are properly in place, there is a recipe for disaster. All three types of controls must be in place, in a balanced way.

3. How does change management interact with SHE?

Assuming an organization has SHE management properly in place, any change is by nature a risk. It represents a change to a well-controlled status quo. Changes are always intended to be improvements, but unforeseen implications, effects and interactions may have negative side-effects on SHE. In fact across industry many, many cases of injuries and even major catastrophes are known to be a result of poorly managed changes.

CASE STUDY

One example of an unintended negative side-effect was seen directly by the author. In a hospital emergency room doctors introduced a new type of stretcher that was intended to increase the comfort of patients (a softer, less cold feel). When used for the very first time, coincidentally with a patient suspected to have severe back damage, the stretcher bent in the middle by about half a metre.

Negative effects of changes on SHE are, unfortunately, not limited to major projects such as building or changing an industrial plant. Negative side effects can also occur in organizational change management projects, where changes can have negative impact on existing SHE controls. For example:

- work instructions or procedures may not be properly amended to reflect a change in the organization, so that staff no longer execute the right steps;
- feelings of insecurity resulting from the change may lead to unacceptable levels of stress for staff;
- excessive workload demanded in a transition phase may also cause high stress levels.

4. Managing SHE during change

4.1 A management of change process (MoC)

A change sponsor is *accountable* for the outcomes of the intended change. However, someone is typically made *responsible* for implementing (managing) the change on behalf of the sponsor. Depending on the governance structure that is in place this may be a project manager, programme manager, change manager or a combination of these. The *responsible* person must ensure that the change is implemented within all internal and external SHE boundary conditions.

As described above, the appropriate process is:

- to assess any risks related to the change;
- to compare these to what is specified as an 'acceptable level';
- to define any mitigating actions where required.

In safety literature, this is called the process of *management of change* (MoC). An effective MoC process includes the following steps:

- Establish a clear scope of the change.
- Convene a multidisciplinary team to assess risks associated with the change.
- Document identified risks, proposed control measures and residual risks.
- Obtain formal management approval (change sponsor) of the risk profile.
- Create a managed list of actions to implement the control measures.
- Check on the control measures just before applying the change.
- Review the effectiveness of control measures.

The person *responsible* for managing this MoC process will use the organization's resources to build the process. In most cases the appropriate resource will be the SHE manager or other specialist support.

CASE STUDY

Organizational restructuring

A division of a global business-to-business company decided to restructure its headquarters activities, including staff departments and its global marketing and sales (M&S) function. This involved reshuffling departments, reducing management layers, reducing overall headcount and introducing different work processes.

The change sponsor appointed a project manager, who asked the local SHE manager to support him in the MoC process. A multidisciplinary team was formed consisting of senior managers, middle managers, the HR business partner, works council representatives, the SHE manager and the project manager. The risk assessment was conducted in a workshop format for which three hours was scheduled.

The workshop began with 15–30 minutes' individual brainstorming. All participants were asked to write down as many risks as they could each envisage, writing each risk on a separate sticky note.

All risks were then put on a whiteboard and grouped. Some risks identified were: risk of high workload due to reduced workforce, health risk due to increased travelling for senior M&S manager, health risks due to job insecurity, and health risks due to increased workload during the transition. Risks were classified pragmatically as low, medium or high. This proved precise enough for the purpose; most of the value was in the group discussion to understand the risk.

It was agreed to focus on the high and mediums risks only. Those classified as 'low' were considered 'acceptable risks', and sufficiently under control. For the high and medium risks, control measures were suggested, based on group discussion. It was also agreed to review the effectiveness of controls three months after the change came into effect.

The SHE manager reported the outcome to the project manager, who sought approval from the change sponsor. The project manager then ensured that the defined controls were included in the change process. The approach proved successful in managing the safety and health risks related to the change. A review concluded that one of the key success factors was the joint risk-assessment process involving both senior management and shop floor representatives (works council).

4.2 Making a MoC process work

Based on the author's experience here are some key elements for each step of the generic MoC process mentioned above.

Establish a clear scope of the change

A clear definition of scope is a prerequisite for proper identification of potential risks involved. The existing situation and the new situation resulting from the proposed change must be clearly described. This should include technical diagrams, procedural changes and other relevant information. The scope of the change is to be factual, not based on interpretations or judgements.

Convene a risk assessment team

Convene a multidisciplinary team to assess risks associated with the change. In organizations with a high SHE maturity level this team is seen as important, requiring the best input, and team members are normally more senior and seasoned employees. A team consisting mainly of newer, less experienced staff is not a good sign. This is not primarily a learning opportunity:

- The team should be competent to assess all aspects of the change. Depending on the change at hand, it may be very beneficial to include end users (those who are directly confronted with the new situation).
- External specialists should be invited if the change involves matters where appropriate expertise is not available in-house.
- Assessing the potential risks requires team members to adopt a state of mind that asks: 'What could go wrong?' and 'How could someone get hurt?' This is not how people normally operate; it is normal to assume that things will *not* go wrong.
- The team atmosphere and chemistry is important; participants should feel free to discuss any points they like.

Document the team's work

Document identified risks, proposed control measures and residual risks. The outcome of the risk assessment is an expert opinion on related risks, their magnitude and controls necessary in order to meet 'acceptable risk' standards. Identified risks can be rated using well-established models; many of them are based on the work of Kinney and Wiruth (1976). The complexity of the model is not a goal in itself, as was shown in the restructuring case above.

Figure 13.2 shows an example of a risk matrix. Probability and impact scales have to be defined before the assessment. This can be qualitative (eg risk: low, medium or high) or quantitative (eg impact: emissions below 1 kilogramme, emissions between 1 and 100 kilogrammes, emissions above 100 kilogrammes). The identified risk associated with scenario 2 in the diagram would require control measures to reduce the risk to an acceptable level.

Obtain approval

Obtain formal management approval (change sponsor) of the risk profile. Identified risks are reported to the change sponsor for approval. If any 'residual risks' still fall outside an 'acceptable standard', the sponsor must decide either: 1) to accept this explicitly (with clear, documented reasons for accepting a higher-than-normal risk exposure for the organization); or 2) to implement additional controls.

FIGURE 13.2 Example risk matrix

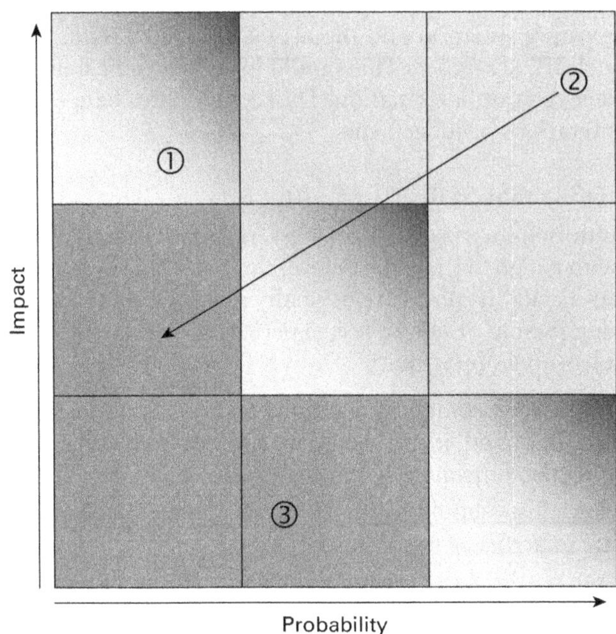

Produce an action list

Create a managed list of actions to implement the control measures. Defining controls intended to manage risks at an acceptable level does not in itself make the world safe. SHE risks are not run in the 'paper world'; they are present in the real world. It is therefore vital that the implementation of these controls is managed actively, and a 'managed action list' is a key tool to achieve this. No one will object to this in principle, but in the hectic world of a change process it can easily be overlooked.

Check the controls

Check on the control measures just before applying the change. This is your 'pre-flight check'. Do it – just like airline pilots do.

Review to improve

Review the effectiveness of control measures. This final step closes the well-known Deming circle of plan–do–check–act. The 'check' (review what has happened), and 'act' (do something to improve things next time around) steps are crucial to ensure that the intended effect is actually achieved. The author's own experience confirms that these steps lead to important learning and improvements.

Summary

Change processes are intended to make things better. However, it is important to realize that any change is a deviation from an (assumed) well-controlled situation and hence possesses SHE risks. All the SHE boundary conditions – external and internal – must be respected. As a result, SHE risks of change must be professionally assessed, and where risks rise above an 'acceptable level', additional controls must be defined and implemented. This section has offered some guidelines on how to do this in an effective way.

Questions to think about

1. For an activity you know well, make a table showing the hardware, software and mindware controls that relate to safety. Is any type of control over-represented? Which type requires more focus?
2. For a set of activities, draw a risk matrix showing the impact and probability of risk scenarios you can imagine (Section B4.2). For what risks would you like to install risk mitigation measures? What mitigation measures would you use?

Further reading

Cameron, I T and Raman, R (2005) *Process Systems Risk Management*, Elsevier, Oxford

Hopkins, A (2005) *Safety, Culture and Risk: The organisational causes of disasters*, CCH, Australia

Perrow, C (1984) *Normal Accidents*, Basic Books, London

Scott, G E (2001) *The Psychology of Safety Handbook*, CRC Press, Florida

References

Energy Institute (2003) [accessed 25 February 2014] *HP PDF Roadmap*, [online] http://www.eimicrosites.org/heartsandminds/userfiles/file/Homepage/HP%20PDF%20roadmap.pdf

Kinney, G F and Wiruth, A D (1976) [accessed 6 May 2014] Practical Risk Analyses for Safety Management, *Naval Weapons Center, China Lake, California, NWC TP 5865* [Online] http://www.dtic.mil/dtic/tr/fulltext/u2/a027189.pdf

Section C: Process optimization in organizations

Martin Lunn

Introduction

Process optimization describes the systematic improvement of material and information flow processes to achieve business goals and ultimately create competitive advantage for an organization. This is not a new approach. Modern-day concepts draw on learning from historical thought leaders such as Fredrick Winslow Taylor's Scientific Management (1911), Henry Ford's Mass Assembly Manufacturing System (1915) and, more recently, Taiichi Ohno's Toyota Production System (1980).

Today, approaches such as Total Quality Management (TQM), Continuous Improvement (CI), Lean and Six Sigma all aim to involve and engage people. They use a set of enabling tools to help identify and then reduce or eliminate wasteful elements of an organization's processes.

1. Process mapping

1.1 Establishing the scope of process mapping

Competitive advantage is improved by closing the performance gaps that inhibit business growth. This is achieved where organizations improve their business processes to add more value to the customer. Process mapping tools help people with such improvements.

The first big challenge is to identify what processes to improve and why. Two questions must be answered satisfactorily:

- Does the selected process have a proven and significant impact on business performance, the identified benefits being aligned with declared business goals and objectives?
- Is there full buy-in from leadership to the process being mapped, to the expected resource commitment and to implementing the expected improvements that are being targeted?

Without these two key prerequisites a process mapping activity will be less accurate. Moreover, if it is not improving the business in the right direction it is likely to fail in implementation, as leaders move on to the next problem. The easiest way to capture this commitment is through the creation of a project scope clearly stating:

- the process to be improved;
- the start and finish of the process to be mapped;
- the expected outcome or improvement.

The approval or sign-off of this scope is an excellent way to check understanding. It also confirms buy-in to the project from all those involved.

1.2 The process mapping activity

Mapping a process creates agreement on what the current state (as-is) process looks like, the waste or non-added value within the process that can be removed and what a future state (to-be) process should be. The value in creating process maps arises from visualizing the flow of value through a process. This can be very difficult to express in words, but creating a picture gets everyone involved, and once complete all can 'see' the process steps from start to finish.

In some cases a current-state process either does not exist or is seen to be so unclear that there is no opportunity to model it on a process map. Process mapping is then used only to aid the creation of a future-state process map and implementation plan. It can also be appropriate to skip the analysis of the current state when a radical change of process is intended, perhaps to strive for an 'ideal state' or 'best-in-class' solution. In these circumstances, skipping the current state can help people to distance their thinking from the way things are currently done.

Process mapping is carried out as a workshop event and is best done manually using paper, pens, sticky notes and flipcharts. Sometimes pre-printed sheets are also used. One risk of using information technology to do process mapping is that it gives editorial power to the person with the keyboard and mouse. Interactive whiteboards (or web-based tools for remote teams) are one solution to this but care must be taken to ensure the engagement and participation of all those involved (see notes on facilitation in Chapter 10). To achieve full engagement from all concerned, people must be encouraged to get up, get involved and create the process maps as a group. The final maps should represent a piece of work that the mapping team is proud of. They can be used to communicate initially to the organization's leadership and then to other stakeholders the work that has been done and the opportunities the group has seen.

By involving everyone who touches the process, all stakeholders have the opportunity to express what the process steps are and how they are done today. Processes often have much local optimization. People improve their own piece of the process and as a result few people, if any, have a clear view of the entire process and all of its steps. A finished 'current state' process map has a high level of accuracy, showing improvement opportunities resulting from current delays, duplication of work, high inventory and rework loops – to name just a few typical issues! This situation arises because people are normally keen to talk only about the problems they are having today.

The 'future state' map is then created. Because this is based in the future it is difficult to argue against, provided it meets any limiting criteria set out in the original process improvement scope. This is where the power of employee involvement shows, as there is now a group of people who enthusiastically believe they can make change and improvements to their process that will deliver improved customer value. This value normally shows in improved lead time, quality or cost.

Once the 'future state' map is created, it is important that the project group checks that the result meets the expectation agreed in the project scope. Hopefully the contribution to business results made from the future state implementation is in line with the organization's needs. If not, the organization's leadership needs to be aware of the gap in contribution, as this may need to be closed through other improvement activities.

2. Mapping techniques

Process maps help people to understand process flow. By visualizing the process start, process end, process steps, the links and relationships it is possible to see very quickly what would take significant time to explain verbally. Visualizing a process makes it very easy for a group to reach a common understanding, and to discuss and agree common interpretation of it.

2.1 Process block diagrams

Block diagrams are the simplest of process maps, an example of which can be seen in Figure 13.3. Blocks are used to represent process steps and are connected using arrows to show process flow. The benefit of this technique is that it is very quick to do and is highly visual, giving all stakeholders an overview of how the process flows from start to finish. Previously this has often been unknown or misunderstood if the line of sight is limited by functional or departmental boundaries.

FIGURE 13.3 Example of a simple block diagram

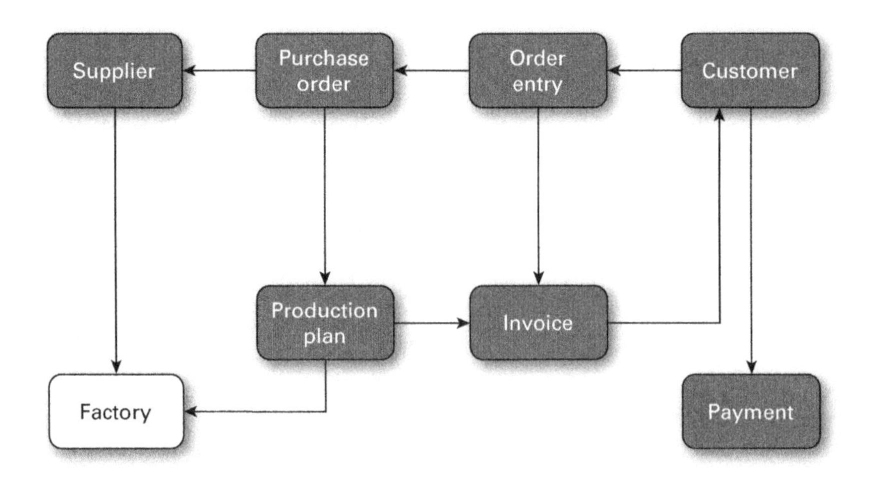

2.2 Process flowcharting

Process flowcharting takes block diagrams one step further by using basic flowchart symbols to represent process flow in more detail. This includes process attributes such as decisions, delays, documents, storage and transportation. An example of a process flowchart can be seen in Figure 13.4. This type of process mapping is used to create basic standards of how departmental- or cell-level processes work and gives greater opportunity to see waste within the process flow. Process flowcharting is still a basic type of process and does not offer visibility of lead time, processing time, ownership or distance.

FIGURE 13.4 Example of a process flowchart

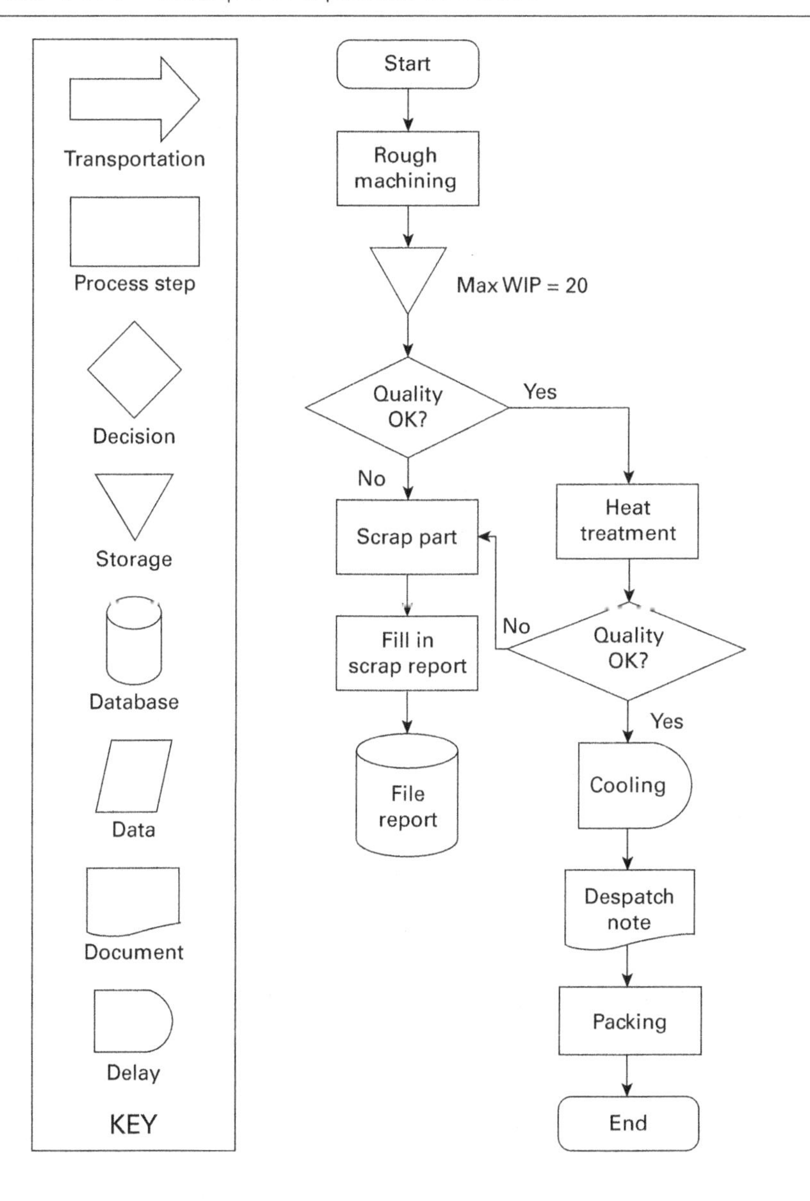

2.3 Value-stream mapping

Value-stream mapping (VSM) focuses on the flow of material value, typically from supplier to customer, for a particular value stream. Icons are used to represent process steps, inventory, key process data and transport, as well as the information and communication flows that support and drive the value stream. An example of a value stream map can be seen in Figure 13.5. This is a tool that places emphasis on meeting customer demands and on developing the whole system, based on flow principles rather than point improvements. Data is used to calculate customer demand, process lead time, cycle times and other inputs to the process flow such as changeover times. Full team involvement in the VSM workshop is the best way to engage people, and to create understanding and agreement with both the current state and future state proposals.

VSM excels at optimizing the material flow process to meet customer demand. This improves delivery performance and, in doing so, ensures the system carries only the minimum amount of inventory for it to work smoothly. More complex value streams with erratic customer demand require a high degree of data collection and a

FIGURE 13.5 Example of a value stream map

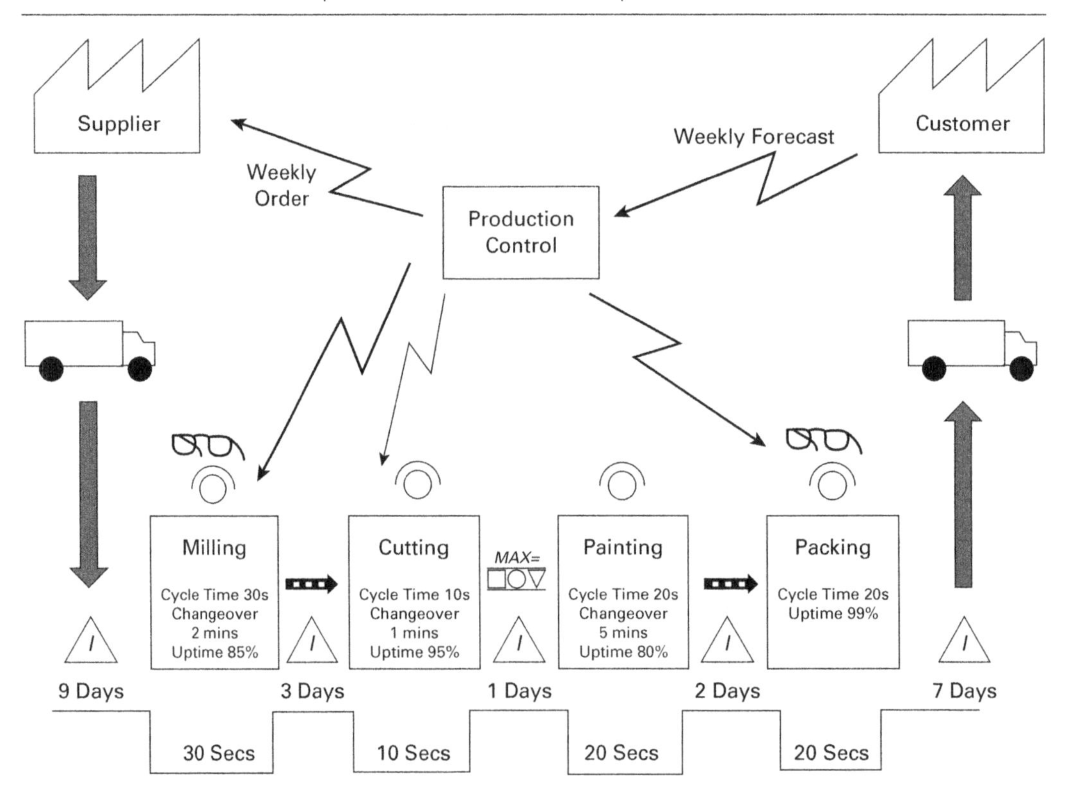

deep understanding of the influencing factors between process steps. Significant time should be allowed for this. Where multiple value streams share the same resources more specialized 'mixed model' VSM knowledge is required to support the mapping process.

2.4 Four-field mapping

Four-field mapping focuses on the flow of information rather than material. It is a tool to follow a document and its experience through the process rather than the people or individual process steps. Four defined fields are used on the process-mapping template:

- process phases;
- process participants/stakeholders;
- process timeline and resource time data;
- process criteria/standards.

An example of a four-field map can be seen in Figure 13.6. Each stakeholder is allocated a separate vertical 'lane' in the 'participant/stakeholder' field. Icons for process steps, decisions, documents and meetings are used to map the relationships and process flow from the nominated starting step to the nominated finish step. Timeline and resource-time data is used to compare how much time has passed on the clock against the amount of time actually spent working on the process. Often there is much improvement opportunity in the difference between these two times as processes stop and the resulting delays incur waiting time. Time data is usually best collected in advance of a mapping workshop, but it may be possible to do so from the mapping team during the workshop. Process steps are identified that are adding value in that:

- they are wanted by the customer;
- are right first time;
- change the process in some way.

This allows the workshop team to create a 'future state' map that reduces or eliminates the non-value-added time.

As with value-stream mapping, maximum benefits are gained from striving to improve the overall process flow rather than simply identifying point improvements. There is typically more scope for improvement in business processes than in material flow processes. This is due to a longer history of focus and measurement of material flows. A mapping team should target at least a 70 per cent improvement in the process time if a business process has not been mapped before. This prevents the team being satisfied with only minor 'future state' changes.

FIGURE 13.6 Example of a four-field map

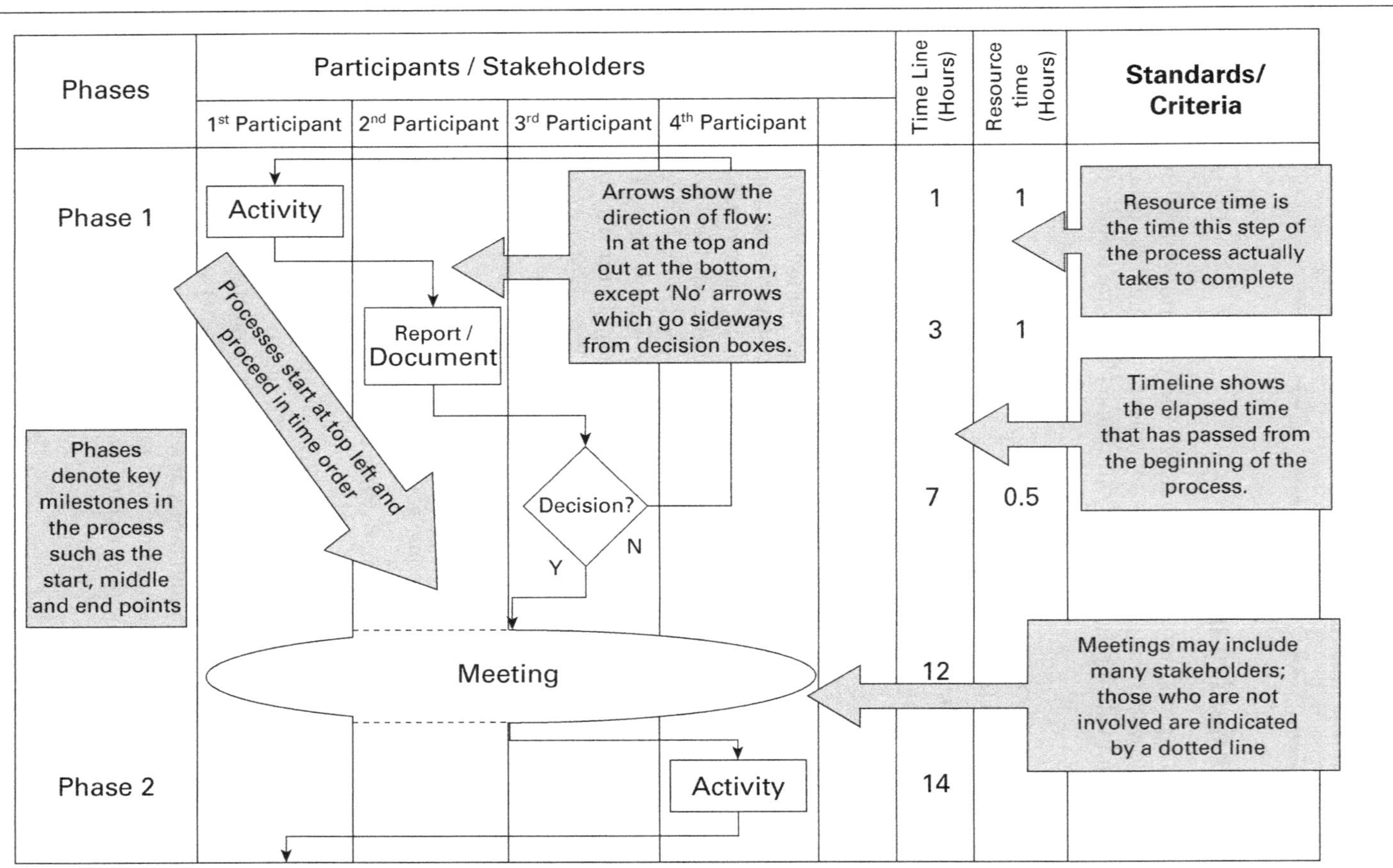

3. Interpretation of process maps

The interpretation of a process map depends largely on what you are trying to achieve. The focus of any process improvement must be achieving customer value, the customer being the person who receives the output of the process. This could equally well be an internal customer (eg a colleague or function within the business) or external customer (eg a person or company outside of the business). The customer is ideally involved as part of the mapping process to obtain a clear value statement. Typical customer value attributes are:

- response times they experience;
- information accuracy;
- lower cost;
- consistent information or material availability;
- good customer focus or service level.

Internal goals and objectives are also a consideration. Achieving competitive advantage may mean exceeding not only the customers' expectations but also the performance of industry competitors to become best in class. Setting challenging targets for process improvement gets the process-mapping team to think harder and more radically about change when creating a future state map.

Common opportunities to look for when interpreting a future state map are:

1. Long periods of elapsed time between process steps (see 'Time Line' column on Figure 13.6) causes a long overall process time, symptomized by late deliveries, excessive waiting times and batch processing. Applying flow principles while matching capacity to the pace of customer demand improves this.
2. Large variations in time required for individual process steps (see 'resource time' column on Figure 13.6) leads to line imbalance and poor process flow. The bottlenecks created cause high levels of waiting and batch processing. This can create overburden within the process. Improving individual process steps and using workload balancing techniques to balance process resource times are helpful here.
3. Unclear roles and responsibilities. Processes that 'just happen' or individual process steps that do not have clear ownership are symptomized by time delays. Clear understanding of who is responsible, accountable, consulted and informed at each process step avoids unnecessary confusion.
4. The shape of the process. A series process with steps following each other in a single line or chain, as shown in Figure 13.7, especially one that is performed by a single stakeholder, has many single points of failure.

   Parallel processing as shown in Figure 13.8 and multiskilling a process team can reduce process step-cycle time and reduces risk of delays due to unforeseen circumstances. Multiple stakeholders complete process steps at the same time rather than each waiting for the preceding steps to be completed.

   Decisions. Every decision is an opportunity for delay. Ideally decisions are eliminated, being taken automatically within the process. Where this is not

FIGURE 13.7 Example of a series process

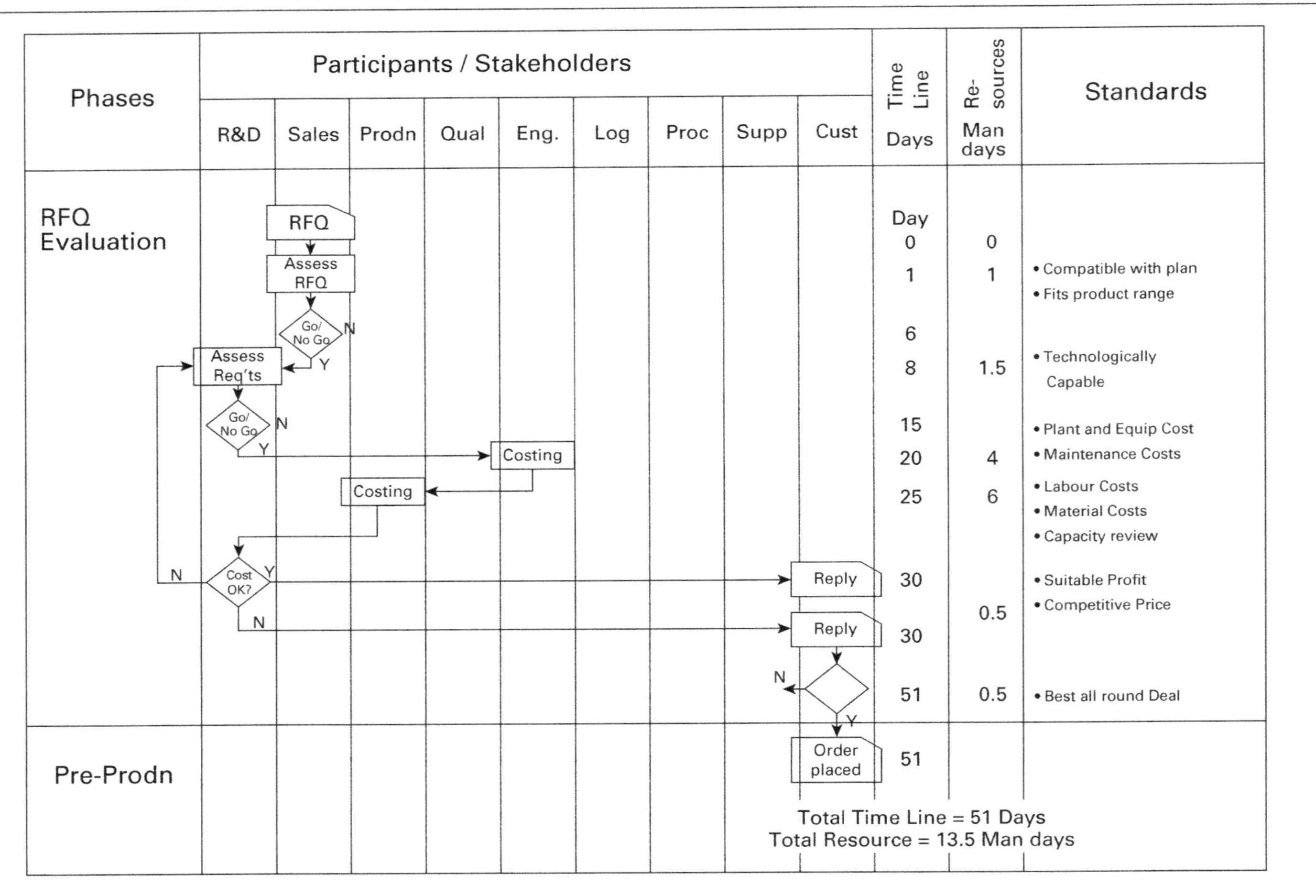

FIGURE 13.8 Example of the same process improved with steps in parallel

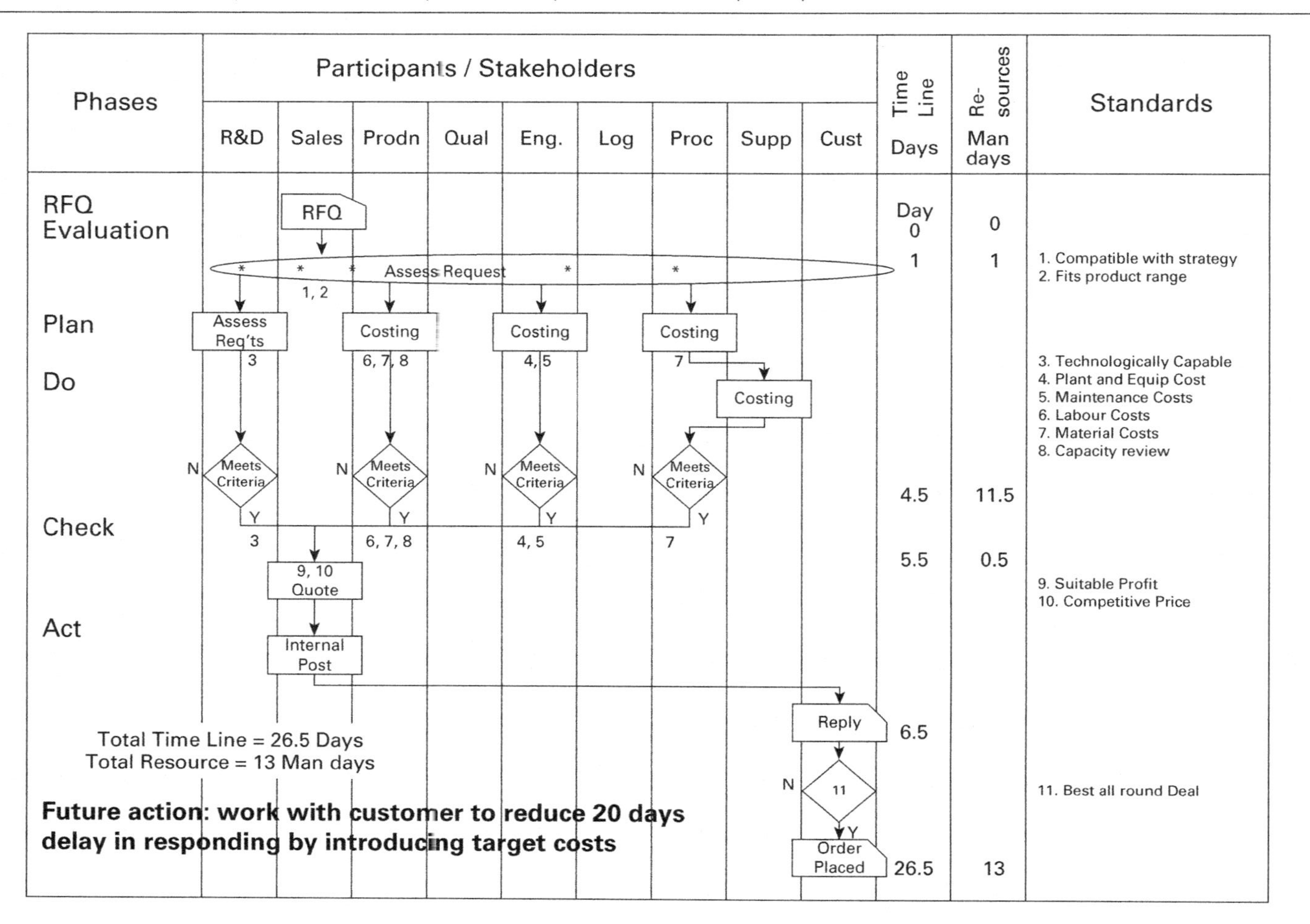

possible, process rules can often be set, allowing decisions to be made more quickly and more locally. This promotes empowerment within an organization and leads to greater employee engagement.

5 Rework loops. Rework, shown as a returning loop on a process map, is the result of not doing the process right the first time. Elimination of the rework loop by problem solving why the error occurs has two benefits: 1) lead-time is improved; and 2) output quality goes up.

6 The process 'issues' list. A process map can convey only some aspects of the process. To understand what is really happening in a process the mapping team must 'go see' the process and walk it from start to finish, talking to the stakeholders. Identifying the 'pain' that stakeholders are experiencing in the process (examples such as printers jamming, difficult-to-read instructions and distractions) helps the future state map to tackle the issues that are most important to those directly involved in the process.

4. The value of a specialist in process mapping

Process-mapping techniques provide a structured approach to communicating what a process looks like, and then challenging it in order to create a future state. It is only when change is implemented that business benefit is created. Any change is challenging both physically and emotionally and a process-mapping specialist can help to prepare for this:

- *The specialist brings facilitation skills*
  As the mapping team work together issues may arise in group or individual behaviours, or in participation levels. Skilled use of facilitation techniques (Chapter 10) keeps everyone involved while creating a productive, respectful environment in which to do the process mapping. This delivers the best results. A future state map that does not have genuine understanding and agreement from all of the mapping team is likely to meet resistance and delays during implementation.
- *The specialist brings a depth of specialist knowledge*
  This can help to ensure that the process-mapping activity follows an appropriate structure. Omitting key tasks in the process-mapping workshop has a detrimental effect on either the implementation or the sustainability of the future state. The specialist knows what the team has to accomplish and how long they need to spend doing it in order to get the result most likely to achieve customer and stakeholder goals.
- *The specialist brings experience*
  Process-mapping techniques focus on the process flow, not individual process steps or what is going through it. The specialist, having mapped many processes, will be able to draw on the experiences of other mapping teams, which may have found good solutions to the complex problems that can arise during process mapping. This can help the current mapping team create ideas and formulate 'future state' solutions they may not otherwise consider.

- *The specialist brings impartiality*
  The process-mapping specialist will be unlikely to know the particular process in detail. This allows the specialist to ask the group difficult and challenging questions about the process flow without suffering from assumptions, prejudice or bias. The specialist remains impartial, leaving the mapping team empowered as the knowledge experts, so participation levels remain high.

Summary

Process mapping helps you to see. The map is a visualization of how a process flows. At the right level of detail it will show you non-adding-value steps that can either be reduced or eliminated. The people involvement aspect of process mapping should be considered carefully to ensure full understanding, buy-in and involvement from leadership and all process stakeholders. This will greatly enhance the chances of a successful future-state implementation.

Questions to think about

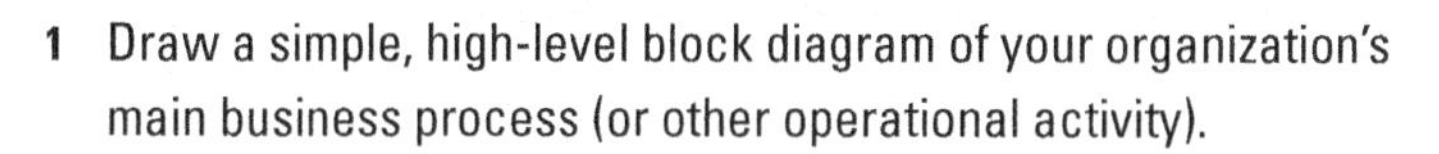

1. Draw a simple, high-level block diagram of your organization's main business process (or other operational activity).
2. Taking a work process that you 'own', draft a process flowchart to describe it.
3. Consider a work process you know well. Which of the approaches to mapping described in this section would offer the most useful insights into it? Why?
4. Find a process-optimization specialist and discuss your responses with him/her.

Further reading

Bicheno, J and Holweg, M (2008) *The Lean Toolbox: The essential guide to lean transformation*, Picsie Books, Buckingham

Lareau, W (2003) *Office Kaizen: Transforming office operations into strategic competitive advantage*, ASQ Quality Press, Milwaukee, WI

Panagacos, T (2012) *The Ultimate Guide to Business Process Management: Everything you need to know and how to apply it in your organization*, CreateSpace Independent Publishing Platform

Rother, M and Shook, J (2003) *Learning to See: Value stream mapping to add value and eliminate* MUDA, The Lean Enterprise Institute Inc., Cambridge, MA

Section D: Financial management for change managers

Tim Cole

Introduction

What does business finance have to do with managing change?

Other chapters in this book show how changes in an organization can impact productivity, employee engagement, employee retention and customer satisfaction. Each stage of change, and the effect of each change, is likely to have a commercial impact too. Chapter 3 traces some of these connections. The purpose of this section is to offer those with limited formal understanding of business finance an introduction to some key terms and concepts. It will also show how they relate to change initiatives. This section does not explore the distinctive financial issues specific to public sector and 'third sector' organizations.

The use of management accounting information is critical at each phase of change to ensure a commercially successful change or, at the very least, to mitigate any financial problems that may result from it. Discussion of some of these concepts with the organization's management accountants will help to deepen understanding.

This chapter will help you to understand:

- how financial information is reported;
- how financial reporting can be used in the change process;
- management accounting and financial analysis tools that can be used in decision making.

1. An introduction, a picture and some common terms

1.1 How money moves in a business

In the end all business is about money and how it moves. To have a reasonable grasp of how financial information is reported it is important to understand how this process operates. Figure 13.9 sets out a business model showing how money moves in a business. The diagram consists of three key areas:

FIGURE 13.9 How money moves – a financial model

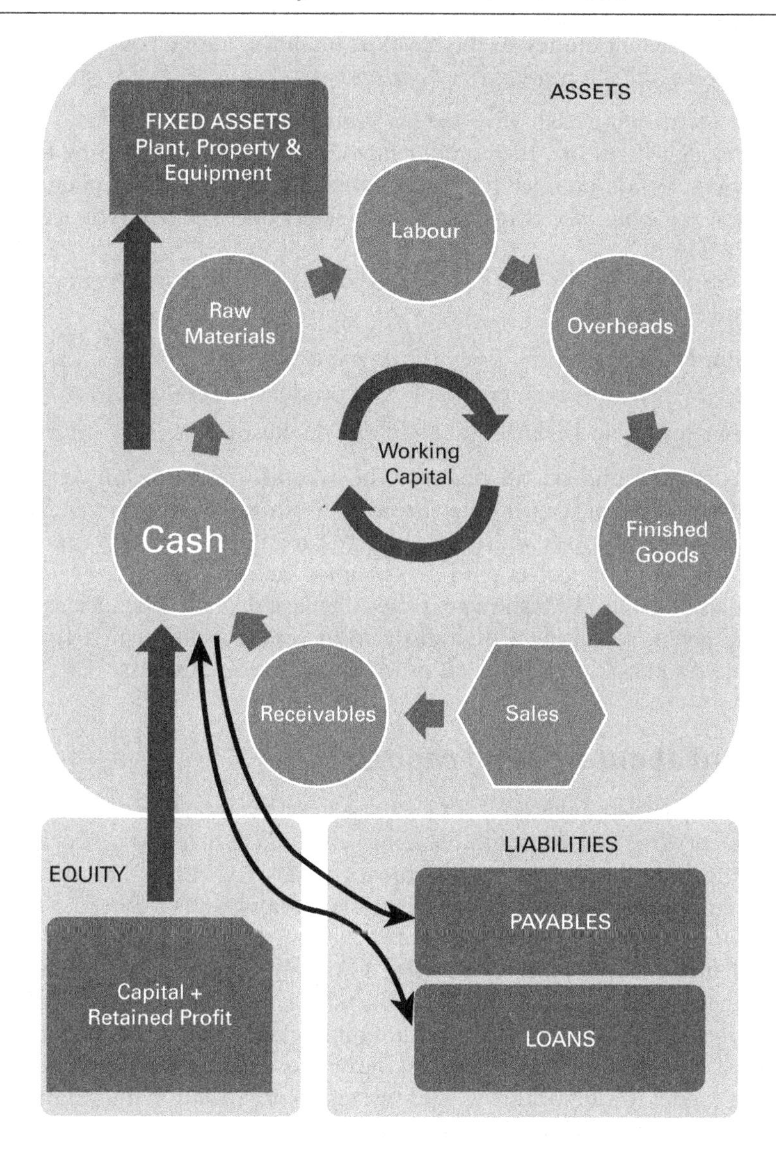

- The top area represents the things of value *owned* by the business, your organization's *assets*.
- The lower area shows the funding of the business – what it *owes* – in two categories:
  - The bottom left area shows the investors' (owners') current stake in the business, known as their *equity*. This is the total of what they contributed to the business (for example, by buying shares) and any accumulated profits (or losses) the business has made.

- The lower right area shows the *liabilities* of the business – money owed by the business to other parties. These may be other people (such as banks) who have lent money to the business (*loans*) or money owed for invoices not yet paid – '*payables*' or '*creditors*'.

A business starts with cash invested as *capital* by the owners, and other cash obtained through *loans* or other similar financing. Cash is invested by the business into items that are not intended for resale (typically land, buildings, plant and equipment). These are called *fixed assets*. Money spent on fixed assets is called *capital expenditure* (CAPEX).

Cash is also invested by the business through *operating (revenue) expenditure*, which includes:

- items intended for resale (such as *raw materials*);
- the *wages* of people who create the end product or service (*direct labour*);
- other materials and salaries that support the business activity (*overheads*).

These items of expenditure contribute to the organization's *working capital*. Other components of working capital are *inventories* (stores of *raw materials*, *work in progress* and *finished goods* waiting to be sold), together with the value of invoices issued to customers but not yet paid ('*receivables*' or '*debtors*').

The arrows on Figure 13.9 show that any change in the business, such as investment in new equipment, recruitment of staff or an increase in sales, will affect *cash*, and therefore have a knock-on impact on other areas of your business.

1.2 A word about working capital

From the model set out in Figure 13.9 it can be seen that money is continually moving through our production, sales and back into cash. Cash invested in working capital may generate a surplus: more is raised through sales and receivables than is needed to sustain current expenditure on raw material, labour and overheads. This can be used to fund expansion (increased expenditure on raw material, labour and overheads), or to fund future developments (through CAPEX). Some may be returned to the owners of the business (perhaps through dividends). The alternative is of course possible, with working capital demanding more and more cash until the organization fails.

Increased sales and increased business activity usually require increased amounts of working capital to support growth. However, an organization must aim constantly at holding the money tied up in working capital to the minimum necessary to sustain its operations. This gives the maximum return on capital invested. In practice, minimizing working capital usually means:

1. reducing inventory (high stock levels represent money sitting on shelves, in addition to storage costs involved);
2. turning resources (such as raw materials) into something that can be sold – a product or service – as quickly as possible;
3. converting the sale speedily back into cash (getting prompt payment from customers);
4. taking full advantage of long payment terms from suppliers (this credit is a valuable source of funding for the organization).

Note that process optimization activity (Section C) is often aimed at creating improvements in the first two of these items.

2. How financial information is reported

Financial information is designed to address the 'money' questions raised by a business. These generally concern profit, capital and cash. Such questions include:

- Has our investment grown in value? If so, by how much (the *return on investment*, or ROI)?
- What are the *chances (or risk) of making a return*?
- Where has the business *generated cash*?

To help answer these questions, financial reporting statements are produced:

- The *income statement*, also commonly known as the *profit-and-loss account*. It summarizes sales revenue and expenses and ends with bottom-line profit for the period.
- The *statement of financial position* commonly known as the *balance sheet*. It summarizes the financial condition of the organization, reporting where capital has come from (including liabilities) and where it is invested in assets.
- The *statement of cash flows* combining both statements and showing cash generated from trading operations and the investments made. Where cash has come from and where it has gone.
- The *cash flow forecast* or *cash budget*, which helps the organization to foresee any problems with funding its activities.

2.1 The income statement

The income statement, also known as the profit-and-loss (P&L) account (Figure 13.10) documents the change in the organization's value over a specified period of time, often a year. The profit (or loss) it shows connects the value of the organization's balance sheet at the beginning of the period with that at the end of it. It does this by taking the organization's *revenue* (the value of goods and services it has invoiced) and deducting in sequence:

- the costs of those sales, which leaves the gross profit;
- *then* the overhead costs of the organization over the period, in various categories, which leaves the 'profit before interest and tax' (PBIT) also called 'earnings before interest and tax' (EBIT);
- *then* the financing costs of the organization over that period (such as interest on loans), leaving the 'profit (or earnings) before tax' (PBT or EBT);
- *then* the organization's tax liability, leaving a 'net profit'.

The format used for an income statement can vary widely, but all contain fundamentally the same information.

FIGURE 13.10 Layout of a simple income statement (P&L)

	Item			
Revenue	**Sales** (value of goods/services shipped and invoiced)			100
Direct costs of these sales	*less*	Raw materials	15	
		Direct labour costs	15	30
	Contribution margin			70
Indirect costs of these sales	*less*	Depreciation	2	
		Other costs related to these sales	3	5
	Gross Profit			65
Overhead costs of running the business: *Distribution*	*less*	Distribution	10	
Marketing and sales costs		Marketing and sales	10	
		Market research	5	
Research and development costs		Innovation (research etc.)	10	
General administration costs		Administration costs	2	
		Rent	3	
		Recruitment and training costs	5	45
	Profit (Earnings) before interest and tax (EBIT)			20
Financing costs	*less*	Interest on loans		4
	Profit (Earnings) Before Tax (EBT)			16
Taxation	*less*	Tax (eg 25% of profit before tax)		4
	Net Profit (Net Earnings)			12

2.2 The balance sheet

The balance sheet simply presents a financial snapshot at a point in time (eg midnight on 31 December) of:

- the things the organization *owns* – its assets (the upper part of Figure 13.9);
- how it has been funded and what it *owes* – to external entities (such as unpaid invoices and bank loans) and to its owners: its liabilities (the lower part of Figure 13.9).

The balance sheet can be presented in various formats, according to different accounting standards, but this description is fundamentally correct. One common historical variant, as shown in Figure 13.11, is to remove the *current liabilities* (such as unpaid invoices) from the 'liabilities'. The figure is deducted instead from the *current assets* (inventories, payables and cash) to create *net working capital.*

FIGURE 13.11 Layout of a simple balance sheet

Balance Sheet		
Fixed Assets		480
Current Assets	195	
Current Liabilities	(190)	
Net Working Capital		5
Net Assets		**485**
Long-term Liabilities (loans etc.)		200
Equity		285
Total		**485**

2.3 *The statement of cash flows*

The statement of cash flows looks back and shows business activity solely in terms of inflows and outflows of cash. It is very useful in understanding what management have done with cash while growing the profits of the business or, in more difficult times, while making losses. This is key when looking at the overall performance of a business, especially in the context of significant change programmes and reviewing business performance.

It considers business activities relating to cash in three broad categories:

- *Operating activities*: the cash generated from sales and operations. If a business is effective here it is organically generating cash and can support investment activities without using other sources of finance. The positive impact of a revenue- and cost-focused change initiative will show here as improved cash generation.
- *Investing activities*: the acquisition and disposal of tangible and fixed assets. This includes the capital investment relating to change initiatives.
- *Financing activities*: the generation and repayment of funds provided by investors (internal funding by owners looking for growth and dividends) and loans (external funding that must be repaid over a term and with interest). This information can be useful to understand how change initiatives have been funded and provide context.

An example of this document is beyond the scope of this introduction to finance. It is something to discuss with your management accountant.

Tip

When building a case for a change initiative, discuss with your accountant how it will be financed. Consider the cost to the business of this form of finance. The initiative must repay this financing cost, as well as other more obvious costs.

Then consider the cost of the initiative compared to other investments in fixed assets and processes.

Finally consider its impact on trade (revenues and costs, reported as profit), and on the efficiency with which working capital is used (perhaps due to improved business processes).

It all comes back to generating more cash!

2.4 The cash-flow forecast

The cash-flow forecast assesses the ability of a business to arrive at its financial objectives. Will there be enough cash at the critical moments to fund its plans? In principle it is like writing on to a calendar every occasion where cash will be spent or received. In practice it uses a table (spreadsheet or similar) to show these inflows and outflows of cash on a monthly basis. The cash-flow forecast is used in conjunction with a budgeted income statement and planned investments (shown on a balance sheet). A simple and stylized example is shown in Figure 13.12.

Remember that accountants prefer to use brackets for negative figures. In the simple example shown in Figure 13.12, it is clear that current plans will lead to insolvency in May or soon afterwards. The organization has a number of options, which include:

- take steps to increase sales revenue during the February to May period;
- arrange additional finance from May to July/August (though this will increase interest charges);
- obtain earlier payments of customer invoices;
- obtain longer credit terms from suppliers;
- delay the CAPEX or spread it over a longer period.

Whatever steps are taken, the cash-flow forecast helps to ensure that there are no nasty surprises! In large organizations there will be a treasury function to manage the cash resources against a clear policy framework. Even here it is appropriate for all managers making decisions to bear in mind the principles of cash management.

A particular application of the cash-flow forecast is discussed in Section D4 in relation to evaluating a change initiative.

FIGURE 13.12 Example cash-flow format

	Jan	Feb	Mar	Apr	May	June	Jul	etc
Cash balance at start of month	100	110	115	100	25	(25)	(30)	
CASH IN:								
Cash sales	50	45	40	40	40	50	60	
Invoices paid by customers	50	50	45	40	40	50	60	
TOTAL CASH IN	100	95	85	80	80	100	120	
CASH OUT:								
Wages and salaries	30	30	30	30	30	30	30	
Payments of suppliers' invoices	40	40	40	35	35	40	40	
Payments of CAPEX project invoices	0	0	10	40	40	10	0	
Interest to be paid on loans etc.	20	20	20	20	25	25	25	
Tax payments	0	0	0	30	0	0	0	
TOTAL CASH OUT	90	90	100	155	130	105	95	
NET CASH FLOW ON MONTH	10	5	(15)	(75)	(50)	(5)	25	
CASH BALANCE AT END OF MONTH	110	115	100	25	(25)	(30)	(5)	

3. Planning the organization's finances

3.1 Budgeting and forecasting

Budgeting and forecasting are two vital tools for planning change. They help change managers to be proactive in managing potential issues with business resources.

A *budget* is a financial action plan. It helps managers to allocate their organization's resources effectively in order to achieve its financial goals. It estimates the expected income and expenditure for a specific period and quantifies financial targets. This provides a reference point against which to check progress and allows managers to compare actual results against the plan. Budgets should be compiled and evaluated regularly during the change process.

Forecasting is the process of using historic data and future plans to predict an organization's performance and likely changes in its financial position:

- *Profit-and-loss forecasts* are a projection of whether or not a company will make a profit. They are based on projected sales and costs for a specified future period.

- *Projected balance sheets* are useful tools for gaining financing as they list a company's assets, liabilities and equity at a specified future point. Additional fixed assets will be seen here.
- *Cash-flow forecasts* predict a company's future liquidity based on these planned changes (Section D2.4).

Using budgeting and forecasting tools, change managers can communicate expectations, avoid foreseeable issues and take action to mitigate problems.

3.2 Decision making

The analysis of management accounting information helps change managers to evaluate possible strategies and action and make informed decisions.

Some of the techniques and tools used in decision making include:

- *Investment appraisal techniques*: these help managers to assess the expected future costs and returns of investments. Factors in an appraisal may include the time an investment takes to pay for itself, the average rate of return or difference between the cash inflows and outflows.
- *Cost–volume–profit analysis*: this helps managers to identify how changes in costs or sales volumes will impact their profits. A useful output of this analysis is the *break even point*, which shows the required volume of sales required to cover your costs.
- *Relevant costing analysis*: costs differ from expenses in that they are the resources that a company sacrifices in order to achieve an objective. Analysing the relevant costs of different strategies can help managers to choose the most appropriate course of action.

Only the first of these is discussed further in this chapter. Further reading (and discussion with your management accountant) will allow you to explore the other topics mentioned.

3.3 Management and accountability

In order to measure progress and performance, clearly defined standards are required. Management accounting provides financial standards with which to compare actual results. Any variances can be analysed and, if necessary, corrective action taken. A common approach is to show in adjacent columns on a spreadsheet:

- the budgeted figures for a specified period;
- actual figures for the same period;
- the amount of variance, positive or negative (remember brackets!).

Ideally the reasons for the actual performance on each line are analysed. Even a positive variance (lower costs or increased income) may be an underachievement in the circumstances. Looking at Figure 13.13 some of the questions it would be reasonable to ask are:

- What factors led to the unexpected high level of sales?
- How were direct labour costs maintained at this level when sales increased by 20 per cent?
- What led to the underspend on marketing and sales activity? How can this be in view of the high level of sales? What is the likely impact of this low level of spending on future sales?

FIGURE 13.13 Example of a budget variance analysis

Budget variance analysis for October 2014	Budget	Actual	Variance	Var %
Sales (value of goods/services shipped and invoiced)	100	120	+20	+20
Costs				
Raw materials	15	18	+3	+20
Labour costs	15	15	0	0
Distribution	10	12	+2	+20
Marketing and sales	10	5	(5)	(50)
Administration	5	6	+1	+20

CASE STUDY

A large organization making and selling ice cream formed a sales budget on the basis of a summer in which 40 days would have a temperature above 22°C. In the event an unusually hot summer meant that 60 days exceeded this temperature, leading to record value sales of ice cream. The sales team claimed a great success, but variance analysis showed that a high level of discounts had been given to customers. Given the actual seasonal conditions, a higher level of profitability should have been achieved.

Management accounting can help to assign responsibility and ensure accountability for performance by providing clear targets for departments and individuals, measuring progress and communicating results.

4. The value of a change initiative

Projects usually involve investing money for significant periods of time before any benefit is received. Examples of this include automation of a production process, an organizational restructuring or a research and development initiative. It is vital that capital should be invested with due care and consideration to ensure a reasonable return on investment.

Project appraisal techniques are means of 'looking before you leap' – that is, to examine the investment proposition before a commitment is made. All financial techniques used to access projects involve collating financial information about the investment. This will be used to assess the costs of the investment, and the projected financial benefits once the investment is made.

The discussion below will refer to the following example (Figure 13.14): a four-year initiative is proposed where investment will be made in new technology to improve efficiency in operations/production. The total capital investment required is expected to be £500,000, including installation. It is estimated it will generate cost savings diminishing each year across four years (£300,000, £200,000, £100,000 and £25,000). At the end of that period the technology will become fully depreciated and an 'end of life' scrap value for the equipment is estimated at £25,000. How would you assess this change initiative/proposal? Is it a viable financial investment?

FIGURE 13.14 Cash flows from a capital project

Cash Flow in Year (£000s)	0	1	2	3	4
Capital investment	(500)				25
Operating cash flow		300	200	100	25
Annual net cash flow	(500)	300	200	100	50
Cumulative net cash flow	(500)	(200)	0	100	150

Questions to think about

Questions you may ask of a proposed change project:

1. How long will it take to recover the initial investment?
2. How much are we likely to get back from this project?
3. By the time I get the money back/the projected profit, what will it be worth?
4. How accurate are our predicted future returns?

4.1 Payback period

This approach answers the question: 'How long will it take to recover the initial investment?' In organizations where cash is tight, payback becomes a critical deciding factor in which projects receive investment. In Figure 13.14 we can see that 'payback' happens in year two. A total of £500,000 has now been saved and the cumulative net cash flow becomes zero. While payback can be useful, it does not tell us anything about the benefits gained from this project as it does not acknowledge late or lagging returns. For this we look at *total net cash flows*.

4.2 Net cash flows

This approach answers the question: 'How much are we likely to get back from this project?'

To answer this question in terms of cash we would look at net cash flows.

Cash in – cash out = net cash flow

In our scenario, we make an immediate ('Year 0') capital expenditure of £500,000 cash to set up the equipment, including all related investment costs. In each of the next four years there is an expected improvement in costs and so in cash inflow. At the end of year four £25,000 is expected to be recovered from scrapping the equipment.

The cumulative net cash flow at the end of the project (year four) is £150,000 (Figure 13.14). This gives us a bigger picture of the project than simply assessing payback.

4.3 Accounting rate of return (ARR)

ARR is a method of specifying the profit that the company can expect from an investment. It divides the profit (before interest and tax) by the investment to get the ratio of return (assuming there are no other expenses arising from the project). For our scenario the calculation is shown in Figure 13.15.

FIGURE 13.15 Accounting rate of return example

Total of the Annual Net Cash Flows	£650,000
less Total accounting depreciation (initial investment – scrap value)	£475,000
Cash profit	£175,000
Accounting rate of return $\frac{\textit{cash profit}}{\textit{investment}} \times \frac{1}{\textit{number of years}} \times 100$	$\frac{175{,}000}{500{,}000} \times \frac{1}{4} \times 100 = 8.75\%$

Change managers should take care when comparing projects using the ARR. The percentages alone give no indication of size of investments, project durations or timings. These factors need to be considered when comparing a portfolio of project choices using this method. For example, in the above scenario we have taken an average of the profit over four years. ARR remains the same, regardless of when the cash came in during that four-year period.

4.4 The time value of money

Questions to think about

Would you prefer £1,000 today or in four years' time? Why? (List some of the reasons.)

Your responses to the above questions may have included concerns about rising levels of prices (inflation), the interest you could gain by investing the money for four years, how sure you can be about the promise four years' from now, and other factors. Most will stem from the comparative certainty of 'money today' and the additional options you have if you are given the money now.

Organizations and those who invest in them are also concerned about the 'time value of money'. As a result, change initiatives must also consider the value of future returns in terms of how much will arrive and when. It is important to be able to value future cash flows in today's terms – because we are looking to invest today!

Figure 13.16 takes the example already outlined (Figure 13.14) and adds information about the future value of money. This will provide the basis for some additional ways to assess the value of a change initiative.

Discounting future cash flows allows us to assess their 'true' value (based on clear assumptions) and to consider associated risks. Understanding the principles involved allows managers to raise relevant questions and reach better decisions.

4.5 Net present value

We can use 'discounting' to look at the 'present value' of cash – ie how much is future years' money worth to me today? The 'discount rate' to be used is one that an organization will decide on as a policy. It represents the cost of borrowing, investor expectations about risk factors and alternative opportunities, and inflation.

Here we are using a 'discount rate' of 15 per cent. Put simply, the 15 per cent discount rate shown in Figure 13.16 implies that the organization would be equally content to receive £100 in one year's time or £87 today (£100 / 1.15 = £87). The

FIGURE 13.16 Discounted cash flows

Cash Flow in Year (£000s)	0	1	2	3	4
Capital investment	(500)				25
Operating cash flow		300	200	100	25
Annual net cash flow	(500)	300	200	100	50
Cumulative net cash flow	(500)	(200)	0	100	150

Above cash flows are as shown in Figure 13.14

Discount Rate @ 15%	1.00	0.87	0.76	0.66	0.57
Annual net cash flow, in **Present Value,** @15%	(500)	261	152	66	29
Cumulative Net Cash Flows, Discounted @15% = **Net Present Value**	(500)	(239)	(87)	(21)	8

same 15 per cent applied to an income of £100 in two years' time 'discounts' the £100 by 15 per cent twice ($£100 / 1.15^2 = £76$) – and so on. This allows us to answer the question: 'By the time we receive the projected income or profit streams, what will they be worth?' In our example it shows us that the investment does not become cash positive (in today's money) until year four, when the 'net present value' (NPV) of the cash flows is just £8,000.

This technique is usually a more appropriate investment appraisal technique than payback or ARR, which do not recognize the time value of money.

4.6 Internal rate of return (IRR)

The discount rate can be used in a different way. We can total the future net cash flows of the project (as in Section D4.2), and then calculate the 'discount rate', which would make the value of these cash flows zero. This is called the *internal rate of return* (IRR) of the project. As a rule, the higher the IRR, the more desirable it is to undertake the investment. Comparing the IRRs of projects is rather like comparing the interest rates available from different types of bank accounts – you will take the highest rates available until you have used up all your investment funds.

When evaluating proposed changes, it is important to set benchmarks. Organizations often set 'hurdle rates' for projects. For a project to be accepted, the IRR must be greater than or equal to the hurdle rate set. When evaluating multiple possible projects, the project with the highest IRR is generally recommended and progressed.

In our scenario (Figure 13.16) the IRR for this project is actually a little over 15 per cent. After four years the NPV is still positive at 15 per cent, but if we discounted using 16 per cent the NPV would become negative.

4.7 *The act of interpretation*

It is only after all the facts and data are understood, measured, collected and organized that review and interpretation should take place. Only then can conclusions be drawn or, more commonly, better questions asked.

It is worth noting that the methods introduced in this section are simply forecasting tools. The figures they generate reflect just part of a project's potential impact. The financial evaluation of proposals should be carried out in conjunction with an evaluation of the human and organizational impacts to assess the full range of outcomes of any proposed change.

Tip

Remember: garbage in = garbage out!

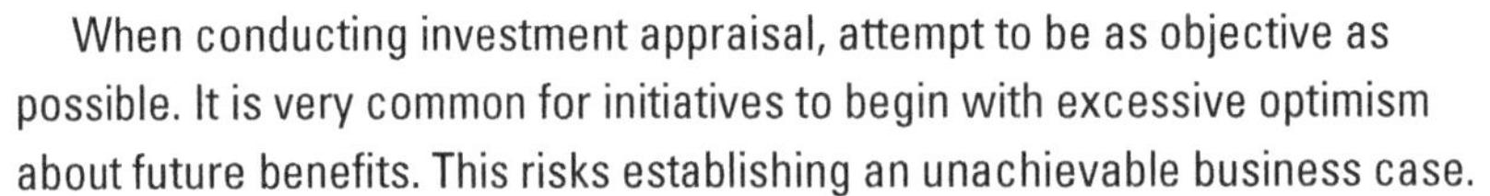

When conducting investment appraisal, attempt to be as objective as possible. It is very common for initiatives to begin with excessive optimism about future benefits. This risks establishing an unachievable business case.

Summary

Almost all organizations have access to professional accounting expertise. The brief overview of finance here is designed to help change managers to engage more effectively with these professionals. This leads to changes that are well founded in the commercial realities of the organization.

Questions to think about

1. In your organization, who gathers all the relevant financial data for the costs and income from a change initiative? Where is this documented?
2. When you study the financial forecasts for a change initiative, how reliable are the future estimates for income, cost and timing?
3. Often the initial plans for change initiatives evolve over time. How does your organization ensure that these changes are reflected in financial forecasts?

Further reading

Warner, S (2010) *Finance Basics Secrets* (Collins Business Secrets series), HarperCollins, London

Online resources:

Accounting-Simplified.com: http://accounting-simplified.com/financial/users-of-accounting-information.html

CKT Solutions Ltd: http://www.cktsolutions.com/business-acumen-development.html

Financial Fluency Ltd: http://www.financial-fluency.co.uk/financial-fluency-publications/

Investopedia LLC, A Division of IAC: http://www.investopedia.com/tags/cash_flow/

Kaplan Financial Limited: http://kfknowledgebank.kaplan.co.uk/wiki%20pages/home.aspx

ReadyRatios Software, Financial Analysis, IFRS Disclosure Guide, *Audit*: http://www.readyratios.com/faq/

References

Deloitte Touche Tohmatsu Limited ('DTTL'): http://www.iasplus.com/en/publications/global/models-checklists/2013/ifrs-mfs-2013

International Financial Reporting Standards Foundation (IFRS Foundation): http://www.ifrs.org/The-organisation/Pages/IFRS-Foundation-and-the-IASB.aspx and www.iasb.org

Professional Accountants in Business International Good Practice Guidance, Project and Investment Appraisal for Sustainable Value Creation, Exposure Draft (2012) November, p 13 [Online] https://www.ifac.org/sites/default/files/publications/files/PAIB-IGPG-ED-Project-and-Investment-Appraisal-for-Sustainable-Value-Creation_0.pdf

Warner, S (2010) *Finance Basics*, HarperCollins, London

INDEX

Note: *italics* indicate a Figure or Table in the text.

CPSIA information can be obtained at www.ICGtesting.com
Printed in the USA
BVOW09s1530021215

429155BV00016B/105/P